MPLS Fundamentals

Luc De Ghein, CCIE
No. 1897

D1580640

Cisco Press

800 East 96th Street
Indianapolis, IN 46240 USA

MPLS Fundamentals

Luc De Ghein

Copyright© 2007 Cisco Systems, Inc.

Published by:
Cisco Press
800 East 96th Street
Indianapolis, IN 46240 USA

Printed in the United States of America   7 8 9 0

First Printing November 2006

Library of Congress Number: 2004101984

ISBN: 1-58705-197-4

Warning and Disclaimer

This book is designed to provide information about Multiprotocol Label Switching (MPLS). Every effort has been made to make this book as complete and as accurate as possible, but no warranty or fitness is implied.

The information is provided on an "as is" basis. The authors, Cisco Press, and Cisco Systems, Inc., shall have neither liability nor responsibility to any person or entity with respect to any loss or damages arising from the information contained in this book or from the use of the discs or programs that may accompany it.

The opinions expressed in this book belong to the author and are not necessarily those of Cisco Systems, Inc.

Feedback Information

At Cisco Press, our goal is to create in-depth technical books of the highest quality and value. Each book is crafted with care and precision, undergoing rigorous development that involves the unique expertise of members from the professional technical community.

Readers' feedback is a natural continuation of this process. If you have any comments regarding how we could improve the quality of this book, or otherwise alter it to better suit your needs, you can contact us through e-mail at feedback@ciscopress.com. Please make sure to include the book title and ISBN in your message.

We greatly appreciate your assistance.

Corporate and Government Sales

Cisco Press offers excellent discounts on this book when ordered in quantity for bulk purchases or special sales. For more information, please contact: **U.S. Corporate and Government Sales**   1-800-382-3419   corpsales@pearsontechgroup.com

For sales outside of the U.S. please contact: **International Sales**   1-317-581-3793   international@pearsontechgroup.com

Safari®
BOOKS ONLINE
ENABLED

THIS BOOK IS SAFARI ENABLED

INCLUDES FREE 45-DAY ACCESS TO THE ONLINE EDITION

The Safari® Enabled icon on the cover of your favorite technology book means the book is available through Safari Bookshelf. When you buy this book, you get free access to the online edition for 45 days.

Safari Bookshelf is an electronic reference library that lets you easily search thousands of technical books, find code samples, download chapters, and access technical information whenever and wherever you need it.

TO GAIN 45-DAY SAFARI ENABLED ACCESS TO THIS BOOK:

- Go to **http://www.ciscopress.com/safarienabled**

- Complete the brief registration form

- Enter the coupon code found in the front of this book before the "Contents at a Glance" page

If you have difficulty registering on Safari Bookshelf or accessing the online edition, please e-mail customer-service@safaribooksonline.com.

Trademark Acknowledgments

All terms mentioned in this book that are known to be trademarks or service marks have been appropriately capitalized. Cisco Press or Cisco Systems, Inc. cannot attest to the accuracy of this information. Use of a term in this book should not be regarded as affecting the validity of any trademark or service mark.

Publisher: Paul Boger

Cisco Representative: Anthony Wolfenden

Cisco Press Program Manager: Jeff Brady

Executive Editor: Mary Beth Ray

Managing Editor: Patrick Kanouse

Development Editor: Allison Beaumont Johnson

Project Editor: Seth Kerney

Copy Editor: Karen A. Gill

Technical Editors: Mohammad Miri, Ivan Pepelnjak, Hari Rakotoranto

Team Coordinator: Vanessa Evans

Book Designer: Louisa Adair

Cover Designer: Louisa Adair

Composition: Tolman Creek

Indexer: Tim Wright

This Book Is Safari Enabled

The Safari® Enabled icon on the cover of your favorite technology book means the book is available through Safari Bookshelf. When you buy this book, you get free access to the online edition for 45 days.

Safari Bookshelf is an electronic reference library that lets you easily search thousands of technical books, find code samples, download chapters, and access technical information whenever and wherever you need it.

To gain 45-day Safari Enabled access to this book:

- Go to http://safari.ciscopress.com/
- Complete the brief registration form
- Enter the coupon code VBAI-CBFC-2HXC-GZCB-CGH8

If you have difficulty registering on Safari Bookshelf or accessing the online edition, please e-mail customer-service@safaribooksonline.com.

CISCO

Americas Headquarters
Cisco Systems, Inc.
170 West Tasman Drive
San Jose, CA 95134-1706
USA
www.cisco.com
Tel: 408 526-4000
800 553-NETS (6387)
Fax: 408 527-0883

Asia Pacific Headquarters
Cisco Systems, Inc.
168 Robinson Road
#28-01 Capital Tower
Singapore 068912
www.cisco.com
Tel: +65 6317 7777
Fax: +65 6317 7799

Europe Headquarters
Cisco Systems International BV
Haarlerbergpark
Haarlerbergweg 13-19
1101 CH Amsterdam
The Netherlands
www-europe.cisco.com
Tel: +31 0 800 020 0791
Fax: +31 0 20 357 1100

Cisco has more than 200 offices worldwide. Addresses, phone numbers, and fax numbers are listed on the Cisco Website at **www.cisco.com/go/offices.**

About the Author

Luc De Ghein, CCIE No. 1897, is an escalation engineer for Cisco Systems in EMEA. Luc has been in the networking industry for 13 years and has been with Cisco for more than 11 years. He provides escalation support to Cisco engineers worldwide and teaches others about IP routing protocols and MPLS technologies. Luc has been a speaker at several Networkers conferences. During the past 7 years, Luc has specialized in the area of MPLS technologies. Before moving to his current position, Luc was a Technical Assistance Center (TAC) customer support engineer for two and a half years, specializing in routing. He has been an escalation engineer for routing and MPLS technologies for more than eight years. Since 1996, Luc has been a Cisco Certified Internetwork Expert (CCIE). He is certified as both a Routing and Switching CCIE and as a Service Provider CCIE.

About the Technical Reviewers

Mohammad Miri is currently employed by Alcatel NA. He has more than 14 years of experience in design and implementation of IP networks for Telecom and Mobile providers involving broadband, narrowband, and MPLS and traffic engineering applications over IP. He received his computer science degree in 1989.

Ivan Pepelnjak, CCIE No. 1354, is a 25-year veteran of the networking industry. He has more than 10 years of experience in designing, installing, troubleshooting, and operating large service provider and enterprise WAN and LAN networks and is currently chief technology advisor at NIL Data Communications focusing on advanced IP-based networks and web technologies. His books published by Cisco Press include *EIGRP Network Design Solutions* and *MPLS and VPN Architectures* (volumes I and II).

Hari Rakotoranto is currently product manager for GMPLS in ITD at Cisco Systems, Inc. He also works closely with service providers and interoperability bodies (ISOCORE and EANTC) in the field of MPLS on technology deployment and overseeing of future directions. Hari has worked as a software engineer and pre- and post-sales technical consultant on different technologies, including Layer 2/3 switches, routing protocols, network management, and UNIX kernel design. He is an active member of ITU-T SG13, focusing mainly on MPLS, MPLS OAM, and MPLS Management.

Dedication

This book is dedicated to my wife Ania, and to my sons Robbe and Lander.

Acknowledgments

I wish to acknowledge a few people who made this book possible. First, I wish to acknowledge my employer Cisco Systems for providing a great working and learning place. Second, I wish to express my gratitude to the technical reviewers, Mohammad Miri, Ivan Pepelnjak, and Hari Rakotoranto, for their feedback, guidance, suggestions, time, and effort in reviewing this book and ensuring its technical accuracy. Third, I'm grateful for the Cisco Press team—Jim Schachterle, Raina Han, Dayna Isley, Mary Beth Ray, Jill Batistick, Karen A. Gill, Seth Kerney, and Allison Johnson—for their support in getting this book published and for their patience with me. Last, but not least, I'd like to thank my family for their support and understanding.

Contents at a Glance

Contents

Icons Used in This Book

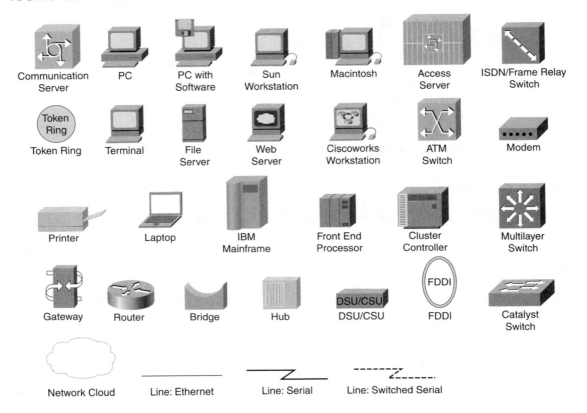

Command Syntax Conventions

The conventions used to present command syntax in this book are the same conventions used in the Cisco IOS Command Reference. The Command Reference describes these conventions as follows:

- **Boldface** indicates commands and keywords that are entered literally as shown. In actual configuration examples and output (not general command syntax), boldface indicates commands that are manually input by the user (such as a **show** command).

- *Italics* indicate arguments for which you supply actual values.

- Vertical bars (|) separate alternative, mutually exclusive elements.

- Square brackets [ ] indicate optional elements.

- Braces { } indicate a required choice.

- Braces within brackets [{ }] indicate a required choice within an optional element.

Introduction

As an escalation engineer, I experienced the boom of Multiprotocol Label Switching (MPLS) networking first hand. I saw the first trials of MPLS in service provider networks and saw MPLS successfully expanding further into enterprise networks. In addition, I witnessed new MPLS technologies coming into existence, which the networking industry embraced quickly. The first deployments of these new MPLS technologies were not always flawless, but they were always interesting.

The success of MPLS is undoubtedly a result of the fact that it enables the network to carry all kinds of traffic, ranging from IP traffic to Voice over IP (VoIP) traffic to Layer 2 traffic. MPLS is the means for an IP network to consolidate many networks into one. MPLS can consolidate the ATM, Frame Relay, Voice, and IP networks into one unified network infrastructure, thereby generating a huge cost advantage.

MPLS has matured a lot and is a stable technology, seeing many new deployments and new features. Given the fact that MPLS is based on IP, and the Internet is based on IP technology, it seems that the future of MPLS is ensured for quite a while to come.

Configuring MPLS on Cisco IOS is relatively simple, but much knowledge is needed to understand what to configure and how to troubleshoot when the MPLS network has problems. This book gives you this knowledge and highlights things from my own experience to warn you of pitfalls.

Goals and Methods

The purpose of this book is to make a network engineer a qualified MPLS network engineer. To accomplish this goal, this book starts by explaining the fundamentals of MPLS. It covers the principles and theory of MPLS thoroughly. It continues by explaining the MPLS applications that made MPLS so popular, including MPLS VPN, MPLS traffic engineering (TE), Any Transport over MPLS (AToM), and Virtual Private LAN Service (VPLS). The theory is accompanied by configuration examples, detailing how to implement and troubleshoot MPLS and its applications in Cisco IOS. When you have finished reading this book, you will have a comprehensive and useable MPLS knowledge. This book contains theory, Cisco IOS commands, and troubleshooting information so that you can deploy, administrate, design, and troubleshoot any MPLS network.

This book was written in a progressive manner, so if in doubt, read this book from beginning to end. That is the logical way of reading this book. Only the reader who already has some MPLS background should jump to any chapter and start reading it.

Who Should Read This Book?

This book lays down the fundamentals of the operation of MPLS and its deployment. As such, it introduces the networking professional to all facets of MPLS. I also tried to cover many MPLS applications and write down the things I learned and experienced the hard way. The aim of this book is to be both an introduction to MPLS for people who have had some networking experience but have not mastered MPLS yet and an opportunity to explain some of the more difficult and lesser-known aspects of MPLS. As such, this book can be used by network engineers, network administrators, network analysts, students, teachers, network managers, and network designers alike.

I tried to find a balance between theory and practical examples. The book was written with Cisco IOS in mind, and there are many configuration examples of Cisco IOS. However, even for the people who are not familiar with Cisco IOS, this book can be a great help in getting to understand MPLS thoroughly.

The reader should be familiar with IP and IP routing, because having a basic knowledge of those is a prerequisite to this book.

Finally, this book is especially useful to people who are preparing for the CCIE Service Provider written exam and the CCIE Service Provider lab exam, because they have a heavy emphasis on MPLS.

How This Book Is Organized

This book has 15 chapters and one appendix and is organized in two parts. Also available are online supplemental materials that you can find on the website, including an appendix on static MPLS labels.

Although each chapter has its own topic and stands alone, it is best to read this book in sequential order. Only if you are an MPLS-experienced reader will you be able to jump to any chapter from Part II without problem. Even if you fit into that category, you might want to browse through the chapters of Part I to refresh your memory and then proceed to Part II, which holds the chapters that require a thorough understanding of the MPLS fundamentals. If you cannot get enough of MPLS, you can find online supplements of Chapters 4, 7, 8, 9, and 10 at http://www.ciscopress.com/title/1587051974. Make sure you read the corresponding chapter in this book before reading the online chapter supplement. Appendix B, "Static MPLS Labels," is available only on this website.

Part I, "Fundamentals of MPLS," discusses how MPLS came about and explains its fundamentals.

- **Chapter 1, "The Evolution of MPLS"**—This chapter is an introduction to MPLS and how it came about. It also covers a brief overview of the most important applications of MPLS.

Chapters 2 through 6, on the fundamentals of MPLS, cover the following topics:

- **Chapter 2, "MPLS Architecture"**—This chapter focuses on the basic building blocks of MPLS.

- **Chapter 3, "Forwarding Labeled Packets"**—This chapter describes the label forwarding and the usage of the reserved MPLS labels.

- **Chapter 4, "Label Distribution Protocol"**—This chapter describes the Label Distribution Protocol (LDP) and how a router uses it to advertise MPLS labels.

- **Chapter 5, "MPLS and ATM Architecture"**—This chapter describes all the specifics of having an MPLS-enabled ATM network.

- **Chapter 6, "Cisco Express Forwarding"**—This chapter describes the Cisco Express Forwarding (CEF) architecture, which is a packet forwarding or switching method that Cisco IOS uses and MPLS needs.

Part II, "Advanced MPLS Topics," covers the MPLS applications, quality of service (QoS), and troubleshooting:

- **Chapter 7, "MPLS VPN"**—This chapter discusses the most popular of all MPLS appications: MPLS VPN. It explains the complete architecture of MPLS VPN.

- **Chapter 8, "MPLS Traffic Engineering"**—This chapter looks at how traffic engineering (TE) is implemented with the MPLS technology.

- **Chapter 9, "IPv6 over MPLS"**—This chapter looks at how the IPv6 protocol can be transported across an MPLS backbone network.

- **Chapter 10, "Any Transport over MPLS"**—This chapter discusses how the MPLS network can transport Layer 2 services.

- **Chapter 11, "Virtual Private LAN Service"**—This chapter describes how an Ethernet LAN can be emulated across an MPLS backbone network.

- **Chapter 12, "MPLS and Quality of Service"**—This chapter discusses how the MPLS network can provide QoS and how the QoS information is propagated in MPLS networks.

- **Chapter 13, "Troubleshooting MPLS Networks"**—This chapter looks at various troubleshooting techniques and tools that you can use in MPLS networks.

- **Chapter 14, "MPLS Operation and Maintenance"**—This chapter focuses on MPLS Operation and Maintenance (OAM) and how it is used to detect operational failures, accounting, and performance measurement in the MPLS network.

- **Chapter 15, "The Future of MPLS"**—This chapter provides a brief insight into the future of MPLS and likely enhancements and developments that could be made to MPLS.

- **Appendix A, "Answers to the Chapter Review Questions"**—This appendix provides the answers to the questions at the end of each chapter.

About the Cisco Press Website for This Book

Cisco Press provides additional content that you can access by registering your individual book at the Ciscopress.com website. To register this book, go to http://www.ciscopress.com/bookstore/register.asp and enter the book ISBN, which is located on the back cover. You are then prompted to log in or join Ciscopress.com to continue registration. After you register this book, you see a link to this book listed on your My Registered Books page. Becoming a member and registering is free.

The following supplemental chapters and online appendix are available at this website. These chapters provide more advanced topics to support the concepts in the book.

- Chapter 4 Supplement, "Label Distribution Protocol"

- Chapter 7 Supplement, "MPLS VPN"

- Chapter 8 Supplement, "MPLS Traffic Engineering"

- Chapter 9 Supplement, "IPv6 over MPLS"

- Chapter 10 Supplement, "Any Transport over MPLS"

- Appendix B, "Static MPLS Labels"

Fundamentals of MPLS

What You Will Learn

After completing this chapter, you will be able to do the following:

- Explain the driving factors behind MPLS

- List the benefits of forwarding labeled packets instead of forwarding IP packets

- Explain the applications of MPLS that have received widespread acceptance

CHAPTER 1

The Evolution of MPLS

Multiprotocol Label Switching (MPLS) has been around for several years. It is a popular networking technology that uses labels attached to packets to forward them through the network. This chapter explains why MPLS became so popular in such a short time.

This chapter starts with a definition of MPLS. It also provides a short overview of pre-MPLS network solutions. The benefits of MPLS are listed, and the end of the chapter explains briefly the history of MPLS in Cisco IOS.

Definition of MPLS

The MPLS labels are advertised between routers so that they can build a label-to-label mapping. These labels are attached to the IP packets, enabling the routers to forward the traffic by looking at the label and not the destination IP address. The packets are forwarded by label switching instead of by IP switching.

The label switching technique is not new. Frame Relay and ATM use it to move frames or cells throughout a network. In Frame Relay, the frame can be any length, whereas in ATM, a fixed-length cell consists of a header of 5 bytes and a payload of 48 bytes. The header of the ATM cell and the Frame Relay frame refer to the virtual circuit that the cell or frame resides on. The similarity between Frame Relay and ATM is that at each hop throughout the network, the "label" value in the header is changed. This is different from the forwarding of IP packets. When a router forwards an IP packet, it does not change a value that pertains to the destination of the packet; that is, it does not change the destination IP address of the packet. The fact that the MPLS labels are used to forward the packets and no longer the destination IP address have led to the popularity of MPLS. These benefits—such as the better integration of IP over ATM and the popular MPLS virtual private network (VPN) application—are explained in the "Benefits of MPLS" section of this chapter.

Pre-MPLS Protocols

Before MPLS, the most popular WAN protocols were ATM and Frame Relay. Cost-effective WAN networks were built to carry various protocols. With the popularity of the Internet, IP became the most popular protocol. IP was everywhere. VPNs were created over these WAN protocols. Customers leased ATM links and Frame Relay links or used leased lines and built their own private network over it. Because the routers of the provider supplied a Layer 2 service toward the Layer 3 customer routers, the separation and isolation between different customer networks were guaranteed. These kinds of networks are referred to as *overlay networks*.

Overlay networks are still used today, but many customers are now using the MPLS VPN service. The next section details the benefits of MPLS. It will help you understand why MPLS is a great benefit to the service providers that deploy it and to their customers.

Benefits of MPLS

This section explains briefly the benefits of running MPLS in your network. These benefits include the following:

- The use of one unified network infrastructure

- Better IP over ATM integration

- Border Gateway Protocol (BGP)-free core

- The peer-to-peer model for MPLS VPN

- Optimal traffic flow

- Traffic engineering

Consider first a bogus reason to run MPLS. This is a reason that might look reasonable initially, but it is not a good reason to deploy MPLS.

Bogus Benefit

One of the early reasons for a label-swapping protocol was the need for speed. Switching IP packets on a CPU was considered to be slower than switching labeled packets by looking up just the label on top of a packet. A router forwards an IP packet by looking up the destination IP address in the IP header and finding the best match in the routing table. This lookup depends on the implementation of the specific vendor of that router. However, because IP addresses can be unicast or multicast and have four octets, the lookup can be complex. A complex lookup means that a forwarding decision for an IP packet can take some time.

Although some people thought that looking up a simple label value in a table rather than looking up the IP address would be a faster way of switching packets, the progress made in switching IP packets in hardware made this argument a moot one. These days, the links on routers can have a bandwidth up to 40 Gbps. A router that has several high-speed links would not be able to switch all the IP packets just by using the CPU to make the forwarding decision. The CPU exists mainly to handle the control plane.

The *control plane* is the set of protocols that helps to set up the data or forwarding plane. The main components of the control plane are the routing protocols, the routing table, and other control or signaling protocols used to provision the data plane. The *data plane* is the packet forwarding path through a router or switch. The switching of the packets—or the forwarding plane—these days is done on specifically built hardware, or application-specific integrated circuits (ASIC). The use of ASICs in the forwarding plane of a router has led to IP packets being switched as fast as labeled packets. Therefore, if your sole reason for implementing MPLS in your network is to pursue the faster switching of packets through the network, it is a bogus reason.

The Use of One Unified Network Infrastructure

With MPLS, the idea is to label ingress packets based on their destination address or other preconfigured criteria and switch all the traffic over a common infrastructure. This is the great advantage of MPLS. One of the reasons that IP became the only protocol to dominate the networking world is because many technologies can be transported over it. Not only is data transported over IP, but also telephony.

By using MPLS with IP, you can extend the possibilities of what you can transport. Adding labels to the packet enables you to carry other protocols than just IP over an MPLS-enabled Layer 3 IP backbone, similarly to what was previously possible only with Frame Relay or ATM Layer 2 networks. MPLS can transport IPv4, IPv6, Ethernet, High-Level Data Link Control (HDLC), PPP, and other Layer 2 technologies.

The feature whereby any Layer 2 frame is carried across the MPLS backbone is called *Any Transport over MPLS* (AToM). The routers that are switching the AToM traffic do not need to be aware of the MPLS payload; they just need to be able to switch the labeled traffic by looking at the label on top of it. In essence, MPLS label switching is a simple method of switching multiple protocols in one network. You need to have a forwarding table consisting of incoming labels to be swapped by outgoing labels and a next hop. Refer to Chapter 3, "Forwarding Labeled Packets," for further details on forwarding labeled traffic.

In short, AToM enables the service provider to provide the same Layer 2 service toward the customers as with any specific non-MPLS network. At the same time, the service provider needs only one unified network infrastructure to carry all kinds of customer traffic.

Better IP over ATM Integration

In the previous decade, IP won the battle over all other networking Layer 3 protocols, such as AppleTalk, Internetwork Packet Exchange (IPX), and DECnet. IP is relatively simple and omnipresent. A much-hyped Layer 2 protocol at the time was ATM. Although ATM as an end-to-end protocol—or desktop-to-desktop protocol—as some predicted, never happened, ATM did have plenty of success, but the success was limited to its use as a WAN protocol in the core of service provider networks. Many of these service providers also deployed IP backbones. The integration of IP over ATM was not trivial. To better integrate IP over ATM, the networking community came up with a few solutions.

One solution was to implement IP over ATM according to the well-known RFC 1483, "Multiprotocol Encapsulation over ATM Adaptation Layer 5," which specifies how to encapsulate multiple routed and bridged protocols over ATM adaptation Layer (AAL) 5. In this solution, all ATM circuits had to be manually established, and all mappings between IP next hops and ATM endpoints had to be manually configured on every ATM-attached router in the network.

> **NOTE**   RFC 1483 became obsolete by RFC 2684.
> You can find all RFCs online at http://www.ietf.org/rfc/rfc*NNNN*.txt, where *NNNN* is the RFC number prefixed with zeroes as necessary to make a four-digit number. If you do not know the number of the RFC, you can find it at the IETF RFC index at http://www.ietf.org/iesg/1rfc_index.txt.

Another method was to implement LAN Emulation (LANE). Ethernet had become a popular Layer 2 technology at the edge of the network, but it never achieved the scalability or reliability requirements of large service provider networks. LANE basically makes your network look like an emulated Ethernet network. This means that several Ethernet segments were bridged together as if the ATM WAN network in the middle were an Ethernet switch.

Finally, Multiprotocol over ATM (MPOA), which is a specification by the ATM Forum, gives you the tightest integration of IP over ATM but also the most complex solution.

All these methods were cumbersome to implement and troubleshoot. A better solution for integrating IP over ATM was one of the driving reasons for the invention of MPLS. The prerequisites for MPLS on ATM switches were that the ATM switches had to become more intelligent. The ATM switches had to run an IP routing protocol and implement a label distribution protocol. Refer to Chapter 5, "MPLS and ATM Architecture," for more details on MPLS on ATM switches.

BGP-Free Core

When the IP network of a service provider must forward traffic, each router must look up the destination IP address of the packet. If the packets are sent to destinations that are external to the service provider network, those external IP prefixes must be present in the routing table of each router. BGP carries external prefixes, such as the customer prefixes or the Internet prefixes. This means that all routers in the service provider network must run BGP.

MPLS, however, enables the forwarding of packets based on a label lookup rather than a lookup of the IP addresses. MPLS enables a label to be associated with an egress router rather than with the destination IP address of the packet. The label is the information attached to the packet that tells every intermediate router to which egress edge router it must be forwarded. The core routers no longer need to have the information to forward the packets based on the destination IP address. Thus, the core routers in the service provider network no longer need to run BGP.

The router at the edge of the MPLS network still needs to look at the destination IP address of the packet and hence still needs to run BGP. Each BGP prefix on the ingress MPLS routers has a BGP next-hop IP address associated with it. This BGP next-hop IP address is an IP address of an egress MPLS router. The label that is associated with an IP packet is the label that is associated with this BGP next-hop IP address. Because every core router forwards a packet based on the attached MPLS label that is associated with the BGP next-hop IP address, each BGP next-hop IP address of an egress MPLS router must be known to all core routers. Any interior gateway routing protocol, such as OSPF or ISIS, can accomplish this task.

Figure 1-1 shows the MPLS network with BGP on the edge routers only.

Figure 1-1 *BGP-Free MPLS Network*

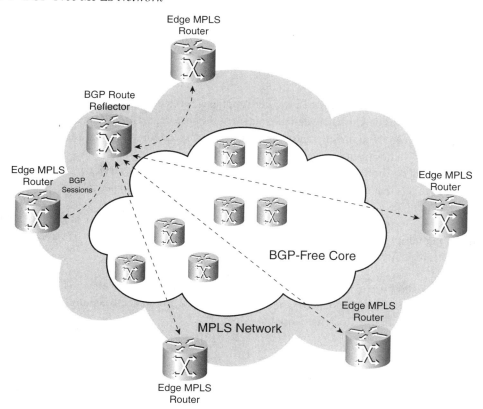

An Internet service provider (ISP) that has 200 routers in its core network needs to have BGP running on all 200 routers. If MPLS is implemented on the network, only the edge routers—which might be 50 or so routers—need to run BGP.

All routers in the core of the network are now forwarding labeled packets, without doing an IP lookup, so they are now relieved from the burden of running BGP. Because the full Internet routing table is well above 150,000 routes, not having to run BGP on all routers is a serious consideration. Routers without the full Internet routing table need a lot less memory. You can run the core routers without the complexity of having to run BGP on them.

Peer-to-Peer VPN Model Versus Overlay VPN Model

A VPN is a network that emulates a private network over a common infrastructure. The private network requires all customer sites to be able to interconnect and be completely separate from other VPNs. The VPN usually belongs to one company and has several sites interconnected across the common service provider infrastructure.

Service providers can deploy two major VPN models to provide VPN services to their customers:

- Overlay VPN model

- Peer-to-peer VPN model

Overlay VPN Model

In the overlay model, the service provider supplies a service of point-to-point links or virtual circuits across his network between the routers of the customer. The customer routers form routing peering between them directly across the links or virtual circuits from the service provider. The routers or switches from the service provider carry the customer data across the service provider network, but no routing peering occurs between a customer and a service provider router. The result of this is that the service provider routers never see the customer routes.

These point-to-point services could be of Layer 1, 2, or even 3. Examples of Layer 1 are time-division multiplexing (TDM), E1, E3, SONET, and SDH links. Examples of Layer 2 are virtual circuits created by X.25, ATM, or Frame Relay.

Figure 1-2 shows an example of an overlay network build on Frame Relay. In the service provider network are Frame Relay switches that set up the virtual circuits between the customer routers on the edge of the Frame Relay network.

Figure 1-2 *Overlay Network on Frame Relay*

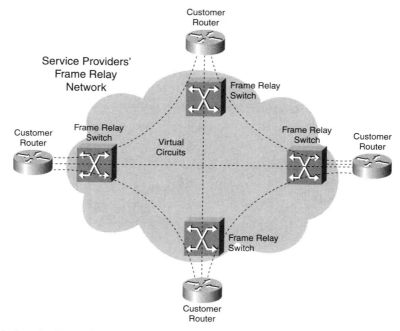

Considering the Layer 3 routing (IP) and peering from the customer viewpoint, the customer routers appear to be directly connected. Figure 1-3 shows this.

Figure 1-3 *Overlay Network: Customer Routing Peering*

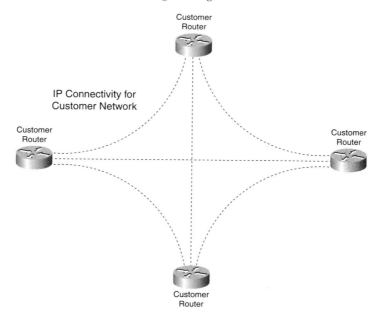

The overlay service can also be provided over the IP Layer 3 protocol. Most commonly used tunnels to build the overlay network on IP are generic routing encapsulation (GRE) tunnels. These tunnels encapsulate the traffic with a GRE header and an IP header. The GRE header, among other things, indicates what the transported protocol is. The IP header is used to route the packet through the service provider network. Figure 1-4 shows an example of an overlay network with GRE tunnels. One advantage of GRE tunnels is that they can route traffic other than IP traffic.

Figure 1-4 *Overlay Network on GRE Tunnels*

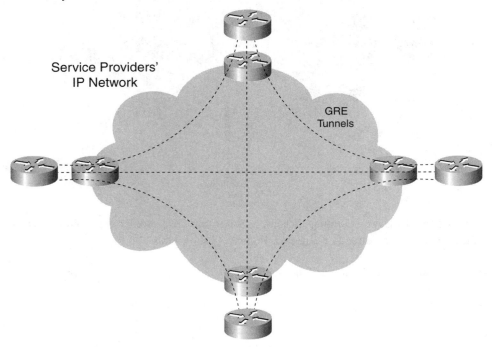

It is possible to use IPsec on the GRE tunnels and thus provide security as the data is encrypted.

Peer-to-Peer VPN Model

In the peer-to-peer VPN model, the service provider routers carry the customer data across the network, but they also participate in the customer routing. In other words, the service provider routers peer directly with the customer routers at Layer 3. The result is that one routing protocol neighborship or adjacency exists between the customer and the service provider router. Figure 1-5 shows the concept of the peer-to-peer VPN model.

Figure 1-5 *Peer-to-Peer VPN Model*

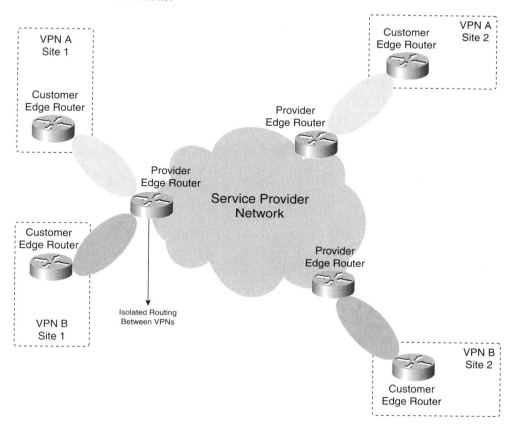

Before MPLS existed, the peer-to-peer VPN model could be achieved by creating the IP routing peering between the customer and service provider routers. The VPN model also requires privateness or isolation between the different customers. You can achieve this by configuring packet filters (access lists) to control the data to and from the customer routers. Another way to achieve a form of privateness is to configure route filters to advertise routes or stop routes from being advertised to the customer routes. Or, you can deploy both methods at the same time.

Before MPLS came into being, the overlay VPN model was deployed much more commonly than the peer-to-peer VPN model. The peer-to-peer VPN model demanded a lot from provisioning because adding one customer site demanded many configuration changes at many sites. MPLS VPN is one application of MPLS that made the peer-to-peer VPN model much easier to implement. Adding or removing a customer site is now easier to configure and thus demands much less time and effort. With MPLS VPN, one customer router, called the *customer edge* (CE) *router*, peers at the IP Layer with at least one service provider router, called the *provider edge* (PE) *router*.

The privateness in MPLS VPN networks is achieved by using the concept of virtual routing/ forwarding (VRF) and the fact that the data is forwarded in the backbone as labeled packets. The VRFs ensure that the routing information from the different customers is kept separate, and the MPLS in the backbone ensures that the packets are forwarding based on the label information and not the information in the IP header. Figure 1-6 shows the concept of VRFs and forwarding labeled packets in the backbone of a network that is running MPLS VPN.

Figure 1-6 *MPLS VPN with VRF*

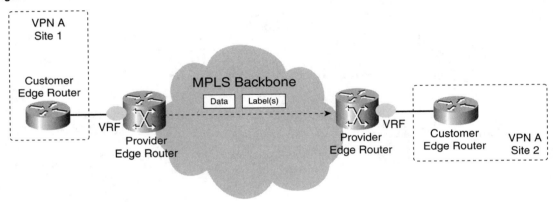

Figure 1-7 shows the concept of the peer-to-peer VPN model applied to MPLS VPN.

Figure 1-7 *Peer-to-Peer MPLS VPN Model*

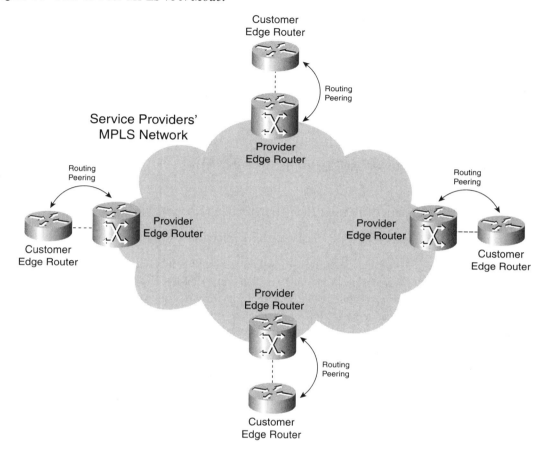

Adding one customer site means that on the PE router, only the peering with the CE router must be added. You do not have to hassle with creating many virtual circuits as with the overlay model or with configuring packet filters or route filters with the peer-to-peer VPN model over an IP network. This is the benefit of MPLS VPN for the service provider.

Most service provider customers have a hub-and-spoke network, whereas some have a fully meshed network around the service provider backbone. Others have something in between. The benefit of MPLS VPN for the customer is at its greatest when the customer has a fully meshed network. Refer to Figure 1-2 to see a fully meshed customer network around a Frame Relay network, and compare that to the same customer network with MPLS VPN in Figure 1-7. In Figure 1-2, each customer edge router peers with $n-1$ other customer edge routers—where n is the total number of customer edge routers. In Figure 1-7, each customer edge router peers with only one service provider edge router.

Another benefit for the service provider is that it only needs to provision the link between the PE and CE routers. With the overlay model, the service provider needs to provision the links or virtual circuits between the sites. It is much easier to predict the traffic and thus the bandwidth requirement of one site than to predict the complete traffic model between all the customer sites.

It is only fair to list the disadvantages of the peer-to-peer VPN model compared to the overlay VPN model:

- The customer must share the routing responsibility with the service provider.

- The edge devices of the service provider have an added burden.

The first disadvantage is that the customer must have a routing peer with the service provider. The customer does not control its network end to end anymore on Layer 3 and regarding the IP routing, as with the overlay model. The second disadvantage is for the service provider. The burden for the service provider is the added task of the edge device—the PE router. The service provider is responsible for the scalability and routing convergence of the customer networks because the PE routers must be able to carry all the routes of the many customers while providing timely routing convergence.

Optimal Traffic Flow

Because the ATM or Frame Relay switches are purely Layer 2 devices, the routers interconnect through them by means of virtual circuits created between them. For any router to send traffic directly to any other router at the edge, a virtual circuit must be created between them directly. Creating the virtual circuits manually is tedious. In any case, if the requirement is the any-to-any connection between sites, it is necessary to have a full mesh of virtual circuits between the sites, which is cumbersome and costly. If the sites are only interconnected as in Figure 1-8, the traffic from CE1 to CE3 must first go through CE2.

Figure 1-8 *Non-Fully Meshed Overlay ATM Network*

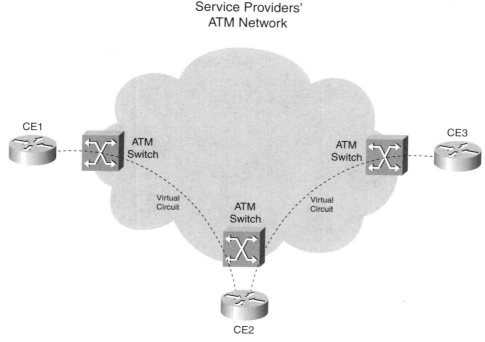

The result is that the traffic crosses the ATM backbone twice and takes a detour through the router CE2. When using MPLS VPN as discussed in the previous section, the traffic flows directly—thus optimally—between all customer sites. For the traffic to flow optimally between the sites in the case of an overlay VPN model, all sites must be interconnected, thus demanding a fully meshed design of links or virtual circuits.

Traffic Engineering

The basic idea behind traffic engineering is to optimally use the network infrastructure, including links that are underutilized, because they do not lie on the preferred path. This means that traffic engineering must provide the possibility to steer traffic through the network on paths different from the preferred path, which is the least-cost path provided by IP routing. The least-cost path is the shortest path as computed by the dynamic routing protocol. With traffic engineering implemented in the MPLS network, you could have the traffic that is destined for a particular prefix or with a particular quality of service flow from point A to point B along a path that is different from the least-cost path. The result is that the traffic can be spread more evenly over the available links in the network and make more use of underutilized links in the network. Figure 1-9 shows an example of this.

Figure 1-9 *Traffic Engineering Example 1*

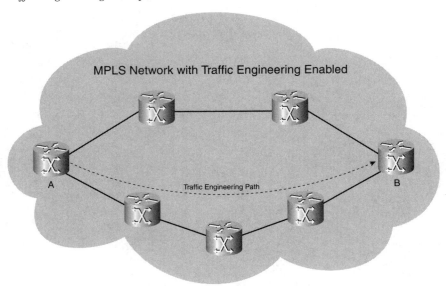

As the operator of the MPLS-with-traffic-engineering-enabled network, you can steer the traffic from A to B over the bottom path, which is not the shortest path between A and B (four hops versus three hops on the top path). As such, you can send the traffic over links that might otherwise not be used much. You can guide the traffic in this network onto the bottom path by changing the routing protocols metrics. Examine Figure 1-10.

Figure 1-10 *Traffic Engineering Example 2*

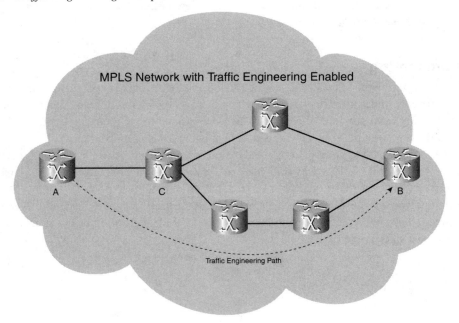

If this network is an IP-only network, you cannot have router C send the traffic along the bottom path by configuring something on router A. The router C decision to send traffic on the top or bottom path is solely its own decision. If you enable MPLS traffic engineering in this network, you can have router A send the traffic toward router B along the bottom path. The MPLS traffic engineering forces router C to forward the traffic A-B onto the bottom path. This can be done in MPLS because of the label forwarding mechanism. The head end router of a traffic-engineered path—here router A—is the router that specifies the complete path that the traffic will take through the MPLS network. Because it is the head end router that specifies the path, traffic engineering is also referred to as a form of *source-based routing*. The label that is attached to the packet by the head end router makes the packet flow along the path as specified by the head end router. No intermediate router forwards the packet onto another path.

An extra advantage of running MPLS traffic engineering is the possibility of Fast ReRouting (FRR). FRR allows you to reroute labeled traffic around a link or router that has become unavailable. The rerouting of traffic happens in less than 50 ms, which is fast even for standards of today.

History of MPLS in Cisco IOS

This section gives you a brief chronological overview of the MPLS implementation in Cisco IOS from its start in 1998.

Tag Switching to MPLS

Cisco Systems started off with putting labels on top of IP packets in what was then called *tag switching*. The first implementation was released in Cisco IOS 11.1(17)CT in 1998. A tag was the name for what is now known as a *label*. This implementation could assign tags to networks from the routing table and put those tags on top of the packet that was destined for that network. Tag switching built a Tag Forwarding Information Base (TFIB), which is, in essence, a table that stores input-to-output label mappings. Each tag-switching router had to match the tag on the incoming packet, swap it with the outgoing tag, and forward the packet.

Later on, the IETF standardized tag switching into MPLS. The IETF released the first RFC on MPLS—RFC 2547, "BGP/MPLS VPNs"—in 1999. The result of this was that much of the terminology changed. Table 1-1 shows an overview of the old and new terminology.

Table 1-1 *Old and New Terminology for Tag Switching/MPLS*

Old Terminology	New Terminology
Tag switching	MPLS
Tag	Label
TDP[1]	LDP[2]
TFIB[3]	LFIB[4]
TSR[5]	LSR[6]
TSC[7]	LSC[8]
TSP[9]	LSP[10]

[1] TDP = Tag Distribution Protocol
[2] LDP = Label Distribution Protocol
[3] TFIB = tag forwarding information base
[4] LFIB = label forwarding information base
[5] TSR = tag switching router
[6] LSR = label switching router
[7] TSC = tag switch controller
[8] LSC = label switch controller
[9] TSP = tag switched path
[10] LSP = label switched path

NOTE Most of the tag switching technology was adopted into MPLS standards. TDP was used as the basis for LDP. LDP has the same functionality as TDP, but they are different protocols.

The purpose of Table 1-1 is to make you aware of the change in terminology. At this point, you do not need to be aware what each acronym means. The acronyms are explained further in the following chapters.

This book uses the new terminology. However, you might still come across the old terminology from time to time, especially in the output taken from the routers.

MPLS Applications

The first release of tag switching in Cisco IOS allowed for traffic engineering, but it was first called Routing with Resource Reservation (RRR or R^3). The first implementation of traffic engineering in Cisco IOS was static. This meant that you as the operator of the router had to configure all the hops that a certain flow of traffic had to follow through the network. A later implementation made traffic engineering more dynamic by using extensions to the link state routing protocols. The operator no longer had to statically configure the traffic engineering tunnels hop by hop. The link state routing protocol carried extra information, so that the tunnels could be created in a more dynamic way. This greatly reduced the amount of work the operator had to do, which made MPLS traffic engineering more popular.

Until the coming of MPLS VPN, tag switching or MPLS was not widespread. When Cisco came out with Cisco IOS Software Release 12.0(5)T, the first Cisco IOS release containing support for MPLS VPN in 1999, it became an instant success because many service providers immediately started to implement MPLS VPN. To date, the MPLS VPN application is still the most popular of all the MPLS applications.

The next big addition to the family of MPLS applications was AToM. Cisco implemented AToM in Cisco IOS Release 12.0(10)ST, released in 2000, to carry ATM AAL 5 over an MPLS backbone. Later, many more encapsulation types were added to AToM in Cisco IOS. Examples of Layer 2 encapsulation types that can be carried over an AToM network today are Frame Relay, ATM, PPP, HDLC, Ethernet, and 802.1Q. Particularly, the transport of Ethernet across the MPLS backbone has seen a growing success today. However, AToM is restricted in that it carries these Ethernet frames across the MPLS backbone in a point-to-point fashion only. Virtual Private LAN Service (VPLS) enables the forwarding of the Ethernet frames in a point-to-multipoint fashion. In essence, VPLS is the Layer 2 service that emulates a LAN across an MPLS-enabled network. The first implementation of VPLS in Cisco IOS was released in early 2004 on the 7600 platform in Cisco IOS release 12.2(17d)SXB. VPLS is explained in detail in Chapter 11, "Virtual Private LAN Service."

Summary

This chapter introduced you to the world of MPLS and gave you an overview of the history of MPLS in Cisco IOS. The forwarding of labeled packets has advantages over the forwarding of IP packets because it combines the benefits of label switching that are well established in Frame Relay and ATM technologies with the ease of deployment of IP networks. This new method of forwarding packets fueled the invention of successful new applications using the forwarding based on labels: MPLS VPN, traffic engineering, AToM, and VPLS.

Chapter Review Questions

1.   What are the MPLS applications mentioned in this chapter?

2.   Name three advantages of running MPLS in a service provider network.

3.   What are the advantages of the MPLS VPN solution for the service provider over all the other VPN solutions?

4.   Name the four technologies that can be used to carry IP over ATM.

5.   Name two pre-MPLS protocols that use label switching.

6.   What do the ATM switches need to run so that they can operate MPLS?

7.   How do you ensure optimal traffic flow between all the customer sites in an ATM or Frame Relay overlay network?

What You Will Learn

After completing this chapter, you will be able to do the following:

- Explain the format of an MPLS label

- Describe a stack of MPLS labels and explain where it resides in the frame

- Tell what a label switch router is and what functions it needs to perform

- Describe what a label switched path and a Forwarding Equivalence Class are

- Explain the difference between LIB and LFIB and how they are used in MPLS networks

- Determine how labels are distributed in an MPLS network

CHAPTER 2

MPLS Architecture

This chapter helps you to understand how MPLS operates. By the time you finish this chapter, you will have a solid understanding of the building blocks of MPLS and an excellent start for the other chapters in this book.

MPLS stands for Multiprotocol Label Switching. The *multiprotocol* aspect of MPLS was fulfilled after the initial implementation of MPLS in Cisco IOS. Although at first only IPv4 was being label switched, later on more protocols followed. In Cisco IOS, you can now label IPv6 packets, too, as described in Chapter 9, "IPv6 over MPLS." Chapter 10, "Any Transport over MPLS," describes how to label and transport Layer 2 frames over an MPLS backbone.

Label switching indicates that the packets switched are no longer IPv4 packets, IPv6 packets, or even Layer 2 frames when switched, but they are labeled. The most important item to MPLS is the label. This chapter explains what the label is used for, how it is used, and how it is distributed in a network.

Introducing MPLS Labels

One MPLS label is a field of 32 bits with a certain structure. Figure 2-1 shows the syntax of one MPLS label.

Figure 2-1 *Syntax of One MPLS Label*

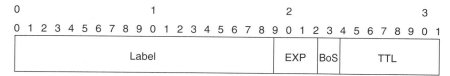

The first 20 bits are the label value. This value can be between 0 and $2^{20}-1$, or 1,048,575. However, the first 16 values are exempted from normal use; that is, they have a special meaning. The bits 20 to 22 are the three experimental (EXP) bits. These bits are used solely for quality of service (QoS).

> **NOTE** These bits are named "experimental" for historical reasons. At one time, nobody knew what they were going to be used for. Chapter 12, "MPLS and Quality of Service," is devoted to ways you can use these three experimental bits.

Bit 23 is the Bottom of Stack (BoS) bit. It is 0, unless this is the bottom label in the stack. If so, the BoS bit is set to 1. The stack is the collection of labels that are found on top of the packet. The stack can consist of just one label, or it might have more. The number of labels (that is, the 32-bit field) that you can find in the stack is limitless, although you should seldom see a stack that consists of four or more labels.

Bits 24 to 31 are the eight bits used for Time To Live (TTL). This TTL has the same function as the TTL found in the IP header. It is simply decreased by 1 at each hop, and its main function is to avoid a packet being stuck in a routing loop. If a routing loop occurs and no TTL is present, the packet loops forever. If the TTL of the label reaches 0, the packet is discarded.

The next sections describe label stacking and the placement of the label stack in a frame.

Label Stacking

MPLS-capable routers might need more than one label on top of the packet to route that packet through the MPLS network. This is done by packing the labels into a stack. The first label in the stack is called the *top label*, and the last label is called the *bottom label*. In between, you can have any number of labels. Figure 2-2 shows you the structure of the label stack.

Figure 2-2 *Label Stack*

Label	EXP	0	TTL
Label	EXP	0	TTL
...			
Label	EXP	1	TTL

Notice that the label stack in Figure 2-2 shows that the BoS bit is 0 for all the labels, except the bottom label. For the bottom label, the BoS bit is set to 1.

Some MPLS applications actually need more than one label in the label stack to forward the labeled packets. Two examples of such MPLS applications are MPLS VPN and AToM. Both MPLS VPN and AToM put two labels in the label stack. The reason for doing so is explained in Chapters 7, "MPLS VPN," and 10.

Encoding of MPLS

Where does this label stack reside? The label stack sits in front of the Layer 3 packet—that is, before the header of the transported protocol, but after the Layer 2 header. Often, the MPLS label stack is called the *shim header* because of its placement.

Figure 2-3 shows you the placement of the label stack for labeled packets.

Figure 2-3 *Encapsulation for Labeled Packet*

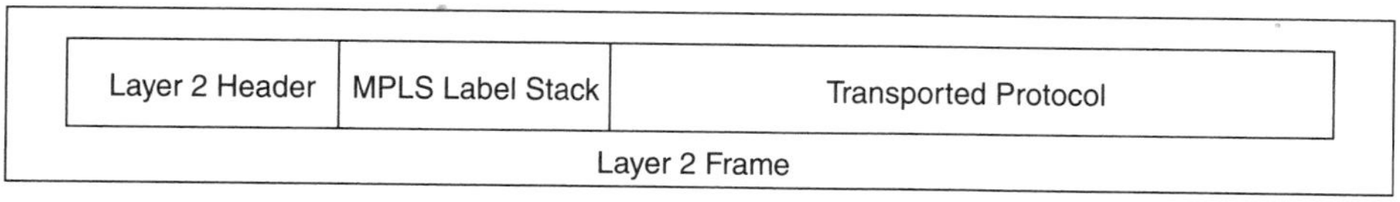

Layer 2 Header	MPLS Label Stack	Transported Protocol
		Layer 2 Frame

The Layer 2 encapsulation of the link can be almost any encapsulation that Cisco IOS supports: PPP, High-Level Data Link Control (HDLC), Ethernet, and so on. Assuming that the transported protocol is IPv4, and the encapsulation of a link is PPP, the label stack is present after the PPP header but before the IPv4 header. Because the label stack in the Layer 2 frame is placed before the Layer 3 header or other transported protocol, you must have new values for the Data Link Layer Protocol field, indicating that what follows the Layer 2 header is an MPLS labeled packet. The Data Link Layer Protocol field is a value indicating what payload type the Layer 2 frame is carrying. Table 2-1 shows you what the names and values are for the Protocol Identifier field in the Layer 2 header for the different Layer 2 encapsulation types.

Table 2-1   *MPLS Protocol Identifier Values for Layer 2 Encapsulation Types*

Layer 2 Encapsulation Type	Layer 2 Protocol Identifier Name	Value (hex)
PPP	PPP Protocol field	0281
Ethernet/802.3 LLC/SNAP encapsulation	Ethertype value	8847
HDLC	Protocol	8847
Frame Relay	NLPID (Network Level Protocol ID)	80

ATM is absent from Table 2-1 because it uses a unique way of encapsulating the label. Refer to Chapter 5, "MPLS and ATM Architecture," for the encapsulation of a labeled packet in ATM. For Frame Relay, the NLPID is 0x80, indicating that an IEEE Subnetwork Access Protocol (SNAP) header is used. The SNAP header is used here in Frame Relay to tell the receiver what protocol Frame Relay carries. The SNAP header contains an Organizationally Unique Identifier (OUI) of 0x000000 and an Ethertype of 0x8847, indicating that the transported protocol is MPLS.

The transported protocol can theoretically be anything; Cisco IOS supports IPv4 and IPv6. In the case of AToM (Chapter 10), you will see that the transported protocol can be any of the most popular Layer 2 protocols, such as Frame Relay, PPP, HDLC, ATM, and Ethernet.

MPLS and the OSI Reference Model

The OSI reference model consists of seven layers. Refer to Figure 2-4 for the OSI reference model.

Figure 2-4 *OSI Reference Model*

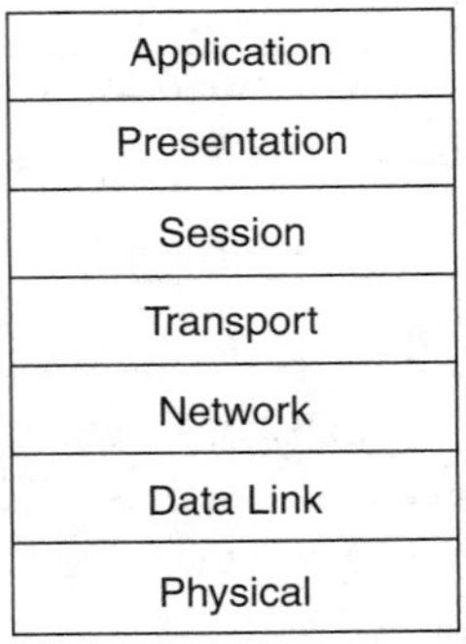

Application
Presentation
Session
Transport
Network
Data Link
Physical

The bottom layer is Layer 1, or the physical layer, and the top layer is Layer 7, or the application layer. Whereas the physical layer concerns the cabling, mechanical, and electrical characteristics, Layer 2, the data link layer, is concerned with the formatting of the frames. Examples of the data link layer are Ethernet, PPP, HDLC, and Frame Relay. The significance of the data link layer is only on one link between two machines, but not beyond. This means that the data link layer header is always replaced by the machine at the other end of the link. Layer 3, the network layer, is concerned with the formatting of packets end to end. It has significance beyond the data link. The most well-known example of a protocol operating at Layer 3 is IP.

Where does MPLS fit in? MPLS is not a Layer 2 protocol because the Layer 2 encapsulation is still present with labeled packets. MPLS also is not really a Layer 3 protocol because the Layer 3 protocol is still present, too. Therefore, MPLS does not fit in the OSI layering too well. Perhaps the easiest thing to do is to view MPLS as the 2.5 layer and be done with it.

Label Switch Router

A label switch router (LSR) is a router that supports MPLS. It is capable of understanding MPLS labels and of receiving and transmitting a labeled packet on a data link. Three kinds of LSRs exist in an MPLS network:

- **Ingress LSRs**—Ingress LSRs receive a packet that is not labeled yet, insert a label (stack) in front of the packet, and send it on a data link.

- **Egress LSRs**—Egress LSRs receive labeled packets, remove the label(s), and send them on a data link. Ingress and egress LSRs are edge LSRs.

- **Intermediate LSRs**—Intermediate LSRs receive an incoming labeled packet, perform an operation on it, switch the packet, and send the packet on the correct data link.

An LSR can do the three operations: pop, push, or swap.

It must be able to pop one or more labels (remove one or more labels from the top of the label stack) before switching the packet out. An LSR must also be able to push one or more labels onto the received packet. If the received packet is already labeled, the LSR pushes one or more labels onto the label stack and switches out the packet. If the packet is not labeled yet, the LSR creates a label stack and pushes it onto the packet. An LSR must also be able to swap a label. This simply means that when a labeled packet is received, the top label of the label stack is swapped with a new label and the packet is switched on the outgoing data link.

An LSR that pushes labels onto a packet that was not labeled yet is called an *imposing LSR* because it is the first LSR to impose labels onto the packet. One that is doing imposition is an ingress LSR. An LSR that removes all labels from the labeled packet before switching out the packet is a *disposing LSR*. One that does disposition is an egress LSR.

In the case of MPLS VPN (see Chapter 7), the ingress and egress LSRs are referred to as provider edge (PE) routers. Intermediate LSRs are referred to as provider (P) routers. The terms PE and P routers have become so popular that they are also used when the MPLS network does not run MPLS VPN.

Label Switched Path

A label switched path (LSP) is a sequence of LSRs that switch a labeled packet through an MPLS network or part of an MPLS network. Basically, the LSP is the path through the MPLS network or a part of it that packets take. The first LSR of an LSP is the ingress LSR for that LSP, whereas the last LSR of the LSP is the egress LSR. All the LSRs in between the ingress and egress LSRs are the intermediate LSRs.

In Figure 2-5, the arrow at the top indicates the direction, because an LSP is unidirectional. The flow of labeled packets in the other direction—right to left—between the same edge LSRs would be another LSP.

Figure 2-5 *An LSP Through an MPLS Network*

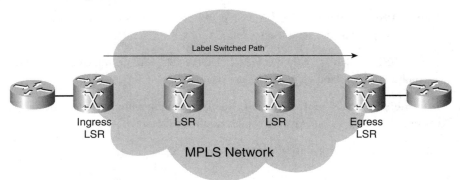

The ingress LSR of an LSP is not necessarily the first router to label the packet. The packet might have already been labeled by a preceding LSR. Such a case would be a *nested LSP*—that is, an LSP inside another LSP. In Figure 2-6, you can see an LSP spanning the whole width of the MPLS network. Another LSP starts at the third LSR and ends on the next-to-last LSR. Therefore, when the packet enters the second LSP on its ingress LSR (this means the third LSR), it is already labeled. This ingress LSR of the nested LSP then pushes a second label onto the packet. The label stack of the packet on the second LSP has two labels now. The top label belongs to the nested LSP, and the bottom label belongs to the LSP that spans the entire MPLS network. In Chapter 8, "MPLS Traffic Engineering," you will see an example of a nested LSP. A backup traffic engineering (TE) tunnel is an example of such a nested LSP.

Figure 2-6 *Nested LSP*

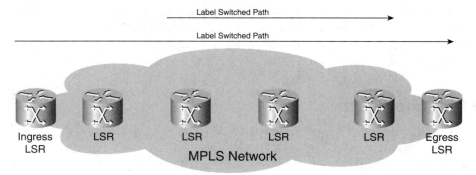

Forwarding Equivalence Class

A Forwarding Equivalence Class (FEC) is a group or flow of packets that are forwarded along the same path and are treated the same with regard to the forwarding treatment. All packets belonging to the same FEC have the same label. However, not all packets that have the same label belong to the same FEC, because their EXP values might differ; the forwarding treatment could be different, and they could belong to a different FEC. The router that decides which packets belong to which FEC is the ingress LSR. This is logical because the ingress LSR classifies and labels the packets. Following are some examples of FECs:

- Packets with Layer 3 destination IP addresses matching a certain prefix

- Multicast packets belonging to a certain group

- Packets with the same forwarding treatment, based on the precedence or IP DiffServ Code Point (DSCP) field

- Layer 2 frames carried across an MPLS network received on one VC or (sub)interface on the ingress LSR and transmitted on one VC or (sub)interface on the egress LSR

- Packets with Layer 3 destination IP addresses that belong to a set of Border Gateway Protocol (BGP) prefixes, all with the same BGP next hop

This last example of a FEC is a particularly interesting one. All packets on the ingress LSR for which the destination IP address points to a set of BGP routes in the routing table—all with the same BGP next-hop address—belong to one FEC. It means that all packets that enter the MPLS network get a label depending on what the BGP next hop is. Figure 2-7 shows an MPLS network in which all the edge LSRs run internal BGP (iBGP).

Figure 2-7 *An MPLS Network Running iBGP*

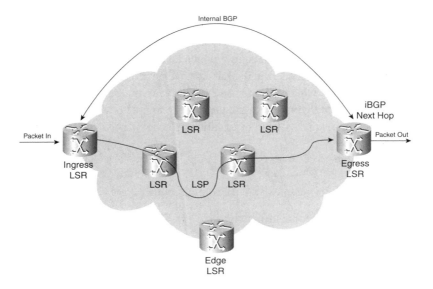

The destination IP address of all IP packets entering the ingress LSR will be looked up in the IP forwarding table. All these addresses belong to a set of prefixes that are known in the routing table as *BGP prefixes*. Many BGP prefixes in the routing table have the same BGP next-hop address, namely one egress LSR. All packets with a destination IP address for which the IP lookup in the routing table recurses to the same BGP next-hop address will be mapped to the same FEC. As already mentioned, all packets that belong to the same FEC get the same label imposed by the ingress LSR.

Label Distribution

The first label is imposed on the ingress LSR and the label belongs to one LSP. The path of the packet through the MPLS network is bound to that one LSP. All that changes is that the top label in the label stack is swapped at each hop. The ingress LSR imposes one or more labels on the packet. The intermediate LSRs swap the top label (the incoming label) of the received labeled packet with another label (the outgoing label) and transmit the packet on the outgoing link. The egress LSR of the LSP strips off the labels of this LSP and forwards the packet.

Consider the example of plain IPv4-over-MPLS, which is the simplest example of an MPLS network. Plain IPv4-over-MPLS is a network that consists of LSRs that run an IPv4 Interior Gateway Protocol (IGP) (for example, Open Shortest Path First [OSPF], Intermediate System-to-Intermediate System [IS-IS], and Enhanced Interior Gateway Routing Protocol [EIGRP]). The ingress LSR looks up the destination IPv4 address of the packet, imposes a label, and forwards the packet. The next LSR (and any other intermediate LSR) receives the labeled packet, swaps the incoming label with an outgoing label, and forwards the packet. The egress LSR pops the label and forwards the IPv4 packet without labels on the outgoing link. For this to work, adjacent LSRs must agree on which label to use for each IGP prefix. Therefore, each intermediate LSR must be able to figure out with which outgoing label the incoming label should be swapped. This means that you need a mechanism to tell the routers which labels to use when forwarding a packet. Labels are local to each pair of adjacent routers. Labels have no global meaning across the network. For adjacent routers to agree which label to use for which prefix, they need some form of communication between them; otherwise, the routers do not know which outgoing label needs to match which incoming label. A label distribution protocol is needed.

You can distribute labels in two ways:

- Piggyback the labels on an existing IP routing protocol

- Have a separate protocol distribute labels

Piggyback the Labels on an Existing IP Routing Protocol

The first method has the advantage that a new protocol is not needed to run on the LSRs, but every existing IP routing protocol needs to be extended to carry the labels. This is not always an easy thing to do. The big advantage of having the routing protocol carry the labels is that the routing and label distribution are always in sync, which means that you cannot have a label if the prefix is missing or vice versa. It also eliminates the need of another protocol running on the LSR to do the label distribution. The implementation for distance vector routing protocols (such as EIGRP) is straightforward, because each router originates a prefix from its routing table. The router then just binds a label to that prefix.

Link state routing protocols (such as IS-IS and OSPF) do not function in this way. Each router originates link state updates that are then forwarded unchanged by all routers inside one area. The problem is that for MPLS to work, each router needs to distribute a label for each IGP prefix—even the routers that are not originators of that prefix. Link state routing protocols need to be enhanced in an intrusive way to be able to do this. The fact that a router needs to advertise a label for a prefix it does not originate is counterintuitive to the way link state routing protocols work anyway. Therefore, for link state routing protocols, a separate protocol is preferred to distribute the labels.

None of the IGPs has been changed to deploy the first method. However, BGP is a routing protocol that can carry prefixes and distribute labels at the same time. However, BGP is not an IGP; it is used to carry external prefixes. BGP is used primarily for label distribution in MPLS VPN networks; you can read about it in Chapter 7.

Running a Separate Protocol for Label Distribution

The second method—running a separate protocol for label distribution—has the advantage of being routing protocol independent. Whatever the IP routing protocol is, whether it is capable of distributing labels or not, a separate protocol distributes the labels and lets the routing protocol distribute the prefixes. The disadvantage of this method is that a new protocol is needed on the LSRs.

The choice of all router vendors was to have a new label distribution protocol distribute the labels for IGP prefixes. This is the Label Distribution Protocol (LDP). LDP, however, is not the only protocol that can distribute MPLS labels.

Several varieties of protocols distribute labels:

- Tag Distribution Protocol (TDP)

- Label Distribution Protocol (LDP)

- Resource Reservation Protocol (RSVP)

TDP, which predates LDP, was the first protocol for label distribution developed and implemented by Cisco. However, TDP is proprietary to Cisco. The IETF later formalized LDP. LDP and TDP are similar in the way they operate, but LDP has more functionality than TDP. With the widespread availability of LDP in general-deployment Cisco IOS releases, TDP was quickly replaced by LDP. The result is that TDP is becoming obsolete. Therefore, the remainder of this book refers to LDP only.

Label distribution by RSVP is used for MPLS TE only. Refer to Chapter 8 for more information about MPLS TE and to find out how RSVP does the label distribution. LDP is explained in detail in Chapter 4, "Label Distribution Protocol."

Label Distribution with LDP

For every IGP IP prefix in its IP routing table, each LSR creates a local binding—that is, it binds a label to the IPv4 prefix. The LSR then distributes this binding to all its LDP neighbors. These received bindings become remote bindings. The neighbors then store these remote and local bindings in a special table, the label information base (LIB). Each LSR has only one local binding per prefix, at least when the label space is per platform. If the label space is per interface, one local label binding can exist per prefix per interface. Therefore, you can have one label per prefix or one label per prefix per interface, but the LSR gets more than one remote binding because it usually has more than one adjacent LSR.

> **NOTE** The difference between per-platform and per-interface label space is explained in the later section "MPLS Label Spaces."

Out of all the remote bindings for one prefix, the LSR needs to pick only one and use that one to determine the outgoing label for that IP prefix. The routing table (sometimes called the routing instance base, or RIB) determines what the next hop of the IPv4 prefix is. The LSR chooses the remote binding received from the downstream LSR, which is the next hop in the routing table for that prefix. It uses this information to set up its label forwarding information base (LFIB) where the label from the local binding serves as the incoming label and the label from the one remote binding chosen via the routing table serves as the outgoing label. Therefore, when an LSR receives a labeled packet, it is now capable of swapping the incoming label it assigned, with the outgoing label assigned by the adjacent next-hop LSR. Figure 2-8 shows the advertisement by LDP of the bindings between the LSRs for the IPv4 prefix 10.0.0.0/8. Each LSR allocates one label per IPv4 prefix. The local binding is this one prefix and its associated label.

Figure 2-8 *An IPv4-over-MPLS Network Running LDP*

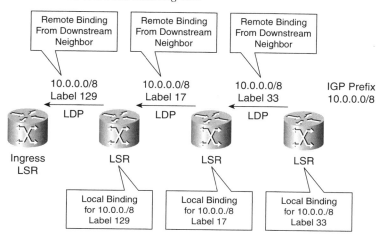

Figure 2-9 shows the IPv4 packet—destined for 10.0.0.0/8—entering the MPLS network on the ingress LSR, where it is imposed with the label 129 and switched toward the next LSR. The second LSR swaps the incoming label 129 with the outgoing label 17 and forwards the packet toward the third LSR. The third LSR swaps the incoming label 17 with the outgoing label 33 and forwards the packet to the next LSR and so on.

Figure 2-9 *An IPv4-over-MPLS Network Running LDP: Packet Switching*

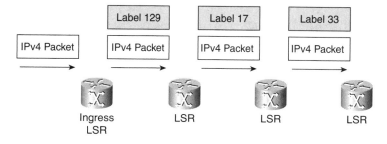

NOTE   In Cisco IOS, LDP does not bind labels to BGP IPv4 prefixes.

Label Forwarding Instance Base

The LFIB is the table used to forward labeled packets. It is populated with the incoming and outgoing labels for the LSPs. The incoming label is the label from the local binding on the particular LSR. The outgoing label is the label from the remote binding chosen by the LSR from all possible remote bindings. All these remote bindings are found in the LIB. The LFIB chooses only one of the possible outgoing labels from all the possible remote bindings in the LIB and installs it in the LFIB. The remote label chosen depends on which path is the best path found in the routing table.

In the example of IPv4-over-MPLS, the label is bound to an IPv4 prefix. However, the LFIB can be populated with labels that LDP does not assign. In the case of MPLS traffic engineering, the labels are distributed by RSVP. In the case of MPLS VPN, the VPN label is distributed by BGP. In any case, the LFIB is always used to forward an incoming labeled packet.

MPLS Payload

The MPLS label has no Network Level Protocol identifier field. This field is present in all Layer 2 frames to indicate what the Layer 3 protocol is. How does the LSR know what the protocol is behind the label stack? Or, in other words, how does the LSR know what the MPLS payload is? Most LSRs do not need to know, because they will receive a labeled packet, swap the top label, and send the packet on the outgoing link. This is the case for intermediate LSRs or P routers.

Intermediate LSRs do not need to know what the MPLS payload is because all the information needed to switch the packet is known by looking at the top label only. If the label stack consists of more than one label, the labels below the top label might not be assigned by the LSR and thus the intermediate LSR might have no knowledge what they are. Furthermore, the LSR might not know what the transported MPLS payload is. Because intermediate LSRs look only at the top label to make a forwarding decision, this is not a problem. For the forwarding based on the top label to be correct, the intermediate LSR must have a local and remote binding for the top label.

An egress LSR that is removing all labels on top of the packet must know what the MPLS payload is, because it must forward the MPLS payload further on. The egress LSR must know what value to use for the Network Level Protocol identifier field in the outgoing frame. That egress LSR is the one that made the local binding, which means that that LSR assigned a local label to that FEC, and it is that label that is used as an incoming label on the packet. Therefore, the egress LSR knows what the MPLS payload is by looking at the label, because it is the egress LSR that created the label binding for that FEC, and it knows what that FEC is.

MPLS Label Spaces

In Figure 2-10, LSR A can advertise label L1 for FEC 1 to LSR B and label L1 for FEC 2 to LSR C, but only if LSR A can later distinguish from which LSR the packet with label L1 was received. In the case that LSR B and LSR C are directly connected to LSR A via point-to-point links, this can easily be achieved by the MPLS implementation on the LSR. The fact that the label L1 is only unique per interface lends its name to this label scope: per-interface label space. If per-interface label space is used, the packet is not forwarded solely based on the label, but based on both the incoming interface and the label.

Figure 2-10 *Per-Interface Label Space*

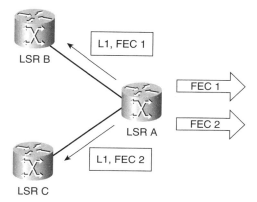

The other possibility is that the label is not unique per interface, but over the LSR assigning the label. This is called *per-platform label space*. In that case, LSR A distributes FEC 1 with label L1 to LSRs B and C, as you can see in Figure 2-11. When LSR A distributes a label for FEC 2, this label must be a different label than label L1. If per-platform label space is used, the packet is forwarded solely based on the label, independently from the incoming interface.

Figure 2-11 *Per-Platform Label Space*

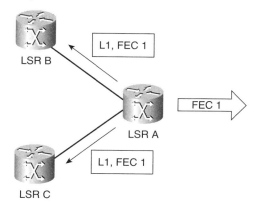

In Cisco IOS, all Label Switching Controlled-ATM (LC-ATM) interfaces have a per-interface label space, whereas all ATM frame-based and non-ATM interfaces have a per-platform label space. Refer to Chapter 5 for more details on LC-ATM interfaces.

Different MPLS Modes

An LSR can use different modes when distributing labels to other LSRs. This section covers three distinct modes, as follows:

- Label distribution mode

- Label retention mode

- LSP control mode

Each mode has its own characteristics. This section explains the advantages of each.

Label Distribution Modes

The MPLS architecture has two modes to distribute label bindings:

- Downstream-on-Demand (DoD) label distribution mode

- Unsolicited Downstream (UD) label distribution mode

In the DoD mode, each LSR requests its next-hop (that is, downstream) LSR on an LSP, a label binding for that FEC. Each LSR receives one binding per FEC only from its downstream LSR on that FEC. The downstream LSR is the next-hop router indicated by the IP routing table.

In the UD mode, each LSR distributes a binding to its adjacent LSRs, without those LSRs requesting a label. In the UD mode, an LSR receives a remote label binding from each adjacent LSR.

In the case of DoD, the LIB shows only one remote binding, whereas in the case of UD, you are likely to see more than one. The label distribution mode used depends on the interface and the implementation. In Cisco IOS, all interfaces—except LC-ATM interfaces—use the UD label distribution mode. All LC-ATM interfaces use the DoD label distribution mode.

Label Retention Modes

Two label retention modes are possible:

- Liberal Label Retention (LLR) mode

- Conservative Label Retention (CLR) mode

In LLR mode, an LSR keeps all received remote bindings in the LIB. One of these bindings is the remote binding received from the downstream or next hop for that FEC. The label from that remote binding is used in the LFIB, but none of the labels from the other remote bindings are put in the

LFIB; therefore, not all are used to forward packets. Why keep the labels around that are not used? Routing is dynamic in a network. At any time, the routing topology can change—for example, due to a link going down or a router being removed—therefore, the next-hop router for a particular FEC can change. At that time, the label for the new next-hop router is already in the LIB and the LFIB can be quickly updated with the new outgoing label.

The second label retention mode is CLR mode. An LSR that is running this mode does not store all remote bindings in the LIB, but it stores only the remote binding that is associated with the next-hop LSR for a particular FEC.

In short, the LLR mode gives you quicker adaptation to routing changes, whereas CLR mode gives you fewer labels to store and a better usage of the available memory on the router. In Cisco IOS, the retention mode for LC-ATM interfaces is the CLR mode. It is the LLR mode for all other types of interfaces.

LSP Control Modes

LSRs can create a local binding for a FEC in two ways:

■   Independent LSP Control mode

■   Ordered LSP Control mode

The LSR can create a local binding for a FEC independently from the other LSRs. This is called *Independent LSP Control mode*. In this control mode, each LSR creates a local binding for a particular FEC as soon as it recognizes the FEC. Usually, this means that the prefix for the FEC is in its routing table.

In Ordered LSP Control mode, an LSR only creates a local binding for a FEC if it recognizes that it is the egress LSR for the FEC or if the LSR has received a label binding from the next hop for this FEC.

The disadvantage of Independent LSP Control is that some LSRs begin to label switch packets before the complete LSP is set up end to end; therefore, the packet is not forwarded in the manner it should be. If the LSP is not completely set up, the packet might not receive the correct forwarding treatment everywhere or it might even be dropped. As an example for both control methods, you can look at LDP as the distribution method for label bindings of IGP prefixes. If the LSR were running in Independent LSP Control mode, it would assign a local binding for each IGP prefix in the routing table. If the LSR were running in Ordered LSP Control mode, this LSR would only assign a local label binding for the IGP prefixes that are marked as connected in its routing table and also for the IGP prefixes for which it has already received a label binding from the next-hop router (as noted in the routing table). Cisco IOS uses Independent LSP Control mode. ATM switches that are running Cisco IOS use Ordered LSP Control mode by default.

Summary

In this chapter, you have seen what a label is and that labels can be stacked in a label stack. The label stack sits in front of the transported packet. If the transported packet is an IP packet, the label stack is behind the Layer 2 header but before the IP header.

You have seen how the labels are switched at each LSR in the MPLS network, thus providing label switching. An ordered sequence of LSRs is a label switched path (LSP). A Forwarding Equivalence Class (FEC) is a group or flow of packets that receive the same forwarding treatment throughout the MPLS network. The FEC is thus determined by the label stack and the EXP bits in the label. A distribution protocol is needed to distribute the labels between LSRs in the MPLS network.

This chapter briefly explained the difference between the label information base (LIB) and the label forwarding information base (LFIB) and what they are used for. The LIB is the table that stores the label bindings, whereas the LFIB is the lookup table that forwards labeled packets.

This chapter explained the different MPLS modes: Unsolicited Downstream (UD) and Downstream-on-Demand (DoD) label distribution, Liberal Label Retention (LLR) and Conservative Label Retention (CLR), and finally, Independent LSP Control and Ordered LSP Control.

Chapter Review Questions

1. Name the four fields that are part of a label.

2. How many labels can reside in a label stack?

3. In which layer does MPLS fit in the OSI reference model?

4. Which table does an LSR use to forward labeled packets?

5. What type of interfaces in Cisco IOS uses the Downstream-on-Demand label distribution mode and the per-interface label space?

6. Why does the MPLS label have a Time To Live (TTL) field?

What You Will Learn

After completing this chapter, you will be able to do the following:

- Explain how labeled packets are forwarded

- Name the reserved MPLS labels and know what they are used for

- Determine the importance of MPLS MTU in MPLS networks

- Explain what happens to labeled packets that have TTL expiring

- Explain what happens with labeled packets that need to be fragmented

CHAPTER **3**

Forwarding Labeled Packets

Chapter 2, "MPLS Architecture," focused on what an MPLS label is and how it is used. This chapter specifically focuses on how labeled packets are forwarded. Forwarding labeled packets is quite different from forwarding IP packets. Not only is the IP lookup replaced with a lookup of the label in the label forwarding information base (LFIB), but different label operations are also possible. These operations refer to the pop, push, and swap operations of MPLS labels in the label stack.

When reading this chapter, note the existence of the reserved MPLS labels that have a special function. These reserved labels are already introduced here, because they are mentioned throughout the book.

Forwarding of Labeled Packets

This section looks at how labeled packets are forwarded in MPLS networks, how forwarding labeled packets is different from forwarding IP packets, how labeled packets are load-balanced, and what a label switching router (LSR) does with a packet with an unknown label.

Label Operation

The possible label operations are swap, push, and pop. Look at Figure 3-1 to see the possible operations on labels.

Figure 3-1 *Operations on Labels*

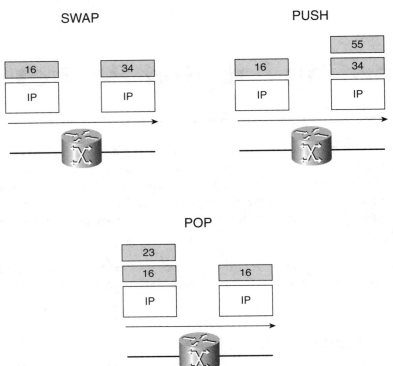

By looking at the top label of the received labeled packet and the corresponding entry in the LFIB, the LSR knows how to forward the packet. The LSR determines what label operation needs to be performed—swap, push, or pop—and what the next hop is to which the packet needs to be forwarded. The swap operation means that the top label in the label stack is replaced with another, and the push operation means that the top label is replaced with another and then one or more additional labels are pushed onto the label stack. The pop operation means that the top label is removed.

> **NOTE** The LSR sees the 20-bit field in the top label, looks up this value in the LFIB, and tries to match it with a value in the local labels list.

IP Lookup Versus Label Lookup

When a router receives an IP packet, the lookup done is an IP lookup. In Cisco IOS, this means that the packet is looked up in the CEF table. When a router receives a labeled packet, the lookup is done in the LFIB of the router. The router knows that it receives a labeled packet or an IP packet by looking at the protocol field in the Layer 2 header. If a packet is forwarded by either Cisco Express Forwarding (CEF) (IP lookup) or by LFIB (label lookup), the packet can leave the router either labeled or unlabeled. Look at Figure 3-2 to see the difference between a lookup in the CEF table and in the LFIB.

Figure 3-2 *CEF or LFIB Lookup*

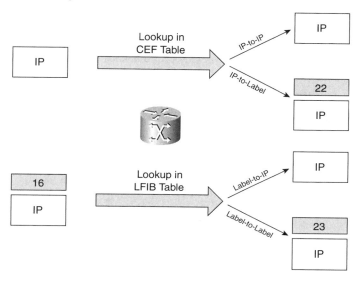

If an ingress LSR receives an IP packet and forwards it as labeled, it is called the IP-to-label forwarding case. If an LSR receives a labeled packet, it can strip off the labels and forward it as an IP packet, or it can forward it as a labeled packet. The first case is referred to as the label-to-IP forwarding case; the second is referred to as the label-to-label forwarding case.

> **NOTE**   For more information on CEF and its interaction with MPLS, refer to Chapter 6, "Cisco Express Forwarding."

Example 3-1 shows an IP-to-label forwarding case—that is, the forwarding of an IP packet by the CEF table.

Example 3-1 *Example of an Entry in the CEF table*

```
lactometer#show ip cef 10.200.254.4
10.200.254.4/32, version 44, epoch 0, cached adjacency 10.200.200.2
0 packets, 0 bytes
  tag information set, all rewrites owned
```
continues

Example 3-1   *Example of an Entry in the CEF table (Continued)*

```
   local tag: 20
   fast tag rewrite with Et0/0/0, 10.200.200.2, tags imposed {18}
 via 10.200.200.2, Ethernet0/0/0, 0 dependencies
   next hop 10.200.200.2, Ethernet0/0/0
   valid cached adjacency
   tag rewrite with Et0/0/0, 10.200.200.2, tags imposed {18}
```

IP packets that enter the LSR destined for 10.200.254.4/32 go out on interface Ethernet0/0/0 after being imposed with the label 18. The next hop of this packet is 10.200.200.2. The IP-to-label forwarding is done at the imposing LSR. In Cisco IOS, CEF switching is the only IP switching mode that you can use to label packets. Other IP switching modes, such as fast switching, cannot be used, because the fast switching cache does not hold information on labels. Because CEF switching is the only IP switching mode that is supported in conjunction with MPLS, you must turn on CEF when you enable MPLS on the router.

In Example 3-2, you can see an extract from the LFIB, by issuing the command **show mpls forwarding-table**.

Example 3-2   *Extract of the LFIB*

```
lactometer#show mpls forwarding-table
Local  Outgoing     Prefix           Bytes tag  Outgoing   Next Hop
tag    tag or VC    or Tunnel Id     switched   interface
16     Untagged     10.1.1.0/24      0          Et0/0/0    10.200.200.2
17     16           10.200.202.0/24  0          Et0/0/0    10.200.200.2
18     Pop tag      10.200.203.0/24  0          Et0/0/0    10.200.200.2
19     Pop tag      10.200.201.0/24  0          Et0/0/0    10.200.200.2
20     18           10.200.254.4/32  0          Et0/0/0    10.200.200.2
21     Pop tag      10.200.254.2/32  0          Et0/0/0    10.200.200.2
22     17           10.200.254.3/32  0          Et0/0/0    10.200.200.2
24     Untagged     l2ckt(100)       4771050    Fa9/0/0    point2point
```

The local label (or tag) is the label that this LSR assigns and distributes to the other LSRs. As such, this LSR expects labeled packets to come to it with these labels as the top ones in the label stack. If this LSR were to receive a labeled packet with the top label 22, it would swap the label with label 17 and then forward it on the Ethernet0/0/0 interface. This is an example of the label-to-label forwarding case.

If this LSR receives a packet with top label 16, it removes all labels and forwards the packet as an IP packet, because the outgoing label (tag) is Untagged. This is an example of the label-to-IP case. If the LSR receives a packet with top label 18, it removes the top label (pop one label) and forwards the packet as a labeled packet or as an IP packet. You can see in this output some examples of the swap and pop operation. Example 3-3 shows an example of a push operation. The incoming label 23 is swapped with label 20, and label 16 is pushed onto label 20.

Example 3-3   *Example of Show MPLS Forwarding-Table (Detail)*

```
lactometer#show mpls forwarding-table 10.200.254.4
Local  Outgoing    Prefix          Bytes tag  Outgoing    Next Hop
tag    tag or VC   or Tunnel Id    switched   interface
23     16       [T] 10.200.254.4/32  0           Tu1         point2point

[T]      Forwarding through a TSP tunnel.
         View additional tagging info with the 'detail' option

lactometer#show mpls forwarding-table 10.200.254.4 detail
Local  Outgoing    Prefix          Bytes tag  Outgoing    Next Hop
tag    tag or VC   or Tunnel Id    switched   interface
23     16          10.200.254.4/32  0           Tu1         point2point
       MAC/Encaps=14/22, MRU=1496, Tag Stack{20 16}, via Et0/0/0
       00604700881D00024A4008008847 0001400000010000
       No output feature configured
```

To see all the labels that change on an already labeled packet, you must use the show mpls **forwarding-table** [*network* {*mask* | *length*}] [**detail**] command. In Example 3-3, you can see the difference between the output of this command with and without the **detail** keyword. If the **detail** keyword is specified, you can see all the labels that change in the label stack. From left to right between { }, you see the first label, which is the swapped label (20), and then the pushed label (16) onto the swapped label. Without the **detail** keyword, you see only the pushed label (16).

The aggregate operation remains. When you perform an aggregation (or summarization) on an LSR, it advertises a specific label for the aggregated prefix, but the outgoing label in the LFIB shows "Aggregate." Because this LSR is aggregating a range of prefixes, it cannot forward an incoming labeled packet by label-swapping the top label. The outgoing label entry showing "Aggregate" means that the aggregating LSR needs to remove the label of the incoming packet and must do an IP lookup to determine the more specific prefix to use for forwarding this IP packet. Example 3-4 shows an entry in the LFIB on an egress PE router in an MPLS VPN network.

The egress LSR receiving a packet with label 23 would remove that label and perform an IP lookup on the destination IP address in the IP header.

Example 3-4 *Example of an Entry in the LFIB for an MPLS VPN Prefix*

```
singularity#show mpls forwarding-tablevrf cust-one
Local  Outgoing    Prefix         Bytes tag  Outgoing    Next Hop
tag    tag or VC   or Tunnel Id    switched   interface
23     Aggregate   10.10.1.0/24[V]  0
```

You know now how the labeled packet is forwarded to a specific next hop after a label operation. The CEF adjacency table, however, determines the outgoing data link encapsulation. The adjacency table provides the necessary Layer 2 information to forward the packet to the next-hop LSR. This is explained in greater detail in Chapter 6.

Example 3-5 shows an adjacency table on an LSR. The adjacency table holds the Layer 2 information needed to switch out a frame on the outgoing data link.

Example 3-5 *Example of an Adjacency Table*

```
lactometer#show adjacency detail
Protocol Interface            Address
IP       Ethernet0/0/0        10.200.200.2(13)
                              0 packets, 0 bytes
                              epoch 0
                              sourced in sev-epoch 4
                              Encap length 14
                              00604700881D00024A4008000800
                              ARP
TAG      Ethernet0/0/0        10.200.200.2(9)
                              231 packets, 22062 bytes
                              epoch 0
                              sourced in sev-epoch 4
                              Encap length 14
                              00604700881D00024A4008008847
                              ARP
IP       Serial0/1/0          point2point(10)
                              258 packets, 35612 bytes
                              epoch 0
                              sourced in sev-epoch 4
                              Encap length 4
                              0F000800
                              P2P-ADJ
```

Example 3-5 *Example of an Adjacency Table (Continued)*

```
TAG       Serial0/1/0                     point2point(5)
                                          0 packets, 0 bytes
                                          epoch 0
                                          sourced in sev-epoch 4
                                          Encap length 4
                                          0F008847
                                          P2P-ADJ
```

To recap the label operations:

- **Pop**—The top label is removed. The packet is forwarded with the remaining label stack or as an unlabeled packet.

- **Swap**—The top label is removed and replaced with a new label.

- **Push**—The top label is replaced with a new label (swapped), and one or more labels are added (pushed) on top of the swapped label.

- **Untagged/No Label**—The stack is removed, and the packet is forwarded unlabeled.

- **Aggregate**—The label stack is removed, and an IP lookup is done on the IP packet.

Load Balancing Labeled Packets

If multiple equal-cost paths exist for an IPv4 prefix, the Cisco IOS can load-balance labeled packets, as illustrated in the Cisco IOS output of Example 3-6. You can see that the incoming/local labels 17 and 18 have two outgoing interfaces. If labeled packets are load-balanced, they can have the same outgoing labels, but they can also be different. The outgoing labels are the same if the two links are between a pair of routers and both links belong to the platform label space. If multiple next-hop LSRs exist, the outgoing label for each path is usually different, because the next-hop LSRs assign labels independently.

Example 3-6 *Example of Load Balancing Labeled Packets*

```
horizon#show mpls forwarding-table
Local   Outgoing     Prefix          Bytes tag   Outgoing    Next Hop
tag     tag or VC    or Tunnel Id    switched    interface
17      Pop tag      10.200.254.3/32  252        Et1/3       10.200.203.2
        Pop tag      10.200.254.3/32  0          Et1/2       10.200.201.2
18      16           10.200.254.4/32  10431273   Et1/2       10.200.201.2
        16           10.200.254.4/32  238        Et1/3       10.200.203.2
```

If a prefix is reachable via a mix of labeled and unlabeled (IP) paths, Cisco IOS does not consider the unlabeled paths for load-balancing labeled packets. That is because in some cases, the traffic going over the unlabeled path does not reach its destination. In the case of plain IPv4-over-MPLS (MPLS running on an IPv4 network), the packets reach the destination even if they become unlabeled. The packets become unlabeled at the link where MPLS is not enabled, and become labeled again at the next link where MPLS is enabled. At the place where the packets become unlabeled, an IP lookup has to occur. Because the network is running IPv4 everywhere, it should be able to deliver the packet to its destination without a label. However, in some scenarios, as with MPLS VPN or Any Transport over MPLS (AToM), a packet that becomes unlabeled in the MPLS network at a certain link does not make it to its final destination.

In the example of MPLS VPN, the MPLS payload is an IPv4 packet, but the P routers do not normally have the VPN routing tables, so they cannot route the packet to its destination. In the case of AToM, the MPLS payload is a Layer 2 frame; therefore, if the packet loses its label stack on a P router, the P router does not have the Layer 2 forwarding tables present to forward the frame further. This is why in an MPLS network labeled packets are not load-balanced over an IP and a labeled path. In general, the intelligence to forward the MPLS payload is on the edge LSRs (or PEs) only. Therefore, a P router cannot—in most cases—forward a packet that becomes unlabeled.

Example 3-7 shows load balancing via two labeled paths. Then Label Distribution Protocol (LDP) is disabled over one of the two outgoing links, and that link is removed as a next hop in the LFIB. The command **no mpls ip** on an interface disables LDP on that interface.

Example 3-7   *Changing One Path to Unlabeled*

```
horizon#show mpls forwarding-table 10.200.254.4
Local   Outgoing     Prefix           Bytes tag   Outgoing     Next Hop
tag     tag or VC    or Tunnel Id     switched    interface
18      18           10.200.254.4/32  56818       Et1/2        10.200.201.2
        18           10.200.254.4/32  160         Et1/3        10.200.203.2
horizon#conf t
Enter configuration commands, one per line.  End with CNTL/Z.
horizon(config)#interface ethernet 1/3
horizon(config-if)#no mpls ip
horizon(config-if)#^Z
horizon#horizon#show mpls forwarding-table 10.200.254.4
Local   Outgoing     Prefix           Bytes tag   Outgoing     Next Hop
tag     tag or VC    or Tunnel Id     switched    interface
18      18           10.200.254.4/32  57270       Et1/2        10.200.201.2
```

Unknown Label

In normal operation, an LSR should receive only a labeled packet with a label at the top of the stack that is known to the LSR, because the LSR should have previously advertised that label. However, it is possible for something to go wrong in the MPLS network and the LSR to start receiving labeled packets with a top label that the LSR does not find in its LFIB. The LSR can theoretically try two things: strip off the labels and try to forward the packet, or drop the packet. The Cisco LSR drops the packet. This is the right thing to do, because this LSR did not assign the top label, and it does not know what kind of packet is behind the label stack. Is it an IPv4, IPv6 packet, a Layer 2 frame, or something else? The LSR can try to figure that out by performing an inspection of the MPLS payload. But then the same problem as described in the previous section occurs: The LSR on which the packet or frame becomes unlabeled is likely not able to look up the destination of the packet or frame. Even if the LSR tries to forward the packet, it is not guaranteed that the packet will not get dropped at a router downstream. The only right thing to do is to drop an incoming packet with an unknown top label.

Reserved Labels

Labels 0 through 15 are reserved labels. An LSR cannot use them in the normal case for forwarding packets. An LSR assigns a specific function to each of these labels. Label 0 is the explicit NULL label, whereas label 3 is the implicit NULL label. Label 1 is the router alert label, whereas label 14 is the OAM alert label. The other reserved labels between 0 and 15 have not been assigned yet.

Implicit NULL Label

The implicit NULL label is the label that has a value of 3. An egress LSR assigns the implicit NULL label to a FEC if it does not want to assign a label to that FEC, thus requesting the upstream LSR to perform a pop operation. In the case of a plain IPv4-over-MPLS network, such as an IPv4 network in which LDP distributes labels between the LSRs, the egress LSR—running Cisco IOS—assigns the implicit NULL label to its connected and summarized prefixes. The benefit of this is that if the egress LSR were to assign a label for these FECs, it would receive the packets with one label on top of it. It would then have to do two lookups. First, it would have to look up the label in the LFIB, just to figure out that the label needs to be removed; then it would have to perform an IP lookup. These are two lookups, and the first is unnecessary.

The solution for this double lookup is to have the egress LSR signal the last but one (or penultimate) LSR in the label switched path (LSP) to send the packets without a label. The egress LSR signals the penultimate LSR to use implicit NULL by not sending a regular label, but by sending the special label with value 3. The result is that the egress LSR receives an IP packet and only needs to perform an IP lookup to be able to forward the packet. This enhances the performance on the egress LSR.

The use of implicit NULL at the end of an LSP is called *penultimate hop popping* (PHP). The LFIB entry for the LSP on the PHP router shows a "Pop Label" as the outgoing label. Figure 3-3 shows penultimate hop popping.

Figure 3-3 *Penultimate Hop Popping*

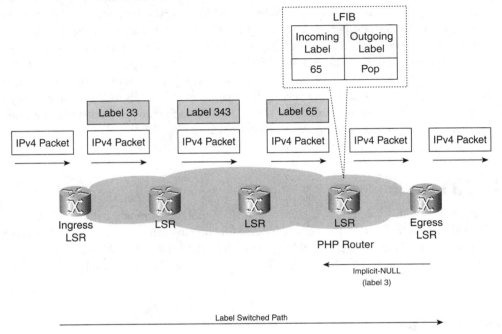

The use of implicit NULL is widespread and not confined only to the example in Figure 3-3. It could be that the packets have two or three or more labels in the label stack. Then the implicit NULL label used at the egress LSR would signal the penultimate hop router to pop one label and send the labeled packet with one label less to the egress LSR. Then the egress LSR does not have to perform two label lookups. The use of the implicit NULL label does not mean that all labels of the label stack must be removed. Only one label is popped off. In any case, the use of the implicit NULL label prevents the egress LSR from having to perform two lookups. Although the label value 3 signals the use of the implicit NULL label, the label 3 will never be seen as a label in the label stack of an MPLS packet. That is why it is called the *implicit* NULL label.

Explicit NULL Label

The use of implicit NULL adds efficiency when forwarding packets. However, it has one downside: The packet is forwarded with one label less than it was received by the penultimate LSR or unlabeled if it was received with only one label. Besides the label value, the label also holds the Experimental (EXP) bits. When a label is removed, the EXP bits are also removed. Because the EXP bits are exclusively used for quality of service (QoS), the QoS part of the packet is lost when the top label is removed. In some cases, you might want to keep this QoS information and have it delivered to the egress LSR. Implicit NULL cannot be used in that case.

The explicit NULL label is the solution to this problem, because the egress LSR signals the IPv4 explicit NULL label (value 0) to the penultimate hop router. The egress LSR then receives labeled packets with a label of value 0 as the top label. The LSR cannot forward the packet by looking up the value 0 in the LFIB because it can be assigned to multiple FECs. The LSR just removes the explicit NULL label. After the LSR removes the explicit NULL label, another lookup has to occur, but the advantage is that the router can derive the QoS information of the received packet by looking at the EXP bits of the explicit NULL label.

NOTE   The explicit NULL label for IPv6 has the value 2.

You can copy the EXP bits value to the precedence or DiffServ bits when performing PHP and thus preserve the QoS information. Or, if the label stack has multiple labels and the top label is popped off, you can copy the EXP bits value to the EXP field of the new top label. However, Chapter 12, "MPLS and Quality of Service," gives you two examples where this is not wanted; thus, the use of the explicit NULL label is warranted.

Router Alert Label

The Router Alert label is the one with value 1. This label can be present anywhere in the label stack except at the bottom. When the Router Alert label is the top label, it alerts the LSR that the packet needs a closer look. Therefore, the packet is not forwarded in hardware, but it is looked at by a software process. When the packet is forwarded, the label 1 is removed. Then a lookup of the next label in the label stack is performed in the LFIB to decide where the packet needs to be switched to. Next, a label action (pop, swap, push) is performed, the label 1 is pushed back on top of the label stack, and the packet is forwarded. Refer to Chapter 14, "MPLS Operation and Maintenance," for more details on the Router Alert label.

Example 3-8 shows the output of **debug mpls packet** on a router for a labeled packet with the Router Alert label on it.

Example 3-8 *Debug MPLS Packet Showing Label 1*

```
00:39:14: MPLS: Et1/1: recvd: CoS=6, TTL=255, Label(s)=1/21
00:39:14: MPLS: Et1/3: xmit: CoS=6, TTL=254, Label(s)=1/18

00:38:13: MPLS turbo: Se4/0: rx: Len 76 Stack {1 6 255} {20 6 255} - ipv4 data
00:38:13: MPLS les: Se4/0: rx: Len 76 Stack {1 6 255} {20 6 255} - ipv4 data
```

Example 3-8 shows two possible formats in the output. Both formats have the labels sorted from left to right or topmost label to bottommost label. The first format is the old format, with the slash separating the labels. The second format is the new format with the *{label EXP TTL}* format.

OAM Alert Label

The label with value 14 is the Operation and Maintenance (OAM) Alert label as described by the ITU-T Recommendation Y.1711 and RFC 3429. OAM is basically used for failure detection, localization, and performance monitoring. This label differentiates OAM packets from normal user data packets. Cisco IOS does not use label 14. It does perform MPLS OAM, but not by using label 14. Chapter 14 covers MPLS OAM in greater detail.

Unreserved Labels

Except for the reserved labels of 0 through 15, you can use all the label values for normal packet forwarding. Because the label value has 20 bits, the labels from 16 through 1,048,575 ($2^{20} - 1$) are used for normal packet forwarding. In Cisco IOS, the default range is 16 through 100,000. This is more than enough for labeling all the IGP prefixes you have, but if you want to label the BGP prefixes, this number might be insufficient. You can change the label range with the **mpls label range** *min max* command. Example 3-9 shows how to change the default mpls label range.

Example 3-9 *Changing the MPLS Label Range*

```
event#show mpls label range
Downstream Generic label region: Min/Max label: 16/100000

event#conf t
Enter configuration commands, one per line.  End with CNTL/Z.
event(config)#mpls label range ?
<16-1048575>  Minimum label value
event(config)#mpls label range 16 ?
  <16-1048575>  Maximum label value
event(config)#mpls label range 16 1048575

event#show mpls label range
Downstream Generic label region: Min/Max label: 16/1048575
```

TTL Behavior of Labeled Packets

Time To Live (TTL) is a well-known mechanism thanks to IP. In the IP header is a field of 8 bits that signifies the time that a packet still has before its life ends and is dropped. When an IP packet is sent, its TTL is usually 255 and is then decremented by 1 at each hop. If the TTL reaches 0, the packet is dropped. In such a case, the router that dropped the IP packet for which the TTL reached 0 sends an Internet Control Message Protocol (ICMP) message type 11 and code 0 (time exceeded) to the originator of the IP packet.

With the introduction of MPLS, labels are added to IP packets. This calls for a mechanism in which the TTL is propagated from the IP header into the label stack and vice versa. This ensures that packets do not live forever when entering and leaving the MPLS cloud, if there is a routing loop.

TTL Behavior in the Case of IP-to-Label or Label-to-IP

In MPLS, the usage of the TTL field in the label is the same as the TTL in the IP header. When an IP packet enters the MPLS cloud—such as on the ingress LSR—the IP TTL value is copied (after being decremented by 1) to the MPLS TTL values of the pushed label(s). At the egress LSR, the label is removed, and the IP header is exposed again. The IP TTL value is copied from the MPLS TTL value in the received top label after decrementing it by 1. In Cisco IOS, however, a safeguard guards against possible routing loops by not copying the MPLS TTL to the IP TTL if the MPLS TTL is greater than the IP TTL of the received labeled packet. If the MPLS TTL would be copied to the IP header, the smaller IP TLL value would be overwritten by a newer but higher value. If the IP packet would be injected into the MPLS cloud again—such as the result of a routing loop—the packet could live forever because the TTL would never reach 0. Figure 3-4 shows the default behavior of copying or propagating the TTL between the IP header and the MPLS labels and vice versa.

Figure 3-4 *Propagation Behavior of TTL Between IP Header and MPLS Labels*

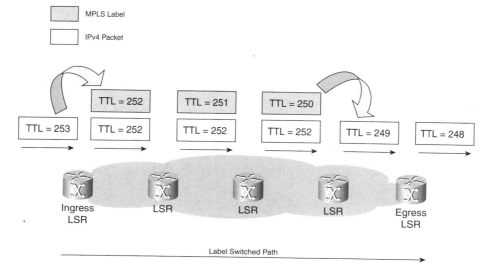

TTL Behavior in the Case of Label-to-Label

If the operation that is performed on the labeled packet is a swap, the TTL of incoming label –1 is copied to the swapped label. If the operation that is performed on the labeled packet is to push one or more labels, the received MPLS TTL of the top label –1 is copied to the swapped label and all pushed labels. If the operation is pop, the TTL of the incoming label –1 is copied to the newly exposed label unless that value is greater than the TTL of the newly exposed label, in which case the copy does not happen. Figure 3-5 shows examples of TTL propagation in the case of Label-to-Label operation for a swap, push, and pop operation.

Figure 3-5   *TTL Propagation in Label-to-Label Operation in the Case of a Swap, Push, and Pop Operation*

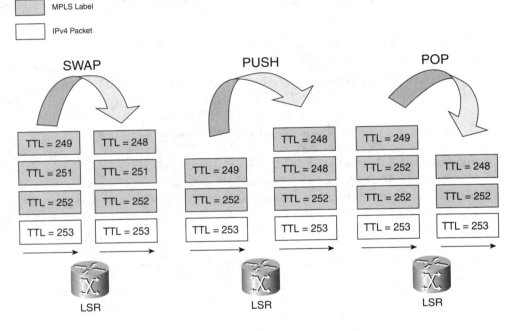

The intermediate LSR does not change the TTL field in underlying labels or the TTL field in the IP header. An LSR only looks at or only changes the top label in the label stack of a packet.

NOTE   The TTL behavior of labeled packets described here refers to the TTL operation in Cisco IOS.

TTL Expiration

When a labeled packet is received with a TTL of 1, the receiving LSR drops the packet and sends an ICMP message "time exceeded" (type 11, code 0) to the originator of the IP packet. This is the same behavior that a router would exhibit with an IP packet that had an expiring TTL. However, the ICMP message is not immediately sent back to the originator of the packet because an interim LSR might not have an IP path toward the source of the packet. The ICMP message is forwarded along the LSP the original packet was following.

Figure 3-6 shows a router sending the ICMP message "time exceeded" to the originator of the packet in the case of an IP network.

Figure 3-6   *ICMP "Time Exceeded" Sent Back by a Router in an IP Network*

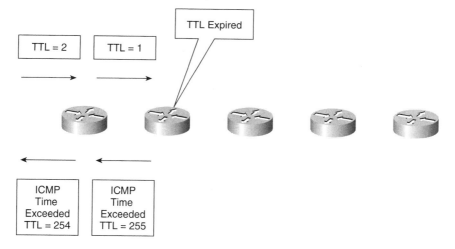

Figure 3-7 shows an LSR forwarding the ICMP "time exceeded" message along the LSP of the original packet.

Figure 3-7 *ICMP "Time Exceeded" Sent by a Router in an MPLS Network*

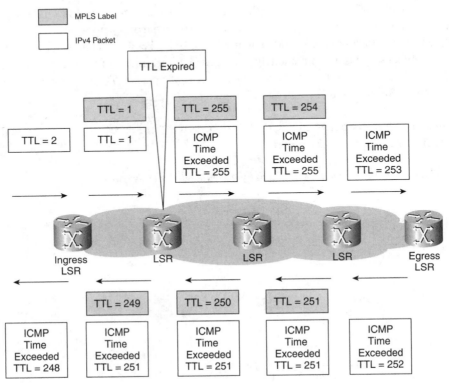

The reason for this forwarding of the ICMP message along the LSP that the original packet with the expiring TTL was following is that in some cases the LSR that is generating the ICMP message has no knowledge of how to reach the originator of the original packet. Equally so, an intermediate LSR closer to the originator of the packet might not have that knowledge. One such case is a network with MPLS VPN. In this scenario, the P router does not have the knowledge to send back the ICMP messages to the originator of the VPN packet, because the P router does not have a route to directly return the ICMP message. (In general, the P routers do not hold the VPN routing tables.) Hence, the P router builds the ICMP message and forwards the packet along the LSP, in the hope that the ICMP message reaches a router at the end of the LSP that can return the packet to the originating routing. In the case of MPLS VPN, the ICMP message is returned by the egress PE or the CE that is attached to that PE, because these routers certainly have the route to correctly return the packet.

It is important that the P router—where the TTL expires—notes what the MPLS payload is. The P router checks whether the payload is an IPv4 (or IPv6) packet. If it is, it can generate the ICMP "time exceeded" message and forward it along the LSP. However, if the payload is not an IPv4 (or IPv6) packet, the P router cannot generate the ICMP message. Therefore, the P router drops the packet in all cases, except if it is an IPv4 (or IPv6) packet. A case in which the LSR drops a packet with the TTL expiring is AToM. The MPLS payload in the case of AToM is a Layer 2 frame and not an IP packet. Hence, if the TTL in the top label of an AToM packet expires at a P router, the only action that the P router can undertake is to drop the packet, because an IP lookup is not possible. The packet is also dropped if the payload is an IPv6 packet. However, if the P router runs newer Cisco IOS code—which understands the IPv6 protocol—that router can generate the ICMP IPv6 time exceeded packet. Whether the P router actually has an IPv6 route pointing to the originator of the packet is irrelevant. This is so because the ICMP message is always forwarded along the LSP of the packet with the expiring TTL.

NOTE   Chapter 13, "Troubleshooting MPLS Networks," has a more detailed description of what happens when the TTL expires. Tracerouting—which relies on expiring TTL to function properly—in an MPLS network is explained there, too.

MPLS MTU

Maximum transmission unit (MTU) is a well-known parameter in the IP world. It indicates the maximum size of the IP packet that can still be sent on a data link, without fragmenting the packet. Data links in MPLS networks also have a specific MTU, but for labeled packets. Take the case of an IPv4 network implementing MPLS. All IPv4 packets have one or more labels. This does imply that the labeled packets are slightly bigger than the IP packets, because for every label, four bytes are added to the packet. So, if n is the number of labels, $n * 4$ bytes are added to the size of the packet when the packet is labeled.

This section explains that an MPLS MTU parameter pertains to labeled packets. Furthermore, it explains what giant and baby giant frames are and how to ensure that Ethernet switches can handle them. Finally, a new parameter is introduced: MPLS Maximum Receive Unit. This parameter is used in the LFIB to keep track of how big labeled packets can be and still be forwarded without needing to fragment them.

MPLS MTU Command

The interface MTU command in Cisco IOS specifies how big a Layer 3 packet can be without having to fragment it when sending it on a data link. For the Ethernet encapsulation, for example, MTU is by default set to 1500. However, when *n* labels are added, *n* * 4 bytes are added to an already maximum sized IP packet of 1500 bytes. This would lead to the need to fragment the packet.

Cisco IOS has the **mpls mtu** command that lets you specify how big a labeled packet can be on a data link. If, for example, you know that all packets that are sent on the link have a maximum of two labels and the MTU is 1500 bytes, you can set the MPLS MTU to 1508 (1500 + 2 * 4). Thus, all labeled packets of size 1508 bytes (labels included) can be sent on the link without fragmenting them. The default MPLS MTU value of a link equals the MTU value. Look at Example 3-10 to see how you can change the MPLS MTU on an interface in Cisco IOS.

Example 3-10 *Changing MPLS MTU*

```
london#show mpls interfaces fastEthernet 2/6 detail
Interface FastEthernet2/6:
        IP labeling enabled
        LSP Tunnel labeling not enabled
        BGP labeling not enabled
        MPLS not operational
        MTU = 1500
london#configure terminal
Enter configuration commands, one per line.  End with CNTL/Z.
london(config)#interface FastEthernet2/6
london(config-if)#mpls mtu 1508
london(config-if)#^Z
london#
london#show mpls interfaces fastEthernet 2/6 detail
Interface FastEthernet2/6:
        IP labeling enabled
        LSP Tunnel labeling not enabled
        BGP labeling not enabled
        MPLS not operational
        MTU = 1508
```

Giant and Baby Giant Frames

When a packet becomes labeled, the size increases slightly. If the IP packet was already at the maximum size possible for a certain data link (full MTU), it becomes too big to be sent on that data link because of the added labels. Therefore, the frame at Layer 2 becomes a giant frame. Because the frame is only slightly bigger than the maximum allowed, it is called a baby giant frame.

Take the example of Ethernet: The payload can be a maximum of 1500 bytes. However, if the packet is a maximum sized packet and labels are added, the packet becomes slightly too big to be sent on the Ethernet link. It is possible to close one eye and allow frames that are bigger (perhaps by just a few bytes) to be sent on the Ethernet link, even though it is not the correct thing according to the Ethernet specifications, which say that such frames should be dropped. This is, of course, possible only if the Ethernet hardware in the router and all switches in the Ethernet network support receiving and sending baby giant frames.

On Ethernet data links on LSRs, you can set the MPLS MTU to 1508 bytes to allow IP packets with a size of 1500 bytes with two labels to be received and forwarded. If, however, the hardware of the router does not support this, or if an Ethernet switch exists in between, dropping baby giant frames, you can lower the MPLS MTU parameter on the LSRs. When you set the MPLS MTU to 1500, all the IP packets with a size of 1492 bytes are still forwarded, because the size of the labeled packet then becomes 1500 (1492 plus 8) bytes at Layer 3. However, all IP packets sized between 1493 through 1500 bytes (or more) are fragmented. Because of the performance impact of fragmentation, you should use methods to avoid it, such as path MTU discovery.

> **NOTE**   In some Cisco IOS releases, you cannot configure the MPLS MTU to be bigger than the interface MTU.

Giant Frames on Switches

You can also see giant and baby giant frames on Layer 2 switches because the maximum Ethernet frame has increased by as many bytes as are in the label stack. Configuration might be needed on the Ethernet switches to allow them to switch giant and baby giant frames. Example 3-11 shows examples on how to enable jumbo Ethernet frames on an Ethernet switch.

Example 3-11   *Allowing Jumbo Frames on Ethernet Switches*

```
Cluster#conf t
Enter configuration commands, one per line.  End with CNTL/Z.
Cluster(config)#system jumbomtu ?
  <1500-9216>  Jumbo mtu size in Bytes, default is 9216

donquijote-msfc#conf t
Enter configuration commands, one per line.  End with CNTL/Z.
donquijote-msfc(config)#int vlan 1
donquijote-msfc(config-if)#mtu ?
  <64-9216>  MTU size in bytes

Lander#conf t
Enter configuration commands, one per line.  End with CNTL/Z.
Lander(config)#system mtu ?
  <1500-2000>  MTU size in bytes
```

MPLS Maximum Receive Unit

Maximum receive unit (MRU) is a parameter that Cisco IOS uses. It informs the LSR how big a received labeled packet of a certain FEC can be that can still be forwarded out of this LSR without fragmenting it. This value is actually a value per FEC (or prefix) and not just per interface. The reason for this is that labels can be added to or removed from a packet on an LSR.

Think of the example of a router in which all the interfaces have an MTU of 1500 bytes. This means that the biggest IP packet that can be received and transmitted on all interfaces is 1500 bytes. Imagine that the packets can be labeled by adding a maximum of two labels. (Typically, MPLS VPN and AToM networks label the packets respectively the frames with two labels.) Also assume that the MPLS MTU is set to 1508 on all links to accommodate for the extra 8 bytes (2 times 4 bytes) for the labels. A labeled packet that is transmitted on any of the links can now be 1508 bytes. If, however, the operation on the incoming packet were POP, the packet could have been 4 bytes or 1 label bigger (thus 1512 bytes) when it was received, because one label would have been popped off before transmitting the packet. If the label operation were a push, however, and one label was added, the incoming packet could only have been 1504 bytes, because 4 bytes or one label would have been added—making the packet 1508 bytes—before switching the packet out.

As you can see, the label operation plays a role in determining the MRU. Because the label operation is determined per FEC or prefix, the MRU can change per FEC or prefix. Notice how in Example 3-12, the MRU changes per prefix according to the specific label operation performed on the packets. The LFIB shows you the value of the MRU per prefix.

Example 3-12 *Example of MRU*

```
lactometer#show mpls forwarding-table 10.200.254.2 detail
Local  Outgoing    Prefix          Bytes tag  Outgoing   Next Hop
tag    tag or VC   or Tunnel Id    switched   interface
21     Pop tag     10.200.254.2/32  0          Et0/0/0    10.200.200.2
         MAC/Encaps=14/14, MRU=1512, Tag Stack{}
         00604700881D00024A4008008847
         No output feature configured


lactometer#show mpls forwarding-table 10.200.254.3 detail
Local  Outgoing    Prefix          Bytes tag  Outgoing   Next Hop
tag    tag or VC   or Tunnel Id    switched   interface
19     17          10.200.254.3/32  0          Et0/0/0    10.200.200.2
         MAC/Encaps=14/18, MRU=1508, Tag Stack{17}
         00604700881D00024A4008008847 00011000
         No output feature configured


lactometer#show mpls forwarding-table 10.200.254.4 detail
Local  Outgoing    Prefix          Bytes tag  Outgoing   Next Hop
tag    tag or VC   or Tunnel Id    switched   interface
20     18          10.200.254.4/32  0          Tu1        point2point
         MAC/Encaps=14/22, MRU=1504, Tag Stack{20 18}, via Et0/0/0
         00604700881D00024A4008008847 0001400000012000
         No output feature configured
```

The MRU for the prefix 10.200.254.2/32 is 1512. The packet received can be 1512 bytes, because one label is popped off before it is forwarded. The MRU for prefix 10.200.254.3/32 is 1508. The size of the packet does not change, because only the top label is swapped. The MRU for prefix 10.200.254.4/32 is 1504. The packet received can be only 1504 bytes because one extra label is pushed onto the label stack before the packet is forwarded; therefore, the packet size increases by 4 bytes. The "Tag Stack" shows that one label is pushed onto the label stack after the incoming label is swapped.

Fragmentation of MPLS Packets

If an LSR receives a labeled packet that is too big to be sent out on a data link, the packet should be fragmented. This is similar to fragmenting an IP packet. If a labeled packet is received and the LSR notices that the outgoing MTU is not big enough for this packet, the LSR strips off the label stack, fragments the IP packet, puts the label stack (after the pop, swap, or push operation) onto all fragments, and forwards the fragments. Only if the IP header has the Don't Fragment (DF) bit set does the LSR not fragment the IP packet, but it drops the packet and returns an ICMP error message "Fragmentation needed and do not fragment bit set" (ICMP type 3, code 4) to the originator of the IP packet. As with the ICMP message "time exceeded" (type 11, code 0), which is sent when the TTL expires of a labeled packet, the "Fragmentation needed and do not fragment bit set" ICMP message is sent, using a label stack that is the outgoing label stack for the packet that caused the ICMP message to be created. This means that the ICMP message travels further down the LSP until it reaches the egress LSR of that LSP. Then it is returned to the originator of the packet with the DF bit set.

In general, fragmentation causes a performance impact and should be avoided. A good method to avoid fragmentation is using the Path MTU Discovery method as described in the next section.

Path MTU Discovery

One method to avoid fragmentation is Path MTU Discovery, which most modern IP hosts perform automatically. In that case, the IP packets sent out have the "Don't Fragment" (DF) bit set. When a packet encounters a router that cannot forward the packet without fragmenting it, the router notices that the DF bit is set, drops the packet, and sends an ICMP error message "Fragmentation needed and do not fragment bit set" (ICMP type 3, code 4) to the originator of the IP packet. The originator of the IP packet then lowers the size of the packet and retransmits the packet. If a problem still exists, the host can lower the size of the packet again. This continues until no ICMP message is received for the IP packet. The size of the last IP packet successfully sent is then used as maximum packet size for all subsequent IP traffic between the specific source and destination; hence, it is the MTU of the path.

> **NOTE**   Path MTU Discovery is not guaranteed to work in all cases; sometimes the ICMP message does not make it back to the originator. Possible causes for the ICMP message not making it to the originator of the packet are firewalls, access lists, and routing problems.

Summary

In this chapter, you have learned how a packet is forwarded in an MPLS network. You have seen that CEF can label an incoming IP packet. An incoming labeled packet is forwarded by looking up the top label value in the LFIB and finding the label operation and next hop to forward the packet to. You have learned that several specially reserved labels (implicit NULL label, explicit NULL label, and Router Alert label) exist and what their function is. MPLS has its own MTU, which is important because the labeled packet is slightly bigger than the unlabeled one. That is because only a few labels add to the packet. You have seen that MPLS has a TTL field in the labels that is used in the same way as it is used for IP packets, but there is a specific behavior in copying the IP TTL to the label TTL fields and vice versa. Finally, you have seen that MPLS also supports fragmenting labeled packets.

Chapter Review Questions

1. What does the push operation do on a labeled packet?

2. Which Cisco IOS command do you use to see what the swapped label is and which labels are pushed onto a received packet for a certain prefix?

3. What does the outgoing label entry of "Aggregate" in the LFIB of a Cisco IOS LSR mean?

4. What label value signals the penultimate LSR to use penultimate hop popping (PHP)?

5. What are the value and the function of the Router Alert label?

6. Why does an LSR forward the ICMP message "time exceeded" along the LSP of the original packet with the TTL expiring instead of returning it directly?

7. Is using Path MTU Discovery a guarantee that there will be no MTU problems in the MPLS network?

8. Why is MTU or MRU such an important parameter in MPLS networks?

What You Will Learn

By the end of this chapter, you should know and be able to explain the following:

- The need for LDP

- The operation of LDP

- Specific Cisco IOS LDP features

In addition, this chapter gives you an overview of the Cisco IOS LDP commands and how to use them. Some examples are given to better illustrate the use of these commands.

CHAPTER **4**

Label Distribution Protocol

The fundamental story on MPLS is that packets are labeled, and each label switching router (LSR) must perform label swapping to forward the packet. This means that in all cases, labels need to be distributed. You can achieve this in two ways: piggyback the labels on an existing routing protocol, or develop a new protocol to do just that. If you want to adjust the Interior Gateway Protocol (IGP)—such as Open Shortest Path First (OSPF), Intermediate System-to-Intermediate System (IS-IS), Enhanced Interior Gateway Routing Protocol (EIGRP), and Routing Information Protocol (RIP)—to carry the labels, you must do it for all IGPs, because all of them are being used as routing protocols in the networks today. If you write a new protocol from the ground up, you could make it routing independent and able to work with any IGP. That is exactly the reason why Label Distribution Protocol (LDP) was invented: It carries the label bindings for the Forwarding Equivalence Classes (FECs) in the MPLS network. One exception is Border Gateway Protocol (BGP). Because BGP carries exterior routes, it is deemed more efficient if it carries the labels, too, next to the prefixes. Because BGP is already multiprotocol anyway, it can be made to carry label information with little effort. A second reason for choosing BGP to carry the label information is the fact that BGP is the only protocol distributing prefixes between autonomous systems; as such, it is a trusted protocol to function between different companies.

> **NOTE** Multiprotocol BGP (MP-BGP) is defined in RFC 2283.

That is why the label bindings for all IGP prefixes in the routing table are distributed by LDP and all label bindings for BGP routes in the routing table are distributed by BGP in Cisco IOS. Chapter 2, "MPLS Architecture," briefly touched on LDP and exchanging label bindings. It explained why the label information base (LIB) and label forwarding information base (LFIB) are necessary and how they are created. Other basics like label operations have already been explained; this means it is necessary to explain the function and operation of LDP more in depth.

> **NOTE** The full specification of LDP is quite lengthy. Please refer to RFC 3036, "LDP Specification," to learn the complete protocol specification, specifically the packet encodings and the procedures for advertising and processing the LDP messages.

Look at Figure 4-1, which is the network used throughout this chapter.

Figure 4-1   *Network Used Throughout Chapter 4*

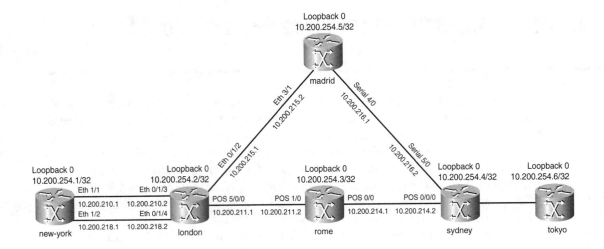

LDP Overview

To get packets across a label switched path (LSP) through the MPLS network, all LSRs must run a label distribution protocol and exchange label bindings. When all the LSRs have the labels for a particular Forwarding Equivalence Class (FEC), the packets can be forwarded on the LSP by means of label switching the packets at each LSR. The label operation (swap, push, pop) is known to each LSR by looking into the LFIB. The LFIB—which is the table that forwards labeled packets—is fed by the label bindings found in the LIB. The LIB is fed by the label bindings received by LDP, Resource Reservation Protocol (RSVP), MP-BGP, or statically assigned label bindings. Because RSVP distributes the labels only for MPLS traffic engineering and MP-BGP distributes the labels only for BGP routes, you are left with LDP for distributing all the labels for interior routes. Therefore, all directly connected LSRs must establish an LDP peer relationship or LDP session between them. The LDP peers exchange the label mapping messages across this LDP session. A label mapping or binding is a label that is bound to a FEC. The FEC is the set of packets that are mapped to a certain LSP and are forwarded over that LSP through the MPLS network. For now, this chapter will look at label bindings only for IGP IPv4 prefixes. Other possibilities exist (Chapter 10, "Any Transport over MPLS," deals with labels that are bound to pseudowires), but it is easier to explain the functioning of LDP with IGP IPv4 prefixes only. LDP has four major functions:

- The discovery of LSRs that are running LDP

- Session establishment and maintenance

- Advertising of label mappings

- Housekeeping by means of notification

When two LSRs are running LDP and they share one or more links between them, they should discover each other by means of Hello messages. The second step is for them to establish a session across a TCP connection. Across this TCP connection, LDP advertises the label mapping messages between the two LDP peers. These label mapping messages are used to advertise, change, or retract label bindings. LDP provides the means to notify the LDP neighbor of some advisory and error messages by sending notification messages.

LDP Operation

This section explains the four major functions of LDP in more detail.

The Discovery of LSRs That Are Running LDP

LSRs that are running LDP send LDP Hello messages on all links that are LDP enabled. These are all the interfaces with **mpls ip** configured on them. First, however, you must enable CEF with the global **ip cef** command. Then you must enable LDP globally with the **mpls ip** command. Example 4-1 shows you the basic global and interface commands to enable LDP.

Example 4-1 *Basic MPLS LDP Configuration*

```
!
hostname london
!
ip cef
!
mpls ldp router-id Loopback0 force
mpls label protocol ldp
!
interface Loopback0
 ip address 10.200.254.2 255.255.255.255
!
interface Ethernet0/1/3
 ip address 10.200.210.2 255.255.255.0
mpls ip
!
```

> **NOTE**   Some Cisco IOS commands still have the old "tag-switching" instead of "mpls" in them. They are functionally the same. In the same way, there are still Tag Distribution Protocol (TDP) references in the commands, although the command can refer to LDP, too.

LDP Hello messages are UDP messages that are sent on the links to the "all routers on this subnet" multicast IP address—in other words, to the 224.0.0.2 group IP multicast address. The UDP port used for LDP is 646. The LSR that is receiving this LDP Hello message on a certain interface is then aware of the presence of this LDP router on that interface. The Hello message contains a *Hold time*. If no Hello message is received from that LSR before the Hold time expires, the LSR removes that LSR from the list of discovered LDP neighbors. To discover whether the LSR sends and receives LDP Hellos, the Hello interval, and the Hold time, use the **show mpls ldp discovery [detail]** command. If LDP Hello messages are sent and received on an interface, there is an LDP adjacency across the link between two LSRs that are running LDP. Example 4-2 shows the LDP discovery on links.

Example 4-2   *LDP Discovery*

```
london#show mpls ldp discovery detail
 Local LDP Identifier:
    10.200.254.2:0
    Discovery Sources:
    Interfaces:
        Ethernet0/1/2 (ldp): xmit/recv
            Enabled: Interface config
            Hello interval: 5000 ms; Transport IP addr: 10.200.254.2
            LDP Id: 10.200.254.5:0
              Src IP addr: 10.200.215.2; Transport IP addr: 10.200.254.5
              Hold time: 15 sec; Proposed local/peer: 15/15 sec
              Reachable via 10.200.254.5/32
        Ethernet0/1/3 (ldp): xmit/recv
            Enabled: Interface config
            Hello interval: 5000 ms; Transport IP addr: 10.200.254.2
            LDP Id: 10.200.254.1:0
              Src IP addr: 10.200.210.1; Transport IP addr: 10.200.254.1
              Hold time: 15 sec; Proposed local/peer: 15/15 sec
              Reachable via 10.200.254.1/32
        Ethernet0/1/4 (ldp): xmit/recv
            Enabled: Interface config
            Hello interval: 5000 ms; Transport IP addr: 10.200.254.2
            LDP Id: 10.200.254.1:0
              Src IP addr: 10.200.218.1; Transport IP addr: 10.200.254.1
              Hold time: 15 sec; Proposed local/peer: 15/15 sec
              Reachable via 10.200.254.1/32
        POS5/0/0 (ldp): xmit/recv
            Enabled: Interface config
            Hello interval: 5000 ms; Transport IP addr: 10.200.254.2
            LDP Id: 10.200.254.3:0
```

Example 4-2 *LDP Discovery (Continued)*

```
            Src IP addr: 10.200.211.2; Transport IP addr: 10.200.254.3
            Hold time: 15 sec; Proposed local/peer: 15/15 sec
            Reachable via 10.200.254.3/32
```

The **show mpls interfaces** command allows you to quickly see which interfaces are running LDP. Look at Example 4-3 to view the output of the **show mpls interfaces** command.

Example 4-3 *show mpls interfaces*

```
london#show mpls interfaces
Interface            IP              Tunnel    Operational
Ethernet0/1/2        Yes (ldp)       Yes       Yes
Ethernet0/1/3        Yes (ldp)       Yes       Yes
Ethernet0/1/4        Yes (ldp)       No        Yes
POS5/0/0             Yes (ldp)       Yes       Yes
```

To change the interval between sending Hello messages or to change the LDP Hold time, you can use the command **mpls ldp discovery** {**hello** {**holdtime** | **interval**} *seconds*.

The default value for the **holdtime** keyword is 15 seconds for link Hello messages, and the default value for the **interval** keyword is 5 seconds. Example 4-2 has three discovered LDP neighbors: 10.200.254.1, 10.200.254.3, and 10.200.254.5. As you can see, the LSR 10.200.254.1 is discovered on two interfaces: Ethernet 0/1/3 and Ethernet 0/1/4. The Hello interval and Hold time are set to the defaults of 5 and 15 seconds. If the two LDP peers have different LDP Hold times configured, the smaller of the two values is used as the Hold time for that LDP discovery source. Cisco IOS might overwrite the configured LDP Hello interval. It will choose a smaller LDP Hello interval than configured so that it can send at least three LDP Hellos before the Hold time expires. (At least nine Hellos are sent in the case of a targeted LDP session; see the section "Targeted LDP Session" for more information on targeted LDP sessions.) If the Hold time expires for one link, that link is removed from the LDP discovery sources list. If the last link from the LDP discovery sources is removed for one LDP neighbor, the LDP session is torn down. If you do change the Hello interval and Hold time for LDP discovery sources, make sure you do not set the Hold time too small or too big. If the Hold time is too small, the session can be lost immediately even when only a few packets are lost, for example due to congestion on the link. If the Hold time is set too big, the LDP session might be up too long in the case of a serious problem, and the reaction might be too slow. As a result, too many labeled packets are lost.

Notice that LSRs that are running LDP have an LDP Identifier, or LDP ID. This LDP ID is a 6-byte field that consists of 4 bytes identifying the LSR uniquely and 2 bytes identifying the label space that the LSR is using. If the last two bytes are 0, the label space is the platform-wide or per-platform label space. If they are non-zero, a per-interface label space is used. If that is the case, multiple LDP IDs are used, where the first 4 bytes are the same value, but the last two bytes indicate a different label space. Per-interface label space is used for LC-ATM links. Refer to Chapter 5, "MPLS and ATM Architecture," for an example depicting per-interface label spaces. The first 4 bytes of the LDP ID are an IP address taken from an operational interface on the router. If loopback interfaces exist, the highest IP address of the loopback interfaces is taken for the LDP ID or LDP router ID. If no loopback interfaces exist, the highest IP address of an interface is taken. In Example 4-2, the local LDP ID or LDP router ID of the router is 10.200.254.2:0, where 10.200.254.2 happens to be the highest IP address of any loopback interface and :0 refers to the platform-wide label space. You can change the LDP router ID manually by using the command **mpls ldp router-id** *interface* [**force**]. If you use the *force* keyword, the LDP router ID is changed immediately. Without this keyword, the LDP router ID is changed only the next time it is necessary to select the router ID after configuring this command. This happens when the interface that determines the current LDP router ID is shut down.

In Cisco IOS, the MPLS LDP router ID needs to be present in the routing table of the LDP neighboring routers. If it is not, the LDP session is not formed. Therefore, the IP address that is the LDP router ID on the router must be included in the routing protocol of the LSR. If for that IP address there is no route in the routing table, the LDP session is not established. In Example 4-4, the route to the IP address 10.200.254.3 is not in the routing table of the router london. The result is that the LSR london does not form an LDP neighborship/session with the LSR rome, which has 10.200.254.3 as the LDP router ID.

Example 4-4   *"No Route" Problem*

```
london#show mpls ldp discovery
 Local LDP Identifier:
    10.200.254.2:0
    Discovery Sources:
    Interfaces:
        Ethernet0/1/2 (ldp): xmit/recv
            LDP Id: 10.200.254.5:0
        Ethernet0/1/3 (ldp): xmit/recv
            LDP Id: 10.200.254.1:0
        Ethernet0/1/4 (ldp): xmit/recv
            LDP Id: 10.200.254.1:0
        POS5/0/0 (ldp): xmit/recv
            LDP Id: 10.200.254.3:0; no route

london#show mpls ldp discovery detail
 Local LDP Identifier:
    10.200.254.2:0
    Discovery Sources:
    Interfaces:
    ...
        POS5/0/0 (ldp): xmit/recv
            Enabled: Interface config
            Hello interval: 5000 ms; Transport IP addr: 10.200.254.2
            LDP Id: 10.200.254.3:0; no route to transport addr
```

Example 4-4 *"No Route" Problem (Continued)*

```
                    Src IP addr: 10.200.211.2; Transport IP addr: 10.200.254.3
                    Hold time: 15 sec; Proposed local/peer: 15/15 sec

london#show ip route 10.200.254.3 255.255.255.255
% Subnet not in table
```

LDP Session Establishment and Maintenance

If two LSRs have discovered each other by means of the LDP Hellos, they attempt to establish an LDP session between them. One LSR tries to open a TCP connection—to TCP port 646—to the other LSR. If the TCP connection is set up, both LSRs negotiate LDP session parameters by exchanging LDP Initialization messages. These parameters include such things as the following:

- Timer values

- Label distribution method

- Virtual path identifier (VPI)/virtual channel identifier (VCI) ranges for Label Controlled ATM (LC-ATM)

- Data-link connection identifier (DLCI) ranges for LC-Frame Relay

If the LDP peers agree on the session parameters, they keep the TCP connection between them. If not, they retry to create the LDP session between them, but at a throttled rate. In Cisco IOS, the LDP backoff command controls this throttling rate:

```
    mpls ldp backoff initial-backoff maximum-backoff
```

The initial-backoff parameter is a value between 5 and 2,147,483, with a default of 15 seconds. The maximum-backoff is a value between 5 and 2,147,483, with a default of 120 seconds. This command slows down the LDP session setup attempts of two LDP LSRs, when the two neighboring LDP peers are incompatible in terms of the parameters they exchange. If the session setup attempt fails, the next attempts are undertaken at an exponentially increased time, until the maximum backoff time is reached. One example in which the two LDP peers might disagree on the parameters and not form an LDP session is the case of LC-ATM, where the two peers are using different ranges of VPI/VCI values for the labels.

After the LDP session has been set up, it is maintained by either the receipt of LDP packets or a periodic keepalive message. Each time the LDP peer receives an LDP packet or a keepalive message, the keepalive timer is reset for that peer. The keepalive timer or Hold time for the LDP session can be configured, too. The command to change the LDP session keepalive timer is **mpls ldp holdtime** *seconds*. You can configure the value of the Hold time to be between 15 and 2,147,483 seconds, with a default of 180 seconds.

Example 4-5 shows an LDP peer with LDP router ID 10.200.254.2. The local TCP port used is 646, and the remote TCP port used is 11537. The session Hold time is 180 seconds, and the keepalive (KA) messages are sent with a 60-second interval.

Example 4-5 *LDP Neighbor Hold Time and KA Interval*

```
london#show mpls ldp neighbor 10.200.254.5 detail
    Peer LDP Ident: 10.200.254.5:0; Local LDP Ident 10.200.254.2:0
        TCP connection: 10.200.254.5.11537 - 10.200.254.2.646
        State: Oper; Msgs sent/rcvd: 16/19; Downstream; Last TIB rev sent 50
        Up time: 00:00:36; UID: 9; Peer Id 1;
        LDP discovery sources:
          Ethernet0/1/2; Src IP addr: 10.200.215.2
            holdtime: 15000 ms, hello interval: 5000 ms
        Addresses bound to peer LDP Ident:
          10.200.254.5    10.200.215.2    10.200.216.1
          Peer holdtime: 180000 ms; KA interval: 60000 ms; Peer state: estab
```

You can also see the discovery and session timers with the command **show mpls ldp parameters**, as in Example 4-6.

Example 4-6 *show mpls ldp parameters*

```
london#show mpls ldp parameters
Protocol version: 1
Downstream label generic region: min label: 16; max label: 100000
Session hold time: 180 sec; keep alive interval: 60 sec
Discovery hello: holdtime: 15 sec; interval: 5 sec
Discovery targeted hello: holdtime: 90 sec; interval: 10 sec
Downstream on Demand max hop count: 255
LDP for targeted sessions
LDP initial/maximum backoff: 15/120 sec
LDP loop detection: off
```

The LDP session is a TCP connection that is established between two IP addresses of the LSRs. Usually these IP addresses are used to create the LDP router Identifier on each router. However, if you do not want to use this IP address to create the LDP session, you can change it. To change the IP address, configure the command **mpls ldp discovery transport-address {interface |** *ip-address***}** on the interface of the router and specify an interface or IP address to be used to create the LDP session. This transport IP address is advertised in the LDP Hellos that are sent on the LDP-enabled interfaces.

> **NOTE** When a router has multiple links toward another LDP router, the same transport address must be advertised on all the parallel links that use the same label space.

In Figure 4-2, two routers are connected via two Ethernet links. On router new-york, the transport-address is changed to the loopback 1000 IP address. Notice in Example 4-7 that the used address for the TCP connection has changed from the IP address found in the LDP router ID to the IP address 10.200.255.1 of loopback 1000.

Figure 4-2   *Changing the Default LDP Transport Address*

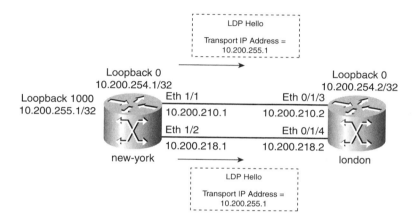

Example 4-7   *Changing the Default LDP Transport Address*

```
!
hostname new-york
!
interface Ethernet1/1
 ip address 10.200.210.1 255.255.255.0
 mpls ldp discovery transport-address 10.200.255.1
 mpls ip
!
interface Ethernet1/2
 ip address 10.200.218.1 255.255.255.0
 mpls ldp discovery transport-address 10.200.255.1
 mpls ip
!

london#show mpls ldp discovery detail
 Local LDP Identifier:
    10.200.254.2:0
    Discovery Sources:
    Interfaces:
        Ethernet0/1/3 (ldp): xmit/recv
            Enabled: Interface config
            Hello interval: 5000 ms; Transport IP addr: 10.200.254.2
```

continues

Example 4-7 *Changing the Default LDP Transport Address (Continued)*

```
          LDP Id: 10.200.254.1:0
            Src IP addr: 10.200.210.1; Transport IP addr: 10.200.255.1
            Hold time: 15 sec; Proposed local/peer: 15/15 sec
            Reachable via 10.200.255.1/32
      Ethernet0/1/4 (ldp): xmit/recv
          Enabled: Interface config
          Hello interval: 5000 ms; Transport IP addr: 10.200.254.2
          LDP Id: 10.200.254.1:0
            Src IP addr: 10.200.218.1; Transport IP addr: 10.200.255.1
            Hold time: 15 sec; Proposed local/peer: 15/15 sec
            Reachable via 10.200.255.1/32
```

NOTE When a router has multiple links toward another LDP router and a different transport address is advertised on those links, the TCP session is still formed, but there is a missing link from the LDP "discovery sources" on the other router. In the previous example, the LDP session is formed, but Ethernet 0/1/3 or Ethernet 0/1/4 is missing from the LDP discovery sources in the output of router london. As such, the traffic from router london toward router new-york is not load-balanced but uses only one outgoing Ethernet link.

Number of LDP Sessions

You might think that one LDP session between a pair of LSRs is enough to do the job. You might be right in most cases! When the per-platform label space is the only label space used between a pair of LSRs, one LDP session suffices. This is so because only one set of label bindings is exchanged between the two LSRs, no matter how many links are between them. Basically, the interfaces can share the same set of labels when the per-platform label space is used. The reason for this is that all the label bindings are relevant to all the links between the two LSRs, because they all belong to the same label space. Interfaces belong to the per-platform label space when they are frame-mode interfaces. Interfaces that are not frame-mode interfaces—such as LC-ATM interfaces—have a per-interface label space. With per-interface label space, each label binding has relevance only to that interface. Therefore, for each interface that has a per-interface label space, one LDP session must exist between the pair of routers. Look at Figure 4-3 to see some examples of the number of LDP sessions between a pair of LSRs.

Figure 4-3   *Examples of the Number of LDP Sessions Between a Pair of LSRs*

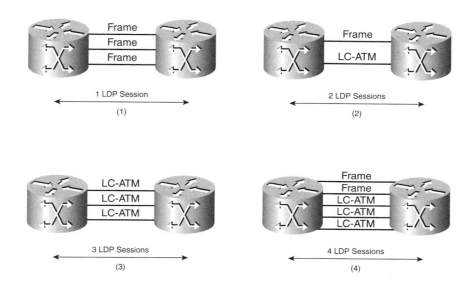

For *all* frame-mode links, only one LDP session should exchange the labels in per-platform label space. For *each* LC-ATM link, an LDP session should exchange the labels in the per-interface label space. In (1) of Figure 4-3, you see three frame links, so only one LDP session is required between the two LSRs. In (2), you see one frame link and one LC-ATM link. Because each LC-ATM link requires its own LDP session, there are two LDP sessions. (3) shows three LC-ATM links—therefore, the number of LDP sessions is three. (4) shows two frame links and three LC-ATM links. The two frame links have one LDP session, and the LC-ATM links have three LDP sessions.

Advertising of Label Mappings

Advertising label mappings or label bindings is the main purpose of LDP. Chapter 2 explains the three different modes in which the LSRs can behave: advertisement, label retention, and LSP control mode. Each of the three modes has two possibilities, which leads to the following six modes:

■   Unsolicited Downstream (UD) versus Downstream-on-Demand (DoD) advertisement mode

■   Liberal Label Retention (LLR) versus Conservative Label Retention (CLR) mode

■   Independent LSP Control versus Ordered LSP Control mode

No matter what mode the LDP peers operate in, the purpose is to advertise label bindings. In UD advertisement mode, the LDP peer distributes the label bindings unsolicited to its LDP peers. However, the label bindings are a set of (LDP Identifier, label) per prefix. An LDP router receives multiple label bindings for each prefix—namely, one per LDP peer. All these label bindings are stored in the LIB of the router. However, only one LDP peer is the downstream LSR for that particular prefix. Of course, if load balancing exists, it is possible to have more than one downstream LSR.

The downstream LSR is found by looking up the next hop for that prefix in the routing table. Only the remote binding associated with that next-hop LSR should be used to populate the LFIB. This means that only one label from all the advertised label bindings from all the LDP neighbors of this LSR should be used as outgoing label in the LFIB for that prefix. The problem is that the label bindings are advertised as (LDP Identifier, label) without the IP addresses of the interfaces. This means that to find the outgoing label for a particular prefix, you must map to the LDP Identifier the IP address of the interface—pointing back to this LSR—on the downstream LSR. You can only do this if each LDP peer advertises all its IP addresses. These IP addresses are advertised by the LDP peer with Address messages and withdrawn with Withdraw Address messages. You can find these addresses when you are looking at the LDP peer. They are called the *bound addresses* for the LDP peer. Example 4-8 shows the bound addresses to peer 10.200.254.2 (london) on LSR new-york.

Example 4-8 *LDP Bound IP Addresses*

```
new-york#show mpls ldp neighbor detail
    Peer LDP Ident: 10.200.254.2:0; Local LDP Ident 10.200.254.1:0
        TCP connection: 10.200.254.2.646 - 10.200.255.1.64481
        State: Oper; Msgs sent/rcvd: 1303/1289; Downstream; Last TIB rev sent 743
        Up time: 17:20:24; UID: 101; Peer Id 0;
        LDP discovery sources:
          Ethernet1/1; Src IP addr: 10.200.210.2
            holdtime: 15000 ms, hello interval: 5000 ms
          Ethernet1/2; Src IP addr: 10.200.218.2
            holdtime: 15000 ms, hello interval: 5000 ms
        Addresses bound to peer LDP Ident:
          10.200.254.2    10.200.210.2    10.200.218.2    10.200.211.1
          10.200.215.1
        Peer holdtime: 180000 ms; KA interval: 60000 ms; Peer state: estab
```

Each LSR assigns one local label to each IGP prefix in the routing table. This is the local label binding. These local bindings are stored in the LIB on the router. Each of these labels and the prefixes they are assigned to are advertised via LDP to all the LDP peers. These label bindings are the remote bindings on the LDP peers and are stored in the LIB. Example 4-9 shows the LIB on an LSR.

Example 4-9 *Example of a LIB*

```
london#show mpls ldp bindings
  lib entry: 10.200.210.0/24, rev 4
        local binding:  label: imp-null
        remote binding: lsr: 10.200.254.5:0, label: 16
        remote binding: lsr: 10.200.254.1:0, label: imp-null
        remote binding: lsr: 10.200.254.3:0, label: 19
  lib entry: 10.200.211.0/24, rev 12
        local binding:  label: imp-null
        remote binding: lsr: 10.200.254.5:0, label: 18
        remote binding: lsr: 10.200.254.1:0, label: 32
        remote binding: lsr: 10.200.254.3:0, label: imp-null
  lib entry: 10.200.254.1/32, rev 31
        local binding:  label: 24
        remote binding: lsr: 10.200.254.5:0, label: 22
        remote binding: lsr: 10.200.254.1:0, label: imp-null
        remote binding: lsr: 10.200.254.3:0, label: 26
…
```

As you can see, for each prefix, the LSR always has one local binding and one remote binding per LDP peer.

Example 4-10 shows another command to have a look at the LIB on the LSR. The one "in label" entry refers to the local binding. The "out label" entries refer to the remote bindings. Each time, you can see the label and the LDP Identifier of the LSR that sent the remote binding.

Example 4-10 *Example of a LIB*

```
london#show mpls ip binding
  10.200.210.0/24
        in label:     imp-null
        out label:    16        lsr: 10.200.254.5:0
        out label:    imp-null  lsr: 10.200.254.1:0
        out label:    19        lsr: 10.200.254.3:0
  10.200.211.0/24
        in label:     imp-null
        out label:    18        lsr: 10.200.254.5:0
        out label:    32        lsr: 10.200.254.1:0
        out label:    imp-null  lsr: 10.200.254.3:0
  10.200.254.1/32
        in label:     24
        out label:    22        lsr: 10.200.254.5:0
        out label:    imp-null  lsr: 10.200.254.1:0    inuse
        out label:    26        lsr: 10.200.254.3:0
...
```

The advantage of the command **show mpls ip binding** is that it also shows which label from all possible remote bindings is used to forward traffic by indicating *inuse*. Inuse indicates the outgoing label in the LFIB for that prefix.

Look at Figure 4-4 to see the association among the RIB, the bound addresses from the LDP peers, the LIB, and the LFIB.

Figure 4-4   *Relationship Among Bound Addresses, RIB, LIB, and LFIB*

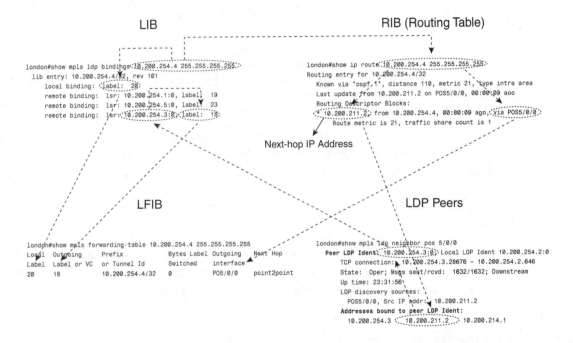

Figure 4-4 shows the example of building the LFIB entry for one FEC bound to the prefix 10.200.254.4/32. The incoming/local label for the prefix is found directly in the LIB, but the outgoing label is found through the RIB, the bound addresses of the LDP peers, and the LIB.

Note that LDP assigns local labels to *all* IGP prefixes and advertises the bindings to *all* LDP peers. The concept of split horizon does not exist; an LDP peer assigns its own local label to a prefix and advertises that back to the other LDP peer, even though that other LDP peer owns the prefix (it is a connected prefix) or that other LDP peer is the downstream LSR. Look at Figure 4-5, which shows a simple network with two LSRs. Router london owns the prefix 10.200.254.2/32 because it is the prefix on the loopback 0. This router advertises its binding for the prefix to rome. The advertised label is label implicit NULL. In turn, router london receives the remote binding for the prefix 10.200.254.2/32 from router rome, even though the router london owns the prefix.

Figure 4-5 *No LDP Split Horizon*

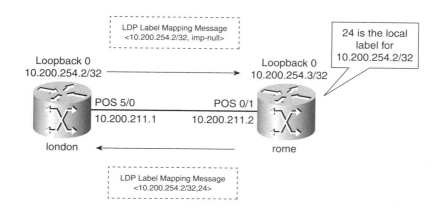

Look at Example 4-11 for the label bindings for that prefix on routers london and rome.

Example 4-11 *Bindings for 10.200.254.2/32 for Figure 4-5*

```
london#show interfaces loopback 0
Loopback0 is up, line protocol is up
  Hardware is Loopback
  Internet address is 10.200.254.2/32

london#show mpls ldp bindings 10.200.254.2 255.255.255.255
  lib entry: 10.200.254.2/32, rev 8
        local binding:  label: imp-null
        remote binding: lsr: 10.200.254.5:0, label: 21
        remote binding: lsr: 10.200.254.1:0, label: 25
        remote binding: lsr: 10.200.254.3:0, label: 24

rome#show mpls ldp bindings 10.200.254.2 255.255.255.255
 . lib entry: 10.200.254.2/32, rev 787
        local binding:  label: 24
        remote binding: lsr: 10.200.254.4:0, label: 23
        remote binding: lsr: 10.200.254.2:0, label: imp-null
```

Label Withdrawing

When an LDP peer advertises a label binding, the receiving LDP peers keep it until the LDP session goes down or until the label is withdrawn. The label might be withdrawn if the local label changes. The local label might change if, for example, the interface with a certain prefix on it goes down, but another LSR still advertises the prefix. Therefore, the local label for that prefix changes from implicit NULL to a non-reserved label. If this happens, the implicit NULL label is immediately withdrawn by sending a Label Withdraw message to the LDP peers. The new label is advertised in a Label Mapping message. In Example 4-12, the Ethernet interface with IP prefix 10.200.210.0/24 goes down on the LSR london. That is why london withdraws the prefix with the label implicit NULL. The LSR new-york still announces the prefix, though, assuming that there is a Layer 2 switch between new-york and london, so that the new-york side of the Ethernet link remains up. LSR london assigns a new local label (27) to the prefix and announces that new label in a label mapping message to the LSR madrid.

Example 4-12 *Label Withdraw*

```
madrid#debug mpls ldp messages received
LDP received messages, excluding periodic Keep Alives debugging is on
madrid#debug mpls ldp bindings
LDP Label Information Base (LIB) changes debugging is on
madrid#show debugging
MPLS ldp:
  LDP Label Information Base (LIB) changes debugging is on
  LDP received messages, excluding periodic Keep Alives debugging is on

madrid#
00:06:29: ldp: Rcvd address withdraw msg from 10.200.254.2:0 (pp 0x63E3C128)
00:06:29: tagcon: 10.200.254.2:0: 10.200.210.2 removed from addr<->ldp ident map
00:06:34: tagcon: rib change: 10.200.210.0/24; event 0x4; ndb attrflags 0x1000000; ndb-
>pdb_index 0x2
00:06:34: tagcon: rib change: 10.200.210.0/255.255.255.0; event 0x4; ndb attrflags
0x1000000; ndb->pdb_index 0x2/undef
00:06:36: ldp: Rcvd label withdraw msg from 10.200.254.2:0 (pp 0x63E3C128)
00:06:36: tagcon: tibent(10.200.210.0/24): label imp-null from 10.200.254.2:0 removed
00:06:36: tib: get path labels: 10.200.210.0/24, tableid: 0, Et3/1, nh 10.200.215.1
00:06:36: tagcon: announce labels for: 10.200.210.0/24; nh 10.200.215.1, Et3/1, inlabel 17,
outlabel unknown (from 10.200.254.2:0), get path labels
00:06:36: ldp: Rcvd label mapping msg from 10.200.254.2:0 (pp 0x63E3C128)
00:06:36: tagcon: tibent(10.200.210.0/24): label 27 from 10.200.254.2:0 added
00:06:36: tib: get path labels: 10.200.210.0/24, tableid: 0, Et3/1, nh 10.200.215.1
00:06:36: tagcon: announce labels for: 10.200.210.0/24; nh 10.200.215.1, Et3/1, inlabel 17,
outlabel 27 (from 10.200.254.2:0), get path labels
```

In older Cisco IOS software (pre 12.0(21)ST), the default behavior was not to send a Label Withdraw message to withdraw the label before advertising the new label for the FEC. The new label advertisement was also an implicit label withdraw. If you want to keep the old behavior, you must configure the command **mpls ldp neighbor** *neighbor* **implicit-withdraw**. Example 4-13 shows what happens when a new label is advertised for the prefix 10.200.210.0/24 with implicit-withdraw configured on the LDP peer london. The label withdraw message is missing from the debug output. The advantage of this command is the avoidance of sending the Label Withdraw messages, which equates to less overhead.

Example 4-13 *Label Implicit-Withdraw*

```
!
hostname london
!
mpls ldp neighbor 10.200.254.5 implicit-withdraw
mpls ldp router-id Loopback0 force
mpls label protocol ldp
!

madrid#
00:15:03: ldp: Rcvd address withdraw msg from 10.200.254.2:0 (pp 0x63E3C128)
00:15:03: tagcon: 10.200.254.2:0: 10.200.210.2 removed from addr<-->ldp ident map
00:15:06: ldp: Rcvd label mapping msg from 10.200.254.2:0 (pp 0x63E3C128)
00:15:06: tagcon: tibent(10.200.210.0/24): label imp-null from 10.200.254.2:0 impl
withdraw
00:15:06: tagcon: tibent(10.200.210.0/24): label 27 from 10.200.254.2:0 added
00:15:06: tib: get path labels: 10.200.210.0/24, tableid: 0, Et3/1, nh 10.200.215.1
00:15:06: tagcon: announce labels for: 10.200.210.0/24; nh 10.200.215.1, Et3/1, inlabel
17, outlabel 27 (from 10.200.254.2:0), get path labels
00:15:08: tagcon: rib change: 10.200.210.0/24; event 0x4; ndb attrflags 0x1000000; ndb-
>pdb_index 0x2
00:15:08: tagcon: rib change: 10.200.210.0/255.255.255.0; event 0x4; ndb attrflags
0x1000000; ndb->pdb_index 0x2/undef
```

Housekeeping by Means of Notification

Notification messages are needed for the housekeeping of LDP sessions. The notification messages signal significant events to the LDP peer. These events might be fatal errors (Error Notifications) or simple advisory information (Advisory Notifications). If a fatal error occurs, the sending LSR and receiving LSR should terminate the LDP session immediately. Advisory Notifications are used to send information about the LDP session or a message received from the peer. The following events can be signaled by sending notification messages:

- Malformed protocol data unit (PDU) or message

- Unknown or malformed type-length-value (TLV)

- Session keepalive timer expiration

- Unilateral session shutdown

- Initialization message events

- Events resulting from other messages

- Internal errors

- Loop detection

- Miscellaneous events

Targeted LDP Session

Normally, LDP sessions are set up between directly connected LSRs. In a network in which the IGP routes need to be labeled, this is sufficient, because the label switching of packets is hop per hop. Therefore, if the label bindings are advertised hop per hop for the IGP routes, the LSPs are set up. However, in some cases, a remote or targeted LDP session is needed. This is an LDP session between LSRs that are not directly connected. Examples in which the targeted LDP session is needed are AToM networks and TE tunnels in an MPLS VPN network. In the case of AToM, an LDP session must exist between each pair of PE routers. The remote LDP session is set up when configuring the **xconnect** command on the PE routers of the AToM network. In the case of TE tunnels in an MPLS VPN network, with the TE tunnels ending on a P router, the head-end and the tail-end LSR of the TE tunnel need a targeted LDP session between them to get the MPLS VPN traffic correctly label-switched through the MPLS VPN network. Refer to Chapter 8, "MPLS Traffic Engineering," for a detailed explanation on this. For directly connected neighbors, you only need to enable **mpls ip** on the interface; the LDP peers discover each other and create the LDP TCP session between them. For LDP neighbors that are not directly connected, the LDP neighborship needs to be configured manually on both the routers with the **mpls ldp neighbor targeted** command.

The syntax of the command is as follows:

```
mpls ldp neighbor [vrf vpn-name] ip-addr targeted [ldp | tdp]
```

The vrf refers to the Carrier's Carrier (CsC) scenarios in which the LDP sessions are established across VRF interfaces.

A targeted LDP neighbor can improve the label convergence time compared to the convergence time with directly connected LDP peers when there are flapping links. That is because when the link between two LSRs goes down, the LDP session is lost. With a targeted LDP session and an alternative path to get the LDP TCP packets from one LSR to the other, the LDP session stays up when the link between the two LSRs goes down. If the LDP session stays up, the labels are retained, improving the installment of the labels from the LIB into the LFIB when the link comes back up. Refer to the section "MPLS LDP Session Protection" later in this chapter to configure targeted LDP sessions with one command to protect the LDP sessions.

To change the LDP Hello interval and the Hold time for targeted LDP sessions, you can use the following command:

```
mpls ldp discovery {hello {holdtime | interval} seconds | targeted-hello {holdtime |
interval} seconds | accept [from acl]}
```

Look at Figure 4-6. The routers new-york and sydney are not directly connected; however, you want them to have an LDP session between them. You can configure on both routers the LDP neighbor as targeted. Another way of achieving the same result is to configure the targeted LDP neighbor on one router only and to configure the other router to accept targeted LDP sessions from specific LDP routers. You do this by configuring the **mpls ldp discovery targeted-hello accept [from** *acl*] command. To prevent just any router from setting up an LDP session with this router, you can use the command with an access list so that you can specify which routers are allowed to set up a targeted LDP session.

Figure 4-6 *Targeted Hello Accept Example Network*

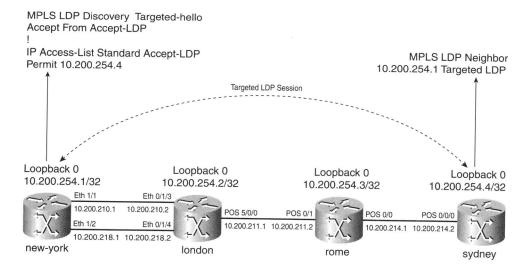

Examples 4-14 and 4-15 show the configuration needed on the new-york and sydney routers to set up a targeted LDP session between them.

Example 4-14 *Sydney Configuration for Targeted LDP*

```
!
hostname sydney
!
mpls label protocol ldp
mpls ldp neighbor 10.200.254.1 targeted ldp
mpls ldp router-id Loopback0 force
!
```

Example 4-15 *New-York Configuration for Targeted LDP*

```
new-york#conf t
new-york(config)#mpls ldp discovery targeted-hello accept from accept-ldp
new-york(config)#ip access-list standard accept-ldp
new-york(config-std-nacl)#permit host 10.200.254.4
new-york(config-std-nacl)#^Z
new-york#


!
mpls ldp discovery targeted-hello accept from accept-ldp
mpls ldp router-id Loopback0 force
mpls label protocol ldp
!


!
ip access-list standard accept-ldp
 permit 10.200.254.4
!
```

Example 4-16 shows the output of the **show mpls ldp neighbor** command for the targeted LDP session.

Example 4-16 *Targeted LDP Session on Router New-York*

```
new-york#show mpls ldp neighbor 10.200.254.4 detail
    Peer LDP Ident: 10.200.254.4:0; Local LDP Ident 10.200.254.1:0
        TCP connection: 10.200.254.4.22262 - 10.200.254.1.646
        State: Oper; Msgs sent/rcvd: 20/20; Downstream; Last TIB rev sent 120
        Up time: 00:03:10; UID: 5; Peer Id 1;
        LDP discovery sources:
          Targeted Hello 10.200.254.1 -> 10.200.254.4, passive;
            holdtime: 90000 ms, hello interval: 10000 ms
        Addresses bound to peer LDP Ident:
          10.200.254.4    10.200.214.2    10.200.217.1    10.200.216.2
        Peer holdtime: 180000 ms; KA interval: 60000 ms; Peer state: estab
```

LDP Authentication

LDP sessions are TCP sessions. TCP sessions can be attacked by spoofed TCP segments. To protect LDP against such attacks, you can use Message Digest 5 (MD5) authentication. MD5 adds a signature—called the MD5 digest—to the TCP segments. The MD5 digest is calculated for the particular TCP segment using the configured password on both ends of the connection. The configured MD5 password is never transmitted. This would leave a potential hacker having to guess the TCP sequence numbers and the MD5 password. In Cisco IOS, you can configure MD5 for LDP by configuring a password for the LDP peer with the following command:

```
mpls ldp neighbor [vrf vpn-name] ip-addr password [0-7] pswd-string
```

MD5 adds a digest to every TCP segment sent out. This digest can be verified only by both LDP peers that are configured with the correct password. If one LSR has MD5 configured for LDP and the other not, the following message is logged:

```
%TCP-6-BADAUTH: No MD5 digest from 10.200.254.4(11092) to 10.200.254.3(646)
```

If both LDP peers have a password configured for MD5 but the passwords do not match, the following message is logged:

```
%TCP-6-BADAUTH: Invalid MD5 digest from 10.200.254.4(11093) to 10.200.254.3(646)
```

Controlling the Advertisement of Labels via LDP

LDP lets you control the advertisement of labels. You can configure LDP to advertise or not to advertise certain labels to certain LDP peers. You can then use the locally assigned labels that are advertised to the LDP peers as outgoing label on those LSRs. The syntax for this command is as follows:

```
mpls ldp advertise-labels [vrf vpn-name] [interface interface |
  for prefix-access-list [to peer-access-list]]
```

The *prefix-access-list* is a standard numbered access list (1–99) or named access list that lets you specify which prefixes should have a label advertised. The *peer-access-list* is a standard numbered access list (1–99) or named access list that lets you specify which LDP peers should receive the label advertisements. The LDP peers are matched by this access list if the first 4 bytes of the LDP router ID are covered by the prefixes listed in that access list. The usage of this command is to restrict in many cases the number of labels advertised to the prefixes that are really used for forwarding traffic through the MPLS network. For instance, in the case of MPLS VPN, the important prefixes to get the customer VPN traffic through the MPLS network are the BGP next-hop prefixes, which are usually the loopback interfaces on the PE routers. In that case, you can choose not to advertise the label bindings for the prefixes belonging to the other interfaces on the PE or P routers.

> **NOTE**   You do not have to clear the LDP neighbor to which you apply the **mpls ldp advertise-labels** command for it to take effect.

You cannot control the LDP advertisement of labels for LC-ATM networks with LDP deployed with the **mpls ldp advertise-labels** command. That is because LC-ATM networks use DoD instead of UD label advertisement mode. DoD has its own command to limit LDP label advertisement. The command **mpls ldp request-labels** is used instead of **mpls ldp advertise-labels** for LC-ATM interfaces.

In Figure 4-7, you can see the sample network again. Router sydney only advertises its own loopback 0 prefix and the one from router rome (prefixes 10.200.254.4/32 and 10.200.254.3/32) toward LDP peer madrid (LDP router ID 10.200.254.5).

Figure 4-7 *Controlling LDP Advertisement*

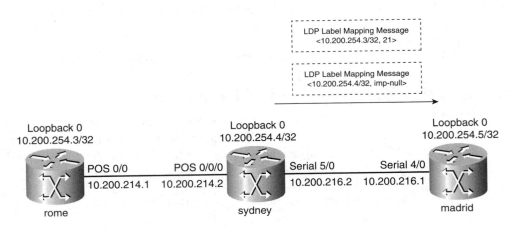

The needed configuration for this is printed in Example 4-17. Do not forget to configure **no mpls ldp advertise-labels**, too. If you forget this command and only configure the **mpls ldp advertise-labels for** *prefix-access-list* **to** *peer-access-list* command, the LSR sydney still sends labels for all prefixes via LDP.

Example 4-17 *Controlling LDP Advertisement: Configuration*

```
!
hostname sydney
!
mpls ldp router-id Loopback0 force
no mpls ldp advertise-labels
mpls ldp advertise-labels for 1 to 2
mpls label protocol ldp
!
access-list 1 permit 10.200.254.4
access-list 1 permit 10.200.254.3
access-list 1 deny    any
access-list 2 permit 10.200.254.5
access-list 2 deny    any
!
```

Only prefixes 10.200.254.3/32 and 10.200.254.4/32 are advertised to LDP peer 10.200.254.5 (router madrid). Example 4-18 shows the bindings on router sydney as a result of this filtering on label bindings.

Example 4-18 *Controlling LDP Advertisement*

```
sydney#show mpls ldp bindings advertisement-acls
Advertisement spec:
        Prefix acl = 1; Peer acl = 2

  lib entry: 10.10.100.33/32, rev 28
  lib entry: 10.200.211.0/24, rev 15
  lib entry: 10.200.254.3/32, rev 21
        Advert acl(s): Prefix acl 1; Peer acl 2
  lib entry: 10.200.254.4/32, rev 2
        Advert acl(s): Prefix acl 1; Peer acl 2
  lib entry: 10.200.254.5/32, rev 23
  lib entry: 10.200.254.6/32, rev 25

 …
```

Notice in Example 4-19 that all the other prefixes advertised from the router sydney to the router madrid have no more remote binding associated with them.

Example 4-19 *Bindings on LSR Madrid for Neighbor 10.200.254.4*

```
madrid#show mpls ldp bindings neighbor 10.200.254.4 detail
  lib entry: 10.200.210.0/24, rev 34
  lib entry: 10.200.211.0/24, rev 14
  lib entry: 10.200.254.3/32, rev 24, chkpt: none
        remote binding: lsr: 10.200.254.4:0, label: 21
  lib entry: 10.200.254.4/32, rev 26, chkpt: none
        remote binding: lsr: 10.200.254.4:0, label: imp-null
  lib entry: 10.200.254.5/32, rev 7
  lib entry: 10.200.254.6/32, rev 28

 …
```

In the LFIB of router madrid, the two prefixes 10.200.254.3/32 and 10.200.254.4/32 have a valid outgoing label, whereas the other prefixes have 'No label' associated with them as outgoing labels. You can see the LFIB on router madrid in Example 4-20.

Example 4-20 *LFIB on LSR Madrid*

```
madrid#show mpls forwarding-table
Local  Outgoing      Prefix          Bytes Label  Outgoing    Next Hop
Label  Label or VC   or Tunnel Id    Switched     interface
16     No Label      10.200.218.0/24  0           Se4/0       point2point
17     No Label      10.200.211.0/24  0           Se4/0       point2point
```

continues

Example 4-20 *LFIB on LSR Madrid (Continued)*

```
20    No Label    10.200.254.1/32   0         Se4/0    point2point
21    No Label    10.200.254.2/32   0         Se4/0    point2point
22    21          10.200.254.3/32   0         Se4/0    point2point
23    Pop Label   10.200.254.4/32   73537     Se4/0    point2point
24    No Label    10.200.254.6/32   0         Se4/0    point2point
```

The Cisco IOS LDP implementation allows you to specify more than one **mpls ldp advertise-labels for** *prefix-access-list* **to** *peer-access-list* command. This brings greater flexibility when you are deciding which label bindings to send to which LDP peers.

Example 4-21 is the same as the previous one, with the addition of another **mpls ldp advertise-labels for** *prefix-access-list* **to** *peer-access-list* command in the configuration of the router. Now the router sydney advertises only the label bindings for the two prefixes to 10.200.254.5 and all label bindings for all prefixes to all the other LDP peers.

Example 4-21 *Controlling LDP Advertisement: Example 2*

```
!
hostname sydney
!
mpls ldp router-id Loopback0 force
no mpls ldp advertise-labels
mpls ldp advertise-labels for 1 to 2
mpls ldp advertise-labels for other-prefixes to other-ldp-peers
mpls label protocol ldp
!
ip access-list standard other-ldp-peers
 deny    10.200.254.5
 permit any
ip access-list standard other-prefixes
 permit any
access-list 1 permit 10.200.254.4
access-list 1 permit 10.200.254.3
access-list 1 deny    any
access-list 2 permit 10.200.254.5
access-list 2 deny    any
!
```

MPLS LDP Inbound Label Binding Filtering

You can filter out incoming label bindings from an LDP neighbor. In effect, this is the opposite of the feature that prevents the advertising of label bindings. You can use the inbound label binding filtering on the receiving LDP peer if you cannot apply the outbound filtering of label bindings, as described in the previous section. This feature can limit the number of label bindings stored in the

LIB of the router. For instance, you can filter out all received label bindings from the LDP peers, except for the label bindings of the loopback interfaces of PE routers in an MPLS VPN network. Usually, these loopback interfaces have the BGP next-hop IP addresses, and the LSRs can use the label associated with that prefix to forward the labeled customer VPN traffic.

Following is the command to enable the inbound label binding filtering:

```
mpls ldp neighbor [vrf vpn-name] nbr-address labels accept acl
```

Example 4-22 shows the madrid LSR that applies this LDP inbound label binding filtering to LDP peer 10.200.254.4. It limits the accepted label bindings to 10.200.254.3/32 and 10.200.254.4/32, the loopback prefixes of PE routers. You can verify that the LSR has remote label bindings only from the specified LDP peer for the prefixes permitted by the access list with the command **show mpls ldp bindings**. The effect of this inbound label binding filtering is the same as the outbound label binding filtering in Example 4-17.

Example 4-22 *Example of LDP Inbound Label Binding Filtering*

```
!
hostname madrid
!
mpls ldp neighbor 10.200.254.4 labels accept 1
mpls ldp router-id Loopback0 force
mpls label protocol ldp
!
access-list 1 permit 10.200.254.4
access-list 1 permit 10.200.254.3
!
madrid#show mpls ldp bindings
  lib entry: 10.200.211.0/24, rev 61
        local binding:  label: 26
  lib entry: 10.200.254.2/32, rev 69
        local binding:  label: 27
  lib entry: 10.200.254.3/32, rev 71
        local binding:  label: 19
        remote binding: lsr: 10.200.254.4:0, label: 21
  lib entry: 10.200.254.4/32, rev 28
        local binding:  label: 24
        remote binding: lsr: 10.200.254.4:0, label: imp-null
  lib entry: 10.200.254.5/32, rev 7
        local binding:  label: imp-null

...
```

LDP Autoconfiguration

LDP is enabled on an interface by configuring the interface command **mpls ip**. On an LSR, LDP is usually enabled on all the interfaces on which the IGP is enabled. Much easier than configuring **mpls ip** on every interface separately is enabling LDP Autoconfiguration for the IGP. Every interface on which the IGP is running then has LDP enabled. The OSPF router command to enable LDP Autoconfiguration is this:

```
mpls ldp autoconfig [area area-id]
```

As you can see, it can be enabled for just a specific OSPF area. You can also disable it from specific interfaces if you want to. The interface command to disable LDP Autoconfiguration on an interface is as follows:

```
no mpls ldp igp autoconfig
```

Look at Example 4-23. "Interface config" indicates that LDP is enabled through the interface **mpls ip** command. "IGP config" indicates that LDP is enabled through the router **mpls ldp autoconfig** command.

Example 4-23 *Configuration Example of LDP Autoconfiguration*

```
!
hostname madrid
!
router ospf 1
 mpls ldp autoconfig area 0
 router-id 10.200.254.5
 log-adjacency-changes
 network 10.200.254.0 0.0.0.255 area 0
 network 10.200.0.0 0.0.255.255 area 0
!
madrid#show mpls interfaces detail
Interface Ethernet3/1:
        IP labeling enabled (ldp):
          Interface config
          IGP config
        LSP Tunnel labeling enabled
        BGP labeling not enabled
        MPLS operational
...
Interface Serial4/0:
        IP labeling enabled (ldp):
          Interface config
          IGP config
        LSP Tunnel labeling enabled
        BGP labeling not enabled
        MPLS operational
```

Example 4-23   *Configuration Example of LDP Autoconfiguration (Continued)*

```
...

madrid#show mpls ldp discovery detail
 Local LDP Identifier:
    10.200.254.5:0
    Discovery Sources:
    Interfaces:
        Ethernet3/1 (ldp): xmit/recv
            Enabled: Interface config, IGP config;
            Hello interval: 5000 ms; Transport IP addr: 10.200.254.5
            LDP Id: 10.200.254.2:0
              Src IP addr: 10.200.215.1; Transport IP addr: 10.200.254.2
              Hold time: 15 sec; Proposed local/peer: 15/15 sec
              Reachable via 10.200.254.2/32
        Serial4/0 (ldp): xmit/recv
            Enabled: Interface config; IGP config;
            Hello interval: 5000 ms; Transport IP addr: 10.200.254.5
            LDP Id: 10.200.254.4:0
              Src IP addr: 10.200.216.2; Transport IP addr: 10.200.254.4
              Hold time: 15 sec; Proposed local/peer: 15/15 sec
              Reachable via 10.200.254.4/32
```

MPLS LDP-IGP Synchronization

A problem with MPLS networks is that LDP and the IGP of the network are not synchronized. Synchronization means that the packet forwarding out of an interface happens only if both the IGP and LDP agree that this is the outgoing link to be used. A common problem with MPLS networks that are running LDP is that when the LDP session is broken on a link, the IGP still has that link as outgoing; thus, packets are still forwarded out of that link. This happens because the IGP installs the best path in the routing table for any prefix. Therefore, traffic for prefixes with a next hop out of a link where LDP is broken becomes unlabeled. This is not a big problem for networks that are running IPv4-over-MPLS only. At the point where LDP is broken, the packets become unlabeled. The packets are forwarded as IPv4 packets until they become labeled again on the next LSR. However, this is a problem for more than just the IPv4-over-MPLS case. With MPLS VPN, AToM, Virtual Private LAN Switching (VPLS), or IPv6 over MPLS, the packets must not become unlabeled in the MPLS network. If they do become unlabeled, the LSR does not have the intelligence to forward the packets anymore and drops them.

In the case of MPLS VPN, the packets are IPv4 packets, but they should be forwarded according to a VRF routing table. This table is private for one customer and is present only on the edge LSRs or PE routers. Therefore, when the MPLS VPN packets become unlabeled on the core LSRs—the P routers—they are dropped. The same is true for AToM and IPv6 traffic. The core LSRs cannot forward them unlabeled. One LDP session being down while the IGP adjacency is up between two LSRs can result in major problems because much traffic can be lost. Figure 4-8 illustrates an LDP session being down between two LSRs in the MPLS core and labeled packets being dropped.

Figure 4-8 *LDP Session Down Between LSRs*

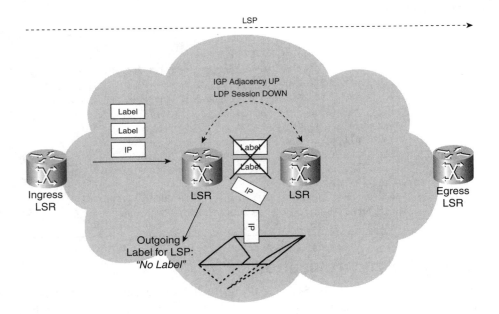

The same problem can occur when LSRs restart. The IGP can be quicker in establishing the adjacencies than LDP can establish its sessions. This means that the IGP forwarding is already happening before the LFIB has the necessary information to start the correct label forwarding. The packets are incorrectly forwarded (unlabeled) or dropped until the LDP session is established.

The solution is MPLS LDP-IGP Synchronization. This feature ensures that the link is not used to forward (unlabeled) traffic when the LDP session across the link is down. Rather, the traffic is forwarded out another link where the LDP session is still established.

NOTE   At the time of writing this book, the only IGP that is supported with MPLS LDP-IGP Synchronization is OSPF.

The problem that LDP-IGP Synchronization solves cannot happen with BGP and label distribution. Because BGP takes care of the binding advertisement and the control plane for IP routing, the before-mentioned problem cannot happen. Although it is possible for the IGP adjacency to be up while LDP is down on a link, BGP is either up or down, meaning that the installation of the IP prefix in the routing table by BGP is linked to the advertisement of the label binding for that prefix by BGP.

How MPLS LDP-IGP Synchronization Works

When the MPLS LDP-IGP synchronization is active for an interface, the IGP announces that link with maximum metric until the synchronization is achieved, or until the LDP session is running across that interface. The maximum link metric for OSPF is 65536 (hex 0xFFFF). No path through the interface where LDP is down is used unless it is the only path. (No other paths have a better metric.) After the LDP session is established and label bindings have been exchanged, the IGP advertises the link with its normal IGP metric. At that point, the traffic is label-switched across that interface. Basically, OSPF does not form an adjacency across a link if the LDP session is not established first across that link. (OSPF does not send out Hellos on the link.)

Until the LDP session is established or until the synchronization Holddown timer has expired, the OSPF adjacency is not established. Synchronized here means that the local label bindings have been sent over the LDP session to the LDP peer. However, when the synchronization is turned on at router A and that router has only one link to router B and no other IP connectivity to router B via another path (this means via other routers), the OSPF adjacency never comes up. OSPF waits for the LDP session to come up, but the LDP session cannot come up because router A cannot have the route for the LDP router ID of router B in its routing table. The OSPF and LDP adjacency can stay down forever in this situation! If router A has only router B as a neighbor, the LDP router ID of router B is not reachable; this means that no route exists for it in the routing table of router A. In that case, the LDP-IGP synchronization detects that the peer is not reachable and lets OSPF bring up the adjacency anyway. In this case, the link is advertised with maximum metric until the synchronization occurs. This makes the path through that link a path of last resort.

In some cases, the problem with the LDP session might be a persistent one; therefore, it might not be desirable to keep waiting for the IGP adjacency to be established. The solution for this is to configure a Holddown timer for the synchronization. If the timer expires before the LDP session is established, the OSPF adjacency is built anyway. If everything is fine with LDP across that link, LDP also forms a session across the link. While OSPF is waiting to bring up its adjacency until LDP synchronizes, the OSPF interface state is down and OSPF does not send Hellos onto that link.

MPLS LDP-IGP Synchronization Configuration

MPLS LDP-IGP Synchronization is enabled for the IGP process. This means that it is configured for an IGP, and it applies to all the interfaces on which the IGP is running. The command to enable it for the IGP is **mpls ldp sync**, and it is configured under the router process. You can disable MPLS LDP-IGP Synchronization on one particular interface with the command **no mpls ldp igp sync**. By default, if synchronization is not achieved, the IGP waits indefinitely to bring up the adjacency. You can change this with the global command **mpls ldp igp sync holddown** *msecs*, which instructs the IGP to wait only for the configured time. After the synchronization Holddown timer expires, the IGP forms an adjacency across the link. As long as the IGP adjacency is up, while the LDP session is not synchronized, the IGP advertises the link with maximum metric.

When OSPF is waiting for LDP to synchronize, it says "Interface is down and pending LDP." In that state, OSPF does not form an adjacency. When the OSPF adjacency is up but the LDP session is not, OSPF says "Interface is up and sending maximum metric." The interface is not used to forward traffic in this case unless it is the only path out of the LSR. Example 4-24 shows the configuration for MPLS LDP-IGP Synchronization.

Example 4-24 *Configuration Example of MPLS LDP-IGP Synchronization*

```
!
hostname madrid
!
router ospf 1
 mpls ldp sync
 router-id 10.200.254.5
 log-adjacency-changes
 network 10.200.254.0 0.0.0.255 area 0
 network 10.200.0.0 0.0.255.255 area 0
!
madrid#show ip ospf mpls ldp interface serial 4/0
Serial4/0
  Process ID 1, Area 0
  LDP is not configured through LDP autoconfig
  LDP-IGP Synchronization : Required
  Holddown timer is not configured
  Interface is up
```

Example 4-25 shows the output of the command **show ip ospf mpls ldp interface** when the interface is back up after it went down, but LDP has a problem, and the LDP session does not come up. As a result, OSPF does not form an adjacency. In fact, the OSPF state of the interface is DOWN.

Example 4-25 *MPLS LDP-IGP Synchronization*

```
madrid#show ip ospf mpls ldp interface serial 4/0
Serial4/0
  Process ID 1, Area 0
  LDP is not configured through LDP autoconfig
  LDP-IGP Synchronization : Required
  Holddown timer is not configured
  Interface is down and pending LDP
```

Example 4-25 *MPLS LDP-IGP Synchronization (Continued)*

```
madrid#show ip ospf interface serial 4/0
Serial4/0 is up, line protocol is up
  Internet Address 10.200.216.1/24, Area 0
  Process ID 1, Router ID 10.200.254.5, Network Type POINT_TO_POINT, Cost: 10
  Transmit Delay is 1 sec, State DOWN,
  Timer intervals configured, Hello 10, Dead 40, Wait 40, Retransmit 5
    oob-resync timeout 40

madrid#show interfaces serial 4/0
Serial4/0 is up, line protocol is up
  Hardware is M4T
  Internet address is 10.200.216.1/24
```

To prevent OSPF from waiting indefinitely for LDP to come up, you can configure a Holddown timer as in Example 4-26. After the Holddown timer expires, OSPF forms an adjacency, even when LDP is not synchronized yet.

Example 4-26 *Example of MPLS LDP-IGP Synchronization with Holddown Timer*

```
!
hostname madrid
!
mpls label protocol ldp
mpls ldp igp sync holddown 30000
!
madrid#show ip ospf mpls ldp interface serial 4/0
Serial4/0
  Process ID 1, Area 0
  LDP is not configured through LDP autoconfig
  LDP-IGP Synchronization : Required
  Holddown timer is configured : 30000 msecs
  Holddown timer is running and is expiring in 1708 msecs
  Interface is down and pending LDP

madrid#
22:21:00: %OSPF-5-ADJCHG: Process 1, Nbr 10.200.254.4 on Serial4/0 from LOADING to FULL,
 Loading Done
```

After the Holddown timer expires, the OSPF adjacency is formed, but the LDP session is still down because of a persisting LDP problem on the link. As long as this state remains, OSPF is advertising the link with the maximum OSPF metric of 65535. Look at Example 4-27 to see this. The sync status is "sync not achieved."

Example 4-27 *MPLS LDP-IGP Synchronization: Advertising Maximum Metric*

```
madrid#show ip ospf mpls ldp interface serial 4/0
Serial4/0
  Process ID 1, Area 0
  LDP is not configured through LDP autoconfig
  LDP-IGP Synchronization : Required
  Holddown timer is configured : 30000 msecs
  Holddown timer is not running
  Interface is up and sending maximum metric

madrid#show ip ospf database router 10.200.254.5

            OSPF Router with ID (10.200.254.5) (Process ID 1)

            Router Link States (Area 0)

  LS age: 276
  Options: (No TOS-capability, DC)
  LS Type: Router Links
  Link State ID: 10.200.254.5
  Advertising Router: 10.200.254.5
  LS Seq Number: 800000CA
  Checksum: 0x43D7
  Length: 72
  Number of Links: 4

    Link connected to: another Router (point-to-point)
     (Link ID) Neighboring Router ID: 10.200.254.4
     (Link Data) Router Interface address: 10.200.216.1
      Number of TOS metrics: 0
      TOS 0 Metrics: 65535

    Link connected to: a Stub Network
     (Link ID) Network/subnet number: 10.200.216.0
     (Link Data) Network Mask: 255.255.255.0
      Number of TOS metrics: 0
      TOS 0 Metrics: 10
...

madrid#show mpls ldp igp sync serial 4/0
    Serial4/0:
        LDP configured; LDP-IGP Synchronization enabled.
        Sync status: sync not achieved; peer reachable.
        IGP holddown time: 30000 milliseconds.
        IGP enabled: OSPF 1
```

The result of advertising the link with a maximum metric is that the LSR cannot use the link to forward packets. If an MPLS AToM, IPv6, VPLS packet, or any labeled packet with two or more labels were to arrive on router madrid and need to be forwarded on interface serial 4/0 while LDP is down and LDP-IGP Synchronization does not exist, those packets would be dropped. With LDP-IGP synchronization, these packets would be routed onto another interface, where the LDP session is established.

The following **debug** command provides debug information on the LDP synchronization.

```
debug mpls ldp sync [interface <name>] [peer-acl <acl>]
```

Example 4-28 shows the output of the **debug mpls ldp igp sync** command.

Example 4-28 *MPLS LDP-IGP Debug Information*

```
madrid#debug mpls ldp igp sync interface serial 4/0
LDP-IGP Synchronization debugging is on for interface Serial4/0
madrid#
22:42:34: %LINK-3-UPDOWN: Interface Serial4/0, changed state to up
22:42:34: LDP-SYNC: Se4/0: queue swif_updown, set INTFADDR_PENDING.
22:42:34: LDP-SYNC: Se4/0: process swif_updown, clear INTFADDR_PENDING.
22:42:35: %LINEPROTO-5-UPDOWN: Line protocol on Interface Serial4/0, changed state to up
22:43:14: %OSPF-5-ADJCHG: Process 1, Nbr 10.200.254.4 on Serial4/0 from LOADING to FULL,
 Loading Done
madrid#
22:44:31: LDP-SYNC: Se4/0: No session or session has not send initial update, ignore adj
joining event.
22:44:31: %LDP-5-NBRCHG: LDP Neighbor 10.200.254.4:0 is UP
22:44:31: LDP-SYNC: Se4/0: session 10.200.254.4:0 came up, sync_achieved up
22:44:31: LDP-SYNC: Se4/0, OSPF 1: notify status (required, achieved, no delay, holddown
 30000)
22:44:31: OSPF: schedule to build router LSA after notification from LDP
```

If the peer is not reachable, as in Example 4-29, the IGP forms an adjacency anyway to give LDP the opportunity to build an LDP session across that link. This happens when this link is the only path (still working) to the peer router.

Example 4-29 *Peer Not Reachable*

```
madrid#show mpls ldp igp sync interface serial 4/0
    Serial4/0:
        LDP configured; LDP-IGP Synchronization enabled.
        Sync status: sync not achieved; peer not reachable.
        IGP holddown time: infinite.
        IGP enabled: OSPF 1
```

MPLS LDP Session Protection

A common problem in networks is flapping links. The flapping of links can have several causes, but it is not the goal of this book to look deeper into this. Flapping links do have an important impact on the convergence of the network. Because the IGP adjacency and the LDP session are running across the link, they go down when the link goes down. This is unfortunate, especially because the link is usually not down for long. The impact is pretty severe though, because the routing protocol and LDP can take time to rebuild the neighborship. LDP has to rebuild the LDP session and must exchange the label bindings again. To avoid having to rebuild the LDP session altogether, you can protect it. When the LDP session between two directly connected LSRs is protected, a targeted LDP session is built between the two LSRs. When the directly connected link does go down between the two LSRs, the targeted LDP session is kept up as long as an alternative path exists between the two LSRs. The LDP link adjacency is removed when the link goes down, but the targeted adjacency keeps the LDP session up. When the link comes back up, the LSR does not need to re-establish the LDP session; therefore, the convergence is better. The global command to enable LDP Session Protection is this:

```
mpls ldp session protection [vrf vpn-name] [for acl] [duration seconds]
```

The *access list (acl)* you can configure lets you specify the LDP peers that should be protected. It should hold the LDP Router Identifier of the LDP neighbors that need protection. The duration is the time that the protection (the targeted LDP session) should remain in place after the LDP link adjacency has gone down. The default value is infinite.

For the protection to work, you need to enable it on both the LSRs. If this is not possible, you can enable it on one LSR, and the other LSR can accept the targeted LDP Hellos by configuring the command **mpls ldp discovery targeted-hello accept**.

Look at Figure 4-9 to see an example. LDP Session Protection is enabled on all four routers. The LSR madrid has two LDP sessions: one with london and one with sydney. When the link madrid-sydney fails, the targeted LDP session is held up as it reroutes over the path madrid-london-rome-sydney. Example 4-30 shows the LDP session on madrid to router sydney before the link went down. The link madrid-sydney then goes down. You can see a logging message for the LDP session when the link goes down and when the link comes back up. The first logging message indicates that the LDP session has gone into protecting state; the second indicates that the LDP session has been recovered successfully.

Figure 4-9   *LDP Session Protection*

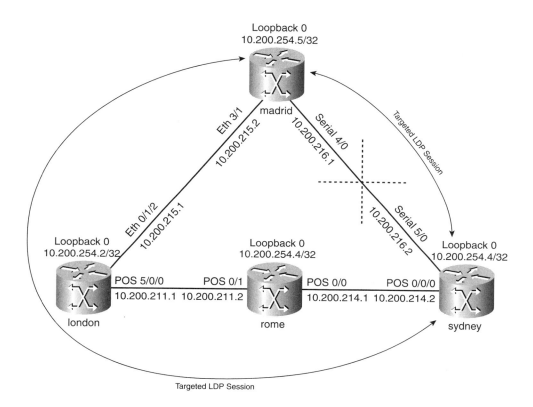

Example 4-30   *Example of LDP Session Protection*

```
madrid#show mpls ldp neighbor serial 4/0 detail
     Peer LDP Ident: 10.200.254.4:0; Local LDP Ident 10.200.254.5:0
         TCP connection: 10.200.254.4.646 - 10.200.254.5.21396
         State: Oper; Msgs sent/rcvd: 43/42; Downstream; Last TIB rev sent 63
         Up time: 00:15:32; UID: 18; Peer Id 0;
         LDP discovery sources:
           Targeted Hello 10.200.254.5 -> 10.200.254.4, active, passive;
            holdtime: infinite, hello interval: 10000 ms
           Serial4/0; Src IP addr: 10.200.216.2
             holdtime: 15000 ms, hello interval: 5000 ms
```

continues

Example 4-30 *Example of LDP Session Protection (Continued)*

```
            Addresses bound to peer LDP Ident:
                10.200.254.4    10.200.214.2    10.200.217.1    10.200.216.2
            Peer holdtime: 180000 ms; KA interval: 60000 ms; Peer state: estab
            Clients: Dir Adj Client
            LDP Session Protection enabled, state: Ready
                duration: infinite


madrid#show mpls ldp discovery
 Local LDP Identifier:
    10.200.254.5:0
    Discovery Sources:
    Interfaces:
        Ethernet3/1 (ldp): xmit/recv
            LDP Id: 10.200.254.2:0
        Serial4/0 (ldp): xmit/recv
            LDP Id: 10.200.254.4:0
    Targeted Hellos:
        10.200.254.5 -> 10.200.254.4 (ldp): active/passive, xmit/recv
            LDP Id: 10.200.254.4:0
        10.200.254.5 -> 10.200.254.2 (ldp): active/passive, xmit/recv
            LDP Id: 10.200.254.2:0
madrid#
02:48:38: %OSPF-5-ADJCHG: Process 1, Nbr 10.200.254.4 on Serial4/0 from FULL to DOWN,
Neighbor Down: Interface down or detached
02:48:39: %LINK-3-UPDOWN: Interface Serial4/0, changed state to down
02:48:39: %LDP-5-SP: 10.200.254.4:0: session hold up initiated
02:48:40: %LINEPROTO-5-UPDOWN: Line protocol on Interface Serial4/0, changed state to down
madrid#show mpls ldp neighbor 10.200.254.4 detail
    Peer LDP Ident: 10.200.254.4:0; Local LDP Ident 10.200.254.5:0
        TCP connection: 10.200.254.4.646 - 10.200.254.5.21396
        State: Oper; Msgs sent/rcvd: 55/51; Downstream; Last TIB rev sent 69
        Up time: 00:17:18; UID: 18; Peer Id 0;
        LDP discovery sources:
          Targeted Hello 10.200.254.5 -> 10.200.254.4, active, passive;
            holdtime: infinite, hello interval: 10000 ms
        Addresses bound to peer LDP Ident:
            10.200.254.4    10.200.214.2    10.200.217.1    10.200.216.2
        Peer holdtime: 180000 ms; KA interval: 60000 ms; Peer state: estab
        Clients: Dir Adj Client
        LDP Session Protection enabled, state: Protecting
            duration: infinite


madrid#
02:49:10: %LINK-3-UPDOWN: Interface Serial4/0, changed state to up
02:49:11: %LINEPROTO-5-UPDOWN: Line protocol on Interface Serial4/0, changed state to up
02:49:15: %LDP-5-SP: 10.200.254.4:0: session recovery succeeded
```

Finally, a useful LDP feature is LDP Graceful Restart. It specifies a mechanism for LDP peers to preserve the MPLS forwarding state when the LDP session goes down. As such, traffic can continue to be forwarded without interruption, even when the LDP session restarts. You can find more information on LDP Graceful Restart in "Chapter 4 Supplement" at http://www.ciscopress.com/title/1587051974.

Summary

In this chapter, you have seen what the purpose of the Label Distribution Protocol (LDP) is. This chapter included an in-depth look at the four main functions of LDP:

- The discovery of LSRs that are running LDP

- Session establishment and maintenance

- Advertising of label mappings

- Housekeeping by means of notification

Some LDP-specific features were covered. You learned about the controlling of label advertisements with LDP, the inbound filtering of label bindings, LDP Autoconfiguration, MPLS LDP-IGP Synchronization, and LDP Session Protection. The functions of LDP and the LDP features were illustrated with configuration examples and the commands to troubleshoot and verify the correct operation of LDP.

Chapter Review Questions

You can find answers to the following questions in Appendix A, "Answers to the Chapter Review Questions."

1.   What is the fundamental purpose of LDP?

2.   Name the four main functions that LDP takes care of.

3.   How can you reduce the number of label bindings on an LSR?

4.   What problem does MPLS LDP-IGP synchronization solve?

5.   How many LDP sessions are established between two LSRs that have six links between them, of which two links are LC-ATM links and four are frame links?

6.   What do you need to configure to protect the LDP sessions against attacks?

7.   What trick does MPLS LDP-IGP Synchronization employ to ensure that the link is not used to forward traffic while the LDP session is unsynchronized?

8.   What does LDP Session Protection use to protect an LDP session?

What You Will Learn

By the end of this chapter, you should know and be able to explain the following:

- The difference between MPLS operating in Frame mode and Cell mode

- How LDP advertises label bindings in an ATM network

- How the Label Virtual Circuits are set up

- How LDP behaves differently with ATM LSRs

- How LDP can provide loop detection

- What VC-Merge is, and what its benefit is for ATM LSRs

- How to deal with ATM switches that are not aware of MPLS

- What a label switch controller is

- How to provide CoS with Label Virtual Circuits

The chapter ends with an important note on how to keep the number of Label Virtual Circuits to a minimum.

MPLS and ATM Architecture

ATM is a connection-oriented protocol that the ITU-T developed. It is connection-oriented because virtual circuits are signaled that carry the ATM traffic. The ATM traffic consists of fixed-sized cells of 53 bytes. Of those 53 bytes, 5 are the cell header and 48 are the cell data. The success of ATM was predominantly in the WAN network. Many vendors built ATM switches that could set up virtual circuits in the WAN network. The advantages of ATM are the following:

- A fixed packet size, resulting in a transmission with low jitter

- Guaranteed quality of service (QoS)

- Great flexibility

The success of ATM was limited to its use in the WAN network. As IP became the de facto standard networking protocol that almost everyone used, much effort was spent on getting IP traffic across the ATM core network. Several schemes were devised:

- Encapsulation according to RFC 1483

- Lane Emulation (LANE)

- Multiprotocol over ATM (MPOA)

RFC 1483 (made obsolete by RFC 2684) specified how to encapsulate multiple routed and bridged protocols over ATM adaptation layer (AAL) 5. LANE specified how to carry Ethernet frames across the ATM cloud. MPOA provided a tight integration of IP over ATM, but it was a complex solution. None of these solutions was perfect in providing a better fit between IP and ATM. One of the driving reasons for MPLS was just that: a better integration between IP and ATM. With MPLS, the ATM switches would need to run an IP routing protocol and a label distribution protocol to exchange IP prefixes and labels between themselves and to the routers. The result would be that the overlay model of IP over ATM would no longer be needed. With MPLS, it became a peer model.

Brief Introduction to ATM

An ATM cell is 5 bytes of header and 48 bytes of data. Look at Figure 5-1 to see the ATM UNI cell format.

Figure 5-1 *ATM UNI Cell Format*

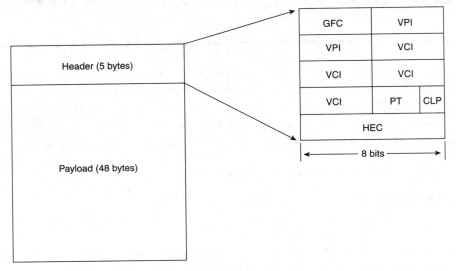

The cell format depicted in Figure 5-1 is the User-Network Interface (UNI) cell. The Network-Node Interface (NNI) header is almost identical to this one, except for the GFC field, which has been omitted. Instead, the VPI field occupies the first 12 bits and is thus 4 bits longer, which allows the ATM switches to assign a larger number of virtual path identifiers (VPI).

Table 5-1 shows the name and meaning of each field of the ATM cell header.

Table 5-1   *ATM Cell Header Fields*

Field	Name	Length (bits)	Meaning
GFC	Generic Flow Control	4	Provides local functions
VPI	Virtual path identifier	8	Identifies the next destination of the cell
VCI	Virtual channel identifier	16	Identifies the next destination of the cell
PT	Payload type	3	Indicates user data or control data
CLP	Cell Loss Priority	1	Indicates whether the cell should be discarded in the event of congestion
HEC	Header Error Control	8	Provides a checksum calculated on the header

The GFC field provides local functions for the ATM cell. Local means that it is not end to end, and the intermediate switches override the field. Local functions might mean flow control and identification of multiple stations on a single ATM interface.

The VPI and VCI fields are used together and identify the next destination of the ATM cell.

The three bits of the PT field are defined as follows:

- The first bit indicates whether the cell contains user data or control data.

- The second bit indicates whether congestion is present.

- The third bit indicates whether the cell is the last cell of an AAL5 frame (PDU).

ATM can have statically defined PVCs, or private network-network interface (PNNI) can assign the virtual circuits dynamically. PNNI is a hierarchical link-state routing protocol that lays out the virtual circuits throughout the ATM network. For the cells to be interpreted correctly and used by upper layer protocols, ITU-T specified a layer between the ATM layer and the upper layer protocols. This layer is called AAL, and it has five categories. AAL1 is connection-oriented and used for delay-sensitive services and circuit emulation. AAL2 is also connection-oriented, but it is used for variable rate services. AAL3/4 is connectionless and used mainly for the older SMDS. AAL5 can be connection-oriented or connectionless and is used for varying bit rate demands. It is used mostly for IP and LANE.

To carry IP traffic across the ATM cloud, the routers on the edge of the ATM WAN cloud are interconnected across ATM PVCs. To connect the routers in the most efficient way, you need to connect them directly to each other across PVCs. This is needed so that the IP traffic does not cross the ATM cloud twice. Therefore, the routers need to be interconnected in a fully meshed way. This is called the overlay model because all the routers have an Interior Gateway Protocol (IGP) adjacency (a peering) with each other across the ATM cloud. Look at Figure 5-2 to see an overlay network of routers across the ATM cloud.

Figure 5-2 *ATM Overlay Network*

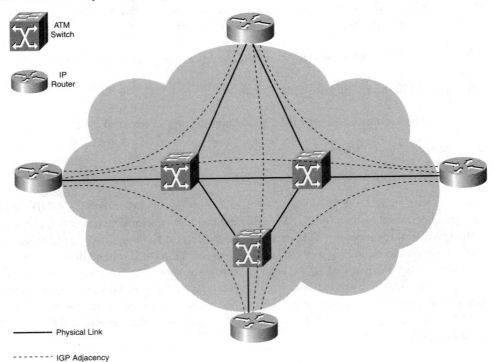

The result is that there is (n–1)/2 number of virtual circuits (VCs) needed for n routers that are connected to the ATM cloud. MPLS solves this problem. When the ATM switches are made aware of routing, they can form an IGP adjacency among themselves and toward the routers. No longer does each router need to form an IGP adjacency to all other routers, but just to the nearest ATM switch(es). Look at Figure 5-3 to see the ATM network where the ATM switches have become label switching routers (LSRs); this means they have become aware of MPLS. This is called the peer model because the routers—which are now edge LSRs—only peer to the nearest ATM switches—which are now LSRs.

Figure 5-3 *ATM LSR Peer Network*

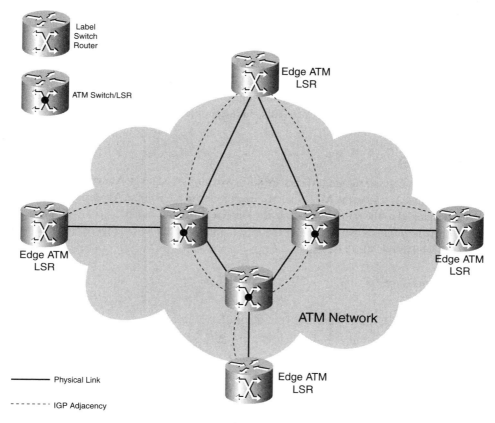

For the traffic to be forwarded correctly through the ATM LSRs, the traffic must be MPLS encapsulated, and the MPLS label value must be mapped to VPI/VCI values. That is because the ATM switches are still switching ATM cells on virtual circuits. Because the ATM switches need to be able to map the MPLS label value to a VC, they must first learn those label values. Hence, the ATM switches must run a label distribution protocol. An ATM LSR consists of the following:

- A routing protocol in the control plane

- A label distribution protocol in the control plane

- Switching ATM cells in the data plane

The Cisco ATM switches support Open Shortest Path First (OSPF) as the routing protocol and LDP as the label distribution protocol. The Cisco ATM LSRs distribute the routes in OSPF and the label bindings associated with the routes with LDP. The incoming and outgoing labels are mapped to incoming and outgoing VPI/VCI pairs. The result is that in the data plane, the ATM switch just needs to switch cells from the incoming virtual circuit to the outgoing virtual circuit, just like regular ATM forwarding. The ATM switch never forwards IP packets. If this is needed, the ATM switch would need to reassemble all incoming ATM cells into frames first. Every ATM switch along the path would need to do this. This is undesirable for performance reasons.

Label Encoding

ATM switches that are running MPLS are still switching ATM cells. As such, they cannot forward labeled frames. Because the MPLS labels are mapped to VCs in the ATM cloud, the MPLS label value is mapped to the VPI/VCI pair. If the labeled packet has a label stack with more than one label, only the value of the top label is mapped to the VPI/VCI fields. Figure 5-4 shows the MPLS label mapped to the VPI/VCI values.

Figure 5-4   *Label Encoding*

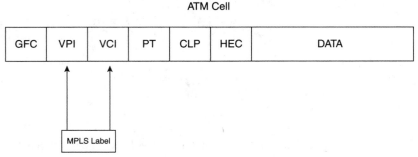

When the edge ATM LSR receives a frame, the frame is chopped up into cells. Only the top label value is encoded as a VPI/VCI value. The rest of the labels in the label stack are not needed to forward the cells. Nevertheless, the complete label stack is present in the frame (now chopped up). These labels will be needed again when the ATM cells are reassembled into a frame and the frame needs further MPLS forwarding outside the ATM network. The label value of the top label is encoded in the VPI/VCI field and changes at every ATM LSR, and the label value of the top label in the label stack is set to 0. The label is kept, however, for the three other fields: TTL, EXP, and End-of-Stack bit. The TTL sets the outgoing TTL when the packet is reassembled on the egress edge ATM LSR. The EXP bits set the QoS of the packet on the egress edge ATM LSR. Even if the label stack consists of only one label, it is still carried across the ATM cloud in the first cell. This enables the egress ATM LSR to figure out whether the packet actually had a label stack or not.

Because the VCI value is 16 bits, there can be 2^{16} or 65,536 labels. Considering that the number of VCs is limited on the ATM switch, this value alone should be enough for all the labels needed on one interface. The VPI value is 12 bits, so there can be 2^{12} or 4096 labels there.

Label Advertisement

The IGP and LDP on the ATM LSRs cannot run directly over the ATM interface and establish a neighborship. A control VC is needed for the IGP and LDP to run on between two adjacent ATM LSRs. When the IGP adjacency is built, the IGP can exchange IP prefixes which are put in the routing table. After LDP forms a session across the control VC, it can exchange label bindings. This in turn enables the ATM LSRs to populate the LIB with bindings. As you recall, a binding is a prefix and an associated label. Each IGP prefix in the routing table must be assigned a label. Each label value is mapped to a VPI/VCI value, and a virtual circuit is built for each label. Such a virtual circuit is called a label switched controlled virtual circuit (LVC) or tag switching controlled virtual circuit (TVC). To create these LVCs, you must configure the ATM interfaces on the ATM switches and routers to be Label Switching Controlled-ATM (LC-ATM) interfaces. Each such LC-ATM interface must have the control virtual circuit. On routers and ATM switches that are running Cisco IOS, this is by default the virtual circuit 0/32. The encapsulation for it must be LLC/SNAP. Figure 5-5 shows a typical MPLS network with ATM LSRs in the core.

Figure 5-5   *ATM LSR Network*

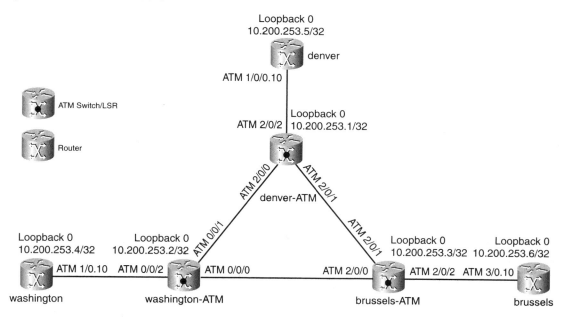

Note the three ATM LSRs: washington-atm, denver-atm, and brussels-atm. Each ATM LSR has one router attached to it via an ATM interface. All six devices are in one OSPF area. The ATM interfaces between the ATM switches are enabled for MPLS with the **mpls ip** command, and they are IP unnumbered to the loopback 0 interface. LDP is running on the ATM interfaces, and LDP sessions are formed between the ATM LSRs over the control VC. On the three interfaces of the routers toward the ATM LSRs are subinterfaces with MPLS enabled and IP unnumbered to their loopback interface 0. Example 5-1 shows the configuration on the ATM LSR denver-atm and the edge LSR denver.

Example 5-1 *Configuration of Denver LSRs*

```
!
hostname denver-atm
!
mpls label protocol ldp
tag-switching tdp router-id Loopback0 force
!
interface Loopback0
 ip address 10.200.253.1 255.255.255.255
!
interface ATM2/0/0
ip unnumbered Loopback0
tag-switching ip
!
interface ATM2/0/1
 ip unnumbered Loopback0
 tag-switching ip
!
interface ATM2/0/2
 ip unnumbered Loopback0
 tag-switching ip
!
router ospf 1
 log-adjacency-changes
 network 10.200.0.0 0.0.255.255 area 0
!


!
hostname denver
!
interface Loopback0
 ip address 10.200.253.5 255.255.255.255
!
interface ATM1/0/0
 no ip address
!
interface ATM1/0/0.10 mpls
 ip unnumbered Loopback0
 mpls ip
!
router ospf 1
 log-adjacency-changes
 network 10.200.0.0 0.0.255.255 area 0
!
```

> **NOTE**   The ATM subinterface with the **mpls** keyword at the end indicates that this is an LC-ATM subinterface on a router LSR.

Look at Example 5-2 to see how to verify that LDP runs over the ATM interfaces and how it uses the control VC 0/32.

Example 5-2   *show mpls interfaces*

```
denver-atm#show mpls interfaces
Interface              IP            Tunnel    Operational
ATM2/0/0               Yes (ldp)     No        Yes        (ATM labels)
ATM2/0/1               Yes (ldp)     No        Yes        (ATM labels)
ATM2/0/2               Yes (ldp)     No        Yes        (ATM labels)

denver-atm#show mpls interfaces detail
Interface ATM2/0/0:
        IP labeling enabled (ldp)
        LSP Tunnel labeling not enabled
        MPLS operational
        MTU = 4470
        ATM tagging: Label VPI = 1
                Label VCI range = 33 - 16383
                Control VC = 0/32
Interface ATM2/0/1:
        IP labeling enabled (ldp)
        LSP Tunnel labeling not enabled
        MPLS operational
        MTU = 4470
        ATM tagging: Label VPI = 1
                Label VCI range = 33 - 16383
                Control VC = 0/32
Interface ATM2/0/2:
        IP labeling enabled (ldp)
        LSP Tunnel labeling not enabled
        MPLS operational
        MTU = 4470
        ATM tagging: Label VPI = 1
                Label VCI range = 33 - 16383
                Control VC = 0/32
```

OSPF is running on the ATM LSRs and the edge LSRs. OSPF neighborships are formed on the ATM links, and a routing table is built with the prefixes. Because all LSRs have only the loopback

0 configured with an IP address, the routing table shows one prefix per LSR in the MPLS network. Example 5-3 shows how to verify the OSPF neighborships and IP routing table.

Example 5-3 *OSPF Neighbors and IP Routing Table*

```
denver-atm#show ip ospf neighbor

Neighbor ID    Pri   State        Dead Time   Address         Interface
10.200.253.2    1    FULL/  -     00:00:31    10.200.253.2    ATM2/0/0
10.200.253.3    1    FULL/  -     00:00:37    10.200.253.3    ATM2/0/1
10.200.253.5    1    FULL/  -     00:00:34    10.200.253.5    ATM2/0/2

denver-atm#show ip route
Codes: C - connected, S - static, I - IGRP, R - RIP, M - mobile, B - BGP
       D - EIGRP, EX - EIGRP external, O - OSPF, IA - OSPF inter area
       N1 - OSPF NSSA external type 1, N2 - OSPF NSSA external type 2
       E1 - OSPF external type 1, E2 - OSPF external type 2, E - EGP
       i - IS-IS, L1 - IS-IS level-1, L2 - IS-IS level-2, ia - IS-IS inter area
       * - candidate default, U - per-user static route, o - ODR
       P - periodic downloaded static route

Gateway of last resort is not set

     10.0.0.0/32 is subnetted, 6 subnets
O       10.200.253.6 [110/3] via 10.200.253.3, 00:14:15, ATM2/0/1
O       10.200.253.5 [110/2] via 10.200.253.5, 00:14:15, ATM2/0/2
O,      10.200.253.4 [110/3] via 10.200.253.2, 00:14:15, ATM2/0/0
O       10.200.253.3 [110/2] via 10.200.253.3, 00:14:15, ATM2/0/1
O       10.200.253.2 [110/2] via 10.200.253.2, 00:14:15, ATM2/0/0
C       10.200.253.1 is directly connected, Loopback0
```

The control VC 0/32 is set up between all devices. OSPF and LDP are running on this control VC on all ATM interfaces between the devices. Example 5-4 shows how to verify the existence of the control VC on the interfaces.

Example 5-4 *Verifying the Control VC*

```
denver-atm#show atm vc interface ATM 2/0/0
Interface    VPI  VCI   Type      X-Interface   X-VPI  X-VCI  Encap   Status
ATM2/0/0     0    5     PVC       ATM0          0      48     QSAAL   UP
ATM2/0/0     0    16    PVC       ATM0          0      35     ILMI    UP
ATM2/0/0     0    18    PVC       ATM0          0      203    PNNI    UP
ATM2/0/0     0    32    PVC       ATM0          0      230    SNAP    UP
ATM2/0/0     1    33    TVC(I)    ATM0          0      231    MUX     UP
ATM2/0/0     1    35    TVC(O)    ATM2/0/2      1      39             UP
ATM2/0/0     1    36    TVC(O)    ATM2/0/2      1      41             UP
ATM2/0/0     1    67    TVC(I)    ATM2/0/2      1      34             UP
```

Example 5-4 *Verifying the Control VC (Continued)*

```
denver-atm#show atm vc interface ATM 2/0/1
Interface      VPI  VCI  Type     X-Interface       X-VPI X-VCI Encap  Status
ATM2/0/1        0    5   PVC      ATM0                0    49    QSAAL  UP
ATM2/0/1        0   16   PVC      ATM0                0    36    ILMI   UP
ATM2/0/1        0   18   PVC      ATM0                0   204    PNNI   UP
ATM2/0/1        0   32   PVC      ATM0                0   221    SNAP   UP
ATM2/0/1        1   33   TVC(I)   ATM0                0   223    MUX    UP
ATM2/0/1        1   35   TVC(O)   ATM2/0/2            1    40           UP
ATM2/0/1        1   36   TVC(O)   ATM2/0/2            1    42           UP
ATM2/0/1        1   75   TVC(I)   ATM2/0/2            1    34           UP
```

To change the LDP control VC from 0/32 to another VPI/VCI pair, you can use the following interface command:

```
mpls atm control-vc vpi vci
```

Example 5-5 shows an example of how to change the control VC for LDP. Obviously, this must be configured on both LDP peers.

Example 5-5 *Changing the Control VC*

```
denver-atm#conf t
Enter configuration commands, one per line.  End with CNTL/Z.
denver-atm(config)#int atm 2/0/2
denver-atm(config-if)#mpls atm control-vc 0 1000
denver-atm(config-if)#^Z
denver-atm#
denver-atm#show mpls interfaces ATM 2/0/2 detail
Interface ATM2/0/2:
        IP labeling enabled (ldp)
        LSP Tunnel labeling not enabled
        MPLS operational
        MTU = 4470
        ATM tagging: Label VPI = 1
                Label VCI range = 33 - 16383
                Control VC = 0/1000
```

On the ATM LSR, you can change the VPI/VCI range that MPLS uses for the LVCs per ATM interface. The default VPI used for MPLS is 1. The Cisco IOS interface command to change the VPI/VCI range is as follows:

```
mpls atm vpi vpi [- vpi] [vci-range low - high]
```

Example 5-6 shows that the VPI range is changed to 2 and the VCI range is changed to 33–2000.

Example 5-6 *Changing the VPI/VCI Range for LVCs*

```
!
interface ATM2/0/0
 ip unnumbered Loopback0
 mpls label protocol ldp
 tag-switching atm vpi 2 vci-range 33-2000
 tag-switching ip
!

brussels-atm#show mpls interfaces ATM 2/0/0 detail
Interface ATM2/0/0:
        IP labeling enabled (ldp)
        LSP Tunnel labeling not enabled
        MPLS not operational
        MTU = 4470
        ATM tagging: Label VPI = 2
                Label VCI range = 33 - 2000
                Control VC = 0/32
```

Remember that each prefix that is present in the routing table creates a virtual circuit through the network. Therefore, in the interest of scalability, it is better to limit the number of prefixes in the routing table. One way of doing this, which is highly advisable, is to have the ATM interfaces as IP unnumbered interfaces. You need a loopback interface anyway as LDP router ID and IGP router ID, and the IP unnumbered interfaces can point to the loopback interface. When you do not use IP unnumbered interfaces, you allocate a label and a virtual circuit to each IP prefix that is configured on a link. These unimportant prefixes do not forward traffic through the ATM network, so unused LVCs are set up.

Downstream-on-Demand Label Advertisement

To avoid unnecessary label advertisement for prefixes in the routing table, the ATM LSR does not operate in Unsolicited Downstream (UD) label advertisement mode. Rather, it operates in Downstream-on-Demand (DoD) label advertisement mode. This means that an ATM LSR only advertises a label (binding) when it is requested to. The upstream LSR requests the downstream LSR for a label for a particular prefix. The upstream ATM LSR knows who the downstream LSR is by looking up the next hop for the prefix in the routing table. ATM LSRs (and routers with LC-ATM interfaces) use the Ordered LSP Control mode (as discussed in Chapter 2, "MPLS Architecture") by default, whereas routers (non-LC-ATM interfaces) use the Independent LSP Control mode.

With Ordered LSP Control mode, the downstream ATM LSR only replies with a label if it has received a label for the prefix from its downstream LSR. The egress LSR at the end of the LSP is the first to allocate a (local) label to the prefix, and it sends this label to the upstream LSR. In turn, this LSR allocates a (local) label and sends it to the upstream LSR. Figure 5-6 shows an example of ATM LSRs and DoD Label Advertisement mode with Ordered LSP Control mode.

Figure 5-6 *DoD Label Advertisement with Ordered LSP Control Mode*

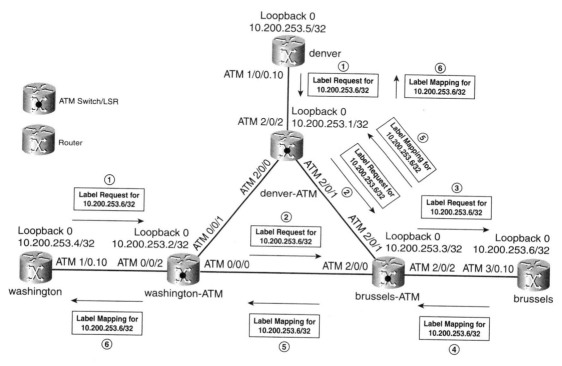

When a new prefix is learned throughout the network via the router brussels, the routers denver and washington send an LDP Label Request message to their downstream ATM LSR neighbor, requesting a label for the prefix. They in turn send an LDP Label Request message to the downstream LSRs. This continues until the Label Request reaches the edge ATM LSR brussels. This router returns an LDP Label Mapping message to its upstream neighbor. The upstream neighbor sends an LDP Label Mapping message upstream and so on, until the edge ATM LSR is reached. At that point, every ATM LSR has the label binding for the destination. Because the ATM LSRs run in DoD mode, they only request a label from the next-hop LSR as indicated by the routing table. Thus, the label retention mode is conservative for LSRs that are running DoD label advertisement mode.

When the routing adjacencies are up, the IP prefixes are propagated, the routing table is built on the LSRs, and LDP forms the LDP neighborships and advertises the label bindings for the prefixes, the ATM LSRs can build the LVCs between them.

> **NOTE**   LVCs and ATM Forum virtual circuits can exist on the same ATM switches and the same ATM interfaces.

Look at Example 5-7. If IP traffic needs to go from the denver edge LSR to the brussels edge LSR (destination 10.200.253.6), it takes the following LVCs (TVCs):

- 1/42 out on denver

- 1/42 in and 1/36 out on denver-atm

- 1/36 in and 1/33 out on brussels-atm

- 1/33 in on brussels (tail end router)

To see the ATM LDP bindings, use the **show mpls atm-ldp bindings** command. Example 5-7 shows you how to use that command to track the LVCs through the ATM LSRs.

Example 5-7   *Checking the LVCs*

```
denver#show mpls forwarding-table
Local   Outgoing      Prefix            Bytes tag   Outgoing      Next Hop
tag     tag or VC     or Tunnel Id      switched    interface
17      1/38          10.200.253.1/32   0           AT1/0/0.10 point2point
18      1/39          10.200.253.2/32   0           AT1/0/0.10 point2point
19      1/40          10.200.253.3/32   0           AT1/0/0.10 point2point
20      1/41          10.200.253.4/32   0           AT1/0/0.10 point2point
21      1/42          10.200.253.6/32   0           AT1/0/0.10 point2point


denver#show atm vc interface ATM 1/0/0.10
                    VCD /                                   Peak Avg/Min Burst
Interface           Name      VPI   VCI Type   Encaps    Kbps   Kbps Cells Sts
1/0/0.10            56        0     32 PVC      SNAP      149760  N/A       UP
1/0/0.10            62        1     34 TVC      MUX       149760  N/A       UP
1/0/0.10            63        1     38 TVC      MUX       149760  N/A       UP
1/0/0.10            66        1     39 TVC      MUX       149760  N/A       UP
1/0/0.10            64        1     40 TVC      MUX       149760  N/A       UP
1/0/0.10            67        1     41 TVC      MUX       149760  N/A       UP
1/0/0.10            65        1     42 TVC      MUX       149760  N/A       UP


denver#show mpls forwarding-table 10.200.253.6 detail
Local   Outgoing      Prefix            Bytes tag   Outgoing      Next Hop
tag     tag or VC     or Tunnel Id      switched    interface
21      1/42          10.200.253.6/32   0           AT1/0/0.10 point2point
        MAC/Encaps=4/8, MRU=4470, Tag Stack{1/42(vcd=65)}
        00418847 00041000
        No output feature configured
```

Example 5-7 *Checking the LVCs (Continued)*

```
denver#show mpls atm-ldp bindings 10.200.253.6 32
  Destination: 10.200.253.6/32
     Headend Router ATM1/0/0.10 (3 hops) 1/42  Active, VCD=65

denver-atm#show mpls atm-ldp bindings 10.200.253.6 32
  Destination: 10.200.253.6/32
     Transit ATM2/0/2 1/42 Active -> ATM2/0/1 1/36 Active

denver-atm#show atm vc interface ATM 2/0/2 1 42

Interface: ATM2/0/2, Type: oc3suni
VPI = 1   VCI = 42
Status: UP
Time-since-last-status-change: 00:18:52
Connection-type: TVC(I)
Cast-type: multipoint-to-point-input
…
Cross-connect-interface: ATM2/0/1, Type: oc3suni
Cross-connect-VPI = 1
Cross-connect-VCI = 36
Cross-connect-UPC: pass
…

brussels-atm#show mpls atm-ldp bindings 10.200.253.6 32
  Destination: 10.200.253.6/32
     Transit ATM2/0/0 1/36 Active -> ATM2/0/2 1/33 Active
     Transit ATM2/0/1 1/36 Active -> ATM2/0/2 1/33 Active

brussels-atm#show atm vc interface ATM 2/0/1 1 36

Interface: ATM2/0/1, Type: oc3suni
VPI = 1   VCI = 36
Status: UP
Time-since-last-status-change: 00:20:00
Connection-type: TVC(I)
Cast-type: multipoint-to-point-input
Packet-discard-option: enabled
Usage-Parameter-Control (UPC): pass
Wrr weight: 2
Number of OAM-configured connections: 0
OAM-configuration: disabled
OAM-states:  Not-applicable
Cross-connect-interface: ATM2/0/2, Type: oc3suni
Cross-connect-VPI = 1
Cross-connect-VCI = 33
Cross-connect-UPC: pass
```

continues

Example 5-7 *Checking the LVCs (Continued)*

```
...

brussels#show mpls atm-ldp bindings 10.200.253.6 32
 Destination: 10.200.253.6/32
    Tailend Router ATM3/0.10 1/33 Active, VCD=597
```

Look at Example 5-8 to see the complete label information base (LIB) for the ATM LSR denver. You can see one entry per IP prefix in the routing table. An ATM switch can be in three positions regarding the LSPs (LVCs): tail end switch, transit, or head end switch. A head end switch means that the ATM LSR is the ingress LSR, and a tail end switch means that the ATM LSR is the egress LSR. A transit LSR is the ATM LSR between the ingress and egress LSR on the LSP. The *Tailend Switch* entries in Example 5-8 are the entries for the prefix 10.200.253.1/32 because this prefix is directly connected on the LSR denver-atm. Three entries exist because the ATM LSR denver-atm has three upstream ATM LSR neighbors for that prefix: denver, washington-atm, and brussels-atm. These LDP label bindings lead to the LVCs (TVCs) set up as in Example 5-4.

Example 5-8 *ATM Label Bindings*

```
denver-atm#show mpls atm-ldp bindings
 Destination: 10.200.253.1/32
    Tailend Switch ATM2/0/1 1/33 Active -> Terminating Active, VCD=223
    Tailend Switch ATM2/0/0 1/33 Active -> Terminating Active, VCD=231
    Tailend Switch ATM2/0/2 1/38 Active -> Terminating Active, VCD=240
 Destination: 10.200.253.5/32
    Transit ATM2/0/1 1/75 Active -> ATM2/0/2 1/34 Active
    Transit ATM2/0/0 1/67 Active -> ATM2/0/2 1/34 Active
 Destination: 10.200.253.2/32
    Transit ATM2/0/2 1/39 Active -> ATM2/0/0 1/35 Active
 Destination: 10.200.253.3/32
    Transit ATM2/0/2 1/40 Active -> ATM2/0/1 1/35 Active
 Destination: 10.200.253.4/32
    Transit ATM2/0/2 1/41 Active -> ATM2/0/0 1/36 Active
 Destination: 10.200.253.6/32
    Transit ATM2/0/2 1/42 Active -> ATM2/0/1 1/36 Active
```

You can see that the LDP-learned labels are VPI/VCI values, and the VCs have been set up in the data plane as a result of the learned MPLS labels. The command **show mpls ip binding** gives another nice overview of the label bindings per prefix. Example 5-9 shows the output of this command.

Example 5-9 *Show MPLS IP Binding*

```
denver-atm#show mpls ip binding
  10.200.253.1/32
        in label:     imp-null
        in vc label:  1/33      lsr: 10.200.253.2:1   ATM2/0/0
                      Active     egress (vcd 231)
        in vc label:  1/38      lsr: 10.200.253.5:1   ATM2/0/2
                      Active     egress (vcd 240)
        in vc label:  1/33      lsr: 10.200.253.3:2   ATM2/0/1
                      Active     egress (vcd 246)
  10.200.253.2/32
        in label:     16
        in vc label:  1/39      lsr: 10.200.253.5:1   ATM2/0/2
                      Active     transit
        out vc label: 1/35      lsr: 10.200.253.2:1   ATM2/0/0
                      Active     transit
  10.200.253.3/32
        in label:     17
        in vc label:  1/91      lsr: 10.200.253.5:1   ATM2/0/2
                      Active     transit
        out vc label: 1/33      lsr: 10.200.253.3:2   ATM2/0/1
                      Active     transit
  10.200.253.4/32
        in label:     18
        in vc label:  1/41      lsr: 10.200.253.5:1   ATM2/0/2
                      Active     transit
        out vc label: 1/36      lsr: 10.200.253.2:1   ATM2/0/0
                      Active     transit
  10.200.253.5/32
        in label:     25
        in vc label:  1/67      lsr: 10.200.253.2:1   ATM2/0/0
                      Active     transit
        in vc label:  1/34      lsr: 10.200.253.3:2   ATM2/0/1
                      Active     transit
        out vc label: 1/34      lsr: 10.200.253.5:1   ATM2/0/2
                      Active     transit
  10.200.253.6/32
        in label:     19
        in vc label:  1/92      lsr: 10.200.253.5:1   ATM2/0/2
                      Active     transit
        out vc label: 1/36      lsr: 10.200.253.3:2   ATM2/0/1
                      Active     transit
```

LDP Control Mode for ATM

Chapter 2 mentioned two possible control modes for label advertisement: Ordered and Independent Control mode. The Independent Control mode means that an LSR immediately responds to a Label Request message from the upstream LSR. Ordered means that the LSR only responds to the Label Request message from the upstream LSR when it received a response to its Label Request message from its downstream LSR. In Figure 5-6, the Control mode was Ordered. Look at Figure 5-7 to see the two different Control modes side by side.

Figure 5-7 *LDP Control Modes*

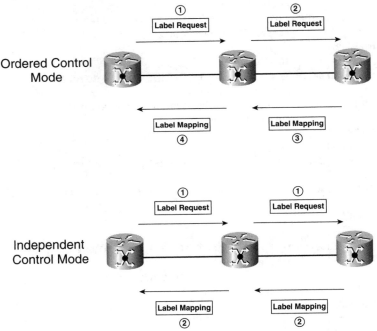

The default Control mode in Cisco IOS on ATM switches is Ordered Control. To change the Control mode, use the following global Cisco IOS command:

```
mpls ldp atm control-mode {ordered | independent}
```

The disadvantage of Ordered Control mode is the delay in receiving a label binding. The advantage is that no packets are lost, because the ingress ATM LSR only has an outgoing label (and hence an outgoing LVC) if all ATM LSRs along the path have one. Packets can be lost in Independent Control mode until all ATM LSRs have the label bindings for that LSP. An ATM LSR that does not have an outgoing LVC must perform an expensive operation—namely, it must reassemble the cells into a packet and then discard the packet.

Look at Example 5-10 to see Label Request and Label Mapping messages received and sent out on the denver-atm LSR running Independent Control mode for a new prefix learned downstream from denver-atm. (The downstream LSR is brussels-atm.)

Example 5-10   *Independent Control Mode*

```
denver-atm#
denver-atm#conf t
Enter configuration commands, one per line.  End with CNTL/Z.
denver-atm(config)#mpls ldp atm control-mode independent
denver-atm(config)#^Z
denver-atm#

denver-atm#deb mpls ldp messages sent
LDP sent PDUs, excluding periodic Keep Alives debugging is on
denver-atm#deb mpls ldp messages received
LDP received messages, excluding periodic Keep Alives debugging is on
denver-atm#show debugging

MPLS ldp:
   LDP received messages, excluding periodic Keep Alives debugging is on
   LDP sent PDUs, excluding periodic Keep Alives debugging is on

ldp: Rcvd label request msg from 10.200.253.5:1 (pp 0x6302D8C4)
ldp: Sent label mapping msg to 10.200.253.5:1 (pp 0x6302D8C4)
ldp: Sent label request msg to 10.200.253.3:2 (pp 0x6302E47C)
ldp: Rcvd label mapping msg from 10.200.253.3:2 (pp 0x6302E47C)
ldp: Rcvd label mapping msg from 10.200.253.3:2 (pp 0x6302E47C)
ldp: Sent label mapping msg to 10.200.253.5:1 (pp 0x6302D8C4)
```

You can see that the LSR denver-atm sends a Label Mapping message immediately in response to the Label request message from the LSR denver (10.200.253.5). In Ordered Control mode, the LSR denver-atm sends a Label Request message to the downstream LSR brussels-atm (10.200.253.3) and awaits the receipt of the Label Mapping message from it before sending a Label Mapping message back to the denver LSR. This is depicted in Example 5-11.

Example 5-11   *Ordered Control Mode*

```
denver-atm#
ldp: Rcvd label request msg from 10.200.253.5:1 (pp 0x6302D8C4)
ldp: Sent label request msg to 10.200.253.3:2 (pp 0x6302E47C)
ldp: Rcvd label mapping msg from 10.200.253.3:2 (pp 0x6302E47C)
ldp: Sent label mapping msg to 10.200.253.5:1 (pp 0x6302D8C4)
```

LDP for LC-ATM

This section covers some specifics on LDP when running on an LC-ATM interface.

Label Space

Per-interface label space is used for LC-ATM interfaces. As you can see in Example 5-12, it means that the peer LDP is not identified with *router-id:0* as in the non-LC-ATM case. The number following the peer LDP router Identifier is now non-zero. If you have multiple links between a pair of ATM LSRs, multiple label spaces will exist between them. Look at Example 5-12 to see that the ATM LSRs washington-atm and brussels-atm have two ATM links between them and two label spaces.

Example 5-12 Per-Interface Label Space

```
washington-atm#show mpls ldp discovery
Local LDP Identifier:
    10.200.253.2:0
Discovery Sources:
    Interfaces:
        ATM0/0/0 (ldp): xmit/recv
            LDP Id: 10.200.253.3:1
        ATM0/0/1 (ldp): xmit/recv
            LDP Id: 10.200.253.1:1
        ATM0/0/2 (ldp): xmit/recv
            LDP Id: 10.200.253.4:1
        ATM0/0/3 (ldp): xmit/recv
            LDP Id: 10.200.253.3:4

washington-atm#show mpls ldp neighbor 10.200.253.3
Peer LDP Ident: 10.200.253.3:1; Local LDP Ident 10.200.253.2:3
        TCP connection: 10.200.253.3.11215 - 10.200.253.2.646
        State: Oper; Msgs sent/rcvd: 471/450; Downstream on demand
        Up time: 04:46:55
        LDP discovery sources:
          ATM0/0/0, Src IP addr: 10.200.253.3
Peer LDP Ident: 10.200.253.3:4; Local LDP Ident 10.200.253.2:4
        TCP connection: 10.200.253.3.11225 - 10.200.253.2.646
        State: Oper; Msgs sent/rcvd: 4/4; Downstream on demand
        Up time: 00:02:02
        LDP discovery sources:
          ATM0/0/3, Src IP addr: 10.200.253.3
```

Loop Detection by LDP

Loop detection in LDP is optional. It consists of the usage of a Hop Count TLV and a Path Vector TLV to find out if an LSP is looping or if Label Request messages are looping. Routing loops can be permanent, but these are rather rare or are the result of a configuration error. Transient loops do occur more often and can be short in nature. They are often the result of the routing protocol converging and one LSR converging faster than the other. If labeled packets are looping, the label TTL eventually reaches 0, and the packet is dropped. However, ATM LSRs forward cells instead of frames. The ATM cells do not have a TTL value, so ATM LSRs cannot use this mechanism. Because an LSP is a VC on ATM LSRs, a mechanism is needed to make sure that the VCs do not loop. Cisco ATM LSRs use both the Hop Count TLV and Path Vector TLV to prevent a looped LSP from being signaled in the first place. When a loop is detected in Cisco IOS, the LSR periodically resends Label Request messages to try to set up the LSP.

Loop Detection by Hop Count TLV

A Hop Count TLV holds the number of LSRs that the LDP message has traversed. Every LSR that sees this TLV must increment the hop count by 1. A loop is detected when a configured maximum hop count value is reached. Following is the command to enable loop detection by means of the Hop Count TLV in Cisco IOS:

```
mpls ldp maxhops number
```

The default value for the maximum hop count argument (number) is 254.

You can configure the maximum hop count to be n. The ingress LSR of a FEC sends an LDP Label Request message with a hop count of 1. The next LSR that receives this request must increase the hop count by 1 in its request, and so on. The same is true for Label Mapping messages. There, the egress LSR must send the first LDP Label Mapping message with a hop count of 1. Subsequent LSRs increase the hop count value by 1. If the MPLS network consists of a part with ATM LSRs and a part with router LSRs, the LSRs at the edge of the ATM domain reset the hop count value to 1, because the ATM LSRs are not "hop count-capable." When an ATM LSR detects that the hop count has reached the maximum configured value n, it returns a Loop Detected Notification message to the source of the Label Request or Label Mapping message. The Label Request or Label Mapping message is not answered with a Label Mapping message. It also is not propagated or used.

Figure 5-8 shows how to use the **mpls ldp maxhops** command. If the routing protocol is in a looped status around the network, the Label Request message can also be looping.

Figure 5-8 *Usage of ldp maxhops Command*

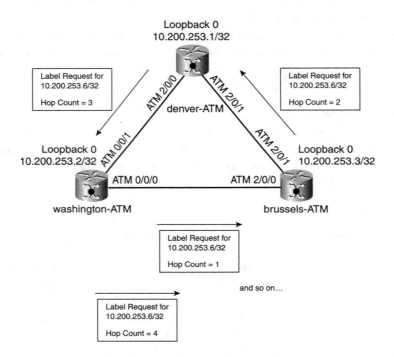

Example 5-13 shows the ATM LSR brussels, which detected a hop count that exceeded the maximum hop count configured. The LSR learns this as soon as it receives an LDP Notification message indicating that the hop count was exceeded.

Example 5-13 *Hop Count Exceeded*

```
brussels#show mpls atm-ldp bindings

Destination: 10.200.253.4/32
    Headend Router ATM3/0.10 (3 hops) 1/36  Active, VCD=748
Destination: 10.200.253.5/32
    Headend Router ATM3/0.10 (hop count exceeded) -/-  BindWait
...
%TDP-4-HOPCOUNT_EXCEEDED: Peer = 10.200.253.3:3 Label Mapping(10.200.253.5/32) Maxhop=10
hopcount=10  ATM3/0.10
```

If the ATM LSRs are running LDP in Independent Control mode, the initial hop count value is set to 0. A hop count of 0 indicates that the real hop count is unknown. If an ATM LSR later receives a Label Mapping message from a downstream neighbor with a non-zero hop count, it sends a new Label Mapping message to the upstream neighbor with an updated hop count. This continues until the ingress ATM LSR receives the Label Mapping message with the real hop count through the ATM network.

Example 5-14 shows the prefix 10.200.253.6/32 with an unknown hop count as a result of the Independent Control mode. The correct hop count is learned later from a downstream LSR.

Example 5-14 *Unknown Hop Count*

```
denver#show mpls atm-ldp bindings
 Destination: 10.200.253.1/32
    Headend Router ATM1/0/0.10 (1 hop) 1/33  Active, VCD=189
 Destination: 10.200.253.2/32
    Headend Router ATM1/0/0.10 (2 hops) 1/34  Active, VCD=190
 Destination: 10.200.253.3/32
    Headend Router ATM1/0/0.10 (2 hops) 1/35  Active, VCD=191
 Destination: 10.200.253.4/32
    Headend Router ATM1/0/0.10 (3 hops) 1/36  Active, VCD=192
 Destination: 10.200.253.6/32
    Headend Router ATM1/0/0.10 (hop count unknown) 1/44  Active, VCD=200
 Destination: 10.200.253.5/32
    Tailend Router ATM1/0/0.10 1/33 Active, VCD=189
```

TTL Manipulation

ATM LSRs cannot decrement the TTL value at each hop. You can use the mechanism described in the previous section by means of the hop count propagated by LDP to set the TTL value of a labeled packet before it enters the ATM domain. As you can see in Example 5-14, the hop count is present for each binding that is received. You can determine the incoming TTL of a packet on the ingress ATM LSR either from the IP TTL if the packet is received as an IP packet or from the TTL in the top label if the packet is received as a labeled packet. This incoming TLL is decremented by 1 to arrive at the new TTL. Then two things are possible: You can use this TTL on the ingress ATM LSR to send the packet, or you can use this TTL minus the reported hop count in the label binding for the prefix to send the packet. The result of the latter is that the TTL set on the packet when it leaves the ingress ATM LSR already has the number of hops through the ATM domain calculated in. If, however, the result of that subtraction is 0 or less, the packet is discarded on the ingress ATM LSR. Look at Figure 5-9. If a packet arrives with a TTL of 3, the ingress ATM LSR does not forward it, because the hop count through the ATM domain is deemed too large. If, however, a packet that has a TTL of 200 arrives on the ingress ATM LSR, it is forwarded with a TTL of 197. The egress ATM LSR then sees an incoming packet with a TTL of 197.

Figure 5-9 *TTL Through ATM Domain*

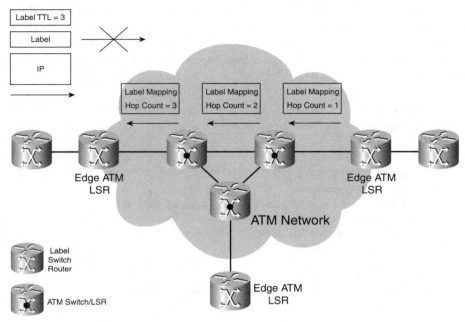

Cisco IOS uses the first possible method. The ingress ATM LSR only decrements the TTL by 1 before sending the packet—as ATM cells—into the ATM cloud. This method has the advantage of a clean traceroute output. If Cisco IOS were to use the second method, the ingress ATM LSR would have to reply to multiple traceroute probes, as many as there are ATM LSRs on the path. That would cause the ingress ATM LSR to show up in multiple lines of the traceroute output.

A traceroute through the MPLS network does not show the ATM part of the network. The ATM part is missing from the traceroute output. The ATM LSRs have the same affect on traceroute as if you were to configure **no mpls ip propagate-ttl** on the edge LSRs of an MPLS network without ATM. Example 5-15 shows a traceroute from the router LSR san-francisco (connected to the LSR denver) to the LSR brussels. As you can see, the ATM switches are not reported in the traceroute output.

Example 5-15 *Traceroute Example*

```
san-francisco#traceroute 10.200.253.6

Type escape sequence to abort.
Tracing the route to 10.200.253.6

  1 10.200.200.2 [MPLS: Label 21 Exp 0] 4 msec 0 msec 0 msec    (LSR denver)
  2 10.200.253.6 4 msec *  0 msec     (LSR brussels)
```

> **NOTE**   Refer to Chapter 13, "Troubleshooting MPLS Networks," to see how tracerouting through an MPLS network operates and what the command **mpls ip propagate-ttl** does.

Loop Detection by Path Vector TLV

A Path Vector TLV holds the list of the LSRs that an LDP message has traversed. The list holds the LSR Identifier—the first four bytes of the LDP Identifier—of the traversed LSRs. Each LSR that propagates the LDP message containing the Path Vector TLV must add its own LSR Identifier to the TLV. A loop is detected when an LSR receives an LDP message with a Path Vector TLV containing its own LSR Identifier. In Cisco IOS, the command to enable loop detection by means of the Path Vector TLV is this:

```
mpls ldp loop-detection
```

When an LSR detects a loop in the received Label Request message or in the Label Mapping message, it must send a Loop Detected Notification message to the source of that LDP message. Example 5-16 shows the result of turning on loop detection with the Path Vector TLV. The path information of the label bindings lists the LSR Identifier of the traversed LSRs.

Example 5-16   *Bindings with Path Information*

```
denver#show mpls atm-ldp bindings path
 Destination: 10.200.253.1/32
    Headend Router ATM1/0/0.10 (1 hop) 1/33  Active, VCD=254
       Path:     10.200.253.5*   10.200.253.1
 Destination: 10.200.253.2/32
    Headend Router ATM1/0/0.10 (2 hops) 1/52  Active, VCD=263
       Path:     10.200.253.5*   10.200.253.1   10.200.253.2
 Destination: 10.200.253.3/32
    Headend Router ATM1/0/0.10 (2 hops) 1/44  Active, VCD=260
       Path:     10.200.253.5*   10.200.253.1   10.200.253.3
 Destination: 10.200.253.4/32
    Headend Router ATM1/0/0.10 (3 hops) 1/53  Active, VCD=264
       Path:     10.200.253.5*   10.200.253.1   10.200.253.2   10.200.253.4
...
```

When the LSRs are running in Independent Control mode, they might need to send multiple Label Mapping messages when either method of loop detection is turned on. As an LSR receives a Label Mapping message from a downstream neighbor with either an updated Hop Count TLV or Path Vector TLV present, it must send a Label Mapping message upstream with that updated TLV. That means many Label Mapping messages might be sent for one LSP. You can avoid this when running Ordered Control mode on the ATM LSRs because the LSRs send only one Label Request and one Label Mapping message per LSP.

For either loop detection method to properly function, it must be turned on for all LSRs that are running LDP. Otherwise, inconsistencies can occur.

LDP Address Messages

An LSR that is running LDP can advertise its IP addresses via LDP. As mentioned in Chapter 2, labels can be advertised in two modes: UD and DoD. LDP can run in both modes. Chapter 4, "Label Distribution Protocol," deals with LDP and explains a bit more the differences in the two modes. It covers why LDP in UD mode must advertise the IP addresses of the LSRs. Without it, the LSRs cannot build the LFIB needed to forward labeled packets, because they need to associate a next hop from the routing table with a peer LDP Router Identifier.

ATM LSRs run in DoD mode and only need to request a label from their downstream neighbor. Furthermore, only one LDP peer exists per LC-ATM interface. Therefore, mapping the received label to the downstream LDP peer is straightforward, and as a result, ATM LSRs really do not need to send their IP addresses to their LDP neighbors. Cisco ATM LSRs run label advertisement in DoD mode and do not advertise their IP addresses. However, you can enable them to advertise their IP addresses anyway. The advantage of doing this is that other vendor ATM LSRs might require the IP addresses to be sent. The Cisco IOS interface command to enable the advertisement of the IP addresses to LC-ATM LDP peers is this:

```
mpls ldp address-message
```

When this command is enabled on the brussels-atm LSR, it advertises its IP addresses to its neighbors. Example 5-17 shows that the neighboring LSR brussels has the one IP address of brussels-atm as a bound IP address to that LDP peer.

Example 5-17   *Advertised Addresses*

```
brussels#show mpls ldp neighbor
    Peer LDP Ident: 10.200.253.3:3; Local LDP Ident 10.200.253.6:1
        TCP connection: 10.200.253.3.646 - 10.200.253.6.47852
        State: Oper; Msgs sent/rcvd: 75/93; Downstream on demand
        Up time: 00:53:41
        LDP discovery sources:
          ATM3/0.10, Src IP addr: 10.200.253.3
        Addresses bound to peer LDP Ident:
          10.200.253.3
```

Blocking Label Requests

The command **mpls ldp request-labels** is used for LC-ATM interfaces instead of the command **mpls ldp advertise-labels** to block label advertisements.

```
mpls ldp request-labels for acl
```

You can configure this command on the ATM LSRs to stop them from sending Label Requests for IP prefixes that do not need an LSP to be set up. Example 5-18 shows the edge ATM LSR denver with this command and 1 stopping it from sending Label Requests for anything other than IP addresses from the range 10.200.253.0/24.

Example 5-18   *Blocking Label Requests on Edge ATM LSR*

```
!
hostname denver
!
mpls label protocol ldp
mpls ldp router-id Loopback0 force
mpls ldp request-labels for 1
!
!
access-list 1 permit 10.200.253.0 0.0.0.255
access-list 1 deny   any
!
```

In general, you want to block LVCs from being set up for IP prefixes that are not important—IP prefixes that do not carry customer or through traffic. In the example of MPLS VPN, the important prefixes in the MPLS network are the PE loopback IP addresses because they are the BGP next-hop IP addresses. These IP addresses carry the VPN customer traffic across the MPLS cloud. Refer to Chapter 7, "MPLS VPN," to understand why the BGP next-hop IP addresses are important prefixes in MPLS VPN networks.

Aggregate Labels

Aggregate labels can be the result of aggregation or summarization of IP prefixes in the network. You can aggregate multiple IPv4 prefixes into one prefix with a smaller mask capturing all the component prefixes with longer masks. You can do this in an MPLS network, but it might not be a good idea. When the labeled packets arrive at the aggregation router, it removes the label and performs an IP lookup, and then it labels them again and forwards them. Do not aggregate on ATM LSRs for that reason. The aggregation label entails that the labeled packets must become unlabeled on the ATM LSR. For this to happen, the aggregating ATM LSR first reassembles the cells into a frame. When the aggregating ATM LSR forwards the packet by doing an IP lookup, it chops the frame into cells again. This is an expensive operation and has a serious performance impact. That is why you should always avoid aggregation on ATM LSRs.

VC-Merge

As mentioned, the upstream LSR requests a label for a prefix from its downstream LSR and so on, until it reaches the egress LSR. However, without VC-merge, the label requests are propagated from the ingress LSR to the egress LSR, even if an intermediate LSR has already received an outgoing label from its downstream LSR for that prefix. Look at Figure 5-10, where the ATM LSR brussels-atm has already received a label for the prefix 10.200.253.6/32 from its downstream LSR brussels. This first label was outgoing label 1/34 from brussels-atm to brussels. For the traffic from washington-atm to brussels, a second label will be requested from brussels by brussels-atm. This is the label 1/33.

Figure 5-10 *Two Upstream LSRs*

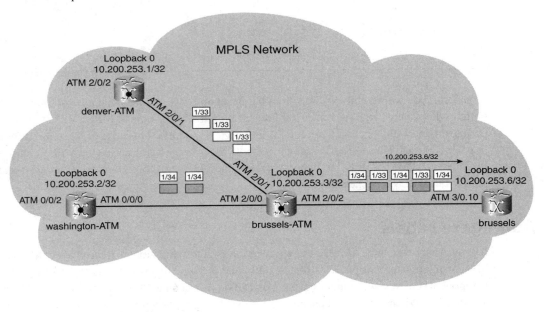

Why does the same destination 10.200.253.6/32 on brussels-atm have a second outgoing label? One VC is from denver-atm to brussels, and the second VC is from washington-atm to brussels. What if the LSR brussels-atm does not request a second label for the second upstream LSR washington-atm but uses the label that it already received from LSR brussels? There would be a problem. Look at Figure 5-11 to see the interleaving of cells problem.

Figure 5-11 *Interleaving of Cells*

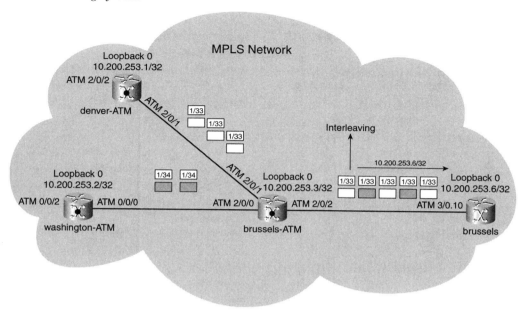

LSR brussels-atm has two incoming labels—one for each upstream LSR and only one outgoing label toward LSR brussels. Therefore, cells from both the LSR denver-atm and the LSR washington-atm are interleaved onto the same LVC; this means they have the same VPI/VCI value toward the LSR brussels. The egress LSR brussels—which needs to reassemble the ATM cells into frames—does not know which cells belong to which of the two streams. That is not a good idea. It might work, however, if the cells forming one frame are not interleaved with cells from another frame from a different upstream LSR. You can do this if the merging LSR (here LSR brussels-atm) buffers the cells until it detects that it has received the last cell from the frame. This detection can be accomplished by looking at the end-of-frame bit in the cell header. The merging LSR can then send the cells without interleaving the cells with cells from another upstream LSR. The cells do need to be buffered, which requires extra memory on the ATM LSR. The procedure of buffering the cells and only using one outgoing label per prefix for all upstream ATM LSRs is called VC-Merge. Different incoming LVCs are merged into one outgoing LVC. Look at Figure 5-12 to see VC-Merge.

Figure 5-12 *VC-Merge*

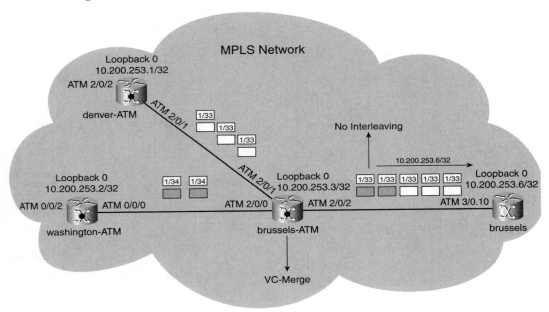

The obvious advantage of VC-Merge is that the number of needed VCs is reduced. If the router brussels-atm had five upstream LSRs for a set of 50 prefixes, there would already be (5 – 1) * 50 = 200 LVCs less in this simple example.

Following is the global Cisco IOS command to enable VC-Merge:

```
mpls ldp atm vc-merge
```

VC-Merge is on by default on Cisco ATM Switches.

Look at Example 5-19 to see the LVCs before disabling VC-Merge on the LSR brussels-atm. Two LVCs are incoming, but only one LVC is outgoing for the prefix 10.200.253.6/32.

Example 5-19 *LVCs Before Disabling VC-Merge*

```
brussels-atm#show mpls atm-ldp bindings 10.200.253.6 32
 Destination: 10.200.253.6/32
    Transit ATM2/0/0 1/36 Active -> ATM2/0/2 1/33 Active
    Transit ATM2/0/1 1/36 Active -> ATM2/0/2 1/33 Active
```

Examine Example 5-20. Notice the VCs after disabling VC-Merge on the LSR brussels-atm. You can see two outgoing LVCs for the prefix 10.200.253.6/32.

Example 5-20   *LVCs After Disabling VC-Merge*

```
brussels-atm#conf t
Enter configuration commands, one per line.  End with CNTL/Z.
brussels-atm(config)#no mpls ldp atm vc-merge
brussels-atm(config)#^Z
brussels-atm#

brussels-atm#show mpls atm-ldp bindings 10.200.253.6 32
 Destination: 10.200.253.6/32
    Transit ATM2/0/1 1/34 Active -> ATM2/0/2 1/33 Active
    Transit ATM2/0/0 1/33 Active -> ATM2/0/2 1/34 Active
```

Non MPLS-Aware ATM Switches

Some ATM switches in the network might not run MPLS. The solution to this problem is to run Virtual Path (VP) tunnels across the non-MPLS-aware ATM switches. Figure 5-13 shows a network with ATM switches that are not MPLS-aware. A VP tunnel is created across those ATM switches to carry the LVCs, which are created as needed on the VP tunnel. The VCIs are mapped to the MPLS labels and carry the "labeled" ATM cells.

Figure 5-13   *MPLS over VP Tunnels*

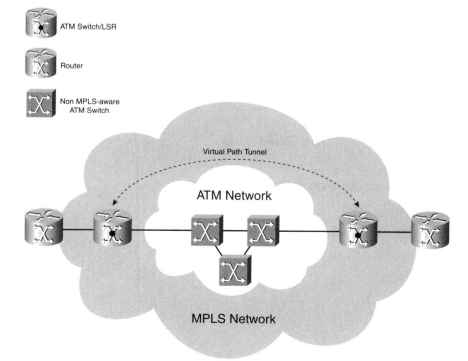

In the example network, the ATM LSR denver-atm is now non-MPLS-aware. Figure 5-14 shows the VP tunnel across the LSR denver-atm.

Figure 5-14 *VP Tunnels Across denver-atm*

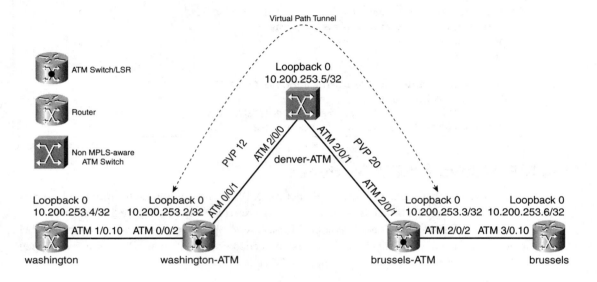

A VP tunnel is created from the LSR washington-atm to the LSR brussels-atm that carries the LVCs across the non-MPLS-aware ATM switch. Look at Example 5-21 to see the configuration needed on the LSRs. An ATM subinterface is created for the VP tunnel.

Example 5-21 *Configuration for MPLS over VP Tunnel*

```
!
hostname washington-atm
!
mpls label protocol ldp
tag-switching tdp router-id Loopback0 force
!
interface Loopback0
 ip address 10.200.253.2 255.255.255.255
!
interface ATM0/0/1
 ip unnumbered Loopback0
```

Example 5-21 *Configuration for MPLS over VP Tunnel (Continued)*

```
 atm pvp 12
  tag-switching ip
 !
 interface ATM0/0/1.12 point-to-point
  ip unnumbered Loopback0
  tag-switching ip
 !


 !
 hostname denver-atm
 !
 interface ATM2/0/0
  ip unnumbered Loopback0
 !
 interface ATM2/0/1
  ip unnumbered Loopback0
  atm pvp 20 interface ATM2/0/0 12
 !


 !
 hostname brussels-atm
 !
 interface ATM2/0/1
  ip unnumbered Loopback0
  atm pvp 20
 !
 interface ATM2/0/1.20 point-to-point
  ip unnumbered Loopback0
  tag-switching ip
 !
```

NOTE PVP stands for permanent virtual path.

The PVP 12 is switched to PVP 20 on the ATM switch denver-atm. The LSR washington-atm now forms an OSPF adjacency and LDP neighborship directly with the LSR brussels-atm across the

VP tunnel. The LVCs (TVCs) are created onto the VP tunnel as they are mapped onto the created subinterface. Example 5-22 shows this.

Example 5-22 *Verifying MPLS over VP Tunnel*

```
denver-atm#show atm vp
Interface        VPI  Type  X-Interface    X-VPI    Status
ATM2/0/0          12  PVP   ATM2/0/1        20      UP
ATM2/0/1          20  PVP   ATM2/0/0        12      UP


washington-atm#show ip ospf neighbor

Neighbor ID      Pri  State         Dead Time  Address        Interface
10.200.253.3      1   FULL/  -      00:00:32   10.200.253.3   ATM0/0/1.12
10.200.253.4      1   FULL/  -      00:00:37   10.200.253.4   ATM0/0/2


washington-atm#show mpls ldp neighbor
Peer LDP Ident: 10.200.253.4:1; Local LDP Ident 10.200.253.2:2
        TCP connection: 10.200.253.4.48103 - 10.200.253.2.646
        State: Oper; Msgs sent/rcvd: 123/122; Downstream on demand
        Up time: 01:13:07
        LDP discovery sources:
          ATM0/0/2, Src IP addr: 10.200.253.4
Peer LDP Ident: 10.200.253.3:2; Local LDP Ident 10.200.253.2:3
        TCP connection: 10.200.253.3.11316 - 10.200.253.2.646
        State: Oper; Msgs sent/rcvd: 29/29; Downstream on demand
        Up time: 00:18:44
        LDP discovery sources:
          ATM0/0/1.12, Src IP addr: 10.200.253.3


washington-atm#show atm vc interface ATM 0/0/1.12
Interface      VPI  VCI  Type    X-Interface   X-VPI  X-VCI  Encap  Status
ATM0/0/1.12     12   3   PVC     ATM0           0     169    SNAP   UP
ATM0/0/1.12     12   4   PVC     ATM0           0     170    SNAP   UP
ATM0/0/1.12     12   5   PVC     ATM0           0     168    QSAAL  UP
ATM0/0/1.12     12  16   PVC     ATM0           0     167    ILMI   UP
ATM0/0/1.12     12  18   PVC     ATM0           0     213    PNNI   UP
ATM0/0/1.12     12  32   PVC     ATM0           0     197    SNAP   UP
ATM0/0/1.12     12  33   TVC(I)  ATM0           0     218    MUX    UP
ATM0/0/1.12     12  33   TVC(O)  ATM0/0/2       1      47           UP
ATM0/0/1.12     12  34   TVC(I)  ATM0/0/2       1      39           UP
ATM0/0/1.12     12  34   TVC(O)  ATM0/0/2       1      48           UP
```

Label Switch Controller

The label switch controller (LSC) is a piece of hardware designed to perform the control plane functions needed to make the ATM switch an ATM LSR. The Cisco BPX is an ATM switch that needs an LSC to become an ATM LSR. The LSC takes care of the control plane functions like the IGP, the routing table, and LDP. The PBX still performs the switching of the ATM cells in the data plane. In the case of the BPX, the LSC is a Cisco 7200 router. The LSC controls the BPX through an ATM interface over which the Virtual Switch Interface (VSI) protocol is running. VSI allows the router to control the ports, trunks, or virtual trunks on the BPX. The result is the same as if the LSC were internal to the ATM switch. When a PBX has an LSC attached to it, it becomes an ATM LSR for all intents and purposes. The LSC creates cross-connects in the switching fabric of the BPX for the LVCs. The interfaces are presented to Cisco IOS as XTagATM (extended label ATM) interfaces on the LSC.

Multi-Virtual Circuit Tagged Bit Rate

With Multi-Virtual Circuit Tagged Bit Rate (Multi-VC TBR), multiple VCs are set up for the same destination to provide different class of service (CoS). Up to four parallel LVCs can go toward the same destination. The switches can then treat the cells differently based on which LVC they are on. The incoming IP packets are mapped with their IP precedence/DiffServ bits to the corresponding outgoing LVC. The labeled packets are mapped based on the EXP bits value of the top label onto the corresponding LVCs. On the ingress edge ATM LSRs are multiple outgoing VCs out of the LC-ATM interface. All of these VCs take the same path, which the least-cost route of the IGP determines.

Multiple VCs out of an interface are enabled with the interface **mpls atm multi-vc** command. This is configured on the edge ATM LSR so that it requests four LVCs set up per prefix. The default mapping of incoming packets onto the parallel outgoing LVCs is depicted in Table 5-2.

Table 5-2   *Multi-VC Default Mapping*

LVC Type	CoS	IP Precedence/MPLS EXP
Available	0	0 and 4
Standard	1	1 and 5
Premium	2	2 and 6
Control	3	3 and 7

You can change the IP precedence/DiffServ of the incoming IP packets or the EXP bits value of the incoming labeled packets through Modular QoS Command Line Interface (MQC). MQC is a flexible and feature-rich component of Cisco IOS that controls QoS. Here it is used to set or change the QoS of the packets before they are sent into the ATM core. Besides classifying the packets, MQC can police and shape the traffic at ingress.

To support the Multi-VC TBR LVCs on the ATM switches, four classes of CoS have been defined. These four TBR classes are best-effort, which means that bandwidth is not guaranteed. These four TBR service classes are depicted in Table 5-3.

Table 5-3   *TBR Classes*

ATM Forum Service Class	CoS	Relative Class Weight	LVC Type
CBR	2	—	
VBR-RT	2	8	
VBR-nRT	3	1	
UBR	4	1	
ABR	5	1	
TBR_1 (WRR_1)	1	1	Available
TBR_2 (WRR_2)	6	2	Standard
TBR_3 (WRR_3)	7	3	Premium
TBR_4 (WRR_4)	8	4	Control

NOTE   No connection admission control (CAC) exists for LVCs because they are best-effort virtual circuits and have no bandwidth guarantees.

You can see that the LVCs do not share the same CoS as the ATM Forum VCs (VBR-RT, VBR-nRT, ABR, and UBR). Each TBR class indicates the CoS treatment that the ATM cells will get at each ATM LSR. Because the cells are on different VCs, they end up in different queues. The ATM cells receive the CoS treatment in two ways:

■ Scheduling based on the relative class weight

■ Discard treatment according to Weighted Early Packet Discard (WEPD)

The command to change the relative class weight for a particular service class is as follows:

```
atm service-class service-class wrr-weight weight
```

You can assign each service class (1–8) a weight of 1 to 15. Example 5-23 shows the configuration needed on the edge ATM LSR brussels for Multi-VC TBR. The output shows four LVCs set up for the prefix 10.200.253.5/32. Four LVCs are set up for all prefixes.

Example 5-23 *Multi-VC TBR Configuration*

```
!
hostname brussels
!
interface ATM3/0.10 mpls
 ip unnumbered Loopback0
 mpls atm multi-vc
 mpls ip
!
brussels#show mpls atm-ldp bindings 10.200.253.5 32
 Destination: 10.200.253.5/32
    Headend Router ATM3/0.10 (3 hops) 1/53  Active, VCD=289, CoS=available
    Headend Router ATM3/0.10 (3 hops) 1/54  Active, VCD=290, CoS=standard
    Headend Router ATM3/0.10 (3 hops) 1/55  Active, VCD=291, CoS=premium
    Headend Router ATM3/0.10 (3 hops) 1/56  Active, VCD=292, CoS=control

brussels#show ip cef 10.200.253.5 255.255.255.255
10.200.253.5/32, version 50, epoch 0, cached adjacency to ATM3/0.10
0 packets, 0 bytes
  tag information set
    local tag: 29
    fast tag rewrite with AT3/0.10, point2point, tags imposed:
        available 1/53(289), standard 1/54(290),
        premium 1/55(291), control 1/56(292)
        {Multi-VC}
  via 10.200.253.3, ATM3/0.10, 0 dependencies
    next hop 10.200.253.3, ATM3/0.10
    valid cached adjacency
    tag rewrite with AT3/0.10, point2point, tags imposed:
        available 1/53(289), standard 1/54(290),
        premium 1/55(291), control 1/56(292)
        {Multi-VC}

brussels#show mpls forwarding-table 10.200.253.5 32 detail
Local  Outgoing    Prefix         Bytes tag Outgoing   Next Hop
tag    tag or VC   or Tunnel Id   switched  interface
29     Multi-VC    10.200.253.5/32 0        AT3/0.10   point2point
        available 1/53(289), standard 1/54(290),
        premium 1/55(291), control 1/56(292)
        MAC/Encaps=4/8, MRU=4470, Tag Stack{Multi-VC}
        00008847 00000000
        Feature Quick flag set
    Per-packet load-sharing
```

Example 5-24 shows that the outgoing VCD 289 matches the VPI/VCI 1/53 on the downstream neighbor—the ATM switch brussels-atm—and that this LVC has service class WRR_1.

Example 5-24 *Service Class of LVC*

```
brussels-atm#show atm vc interface ATM 2/0/2 1 53

Interface: ATM2/0/2, Type: oc3suni
VPI = 1   VCI = 53
Status: UP
Time-since-last-status-change: 00:19:31
Connection-type: TVC(I)
...
Rx service-category: WRR_1 (WRR Bit Rate)
…
Tx service-category: WRR_1 (WRR Bit Rate)
```

Unless you use Multi-VC TBR, each prefix has only one LVC, and you cannot use WEPD. However, you can use weighted random early detection (WRED) on the edge LSRs.

MPLS CoS

You can map CoS classes to LVCs. When using Multi-VC TBR, you might want to map the CoS classes in a different way from the LVCs set up by the Multi-VC TBR feature. Mapping the CoS classes can reduce the VCs set up through the network. You just need to map several classes to one Multi-VC TBR LVC type: available, standard, premium, and control. In Example 5-25, each of the two LVC types—available and premium—get two classes assigned. This reduces the number of LVCs set up from four to two per prefix. With an access list, you can specify for which prefixes the cos-map is applicable.

Example 5-25 *Configuration of MPLS COS*

```
!
hostname washington
!
mpls label protocol ldp
mpls ldp router-id Loopback0 force
mpls prefix-map 1 access-list 10 cos-map 1
mpls cos-map 1
 class 0 available
 class 1 available
 class 2 premium
 class 3 premium
!
access-list 10 permit any
!
washington#show mpls atm-ldp bindings 10.200.253.2 32
```

Example 5-25 *Configuration of MPLS COS (Continued)*

```
Destination: 10.200.253.2/32
   Headend Router ATM1/0.10 (1 hop) 1/47  Active, VCD=323, CoS=available
   Headend Router ATM1/0.10 (1 hop) 1/48  Active, VCD=324, CoS=premium

washington#show mpls forwarding-table 10.200.253.2 detail
Local  Outgoing    Prefix           Bytes tag  Outgoing   Next Hop
tag    tag or VC   or Tunnel Id     switched   interface
17     Multi-VC    10.200.253.2/32  0          AT1/0.10   point2point
          available 1/47(323), standard 1/47(323),
          premium 1/48(324), control 1/48(324)
          MAC/Encaps=4/8, MRU=4470, Tag Stack{Multi-VC}
          00078847 00007000
          Feature Quick flag set
     Per-packet load-sharing
```

Frame Mode ATM

You can also use ATM in Frame mode on the edge routers. In that case, a PVC is configured between the edge routers. The configuration on the router consists of an ATM subinterface with PVC. LDP is enabled on the subinterface with the command **mpls ip**. The ATM switches in this case are not MPLS-aware. The routers on the edge peer with each other—both for OSPF and LDP—instead of with the ATM switches. This is the overlay model. The label space used on the ATM subinterface is the platform-wide label space instead of the per-interface label space used on the LC-ATM interface. The configuration needed on the edge routers is shown in Example 5-26. A PVC is created between the edge ATM routers washington and brussels.

Example 5-26 *Frame Mode ATM Configuration*

```
!
hostname washington
!
mpls label protocol ldp
mpls ldp router-id Loopback0 force
!
interface ATM1/0
 no ip address
!
interface ATM1/0.100 point-to-point
 ip unnumbered Loopback0
 atm pvc 200 10 200 aal5snap
 mpls ip
!
router ospf 1
 log-adjacency-changes
 network 10.0.0.0 0.255.255.255 area 0
!
```

The OSPF peering and LDP peering is between the two edge routers. The label space used is per-platform. The *:0* output in the LDP Identifier indicates this, as you can see in Example 5-27.

Example 5-27 *OSPF and LDP Peering*

```
washington#show ip ospf neighbor

Neighbor ID      Pri   State        Dead Time   Address        Interface
10.200.253.6       0   FULL/  -     00:00:35    10.200.253.6   ATM1/0.100

washington#show mpls ldp neighbor
    Peer LDP Ident: 10.200.253.6:0; Local LDP Ident 10.200.253.4:0
        TCP connection: 10.200.253.6.22594 - 10.200.253.4.646
        State: Oper; Msgs sent/rcvd: 9/9; Downstream
        Up time: 00:02:36
        LDP discovery sources:
          ATM1/0.100, Src IP addr: 10.200.253.6
        Addresses bound to peer LDP Ident:
          10.200.253.6
```

Reducing the Number of LVCs

You can take the following actions to decrease the number of LVCs:

■ Reduce the number of IP prefixes

■ Use VC-Merge

■ Map CoS classes to LVCs

■ Disable head end VCs on an LSC

■ Block Label Request messages for IP prefixes

You can reduce the number of IP prefixes by using a loopback IP address for the IGP and LDP. Configure all links as IP unnumbered to the loopback interface IP address. Note that IP prefixes that are not configured on the ATM LSR but are still in the same routing domain cause LVCs to be set up. You can also reduce these IP prefixes by using unnumbered interfaces.

VC-Merge causes VCs to be merged at an ATM LSR. Without VC-Merge, one VC is set up per upstream neighbor and per destination. With VC-Merge, this is reduced to one VC per destination, regardless of the number of upstream neighbors on the ATM LSR.

In the case of Multi-VC TBR, four LVCs are set up per destination. You can reduce this by configuring a mapping of CoS classes to LVCs.

When you use an LSC for the BPX/MGX switch, disabling the head end VCs can reduce the number of LVCs. This disables the ATM LSR functioning as an edge ATM LSR. To stop the ATM LSR from acting as an edge ATM LSR, use the command **mpls disable headend-vc**.

You can block Label Request messages from an LSR. This blocks the signaling of the VCs. The command to block the Label Request messages is **mpls ldp request-labels for** *acl*.

Summary

The most important items to remember from this chapter are all the differences between an MPLS network that is running in Frame mode and an MPLS network that is running in Cell mode. An MPLS network with ATM LSRs has LDP functioning differently than in a Frame mode. The Control mode is usually ordered, the Label Advertisement mode is Downstream-on-Demand (DoD), and the Label Retention mode is conservative. Furthermore, each prefix has at least one MPLS label associated with it and leads to at least one LVC set up. Because the number of VCs can grow quite large, it is important to reduce the number of LVCs whenever possible. Possible techniques to reduce the number of prefixes and LVCs were provided in this chapter. They include using IP unnumbered interfaces, blocking the Label Request messages, and using VC-Merge. Multi-Virtual Circuit Tagged Bit Rate (Multi-VC TBR) was explained as a feature that can provide CoS for LVCs on ATM LSRs.

Chapter Review Questions

1. In what ways is an ATM LSR different from a frame-based LSR?

2. What is the default control VC for LDP?

3. What is the preferred control mode for LDP on the ATM LSRs?

4. Name two ways that LDP can detect loops.

5. Which two features must an ATM switch have in the control plane to become an ATM LSR?

6. Which label space is used on an LC-ATM interface?

7. What IP precedence values are by default mapped to the standard LVC type with Multi-VC TBR?

8. What would be the reason to disable the head end VCs on an LSC?

9. Why does the Cisco equipment not advertise bound IP addresses of the LSR on LC-ATM interfaces with LDP?

10. What is the advantage and disadvantage of VC-Merge?

What You Will Learn

By the end of this chapter, you should know and be able to explain the following:

- What kind of switching method CEF is

- Why CEF is needed for the forwarding of packets in MPLS networks

- How CEF load balancing works

- How to troubleshoot CEF problems

Being able to answer these basic questions on CEF helps you to understand how one of the building blocks of MPLS in Cisco IOS works. By the time you finish this chapter, you will have a solid understanding of CEF and why it is essential to the operation of MPLS networks.

CHAPTER 6

Cisco Express Forwarding

Cisco Express Forwarding (CEF) is a packet forwarding or switching method that Cisco IOS uses. It is the latest IP switching method developed in Cisco IOS, and it is the default packet forwarding method being used now. CEF is needed in MPLS networks, which is why this book devotes a chapter to it. This chapter explains the basics of CEF so that you can understand its role in MPLS networks.

Overview of Cisco IOS Switching Methods

The basic function of a router is to move packets through the network. For a router to forward packets, it needs to look up the destination address of the packet in a table and decide which route to use to switch or forward the packet. Each protocol that the router can forward packets for must have a separate forwarding table. Such protocols might include DECnet, Internetwork Packet Exchange (IPX), AppleTalk, IP, and MPLS.

Packets can be forwarded through the router in three basic ways: process switching, interrupt switching, or through an application-specific integrated circuit (ASIC).

In process switching, a special Cisco IOS process that is scheduled to run when the router receives packets is what performs the switching of packets.

A Cisco IOS process does not perform the switching of packets in Interrupt mode. Rather, when packets arrive to the router, the interface processor interrupts the central CPU and asks it to switch the packet according to a route cache or switching table. That cache or table can be built in several ways. Fast switching and CEF switching build such a cache or table.

Finally, the router can program the switching table into an ASIC so that the packets can be switched in hardware. Several Cisco platforms can program the CEF table into ASICs.

Process Switching

Process switching is the slowest of all switching methods. When switching a packet through the router, a Cisco IOS process copies the packet to the CPU memory and looks up the destination IP address in the IP routing table. Based on the outcome of this lookup, the process switches out the packet on a particular interface after it does some housekeeping on the IP header. This housekeeping includes the lowering of the Time To Live (TTL) field and the recalculation of the cyclic redundancy check (CRC) of the IP header. The central CPU of the router always looks at the packet; no other intelligent hardware decides how the packet is forwarded. The opposite to process switching is the switching of packets in Interrupt mode, in which the central CPU might be involved, but the switching decision is performed within the interrupt context, not by a dedicated Cisco IOS process.

Fast Switching

Fast switching is a switching method that builds an *on-demand* forwarding table. The first packet for a destination that arrives is process switched. The switching of the first packet by the central CPU gives the CPU the opportunity to build a cache. This cache is called the *IP fast switching route cache* and is used by the interrupt code to switch subsequent packets for the same destination. This cache is not permanent. Some timers govern the fast switching route cache, and from time to time, some entries are deleted, freeing memory. As long as packets are switched for certain destinations, these destinations remain in the route cache. However, if for some time, no more packets for a certain destination are switched, the entry for that destination in the route cache is deleted. With fast switching, a change in the routing table has an intrusive effect: If a prefix changes in the routing table, the entry in the fast switching cache is invalidated, and the first packet for a destination has to be process-switched again to build the new entry in the route cache.

Each IP prefix entry in the route cache has an outgoing interface, next hop, and Layer 2 rewrite field. This Layer 2 rewrite (or MAC rewrite) is the information that the router needs to change in the Layer 2 frame header when the frame is rebuilt so that it can be sent on the outgoing interface. The command to enable fast switching on the interface is **ip route-cache**. Example 6-1 shows the IP fast switching route cache of a router.

Example 6-1 *IP Fast Switching Route Cache*

```
new-york#show ip cache verbose
IP routing cache 3 entries, 492 bytes
   3 adds, 0 invalidates, 0 refcounts
Cache aged by 1/3 every 600 seconds (1/2 when memory is low).
Minimum invalidation interval 2 seconds, maximum interval 5 seconds,
   quiet interval 3 seconds, threshold 0 requests
Invalidation rate 0 in last second, 0 in last 3 seconds
Last full cache invalidation occurred 00:02:57 ago
```

Example 6-1 *IP Fast Switching Route Cache (Continued)*

```
Prefix/Length            Age       Interface       Next Hop
10.200.202.2/32-24       00:00:46  Serial4/0       10.200.202.2
                   4     0F000800
10.200.254.1/32-32       00:01:54  Ethernet3/3     10.200.203.1
                  14     00604700881F00036CC898570800
10.200.254.4/32-32       00:01:54  Serial4/0       10.200.202.2
                   4     0F000800
```

In Example 6-1, you see for each prefix in the fast switching cache the following parameters: age, interface, next hop, and the Layer 2 rewrite. For the serial interface, you see a Layer 2 rewrite of 0F00800, where 0F00 indicates the High-Level Data Link Control (HDLC) encapsulation and 0800 is the IPv4 protocol number. For the Ethernet interface, the Layer 2 rewrite consists of 48 bits for the destination MAC address, 48 bits for the source MAC address, and 16 bits for the protocol number (0800).

CEF Switching

A compelling reason for a new and better switching method was that the fast switching cache was only built on demand. Therefore, to fast-switch packets, the first packet to a destination had to be process-switched, which is inherently time consuming, especially on routers that have a huge number of potential destinations, such as routers with the Internet routing table. To avoid this, a pre-built switching table was needed. Out of the need of such a pre-built switching table, CEF was born.

In short, the switching table is no longer built on demand, but it is built in advance. As such, each prefix in the routing table has an entry in the CEF switching table at the same time. Only when the routing table changes does the CEF switching table change. However, in some cases, the other switching methods might still be needed. One example of this is packets that have IP options. If an IP packet has IP options trailing the IP header, the packet is process–switched. That is because the treatment of IP options is not straightforward and cannot be done easily in Interrupt mode or in hardware and is thus handled by the central CPU.

Why Is CEF Needed in MPLS Networks?

Concerning MPLS, CEF is special for a certain reason; otherwise, this book would not explicitly cover it. Labeled packets that enter the router are switched according to the label forwarding information base (LFIB) on the router. IP packets that enter the router are switched according to the CEF table on the router. Regardless of whether the packet is switched according to the LFIB or the CEF table, the outgoing packet can be a labeled packet or an IP packet. Figure 6-1 shows the difference between a lookup in the CEF table and in the LFIB.

Figure 6-1 *Lookup in CEF Table Versus Lookup in LFIB*

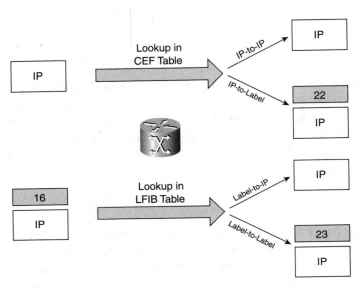

When an IP packet enters the router and the packet is forwarded out of the router labeled, CEF needs to label the packet with a label stack. That label stack can have any number of labels in it. CEF is the only switching method in Cisco IOS that can label an incoming IP packet and forward it. (This is the IP-to-label forwarding case.)

What Are the Components of CEF?

CEF has two main data structures: the Forwarding Information Base (FIB) and the adjacency table. The FIB is also referred to as just the CEF table. Look at Figure 6-2 to see an overview of CEF and its components.

Figure 6-2 *Overview of CEF*

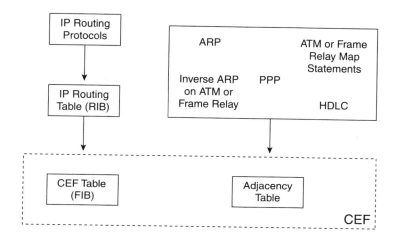

The Adjacency Table

The adjacency table is the CEF component that is responsible for the MAC or Layer 2 rewrite. When routers and hosts are adjacent, they learn about each other by some means. They can discover each other dynamically or by means of configuration. If routers are adjacent across a point-to-point connection, they discover each other trivially. However, on a multiaccess medium such as Ethernet, it is necessary for the routers to use a dynamic mechanism to discover each other. This mechanism is ARP, which maps Layer 2 (for example, Ethernet MAC) addresses to IP addresses.

Because routers usually run routing protocols among each other, the ARP table is built with the MAC addresses of the connecting routers on the Ethernet interfaces. If the interface is Frame Relay or ATM, it can be point-to-point or multipoint. In the first case, only one adjacency exists per interface; in the second case, multiple adjacencies can exist per interface. The adjacency table holds one adjacency or Layer 2 rewrite structure per router that is connected to that multipoint interface. This adjacency can be built from information learned from Address Resolution Protocol (ARP), ATM, or Frame Relay map statements, and inverse ARP on ATM or Frame Relay. Although the FIB decides where to forward the packet, the Layer 2 rewrite of the frame is done with the information found in the adjacency table. The Layer 2 rewrite string contains the new Layer 2 header that is used on the forwarded frame. For Ethernet, this is the new destination and source MAC address and the Ethertype (the protocol number for the Layer 3 payload). For PPP, the Layer 2 header is the complete PPP header, including the Layer 3 protocol ID. Example 6-2 shows an adjacency table holding one adjacency for a point-to-point interface and one for a multipoint interface (Ethernet). The highlighted section shows the Layer 2 rewrite string and how it was learned.

Example 6-2   *CEF Adjacency Table*

```
new-york#show adjacency
Protocol Interface              Address
IP       Ethernet3/3            10.200.203.1(12)
IP       Serial4/0              point2point(11)

new-york#show adjacency detail
Protocol Interface              Address
IP       Ethernet3/3            10.200.203.1(12)
                                48 packets, 3673 bytes
                                epoch 0
                                sourced in sev-epoch 6
                                Encap length 14
                                00604700881F00036CC898570800
                                ARP
IP       Serial4/0              point2point(11)
                                41 packets, 2637 bytes
                                epoch 0
                                sourced in sev-epoch 6
                                Encap length 4
                                0F000800
                                P2P-ADJ
```

The CEF Table

The CEF table or FIB is the CEF component that is responsible for the Layer 3 forwarding decision that is made. The CEF table looks similar to the IP routing table on the router. In fact, each prefix in the routing table has the same prefix in the CEF table. The CEF table holds the essential information—taken from the routing table—to be able to make a forwarding decision for a received IP packet. This information is the IP prefix, the recursively evaluated next hop, and the outgoing interface. Information such as distance and metric of the protocol that put the prefix in the routing table are used to decide which paths are put into the routing table. However, they are not essential to forward a packet, so they are omitted from the CEF table. Example 6-3 shows the FIB on a router.

Example 6-3   *CEF Table or FIB*

```
new-york#show ip cef
Prefix                Next Hop         Interface
0.0.0.0/32            receive
10.200.200.0/24       10.200.203.1     Ethernet3/3
10.200.201.0/24       10.200.203.1     Ethernet3/3
10.200.203.0/24       attached         Ethernet3/3
```

Example 6-3 *CEF Table or FIB (Continued)*

```
10.200.203.0/32      receive
10.200.203.1/32      attached             Ethernet3/3
10.200.203.2/32      receive
10.200.203.255/32    receive
10.200.254.1/32      10.200.203.1         Ethernet3/3
10.200.254.2/32      10.200.203.1         Ethernet3/3
10.200.254.3/32      receive
224.0.0.0/4          drop
224.0.0.0/24         receive
255.255.255.255/32   receive
```

An important aspect of the CEF table is that recursive prefixes are immediately resolved. If, for instance, a Border Gateway Protocol (BGP) prefix is in the routing table, and it points to a BGP next hop—which is learned via an Interior Gateway Protocol (IGP)—the BGP prefix is inserted into the CEF table with a next hop that is learned from recursing to the BGP next hop. In Example 6-4, a BGP prefix 10.99.1.1/32 with a next hop of 10.200.254.4 recurses to the IGP prefix 10.200.254.4. Therefore, the prefix 10.99.1.1/32 inherits the next-hop 10.200.200.2 from the IGP prefix 10.200.254.4. The CEF table immediately shows that the next hop of 10.99.1.1/32 is 10.200.200.2. This recursion is not done in the routing table. The next hop of the BGP prefix 10.99.1.1/32 is 10.200.254.4 in the routing table.

Example 6-4 *Example of Recursion*

```
london#show ip bgp 10.99.1.1
BGP routing table entry for 10.99.1.1/32, version 13
Paths: (1 available, best #1, table Default-IP-Routing-Table)
  Not advertised to any peer
  Local
    10.200.254.4 (metric 85) from 10.200.254.4 (10.200.254.4)
      Origin IGP, metric 0, localpref 100, valid, internal, best

london#show ip cef 10.99.1.1
10.99.1.1/32
  nexthop 10.200.200.2 Ethernet0/0/0 label 23

london#show ip cef 10.200.254.4
10.200.254.4/32
  nexthop 10.200.200.2 Ethernet0/0/0 label 23
```

Operation of CEF

When a packet enters the router, the router strips off the Layer 2 information. The router looks up the destination IP address in the CEF table (FIB), and it makes a forwarding decision. The result of this forwarding decision points to one adjacency entry in the adjacency table. The information retrieved from the adjacency table is the Layer 2 rewrite string, which enables the router to put a new Layer 2 header onto the frame, just before switching the packet out onto the outgoing interface toward the next hop. Figure 6-3 shows CEF forwarding an IP packet and the role of both the Layer 3 lookup of the destination IP address and the Layer 2 rewrite on the frame.

Figure 6-3   *Layer 3 Lookup and Layer 2 Rewrite When Forwarding an IP Packet*

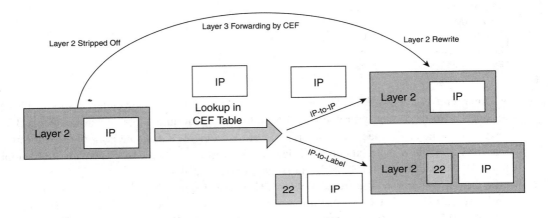

Distributed CEF (DCEF)

One of the main advantages of CEF is that it can be used in a distributed manner. Some Cisco routers use a central CPU without any form of decentralized or distributed intelligence. An example of such a router is the 7200 series router. CEF in this platform can only use the central CPU and as such can forward traffic by the CPU or in interrupt mode. Other hardware—such as the 7500 or GSR 12000 series router—has distributed intelligence and CPUs. Therefore, the router can distribute the burden of forwarding traffic through CEF by using the distributed CPUs to forward traffic without interrupting the central CPU. To achieve the distributed forwarding, both the CEF and adjacency table have to be distributed to these distributed CPUs. For the 7500 series router, the distributed intelligence is present on a Versatile Interface Processor (VIP), and for the GSR 12000 series router, the distributed intelligence is present on the line cards. Figure 6-4 shows a diagram depicting the main CPU of a router with the distributed intelligence on VIPs/line cards. They are all interconnected by means of a bus or switching fabric architecture, which can distribute the CEF and adjacency table.

Figure 6-4 *Distributed Architectures*

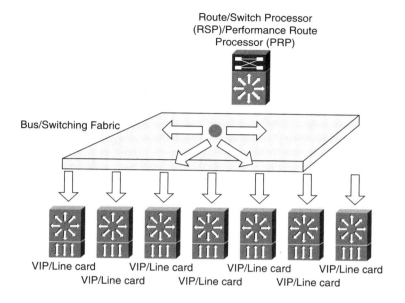

To enable distributed CEF on a router, configure the command **ip cef distributed**.

The router only uses the CEF table to forward IP packets. The router forwards labeled packets through a lookup in the LFIB. In addition, the router can distribute the LFIB. However, no specific command makes the LFIB distributed or not. Rather, if you use CEF in the Distributed mode, LFIB is also distributed. If you do not distribute CEF, LFIB is not distributed either. You can use the command **show mpls forwarding-table** to view the LFIB.

CEF Switching Packets in Hardware

To achieve high rate packet forwarding, the router can use ASICs on the boards or line cards. These ASICs are specially built chips that can forward packets at the highest rate. To have the ASICs forward the packets per the routing table, the router distills the CEF table into the ASIC so that it is correctly programmed to forward the packets. Example 6-5 shows the Packet Switching ASIC

(PSA) on an engine 2 line card of the GSR 12000 series, programmed to switch packets. You see the forwarding entry for the prefix 10.1.2.5/32.

Example 6-5 *CEF Table (FIB) in ASIC*

```
berlin#execute-on slot 7 show ip psa-cef 10.1.2.5 255.255.255.255 detail
========= Line Card (Slot 7) =======

Leaf FCR 7 0x7006F1E0 found 3 deepFast Tag Rewrite for Prefix 10.1.2.5

        [0-7] loq 8800 mtu 4470  oq 4000 ai 13 oi 04019110 oacl FFFF (encaps size 4)
        gather 6B1 (bufhdr size 0 ip to tag profile 53) 1 tag 12312
        counters 0, 0 reported 0, 0.
Local OutputQ (Unicast):      Slot:2  Port:0  RED queue:0  COS queue:0
Output Q (Unicast):           Channel:0       RED queue:0  COS queue:0
```

> **NOTE** The generalized command to see the CEF table in hardware for any ASIC is **show ip hardware-cef**.

The router can also distribute the LFIB and load it into ASICs. The command to see the LFIB in the ASIC is **show tag-switching hardware-tag**.

Load Balancing in CEF

CEF allows for load balancing or load sharing of traffic among multiple outgoing links. CEF needs multiple outgoing links as next hops in the routing table to perform load balancing. The command **maximum-paths** specifies how many paths or next hops are allowed per prefix in the routing table for the specific routing protocol. For instance, if you configure **maximum-path 2** under the routing protocol Open Shortest Path First (OSPF), only two OSPF paths per prefix are allowed in the routing table. Those two paths are then shown in the CEF table as outgoing paths.

In CEF, the two main load balancing schemes are per-packet or per-destination. If you configure the per-packet load balancing scheme, the load balancing of all packets is round-robin packet per packet on the outgoing links. The per-packet load balancing is configured with the interface command **ip load-sharing per-packet**. You need to configure this command on all the outbound interfaces if you want to configure per-packet CEF load balancing.

The default CEF load balancing scheme is per-destination. This terminology is a bit misleading, though, because the CEF per-destination load balancing is done by hashing the destination and *source* IP address. In contrast, the per-destination load balancing that fast switching does is strictly by looking at the destination IP address. Per-destination load sharing is the default load sharing scheme for CEF. It is the default load sharing method for CEF because the per-packet load sharing scheme can send consecutive packets of the same flow (this means the same source/destination IP address pair) across different paths and hence might lead to a reordering problem of the IP packets at the destination. This can lead to problems for traffic such as VoIP because a performance hit or quality degradation can occur if the packets arrive out of sequence, as packets might be considered lost. In addition, it adds jitter.

Per-packet load sharing, however, gives a perfect load sharing distribution on the outgoing paths, whereas the per-destination load sharing is only a statistical method of distributing flows per pairs of (source IP address, destination IP address). Therefore, the load sharing of traffic with the per-destination method can only give a good result (a good distribution among all possible outgoing links) if enough different pairs of source and destination addresses make up the traffic toward the different destinations that are outbound on the outgoing links. Even then, if some flows are present, with considerably more traffic on than some others, which are on one path, the distribution might still be uneven. Look at Example 6-6 to see how to change the CEF load balancing scheme.

Example 6-6 *Per-Destination Versus Per-Packet CEF Load Sharing Example*

```
paris#show cef interface ethernet 1/2
Ethernet1/2 is up (if_number 5)
  Corresponding hwidb fast_if_number 5
  Corresponding hwidb firstsw->if_number 5
  Internet address is 10.200.201.1/24
  ICMP redirects are always sent
  Per packet load-sharing is disabled
  IP unicast RPF check is disabled
…


paris#conf t
Enter configuration commands, one per line.  End with CNTL/Z.
paris(config)#int et 1/2
paris(config-if)#ip load-sharing per-packet
paris(config-if)#^Z
paris#
paris#show cef interface ethernet 1/2
Ethernet1/2 is up (if_number 5)
  Corresponding hwidb fast_if_number 5
  Corresponding hwidb firstsw->if_number 5
  Internet address is 10.200.201.1/24
  ICMP redirects are always sent
  Per packet load-sharing is enabled
  IP unicast RPF check is disabled
…
```

> **NOTE** To restore the CEF default load balancing mode (per-destination load balancing), configure the command **ip load-sharing per-destination**.

Cisco IOS can load-balance in CEF by hashing the source and destination IP address and pointing the result of that hash to a load sharing table. This table holds 16 hash buckets. Each of the 16 hash buckets points to one adjacency, and multiple buckets can point to the same adjacency. Example 6-7 shows that you can verify the hash buckets for the per-destination load sharing scheme with the **show ip cef** [*network* [*mask*]] **internal** command.

Example 6-7 *CEF Load Balancing Example*

```
paris#show ip cef 10.200.254.4 detail
10.200.254.4/32, epoch 0, per-destination sharing
  nexthop 10.200.201.2 Ethernet1/2
  nexthop 10.200.203.2 Ethernet1/3

paris#show ip cef 10.200.254.4 internal
10.200.254.4/32, version 26, epoch 0, RIB, refcount 5, per-destination sharing
  sources: RIB
...
  output chain:
    loadinfo 6327D930, per-session, flags 0003, 6 locks
    flags: Per-session, for-rx-IPv4
    16 hash buckets
      <0  > IP adj out of Ethernet1/2, addr 10.200.201.2 6346B8C0
      <1  > IP adj out of Ethernet1/3, addr 10.200.203.2 6346C640
      <2  > IP adj out of Ethernet1/2, addr 10.200.201.2 6346B8C0
      <3  > IP adj out of Ethernet1/3, addr 10.200.203.2 6346C640
      <4  > IP adj out of Ethernet1/2, addr 10.200.201.2 6346B8C0
      <5  > IP adj out of Ethernet1/3, addr 10.200.203.2 6346C640
      <6  > IP adj out of Ethernet1/2, addr 10.200.201.2 6346B8C0
      <7  > IP adj out of Ethernet1/3, addr 10.200.203.2 6346C640
      <8  > IP adj out of Ethernet1/2, addr 10.200.201.2 6346B8C0
      <9  > IP adj out of Ethernet1/3, addr 10.200.203.2 6346C640
      <10 > IP adj out of Ethernet1/2, addr 10.200.201.2 6346B8C0
      <11 > IP adj out of Ethernet1/3, addr 10.200.203.2 6346C640
      <12 > IP adj out of Ethernet1/2, addr 10.200.201.2 6346B8C0
      <13 > IP adj out of Ethernet1/3, addr 10.200.203.2 6346C640
      <14 > IP adj out of Ethernet1/2, addr 10.200.201.2 6346B8C0
      <15 > IP adj out of Ethernet1/3, addr 10.200.203.2 6346C640
```

To verify which outgoing interface a particular flow of traffic is taking in the case of per-destination load sharing, use the command **show ip cef exact-route** *source-address destination-address*. Example 6-7 shows that prefix 10.200.254.4/32 has two outgoing interfaces in the CEF table: Ethernet 1/2 and Ethernet1/3. Example 6-8 shows that the outgoing interface is Ethernet 1/2 for traffic destined for that IP address 10.200.254.4 and with a source IP address of 10.200.254.1.

Example 6-8 *show ip cef exact-route Example*

```
paris#show ip cef exact-route 10.200.254.1 10.200.254.4
10.200.254.1 -> 10.200.254.4 => IP adj out of Ethernet1/2, addr 10.200.201.2
paris#show ip cef exact-route 10.200.1.2 10.200.254.4
10.200.1.2 -> 10.200.254.4 => IP adj out of Ethernet1/3, addr 10.200.203.2
```

As you can see in Example 6-8, the traffic that is destined to the same destination IP address *can* take a different output interface if the source IP address is different.

Sixteen hash buckets exist. These hash buckets distribute the load of traffic among all possible outgoing paths in the best possible way. For example, in the case of two outgoing paths, eight hash buckets are assigned to each outgoing path. In the case of three outgoing paths, five hash buckets are assigned to each outgoing path, and one hash bucket is unassigned. In short, if 16 is not divisible by the number of paths, the remainder hash buckets are not used and are disabled.

Unequal Cost Load Balancing

It is possible to have unequal cost load balancing in CEF. In that case, the 16 hash buckets are not evenly distributed among all possible paths. Example 6-9 shows a router running Enhanced Interior Gateway Routing Protocol (EIGRP) as the routing protocol and variance being configured for EIGRP. Variance allows EIGRP to perform unequal cost load balancing because it enables routes to be installed in the routing table that are not the best. (These routes do not have the lowest metric.) In short, the variance number allows all routes that have a metric that is smaller than that of the best route multiplied by the variance to be installed in the routing table. One additional check is needed: The reported distance (metric of the route as reported by the EIGRP neighbor) of a route has to be smaller than the feasible distance (FD) in EIGRP for it to be eligible for installation in the routing table.

In Example 6-9, the best route for prefix 10.200.254.4/32 has a metric of 2323456, and the second best route has a metric of 8697856. This latter metric is 3.74 times bigger than the metric of the best route, and this is reflected in the number of hash buckets assigned to each of the two paths. This ratio is also seen in the *traffic share count* in the routing table for the prefix (15/4). The best path pointing to Ethernet 1/2 has 13 hash buckets, whereas the path pointing to Ethernet 1/3 has 3 hash buckets. Obviously, 16 is a small number; as a result, a perfect distribution of the hash buckets according to the metric is not always possible. The distribution will always be approximate.

Example 6-9 *Unequal Cost Load Balancing Example*

```
paris#show running-config | begin router eigrp 1
router eigrp 1
 variance 6
 network 10.0.0.0
 auto-summary
!
paris#show ip route 10.200.254.4
Routing entry for 10.200.254.4/32
  Known via "eigrp 1", distance 90, metric 2323456, type internal
  Redistributing via eigrp 1
  Last update from 10.200.203.2 on Ethernet1/3, 00:00:59 ago
  Routing Descriptor Blocks:
    10.200.203.2, from 10.200.203.2, 00:00:59 ago, via Ethernet1/3
      Route metric is 8697856, traffic share count is 4
      Total delay is 275000 microseconds, minimum bandwidth is 1544 Kbit
      Reliability 255/255, minimum MTU 1500 bytes
      Loading 1/255, Hops 2
  * 10.200.201.2, from 10.200.201.2, 00:00:59 ago, via Ethernet1/2
      Route metric is 2323456, traffic share count is 15
      Total delay is 26000 microseconds, minimum bandwidth is 1544 Kbit
      Reliability 255/255, minimum MTU 1500 bytes
      Loading 1/255, Hops 2

paris#show ip eigrp topology  10.200.254.4 255.255.255.255
IP-EIGRP (AS 1): Topology entry for 10.200.254.4/32
  State is Passive, Query origin flag is 1, 1 Successor(s), FD is 2323456
  Routing Descriptor Blocks:
  10.200.201.2 (Ethernet1/2), from 10.200.201.2, Send flag is 0x0
      Composite metric is (2323456/2297856), Route is Internal
      Vector metric:
        Minimum bandwidth is 1544 Kbit
        Total delay is 26000 microseconds
        Reliability is 255/255
        Load is 1/255
        Minimum MTU is 1500
        Hop count is 2
  10.200.203.2 (Ethernet1/3), from 10.200.203.2, Send flag is 0x0
      Composite metric is (8697856/2297856), Route is Internal
      Vector metric:
        Minimum bandwidth is 1544 Kbit
        Total delay is 275000 microseconds
        Reliability is 255/255
```

Example 6-9 *Unequal Cost Load Balancing Example (Continued)*

```
             Load is 1/255
             Minimum MTU is 1500
             Hop count is 2

paris#show ip cef 10.200.254.4 internal
10.200.254.4/32, version 31, epoch 0, RIB, refcount 5, per-destination sharing
…
  output chain:
    loadinfo 6327D850, per-session, flags 0003, 4 locks
    flags: Per-session, for-rx-IPv4
    16 hash buckets
      <0  > IP adj out of Ethernet1/3, addr 10.200.203.2 6346C640
      <1  > IP adj out of Ethernet1/2, addr 10.200.201.2 6346B8C0
      <2  > IP adj out of Ethernet1/3, addr 10.200.203.2 6346C640
      <3  > IP adj out of Ethernet1/2, addr 10.200.201.2 6346B8C0
      <4  > IP adj out of Ethernet1/3, addr 10.200.203.2 6346C640
      <5  > IP adj out of Ethernet1/2, addr 10.200.201.2 6346B8C0
      <6  > IP adj out of Ethernet1/2, addr 10.200.201.2 6346B8C0
      <7  > IP adj out of Ethernet1/2, addr 10.200.201.2 6346B8C0
      <8  > IP adj out of Ethernet1/2, addr 10.200.201.2 6346B8C0
      <9  > IP adj out of Ethernet1/2, addr 10.200.201.2 6346B8C0
      <10 > IP adj out of Ethernet1/2, addr 10.200.201.2 6346B8C0
      <11 > IP adj out of Ethernet1/2, addr 10.200.201.2 6346B8C0
      <12 > IP adj out of Ethernet1/2, addr 10.200.201.2 6346B8C0
      <13 > IP adj out of Ethernet1/2, addr 10.200.201.2 6346B8C0
      <14 > IP adj out of Ethernet1/2, addr 10.200.201.2 6346B8C0
      <15 > IP adj out of Ethernet1/2, addr 10.200.201.2 6346B8C0
```

Labeling IP Packets by CEF

At the edge of the MPLS network, a router needs to label the IP packets. A stack of at least one label is imposed on the IP packet on the ingress LSR. The imposed label stack is not limited by the number of labels, so the IP packet can receive one, two, three, or more labels at the ingress PE router. When you look at the CEF table on the ingress PE router, you can see for each prefix what the imposed label stack is. Example 6-10 shows an example of labeling the packets that are destined for the prefix 10.200.254.4/32 with one label.

Example 6-10 *CEF Imposing One Label*

```
london#show ip cef 10.200.254.4 detail
10.200.254.4/32, epoch 5
  local label info: global/21
  nexthop 10.200.200.2 Ethernet0/0/0 label 23
```

Example 6-11 shows that the packets destined for a VPN prefix 10.100.103.2/32 in the VRF table *cust-one* are imposed with two labels. The labels are top label to bottom label when read from left to right. In this case, 23 is the top label and 21 is the bottom label. This VPN prefix is an MPLS VPN prefix. Usually two labels are imposed on the ingress PE router for it. Refer to Chapter 7, "MPLS VPN," to learn more about MPLS VPN.

Example 6-11   *CEF Imposing Two Labels*

```
london#show ip cef vrf cust-one 10.100.103.2
10.100.103.2/32
  nexthop 10.200.200.2 Ethernet0/0/0 label 23 21

london#show ip cef vrf cust-one 10.100.103.2 detail
10.100.103.2/32, epoch 5
  recursive via 10.200.254.4 label 21
    nexthop 10.200.200.2 Ethernet0/0/0 label 23
```

An LSR can add labels to an already labeled packet along the LSP, but the LSR performs that function according to the LFIB and not the CEF table. CEF labels only the packets that are initially on the ingress PE router; CEF labels only IP packets.

The LSR can use various means to assign each label in the label stack to the IP prefix. The LSR can use Label Distribution Protocol (LDP), BGP, or Resource Reservation Protocol (RSVP). Recursion can also be used to assign the label to a prefix. In Example 6-4, the label 23 is assigned to the BGP prefix 10.99.1.1/32, although a label signaling protocol did not assign it directly to that prefix. The label 23 is assigned to the IGP prefix 10.200.254.4. When the recursion of the BGP prefix 10.99.1.1/32 to the IGP prefix 10.200.254.4 (the BGP next hop) is done, the label 23 is inherited from the IGP prefix and shows up in the CEF table as the imposed label for the BGP prefix 10.99.1.1/32. This is an extremely important feature of MPLS. All the packets that are flowing along the same LSP (in this case, all the packets that are destined for prefixes with the same BGP next hop) are imposed with the same label. Remember this when you reach Chapter 7, which deals with MPLS VPN, because it uses this feature.

Load Balancing Labeled Packets

Chapter 3, "Forwarding Labeled Packets," explained that labeled packets can be load-balanced. If the MPLS payload is an IPv4 or IPv6 packet, Cisco IOS uses the CEF hashing algorithm to determine the outgoing interface, in the case of per-destination load balancing. The load balancing is done only between labeled paths. This means that if an IP (unlabeled) and a labeled path have the same cost, only the labeled path is used to forward the packets. The reason for that was explained in Chapter 3.

As you can see in Example 6-12, **show mpls forwarding-table** shows the possible load balancing done for labeled packets.

Example 6-12 *Load Balancing Labeled Packets*

```
horizon#show mpls forwarding-table
Local   Outgoing     Prefix          Bytes tag  Outgoing   Next Hop
tag     tag or VC    or Tunnel Id    switched   interface
17      Pop tag      10.200.254.3/32 252        Et1/3      10.200.203.2
        Pop tag      10.200.254.3/32 0          Et1/2      10.200.201.2
18      16           10.200.254.4/32 10431273   Et1/2      10.200.201.2
        16           10.200.254.4/32 238        Et1/3      10.200.203.2
```

The command to verify which path a labeled IPv4 packet will take in the case of per-destination load balancing is **show mpls forwarding-table labels** *label* **exact-path ipv4** *source-address destination-address*.

Following are the general rules for load balancing labeled packets on a non-IPv6-capable Cisco IOS router:

■ If the MPLS payload is an IPv4 packet, the load balancing is done by hashing the source and destination IP address of the IPv4 header.

■ If the MPLS payload is not an IPv4 packet, the load balancing is done by looking at the value of the bottom label.

How does an MPLS-enabled router know what the MPLS payload is? The router that assigned the label can figure this out by looking at the label, because this router assigned a label to the particular FEC that the packet belongs to. However, if the stack holds more than one label, the P router in the MPLS network did not assign the bottom label. Because MPLS does not yet have a protocol identifier field in the label stack, the P router cannot easily identify what the MPLS payload is. In Cisco IOS, the router can look at the first nibble following the MPLS label stack. If the first nibble has the value 4, Cisco IOS considers this an IPv4 packet and performs IPv4 CEF hashing. Newer Cisco IOS software that is also capable of running IPv6 can check whether the first nibble is 6. If so, the MPLS payload is considered IPv6, and the router performs IPv6 CEF hashing. The load balancing is then based on the source and destination address in the IPv6 header. The algorithm for load balancing the MPLS packets becomes as follows:

- If the MPLS payload is an IPv4 packet, the load balancing is done by hashing the source and destination IP address of the IPv4 header.

- If the MPLS payload is an IPv6 packet, the load balancing is done by hashing the source and destination IP address of the IPv6 header.

- If the MPLS payload is not an IPv4 or IPv6 packet, the load balancing is done by looking at the value of the bottom label.

Troubleshooting CEF

When packets do not get to their destination in an MPLS network, it might be because CEF failed to label the packets correctly on the ingress PE router or forwarded them to the wrong adjacent router. You should have some technical troubleshooting skills to debug such CEF problems.

You can disable and enable CEF on the interface by using the command **ip route-cache cef**. Toggling CEF on the interface can often indicate whether the problem is with CEF. If the problem lies with the Layer 2 rewrite of the packets, you can check the adjacency information with the **show adjacency** command or clear the adjacency with the **clear adjacency** command. The debug command **debug ip cef drops** [*access-list*] tells you if IP packets are dropped on the ingress PE router. You can specify an access list 1 to 99 to help narrow the debug output to one or more specific prefixes. In Example 6-13, you see the possible debug commands for CEF.

Example 6-13 *debug ip cef and debug cef*

```
london#debug ip cef ?
  accounting      Accounting events
  drops           Packets dropped by CEF
  events          IP CEF table events
  fragmentation   IP CEF fragmentation
  hash            IP CEF hash events
  ipc             IP CEF IPC events
  packet          Packets seen by IP CEF
  prefix-ipc      IP-prefixes related IPC
  receive         Packets received by IP CEF
  subblock        IP CEF subblock events
  table           IP CEF table changes

london#debug cef ?
  all             All CEF events
  assert          CEF assert events
  background      CEF background events
```

Example 6-13 *debug ip cef and debug cef (Continued)*

```
broker              CEF broker events
consistency-check   CEF consistency checker events
elog                CEF enable elog points
epoch               CEF epoch events
fib                 CEF fib entry events
filter              Configure filter
hardware            CEF hardware api debugging
high-availability   CEF high availability events
interest            CEF interest list events
interface           CEF interface events
loadinfo            CEF loadinfo events
memory              CEF memory events
non-ip              CEF non ip entry events
path                CEF path events
switching           Switching infrastructure
table               CEF table events
xdr                 CEF XDR events
```

Example 6-14 shows the interesting command **show ip cef switching statistics**, which tells where packets possibly have been dropped and why.

Example 6-14 *show ip cef switching statistics*

```
london#show ip cef switching statistics

Path    Reason                      Drop      Punt  Punt2Host
RP RIB  Packet destined for us         0     86654          0
RP RIB  Total                          0     86654          0

RP LES  Packet destined for us         0     39003          0
RP LES  TTL expired                    0         0     101049
RP LES  Total                          0     39003     101049

RP RSP  Packet destined for us         0     19491          0
RP RSP  No adjacency                   0         0          1
RP RSP  IP redirects                   0         0       4743
RP RSP  Total                          0     19491       4744

Slot 0  Packet destined for us         0     19491          0
Slot 0  No adjacency                   0         0          1
Slot 0  TTL expired                    0         0          3
Slot 0  IP redirects                   0         0       4743
Slot 0  Total                          0     19491       4747

All     Total                          0    164639     110540
```

Example 6-15 presents an overview of the most interesting **show** CEF commands in Cisco IOS. Notice that the router london has three routing tables and three CEF tables: the global routing table or Default routing table and the two VRF routing tables *cust-one* and *cust-one-ipv4*. A VRF routing table is a routing table used for one virtual private network (VPN) in a network that is running MPLS VPN. See Chapter 7 for a detailed explanation on MPLS VPN.

Example 6-15 *show cef Commands*

```
london#show cef table
Global information:
 MTRIE information:
  TAL: node pools:
   pool[C/8 bits]: 45 allocated (0 failed), 46800 bytes {3 refcount}

3 active IPv4 tables out of a maximum of 2048
VRF                       Prefixes      Memory  Flags
Default                         38        23620
cust-one                        11        14680  LCS
cust-one-ipv4                   11        14680  LCS

1 active IPv6 table out of a maximum of 1
VRF                       Prefixes      Memory  Flags
Default                          0           60

london#show cef table IPv4 cust-one
Table: IPv4:cust-one (id 1)
 ref count:             3
 reset count:           1
 flags (0x01):          LCS
 smp allowed:           yes
 default network:       none
 route count:           11
 route count (fwd):     11
 route count (non-fwd): 0
 Database epoch: 8 (11 entries at this epoch)
 Subblocks:
  None

london#show cef table IPv4 Default
Table: IPv4:Default (id 0)
 ref count:             17
 reset count:           1
 flags (0x00):          none
 smp allowed:           yes
 default network:       0.0.0.0/0
 route count:           38
 route count (fwd):     38
```

Example 6-15 *show cef* Commands

```
route count (non-fwd): 0
Database epoch: 7 (38 entries at this epoch)
Subblocks:
  None
```

The **clear cef table** {**IPv4** | **IPv6** {**vrf** {*vrf-name* |*****}}} command rebuilds the CEF table. On a
12000 series router, you could use the command **clear cef linecard** [*slot-number*] [**adjacency** |
interface | **prefix** | **events**] to resend the CEF table from the Router Processor board to the line
cards, as shown in Example 6-16.

Example 6-16 *clear cef* Commands

```
london#clear cef ?
  interface  CEF interface information
  linecard   CEF information related to linecard
  table      CEF forwarding table

london#clear cef table IPv4 vrf ?
  *          All VRFs
  Default
  cust-one
  cust-one-ipv4


london#clear cef linecard ?
  <0-37>     linecard slot number
  Adjacency  Clear adjacency information
  Interface  Clear interface related information
  Prefix     Clear Cisco Express Forwarding table
  events     Clear the linecard event log
  <cr>
```

Summary

Although this chapter could have covered more about CEF, this book is about MPLS, not CEF.
You did learn the basics of CEF so that you understand how it is used in the context of MPLS. You
also learned the differences among process switching, fast switching, and CEF switching. You
should understand the functioning of CEF and its two main components: the adjacency table and
the CEF table. You discovered how CEF performs equal cost load balancing and unequal cost load
balancing on IP packets. Finally, you found out why CEF is needed for MPLS and how load
balancing of labeled packets is performed.

Chapter Review Questions

1. Name the two components of CEF.

2. Name the three most common packet switching methods in Cisco IOS.

3. Why does MPLS use CEF?

4. What is the adjacency table used for?

5. What fields of the IP header does CEF use to load-balance IP packets?

6. How does CEF perform equal and unequal cost load balancing?

7. How does a prefix in the CEF table get the imposed label stack?

8. How is load balancing of labeled packets performed in Cisco IOS?

9. Name two reasons *not* to use CEF per-packet load balancing.

10. Name two huge differences between the fast switching and the CEF switching methods.

PART 2

Advanced MPLS Topics

What You Will Learn

By the end of this chapter, you should know and be able to explain the following:

- The definition of a VPN

- The operation of MPLS VPN

- What RDs and RTs are

- The role of Multiprotocol BGP in MPLS VPN networks

- The packet forwarding through the MPLS VPN network

- The operation of PE-CE routing protocols and their specifics for MPLS VPNs

CHAPTER 7

MPLS VPN

MPLS VPN, or MPLS Virtual Private Networks, is the most popular and widespread implementation of MPLS technology. Its popularity has grown exponentially since it was invented, and it is still growing steadily. Although most service providers have implemented it as a replacement for the Frame Relay and ATM services that were popular before it, MPLS VPN is now seeing a growing interest from large enterprise companies who view it as the next step in their network design. MPLS VPN can provide scalability and divide the network into separate smaller networks, which is often necessary in the larger enterprise networks, where the common IT infrastructure has to offer isolated networks to individual departments. Many service providers that have run MPLS VPN for years are now looking at interconnecting their network to the MPLS VPN networks of other service providers to improve the scalability and ease of operation of their network. This is where Inter-Autonomous MPLS VPN and Carrier's Carrier (CsC) come into the picture.

Before reading this chapter, make sure you have read the sections "Peer-to-Peer VPN Model Versus Overlay VPN Model" and "Optimal Traffic Flow" from Chapter 1, "The Evolution of MPLS." It is imperative that you understand what the peer-to-peer VPN model entails, because it is the most important concept of MPLS VPN.

Introduction to MPLS VPN

This section introduces virtual private networks (VPN) in general and MPLS VPN specifically.

Definition of a VPN

A VPN is a network that emulates a private network over a common infrastructure. The VPN might provide communication at OSI Layer 2 or 3. The VPN usually belongs to one company and has several sites interconnected across the common service provider infrastructure. The private network requires that all customer sites are able to interconnect and are completely separate from other VPNs. That is the minimum connectivity requirement. However, VPN models at the IP layer might require more than that. They can provide connectivity between different VPNs when that is wanted and even provide connectivity to the Internet. MPLS VPN offers all of this. MPLS VPNs are made possible because the service provider runs MPLS in the backbone network, which supplies a decoupling of forwarding plane and control plane that IP does not.

VPN Models

VPNs did exist before the arrival of MPLS. Most popular were Frame Relay or ATM technologies, providing VPN service at Layer 2. The provider had a Frame Relay or ATM backbone and supplied Layer 2 connectivity to the customer routers. This was commonly referred to as the *overlay model*. The service provider might have actually owned or managed the edge routers that were connected to the customer network. The point is that the routers were physically at the customer premises. Refer to the section "Peer-to-Peer VPN Model Versus Overlay VPN Model" in Chapter 1 for more information on this. Peer-to-peer VPN networks existed, but they were not popular. The main reason is that they were not easy to deploy and maintain because they needed distribute lists, IP packet filters, or GRE tunnels. As explained in Chapter 1, MPLS VPN is an example of a highly scalable peer-to-peer VPN model.

MPLS VPN Model

It is important to become familiar with the terminology concerning MPLS VPN. Look at Figure 7-1 for a schematic overview of the MPLS VPN model. A service provider is providing the common public infrastructure that customers use.

Figure 7-1   *MPLS VPN Schematic Overview*

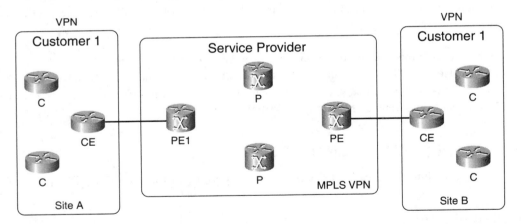

A PE router is a provider edge (PE) router. It has a direct connection with the customer edge (CE) router at Layer 3. A provider (P) router is a router without the direct connection to the routers of the customer. In the MPLS VPN implementation, both P and PE routers run MPLS. This means that they must be able to distribute labels between them and forward labeled packets.

A CE router has a direct Layer 3 connection with the PE router. A customer (C) router is a router without a direct connection with the PE router. A CE router does not need to run MPLS.

Because the CE and PE routers interact at Layer 3, they must run a routing protocol (or static routing) between them. The CE router has only one peer outside of its own site: the PE router. If the CE router is multihomed, it can peer with multiple PE routers. The CE router does not peer with any of the CE routers from the other sites across the service provider network, as with the overlay model. The name *peer-to-peer model* is derived from the fact that the CE and PE form a peer at Layer 3.

The *P* in VPN stands for private. As such, the customers of the service provider are allowed to have their own IP addressing scheme. This means that they can use registered IP addresses but also private IP addresses (see RFC 1918) or even IP addresses that are also used by other customers who are connecting to the same service provider (referred to as *overlapping IP addressing*). If the packets were to be forwarded as IP packets within the service provider network, this would cause problems, because the P routers would be confused. If the private and overlapping IP addressing scheme is not allowed, then every customer must be using a unique address range. In that case, the packets can be forwarded by looking up the destination IP address on every router in the service provider network. This means that all P and PE routers must have the complete routing table of every customer. This would be a large routing table. The only routing protocol that is capable of carrying a large number of routes is Border Gateway Protocol (BGP). This would mean that all P and PE routers would have to run internal BGP (iBGP) among them. However, this is not a VPN scheme, because it is not private to the customers.

Another solution is that every P and PE router has a private routing table for each customer. Several processes of one routing protocol (one process per VPN) could be running on all the routers to distribute the VPN routes. Running one routing process per VPN on every P router is not very scalable. Each time one VPN is added to the network, a new routing process must be added to every P router. Furthermore, if an IP packet enters a P router, how does the P router determine which VPN the packet belongs to to figure out which private routing table to use to forward the packet? If the packet is an IP packet, this is not possible. You could add one extra field to the IP packet indicating which VPN the IP packet belongs to. The P routers could then forward the IP packets by looking at this extra field and at the destination IP address. Again, all P routers would have to be aware of this extra field.

A scalable solution would be to have the P routers completely unaware of the VPNs. Then the P routers would not be burdened with having routing information for VPN routes. Can you achieve this by using MPLS? The answer is yes. The customer IP packets are labeled in the service provider network to achieve a private VPN for each customer. Furthermore, the P routers no longer need to have the routing table of the customers by using two MPLS labels. Therefore, BGP is not needed on the P routers. See the section "BGP-Free Core" in Chapter 1 for an explanation on this. The VPN routes are only known on the PE routers. As such, the VPN knowledge is present only on the edge routers of the MPLS VPN network, which makes the MPLS VPN solution scalable.

Figure 7-2 shows the MPLS VPN model: label switching packets in the service provider network and PE routers that are VPN aware.

Figure 7-2 *MPLS VPN Model*

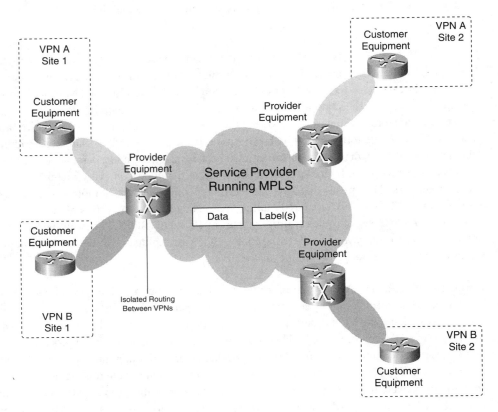

Architectural Overview of MPLS VPN

To achieve MPLS VPN, you need some basic building blocks on the PE routers. These building blocks are the following: VRF, route distinguisher (RD), route targets (RT), route propagation through MP-BGP, and forwarding of labeled packets.

Virtual Routing Forwarding

A virtual routing/forwarding (VRF) is a VPN routing and forwarding instance. It is the name for the combination of the VPN routing table, the VRF Cisco Express Forwarding (CEF) table, and the associated IP routing protocols on the PE router. A PE router has a VRF instance for each attached VPN. Look at Figure 7-3 to see that a PE router holds the global IP routing table, but also a VRF routing table per VPN connected to the PE.

Figure 7-3 *VRFs on a PE Router*

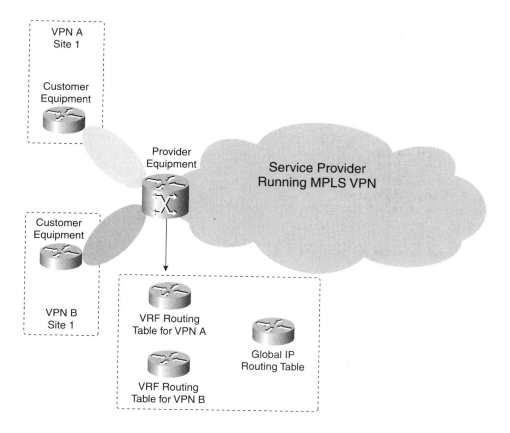

Because the routing should be separate and private for each customer (VPN) on a PE router, each VPN should have its own routing table. This private routing table is called the VRF routing table. The interface on the PE router toward the CE router can belong to only one VRF. As such, all IP packets received on the VRF interface are unambiguously identified as belonging to that VRF. Because there is a separate routing table per VPN, there is a separate CEF table per VPN to forward these packets on the PE router. This is the VRF CEF table. As with the global routing table and the global CEF table, the VRF CEF table is derived from the VRF routing table.

You create the VRF on the PE router with the **ip vrf** command. You use the **ip vrf forwarding** command to assign PE-CE interfaces on the PE router to a VRF. You can assign an interface to only one VRF, but you can assign several interfaces to the same VRF. The PE router then automatically creates a VRF routing table and CEF table. The VRF routing table does not differ from a regular routing table in Cisco IOS other than that it is used for a set of VPN sites only and is completely separated from all other routing tables: The routing table as you have known it to this point will now be referred to as the *global* or the *default routing table*. Look at Example 7-1, where the VRF configured is the VRF *cust-one*.

Example 7-1 *Configuring a VRF*

```
!
ip vrf cust-one
 rd 1:1
 route-target export 1:1
 route-target import 1:1
!
interface Serial5/1
 ip vrf forwarding cust-one
 ip address 10.10.4.1 255.255.255.0
!

sydney#show ip route vrf cust-one

Routing Table: cust-one
Codes: C - connected, S - static, R - RIP, M - mobile, B - BGP
       D - EIGRP, EX - EIGRP external, O - OSPF, IA - OSPF inter area
       N1 - OSPF NSSA external type 1, N2 - OSPF NSSA external type 2
       E1 - OSPF external type 1, E2 - OSPF external type 2, E - EGP
       i - IS-IS, su - IS-IS summary, L1 - IS-IS level-1, L2 - IS-IS level-2
       ia - IS-IS inter area, * - candidate default, U - per-user static route
       o - ODR, P - periodic downloaded static route

Gateway of last resort is not set

     10.0.0.0/8 is variably subnetted, 9 subnets, 2 masks
B       10.10.2.0/24 [200/0] via 10.200.254.2, 00:31:04
C       10.10.4.0/24 is directly connected, Serial5/1
C       10.10.4.2/32 is directly connected, Serial5/1
B       10.10.100.1/32 [200/1] via 10.200.254.2, 00:31:04
B       10.10.100.3/32 [20/0] via 10.10.4.2, 00:13:29

sydney#show ip cef vrf cust-one
Prefix               Next Hop            Interface
0.0.0.0/0            no route
0.0.0.0/32           receive
10.10.2.0/24         10.200.214.1        POS0/1/0
10.10.4.0/24         attached            Serial5/1
10.10.4.0/32         receive
10.10.4.1/32         receive
10.10.4.2/32         attached            Serial5/1
10.10.4.255/32       receive
10.10.100.1/32       10.200.214.1        POS0/1/0
```

Example 7-1   *Configuring a VRF (Continued)*

```
10.10.100.3/32       10.10.4.2           Serial5/1
224.0.0.0/4          drop
224.0.0.0/24         receive
255.255.255.255/32   receive
```

The VRF routing table *cust-one* has prefixes in it that are populated by dynamic routing protocols and static routing, just like the global routing table. The concept of metrics, distance, next hop, and so on does not change. Because the VRF instance is associated with interfaces, only IP packets that are entering the PE router via those VRF interfaces are forwarded according to that VRF CEF table.

> **NOTE**   In Cisco IOS, CEF is the only switching method supported for forwarding IP packets from the VRF interface. As such, CEF must be enabled globally on all PE routers and all VRF interfaces.

RD

The VPN prefixes are propagated across the MPLS VPN network by Multiprotocol BGP (MP-BGP). The problem is that when BGP carries these IPv4 prefixes across the service provider network, they must be unique. If the customers had overlapping IP addressing, the routing would be wrong. To solve this problem, the concept of RDs was conceived to make IPv4 prefixes unique. The basic idea is that each prefix from each customer receives a unique identifier (the RD) to distinguish the same prefix from different customers. A prefix derived from the combination of the IPv4 prefix and the RD is called a vpnv4 prefix. MP-BGP needs to carry these vpnv4 prefixes between the PE routers.

> **NOTE**   MP-BGP is explained in the section "BGP" later in this chapter.

An RD is a 64-bit field used to make the VRF prefixes unique when MP-BGP carries them. The RD does not indicate which VRF the prefix belongs to. The function of the RD is not that of a VPN identifier, because some more complex VPN scenarios might require more than one RD per VPN. Each VRF instance on the PE router must have one RD assigned to it. This 64-bit value can have two formats: *ASN:nn* or *IP-address:nn*, where *nn* represents a number. The most commonly used format is *ASN:nn*, where *ASN* stands for autonomous system number. Usually, the service provider uses *ASN:nn*, where *ASN* is the autonomous system number that the Internet Assigned Numbers Authority (IANA) assigns to the service provider and nn is the number that the service provider uniquely assigns to the VRF. The RD does not impose semantics; it is just used to uniquely identify the VPN routes. This is needed because the IPv4 routes from one customer might be overlapping with the IPv4 routes from another. The combination of the RD with the IPv4 prefix provides a vpnv4 prefix, of which the address is 96 bits long. The mask is 32 bits long, just as it is for an IPv4 prefix. If you take an IPv4 prefix 10.1.1.0/24 and an RD 1:1, the vpnv4 prefix becomes 1:1:10.1.1.0/24.

One customer might use different RDs for the same IPv4 route. When a VPN site is connected to two PE routers, routes from the VPN site might get two different RDs, depending on which PE router the routes are received. Each IPv4 route would get two different RDs assigned and would have two completely different vpnv4 routes. This would allow BGP to see them as different routes and apply a different policy to the routes. Example 7-2 shows how to configure the RD in Cisco IOS.

Example 7-2   *Configuring an RD*

```
sydney#conf t
Enter configuration commands, one per line.  End with CNTL/Z.
sydney(config)#ip vrf ?
  WORD  VPN Routing/Forwarding instance name
sydney(config)#ip vrf cust-one
sydney(config-vrf)#rd ?
  ASN:nn or IP-address:nn  VPN Route Distinguisher
sydney(config-vrf)#rd 1:1
```

RTs

If RDs were just used to indicate the VPN, communication between sites of different VPNs would be problematic. A site of Company A would not be able to talk to a site of Company B because the RDs would not match. The concept of having sites of Company A being able to talk to sites of Company B is called *extranet* VPN. The simple case of communication between sites of the same company—the same VPN—is called *intranet*. The communication between sites is controlled by another MPLS VPN feature called RTs.

An RT is a BGP extended community that indicates which routes should be imported from MP-BGP into the VRF. Exporting an RT means that the exported vpnv4 route receives an additional BGP extended community—this is the RT—as configured under *ip vrf* on the PE router, when the route is redistributed from the VRF routing table into MP-BGP. Importing an RT means that the received vpnv4 route from MP-BGP is checked for a matching extended community—this is the route target—with the ones in the configuration. If the result is a match, the prefix is put into the VRF routing table as an IPv4 route. If a match does not occur, the prefix is rejected. The command to configure RTs for a VRF is **route-target** {**import** | **export** | **both**} *route-target-ext-community*. The keyword *both* indicates both import and export.

Figure 7-4 shows that the RTs control which routes are imported into which VRFs from the remote PE routers and with which RTs the vpnv4 routes are exported toward the remote PE routers. More than one RT might be attached to the vpnv4 route. For the import into the VRF to be permitted, only one RT from the vpnv4 route needs to be matched with the configuration of the imported RTs under the *ip vrf* section on the PE router.

Figure 7-4 *RTs*

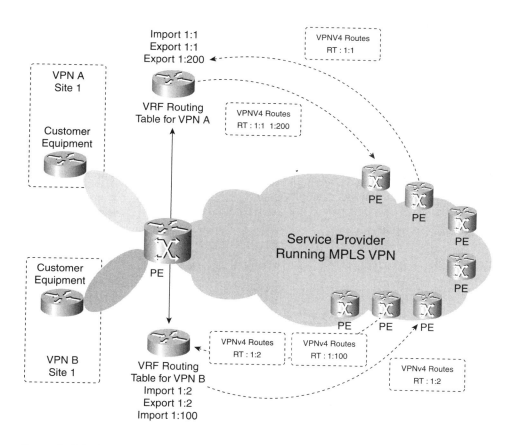

Example 7-3 shows how to configure RTs in Cisco IOS.

Example 7-3 *Configuring RTs*

```
sydney#conf t
Enter configuration commands, one per line.  End with CNTL/Z.
sydney(config)#ip vrf cust-one
sydney(config-vrf)#route-target ?
  ASN:nn or IP-address:nn  Target VPN Extended Community
  both                     Both import and export Target-VPN community
  export                   Export Target-VPN community
  import                   Import Target-VPN community
sydney(config-vrf)#route-target both 1:1
```

The RD and the RTs then define the VRF *cust-one*, as you can see in Example 7-4.

Example 7-4 *VRF Configuration*

```
!
ip vrf cust-one
 rd 1:1
 route-target export 1:1
 route-target import 1:1
!
```

When configuring a VRF with several sites that belong to one VPN, without having to communicate to sites belonging to another VPN, you just need to configure one RT to be imported and exported on all the PE routers with a site belonging to that VRF. This is the simple case of an intranet. When you have sites belonging to one VPN that need to be able to communicate with sites from another VPN (the extranet case), pay attention to the way to configure the RTs correctly. Figure 7-5 shows an extranet example.

Figure 7-5 *Extranet Example*

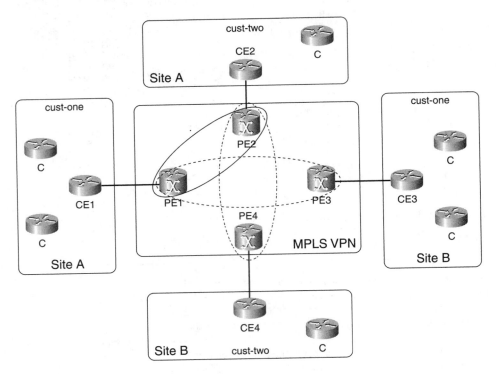

Obviously, Site A and Site B from the VRF *cust-one* should be able to communicate with each other. The same holds true for Sites A and B of the VRF *cust-two*. The RT that VPN *cust-one* uses is 1:1. The RT that VPN *cust-two uses* is 1:2. Now imagine that Site A only of VRF *cust-one* needs to talk to Site A only of VRF *cust-two*. This is perfectly possible and is determined by configuring the RTs accordingly. The RT 100:1 is imported and exported for Site A of vrf *cust-one* and *cust-two* on PE1 and PE2 to achieve this. This is called an *extranet*. Figure 7-6 shows the same network as in Figure 7-5, but with the RTs.

Figure 7-6 *Extranet Example with RTs*

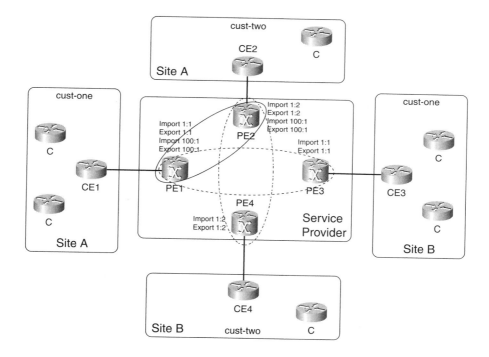

Look at Example 7-5 for the configuration needed on the PE routers.

Example 7-5 *Configuring RTs for Extranet*

```
PE1:
!
ip vrf cust-one
 rd 1:1
 route-target export 1:1
 route-target export 100:1
 route-target import 1:1
 route-target import 100:1
!

PE2:

!
```

continues

Example 7-5 *Configuring RTs for Extranet (Continued)*

```
ip vrf cust-two
 rd 1:2
 route-target export 1:2
 route-target export 100:1
 route-target import 1:2
 route-target import 100:1
!
```

Example 7-6 shows a route 10.10.100.1/32. It is a route with RD 1:1 (VRF *cust-one*) that is imported into the VRF *cust-two* and becomes a vpnv4 route with RD 1:2.

Example 7-6 *Extranet Route*

```
PE1#show ip bgp vpnv4 all 10.10.100.1
BGP routing table entry for 1:1:10.10.100.1/32, version 40
Paths: (1 available, best #1, table cust-one)
  Advertised to update-groups:
      3
  65001
    10.10.2.1 from 10.10.2.1 (192.168.1.1)
      Origin IGP, metric 0, localpref 100, valid, external, best
      Extended Community: RT:1:1 RT:100:1,
      mpls labels in/out 45/nolabel
BGP routing table entry for 1:2:10.10.100.1/32, version 41
Paths: (1 available, best #1, table cust-two)
  Not advertised to any peer
  65001, imported path from 1:1:10.10.100.1/32
    10.10.2.1 from 10.10.2.1 (192.168.1.1)
      Origin IGP, metric 0, localpref 100, valid, external, best
      Extended Community: RT:1:1 RT:100:1
```

You might not want two VRFs to exchange all the routes. The number of routes leaked from one VRF to another can be limited by configuring an import or export map under **ip vrf**, which uses a route map to further filter routes. Refer to the later section "CE Management" for more details on how to set this up.

VPNv4 Route Propagation in the MPLS VPN Network

The VRF separates the customer routes on the PE routers, but how are the prefixes transported across the service provider network? Because, potentially, numerous routes—perhaps hundred of thousands—could be transported, BGP is the ideal candidate because it is a proven and stable routing protocol for carrying that many routes. Just realize that BGP is the standard routing protocol for carrying the complete Internet routing table. Because the customer VPN routes are made unique by adding the RD to each IPv4 route—turning them into vpnv4 routes—all customer routes can safely be transported across the MPLS VPN network.

An overview of the route propagation in an MPLS VPN network is shown in Figure 7-7.

Figure 7-7   *Route Propagation in an MPLS VPN Network*

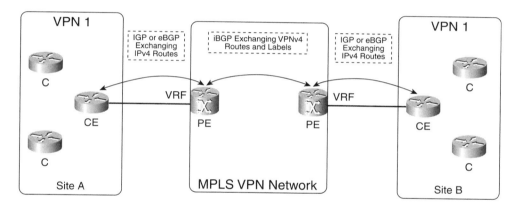

The PE router receives IPv4 routes from the CE router through an Interior Gateway Protocol (IGP) or external BGP (eBGP). These IPv4 routes from the VPN site are put into the VRF routing table. Which VRF is used depends on the VRF that is configured on the interface on the PE router toward the CE router. These routes are appended with the RD that is assigned to that VRF. Thus, they become vpnv4 routes, which are then put into MP-BGP. BGP takes care of distributing these vpnv4 routes to all PE routers in the MPLS VPN network. On the PE routers, the vpnv4 routes are stripped of the RDs and put into the VRF routing table as IPv4 routes. Whether the vpnv4 route, after stripping off the RD, is put into the VRF depends on whether the RTs allow the import into the VRF. These IPv4 routes are then advertised to the CE router through an IGP or eBGP that is running between the PE and CE router. Figure 7-8 shows the steps in the route propagation from CE to CE through the MPLS VPN network.

Figure 7-8 *Route Propagation in an MPLS VPN Network Step by Step*

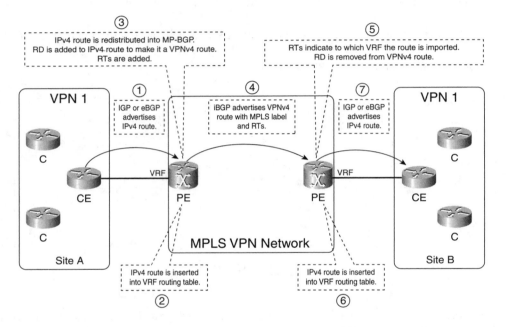

Because the service provider that is running the MPLS VPN network runs BGP in one autonomous system, iBGP is running between the PE routers.

The propagation from eBGP—running between the PE and CE router—to MP-iBGP in the MPLS VPN network and vice versa is automatic and needs no extra configuration. However, the redistribution of MP-iBGP into the IGP that is running between the PE and CE router is not automatic. You need to configure mutual redistribution between MP-iBGP and the IGP.

Packet Forwarding in an MPLS VPN Network

As explained in the previous section, the packets cannot be forwarded as pure IP packets between sites. The P routers cannot forward them because they do not have the VRF information from each site. MPLS can solve this problem by labeling the packets. The P routers must then have only the correct forwarding information for the label to forward the packets. The most common way is to configure Label Distribution Protocol (LDP) between all P and PE routers so that all IP traffic is label-switched between them. You can also use RSVP with extensions for traffic engineering (TE) when implementing MPLS TE, but LDP is the most common for MPLS VPN. The IP packets are then label-forwarded with one label from ingress PE router to egress PE router. A P router never has to perform a lookup of the destination IP address. This is the way the packets are switched between the ingress PE and egress PE router. This label is called the *IGP label*, because it is the label that is bound to an IPv4 prefix in the global routing table of the P and PE router, and the IGP of the service provider network advertises it.

How does the egress PE router know which VRF the packet belongs to? This information is not in the IP header, and it cannot be derived from the IGP label, because this is used solely to forward the packet through the service provider network. The solution is to add another label in the MPLS label stack. This label indicates which VRF the packet belongs to. Therefore, all customer packets are forwarded with two labels: the IGP label as the top label and the VPN label as the bottom label. The VPN label must be put on by the ingress PE router to indicate to the egress PE router which VRF the packet belongs to. How does the egress PE router signal to the ingress PE router which label to use for a VRF prefix? Because MP-BGP is already used to advertise the vpnv4 prefix, it also signals the VPN label (also referred to as the *BGP label*) that is associated with the vpnv4 prefix.

> **NOTE**   Actually, the concept of having one VPN label indicating the VRF that the packet belongs to is not quite correct. This might be true in some cases, but most of the time it is not. A VPN label usually indicates the next hop that the packet should be forwarded onto on the egress PE router. Therefore, most of the time, its purpose is to indicate the correct CE router as the next hop of the packet.

To recap, the VRF-to-VRF traffic has two labels in the MPLS VPN network. The top label is the IGP label and is distributed by LDP or RSVP for TE between all P and PE routers hop by hop. The bottom label is the VPN label that is advertised by MP-iBGP from PE to PE. P routers use the IGP label to forward the packet to the correct egress PE router. The egress PE router uses the VPN label to forward the IP packet to the correct CE router.

Figure 7-9 shows the packet forwarding in an MPLS VPN network. The packet enters the PE router on the VRF interface as an IPv4 packet. It is forwarded throughout the MPLS VPN network with two labels. P routers forward the packet by looking at the top label. The top label is swapped at each P router. The labels are stripped off at the egress PE router and the packet is forwarded as an IPv4 packet onto the VRF interface toward the CE router. The correct CE router is found by looking at the VPN label.

Figure 7-9 *Packet Forwarding in an MPLS VPN Network*

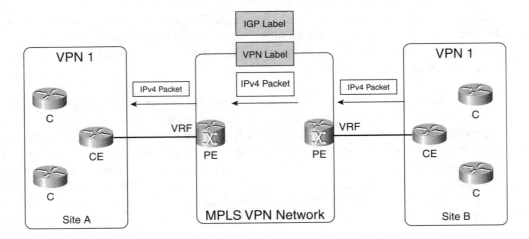

The later section "Packet Forwarding" has a more detailed example of this packet forwarding through the MPLS VPN network. First, however, you must learn more details on the role of BGP in the MPLS VPN network.

BGP

BGP version 4 (BGP-4) has been around for many years and is the standard protocol for interdomain routing. BGP is the protocol that makes the Internet work so well today. The service providers that make up the Internet run BGP between each other. They peer with other service providers through eBGP and run iBGP in their own networks. BGP is a routing protocol that is well suited to carry hundred of thousands of routes and has a proven record to back this up. BGP is also a routing protocol that allows flexible and extended policies to be implemented. That is why it is such a good candidate to carry MPLS VPN routes. As mentioned before, the combination of the RD with the IPv4 prefix makes up the vpnv4 prefix. It is this vpnv4 prefix that iBGP needs to carry between the PE routers.

BGP Multiprotocol Extensions and Capabilities

BGP-4 is described in RFC 1771, but that RFC describes only the use of BGP to carry IPv4 prefixes. BGP can do much more than carry IPv4 prefixes. RFC 2858, "Multiprotocol Extensions for BGP-4," was written to extend BGP as being able to carry other routing information than IPv4. For instance, BGP-4 can carry IPv6 prefixes and thus provide interdomain routing for IPv6. A BGP speaker lets its peers know that multiprotocol extensions for BGP-4 is supported by using capabilities advertisement. BGP peers send each other the capabilities that they support. The capabilities that both peers share can then be used. Examples of capabilities are outbound route filtering (ORF), route refresh capability, and multiprotocol extensions. RFC 3392 (Capabilities Advertisement with BGP-4) describes the functioning of the capabilities advertisement.

When a BGP speaker sends an Open message to its peer, it can include the capability optional parameter, listing all the capabilities of this BGP speaker. The BGP peer can do the same. Either the capabilities match on both peers, or a BGP notification is received from the other BGP speaker indicating what capabilities it does not support. Look at Example 7-7 to see an exchange in BGP capabilities between two BGP peers.

Example 7-7   *BGP Capabilities Exchange*

```
sydney-ce#debug ip bgp
BGP debugging is on
sydney-ce#
*Nov 27 14:49:16.639: BGP: 10.10.4.1 passive open to 10.10.4.2
*Nov 27 14:49:16.639: BGP: 10.10.4.1 went from Idle to Connect
*Nov 27 14:49:16.643: BGP: 10.10.4.1 rcv message type 1, length (excl. header) 34
*Nov 27 14:49:16.643: BGP: 10.10.4.1 rcv OPEN, version 4, holdtime 180 seconds
*Nov 27 14:49:16.643: BGP: 10.10.4.1 went from Connect to OpenSent
*Nov 27 14:49:16.643: BGP: 10.10.4.1 sending OPEN, version 4, my as: 65002, holdtime 180
  seconds
*Nov 27 14:49:16.643: BGP: 10.10.4.1 rcv OPEN w/ OPTION prameter len: 24
*Nov 27 14:49:16.643: BGP: 10.10.4.1 rcvd OPEN w/ optional parameter type 2 (Capability)
  len 6
*Nov 27 14:49:16.643: BGP: 10.10.4.1 OPEN has CAPABILITY code: 1, length 4
*Nov 27 14:49:16.643: BGP: 10.10.4.1 OPEN has MP_EXT CAP for afi/safi: 1/1
*Nov 27 14:49:16.643: BGP: 10.10.4.1 rcvd OPEN w/ optional parameter type 2 (Capability)
  len 6
*Nov 27 14:49:16.643: BGP: 10.10.4.1 OPEN has CAPABILITY code: 1, length 4
*Nov 27 14:49:16.643: BGP: 10.10.4.1 OPEN has MP_EXT CAP for afi/safi: 1/4
*Nov 27 14:49:16.643: BGP: 10.10.4.1 rcvd OPEN w/ optional parameter type 2 (Capability)
  len 2
*Nov 27 14:49:16.647: BGP: 10.10.4.1 OPEN has CAPABILITY code: 128, length 0
*Nov 27 14:49:16.647: BGP: 10.10.4.1 OPEN has ROUTE-REFRESH capability(old) for all
address-families
```

Example 7-7 *BGP Capabilities Exchange (Continued)*

```
*Nov 27 14:49:16.647: BGP: 10.10.4.1 rcvd OPEN w/ optional parameter type 2 (Capability)
  len 2
*Nov 27 14:49:16.647: BGP: 10.10.4.1 OPEN has CAPABILITY code: 2, length 0
*Nov 27 14:49:16.647: BGP: 10.10.4.1 OPEN has ROUTE-REFRESH capability for all address-
  families
BGP: 10.10.4.1 rcvd OPEN w/ remote AS 1
*Nov 27 14:49:16.647: BGP: 10.10.4.1 went from OpenSent to OpenConfirm
*Nov 27 14:49:16.647: BGP: 10.10.4.1 send message type 1, length (incl. header) 53
*Nov 27 14:49:16.651: BGP: 10.10.4.1 went from OpenConfirm to Established
*Nov 27 14:49:16.655: %BGP-5-ADJCHANGE: neighbor 10.10.4.1 Up
```

Example 7-8 shows that you can check the BGP capabilities of the BGP peer with the **show ip bgp neighbors** command.

Example 7-8 *BGP Neighbor Capabilities*

```
sydney-ce#show ip bgp neighbors
BGP neighbor is 10.10.4.1,  remote AS 1, external link
  BGP version 4, remote router ID 10.200.254.5
  BGP state = Established, up for 00:00:37
  Last read 00:00:30, hold time is 180, keepalive interval is 60 seconds
  Neighbor capabilities:
    Route refresh: advertised and received(new)
    Address family IPv4 Unicast: advertised and received
    ipv4 MPLS Label capability: advertised and received
...
```

Multiprotocol Extensions for BGP-4 define two new BGP attributes: Multiprotocol Reachable NLRI and Multiprotocol Unreachable NLRI. These attributes advertise or withdraw routes. Both of them hold two fields: the Address Family Identifier (AFI) and the Subsequent Address Family Identifier (SAFI). Together they describe exactly which kinds of routes BGP is carrying.

Look at Figure 7-10 for the format of this tuple.

Figure 7-10 *AFI/SAFI Format*

Address Family Identifier (2 Octets)
Subsequent Address Family Identifier (1 Octet)

Table 7-1 provides some of the AFI numbers and their descriptions.

Table 7-1   *Some Address Family Numbers*

Number	Description
0	Reserved
1	IP (IP version 4)
2	IP6 (IP version 6)
11	IPX
12	AppleTalk

Table 7-2 lists the SAFI numbers and their descriptions for the IP address family.

Table 7-2   *Subsequent Address Family Numbers*

Number	Description
1	NLRI[1] for unicast forwarding
2	NLRI for multicast forwarding
3	NLRI for both unicast and multicast forwarding
4	NLRI for IPv4 and label forwarding
128	NLRI for labeled VPN forwarding

[1] NLRI = Network Layer Reachability Information

To support the Multiprotocol behavior of BGP in Cisco IOS, the BGP routing process has the concept of address families. The four address families that are currently supported are IPv4, IPv6, vpnv4 (VPN-IPv4), and vpnv6 (VPN-IPv6). The subsequent address families that you can specify are unicast, multicast, and VRF. Look at Example 7-9 for the configuration of BGP address families.

Example 7-9   *Configuring BGP Address Families*

```
sydney#conf t
Enter configuration commands, one per line.  End with CNTL/Z.
sydney(config)#router bgp 1
sydney(config-router)#address-family ?
  ipv4   Address family
  ipv6   Address family
  vpnv4  Address family
  vpnv6  Address family
```
continues

Example 7-9 *Configuring BGP Address Families (Continued)*

```
sydney(config-router)#address-family ipv4 ?
  multicast  Address Family modifier
  unicast    Address Family modifier
  vrf        Specify parameters for a VPN Routing/Forwarding instance
  <cr>
```

You use the address family vpnv4 under the router bgp process to configure the vpnv4 BGP sessions and parameters, which the PE routers need.

You use the address family ipv4 vrf *vrf-name* under the router bgp process on the PE routers to configure the BGP sessions and parameters toward the CE routers, across the VRF interfaces.

BGP Extended Community: RT

The draft ietf-idr-bgp-ext-communities defines the extended community attribute. The community attribute is an optional transitive attribute that is described in RFC 1997. The extended community is also a transitive optional BGP attribute. It came into existence to extend the range of communities and has an enhanced structure over the BGP community attribute. Several BGP extended community attributes are defined, but only one is required for MPLS VPN: the RT extended community. It indicates to the BGP speakers (the PE routers) if the route should be imported into a VRF. Example 7-10 shows the vpnv4 route 1:1:10.10.100.1/32 with the RTs 1:1, 100:100, and 100:101. Only the VRFs that are configured to import at least one of these RTs insert the IPv4 route 10.10.100.1/32 into the VRF routing table.

Example 7-10 *BGP RT Attribute*

```
sydney#show ip bgp vpnv4 rd 1:1 10.10.100.1
BGP routing table entry for 1:1:10.10.100.1/32, version 277
Paths: (1 available, best #1, table cust-one)
Flag: 0xA00
  Advertised to update-groups:
     2
  Local
    10.200.254.2 (metric 3) from 10.200.254.2 (10.200.254.2)
      Origin incomplete, metric 1, localpref 100, valid, internal, best
      Extended Community: RT:1:1 RT:100:100 RT:100:101,
      mpls labels in/out 39/32
```

VPNv4 Routes

The 64-bit field of the RD and the 32-bit IPv4 prefix make up the vpnv4 prefix, which is 96 bits long. MP-iBGP advertises these prefixes between the PE routers. You can see the vpnv4 prefixes that BGP carries with the following command:

```
show ip bgp vpnv4 {all | rd route-distinguisher | vrf vrf-name} [rib-failure]
[ip-prefix/length [longer-prefixes] [output-modifiers]] [network-address [mask]
[longer-prefixes][labels]
```

The *all* keyword for this command shows all vnpv4 routes, or all the routes for all RDs. With the *rd* keyword, you can look at only the vpnv4 routes with that certain RD. You can do the same by using the *vrf* keyword on a PE router. However, if you use the command with the *vrf* keyword on a route reflector (RR), it might not show you routes. The RR might not have VRFs configured, because it is probably just used to reflect the vpnv4 routes. In that case, you should use the command with the *rd* keyword to look at specific vpnv4 routes. Example 7-11 demonstrates the **show ip bgp vpnv4** command with the keywords.

Example 7-11 *Vpnv4 Routes*

```
london#show ip bgp vpnv4 ?
  all  Display information about all VPNv4 NLRIs
  rd   Display information for a route distinguisher
  vrf  Display information for a VPN Routing/Forwarding instance

london#show ip bgp vpnv4 all
BGP table version is 31, local router ID is 10.200.254.2
Status codes: s suppressed, d damped, h history, * valid, > best, i - internal,
              r RIB-failure, S Stale
Origin codes: i - IGP, e - EGP, ? - incomplete

   Network          Next Hop          Metric LocPrf Weight Path
Route Distinguisher: 1:1 (default for vrf cust-one)
*> 10.10.2.0/24     0.0.0.0                0        32768 ?
*> 10.10.100.1/32   10.10.2.1              0            0 65001 i
*> 10.99.1.1/32     0.0.0.0                0        32768 ?
Route Distinguisher: 2:2 (default for vrf cust-two)
*> 10.140.1.1/32    0.0.0.0                0        32768 ?
Route Distinguisher: 9000:1 (default for vrf management)
*> 10.239.9.1/32    10.239.1.1             0            0 65400 i

london#show ip bgp vpnv4 rd ?
  ASN:nn or IP-address:nn  VPN Route Distinguisher

london#show ip bgp vpnv4 rd 1:1
BGP table version is 31, local router ID is 10.200.254.2
Status codes: s suppressed, d damped, h history, * valid, > best, i - internal,
              r RIB-failure, S Stale
Origin codes: i - IGP, e - EGP, ? - incomplete
```

continues

Example 7-11 *Vpnv4 Routes (Continued)*

```
   Network              Next Hop            Metric LocPrf Weight Path
Route Distinguisher: 1:1 (default for vrf cust-one)
*> 10.10.2.0/24      0.0.0.0                   0           32768 ?
*> 10.10.100.1/32    10.10.2.1                 0               0 65001 i
*> 10.99.1.1/32      0.0.0.0                   0           32768 ?


london#show ip bgp vpnv4 vrf cust-one
BGP table version is 31, local router ID is 10.200.254.2
Status codes: s suppressed, d damped, h history, * valid, > best, i - internal,
              r RIB-failure, S Stale
Origin codes: i - IGP, e - EGP, ? - incomplete

   Network              Next Hop            Metric LocPrf Weight Path
Route Distinguisher: 1:1 (default for vrf cust-one)
*> 10.10.2.0/24      0.0.0.0                   0           32768 ?
*> 10.10.100.1/32    10.10.2.1                 0               0 65001 i
*> 10.99.1.1/32      0.0.0.0                   0           32768 ?
```

BGP Carrying the Label

BGP advertises the vpnv4 prefixes in the MPLS VPN network. This is not enough to be able to forward the VPN traffic correctly. For the egress PE router to be able to forward the VPN traffic correctly to the CE router, it must forward the packet based on a label. The egress PE router can map such a label to the vpnv4 prefix, it is called the *VPN label*. The egress PE router must advertise the label along with the vpnv4 prefix to the possible ingress PE routers. The encoding of the label with the prefix is described in RFC 3107, "Carrying Label Information in BGP-4." The label is simply piggybacked along with the vpnv4 prefix and advertised by BGP using the multiprotocol extensions attribute. The label is contained in the NLRI field. The AFI is 1 and the SAFI 128 in the case of MPLS VPN for IPv4.

NOTE MPLS VPN can be done for IPv6 in addition to IPv4. Refer to Chapter 9, "IPv6 over MPLS," for more on this.

That the PE router is capable of advertising labels for vpnv4 prefixes can be seen when the BGP capabilities are exchanged, as in Example 7-12.

Example 7-12 *BGP Label Advertisement Capability*

```
sydney#debug ip bgp
BGP debugging is on for address family: IPv4 Unicast
sydney#
BGP: 10.200.254.2 went from Idle to Active
BGP: 10.200.254.2 open active, delay 9236ms
BGP: 10.200.254.2 passive open to 10.200.254.5
```

Example 7-12   *BGP Label Advertisement Capability (Continued)*

```
BGP: 10.200.254.2 went from Active to Idle
BGP: 10.200.254.2 went from Idle to Connect
BGP: 10.200.254.2 rcv message type 1, length (excl. header) 34
BGP: 10.200.254.2 rcv OPEN, version 4, holdtime 180 seconds
BGP: 10.200.254.2 went from Connect to OpenSent
BGP: 10.200.254.2 sending OPEN, version 4, my as: 1, holdtime 180 seconds
BGP: 10.200.254.2 rcv OPEN w/ OPTION parameter len: 24
BGP: 10.200.254.2 rcvd OPEN w/ optional parameter type 2 (Capability) len 6
BGP: 10.200.254.2 OPEN has CAPABILITY code: 1, length 4
BGP: 10.200.254.2 OPEN has MP_EXT CAP for afi/safi: 1/1
BGP: 10.200.254.2 rcvd OPEN w/ optional parameter type 2 (Capability) len 6
BGP: 10.200.254.2 OPEN has CAPABILITY code: 1, length 4
BGP: 10.200.254.2 OPEN has MP_EXT CAP for afi/safi: 1/128
BGP: 10.200.254.2 rcvd OPEN w/ optional parameter type 2 (Capability) len 2
BGP: 10.200.254.2 OPEN has CAPABILITY code: 128, length 0
BGP: 10.200.254.2 OPEN has ROUTE-REFRESH capability(old) for all address-families
BGP: 10.200.254.2 rcvd OPEN w/ optional parameter type 2 (Capability) len 2
BGP: 10.200.254.2 OPEN has CAPABILITY code: 2, length 0
BGP: 10.200.254.2 OPEN has ROUTE-REFRESH capability(new) for all address-families
BGP: 10.200.254.2 rcvd OPEN w/ remote AS 1
BGP: 10.200.254.2 went from OpenSent to OpenConfirm
BGP: 10.200.254.2 send message type 1, length (incl. header) 53
BGP: 10.200.254.2 went from OpenConfirm to Established
%BGP-5-ADJCHANGE: neighbor 10.200.254.2 Up
```

Look at Figure 7-11 to see the encoding of the NLRI field for MPLS VPN. Notice that the label is encoded as three octets, not four. The three octets contain the 20 bits of the label value encoded into the high-order bits and the Bottom-of-Stack bit as the low-order bit. More than one label can exist, each encoded as three octets. However, for MPLS VPN described here, MP-BGP advertises only one label for each vpnv4 prefix.

Figure 7-11   *Label Encoding*

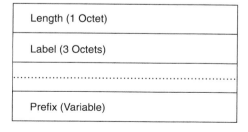

A BGP speaker only assigns a label to a prefix for which it is the next hop. This is an important rule to remember when looking at the behavior of a BGP RR for vpnv4 routes.

Look at Example 7-13 for the address family vpnv4 configuration. First, you need to define the BGP neighbor in the global part of the BGP configuration. Then you need to enable the BGP neighbor in the address family vpnv4 by specifying the *activate* keyword.

> **NOTE** Only BGP extended communities are sent by default to the vpnv4 neighbor. If you want to use standard communities, too, please specify *send-community both* for the BGP neighbor.

Example 7-13 *BGP Address Family vpnv4 Configuration*

```
router bgp 1
 bgp log-neighbor-changes
 neighbor 10.200.254.2 remote-as 1
 neighbor 10.200.254.2 update-source Loopback0
 !
 address-family ipv4
 redistribute rip
 neighbor 10.200.254.2 activate
 exit-address-family
 !
 address-family vpnv4
 neighbor 10.200.254.2 activate
 neighbor 10.200.254.2 send-community both
 exit-address-family
 !
```

Debug ip bgp vpnv4 unicast updates enables the debugging of vpnv4 updates in BGP. Example 7-14 shows this debugging when a vpnv4 prefix is received.

Example 7-14 *debug ip bgp vpnv4 Unicast Updates*

```
sydney#debug ip bgp vpnv4 unicast updates
BGP updates debugging is on for address family: VPNv4 Unicast
sydney#
BGP(2): 10.200.254.2 rcvd UPDATE w/ attr: nexthop 10.200.254.2, origin ?, localpref 100,
  metric
1, extended community RT:1:1
BGP(2): 10.200.254.2 rcvd 1:1:10.10.100.1/32
BGP(2): Revise route installing 1 of 1 routes for 10.10.100.1/32 -> 10.200.254.2(main) to
  cust-
one IP table
```

You can see the labels that BGP receives and advertises for vpnv4 routes in Example 7-15. The In Label is used as an incoming label in the label forwarding information base (LFIB) for this vpnv4 prefix. It is the label that is advertised to the other PE routers for this vpnv4 prefix. The Out Label for vpnv4 prefixes from the other PE routers is the one attached to the vpnv4 prefix. It is the VPN label that this PE uses when forwarding traffic across the MPLS VPN network. For the prefixes with 0.0.0.0 as the next hop in Example 7-15, no outgoing label has been received. This is because the prefixes are learned from VRF interfaces and packets should be forwarded unlabeled toward the CE router.

Example 7-15 *BGP Advertising MPLS Labels*

```
sydney#show ip bgp vpnv4 rd 1:1 labels
   Network           Next Hop        In label/Out label
Route Distinguisher: 1:1 (cust-one)
   10.10.2.0/24      10.200.254.2    29/36
   10.10.4.0/24      0.0.0.0         26/nolabel
   10.10.4.2/32      0.0.0.0         37/nolabel
   10.10.100.1/32    10.200.254.2    32/35
   10.10.100.3/32    10.10.4.2       38/exp-null
   10.88.1.1/32      10.200.254.2    34/34
   10.99.1.1/32      10.200.254.2    28/33
   10.99.1.2/32      0.0.0.0         27/nolabel
   10.200.200.1/32   10.200.254.2    30/32
```

NOTE   Each vpnv4 prefix is assigned a unique MPLS label in Cisco IOS. This is the default Cisco IOS behavior.

RRs

An *RR* is a BGP speaker that reflects routes from other BGP speakers. RRs were invented when networks grew larger. Internal BGP requires that all BGP speakers are in a full mesh with each other. This is fine for a low number of BGP speakers, but it gives the operator of the network problems when the network becomes larger than a certain size. When you have a network with n internal BGP speakers, each BGP speaker has $n-1$ peers, and $n*(n-1)/2$ BGP sessions exist in total. RRs and BGP confederations were invented to alleviate this problem. RRs peer with the BGP speakers in a cluster, but the BGP speakers in the cluster do not need to peer with each other any more if they peer with the RRs. The RRs just forward or reflect all the BGP routes they receive. If you want to use RRs with MPLS VPN, the RRs should reflect vpnv4 prefixes, which carry labels. RRs only change the label if they become the next hop for the routes, which they usually do not. RRs that do become the next hop for the iBGP route are in the forwarding path. This means that they have to forward the traffic for those routes. This could result in a huge amount of traffic flowing through a few RRs, which is definitely not a good idea. The RRs should not be burdened with forwarding traffic. Furthermore, the route of the traffic through the RRs from ingress PE to egress PE is usually not the most optimal route, because the RRs can be anywhere in the network. RRs should not forward traffic, but just reflect BGP routes.

RRs differ in another way from the other BGP speakers (the PE routers) in the MPLS VPN network. They do not reject vnpv4 routes when the RT is not configured for acceptance on the RRs. A PE router that receives a vpnv4 route for which any of the RTs is not imported into a VRF rejects the route. Example 7-16 shows a route that is rejected because the RT 2:2 is not configured to be imported by a VRF on the PE.

Example 7-16 *Rejected vnpv4 Route*

```
sydney#debug ip bgp vpnv4 unicast updates in
BGP updates debugging is on (inbound) for address family: VPNv4 Unicast

sydney#
BGP(2): 10.200.254.2 rcvd UPDATE w/ attr: nexthop 10.200.254.2, origin ?, localpref 100,
  metric
0, extended community RT:2:2
BGP(2): 10.200.254.2 rcvd 2:2:10.140.1.1/32 -- DENIED due to:  extended community not
  supported;
```

The PE router has this default behavior to save memory. Why does it need to store the vpnv4 routes in the BGP table if no VRF is attached to this PE router that imports the route? RRs do not exhibit this behavior because they do not know which RTs the PEs permit or deny. RRs accept and store all BGP routes. To ease the burden, you can implement RR groups to split the load of reflecting vpnv4 routes among several RRs or groups of RRs. Each RR or group of RRs then reflects a subset of all the vpnv4 routes.

NOTE It is a good idea to have at least two RRs for a subset of the vpnv4 prefixes for redundancy reasons.

RR Group

It is unnecessary for one RR or a group of RRs to have all the vpnv4 routes in the BGP table. You can subdivide the vpnv4 routes into groups and allow several RRs or several groups of RRs to carry one of those subsets of routes. Divide and conquer. This increases the scalability of your network. The command needed to implement RR group on the RRs is **bgp rr-group** {*extcom-list-number*} under the address family vpnv4. You must specify an extended community list for the RR group. This extended community list specifies the RTs that you want this RR to permit or deny. Figure 7-12 shows an example of the usage of an RR group. Two RRs are available, with RR group configured for a different set of vpnv4 routes. One RR filters out the vpnv4 updates with the even RTs; the other RR filters out the vpnv4 updates with the odd RTs.

Figure 7-12   *Example of an MPLS VPN Network with RR Groups*

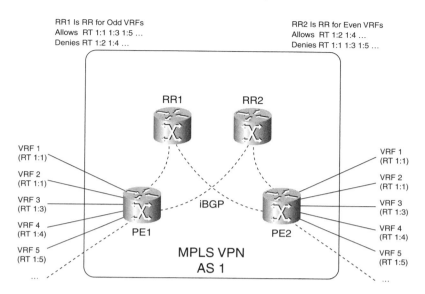

Example 7-17 shows the use of RR groups. An extended community list 1 is created on RR1 permitting the RT 1:1 and denying the RT 1:2 from the RR clients. On the second RR, you swap the permitted and denied RTs.

Example 7-17   *Example of RR Groups*

```
RR1(config-router)#address-family vpnv4
RR1(config-router-af)#bgp rr-group ?
  <1-500>   Extended-Community list number

!
router bgp 1
 neighbor 10.200.254.2 remote-as 1
 neighbor 10.200.254.2 update-source Loopback0
 neighbor 10.200.254.5 remote-as 1
 neighbor 10.200.254.5 update-source Loopback0
 no auto-summary
 !
 address-family vpnv4
 neighbor 10.200.254.2 activate
 neighbor 10.200.254.2 route-reflector-client
 neighbor 10.200.254.2 send-community extended
 neighbor 10.200.254.5 activate
 neighbor 10.200.254.5 route-reflector-client
 neighbor 10.200.254.5 send-community extended
 bgp rr-group 1
 exit-address-family
```

Example 7-17 *Example of RR Groups (Continued)*

```
!
ip extcommunity-list 1 permit rt 1:1
ip extcommunity-list 1 deny rt 1:2
ip extcommunity-list 1 permit rt 1:3
ip extcommunity-list 1 deny rt 1:4
...
!
```

BGP Route Selection

Different BGP speakers can advertise the vpnv4 route when, for instance, a customer site is dual homed to two PE routers. The receiving BGP speaker must then choose one BGP route as the best one. The process for selecting the best vpnv4 route is the same as the one for regular IPv4 BGP routes. The only difference is that now the BGP routes are not 32-bit IPv4 prefixes but 96-bit vpnv4 prefixes. Therefore, if a customer site is dual homed to two PE routers, the ingress PE router receives the vpnv4 route with two different BGP next hops—namely, the two egress PE routers. The ingress PE router applies the BGP best path selection process and installs one of the two BGP paths in the VRF routing table.

> **NOTE** Refer to www.Cisco.com for details on the BGP best path selection process.

BGP Multipath

BGP selects only one best path for each prefix it receives. This means that only one BGP path is installed in the IP routing table, which excludes the possibility of load balancing. BGP Multipath is a BGP feature whereby the selection process still selects one BGP path as the best but allows multiple BGP paths to be installed in the routing table. BGP Multipath comes in three types: iBGP, eBGP, and eiBGP. iBGP Multipath is the installation of two or more internal BGP paths. eBGP Multipath is the installation of two or more external BGP paths. eiBGP Multipath is the installation of one or more internal and one or more external BGP paths. Not just any BGP path can be chosen for Multipath together with the best path. The following criteria must be fulfilled for the BGP path to be a candidate for Multipath. The following BGP attributes of the alternate BGP paths must be identical to the ones of the best path for the alternative paths to be used in parallel:

- Weight

- Local preference

- AS-PATH length

- Origin

- Multi-exit discriminator (MED)

- One of the following:

Neighboring autonomous system (AS) or sub-AS (before the eiBGP Multipath feature was added)

AS-PATH (after the eiBGP Multipath feature was added)

■   IGP metric to the BGP next hop

Table 7-3 shows what command is used under the specific address family of BGP to configure BGP Multipath.

Table 7-3   *BGP Multipath Commands*

BGP Multipath	BGP Address Family Command
eBGP	**maximum-paths** *n*
iBGP	**maximum-paths ibgp** *n*
eiBGP	**maximum-paths eiBGP** *n*

The *n* in the BGP address family **maximum-paths** command indicates how many paths can be installed in the IP routing table. The default value of *n* is 1, so BGP Multipath is disabled by default.

Look at Figure 7-13 to see an example of eiBGP Multipath in an MPLS VPN network.

Figure 7-13   *Example of a MPLS VPN with eiBGP Multipath*

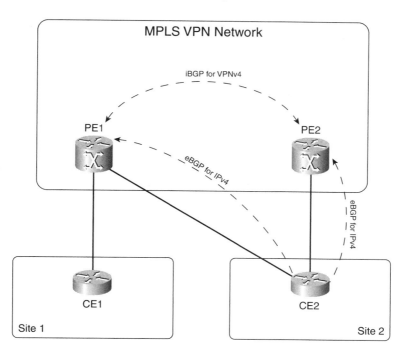

PE1 receives a route from site 2 either directly from the eBGP peering across the VRF interface toward CE2 or indirectly from the iBGP peering to PE2. If eiBGP Multipath is enabled on PE1 under address family ipv4 vrf, PE1 can install both BGP paths into the IP VRF routing table.

If BGP Multipath is used for MPLS VPN, you can configure an additional *import* keyword. The import keyword indicates how many routes can be imported from one VRF into another. This occurs when the RDs are different in the source VRF and the destination VRF. This was true in Example 7-6, where 1:1:10.10.100.1/32 was imported into the VRF with RD 1:2. Therefore, the prefix became 1:2:10.10.100.1/32 in the VRF with RD 1:2.

Figure 7-14 shows iBGP Multipath in an MPLS VPN network with the import keyword.

Figure 7-14 *Example of a MPLS VPN with iBGP Multipath and the Import Keyword*

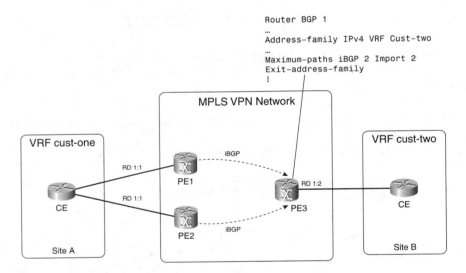

PE1 and PE2 advertise a vpnv4 prefix with RD 1:1. However, the VRF on PE3 has RD 1:2. Importing the appropriate RTs controls the importing of the routes into the VRF *cust-two*. The RDs of the vpnv4 routes that are received on PE3 and the configured RD of VRF *cust-two* differ, though, so the import keyword for iBGP Multipath is needed here.

Using Multiple RDs

When a CE router is dual homed to two PE routers and RRs are used for vpnv4 routes, you will have a problem when trying to use BGP Multipath on the PE routers. BGP Multipath should install multiple paths for the same destination in the routing table. However, when RRs are used, they use the BGP best path selection process to choose the best vpnv4 route. The RRs advertise or reflect only this best path further. The ingress PE router gets only one route to install instead of two. Look at Figure 7-15. The prefix 10.1.1.0/24 is advertised from two PE routers. On each PE router, the same RD 1:1 is attached to the IP prefix. The RR receives two BGP prefix advertisements for this vpnv4 prefix. The RR chooses the best path as the one with PE1 as the next hop. This is the only path advertised from the RR to its clients (the PE routers).

Figure 7-15 *RR Advertises Only the Best BGP Path*

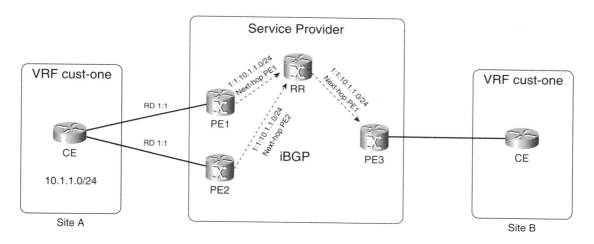

A simple workaround for this problem is to make the vpnv4 prefixes that are advertised by both egress PE routers different. If the two routes are different, the RRs will advertise both of them. The vpnv4 routes can be made different from each other by assigning different RDs to the VRFs on both egress PE routers. By having a different RD under the VRF configuration on the egress PE routers, the routes become unique. In that case, the RRs advertise both routes, and the ingress PE routers can install both paths in the VRF routing table if BGP Multipath is used. Look at Figure 7-16 for the same example as in Figure 7-15, but with two RDs used for the same IPv4 route from the VRF on the egress PE routers. The result is that the RR can forward two vpnv4 routes to the PE routers. PE3 can install both paths if it has iBGP Multipath configured.

Figure 7-16 *Usage of Multiple RDs*

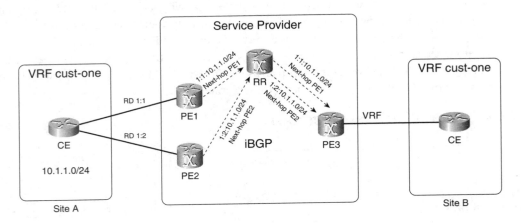

Packet Forwarding

This section, illustrated with a specific example, looks at the life of an IP packet as it traverses the MPLS VPN backbone from one customer site to another. The basic building blocks of MPLS VPN need to be in place first. Multiprotocol iBGP needs to run between the PE routers that are distributing the vpnv4 routes and their associated VPN label. A label distribution protocol needs to exist between all the PE and P routers. This example assumes that the label distribution protocol is LDP. Between the PE and the CE routers, a routing protocol needs to run and put the customer routes into the VRF routing table on the PE routers. Finally, those routes need to be distributed into MP-iBGP and vice versa. Look at Figures 7-17 and 7-18 to better understand the explanation that follows. Figure 7-17 shows the route advertisement of the vpnv4 route and label from egress PE to ingress PE and the advertisement of the IGP route—representing the BGP next hop of the egress PE—and label to the ingress PE. The BGP next-hop address on the egress PE is 10.200.254.2/32, which an IGP advertises to the ingress PE. The label for that IGP route is advertised hop by hop by LDP. The customer IPv4 route 10.10.100.1/32 is advertised by a PE-CE routing protocol from the CE to the egress PE. The egress PE adds the RD 1:1, turns it into vpnv4 route 1:1:10.10.100.1/32, and sends it to the ingress PE with label 30, via Multiprotocol iBGP.

Figure 7-17   *Life of an IPv4 Packet Across the MPLS VPN Backbone: Route and Label Advertisement*

MP-iBGP Update
VPNv4 Route 1:1:10.10.100.1/32
Label 30

LDP Label Binding   LDP Label Binding   LDP Label Binding

Loopback 0   Label Implicit-null For   Label 33 For   Label 16 For
10.200.254.2/32   10.200.254.2/32   10.200.254.2/32   10.200.254.2/32

VRF cust-one
RD 1:1

VRF   VRF

CE   Egress   P   P   Ingress   CE
10.10.100.1/32   PE   PE
VRF cust-one   VRF cust-one

MPLS VPN

Route Update   Route Update   Route Update   Route Update   Route Update
10.10.100.1/32   10.200.254.2/32   10.200.254.2/32   10.200.254.2/32   10.10.100.1/32

Figure 7-18 shows a packet with destination IP address 10.10.100.1 being forwarded with the two labels as advertised in Figure 7-17.

Figure 7-18   *Life of an IPv4 Packet Across the MPLS VPN Backbone: Packet Forwarding*

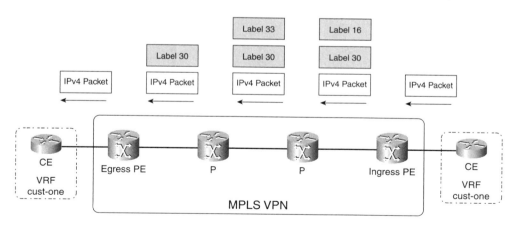

When an IP packet enters the ingress PE router from the CE, the ingress PE router looks up the destination IP address in the VRF *cust-one* CEF table. The ingress PE router finds the correct VRF by looking at which interface the packet entered the PE router, and with which VRF table this interface is associated. The specific entry in the VRF CEF table usually indicates that two labels need to be added.

> **NOTE** When the ingress and egress PE routers are directly connected, the packets will have only one label—the VPN label. This is true because of penultimate hop popping (PHP).

First, the ingress PE router pushes VPN label 30—as advertised by BGP for the vpnv4 route. This becomes the bottom label. Then, the ingress PE router pushes the IGP label as the top label. This label is the label that is associated with the /32 IGP route for the BGP next-hop IP address. This is usually the IP address of the loopback interface on the egress PE. This label is advertised hop by hop between the P routers until it reaches the ingress PE router. Each hop changes the value of the label. The IGP label that the ingress PE pushes is label 16.

The IPv4 packet leaves the ingress PE router with two labels on top of it. The top label—the IGP label for the egress PE router—is swapped at each hop in the path. This label gets the IPv4 VPN packet to the correct egress PE router. Usually—because it is the default behavior in Cisco IOS—PHP behavior takes place between the last P and the egress PE router. Therefore, the IGP label is popped off on the last P router and the packet enters the egress PE router with only the VPN label in the label stack. The egress PE router looks up this VPN label in the LFIB and makes a forwarding decision. Because the outgoing label is *No Label,* the remaining label stack is removed and the packet is forwarded as an IP packet to the CE router. The egress PE router does not have to perform an IP lookup of the destination IP address in the IP header if the outgoing label is *No Label.* The correct next-hop information is found by looking up the VPN label in the LFIB. Only when the outgoing label is *Aggregate* does the egress PE router have to perform an IP lookup in the VRF CEF table after the label lookup in the LFIB.

Look at Examples 7-18 through 7-20 to see the labels advertised by LDP and MP-iBGP and their use in the VRF CEF table and LFIB. These labels correspond with the labels in Figures 7-17 and 7-18.

Example 7-18 *VRF CEF Table Cust-One on Ingress PE*

```
Ingress-PE#show ip cef vrf cust-one 10.10.100.1 255.255.255.255 detail
10.10.100.1/32, epoch 0
  recursive via 10.200.254.2 label 30
    nexthop 10.200.214.1 POS0/1/0 label 16
```

Example 7-19 *Vpnv4 Route on Ingress PE*

```
Ingress-PE#show ip bgp vpnv4 rd 1:1 10.10.100.1
BGP routing table entry for 1:1:10.10.100.1/32, version 81
Paths: (1 available, best #1, table cust-one)
  Not advertised to any peer
  Local
    10.200.254.2 (metric 3) from 10.200.254.2 (10.200.254.2)
      Origin incomplete, metric 1, localpref 100, valid, internal, best
      Extended Community: RT:1:1,
      mpls labels in/out nolabel/30
```

Example 7-20 *LFIB Entry on Egress PE*

```
Egress-PE#show mpls forwarding-table labels 30
Local   Outgoing      Prefix          Bytes Label   Outgoing    Next Hop
Label   Label or VC   or Tunnel Id    Switched      interface
30      No Label      10.10.100.1/32[V] 0           Et0/1/2     10.10.2.1
```

PE-CE Routing Protocols

Routing needs to occur between the PE and CE routers. The PE-CE routing protocols that Cisco IOS supports are static routing, RIPv2, Open Shortest Path First (OSPF), Enhanced Interior Gateway Routing Protocol (EIGRP), Intermediate System-to-Intermediate System (IS-IS), and eBGP.

Connected Routes

Strictly speaking, the connected routes are not a routing protocol. However, to ensure connectivity, it is best practice to redistribute the connected routes on the PE router into BGP. That way, when the user launches a ping from a CE router to the remote CE router, the return packet is routed back. By default, if the user sends a ping and does not specify the source IP address, it takes as the source IP address the IP address of the outgoing interface, which in the case of a CE router is an IP address from the subnet on the PE-CE link. As such, the return packet has this IP address as the destination IP address. Thus, this prefix must be known on the remote sites for the ping to succeed. You can choose not to distribute the connected subnets into BGP, but then you have to launch a ping from CE to CE by specifying a different source IP address on the CE router. Then you must include this IP address in the specific PE-CE routing protocol. The same applies for other applications, such as Telnet. Example 7-21 shows the **redistribute connected** command under the address family ipv4 for the VRF. As mentioned before, you use the address family ipv4 vrf *vrf-name* under the router bgp process on the PE routers to configure the BGP sessions and parameters toward the CE routers, across the VRF interfaces. This is also the place where other VRF routing protocols are redistributed into BGP.

Example 7-21 *Redistribution of Connected Routes into BGP*

```
router bgp 1
...
 !
 address-family ipv4 vrf cust-one
 redistribute connected
 neighbor 10.10.2.1 remote-as 65001
 neighbor 10.10.2.1 activate
 exit-address-family
 !
```

Static Routing

Static routing is the simplest of all routing to configure. It can, however, be tedious when you manually need to configure many static routes. To support VRFs, static routes have been made VRF aware so that they can be configured on the PE router to route traffic in the VRFs. Example 7-22 shows a static route for the prefix 10.88.1.1/32 pointing to a next-hop 10.10.2.1, which is the IP address of the interface of the PE-CE link on the CE router. You can see that the static route applies to the VRF *cust-one* and that the route is installed in the VRF routing table that is associated with VRF *cust-one*.

Example 7-22 *OSPF VRF Configuration*

```
!
ip route vrf cust-one 10.88.1.1 255.255.255.255 10.10.2.1
!

london#show ip route vrf cust-one static
     10.0.0.0/8 is variably subnetted, 7 subnets, 2 masks
S        10.88.1.1/32 [1/0] via 10.10.2.1
```

To ensure that the static route is learned on the other PE routers as a vpnv4 route, you must distribute the static routes into BGP under the address family for the specific VRF. Example 7-23 shows the **redistribute** command for static routes.

Example 7-23 *Distribution of Static Routes into BGP*

```
router bgp 1
...
 !
 address-family ipv4 vrf cust-one
 redistribute connected
 redistribute static
 exit-address-family
 !
```

RIP Version 2

Routing Information Protocol (RIP) is a simple distance vector routing protocol. It is limited in its use and is not a routing protocol that is suited for large networks because of its slowness in converging. However, it is still used often in small networks as a quick-and-dirty routing protocol that gets the job done with respect to basic routing functionality.

RIP version 2 (RIPv2) has seen some improvements over the first RIP specification, but it is still a limited routing protocol. Following are some of the improvements:

■ Including a subnet mask with the prefixes

■ Using the multicast address 224.0.0.9 instead of the broadcast address 255.255.255.255

- Including a next-hop address

- Including a route tag

- Use authentication (optional)

In Cisco IOS, RIPv2 is supported as a PE-CE routing protocol, but RIP version 1 is not. You can see the basic RIPv2 VRF configuration on a PE router in Example 7-24. Only one RIPv2 process exists on the PE router. The specific configuration needed per VRF is configured under the specific address family. Make sure the **default-metric** command is configured for RIP. Otherwise, no routes are distributed from BGP to RIP.

Example 7-24 *RIPv2 VRF Configuration*

```
!
ip vrf cust-one
 rd 1:1
 route-target export 1:1
 route-target import 1:1
!
router rip
 no auto-summary
 !
 address-family ipv4 vrf cust-one
 redistribute bgp 1
 network 10.0.0.0
 default-metric 2
 version 2
 exit-address-family
 !
router bgp 1
 ...
 !
 address-family ipv4 vrf cust-one
 redistribute connected
 redistribute rip
 exit-address-family
 !
```

OSPF

OSPF can be the routing protocol on the PE-CE link. To propagate the customer routes from PE to PE, OSPF is redistributed into iBGP and vice versa on the PE routers. The down side of this is that all OSPF routes become external routes on the remote PE when the routes are redistributed back into OSPF. The result of this would be that all OSPF routes that transverse the MPLS VPN backbone would be less preferable than the routes that did not transverse the backbone but were sent via an intersite link (backdoor link) from one OSPF site to another.

To prevent all redistributed routes from becoming OSPF external prefixes, internal OSPF routes are advertised as summary routes (link-state advertisement [LSA] type 3)—which are interarea routes—on the PE when they are redistributed from BGP back to OSPF. This is not the normal behavior, because the PE routers redistribute BGP routes into OSPF and are autonomous system boundary routers (ASBR) that should advertise the routes as external OSPF routes (LSA type 5). In effect, it is as if the PE routers are area border routers (ABR) that advertise summary routes into another area. However, all OSPF internal routes (intra-area and interarea routes) become interarea (LSA type 3) routes after BGP propagates them, even if the area numbers match on different PE routers. Figure 7-19 shows the propagation of OSPF internal routes across the MPLS VPN backbone.

Figure 7-19 *Internal OSPF Routes Across MPLS VPN Backbone*

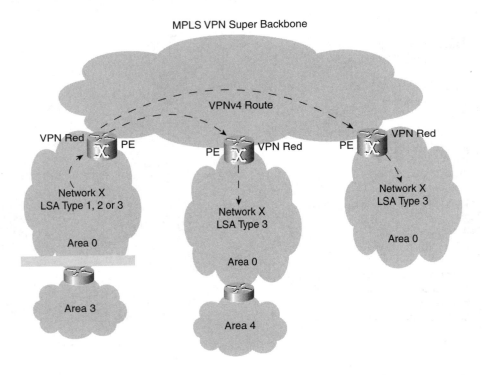

The normal OSPF route preference dictates that intra-area routes are more preferred than interarea OSPF routes. Because all internal OSPF routes become interarea routes at the remote sites, intra-area routes might still cause a problem becoming interarea routes when a backdoor link exists between sites. The intra-area routes remain intra-area routes across the backdoor link but become interarea routes across the MPLS VPN backbone. Therefore, the intra-area routes that are advertised across the backdoor link are always preferred. To avoid this, you must configure a special link, called a sham link, between the PE routers. Read the section "Sham Link" later in this chapter to learn more.

The PE routers have OSPF areas connected to them. These areas can be the backbone area 0 or any other area. The MPLS VPN backbone can be considered an added hierarchy that is higher than the OSPF backbone area: the MPLS VPN super backbone. Figure 7-20 shows this concept.

Figure 7-20 *Possible OSPF MPLS VPN Scenarios*

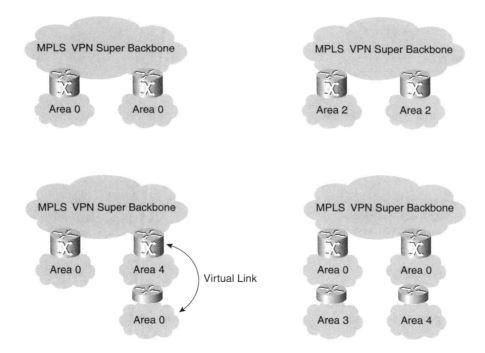

OSPF VRF Configuration

To run OSPF for a VRF, you configure the OSPF process command with the VRF keyword. The syntax is **router ospf** *process-id* **vrf** *vrf-name*. Note that RIPv2 and EIGRP have only one routing process with an address family per VRF configured. OSPF has one separate OSPF process per VRF.

Example 7-25 shows the basic OSPF VRF configuration. Obviously, the OSPF VRF process needs to be redistributed into BGP and vice versa. You can configure all the regular OSPF commands for the OSPF VRF process. Make sure you have the *subnets* keyword on the **redistribute bgp** command under the router ospf process. Otherwise, only classful routes are redistributed. When you are redistributing OSPF into BGP, make sure to configure the appropriate match parameters on the **redistribute** command so that you can redistribute the proper OSPF type of routes.

Example 7-25 *Basic OSPF VRF Configuration*

```
!
ip vrf cust-one
 rd 1:1
 route-target export 1:1
 route-target import 1:1
!
interface Loopback1
 ip vrf forwarding cust-one
 ip address 10.99.1.1 255.255.255.255
!
router ospf 42 vrf cust-one
 router-id 10.99.1.1
 log-adjacency-changes
 redistribute bgp 1 metric 10 subnets
 network 10.10.2.0 0.0.0.255 area 0
!
router bgp 1
 bgp log-neighbor-changes
 neighbor 10.200.254.5 remote-as 1
 neighbor 10.200.254.5 update-source Loopback0
 !
 address-family vpnv4
 neighbor 10.200.254.5 activate
 neighbor 10.200.254.5 send-community extended
 exit-address-family
 !
 address-family ipv4 vrf cust-one
 redistribute connected
 redistribute ospf 42 vrf cust-one metric 10 match internal external 1 external 2
 exit-address-family
 !
```

Example 7-26 shows the OSPF VRF process 42 running on the PE router.

Example 7-26 *Show IP OSPF Command*

```
london#show ip ospf 42
 Routing Process "ospf 42" with ID 10.99.1.1
   Domain ID type 0x0005, value 0.0.0.42
 Supports only single TOS(TOS0) routes
 Supports opaque LSA
 Supports Link-local Signaling (LLS)
 Supports area transit capability
 Connected to MPLS VPN Superbackbone, VRF cust-one
 It is an area border and autonomous system boundary router
 Redistributing External Routes from,
     bgp 1 with metric mapped to 10, includes subnets in redistribution
 …
 Number of areas in this router is 1. 1 normal 0 stub 0 nssa
 Number of areas transit capable is 0
 External flood list length 0
    Area BACKBONE(0)
        Number of interfaces in this area is 2
        Area has no authentication
        SPF algorithm last executed 00:04:35.120 ago
        SPF algorithm executed 25 times
        Area ranges are
        Number of LSA 17. Checksum Sum 0x0E27D6
        Number of opaque link LSA 0. Checksum Sum 0x000000
        Number of DCbitless LSA 0
        Number of indication LSA 0
        Number of DoNotAge LSA 13
        Flood list length 0
```

OSPF Metric Propagation

When you redistribute both internal and external OSPF routes from OSPF into MP-BGP on the PE router, the PE router uses the OSPF metric to set the BGP MED. The MED is often referred to as the *external metric* of a BGP route. It is part of the BGP best path selection process. BGP can use it to select the best path when two or more BGP speakers advertise the same route in BGP. The MED is shown as "metric" in the BGP table in Cisco IOS. Look at Example 7-27, where the prefixes 1:1:10.10.100.1/32 and 1:1:10.200.200.1/32 are advertised with a MED (external metric) of 10. When the PE redistributes the route back from BGP into OSPF, the PE uses the MED to set the OSPF metric of the OSPF internal or external route. When you use the **default-metric** *metric-value* command or **metric** option on the **redistribute** command, it overrides this behavior because it directly sets the metric to the configured value.

BGP Extended Communities for OSPF

To carry the characteristics of the OSPF routes across the MPLS VPN backbone, several additional BGP extended communities were defined. The OSPF characteristics that are transported with MP-BGP include the following:

■   Route type

■   Area number

■   OSPF router ID

■   Domain ID

■   Metric type 1 or 2 for OSPF external routes

The OSPF-specific BGP extended communities allow the OSPF route to be completely reconstructed at the remote PE router. The route type lets the remote PE router figure out what kind of route to advertise in OSPF. If the route type is 1, 2, or 3 (corresponding to LSA types 1, 2, or 3), the remote PE router advertises an interarea summary route (LSA type 3) into the OSPF area.

The domain ID indicates to the remote PE whether an external OSPF route is to be advertised. If the domain ID (by default set equal to the OSPF router process ID) of the route received by a PE router does not match the OSPF process ID of the particular VRF, the route is advertised as an OSPF external route (LSA type 5) type 2 to provide support for networks that are redistributing IP routes between different OSPF processes. If the domain ID does match the OSPF process ID, the route is advertised as an internal route. You can change the domain ID on the PE router with the command **domain-id ospf** *domain ID*.

A route type of 5 indicates that the vpnv4 route that is received is an OSPF external route. As such, the PE floods a type 5 LSA into the OSPF site; by default, the metric type is type 2. The metric that is used for the type 5 LSA is the MED from the BGP vpnv4 route if one is present. If none is present, the default OSPF metric is used.

Example 7-27 shows the BGP extended communities for OSPF. Prefix 10.10.100.1/32 is an OSPF internal route, and prefix 10.200.200.1/32 is an OSPF external route.

Example 7-27   *BGP Extended Communities for OSPF*

```
sydney#show ip bgp vpnv4 rd 1:1 10.10.100.1
BGP routing table entry for 1:1:10.10.100.1/32, version 2045
Paths: (2 available, best #2, table cust-one)
  Advertised to update-groups:
    1
  Local
```

Example 7-27 *BGP Extended Communities for OSPF (Continued)*

```
        10.200.254.2 (metric 3) from 10.200.254.2 (10.200.254.2)
          Origin incomplete, metric 10, localpref 100, valid, internal
          Extended Community: RT:1:1 OSPF DOMAIN ID:0x0005:0x0000002A0200
            OSPF RT:0.0.0.0:2:0 OSPF ROUTER ID:10.10.2.2:512,
          mpls labels in/out 18/28

sydney#show ip bgp vpnv4 rd 1:1 10.200.200.1
BGP routing table entry for 1:1:10.200.200.1/32, version 5649
Paths: (1 available, best #1, table cust-one)
  Not advertised to any peer
  Local
    10.200.254.2 (metric 3) from 10.200.254.2 (10.200.254.2)
      Origin incomplete, metric 10, localpref 100, valid, internal, best
      Extended Community: RT:1:1 OSPF DOMAIN ID:0x0005:0x0000002A0200
        OSPF RT:0.0.0.0:5:1 OSPF ROUTER ID:10.99.1.1:1281,
      mpls labels in/out nolabel/18
```

You can see that the OSPF route type is encoded as *area:route-type:option*. The area is encoded in 4 bytes; the route-type and option are 1 byte each. If the route is external, the area is 0.0.0.0. If the least significant bit of the option field is set, it indicates an external metric type 2. If the least significant bit is not set, it indicates an external metric type 1.

OSPF Network Design

OSPF is designed to work with areas. The special area 0 is the backbone area that connects all other areas. MPLS VPN has another "area" between the OSPF sites: the MPLS VPN backbone. This is not an OSPF area, of course, because it runs iBGP. Nevertheless, it acts as an area as the PE routers act as ABRs. Therefore, you can consider the MPLS VPN backbone as the *super backbone* in the OSPF hierarchy. If multiple sites of one VRF have a PE router with area 0, the backbone area is split into more than one part. Normally, a split backbone area requires a virtual link to interconnect the parts. This is not needed for MPLS VPN, though, because iBGP carries the OSPF routes, OSPF routes are re-created on the PE routers, and the MPLS VPN backbone has no flooding. Refer to the next section for one exception; flooding does occur across the MPLS VPN backbone when a sham link is used.

The PE routers function as ABRs as they advertise type 3 LSAs to the CE routers. The CE routers can be in area 0 or any other area. If, however, a site has more than one area, the PE routers must be in area 0 because they are ABRs. If they are not, a virtual link between the PE router and the nearest ABR in the customer site must bring area 0 up to the PE router. Look again at Figure 7-20 to see the possible scenarios regarding OSPF areas and connections to the MPLS VPN backbone.

Sham Link

If two sites belong to the same area and are interconnected with a backdoor link, they appear as one area to OSPF. Through the backdoor link, all LSAs are flooded unaltered from one site to the other. This means that intra-area routes stay intra-area routes. The intra-area routes (type 1 and 2 LSAs) are flooded across the backdoor link. They are transformed into interarea routes across the MPLS VPN backbone. That means that the preferred path between the two sites is always the backdoor link because OSPF always prefers the intra-area routes over the interarea routes. This reduces the MPLS VPN service to a mere backup solution in case the backdoor link goes down. The concept of sham link was invented to solve this problem. The sham link is not a real link but a fake one between two PE routers. It is an OSPF intra-area link created between the two PE routers so that they can flood this link in the area connected to both the PE routers. The sham link has two endpoints. The sham link endpoint on each PE router is a /32 IPv4 address from the specific VRF. iBGP must advertise this /32 IPv4 address from one PE to the other as a vpnv4 prefix. The sham link is an unnumbered point-to-point intra-area link that is treated as a demand-circuit link. This means that LSAs are flooded across the sham link, but no periodic refresh flooding occurs across the sham link.

The sham link is included in the shortest path first (SPF) computation, just as any link in OSPF. As LSAs are flooded across the sham link, all OSPF route types can be preserved and do not have to be converted into type 3 or 5 LSAs. If the sham link fails, the default mechanism of sending only type 3 and type 5 LSAs into the site occurs. Routing across the MPLS VPN backbone is still possible if the sham link fails, but the backdoor link is the preferred path for intra-area routes because intra-area routes are still learned that way. You configure the sham link by specifying a source IP address in the VRF on the local PE and a destination IP address in the VRF on the remote PE. In addition, you can specify a cost for the sham link to make it more or less preferred than the backdoor link. The syntax of the sham link command is **area** *area-id* **sham-link** *source-address destination-address* **cost** *number.*

Figure 7-21 shows an example of a sham link configured for OSPF process 42 in VRF *cust-one.* Both sites that are attached to the PE routers are in OSPF area 0 of VRF *cust-one.* A sham link is configured between the two PE routers with endpoints in the VRF *cust-one.*

Figure 7-21 *Example of a Sham Link*

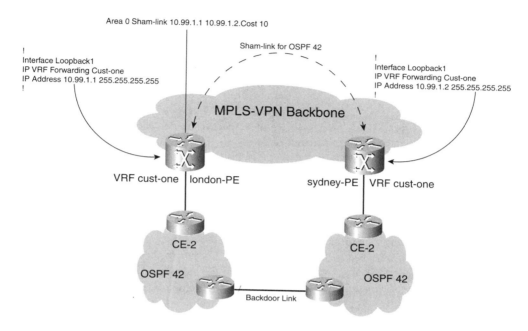

You can see the configuration for the sham link in Figure 7-21 in Example 7-28.

Example 7-28 *OSPF Sham Link*

```
!
router ospf 42 vrf cust-one
 router-id 10.99.1.1
 log-adjacency-changes
 area 0 sham-link 10.99.1.1 10.99.1.2 cost 10
 redistribute bgp 1 metric 10 subnets
 network 10.10.2.0 0.0.0.255 area 0
!
london#show ip ospf 42 neighbor

Neighbor ID     Pri   State         Dead Time   Address       Interface
10.200.200.1     1    FULL/DR       00:00:35    10.10.2.1     Ethernet0/1/2
10.99.1.2        0    FULL/  -         -         10.99.1.2     OSPF_SL2
```

continues

Example 7-28   *OSPF Sham Link (Continued)*

```
london#show ip ospf 42 sham-links
Sham Link OSPF_SL2 to address 10.99.1.2 is up
Area 0 source address 10.99.1.1
  Run as demand circuit
  DoNotAge LSA allowed. Cost of using 10 State POINT_TO_POINT,
  Timer intervals configured, Hello 10, Dead 40, Wait 40,
    Hello due in 00:00:03
    Adjacency State FULL (Hello suppressed)
    Index 2/2, retransmission queue length 0, number of retransmission 1
    First 0x0(0)/0x0(0) Next 0x0(0)/0x0(0)
    Last retransmission scan length is 1, maximum is 1
    Last retransmission scan time is 0 msec, maximum is 0 msec
```

iBGP, not OSPF, must always advertise the sham link endpoints. Otherwise, the sham link flaps. First, iBGP learns the sham link endpoints, and the sham link is created. When the sham link is created, OSPF advertises the sham link endpoints, if the network command includes them. The distance of OSPF is 110, versus 200 for iBGP routes. Therefore, the sham link endpoint routes are in the routing table as OSPF routes, because the distance for OSPF routes is lower than the distance for iBGP routes. As soon as the endpoints are no longer learned in the routing table via iBGP, the sham link goes down and the process starts over again. The result is a continual flapping of the sham link.

Even if a sham link exists and the OSPF routes are flooded across it, iBGP still needs to advertise the OSPF routes as vpnv4 routes from PE to PE router. The reason for this is that iBGP still needs to carry the MPLS VPN label for each OSPF route so that the packets can be correctly forwarded across the MPLS VPN backbone.

If a prefix is learned across the sham link, and the path via the sham link is selected as the best, the PE router does not generate an MP-BGP update for the prefix. This means that OSPF routes learned across the sham link are not redistributed into BGP. The PE router on the other side of the sham link has already redistributed the OSPF routes into BGP, so it does not need to be done a second time.

Down Bit and Domain Tag

The *down bit* is a bit that is set in the Options field of an OSPF LSA type 3. It indicates the direction that the route has been advertised. If the OSPF route has been advertised from a PE router into an OSPF area, the down bit is set. Another PE router in the same area does not redistribute this route into iBGP of the MPLS VPN network if this bit is set. The PE router does not even include the route in the SPF computation. As such, you can avoid a possible routing loop if the site is multihomed or if a backdoor link exists between OSPF sites. Figure 7-22 demonstrates that an OSPF route with the down bit set is not readvertised into iBGP.

Figure 7-22 *Down Bit*

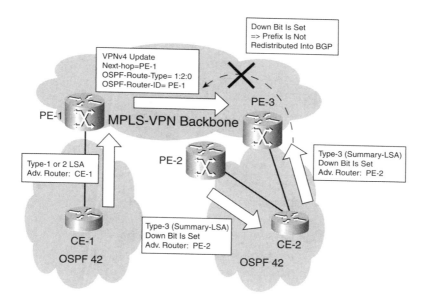

The domain tag (also known as the *VPN route tag*) serves the same purpose as the down bit, but for OSPF external routes. You can set it manually on the PE routers with the command **domain-tag** *tag-value*. If you set the domain tag to a particular value on a PE router, the tag value of the external OSPF route is set to that value. If another PE router that is connected to the same site or another site that is connected through a backdoor link receives this route and it matches the configured domain tag, the route is not redistributed into iBGP. By default, the domain tag is set to a value as determined in RFC 1745. This RFC specifies the interaction between OSPF and BGP and determines how the tag should automatically be set. The autonomous system number of BGP is encoded into the tag of the OSPF external routes in the least significant 16 bits. Figure 7-23 shows that an OSPF route is not readvertised into iBGP if the domain tag of the route matches the configured domain tag on the PE router.

Figure 7-23 *Domain Tag*

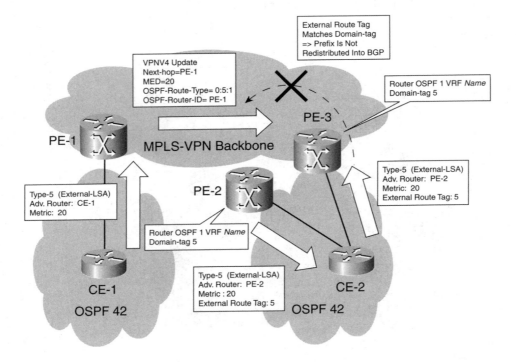

EIGRP

EIGRP can be the PE-CE routing protocol. The usual disadvantage of the redistribution between iBGP and the routing protocol between the PE and CE router is present here, too. This means that redistributing the routes from BGP into EIGRP makes all the routes external EIGRP routes. However, as much EIGRP information as possible is coded in new BGP extended communities to alleviate the problem. This enables the remote PE router to reconstruct the EIGRP route with all its characteristics, including metric components, AS, TAG and, for external routes, the remote AS number, the remote ID, the remote protocol, and the remote metric. These are the EIGRP characteristics of a prefix that you can find in the topology table. If the EIGRP-advertised route is internal, the route is advertised as an internal route into the remote site if the destination AS matches the source AS carried by the BGP extended community. If the AS numbers do not match, the route is reconstructed as an external EIGRP route. Table 7-4 shows the extended BGP communities that convey the EIGRP information.

Table 7-4 *BGP Extended Communities for EIGRP*

Type	Usage	Value
0x8800	General route information	Flags + TAG
0x8801	Route metric information and autonomous system	Autonomous System + Delay
0x8802	Route metric information	Reliability + Hop Count + BW
0x8803	Route metric information	Reserved field + Load + MTU
0x8804	External route information	Remote Autonomous System + Remote ID
0x8805	External route information	Remote Protocol + Remote Metric

Example 7-29 demonstrates how BGP carries these extended communities. The prefix 10.10.100.1/32 is an internal EIGRP prefix, and the prefix 10.200.200.1/32 is an external EIGRP prefix.

Example 7-29 *BGP Extended Communities for EIGRP*

```
amsterdam#show ip bgp vpnv4 all 10.10.100.1
BGP routing table entry for 1:1:10.10.100.1/32, version 28
Paths: (1 available, best #1, table cust-one)
  Advertised to update-groups:
     1
  Local
    10.10.2.1 from 0.0.0.0 (10.200.254.2)
      Origin incomplete, metric 409600, localpref 100, weight 32768, valid, sourced, best
      Extended Community: RT:1:1 Cost:pre-bestpath:128:409600 0x8800:32768:0
        0x8801:42:153600 0x8802:65281:256000 0x8803:65281:1500,
      mpls labels in/out 22/nolabel

sydney#show ip bgp vpnv4 all 10.200.200.1
BGP routing table entry for 1:1:10.200.200.1/32, version 91
Paths: (1 available, best #1, table cust-one)
Flag: 0x820
  Not advertised to any peer
  Local
    10.200.254.2 (metric 4) from 10.200.254.2 (10.200.254.2)
      Origin incomplete, metric 409600, localpref 100, valid, internal, best
      Extended Community: RT:1:1 Cost:pre-bestpath:129:409600 0x8800:0:0
        0x8801:42:153600 0x8802:65281:256000 0x8803:65281:1500
        0x8804:0:168453121 0x8805:11:0,
      mpls labels in/out nolabel/31
```

Figure 7-24 shows how an EIGRP route is propagated across the MPLS VPN backbone from one EIGRP site to another.

Figure 7-24   *Propagation of an EIGRP Route Across the MPLS VPN Backbone*

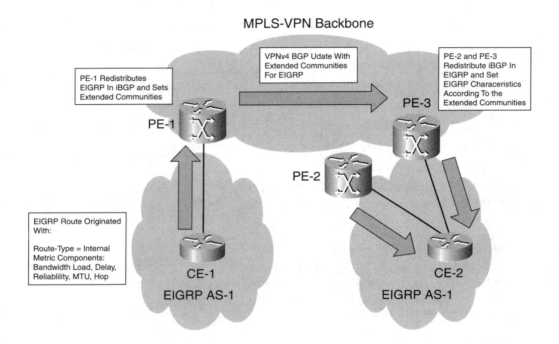

On the right side, PE-2 and PE-3 redistribute the vpnv4 route from iBGP into EIGRP. However, the same route can be received as an EIGRP route from the other PE router in the same site. Nevertheless, the vpnv4 route that is learned from PE-1 is always preferred over the EIGRP route that is learned from the other PE in the same site. That is because the metric of the received routes is compared, and the lowest metric always wins. This is always the vpnv4 route from the remote PE router, if the cost of the EIGRP route is computed from reconstructing the metric components from the extended communities. This is why EIGRP does not need a down bit as OSPF does. The cost of traversing the MPLS VPN backbone is 0 for the EIGRP routes.

Configuration

Similarly to RIPv2, EIGRP has been extended with support for address families so that it can support MPLS VPN. Therefore, the VRF configuration on the PE routers for EIGRP is under address family IPv4 vrf. The regular EIGRP commands are available for each VRF that is configured. Because VPN customers usually use different EIGRP AS numbers (and the AS number has to match between EIGRP neighbors), the new EIGRP command **autonomous-system** *as-number* lets you specify the autonomous system number for the specified VRF. Example 7-30 shows the configuration of one PE router that is configured for two VRFs running EIGRP. Obviously, as with all other PE-CE routing protocols, you need to configure redistribution of BGP into EIGRP and vice versa.

Example 7-30   *EIGRP VRF Configuration Example*

```
!
router eigrp 1
 no auto-summary
 !
 address-family ipv4 vrf cust-two
 redistribute static metric 64 2000 255 1 1500
 redistribute bgp 1 metric 300 40000 255 1 1500
 network 10.10.0.0 0.0.255.255
 no auto-summary
 autonomous-system 33
 exit-address-family
 !
 address-family ipv4 vrf cust-one
 redistribute bgp 1 metric 300 40000 255 1 1500
 network 10.0.0.0
 no auto-summary
 autonomous-system 42
 exit-address-family
 !
```

Pre-Bestpath POI

The cost community in BGP is a nontransitive community that is passed to iBGP and confederation peers, but not beyond. It influences the BGP best path selection process by assigning cost values to specific routes. The cost community is set with the **set extcommunity cost** command in a route map. You can set a cost community ID (0–255) and a cost value (0–4,294,967,295). The cost community ID indicates the preference of this BGP path versus the others. The lower the cost ID, the more preferred it is.

The point of insertion (POI) is the place in the BGP best path selection process where BGP considers the cost community. The pre-bestpath POI indicates that BGP is to consider the cost community before any of the regular BGP comparisons steps in the well-known BGP best path selection process. You can configure a pre-bestpath cost community by configuring the cost community with the *pre-bestpath* keyword in a route map. The cost community is of the form *Cost:POI:ID:value*.

It is the cost community with pre-bestpath that is set when EIGRP is redistributed into BGP. Without the cost community for EIGRP on the PE router, the PE router always prefers the locally sourced BGP route above the route learned from a BGP peer. In the case of having a backdoor link between two EIGRP sites, this means that the backdoor link is the preferred path. With the cost community for EIGRP, the backdoor link and the path learned from iBGP through the MPLS VPN backbone are compared. The path with the lowest EIGRP cost is the preferred path. Cost community for EIGRP over MPLS VPN is turned on automatically in the case of EIGRP as the PE-CE routing protocol, so you do not need to configure it. The *POI* is pre-bestpath. The *cost community ID* is either 128 or 129: 128 for EIGRP internal routes and 129 for EIGRP external routes. Therefore, the EIGRP internal routes are always preferred over the EIGRP external routes. The *value* is the EIGRP composite metric value set on the PE router that redistributes the route into BGP. Routes that have a lower value are preferred over routes that have a greater value. If the cost community ID of the route and the value are the same, Cisco IOS prefers the EIGRP route over the BGP route on the PE router.

Example 7-31 shows the cost community that EIGRP uses in an MPLS VPN scenario. Two PE routers advertise the vpnv4 prefix 10.10.100.1/32, and each sets the cost community to an ID of 128 and a value that represents the composite EIGRP metric as seen by the sydney PE router. The sydney PE can choose the best path based on the cost community value that the PE routers advertise, ignoring the other BGP attributes.

Example 7-31 *Cost Community for EIGRP over MPLS VPN*

```
sydney#show ip bgp vpnv4 all 10.10.100.1
BGP routing table entry for 1:1:10.10.100.1/32, version 1259
Paths: (2 available, best #2, table cust-one)
  Advertised to update-groups:
     1
  Local
    10.200.254.2 (metric 3) from 10.200.254.2 (10.200.254.2)
      Origin incomplete, metric 256384000, localpref 100, valid, internal
      Extended Community: RT:1:1
        Cost:pre-bestpath:128:256384000 (default-1891099647) 0x8800:32768:0
        0x8801:42:256128000 0x8802:65281:256000 0x8803:65281:1500,
      mpls labels in/out 16/16
  Local
    10.10.4.2 from 0.0.0.0 (10.200.254.5)
      Origin incomplete, metric 2323456, localpref 100, weight 32768, valid, sourced, best
      Extended Community: SoO:10:10 RT:1:1
        Cost:pre-bestpath:128:2323456 (default-2145160191) 0x8800:32768:0
        0x8801:42:665600 0x8802:65282:1657856 0x8803:65281:1500,
      mpls labels in/out 16/nolabel
```

EIGRP PE-CE with Backdoor Links

Backdoor links are supported between EIGRP sites that are connected to the MPLS VPN backbone. However, when a route disappears, routing can take longer to reconverge, which is typical in the case of redistribution between routing protocols. The cause of the longer convergence is redistribution between EIGRP and BGP. To help speed up the reconverging, you can use Site-of-Origin (SOO) for EIGRP. It can be defined on the PE routers on the VRF interfaces toward the CE routers and on the routers with a backdoor link. You need to configure **ip vrf sitemap** on the interface, setting the extended community SOO. This route map sets the SOO on the EIGRP route, either on the PE or on the backdoor link router. When the router receives a route across the interface with this route map configured and the SOO of the route matches the configured SOO, the router rejects the route. When the PE router receives a vpnv4 update with the SOO set, it extracts the SOO and adds it to the EIGRP route when it is reconstructed.

Figure 7-25 shows a network with a backdoor link between EIGRP sites and EIGRP SOO configured on the PE and backdoor routers.

Figure 7-25 *Backdoor Link Between EIGRP Sites*

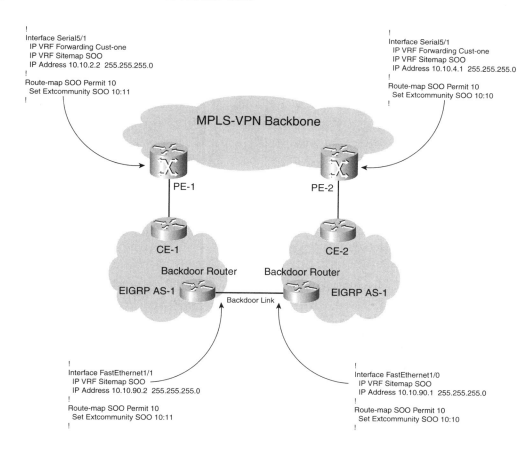

When no SOO for EIGRP is used anywhere, a count-to-infinity problem might exist across the EIGRP sites and across the MPLS VPN backbone. This means that when a route disappears, EIGRP routers see that the hop count slowly increases up to infinity. With EIGRP, infinity is a hop count of 100 by default. That means that it might take quite some time for the route to disappear, while in the meantime traffic is looped. You can lower the default maximum hop count of EIGRP by configuring the command **metric maximum-hops** *hops*. You must take care, however, not to configure this value too low. The value must be big enough for regular operation, but also in case the shortest path is unavailable and a longer path routes the traffic.

The disadvantage of using the SOO for EIGRP on the PE and backdoor routers is that one part of the site cannot reach the other part of the site across the backdoor link and the MPLS VPN backbone if the site is split. The backdoor router or the PE router blocks the route that is needed to get to the other part of the site. To work around this problem, you can configure the sitemap for SOO only on the PE routers and not the backdoor routers. The count-to-infinity problem does not occur in this case, but the routing might take a bit longer to reconverge. Example 7-32 shows the SOO for an EIGRP route.

Example 7-32   *SOO Set for an EIGRP Route*

```
PE-1#show ip eigrp vrf cust-one topology 10.10.100.3 255.255.255.255
IP-EIGRP (AS 42): Topology entry for 10.10.100.3/32
  State is Passive, Query origin flag is 1, 1 Successor(s), FD is 2297856
  Routing Descriptor Blocks:
  10.200.254.5, from VPNv4 Sourced, Send flag is 0x0
      Composite metric is (2297856/0), Route is Internal (VPNv4 Sourced)
      Vector metric:
        Minimum bandwidth is 1544 Kbit
        Total delay is 25000 microseconds
        Reliability is 255/255
        Load is 1/255
        Minimum MTU is 1500
        Hop count is 1
      Extended Community: SoO:10:10
```

IS-IS

Another possible PE-CE routing protocol is IS-IS, which is a link state routing protocol like OSPF. Unlike OSPF, however, IS-IS runs directly over Layer 2, not over IP. Having IS-IS run across the PE–CE link requires ISIS to be VRF aware on the PE routers. You can configure ISIS for a VRF by using the command **vrf** *vrf-name* under the IS-IS process. IS-IS processes on a router are differentiated from each other by the tag as configured with the command **router isis** *process-tag*. You have to associate the PE-CE link with the correct IS-IS VRF process with the interface command **ip router isis** *process-tag*. As with OSPF, each VRF instance has its own IS-IS routing process (and SPF algorithm), IS-IS database, and routing table.

The *up/down* bit performs routing loop prevention when an IS-IS site is dual homed. This bit has the same functionality as the down bit for OSPF over MPLS VPN. However, the up/down bit was not invented to run IS-IS over MPLS VPN. It was introduced earlier to prevent routing loops in the case of advertising IP prefixes from Level 2 to Level 1. (You might call them interarea *routes*.) When an L1L2 router advertises a Level 2 prefix in the Level 1 LSP, it must set the up/down bit. That way, another L1L2 router can see this bit set and does not distribute this prefix back into Level 2. A PE router that is distributing the learned iBGP vpnv4 route into IS-IS sets the up/down bit when advertising the prefix into IS-IS. Another PE router that sees this IS-IS prefix with the up/down bit set never distributes this prefix back into iBGP.

NOTE   The up/down bit is the high order bit in the default metric field of TLV 128 and TLV 130.

Figure 7-26 shows a simple IS-IS network. Two IS-IS sites are connected to each other via the MPLS VPN backbone. The IS-IS process for this VPN customer is *cust-one*.

Figure 7-26   *IS-IS over MPLS VPN*

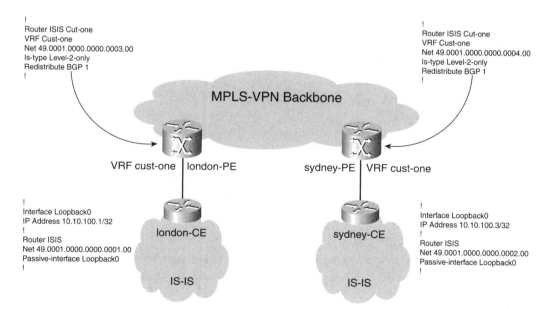

Example 7-33 shows the configuration of the router london-PE.

Example 7-33 *IS-IS Configuration on the Router london-PE*

```
!
ip vrf cust-one
 rd 1:1
 route-target export 1:1
 route-target import 1:1
!
interface Ethernet0/1/2
 ip vrf forwarding cust-one
 ip address 10.10.2.2 255.255.255.0
 ip router isis cust-one
 isis circuit-type level-2-only
!
router isis cust-one
 vrf cust-one
 net 49.0001.0000.0000.0003.00
 is-type level-2-only
 redistribute bgp 1
!
router bgp 1
 neighbor 10.200.254.5 remote-as 1
 neighbor 10.200.254.5 update-source Loopback0
 !
 address-family vpnv4
 neighbor 10.200.254.5 activate
 neighbor 10.200.254.5 send-community extended
 exit-address-family
 !
 address-family ipv4 vrf cust-one
 redistribute connected
 redistribute isis cust-one level-2
 exit-address-family
!
```

Example 7-34 shows the output of some IS-IS commands on the PE routers for the IS-IS VRF process. You can see that the router sydney-PE has one IS-IS adjacency, namely with the sydney-ce. The prefix 10.10.100.1/32 is the loopback IP address on the router london-ce. The VPN label that is used to reach that prefix across the MPLS backbone is label 27. The label is advertised with the vpnv4 route from the router london-PE to the router sydney-PE. This VPN label is installed in the LFIB of the router london-PE to get the traffic from the MPLS VPN backbone switched to the correct CE router (london-ce).

Example 7-34 *IS-IS Output on the PE Routers for VRF Cust-One*

```
sydney#show isis cust-one neighbors

System Id       Type Interface IP Address     State Holdtime Circuit Id
sydney-ce       L2   Se5/1     10.10.4.2       UP    20       00

sydney#show isis cust-one database

IS-IS Level-2 Link State Database:
LSPID                  LSP Seq Num  LSP Checksum  LSP Holdtime   ATT/P/OL
sydney-ce.00-00        0x00000004   0xC80A        1167           0/0/0
sydney.00-00         * 0x00000007   0x1377        1198           0/0/0

sydney#show clns cust-one protocol

IS-IS Router: cust-one
  System Id: 0000.0000.0004.00  IS-Type: level-2-only
  Manual area address(es):
        49.0001
  Routing for area address(es):
        49.0001
  Interfaces supported by IS-IS:
        Serial5/1 - IP
  Redistributing:
    static
  Distance: 110
  RRR level: none
  Generate narrow metrics: level-1-2
  Accept narrow metrics:   level-1-2
  Generate wide metrics:   none
  Accept wide metrics:     none

sydney#show ip bgp vpnv4 rd 1:1
BGP table version is 68, local router ID is 10.200.254.5
Status codes: s suppressed, d damped, h history, * valid, > best, i - internal,
              r RIB-failure, S Stale
Origin codes: i - IGP, e - EGP, ? - incomplete

   Network          Next Hop          Metric LocPrf Weight Path
Route Distinguisher: 1:1 (default for vrf cust-one)
*>i10.10.2.0/24     10.200.254.2           0    100      0 ?
*> 10.10.4.0/24     0.0.0.0                0         32768 ?
*>i10.10.100.1/32   10.200.254.2          10    100      0 ?
*> 10.10.100.3/32   10.10.4.2             10         32768 ?
*>i10.99.1.1/32     10.200.254.2           0    100      0 ?
*> 10.99.1.2/32     0.0.0.0                0         32768 ?
```

continues

Example 7-34 *IS-IS Output on the PE Routers for VRF Cust-One (Continued)*

```
sydney#show ip bgp vpnv4 rd 1:1 10.10.100.1
BGP routing table entry for 1:1:10.10.100.1/32, version 68
Bestpath Modifiers: ignore-cost-community
Paths: (1 available, best #1, table cust-one)
  Not advertised to any peer
  Local
    10.200.254.2 (metric 3) from 10.200.254.2 (10.200.254.2)
      Origin incomplete, metric 10, localpref 100, valid, internal, best
      Extended Community: RT:1:1,
      mpls labels in/out nolabel/27

london#show mpls forwarding-table vrf cust-one 10.10.100.1
Local   Outgoing     Prefix          Bytes tag  Outgoing    Next Hop
tag     tag or VC    or Tunnel Id    switched   interface
27      Untagged     10.10.100.1/32[V] 0        Et0/1/2     10.10.2.1
```

> **NOTE** In Cisco IOS, the IS-IS VRF process cannot run Connectionless Network Service (CLNS) routing.

eBGP

eBGP can be the PE-CE routing protocol. Under the address family ipv4 vrf of the router bgp process on the PE, you need to configure the CE router as the eBGP neighbor and activate it. In Example 7-35, the eBGP neighbor 10.20.2.1 (the CE router) in the autonomous system 65001 in VRF cust-one is configured.

Example 7-35 *Basic BGP Configuration as PE-CE Routing Protocol*

```
!
router bgp 1
 neighbor 10.200.254.5 remote-as 1
 neighbor 10.200.254.5 update-source Loopback0
 !
 address-family vpnv4
 neighbor 10.200.254.5 activate
 neighbor 10.200.254.5 send-community extended
 exit-address-family
 !
 address-family ipv4 vrf cust-one
 redistribute connected
 neighbor 10.10.2.1 remote-as 65001
 neighbor 10.10.2.1 activate
 exit-address-family
!
```

If the customer sites have different autonomous system numbers for every site, BGP can operate with the default behavior regarding the as-path. However, sometimes the default behavior is not enough to have the correct routing for the customer in the VRF. In two scenarios, BGP has to be adapted to get the correct routing: customers who have the same autonomous system number (ASN) at more than one site, and a hub-and-spoke situation.

Autonomous System Override

If the customer has the same ASN at different sites, the CE routers drop the BGP routes. Look at Figure 7-27, where all the customer sites of VPN *cust-one* have AS 65000.

Figure 7-27   *Use of As-Override*

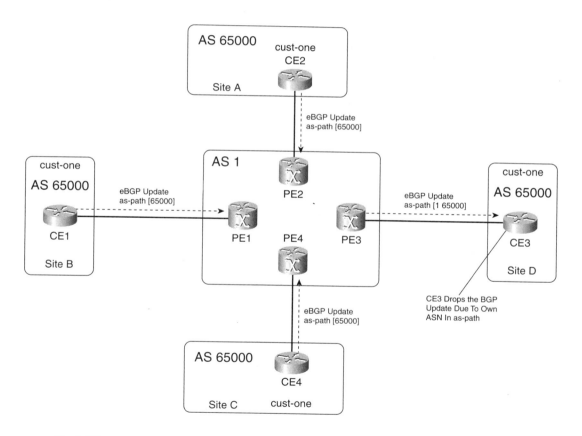

Each PE router sends the VRF cust-one routes with an as-path of [65000] in the vpnv4 update to the other PE routers. The BGP route that is sent to the remote CE router is the vpnv4 route that is converted to an IPv4 route when the RD is stripped off. The route is sent to the CE router via eBGP with an as-path of [1 65000]. The CE router drops the BGP update as it sees that its own ASN 65000 is in the update. This behavior is the default behavior of BGP and is a prevention mechanism against loops in BGP. This means that if the customer had his own private network (with only 1 autonomous system number) before using the MPLS VPN service from the service provider, he would now have to use different autonomous system numbers for each site. This is tedious, and new autonomous system numbers are almost impossible to get. The customer can use ASNs from the private ASN range [64512–65535]. However, an easier solution is available, and it involves having the PE router replace the customer ASN in the as-path with the ASN of the service provider. In the example of Figure 7-27, it means that the PE router sends the BGP prefix to the remote CE router with the as-path [1 1] instead of [1 65000]. The PE router simply checks the ASN of the CE router against the ASNs in the as-path. If a match happens, all occurrences of this ASN in the as-path are replaced with the ASN of the service provider. The remote CE then accepts this route because it no longer sees its own ASN in the as-path of the BGP route.

The command that you need to configure on the PE router to override the ASN is **neighbor** *ip-address* **as-override**. The safeguard against possible routing loops and suboptimal routing that comes from the as-path verification is now gone. Therefore, when using the as-override functionality, it is advisable to deploy the SOO feature for BGP. See the section "SOO" for more information.

allowas-in

You can perform another cheat with the as-path in BGP. Instead of overriding autonomous system numbers in the as-path, you can instruct the PE router to loosen the check of the as-path. In the next section, you can read up on the hub-and-spoke scenario. This scenario needs to permit the routes that are coming from the VRF hub site to re-enter the autonomous system of the service provider. This ensures that the spoke-to-spoke communication happens through the VRF hub site. For BGP, this implies that a route traverses the service provider AS from a VRF spoke site to the VRF hub site and traverses it again on the way to another VRF spoke site. The PE router that connects to the VRF hub site sees its own ASN in the as-path, so the BGP route is rejected. To work around this problem, you can configure the command **neighbor allowas-in** *number* on the PE router that connects to the VRF hub site. The **allowas-in** command permits multiple occurrences of the same ASN (in this case the ASN of the service provider) in the as-path as the ASN of the BGP speaker without BGP denying the route. The number you can configure is from 1 to 10, specifying the number of times that the ASN is allowed in the as-path.

Figure 7-28 shows a hub-and-spoke scenario with BGP as the PE-CE routing protocol at the customer sites.

Figure 7-28 *Hub-and-Spoke with BGP as the PE-CE Routing Protocol*

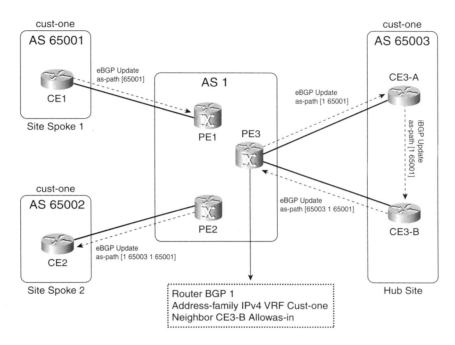

When you need to advertise a route from spoke to spoke, advertise it to the hub site first. When the route arrives at the spoke site 2, it will have traversed the MPLS VPN backbone twice. This is possible only if **neighbor allowas-in** is configured on the PE3 router toward the CE3-B router. PE3 simply ignores seeing its own ASN in the as-path and accepts the BGP route from the CE router CE3-B.

> **NOTE**   Current Cisco IOS does not support internal BGP as the PE-CE routing protocol. It supports only external BGP.

Hub-and-Spoke

Often, customers do not want their sites to have full interconnectivity. This means they do not want or need the sites to be fully meshed. A typical scenario involves one main site at a company with many remote sites. The remote sites or spokes need connectivity to the main or hub site, but they do not need to communicate between them directly. Perhaps the connectivity is possible but not wanted for security reasons. This scenario is commonly referred to as the *hub-and-spoke scenario*. It can also be achieved across MPLS VPN, but care must be taken. The following is needed:

■   The spoke sites can communicate only with the hub site.

■   Spoke-to-spoke traffic needs to be sent to the hub site first.

To achieve this, adhere to the following needs:

■ Two different RTs

■ Different RDs

First, choose the RTs carefully. You need two different RTs: one is attached to the spoke routes when the spoke site sends them to the hub site, and one is attached to the hub routes when the hub site sends them to the spoke sites. At the same time, when a spoke site sends the spoke routes to the other spoke sites, the routes should be rejected because the VRF on the spoke sites does not import the RTs. However, the same PE router might use them for another site, or the automatic inbound filtering might be turned off if this is an ASBR router in the case of Inter-Autonomous MPLS VPN. (See the section on Inter-Autonomous MPLS VPN in the online supplement for how to turn off the automatic inbound filtering.) In those cases, the PE router accepts the route, but the VRF does not import the route because the RT is not configured for import. However, it might be selected as the best vpnv4 route, which means that the PE will not import the other vpnv4 route with the correct RT. Therefore, it is strongly advised that you use one unique RD per spoke site. You might get away with using the same RD for all spoke sites most of the time, but that does not work in all scenarios. You might have two spoke CE routers connected to the same PE router. In that case, the only thing that prevents the spoke routes from being sent directly to the other spoke CE router that is connected to the same PE router is the different RD for each spoke CE router.

Figure 7-29 shows an example of a hub-and-spoke network.

Figure 7-29 *Hub-and-Spoke Scenario*

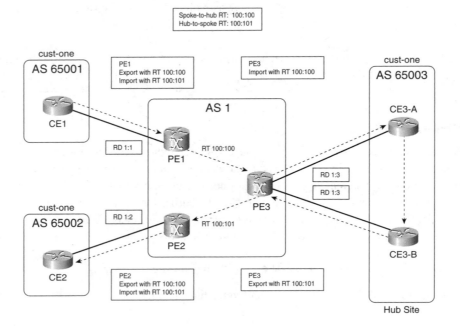

The spoke PE routers advertise the routes with RT=100:100 while the hub PE router imports this RT. The hub PE router advertises the routes from the hub CE router with RT=100:101. The spoke PE routers import RT 100:101, which ensures that spoke-to-spoke traffic goes through the hub site.

SOO

SOO uniquely identifies the site that originates a route. It is a BGP extended community that prevents routing loops or suboptimal routing, specifically when a backdoor is present between VPN sites. SOO provides loop prevention in networks with dual-homed sites (sites that are connected to two or more PE routers). You can use it when an IGP is the PE-CE routing protocol. You can also use it when BGP is used between PE and CE, when the as-path loop prevention cannot be trusted anymore. This happens when BGP uses as-override or allowas-in. If the SOO is configured for a CE router and a vpnv4 route is learned with the same SOO, the route must not be put in the VRF routing table on the PE and advertised to the CE. In Figure 7-30, the vpnv4 prefix is advertised from PE-2 toward the other PE routers with SOO 1:100. This vpnv4 route can be advertised back to the same site and received on PE-3 via MP-BGP. When PE-3 notices the same SOO on the vpnv4 route as the SOO in the configuration, it does not install the prefix in the VRF routing table.

Figure 7-30 *SOO Preventing Routing Loops*

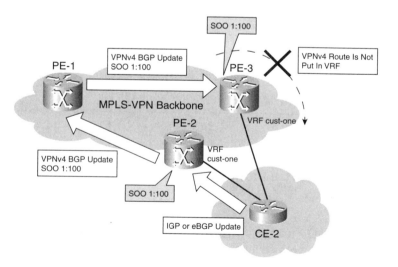

This prevents possible routing loops, but it also prevents suboptimal routing. The suboptimal case that entails that for the routes local to the dual-homed sites, the path across the MPLS VPN backbone is preferred over the local path is blocked.

SOO is set in a route map, as shown in Example 7-36.

Example 7-36 *SOO Route Map Configuration*

```
!
route-map cust-one-soo permit 10
 set extcommunity soo 1:100
!
```

If the SOO is applied for BGP, the route map is configured on the BGP **neighbor** command, as in Example 7-37.

Example 7-37 *Applying SOO Route Map for BGP*

```
!
router bgp 1
...
!
 address-family ipv4 vrf cust-one
 redistribute connected
 neighbor 10.10.2.1 remote-as 65001
 neighbor 10.10.2.1 activate
 neighbor 10.10.2.1 route-map cust-one-soo in
 exit-address-family
!
```

If the SOO is applied for any routing protocol other than BGP, the route map is configured with the **ip vrf sitemap** command on the appropriate VRF interface, as in Example 7-38.

Example 7-38 *Applying SOO Route Map on the VRF Interface*

```
!
interface Ethernet0/1/2
 ip vrf forwarding cust-one
 ip vrf sitemap cust-one-soo
 ip address 10.10.2.2 255.255.255.0
!
```

You can also set the SOO for connected and static routes when they are redistributed into the IGP. Example 7-39 shows the **redistribute** command with an SOO route map.

Example 7-39 *Applying SOO Route Map for Static Routes*

```
!
router bgp 1
...
!
 address-family ipv4 vrf cust-one
```

Example 7-39 *Applying SOO Route Map for Static Routes (Continued)*

```
redistribute static route-map cust-one-soo
neighbor 10.10.2.1 remote-as 65001
neighbor 10.10.2.1 activate
exit-address-family
!
```

VRF Access

On the PE router, Cisco IOS commands were made VRF aware so that the user could communicate with the CE devices or IP addresses on the PE router in the VRF context. The **ping**, **traceroute**, and **telnet** commands have been made VRF aware for troubleshooting purposes and for accessibility to the CE routers and other devices in the VRF sites from the PE router. Example 7-40 shows how these three commands were extended for the VRF context.

Example 7-40 *VRF ping, traceroute, and telnet*

```
london#ping vrf cust-one 10.10.100.1

london#traceroute vrf cust-one 10.10.100.1

london#telnet 10.10.100.1 /vrf cust-one
```

Internet Access

Internet routing is usually done via the BGP table of the MPLS VPN network of the service provider. This BGP table is in the global routing space, not in the VRF context. By default, the VRF sites can communicate only with other VRF sites in the same VPN, not with anything in the global routing space. Therefore, something must be done to provide Internet access (global context) to the CE routers (VRF context). The following sections detail how to provide Internet access to VRF sites. Obviously, Internet access is only possible for the IP subnets of the customer that are not from the private IP addressing space (RFC 1918).

> **NOTE** As soon as the VPN has Internet connectivity, there is a potential security risk. It is important to take the proper steps—such as filtering and using a firewall—to ensure the highest level of security.

Internet in a VPN

One solution that might seem the simplest is actually the worst. The service provider could place the complete Internet routing table in the VRF. However, that would mean that an enormous number of routes would be placed in the VPN. The provider could do this once and put all customers requiring Internet access in this VRF. However, then the point of each customer having his own private network would be completely lost. Another solution could involve the service provider putting the Internet routing table in each VRF of a customer who requires Internet access. That would be even worse, though. The enormous number of Internet routes would be replicated multiple times and cause scaling problems on the PE routers. Therefore, you should avoid this solution.

Internet Access Through the Global Routing Table

An easy way to provide Internet access to CE routers is to have an interface from the PE to the CE router that is in the global routing space. The PE router has a VRF interface toward the CE router, but you can have a second interface that is not in a VRF toward the CE router. The routing on the CE router should then take care of sending the VPN traffic to the VRF interface and the Internet traffic to the interface in the global routing space on the PE router. The obvious disadvantage is that you need a second link between the PE and CE routers, using up an extra interface on both routers. To solve this, you can use subinterfaces when the Layer 2 encapsulation is Frame Relay or 802.1Q encapsulation. However, if the Layer 2 encapsulation does not allow subinterfaces, you can still use a workaround. A possible workaround might be sticking with just the VRF interface on the PE router and creating a GRE tunnel in the global routing space across that VRF interface.

Example 7-41 shows a sample configuration for this solution. The default route on the CE router points to the tunnel interface for the Internet access. Therefore, all traffic that has no specific route is sent to the tunnel interface according to the default route. This traffic ends up in the global routing context of the PE router. All traffic that *does* have a specific route in the routing table of the CE is sent to the physical interface and ends up inside the VRF on the PE router. The traffic from the Internet to the customer routers is forwarded according to a static route on the PE router that points to the tunnel interface. In Example 7-41, the static route for 192.168.1.0/24 takes care of returning the traffic from the Internet to the CE router. The service provider forwards the Internet traffic in the backbone to and from the Internet gateway(s) with BGP. The tunnel interface on the PE router needs the command **tunnel vrf** *vrf-name* because the tunnel end point is not in the global routing space, but in the specified VRF. Because the tunnel does not have the **ip vrf forwarding** *vrf-name* command, it is in the global routing space.

Example 7-41 *Configuration of GRE Tunnel in Global Routing Space on the PE*

```
london#
!
interface Tunnel1
 ip address 10.10.20.1 255.255.255.0
 tunnel source 10.10.2.2
 tunnel destination 10.10.2.1
 tunnel vrf cust-one
!
```

Example 7-41 *Configuration of GRE Tunnel in Global Routing Space on the PE (Continued)*

```
interface Ethernet0/1/2
 ip vrf forwarding cust-one
 ip address 10.10.2.2 255.255.255.0
!
ip route 192.168.1.0 255.255.255.0 Tunnel1

london-ce#
!
interface Tunnel1
 ip address 10.10.20.2 255.255.255.0
 tunnel source 10.10.2.1
 tunnel destination 10.10.2.2
!
ip route 0.0.0.0 0.0.0.0 Tunnel1
```

Internet Access Through the Global Routing Table with Static Routes

You can provide Internet access to the VPN customers by forwarding their traffic to the Internet gateway of the service provider. The Internet gateway is known to all P routers in the MPLS VPN network because the gateway IP address is known in the global routing table of the service provider. It surely is running eBGP with a router of an Internet provider. The PE routers are already running BGP, so they can provide MPLS VPN services. The PE routers can also run an iBGP peering session for IPv4 to the Internet gateway router. To provide Internet access to a VRF, the global routing table must forward the traffic. This occurs by creating a static route in the VRF table on the PE router and specifying a next hop that is in the global routing table. To do this, use the keyword *global* on the static VRF route. This ensures that traffic flowing from the CE router to the PE router via the VRF interface and being forwarded according to the static route is forwarded to the next hop in the global routing table. This next-hop IP address should be on the Internet gateway router. You need to forward to the VRF the traffic that is flowing from the Internet. Configuring a static route on the PE router and specifying the next hop to be the CE router accomplishes this. To ensure that the Internet gateway knows about this route, distribute the static route into BGP or the IGP of the service provider. Because the traffic is no longer VPN-to-VPN but is forwarded in the global routing table, it has only one label in the MPLS VPN network.

Look at Example 7-42 for the configuration on the london PE router where the static route is distributed into BGP. The Internet gateway router is 10.200.254.5, and 192.168.1.0/24 is the subnet of the customer who needs Internet access. All traffic that has no specific route in the VRF *cust-one* routing table is forwarded according to the default route in the VRF with the next-hop 10.200.254.5 in the global routing table. The traffic from the Internet toward the london-ce router

is forwarded according to the static route for 192.168.1.0/24 pointing to the interface Ethernet 0/
1/2 on the PE router toward the CE router.

Example 7-42 *Internet Access Through the Global Routing Table with Static Routes*

```
london#
!
interface Ethernet0/1/2
 ip vrf forwarding cust-one
 ip address 10.10.2.2 255.255.255.0
!
router bgp 1
 bgp log-neighbor-changes
 redistribute static
 neighbor 10.200.254.3 remote-as 1
 no auto-summary
 !
ip route vrf cust-one 0.0.0.0 0.0.0.0 10.200.254.5 global
ip route 192.168.1.0 255.255.255.0 Ethernet0/1/2 10.10.2.1
!
london-ce#show ip route 0.0.0.0 0.0.0.0
Routing entry for 0.0.0.0/0, supernet
  Known via "rip", distance 120, metric 2, candidate default path
  Redistributing via rip
  Last update from 10.10.2.2 on Ethernet1/1, 00:00:14 ago
  Routing Descriptor Blocks:
  * 10.10.2.2, from 10.10.2.2, 00:00:14 ago, via Ethernet1/1
      Route metric is 2, traffic share count is 1
```

Internet Access Through a Central VRF Site

Instead of traffic from each VPN site being forwarded directly to the Internet gateway router, it is
possible to forward all the Internet traffic from the VRF sites to the CE router(s) of a central VRF
site in a VPN. The advantage is that security features—such as firewall services—or other
services—such as Network Address Translation (NAT)—are implemented only once and centrally
in the central VRF site. The Internet traffic between the VRF sites and the VRF central site is then
forwarded across the regular VRF interfaces in the normal manner for MPLS VPN. Look at Figure
7-31 for the network in this scenario. This is most likely the preferred scenario for hub-and-spoke
VPN networks anyway. Note that at the central VRF site, you can deploy a firewall to verify all
Internet traffic.

Figure 7-31 *Internet Access Through a Central VRF Site*

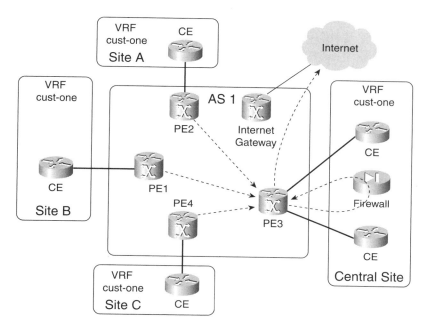

Multi-VRF CE

The Multi-VRF CE feature—also known as VRF-Lite—is a feature whereby the VPN
functionality is extended to the CE router in a cheap way. Assume that you have a company with
a large main site and some smaller sites that are interconnected across an MPLS VPN network.
The main site of the company is rather large and has several departments that need to be separated
from each other for privacy reasons. These departments (finance, human resources, engineering,
and so on) then connect to their respective department remote sites through the MPLS VPN
network. You can separate the departments by implementing VLANs on switches in the main site
and mapping each VLAN to a VRF (sub)interface on the PE router. Instead of using a Layer 2
switch or one CE router per department, you can bring the VPN functionality to the CE router. For
Multi-VRF CE, the separation into VRFs is used on the CE router as it is used on the PE router.
However, the CE does not need the other MPLS VPN functionality, such as labeling packets,
Multiprotocol iBGP, and LDP. The interfaces toward the PE router are VRF interfaces. You need
to configure the appropriate VRFs and VRF routing protocols on the Multi-VRF CE router.

An example of Multi-VRF CE is shown in Figure 7-32.

Figure 7-32 *Example of a Multi-VRF CE*

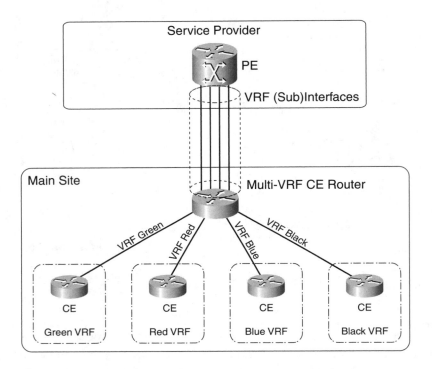

The Multi-VRF CE router has a VRF interface toward each CE router that is connected to it. Each VRF toward a CE router must also have a VRF interface toward the PE router. Of course, if you use an interface for each VRF on the PE and Multi-VRF CE router, it becomes costly. A much cheaper solution is to use a FastEthernet or GigabitEthernet link or a channelized serial link between the PE and Multi-VRF CE and use one subinterface for each VRF.

You need no new MPLS VPN functionality on the Multi-VRF CE router. The Multi-VRF CE feature is defined on the CE router and not on the PE router. The rest of the MPLS VPN network functions the same as regular MPLS VPN.

OSPF VRF-Lite Command

If the Multi-VRF CE router runs OSPF, you need to configure the command **capability vrf-lite** under the OSPF VRF process to make OSPF behave correctly. As discussed in the section "Down Bit and Domain Tag," the PE router uses two checks to ensure that routing loops do not form. With Multi-VRF CE, the CE router acts as a PE router and performs these two checks. The first check involves investigating whether the down bit is set on summary LSAs. If it is, the route is discarded and not advertised further to the CE routers. The second check involves verifying whether the domain tag on the external OSPF routes matches the configured domain tag. If they match, the external OSPF route is discarded. For the Multi-VRF CE router to advertise the OSPF routes from the MPLS VPN backbone further down to the CE routers, you must disable these two checks under the OSPF process with the command **capability vrf-lite**.

CE Management

Often, the service provider, not the customer, owns and manages the CE router. In that situation, the service provider wants management access to the CE router from a central management server. You can do this by having the PE router advertise one prefix from the managed CE router with one RT that is imported into the management VRF by the PE router connected to the management VRF.

You can limit the number of prefixes advertised with this management RT by configuring an export map on each VRF that assigns this management RT to only one prefix on the CE router. You can also advertise the regular VRF RTs used by the VPN with this prefix if the other CE routers need to be able to reach it. Figure 7-33 is an overview of the management setup. The management VRF has a management station. The PE router with the management VRF is importing all routes with the RT 9000:100. The PE router sydney sets the RT of one prefix on the CE router (here prefix 10.10.100.3/32; the loopback prefix on the CE router) to 9000:100.

Figure 7-33 *Example of Management Access*

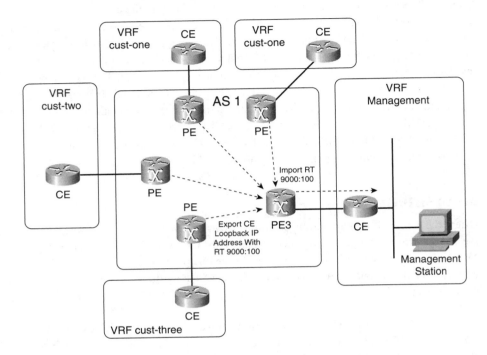

The configuration of a PE router that provides management access to the CE is shown in Example 7-43.

Example 7-43 *Configuration of a PE Router Providing Management Access*

```
!
hostname sydney
!
ip vrf cust-one
 rd 1:1
 export map management
 route-target export 1:1
 route-target import 1:1
!
ip prefix-list CE-management-loopback seq 5 permit 10.10.100.3/32
!
route-map management permit 10
```

Example 7-43 *Configuration of a PE Router Providing Management Access (Continued)*

```
match ip address prefix-list CE-management-loopback
 set extcommunity rt 9000:100
!
```

The configuration of the PE router with the management VRF attached is shown in Example 7-44.

Example 7-44 *Management PE Router Configuration*

```
!
hostname london
!
 ip vrf management
 rd 9000:1
 route-target export 9000:100
 route-target import 9000:100
!
london#show ip bgp vpnv4 rd 9000:1 10.10.100.3
BGP routing table entry for 9000:1:10.10.100.3/32, version 121
Paths: (1 available, best #1, table management)
  Advertised to update-groups:
     4
  65002, imported path from 1:1:10.10.100.3/32
    10.200.254.5 (metric 3) from 10.200.254.3 (194.68.129.9)
      Origin IGP, metric 0, localpref 100, valid, internal, best
      Extended Community: RT:9000:100
      Originator: 10.200.254.5, Cluster list: 194.68.129.9,
      mpls labels in/out 45/41
```

More and more service providers interconnect their MPLS VPN backbones. They can do this in two ways:

- Inter-Autonomous MPLS VPN

- CsC

With Inter-Autonomous MPLS VPN, the MPLS VPN networks peer with each other and exchange the prefixes of customers that have sites connected to each of the service providers. The service providers must then offer the connectivity between the sites of the customers, even when they are not connected to only one MPLS VPN backbone.

CsC is a solution whereby a larger carrier provides MPLS VPN services to other carriers or service providers. The service is hierarchical in nature, whereas Inter-Autonomous MPLS VPN is merely an interconnection between MPLS VPN backbones that are exchanging customer prefixes.

For more information on Inter-Autonomous MPLS VPN and CsC, refer to http://www.ciscopress.com/1587051974.

Summary

You have seen in this chapter what a VPN is and what the building blocks of MPLS VPN are. It explained the operation of MPLS VPN, both in the control plane and in the forwarding plane. It also examined BGP and detailed the enhancements needed for MPLS VPN. This chapter covered intranet, extranet, and hub-and-spoke scenarios. It also reviewed each PE-CE routing protocol and provided its specific operation across the MPLS VPN backbone.

Chapter Review Questions

You can find answers to the following questions in Appendix A, "Answers to the Chapter Review Questions."

1. What is a route distinguisher?

2. How is a packet that is coming from the CE router identified as to which VRF it belongs?

3. What is the purpose of RTs?

4. What is an RR group?

5. What is the BGP neighbor command with as-override used for?

6. When would you use different route distinguishers for routes of the same VPN?

7. What command should you configure on a Multi-VRF CE router that is running OSPF?

8. What three characteristics does an OSPF sham link have?

9. Why do MPLS VPN packets have two MPLS labels?

10. Which BGP extended community can prevent routing loops from occurring in MPLS VPN networks?

What You Will Learn

By the end of this chapter, you should know and be able to explain the following:

■ What the advantages of MPLS TE are

■ How OSPF and IS-IS have been extended for MPLS TE

■ How TE LSPs and their costs are calculated

■ How traffic is mapped to MPLS TE tunnels

■ How Fast ReRoute for link and node protection works

■ How RSVP was extended for MPLS TE

After you have digested these topics, you'll have a thorough understanding of MPLS traffic engineering.

CHAPTER 8

MPLS Traffic Engineering

Traffic engineering (TE), or the ability to steer traffic through a network, has been around for a while, but it was mainly present in ATM or Frame Relay networks. The role of TE is to get the traffic from edge to edge in the network in the most optimal way. In these networks, virtual circuits were laid out to carry traffic from one edge point in the network to another over ATM or Frame Relay switches. The site-to-site traffic was carefully planned and mapped to these virtual circuits. This is referred to as the *overlay model*. These days, the dominant networking protocol is clearly IP. Although early IP networks were implemented with a Frame Relay or an ATM infrastructure, more and more networks rely on a pure IP solution or IP running over an MPLS-enabled network. Therefore, a TE solution was needed for IP networks. Although TE might not yet be possible in a pure IP network, it is possible in an IP/MPLS network with the MPLS TE solution.

The Need for MPLS TE

Routing in IP networks is governed by the need to get the traffic across the network as quickly as possible. That is why IP routing is based on the least-cost routing principle. Every IP routing protocol has a cost associated with the links in the networks. The accumulation of the cost of every link of a path is used to calculate the smallest cost path to forward traffic through the network. That cost is a single metric that is assigned to a link (for instance, Open Shortest Path First [OSPF] and Intermediate System-to-Intermediate System [IS-IS]), a composite metric (for instance, Interior Gateway Routing Protocol [IGRP] and Enhanced Interior Gateway Routing Protocol [EIGRP]), or simply a hop count (for instance, Routing Information Protocol [RIP] and RIP version 2).

The forwarding paradigm of IP is based on this least-cost path forwarding. Furthermore, IP packets are forwarded on every hop (router) based solely on the destination IP address and independently of the way the IP packets were forwarded on the routers before or after this hop. Also, the IP forwarding paradigm does not take into account the available bandwidth capacity of the link, which might differ significantly from the cost that is assigned to the link. Therefore, a router can keep forwarding IP traffic onto a link, even though that link is already dropping packets due to a lack of bandwidth to forward all the traffic flows for which the routing table points to that link. The result of this behavior in forwarding IP packets is that some links might be overutilized in the network, whereas other links might be underutilized. Of course, you can keep an eye on the traffic rates on the links of the network and plan an upgrade of the link capacity to accommodate the increased load. Adding bandwidth to the links is something that does not happen overnight; it needs planning and takes time. Because traffic patterns between sites can shift quite suddenly and are not always permanent, TE can bring a solution by steering the traffic or a portion of it away from the overloaded links. Look at Figure 8-1 for a sample network where IP forwarding is in place.

Figure 8-1 *Network with IP Forwarding*

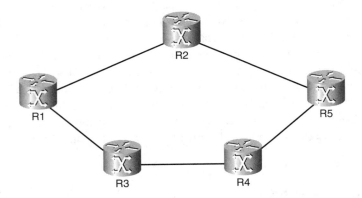

If every link in this sample network has the same cost, the least cost path from router R1 to router R5 is the path R1-R2-R5. Clearly, all traffic from R1 to R5 will use the path R1-R2-R5, and the path R1-R3-R4-R5 will have no traffic. In a real network, things are not as black and white. Many traffic flows can exist, and the load on the links might vary greatly.

You can distribute the load more evenly by playing with the cost of the links for the particular routing protocol. That might distribute the traffic more evenly, but you can never distribute the load perfectly, because in real networks, the links are hardly ever of the same bandwidth capacity. In the network of Figure 8-1, you can ensure that the two paths look equal by making sure that the sum of the costs of the links in the path R1-R2-R5 and the path R1-R3-R4-R5 are equal. The result will be the load balancing of traffic between R1 and R5 on the two paths. This will be fine for the traffic between R1 and R5, but you will surely have traffic entering the network on R2 and leaving it on R4, and so on. This is the same problem, because two paths exist from R2 to R4; one path is two hops, and the other is three. You can have the same problem between the routers R3 and R5 or any of the others. In other words, the problem of loading the links equally with traffic is an impossible task if you just try to adjust the cost of each link in the network.

To further increase the complexity of the problem, at any given day, the speed of any of the links might be upgraded, allowing for more bandwidth on certain links. At that point, you need to plan again from scratch and change the cost of the links manually throughout the network. This is clearly not sustainable from an operational standpoint. MPLS TE is a solution for this problem in the following ways:

- MPLS TE provides efficient spreading of traffic throughout the network, avoiding underutilized and overutilized links.

- MPLS TE takes into account the configured (static) bandwidth of links.

- MPLS TE takes link attributes into account (for instance, delay, jitter).

- MPLS TE adapts automatically to changing bandwidth and link attributes.

- Source-based routing is applied to the traffic-engineered load as opposed to IP destination-based routing.

MPLS TE allows for a TE scheme where the head end router of a label switched path (LSP) can calculate the most efficient route through the network toward the tail end router of the LSP. The head end router can do that if it has the topology of the network. Furthermore, the head end router needs to know the remaining bandwidth on all the links of the network. Finally, you need to enable MPLS on the routers so that you can establish LSPs end to end. The fact that label switching is used and not IP forwarding allows for source-based routing instead of IP destination-based routing. That is because MPLS does forwarding in the data plane by matching an incoming label in the label forwarding information base (LFIB) and swapping it with an outgoing label. Therefore, it is the head end label switching router (LSR) of the LSP that can determine the routing of the labeled packet, after all LSRs agree which labels to use for which LSP. Figure 8-2 shows an example of this source-based routing ability of MPLS TE.

Figure 8-2 *MPLS TE Head End Router*

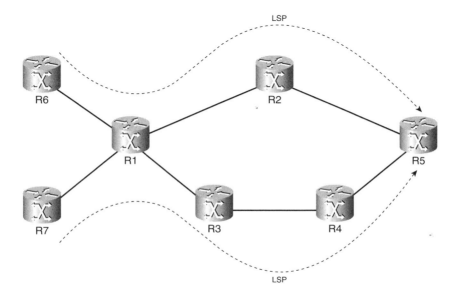

To illustrate this concept, routers R6 and R7 have been added in front of router R1. Assume that routers R6 and R7 want to send traffic to R5. If this network is running IP forwarding only, this traffic follows the path R1-R2-R5 only, no matter what you configured on routers R6 and R7. That is because the forwarding of IP packets is done independently on every hop in the network. Therefore, router R1 does not know what routers R6 and R7 are up to, and it forwards the traffic according to its own forwarding decision based on the IP routing table. R6 and R7 might have different policies, though. R6 might want to send the traffic along the path R6-R1-R2-R5, whereas R7 might want to forward the traffic along the path R7-R1-R3-R4-R5, which is impossible to achieve in a plain IP network. If the network is running MPLS, you can set up these two paths as two different LSPs so that different labels are used. At router R1, the different incoming label value indicates whether the packet belongs to the LSP with R6 as the head end or the LSP with R7 as the head end. R1 then forwards the packet on one of the two LSPs, but it does not forward the packet according to its own will as is the case with plain IP forwarding.

You can deploy MPLS TE in any network that has LSRs. However, because the bandwidth and other attributes of the links have to be known by the head end LSR of the LSPs, the routing protocol used between MPLS TE endpoints (head end and tail end LSRs) has to be a link state routing protocol. With a link state routing protocol, each router builds a state of its own links, which is then flooded to all the other routers in the same area. This means that all routers in the area have all topology information of that area. The head end LSR can thus figure out how to lay out the MPLS traffic-engineered LSP. This allows for source-based routing. This LSP is called an *MPLS TE tunnel*. It is not like a GRE tunnel, however. A TE tunnel is unidirectional, because an LSP is unidirectional, and it has the TE tunnel configuration only on the head end LSR and not on the tail end LSR of the LSP. Furthermore, a TE tunnel must be signaled, whereas a GRE tunnel does not have to be.

If TE is enabled in the network, you can use it in two distinct ways. First, you can create MPLS TE tunnels between each pair of edge LSRs in your network. As such, you can steer all traffic in the network, avoid congestion in it, and give all traffic the characteristics (bandwidth, delay, jitter, and so on) it needs. A good example is MPLS VPN, where you can create one TE tunnel from every PE router to every other PE router. Second, you can enable MPLS TE everywhere in the network but not have TE tunnels until they are needed. You can create the TE tunnels on demand. A good example of this is when you create TE tunnels to steer traffic around a hotspot or overloaded point in the network. Equally important as how to steer traffic with the TE LSPs through the network is how to map traffic onto them. This is explained in the section "Forwarding Traffic onto MPLS TE Tunnels." When no traffic enters the TE tunnels, the TE tunnels are idle.

Overview of the Operation of MPLS TE

Following is what MPLS TE needs to make it work. These are the building blocks of MPLS TE:

■   Link constraints (how much traffic each link can support and which TE tunnel can use the link)

- TE information distribution (by the MPLS TE-enabled link-state routing protocol)

- An algorithm (path calculation [PCALC]) to calculate the best path from the head end LSR to the tail end LSR

- A signaling protocol (Resource Reservation Protocol [RSVP]) to signal the TE tunnel across the network

- A way to forward traffic onto the TE tunnel

Figure 8-3 has the TE building blocks in the network from Figure 8-2. One TE tunnel or LSP extends from R6 to R5.

Figure 8-3 *MPLS TE Building Blocks*

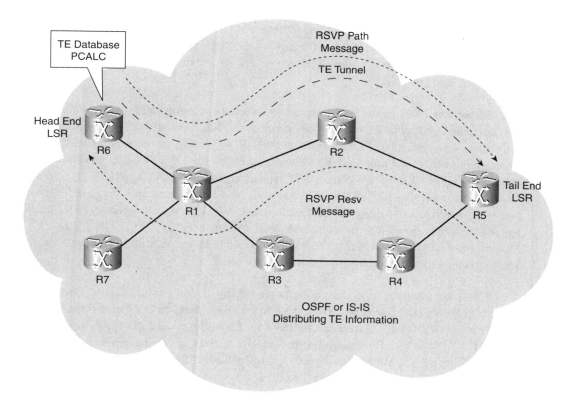

The first name used at Cisco for MPLS TE was Routing with Resource Reservation, also known as RRR or R^3 (read as R cubed). This name indicates that an important reason to have MPLS TE is the routing or steering of traffic according to resources or constraints. These resources are the bandwidth of the links and some attributes of the links that the operator specifies. These attributes are configured on the links and advertised by the link state protocol. (This means OSPF or IS-IS.) Instead of creating a new protocol to carry this information and advertise it to all the LSRs, OSPF and IS-IS were extended to piggyback this information. When you configure a TE tunnel on an LSR, it becomes the head end LSR of that TE tunnel or TE LSP. You then specify the destination LSR of the TE tunnel and the constraints it must adhere to. For example, you can specify the bandwidth requirement of the tunnel.

Inside Cisco IOS, a TE database is built from the TE information that the link state protocol sends. This dataset contains all the links that are enabled for MPLS TE and their characteristics or attributes. From this MPLS TE database, path calculation (PCALC) or constrained SPF (CSPF) calculates the shortest route that still adheres to all the constraints (most importantly the bandwidth) from the head end LSR to the tail end LSR. PCALC or CSPF is a shortest path first (SPF) algorithm modified for MPLS TE, so that constraints can be taken into account. The bandwidth available to TE and the attributes are configurable on all links of the networks. You configure the bandwidth requirement and attributes of the TE tunnel on the tunnel configuration of the head end LSR. PCALC matches the bandwidth requirement and attributes of the TE tunnel with the ones on the links, and from all possible paths, it takes the shortest one. The calculation is done on the head end LSR.

The intermediate LSRs on the LSP need to know what the incoming and outgoing labels are for the particular LSP for that TE tunnel. The intermediate LSRs can only learn the labels if the head end router and intermediate LSRs signal the labels by a signaling protocol. In the past, two signaling protocols were proposed: RSVP with extensions for TE (RSVP-TE) and constraint-based LDP (CR-LDP). Cisco IOS has RSVP with extensions for signaling MPLS TE tunnels and never had an implementation of CR-LDP. At the Internet Engineering Task Force (IETF), consensus was reached to carry on with developing RSVP as the signaling protocol for MPLS TE and to stop further development on CR-LDP. This was documented in RFC 3468, "The Multiprotocol Label Switching (MPLS) Working Group Decision on MPLS Signaling Protocols." The following is a quotation from the abstract of that RFC:

> This document documents the consensus reached by the Multiprotocol Label Switching (MPLS) Working Group within the IETF to focus its efforts on "Resource Reservation Protocol (RSVP)-TE: Extensions to RSVP for Label-Switched Paths (LSP) Tunnels" (RFC 3209) as the MPLS signalling protocol for traffic engineering applications and to undertake no new efforts relating to "Constraint-Based LSP Setup using Label Distribution Protocol (LDP)" (RFC 3212).

Extensions were made to RSVP to allow it to carry the MPLS label information and other TE specifics, such as the Explicit Route and Record Route objects. In essence, RSVP tries to signal the TE tunnel along the path—from head end LSR to tail end LSR—which is the result from the calculation based on the TE database on the head end LSR. RSVP needs to signal it to get the label information set up at each LSR. The RSVP PATH message is sent from head end LSR to tail end LSR and carries a request for an MPLS label. The RSVP RESV message sent back from the tail end LSR to the head end LSR carries the MPLS label that each LSR along the TE tunnel LSP can use to forward the TE traffic. RSVP also verifies that the TE tunnel with the constraints can be set up at each node. The latter part should not be a problem, because OSPF or IS-IS has advertised this information. Thus, the head end should have calculated a feasible path through the network for the TE LSP. However, it might be that another TE tunnel just reserved an amount of bandwidth on a link of an intermediate LSR, and OSPF or IS-IS has not advertised this yet. Therefore, it might be that the remainder of the bandwidth at that link is no longer sufficient for this TE tunnel to be set up—hence the need for a signaling protocol to make sure the bandwidth is reserved at each hop.

How is the RSVP PATH message routed through the network? The Explicit Route object (ERO) details the hops that the RSVP PATH message must follow to signal the TE tunnel. The series of hops or path is the result of the path calculation on the head end router. At each hop, this PATH message temporarily reserves the bandwidth and requests a label. Eventually, the PATH message gets to the tail end of the LSP, which returns a RESV message to the head end of the LSP. This RESV message then returns a label that the MPLS data plane can use to forward the packets of this MPLS TE tunnel along the LSP. The RESV message also tells the intermediate LSR to reserve the resources for the links that the TE LSP uses.

The most important task is for you to ensure that traffic is forwarded on to the TE tunnels. A later section "Forwarding Traffic onto MPLS TE Tunnels" of this chapter explains the different methods to achieve this.

Distribution of TE Information

A link state routing protocol needs to flood the constraints of the links in the network to all routers that are running TE. In the next sections, you can see what link information the routing protocol needs to flood and how OSPF and IS-IS have been extended to carry this TE information.

Requirements for the IGP

The Interior Gateway Protocol (IGP) needs to be capable of sending all the topology information (the state of the links) to all routers in the area in which TE has been enabled. Only a link state protocol can perform this task because it floods the state of all links of a router to all the routers in one area. Therefore, every router in the area knows all alternative paths to get to the destination. A distance vector routing protocol cannot perform this task. It is designed only to forward the best route (the route in the routing table); therefore, the information on alternate paths is lost.

> **NOTE**   The only compelling reason to run a link state routing protocol in an MPLS network is TE. For all other MPLS applications, any routing protocol can do the job. Therefore, you cannot run the distance vector routing protocol EIGRP when deploying MPLS TE, but you can run it for any other MPLS application, such as MPLS VPN.

The head end of the TE tunnel must have all topology information to see all the possible paths, but it must also have all the constraints information of the links available to it. This constraint information is the collection of resource information of the links that are associated with TE. The link state routing protocol must be extended to carry this extra resource information. The TE resources of a link are as follows:

- TE metric

- Maximum bandwidth

- Maximum reservable bandwidth

- Unreserved bandwidth

- Administrative group

The TE metric is a parameter that you can use to construct a TE topology that is different from the IP topology. As such, the TE metric of a link can be different from the OSPF cost or IS-IS metric of the link. The maximum bandwidth is the total bandwidth of the link. In Cisco IOS, this value matches the physical or configured bandwidth value of the link. The maximum reservable bandwidth is obviously the bandwidth available to TE on the link. You set this by using the **ip rsvp bandwidth** command. The unreserved bandwidth is the remainder of the bandwidth that is available to TE. It is the maximum reservable bandwidth minus whatever bandwidth is currently reserved by TE tunnels crossing this link. The administrative group is a 32-bit field with no further syntax. The operator of the network can individually set each bit of this 32-bit field and can have a meaning chosen by him. For example, one bit might mean that the link is a pos link with a speed greater than OC 48, or a link that is intercontinental, or a link that has a delay smaller than 100 ms. One link can have multiple resources associated with it, with a maximum of 32. These resources are flooded throughout the area whenever they change in value or at regular intervals. The flooding of these IGP changes is backward compatible. This means that not all routers must support these changes before you can run MPLS TE. Routers that do not understand the IGP changes for TE just ignore them.

OSPF Extensions for TE

RFC 2370 describes an extension to the OSPF protocol whereby three new link-state advertisements (LSAs) are defined and are called opaque LSAs. These three new LSAs give OPSF a generalized mechanism to extend OSPF. They can carry information to be used by OSPF or directly by any application. These LSAs are exactly what MPLS TE needs to put its information into OSPF. OSPF can then flood this information throughout the network.

Three types of opaque LSAs exist, differing only in the flooding scope. Opaque LSA type 9 has a flooding scope that is link-local only; opaque type 10 has a flooding scope that is area wide, and opaque type 11 has a flooding scope that is autonomous system wide. That means that type 9 LSAs are only sent onto the link but never forwarded beyond; type 10 LSAs are stopped by area border routers, and type 11 LSAs are flooded throughout the OSPF domain, just like type 5 LSAs. Like type 5 LSAs, the type 11 LSAs are flooded into transit areas but not into stub areas. MPLS TE uses type 10 LSAs for intra-area MPLS TE. You can read in the online supplement of this chapter—in the section "Interarea TE"—that TE is also supported in an interarea way, but that opaque type 11 LSAs are not used to achieve this.

A new bit, the O-bit, was defined for use in the Options field of OSPF. This bit can indicate whether a router is capable of sending and receiving the opaque LSAs. The Options field is present in OSPF Hello packets, Database Description packets, and all LSAs. Look at Figure 8-4 for the OSPF Options field.

Figure 8-4 *OSPF Options Field with the O-Bit*

The Options Field

Figure 8-5 shows the opaque LSA format. The LSA type is 9, 10, or 11, and the normal link state ID has been replaced with the Opaque Type and Opaque ID.

Figure 8-5 *Opaque LSA*

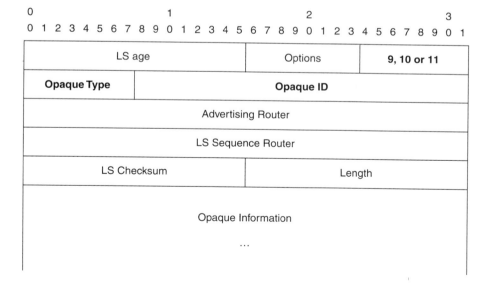

The TE LSA is an opaque LSA type 10 that carries one or more Type Length Values (TLV). A TLV enables OSPF to carry data in a flexible way. Figure 8-6 shows the format of a TLV.

Figure 8-6 *TLV Format*

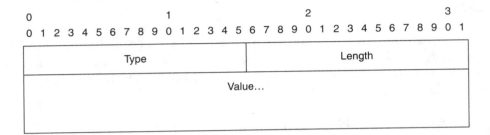

These TLVs carry the specific MPLS TE data. A Router Address TLV and a Link TLV exist. The Router Address TLV carries the router ID for TE. The link TLV carries a set of sub-TLVs describing a single link for MPLS TE. Table 8-1 gives an overview of the Link sub-TLVs. You can see that the link resources—as mentioned in the previous section—are present.

Table 8-1 *OSPF Link TLV Sub-TLVs*

Sub-TLV Number	Name	Length in Octets
1	Link type	1
2	Link ID	4
3	Local interface IP address	4
4	Remote interface IP address	4
5	Traffic engineering metric	4
6	Maximum bandwidth	4
7	Maximum reservable bandwidth	4
8	Unreserved bandwidth	32
9	Administrative group	4

The link type indicates whether the link is a point-to-point link or a multiaccess link. The link ID is set to the router ID of the neighbor or the interface address of the designated router if the link is multiaccess. The bandwidth parameters are expressed in bytes per second. Notice that the parameter unreserved bandwidth has 32 octets, whereas the other bandwidth parameters have only 4 octets. The difference comes from the fact that the unreserved bandwidth is expressed in 4 octets for each priority level. Eight priority levels exist, ranging from 0 to 7. These levels are the eight setup priority levels that TE tunnels use. The use of these priority levels is explained in the section "MPLS TE Tunnel (Trunk) Attributes."

Example 8-1 shows the configuration needed to enable MPLS TE for OSPF. You need to enable MPLS TE globally on the router with the command **mpls traffic-eng tunnels.** Every link that you want to be enabled with TE and thus be able to carry TE tunnels must have the interface command **mpls traffic-eng tunnels**.

Example 8-1 *Configuring MPLS TE for OSPF*

```
!
mpls traffic-eng tunnels
!
interface Loopback0
 ip address 10.200.254.2 255.255.255.255
!
interface pos 10/1
 ip address 10.200.210.1 255.255.255.0
 mpls traffic-eng tunnels
!
router ospf 1
 mpls traffic-eng router-id Loopback0
 mpls traffic-eng area 0
 router-id 10.200.254.2
 network 10.192.0.0 0.63.255.255 area 0
!
```

The command **mpls traffic-eng router-id** *interface-name* allows you to configure a stable IP address as MPLS TE router ID (similar to OSPF router ID). You should use a loopback interface on the router for this purpose. Example 8-2 shows that you can verify that OSPF is enabled to run MPLS TE in area 0, and that opaque LSAs type 10 are in the OSPF database.

Example 8-2 *Verifying MPLS TE for OSPF*

```
paris#show ip ospf
 Routing Process "ospf 1" with ID 10.200.254.2
 Supports only single TOS(TOS0) routes
 Supports opaque LSA
 Supports Link-local Signaling (LLS)
...
Number of areas transit capable is 0
 External flood list length 0
    Area BACKBONE(0)
       Number of interfaces in this area is 7 (2 loopback)
       Area has RRR enabled
       Area has no authentication...
```

Example 8-2 *Verifying MPLS TE for OSPF (Continued)*

```
paris#show ip ospf database

                OSPF Router with ID (10.200.254.2) (Process ID 1)

                   Router Link States (Area 0)

Link ID          ADV Router       Age          Seq#         Checksum Link count
10.200.254.1     10.200.254.1     341          0x800004B8 0x745C    3
10.200.254.2     10.200.254.2     150          0x8000002A 0x9A9D    6
...

                Type-10 Opaque Link Area Link States (Area 0)

Link ID          ADV Router       Age          Seq#         Checksum Opaque ID
1.0.0.0          10.200.254.1     1858         0x80000026 0xF71B    0
1.0.0.0          10.200.254.2     151          0x80000027 0xEC9A    0
1.0.0.0          10.200.254.3     92           0x80000029 0x7B04    0
1.0.0.0          10.200.254.4     1394         0x80000024 0x9EDC    0
1.0.0.0          10.200.254.5     1326         0x80000041 0xBA9F    0
...
```

Example 8-3 shows one opaque LSA in detail. The advertising router is the router with OSPF router ID and MPLS TE ID equal to 10.200.254.2. You can see that the discussed link resources are present for this link. Note that even though the bandwidth interface command and the **ip rsvp bandwidth** command are expressed in kilo*bits* per second, the maximum bandwidth and the maximum reservable bandwidth are expressed in kilo*bytes* per second in the OSPF output. The admin metric is the TE metric of the link.

Example 8-3 *OSPF Opaque LSA in Detail*

```
paris#show ip ospf database opaque-area

                OSPF Router with ID (10.200.254.2) (Process ID 1)

                Type-10 Opaque Link Area Link States (Area 0)

  LS age: 173
  Options: (No TOS-capability, DC)
  LS Type: Opaque Area Link
  Link State ID: 1.0.0.0
  Opaque Type: 1
  Opaque ID: 0
  Advertising Router: 10.200.254.2
  LS Seq Number: 80000027
  Checksum: 0xEC9A
  Length: 140
```

Example 8-3 *OSPF Opaque LSA in Detail (Continued)*

```
Fragment number : 0

  MPLS TE router ID : 10.200.254.2

  Link connected to Point-to-Point network
    Link ID : 10.200.254.3
    Interface Address : 10.200.210.1
    Neighbor Address : 10.200.210.2
    Admin Metric : 1
    Maximum bandwidth : 19375000
    Maximum reservable bandwidth : 19375000
    Number of Priority : 8
    Priority 0 : 19375000      Priority 1 : 19375000
    Priority 2 : 19375000      Priority 3 : 19375000
    Priority 4 : 19375000      Priority 5 : 19375000
    Priority 6 : 19375000      Priority 7 : 19375000
    Affinity Bit : 0x0
    IGP Metric : 1

  Number of Links : 1
```

IS-IS Extensions for TE

RFC 3784 describes the extensions made to IS-IS that enable it to carry the MPLS TE information.
Two new IS-IS TLVs have been defined. They allow the MPLS TE information to be carried by
IS-IS. However, at the same time, some other changes were made regarding these TLVs, such as
extending the link metric from a maximum of 63 to a new maximum of $2^{24}-1$, the usage of sub-
TLVs, and the introduction of the down bit. The first new TLV is the extended IS Reachability
TLV, or TLV type 22. It is the successor of the IS Reachability TLV (TLV type 2). This TLV
describes the IS-IS neighbors, with among others, the cost to them. The second new TLV is the
extended IP Reachability TLV, or TLV type 135. It is the successor of the IP Reachability TLVs
(TLV type 128 and TLV type 130). Both new TLVs have the extended metric format that allows
for greater metrics. The extended IS Reachability TLV is the TLV that carries the sub-TLVs
needed by MPLS TE. The sub-TLVs present are listed in Table 8-2. Again, you can see that the
link resources as mentioned in the earlier section "Requirements for the IGP" are present.

Table 8-2   *IS-IS Sub-TLVs of TLV Type 22*

Sub-TLV Number	Name	Length in Octets
0–2	Unassigned	—
3	Administrative group (color)	4
4–5	Unassigned	
6	IPv4 interface address	4

continues

Table 8-2 *IS-IS Sub-TLVs of TLV Type 22 (Continued)*

Sub-TLV Number	Name	Length in Octets
7	Unassigned	—
8	IPv4 neighbor address	4
9	Maximum link bandwidth	4
10	Reservable link bandwidth	4
11	Unreserved bandwidth	32
12–17	Unassigned	—
18	TE default metric	3
19–254	Unassigned	—
255	Reserved for future expansion	—

The bandwidth parameters are expressed in bytes per second. Notice that the parameter unreserved bandwidth has 32 octets, whereas the other bandwidth parameters have only 4 octets. The difference comes from the fact that unreserved bandwidth is expressed in 4 octets for each priority level. Priority levels range from 0 to 7. These eight priority levels are the eight setup priority levels that TE tunnels use. The use of these priority levels is explained in the section "MPLS TE Tunnel (Trunk) Attributes."

Another new TLV is the TE router ID TLV, or TLV type 134. This TLV describes the MPLS router ID as a 4-octet value.

In Cisco IOS, the router IS-IS configuration needs to have the wide metrics enabled when running MPLS TE. MPLS TE needs to be enabled for level 1 or level 2, and the MPLS TE router ID can be set. Example 8-4 shows how to configure IS-IS with MPLS TE enabled.

Example 8-4 *IS-IS TE Configuration*

```
!
interface POS5/0
 ip address 10.200.202.2 255.255.255.0
 ip router isis bruges
 mpls traffic-eng tunnels
 ip rsvp bandwidth 155000 sub-pool 10000
!
router isis bruges
 net 49.0001.0000.0000.0001.00
 is-type level-2-only
 metric-style wide
 mpls traffic-eng router-id Loopback0
 mpls traffic-eng level-2
!
```

You can verify that the IS-IS database holds the link resources. Use the **show isis database verbose** or the **show isis mpls traffic-eng advertisements** command, as in Example 8-5, for this task.

Example 8-5 *IS-IS Database*

```
rome#show isis database verbose

Tag bruges:
IS-IS Level-2 Link State Database:
LSPID                    LSP Seq Num  LSP Checksum  LSP Holdtime        ATT/P/OL
rome.00-00          * 0x00000002    0xDE1A        1107                0/0/0
  Area Address: 49.0001
  NLPID:        0xCC
  Hostname: rome
  Router ID:    10.200.254.6
  IP Address:   10.200.202.2
  Metric: 10          IS-Extended sydney.00
    Affinity: 0x00000000
    Interface IP Address: 10.200.202.2
    Neighbor IP Address: 10.200.202.1
    Physical BW: 1544 kbits/sec
    Reservable Global Pool BW: 155000 kbits/sec
    Reservable Sub Pool BW: 10000 kbits/sec
    Global Pool BW Unreserved:
      [0]:    155000 kbits/sec, [1]:    155000 kbits/sec
      [2]:    155000 kbits/sec, [3]:    155000 kbits/sec
      [4]:    155000 kbits/sec, [5]:    155000 kbits/sec
      [6]:    155000 kbits/sec, [7]:    155000 kbits/sec
    Sub Pool BW Unreserved:
      [0]:     10000 kbits/sec, [1]:     10000 kbits/sec
      [2]:     10000 kbits/sec, [3]:     10000 kbits/sec
      [4]:     10000 kbits/sec, [5]:     10000 kbits/sec
      [6]:     10000 kbits/sec, [7]:     10000 kbits/sec
    Admin. Weight: 64
  Metric: 10          IP 10.200.202.0/24

rome#show isis mpls traffic-eng advertisements

Tag bruges:
  System ID: rome.00
  Router ID: 10.200.254.6
  Link Count: 1
    Link[1]
      Neighbor System ID: sydney.00 (P2P link)
      Interface IP address: 10.200.202.2
      Neighbor IP Address: 10.200.202.1
      Admin. Weight te: 64 igp: 64
```

continues

Example 8-5 *IS-IS Database (Continued)*

```
        Physical BW: 1544 kbits/sec
        Reservable Global Pool BW: 155000 kbits/sec
        Reservable Sub Pool BW: 10000 kbits/sec
        Global Pool BW unreserved:
          [0]: 155000 kbits/sec, [1]: 155000 kbits/sec
          [2]: 155000 kbits/sec, [3]: 155000 kbits/sec
          [4]: 155000 kbits/sec, [5]: 155000 kbits/sec
          [6]: 155000 kbits/sec, [7]: 155000 kbits/sec
        Sub Pool BW unreserved:
          [0]: 10000 kbits/sec, [1]: 10000 kbits/sec
          [2]: 10000 kbits/sec, [3]: 10000 kbits/sec
          [4]: 10000 kbits/sec, [5]: 10000 kbits/sec
          [6]: 10000 kbits/sec, [7]: 10000 kbits/sec
        Affinity Bits: 0x00000000
```

NOTE The *Sub Pool* in the output of Example 8-5 refers to DiffServ-aware TE tunnels. DiffServ-aware TE tunnels are explained in the online supplement of this chapter.

Flooding by the IGP

The IGP floods the TE information in the following cases:

- Link status change

- Configuration change

- Periodic flooding

- Changes in the reserved bandwidth

- After a tunnel setup failure

As with regular IP routing, OSPF floods the LSA or IS-IS floods the LSP when the state (up or down) of the interface changes or when a manual configuration change alters the characteristics of the interface for the IGP. OSPF and IS-IS also have a periodic flooding mechanism. With OSPF, a periodic flooding occurs every 30 minutes. You can change this interval with the command **timers pacing lsa-group** *seconds*. With IS-IS, the periodic flooding is set to 15 minutes by default, but you can change it with the **lsp-refresh-interval** *seconds* command.

You can also change the periodic flooding for TE specifically. This periodic flooding is used because small changes in the reserved bandwidth do not trigger an immediate flooding. TE information is flooded by default every three minutes. You can change this interval with the global **mpls traffic-eng link-management timers periodic-flooding** *interval* command.

```
london(config)#mpls traffic-eng link-management timers periodic-flooding ?
  <0-3600>  seconds
```

Small changes in reserved bandwidth are not flooded immediately. What are small changes? When the link has a lot of bandwidth unreserved, the chances are relatively greater that a tunnel LSP will find enough bandwidth across that link than when little unreserved bandwidth remains on the link. That is why the triggers in place for flooding the information when bandwidth is reserved on the link are closer to each other at the high end mark than at the low end mark of reserved bandwidth. A link can have 0 percent reserved bandwidth, 100 percent reserved bandwidth, or anything in between. Several triggers are laid out between the 0 and 100 percent mark. Two sets of triggers exist: one for the down movement (this means less reserved bandwidth) and one for the up movement (this means more reserved bandwidth). The default triggers for down are 100, 99, 98, 97, 96, 95, 90, 85, 80, 75, 60, 45, 30, and 15. The default triggers for up are 15, 30, 45, 60, 75, 80, 85, 90, 95, 97, 98, 99, and 100. You can change these, as shown in Example 8-6.

Example 8-6 *Changing the TE Flooding Thresholds*

```
london(config-if)#mpls traffic-eng flooding thresholds ?
  down   Set the thresholds for decreased resource availability
  up     Set the thresholds for increased resource availability

london(config-if)#mpls traffic-eng flooding thresholds down ?
  <0-100>  decreased bandwidth usage (percent)

london(config-if)#mpls traffic-eng flooding thresholds down 20 ?
  <0-100>  decreased bandwidth usage (percent)
  <cr>

london(config-if)#mpls traffic-eng flooding thresholds down 20 30 40 50 60 70 80 90 99

london(config-if)#mpls traffic-eng flooding thresholds up ?
  <0-100>  increased bandwidth usage (percent)
```

The last case when a router floods the link state information is when a tunnel has failed to set up. It is expected that a tunnel that tries to set up the LSP via RSVP succeeds in doing this. This is because the head end LSR has all the information available to it by looking at the TE database to find a path that is suitable for the tunnel LSP. This information in the TE database got there by the IGP. However, RSVP might still be unable to signal that LSP. A reason for this might be that another tunnel just reserved enough bandwidth on a particular link of a router on the path so that the unreserved bandwidth is insufficient for this new tunnel LSP. Of course, this can only happen if the IGP did not flood this link information yet, because the threshold of reserved bandwidth was not crossed. Because of the tunnel setup failure on an intermediate router, that router immediately floods again so that the head end router prunes this link when performing the CSPF. The head end router can then compute a different path through the network for the tunnel LSP.

Routing and Cost of a TE LSP

When the path for a TE tunnel is calculated, several factors come into play. The result of the calculation is the shortest path possible from all paths of which the characteristics of the links match the needed characteristics of the TE tunnel. These characteristics are the resources explained in the following sections. The network depicted in Figure 8-7 is the network—or parts of it—used to illustrate examples for the rest of this chapter.

Figure 8-7 *TE Network Topology*

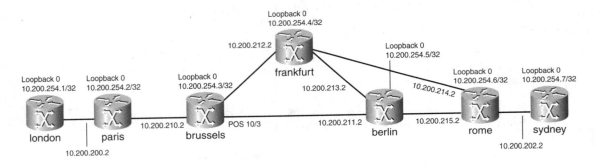

Link TE Attributes

Every link in the MPLS network enabled for TE can have characteristics that need to be flooded so that the head end router can figure out whether the TE tunnel can use a particular link. A link that is enabled for TE can have the following characteristics configured for TE:

- Maximum reservable bandwidth

- Attribute flags

- TE metric

- Shared risk link groups

- Maximum reservable sub-pool bandwidth

Maximum Reservable Bandwidth

You configure the maximum reservable bandwidth on the interface by configuring **ip rsvp bandwidth** *interface-kbps*. It is configured in kpbs. This is the maximum bandwidth reservable in the global pool, which is the pool that all regular TE tunnels use.

Attribute Flags

A link can have attribute flags associated with it by configuring **mpls traffic-eng attribute-flags** *attributes* on it. These attribute flags indicate the resources of the link, the capabilities of the link (for example, whether it is encrypted), or administrative policies. They indicate whether a tunnel that has specific resource needs can cross that link.

```
london(config-if)#mpls traffic-eng attribute-flags ?
  <0x0-0xFFFFFFFF>  Attribute flags
london(config-if)#mpls traffic-eng attribute-flags 0x0000FFFF
```

The attribute flags are 32 bits with no syntax associated with them. Each bit can be set or left cleared and can have any meaning that the operator wants to associate with it. For example, one' bit can indicate a link delay of less than 100 ms; another bit can indicate that the link is transatlantic; and so on.

On the tunnel configuration on the head end router, you can configure affinity bits and a mask to control whether the tunnel is allowed to cross the link with those attribute flags. The affinity bits are also 32 bits in total and are matched one by one with the attribute bits of the links. The mask of the affinity bits indicates whether each specific bit needs to be checked with the corresponding bit in the attribute field of the link. If the *n*th bit in the mask is set, the *n*th bit in the Attribute Flags field must match the *n*th bit in the affinity field of the TE tunnel. If the bit in the mask is not set, it does not matter whether the two bits in the same position in the affinity field and attribute flags match. The tunnel affinity bits are configured with the **tunnel mpls traffic-eng affinity** *properties* [**mask** *mask-value*] command on the tunnel interface on the head end router. The properties and mask are from the range 0x0 to 0xFFFFFFFF. The default value of the properties is 0X00000000; the default value for the mask is 0X0000FFFF.

TE Metric

You can change the TE metric of a link with the command **mpls traffic-eng administrative-weight** *weight*. The *weight* is the user-specified TE metric of a link.

The default TE metric of a link is the IGP cost of the link. A tunnel takes the IGP cost of the links into account when calculating the path through the network. You can configure the head end router of the tunnel(s) to use the TE metric of the links instead of the IGP cost of the links to route the tunnel throughout the network. Refer to the later section "Dual TE Metrics" for more on this.

Shared Risk Link Groups

Shared risk link groups (SRLGs) is a characteristic of a link that the network administrator assigns indicating that links share a common fiber or conduit. Therefore, if the fiber fails or if the conduit is cut, several links are affected at the same time and share the same risk. The SRLG is flooded by the IGP and is used when backup tunnels are deployed. Refer to the section "FRR" for more information on SRLG.

Maximum Reservable Sub-Pool Bandwidth

The *sub-pool* is a pool where the sub-pool or DiffServ-aware TE tunnels obtain their bandwidth. The online supplement of this chapter discusses DiffServ-aware TE tunnels, which use sub-pool bandwidth. This sub-pool bandwidth is a fraction of the global pool bandwidth.

MPLS TE Tunnel (Trunk) Attributes

The TE tunnel attributes are as follows:

- Tunnel destination

- Desired bandwidth

- Affinity

- Setup and holding priorities

- Reoptimization

- Path options

The tunnel destination is the MPLS TE router ID of the tail end LSR that the tunnel LSP should be routed to. The desired bandwidth of the TE tunnel is the bandwidth requirement of the TE tunnel. You can configure it on the tunnel interface with the following command:

tunnel mpls traffic-eng bandwidth [sub-pool | global] *bandwidth*

The **global** keyword indicates a regular TE tunnel, whereas the **sub-pool** keyword indicates a DiffServ-aware TE tunnel. The affinity bits and mask that are configured on the tunnel interface on the head end router were already explained in the section "Link TE Attributes." The setup and holding priorities, reoptimization, and path options are explained in the next section.

TE Tunnel Path Calculation

The way that the TE tunnel is laid out through the network depends on several factors:

- Path setup option

- Setup and holding priority

- Attribute flags and affinity bits

- Reoptimization

Path Setup Option

You can configure the path option on the tunnel configuration on the head end router. You can set up a tunnel in two ways: explicitly or dynamically. In the explicit way, you must specify every router that the TE tunnel must be routed on, up to and including the tail end router. You can either specify the TE router ID or the link IP address of the intermediate routers. In the dynamic way, you let the tunnel head end figure out how the TE tunnel should best be routed throughout the network toward the tail end router. In the dynamic way, you only need to configure the destination of the TE tunnel (this means the tail end router). The path from the head end router to the tail end router is calculated on the head end router. This router figures out how to route the TE tunnel by looking at the MPLS TE database learned from either OSPF or IS-IS. The router takes the topology information and the resources on the links into account. The process in Cisco IOS that is responsible for the path calculation of a TE LSP is called PCALC.

More than one dynamic and explicit path option can be configured, as long as they have a different preference. This preference is a number from 1 to 1000. The lower the number, the more preferred the path option is. The more preferred path option is tried first. Only if the path is not available is the next preferred path option tried. If all of the path options on the tunnel fail, the TE tunnel LSP fails and the tunnel interface on the head end router remains in a down state. Example 8-7 shows how to use path options. On router paris, an explicit path option is configured for a TE tunnel toward the router berlin. You enter the IP addresses of the links paris-brussels and brussels-berlin so that the explicit path becomes paris-brussels-berlin. The network is shown in Figure 8-7. Use the command **show mpls traffic-eng tunnels tunnel** *tunnel-num* to verify the state of the TE tunnel.

Example 8-7 *Explicit Path Option*

```
paris#
!
interface Tunnel1
 ip unnumbered Loopback0
 tunnel destination 10.200.254.5
```

continues

Example 8-7 *Explicit Path Option (Continued)*

```
 tunnel mode mpls traffic-eng
 tunnel mpls traffic-eng autoroute announce
 tunnel mpls traffic-eng path-option 1 explicit name paris-berlin
 tunnel mpls traffic-eng fast-reroute
!
ip explicit-path name paris-berlin enable
 next-address 10.200.210.2
 next-address 10.200.211.2
!

paris#show ip explicit-paths name paris-berlin
PATH paris-berlin (strict source route, path complete, generation 62)
    1: next-address 10.200.210.2
    2: next-address 10.200.211.2

paris#show mpls traffic-eng tunnels tunnel 1

Name: paris_t1                            (Tunnel1) Destination: 10.200.254.5
  Status:
    Admin: up         Oper: up      Path: valid      Signalling: connected
    path option 1, type explicit paris-berlin (Basis for Setup, path weight 2)

  Config Parameters:
    Bandwidth: 0         kbps (Global) Priority: 7  7   Affinity: 0x0/0xFFFF
    Metric Type: TE (default)
    AutoRoute:  enabled   LockDown: disabled Loadshare: 0       bw-based
    auto-bw: disabled
  Active Path Option Parameters:
    State: explicit path option 1 is active
    BandwidthOverride: disabled  LockDown: disabled  Verbatim: disabled

  InLabel  :  -
  OutLabel : POS4/0, 17
  RSVP Signalling Info:
      Src 10.200.254.2, Dst 10.200.254.5, Tun_Id 1, Tun_Instance 799
    RSVP Path Info:
      My Address: 10.200.254.2
      Explicit Route: 10.200.210.2 10.200.211.2 10.200.254.5
      Record   Route:   NONE
      Tspec: ave rate=0 kbits, burst=1000 bytes, peak rate=0 kbits
    RSVP Resv Info:
      Record   Route:  10.200.211.1(17) 10.200.211.2(0)
      Fspec: ave rate=0 kbits, burst=1000 bytes, peak rate=0 kbits
  Shortest Unconstrained Path Info:
    Path Weight: 2 (TE)
    Explicit Route: 10.200.210.2 10.200.211.2 10.200.254.5
```

Example 8-8 shows two configured path options: one explicit and one dynamic. The explicit path option has a lower value and is tried first. If that explicit path is unavailable for the TE tunnel 1, the second best path option (here a dynamic path option) is tried. Because the link brussels-berlin is down, the explicit path option is no longer possible for tunnel 1. The second option—the dynamic path option—is tried and succeeds because CSPF can find a path for tunnel 1. That path is paris-brussels-frankfurt-berlin. You can see which path option has been chosen for a TE tunnel in the Active Path Option Parameters section. The path with all the routers that are crossed by the TE LSP is shown in the RSVP Path Info section.

Example 8-8 *Explicit Path Option*

```
paris#show running-config interface tunnel 1
!
interface Tunnel1
 ip unnumbered Loopback0
 tunnel destination 10.200.254.5
 tunnel mode mpls traffic-eng
 tunnel mpls traffic-eng autoroute announce
 tunnel mpls traffic-eng path-option 1 explicit name paris-berlin
 tunnel mpls traffic-eng path-option 2 dynamic
 tunnel mpls traffic-eng fast-reroute
end


paris#show mpls traffic-eng tunnels tunnel 1

Name: paris_t1                          (Tunnel1) Destination: 10.200.254.5
  Status:
    Admin: up         Oper: up      Path: valid        Signalling: connected
    path option 2, type dynamic (Basis for Setup, path weight 3)
    path option 1, type explicit paris-berlin

  Config Parameters:
    Bandwidth: 0        kbps (Global) Priority: 7  7   Affinity: 0x0/0xFFFF
    Metric Type: TE (default)
    AutoRoute:  enabled   LockDown: disabled Loadshare: 0       bw-based
    auto-bw: disabled
  Active Path Option Parameters:
    State: dynamic path option 2 is active
    BandwidthOverride: disabled  LockDown: disabled  Verbatim: disabled

  InLabel  :  -
  OutLabel : POS4/0, 18
  RSVP Signalling Info:
      Src 10.200.254.2, Dst 10.200.254.5, Tun_Id 1, Tun_Instance 66
    RSVP Path Info:
      My Address: 10.200.254.2
      Explicit Route: 10.200.210.2 10.200.212.2 10.200.213.2 10.200.254.5
```

continues

Example 8-8 *Explicit Path Option (Continued)*

```
   Record   Route:   NONE
   Tspec: ave rate=0 kbits, burst=1000 bytes, peak rate=0 kbits
 RSVP Resv Info:
   Record   Route:   NONE
   Fspec: ave rate=0 kbits, burst=1000 bytes, peak rate=0 kbits
 Shortest Unconstrained Path Info:
   Path Weight: 3 (TE)
   Explicit Route: 10.200.210.2 10.200.212.2 10.200.213.2 10.200.254.5
```

IP Explicit Address Exclusion

Instead of including an IP address in the explicit path option, you can exclude an IP address from the path that the TE LSP will take. This IP address is the address of the link that should *not* be included when the path calculation takes place for the TE tunnel. The head end LSR must never use this link to route the TE tunnel LSP through the network. Instead of the IP address of a link, the IP address can also be the MPLS TE router ID of a node. In that case, the LSR with that MPLS TE router ID is excluded when CSPF runs to calculate the path of a TE LSP, thus avoiding a particular router. Example 8-9 shows such an exclude address in an explicit path option. The router berlin is excluded from the CSPF calculation completely because its TE router ID (10.200.254.5) is put as an excluded address in the explicit path *not-router-berlin* for tunnel 1. The tunnel destination is now the router rome. You can see in the RSVP Path Info that the path of the TE tunnel 1 avoids all links on the router berlin.

Example 8-9 *IP Explicit Address Exclusion*

```
!
interface Tunnel1
 ip unnumbered Loopback0
 tunnel destination 10.200.254.6
 tunnel mode mpls traffic-eng
 tunnel mpls traffic-eng autoroute announce
 tunnel mpls traffic-eng priority 7 7
 tunnel mpls traffic-eng bandwidth  100000
 tunnel mpls traffic-eng path-option 10 explicit name not-router-berlin
!
ip explicit-path name not-router-berlin enable
 exclude-address 10.200.254.5
!

paris#show mpls traffic-eng tunnels tunnel 1

Name: paris_t1                          (Tunnel1) Destination: 10.200.254.6
  Status:
    Admin: up        Oper: up      Path: valid       Signalling: connected
    path option 10, type explicit not-router-berlin (Basis for Setup, path weight 4)
```

Example 8-9 *IP Explicit Address Exclusion (Continued)*

```
Config Parameters:
  Bandwidth: 100000   kbps (Global)  Priority: 7  7   Affinity: 0x0/0xFFFF
  Metric Type: TE (default)
  AutoRoute:  enabled   LockDown: disabled  Loadshare: 100000   bw-based
  auto-bw: disabled
Active Path Option Parameters:
  State: explicit path option 10 is active
  BandwidthOverride: disabled  LockDown: disabled  Verbatim: disabled

InLabel  :  -
OutLabel : POS4/0, 25
RSVP Signalling Info:
    Src 10.200.254.2, Dst 10.200.254.6, Tun_Id 1, Tun_Instance 668
  RSVP Path Info:
    My Address: 10.200.254.2
    Explicit Route: 10.200.210.2 10.200.212.2 10.200.214.2 10.200.254.6
    Record   Route:   NONE
    Tspec: ave rate=100000 kbits, burst=1000 bytes, peak rate=100000 kbits
  RSVP Resv Info:
    Record   Route:   NONE
    Fspec: ave rate=100000 kbits, burst=1000 bytes, peak rate=100000 kbits
Shortest Unconstrained Path Info:
  Path Weight: 4 (TE)
  Explicit Route: 10.200.210.2 10.200.212.2 10.200.214.2 10.200.254.6
```

You can use this method of excluding a router from the path to route TE tunnel LSPs away from that router so that maintenance can occur on it. You must, however, wait until all TE LSPs reoptimize after configuring the path option with the exclude address. Refer to the later section "Reoptimization" for more information.

Setup and Holding Priority

MPLS TE tunnels can have different importance in the network. For example, you can think of tunnels that are longer—in terms of router hops—as being more important than the shorter TE tunnels. Alternatively, you can consider MPLS TE tunnels with a greater bandwidth need as more important than tunnels with a smaller bandwidth need. These more important TE tunnels, however, might be signaled later than the less important ones, or they might be configured later. That can lead to a situation in which the more important TE tunnels are not routed optimally, or they might not find a path that has enough bandwidth. TE tunnels have priorities to avoid such situations and to make sure that the more important TE tunnels can still be routed optimally by preempting the less important TE tunnels.

You can configure two priorities for each TE tunnel: setup and holding. Both the setup priority and holding priority indicate with their relative values whether a TE tunnel can preempt another tunnel. The lower the priority value, the higher the importance. The setup priority indicates how important the tunnel is to preempt the other tunnels, whereas the holding priority indicates how much the weight of that tunnel is to hold on to its reservations on the links. A tunnel that has a lower setup priority than the holding priority of a second tunnel can preempt that second tunnel. This means that the newly signaled tunnel preempts the existing tunnel. The setup and holding priorities are configured on the TE tunnel with the following command:

```
tunnel mpls traffic-eng priority setup-priority [hold-priority]
```

Important TE tunnels have a low setup priority (so that they can preempt other tunnels) and a low holding priority (so that other tunnels do not preempt them). The values that can be configured for both priorities are 0 to 7, with 0 indicating the highest priority. It might be a good idea for the network operator to stick to giving the tunnels that have a big bandwidth requirement a low value for both the priorities because you can imagine that it makes the layout of all tunnels easier if these tunnels are created before the tunnels that have the smaller bandwidth requirement. It is easier to fill the small holes that remain afterward with smaller tunnels. The setup priority of a tunnel should not be lower than its holding priority; otherwise, it can preempt another tunnel, but in turn it can be preempted by that other tunnel. This is why in Cisco IOS, you cannot configure a setup priority that is lower than the holding priority.

Reoptimization

A TE tunnel can end up on a path through the network that is no longer the best or optimal path for it. This can happen if a link that was previously down becomes available again or if a link did not have sufficient unreserved bandwidth at the time the tunnel was signaled, but now the bandwidth reservation on the link has gone down sufficiently for the TE tunnel to be routed across that link. Reoptimization causes a tunnel to be rerouted in the network onto the more optimal path. To understand reoptimization, you must know that three triggers can cause reoptimization of the TE tunnel so that it can be rerouted to the better path. These three triggers are periodic reoptimization, event-driven reoptimization, and manual reoptimization.

Periodic Reoptimization

In Cisco IOS, the reoptimization of a TE tunnel occurs with a frequency of one hour, by default. You can change this with the command **mpls traffic-eng reoptimize timers frequency** *interval*.

The interval that you can specify needs to be between 0 and 604,800 seconds (168 hours, or 7 days). The default value is 1 hour. If you specify 0 for the interval, the periodic reoptimization is turned off globally on the router for all TE tunnels. You can turn off the reoptimization check for an individual TE tunnel by specifying the **lockdown** keyword on the **path-option** command.

```
tunnel mpls traffic-eng path-option number {dynamic | explicit {name path-name |
path-number}} [lockdown]
```

Event-Driven Reoptimization

By default, Cisco IOS does not trigger reoptimization when a link in the network is available to TE again, either by configuration or because its state becomes operational. To enable the reoptimization when a link becomes operational for MPLS TE, configure the following command:

mpls traffic-eng reoptimize events link-up

Manual Reoptimization

To force the immediate reoptimization of all the TE tunnels on the head end router, you must type the **mpls traffic-eng reoptimize** command at the router prompt. You can specify a specific TE tunnel number to reoptimize only a specific tunnel with the command **mpls traffic-eng reoptimize tunnel** *tunnel-number.*

Dual TE Metrics

By default, MPLS TE uses the TE metrics of the links to route the TE tunnels; however, by default the TE link metrics are the same as the IGP link metrics. However, you can override this option when you set the TE metrics. You cannot have two TE metrics, though, to route TE tunnels. One solution, if you want to use two metrics, is to use the IGP metric and TE metric at the same time to route TE tunnels. Network administrators who want one metric for delay and one for bandwidth choose this option. You can use the metric reflecting the delay of the links to indicate what the best paths are for TE tunnels carrying the voice traffic, because the voice traffic needs a small overall delay. You can use the other metric reflecting the bandwidth to indicate the best path for the TE tunnels that are carrying the bulk data traffic. Because the availability of both metric types exists, it is simply a matter of choosing which metric to use for each TE tunnel: the IGP or the TE metric. You do this with the **traffic-eng path-selection metric** {**igp** | **te**} command on the tunnel interface on the head end router. Example 8-10 shows this command.

Example 8-10 *Configuring the **path-selection** Metric*

```
london(config)#interface tunnel 1
london(config-if)#tunnel mpls traffic-eng path-selection ?
  metric  Metric type for path calculation
london(config-if)#tunnel mpls traffic-eng path-selection metric ?
  igp  Use IGP Metric
  te   Use TE Metric
```

Figure 8-8 shows an example of using both metric types.

Figure 8-8 *Using the MPLS* **traffic-eng administrative-weight** *Command*

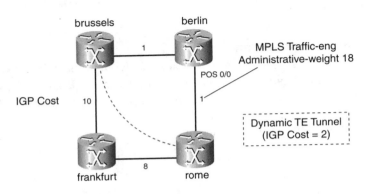

The IGP cost of the links is mentioned next to the links. If traffic is routed from router brussels to router rome, the total IGP cost of the path is 2. The IP traffic that is routed from router brussels to rome takes the path brussels-berlin-rome. A TE tunnel from router brussels to rome also follows the path brussels-berlin-rome, because the TE metrics are the same as the IGP metrics by default. If you want to put the TE tunnel on the path brussels-frankfurt-rome instead, you can increase the IGP cost of the link berlin-rome so that the total TE cost of the path brussels-berlin-rome is higher than the path brussels-frankfurt-rome. However, changing the IGP cost influences all traffic—including the IP traffic. If you change the TE metric of the link berlin-rome to 18, the total cost of the path brussels-berlin-rome becomes 19. The preferred path for the tunnel from router brussels to router rome is now brussels-frankfurt-rome, with a cost of 18. The IP traffic still prefers the path brussels-berlin-rome; however, if you configure the tunnel to prefer the IGP cost, the path becomes brussels-berlin-rome again. Example 8-11 shows you this tunnel when using the TE metric as the basis for path calculation. As you can see, the path weight (metric) is 18.

Example 8-11 *TE Metric*

```
berlin#conf t
Enter configuration commands, one per line.  End with CNTL/Z.
berlin(config)#int pos 0/0
berlin(config-if)#mpls traffic-eng administrative-weight 18

brussels#show mpls traffic-eng tunnels tunnel 1

Name: brussels_t1                     (Tunnel1) Destination: 10.200.254.6
  Status:
     Admin: up         Oper: up      Path: valid      Signalling: connected

     path option 1, type dynamic (Basis for Setup, path weight 18)
```

Example 8-11   *TE Metric (Continued)*

```
    path option 1, delayed clean in progress

  Config Parameters:
    Bandwidth: 0          kbps (Global)  Priority: 7  7    Affinity: 0x0/0xFFFF
    Metric Type: TE (default)
    AutoRoute:  disabled  LockDown: disabled  Loadshare: 0        bw-based
    auto-bw: disabled
  Active Path Option Parameters:
    State: dynamic path option 1 is active
    BandwidthOverride: disabled  LockDown: disabled  Verbatim: disabled

  InLabel  :  -
  OutLabel : POS10/1, 36
  RSVP Signalling Info:
      Src 10.200.254.3, Dst 10.200.254.6, Tun_Id 1, Tun_Instance 3
    RSVP Path Info:
      My Address: 10.200.254.3
      Explicit Route: 10.200.212.2 10.200.214.2 10.200.254.6
      Record   Route:   NONE
      Tspec: ave rate=0 kbits, burst=1000 bytes, peak rate=0 kbits
    RSVP Resv Info:
      Record   Route:   NONE
      Fspec: ave rate=0 kbits, burst=1000 bytes, peak rate=0 kbits
  Shortest Unconstrained Path Info:
    Path Weight: 18 (TE)
    Explicit Route: 10.200.212.2 10.200.214.2 10.200.254.6
```

Look at Example 8-12. When you configure the **path-selection** command to instruct the TE tunnel to use the IGP metric instead of the TE metric, the TE tunnel 1 path weight (metric) becomes 2.

Example 8-12   *Path-Selection Metric IGP*

```
brussels(config)#interface tunnel 1
brussels(config-if)#tunnel mpls traffic-eng path-selection metric igp
brussels(config-if)#^Z

brussels#show mpls traffic-eng tunnels tunnel 1

Name: brussels_t1                        (Tunnel1) Destination: 10.200.254.6
  Status:
    Admin: up       Oper: up      Path: valid      Signalling: connected

    path option 1, type dynamic (Basis for Setup, path weight 2)

  Config Parameters:
    Bandwidth: 0          kbps (Global)  Priority: 7  7    Affinity: 0x0/0xFFFF
```

continues

Example 8-12 *Path-Selection Metric IGP (Continued)*

```
    Metric Type: IGP (interface)
    AutoRoute: disabled  LockDown: disabled  Loadshare: 0          bw-based
    auto-bw: disabled
 Active Path Option Parameters:
   State: dynamic path option 1 is active
   BandwidthOverride: disabled  LockDown: disabled  Verbatim: disabled


 InLabel  :  -
 OutLabel : POS10/3, 22
 RSVP Signalling Info:
      Src 10.200.254.3, Dst 10.200.254.6, Tun_Id 1, Tun_Instance 4
   RSVP Path Info:
     My Address: 10.200.254.3
     Explicit Route: 10.200.211.2 10.200.215.2 10.200.254.6
     Record  Route:   NONE
     Tspec: ave rate=0 kbits, burst=1000 bytes, peak rate=0 kbits
   RSVP Resv Info:
     Record  Route:   NONE
     Fspec: ave rate=0 kbits, burst=1000 bytes, peak rate=0 kbits
   Shortest Unconstrained Path Info:
     Path Weight: 2 (IGP)
     Explicit Route: 10.200.211.2 10.200.215.2 10.200.254.6

brussels#show mpls traffic-eng topology 10.200.254.5

IGP Id: 10.200.254.5, MPLS TE Id:10.200.254.5 Router Node  (ospf 1  area 0) id 46
      link[0]: Point-to-Point, Nbr IGP Id: 10.200.254.6, nbr_node_id:52, gen:602
         frag_id 0, Intf Address:10.200.215.1, Nbr Intf Address:10.200.215.2
         TE metric:18, IGP metric:1, attribute_flags:0x0
         SRLGs: None
         physical_bw: 155000 (kbps), max_reservable_bw_global: 155000 (kbps)
         max_reservable_bw_sub: 10000 (kbps)
```

	Total Allocated BW (kbps)	Global Pool Reservable BW (kbps)	Sub Pool Reservable BW (kbps)
bw[0]:	0	155000	10000
bw[1]:	0	155000	10000
bw[2]:	0	155000	10000
bw[3]:	0	155000	10000
bw[4]:	0	155000	10000
bw[5]:	0	155000	10000
bw[6]:	0	155000	10000
bw[7]:	0	155000	10000

PCALC

PCALC is the special SPF algorithm that MPLS TE uses. SPF is an algorithm that OSPF and IS-IS use to calculate the shortest path to a destination. In short, SPF runs on every router and uses the database built by OSPF or IS-IS to distill a routing table. The only criterion that is important to SPF is the lowest cost for each IP prefix. For TE, however, other criteria play a role: the resources or constraints on the links. Because OSPF and IS-IS have been extended to distribute these resources, too, PCALC can calculate a path not only based on shortest path but also based on these resources. The SPF algorithm becomes a CSPF algorithm. Basically, links that do not have sufficient bandwidth or that do not have the right resources are pruned off while the SPF tree is built. Another difference with regular SPF is that PCALC or CSPF can run upon request—namely, when you configure a TE tunnel. The result of a CSPF calculation is not a routing table, but a path. This path is an explicit route, which is nothing other than a sequence of IP addresses, where each IP address represents one interface on a router. This explicit route is then used to set up or signal the TE LSP. PCALC builds exactly one path for the TE tunnel, never two or more. Therefore, it is important to know what the best path is in case multiple possible paths are presented. If multiple paths have the same cost and adhere to all the constraints, the path with the largest minimum bandwidth is chosen. If multiple paths are still possible, the path that has the fewest hops is chosen. If multiple paths still remain, Cisco IOS picks one for you.

RSVP

You need a signaling protocol for TE tunnels to ensure that link admissions happen at the interfaces of the LSRs that the TE tunnel crosses and for propagation of a label hop by hop that the traffic flowing on the TE tunnel can use. RSVP was enhanced so that it could signal TE tunnels, because RSVP was originally designed for signaling Integrated Services (IntServ). In other words, RSVP signaled quality of service (QoS) throughout the network. This protocol has seen few deployments to provide IntServ because the Differentiated Services (DiffServ) model provides the QoS these days as a result of severe scalability constraints of the IntServ model in large networks. Several new RSVP objects related to TE were defined. The TE extensions for RSVP are detailed in RFC 3209.

RSVP uses PATH and RESV messages to signal a path. The TE head end router sends the PATH messages to the tail end router, whereas the RESV messages take the exact but opposite path back to the head end router. The head end router of a TE tunnel computes the best path that the TE tunnel should take from the TE database, considering bandwidth and other constraints. Alternatively, the path is defined by an explicit path option configured by the user on the tunnel interface. In either case, the head end router knows the exact path that the TE tunnel should take. Each hop (LSR) that the TE tunnel should cross is put into an ERO, which is basically an ordered list of interface IP addresses, with one IP address per LSR. The PATH message is sent from the head end router to the next-hop router. This next-hop router removes his own IP address from the ERO, sees what the next IP address is, and sends the PATH message to that next hop. This continues until the tail end router of the TE tunnel receives the PATH message. Upon receipt of the PATH message, the tail end router returns a RESV (or reservation) message along the same path that the PATH message took, but in the opposite direction. Only when the head end receives the RESV message without an RSVP error message is the path set up or signaled and is the TE tunnel up. It is a bit more complicated than this, as you will see in the next section.

RSVP and Labels

RSVP signals the path for the TE tunnel, but it is also its task to carry the MPLS label so that the packets can be label-switched along the path of the TE tunnel. Look at Figure 8-9 to see the RSVP messages sent for the TE tunnel signaling.

Figure 8-9 *RSVP for TE and Labels*

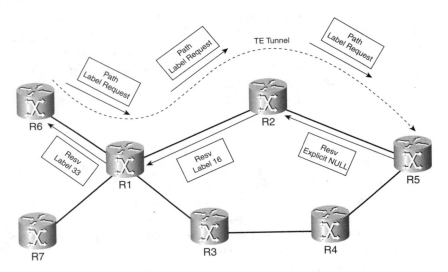

The PATH messages carry a Label Request object. When the tail end router receives this Label Request object, it assigns a label to this TE tunnel LSP and advertises it to the upstream router (the penultimate hop router) in a Label object in the RESV message. This label is the incoming label in the LFIB of the tail end router. The upstream router receives the label from the tail end router and puts this label as the outgoing label in the LFIB for this TE tunnel LSP. The router assigns a label from the global label table to this TE tunnel LSP and sends it in a Label object in the RESV message to its upstream router. This label becomes the incoming label in the LFIB for this TE tunnel LSP. It continues like this until the RESV message reaches the head end router of the TE tunnel LSP. The fact that a label is advertised from tail end router to head end router, hop-by-hop, after being requested by the head end router indicates that TE tunnels use Downstream-on-Demand (DoD) label distribution.

> **NOTE**   Because RSVP with TE extensions takes care of the distribution of the MPLS labels, you do not need to configure Label Distribution Protocol (LDP) on the interfaces. Therefore, the MPLS network does not strictly need to have **mpls ip** on the interfaces, if TE is deployed. However, if you do not deploy TE to carry all traffic from ingress LSRs to egress LSRs, you need LDP to avoid unlabeled traffic in the core network. MPLS VPN traffic, for instance, needs to be labeled at all times in the core network.

The label that the tail end router advertises is the explicit NULL label in the RESV Label object. The receiving router that is running Cisco IOS—the penultimate hop LSR—interprets this as an implicit NULL label by default. So—by default—the packet that is sent on a TE tunnel from the penultimate hop router to the tail end router has no label or the top label is popped off. Therefore, penultimate hop popping (PHP) occurs. Figure 8-10 shows the packet forwarding for packets forwarded on the TE tunnel of Figure 8-9.

Figure 8-10 *Packet Forwarding*

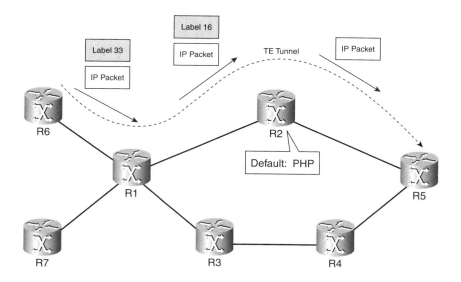

If you want the penultimate hop router to interpret the explicit NULL label as explicit NULL instead of implicit NULL, you must configure the following hidden command on the penultimate hop router:

```
mpls traffic-eng signalling interpret explicit-null verbatim
```

You use explicit NULL when you want to preserve the QoS information. Refer to Chapter 12, "MPLS and Quality of Service," for more information on this.

You can also configure the tail end router to advertise an implicit NULL label (label 3) in the Label object in the RESV message to the penultimate hop router. For this, you need the following command on the tail end router:

```
mpls traffic-eng signalling advertise implicit-null [acl-name | acl-number]
```

You can configure a standard access list or named access list to indicate to which peer routers to send the implicit NULL.

Record Route Object

Another new RSVP object is the Record Route object (RRO). PATH and RESV messages carry this object, which stores the IP addresses of the routers that the TE tunnel traversed. The path in the RSVP Path Info (Explicit Route) is usually the same as the path in the RRO, although it can differ. One example of it differing is when the TE LSP is rerouted temporarily onto a backup tunnel. See the section "FRR" for more information on backup tunnels.

You can record in the RRO the label that is associated with each hop. For an idea of where RRO can be useful to examine, look at Examples 8-13 and 8-14. A TE tunnel is created with the RRO that is enabled on the tunnel interface on the head end router. The output in Example 8-13 is taken when the tunnel is routed normally. The Explicit Route from the RSVP Path Info and the Record Route from the RSVP Resv Info show the same path.

Example 8-13 *Record Route Object*

```
paris#show mpls traffic-eng tunnel tunnel 1

Name: paris_t1                          (Tunnel1) Destination: 10.200.254.5
  Status:
    Admin: up        Oper: up      Path: valid      Signalling: connected
    path option 1, type explicit paris-rome (Basis for Setup, path weight 2)

  Config Parameters:
    Bandwidth: 100000   kbps (Global) Priority: 7  7   Affinity: 0x0/0xFFFF
    Metric Type: TE (default)
    AutoRoute: enabled  LockDown: disabled Loadshare: 100000   bw-based
    auto-bw: disabled
  Active Path Option Parameters:
    State: explicit path option 1 is active
    BandwidthOverride: disabled LockDown: disabled Verbatim: disabled

  InLabel  :  -
  OutLabel : POS4/0, 21
```

Example 8-13 *Record Route Object (Continued)*

```
    RSVP Signalling Info:
         Src 10.200.254.2, Dst 10.200.254.5, Tun_Id 1, Tun_Instance 5805
      RSVP Path Info:
        My Address: 10.200.254.2
        Explicit Route: 10.200.210.2 10.200.211.2 10.200.254.5
        Record    Route:
        Tspec: ave rate=100000 kbits, burst=1000 bytes, peak rate=100000 kbits
      RSVP Resv Info:
        Record    Route: 10.200.211.1(21) 10.200.211.2(0)
        Fspec: ave rate=100000 kbits, burst=1000 bytes, peak rate=100000 kbits
    Shortest Unconstrained Path Info:
      Path Weight: 2 (TE)
      Explicit Route: 10.200.210.2 10.200.211.2 10.200.254.5
    History:
```

The output in Example 8-14 is taken when the TE tunnel LSP is routed over a backup tunnel. (FRR is applied.) Notice the difference in the Explicit Route from the RSVP Path Info and the Record Route from the RSVP Resv Info. The TE tunnel LSP has been rerouted over the backup tunnel brussels-frankfurt-berlin.

Example 8-14 *Record Route Object with Backup Tunnel*

```
paris#show mpls traffic-eng tunnel tunnel 1

Name: paris_t1                             (Tunnel1) Destination: 10.200.254.5
  Status:
    Admin: up          Oper: up      Path: valid      Signalling: connected
    path option 1, type explicit paris-rome (Basis for Setup, path weight 2)
        Change in required resources detected: reroute pending
        Currently Signalled Parameters:
          Bandwidth: 100000    kbps (Global) Priority: 7  7   Affinity: 0x0/0xFFFF
          Metric Type: TE (default)

  Config Parameters:
    Bandwidth: 100000    kbps (Global) Priority: 7  7   Affinity: 0x0/0xFFFF
    Metric Type: TE (default)
    AutoRoute: enabled   LockDown: disabled Loadshare: 100000    bw-based
    auto-bw: disabled
  Active Path Option Parameters:
    State: explicit path option 1 is active
    BandwidthOverride: disabled  LockDown: disabled  Verbatim: disabled

  InLabel  :  -
  OutLabel : POS4/0, 21
  RSVP Signalling Info:
      Src 10.200.254.2, Dst 10.200.254.5, Tun_Id 1, Tun_Instance 5805
```

continues

Example 8-14   *Record Route Object with Backup Tunnel (Continued)*

```
   RSVP Path Info:
     My Address: 10.200.254.2
     Explicit Route: 10.200.210.2 10.200.211.2 10.200.254.5
     Record   Route:
     Tspec: ave rate=100000 kbits, burst=1000 bytes, peak rate=100000 kbits
   RSVP Resv Info:
     Record   Route:  10.200.212.1(21) 10.200.213.2(0)
     Fspec: ave rate=100000 kbits, burst=1000 bytes, peak rate=100000 kbits
 Shortest Unconstrained Path Info:
   Path Weight: 3 (TE)
   Explicit Route: 10.200.210.2 10.200.194.2 10.200.193.1 10.200.254.5
```

Other Information Carried by RSVP

The bandwidth requirement for the TE tunnel is the most important TE tunnel attribute. It is carried in the SENDER_TSPEC as average rate. Note that the value of the average rate is expressed in bytes per second.

The Session object holds the IPv4 address of the egress router, the tunnel ID, and the extended tunnel ID. Look at Figure 8-11, which shows the format of the Session object.

Figure 8-11   *Session Object*

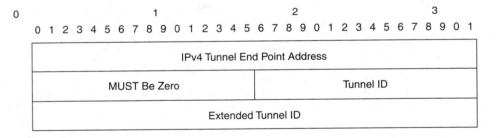

The Session attribute holds the tunnel setup and holding priority and some flags. These flags can indicate that local protection is desired, for example. In addition to that, the Session attribute in an extended format can hold the resource affinity bits. Look at Figure 8-12, which shows the format of the Session attribute.

Figure 8-12 *Session Attribute*

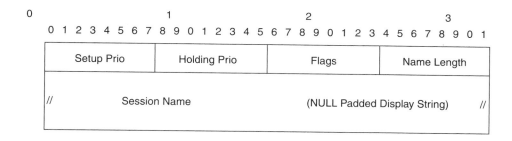

Putting It All Together

Figure 8-13 shows a network with three routers, all enabled for MPLS TE.

Figure 8-13 *RSVP PATH and RESV Advertisements*

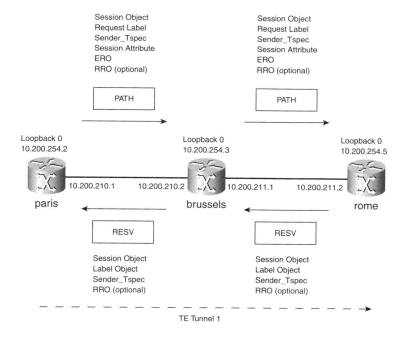

The head end router paris is configured as in Example 8-15.

Example 8-15   *Tunnel Configuration*

```
!
interface Tunnel1
 ip unnumbered Loopback0
 tunnel destination 10.200.254.5
 tunnel mode mpls traffic-eng
 tunnel mpls traffic-eng autoroute announce
 tunnel mpls traffic-eng priority 7 7
 tunnel mpls traffic-eng bandwidth 100000
 tunnel mpls traffic-eng path-option 1 explicit name paris-rome
 tunnel mpls traffic-eng record-route
 tunnel mpls traffic-eng fast-reroute

paris#show mpls traffic-eng tunnels tunnel 1

Name: paris_t1                          (Tunnel1) Destination: 10.200.254.5
  Status:
    Admin: up        Oper: up      Path: valid      Signalling: connected
    path option 1, type explicit paris-rome (Basis for Setup, path weight 2)

  Config Parameters:
    Bandwidth: 100000   kbps (Global)  Priority: 7  7   Affinity: 0x0/0xFFFF
    Metric Type: TE (default)
    AutoRoute: enabled   LockDown: disabled  Loadshare: 100000   bw-based
    auto-bw: disabled
  Active Path Option Parameters:
    State: explicit path option 1 is active
    BandwidthOverride: disabled  LockDown: disabled  Verbatim: disabled


  InLabel  :  -
  OutLabel : POS4/0, 17
  RSVP Signalling Info:
       Src 10.200.254.2, Dst 10.200.254.5, Tun_Id 1, Tun_Instance 5846
    RSVP Path Info:
      My Address: 10.200.254.2
      Explicit Route: 10.200.210.2 10.200.211.2 10.200.254.5
      Record   Route:
      Tspec: ave rate=100000 kbits, burst=1000 bytes, peak rate=100000 kbits
    RSVP Resv Info:
      Record   Route:   10.200.211.1(17) 10.200.211.2(0)
      Fspec: ave rate=100000 kbits, burst=1000 bytes, peak rate=100000 kbits
  Shortest Unconstrained Path Info:
    Path Weight: 2 (TE)
    Explicit Route: 10.200.210.2 10.200.211.2 10.200.254.5
```

Look at Example 8-16. On router paris, the command **debug ip rsvp dump-messages** shows the outgoing PATH messages and the incoming RESV messages. In the PATH message, you can see the ERO, the RRO, the Session attribute (with the tunnel priorities and the local protection desire on), and the bandwidth requested for the TE tunnel as the average rate value under Sender TSPEC. The RESV message that the paris router receives shows the complete path in the RRO and the label to be used for this TE tunnel.

Example 8-16   *debug ip rsvp dump-messages*

```
paris#
*Apr 15 : Outgoing Path:
*Apr 15 :    version:1 flags:0000 cksum:AA19 ttl:255 reserved:0 length:204
*Apr 15 :    SESSION                 type 7 length 16:
*Apr 15 :    Tun Dest:    10.200.254.5  Tun ID: 1  Ext Tun ID: 10.200.254.2
*Apr 15 :    HOP                     type 1 length 12:
*Apr 15 :    Hop Addr: 10.200.210.1 LIH: 0x5D00040E
*Apr 15 :    TIME_VALUES             type 1 length 8 :
*Apr 15 :    Refresh Period (msec): 30000
*Apr 15 :    EXPLICIT_ROUTE          type 1 length 28:
*Apr 15 :    10.200.210.2 (Strict IPv4 Prefix, 8 bytes, /32)
*Apr 15 :    10.200.211.2 (Strict IPv4 Prefix, 8 bytes, /32)
*Apr 15 :    10.200.254.5 (Strict IPv4 Prefix, 8 bytes, /32)
*Apr 15 :    LABEL_REQUEST           type 1 length 8 :
*Apr 15 :    Layer 3 protocol ID: 2048
*Apr 15 :    SESSION_ATTRIBUTE       type 7 length 16:
*Apr 15 :    Setup Prio: 7, Holding Prio: 7
*Apr 15 :    Flags: (0x7) Local Prot desired, Label Recording, SE Style
*Apr 15 :    Session Name: paris_t1
*Apr 15 :    SENDER_TEMPLATE         type 7 length 12:
*Apr 15 :    Tun Sender: 10.200.254.2  LSP ID: 5846
*Apr 15 :    SENDER_TSPEC            type 2 length 36:
*Apr 15 :    version=0, length in words=7
*Apr 15 :    Token bucket fragment (service_id=1, length=6 words
*Apr 15 :      parameter id=127, flags=0, parameter length=5
*Apr 15 :      average rate=12500000 bytes/sec, burst depth=1000 bytes
*Apr 15 :      peak rate   =12500000 bytes/sec
*Apr 15 :      min unit=0 bytes, max pkt size=4294967295 bytes
*Apr 15 :    ADSPEC                  type 2 length 48:
*Apr 15 :    version=0  length in words=10
*Apr 15 :    General Parameters  break bit=0  service length=8
*Apr 15 :                                    IS Hops:1
*Apr 15 :                Minimum Path Bandwidth (bytes/sec):19375000
*Apr 15 :                    Path Latency (microseconds):0
*Apr 15 :                                    Path MTU:4470
*Apr 15 : Controlled Load Service  break bit=0  service length=0
*Apr 15 :    RECORD_ROUTE            type 1 length 12:
*Apr 15 :    10.200.210.1/32, Flags:0x0 (No Local Protection)
```

continues

Example 8-16 *debug ip rsvp dump-messages (Continued)*

```
*Apr 15 : Incoming Resv:
*Apr 15 :   version:1 flags:0000 cksum:E553 ttl:255 reserved:0 length:144
*Apr 15 :   SESSION              type 7 length 16:
*Apr 15 :   Tun Dest:   10.200.254.5  Tun ID: 1  Ext Tun ID: 10.200.254.2
*Apr 15 :   HOP                  type 1 length 12:
*Apr 15 :   Hop Addr: 10.200.210.2 LIH: 0x5D00040E
*Apr 15 :   TIME_VALUES          type 1 length 8 :
*Apr 15 :   Refresh Period (msec): 30000
*Apr 15 :   STYLE                type 1 length 8 :
*Apr 15 :   Shared-Explicit (SE)
*Apr 15 :   FLOWSPEC             type 2 length 36:
*Apr 15 :   version = 0 length in words = 7
*Apr 15 :   service id = 5, service length = 6
*Apr 15 :   tspec parameter id = 127, flags = 0, length = 5
*Apr 15 :   average rate = 12500000 bytes/sec, burst depth = 1000 bytes
*Apr 15 :   peak rate   = 12500000 bytes/sec
*Apr 15 :   min unit = 0 bytes, max pkt size = 0 bytes
*Apr 15 :   FILTER_SPEC          type 7 length 12:
*Apr 15 :   Tun Sender: 10.200.254.2, LSP ID: 5846
*Apr 15 :   LABEL                type 1 length 8 :
*Apr 15 :   Labels: 17
*Apr 15 :   RECORD_ROUTE         type 1 length 36:
*Apr 15 :   10.200.211.1/32, Flags:0x1 (Local Prot Avail/to NHOP)
*Apr 15 :     Label subobject: Flags 0x1, C-Type 1, Label 17
*Apr 15 :   10.200.211.2/32, Flags:0x0 (No Local Protection)
*Apr 15 :     Label subobject: Flags 0x1, C-Type 1, Label 0
```

Shared Explicit Style

The Shared Explicit (SE) RSVP style that is used for TE ensures that make-before-break is issued. SE style is advertised in the PATH message, as shown in Example 8-16. This means that when an LSR needs to reroute a TE LSP, the new TE LSP is built before the old TE LSP is torn down for a specific TE tunnel. The traffic is only switched onto the new LSP when it is completely set up to avoid or reduce traffic loss. The bandwidth reserved on the links that might be used by both the old and the new TE LSP for a particular TE tunnel is not accounted for twice: once for the old LSP and once for the new LSP. The same can happen when the administrator increases the required bandwidth of an existing TE tunnel. The old and new bandwidth requirements are not reserved at the same time on shared links; rather, the highest amount of bandwidth is accounted. In Figure 8-14, one TE tunnel is reoptimizing. While this is happening, the RSVP SE style ensures the absence of bandwidth double booking on the links that are shared between the old and new LSP of this tunnel.

Figure 8-14 *RSVP SE Style*

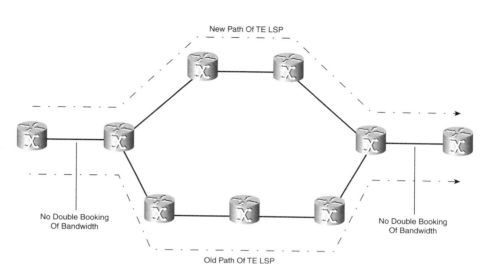

LSP Is Rerouted To More Optimal Path

New Path Of TE LSP

No Double Booking
Of Bandwidth

No Double Booking
Of Bandwidth

Old Path Of TE LSP

RSVP Messages

So far, this chapter has covered only PATH and RESV messages. However, TE can also use other RSVP messages. TE primarily uses these other messages to signal that a problem has occurred.

PathTear

A PathTear message is much like a PATH message, except it is sent when the head end router wants to signal that the TE LSP should be torn down (for instance, after an admin shut on the tunnel interface).

ResvTear

A ResvTear message is much like a RESV message, except it is sent by the tail end router in a response to the receipt of an PathTear message.

PathErr

A PathErr message is actually a message sent in the direction toward the head end router. The most common reason for this error message to be sent is that the link that was in use by a TE LSP has gone down. It could also be that an LSR received a PATH message with bogus information.

ResvErr

A ResvErr message is sent in the direction of the tail end router.

Link Manager

The link manager is a piece of the Cisco IOS TE code that does some necessary housekeeping on every TE-enabled router. It mainly does *link admission control*, which involves keeping track of the bandwidth reserved by RSVP on the links and allowing RSVP to reserve more bandwidth on the link for new tunnel setup requests. It is also the piece of software that determines which TE tunnel LSP can preempt another (by looking at the tunnel priorities) on the links. Finally, it is what triggers the IGP to flood the link state information if the thresholds of the links are crossed. Refer to the earlier section "Flooding by the IGP" for more on this. Example 8-17 shows the **show** and **debug** commands to figure out what the link manager is up to.

Example 8-17 *Checking the TE Link Manager*

```
rome#show mpls traffic-eng link-management ?
  admission-control     Link Management admission-control
  advertisements        Link Management advertisements
  bandwidth-allocation  Link Management bandwidth-allocation
  igp-neighbors         Link Management igp-neighbors
  interfaces            Link Management Traffic Engineering interfaces
  statistics            Link Management Traffic Engineering statistics
  summary               Link Management summary
rome#debug mpls traffic-eng link-management ?
  admission-control     Link admission control
  advertisements        Link state advertisements
  bandwidth-allocation  Link bandwidth allocation
  errors                Link Management errors
  events                Link Management process events
  igp-neighbors         Link IGP-neighbor adjacencies
  links                 Link configuration activity
  preemption            Link Management preemption
  routing               Link local routing decisions
```

> **NOTE**   RSVP for TE does not reserve bandwidth in the data plane on the interface level. What happens is that the link admission software on each node keeps track of how much bandwidth the TE tunnels have reserved on each interface in the control plane. As such, RSVP for TE does not provide QoS on the interface level on the router.

FRR

TE is usually enabled in the core network, where the capacity of the links is high. If a link or a router fails, traffic is rerouted around the failure. This rerouting happens for IP and for MPLS traffic relatively fast. However, even if the rerouting takes only a few seconds, it might mean that a lot of traffic is dropped to the point of failure because of the high capacity of the links. For certain traffic, such as Voice over IP (VoIP), this can be devastating for the service. Although links can potentially be protected at Layer 1—for example, with a mechanism called automatic protection switching (APS)—having a protection at the level of MPLS is best. APS is a well-known mechanism for protecting optical links. A disadvantage of APS is that for every protected link, a backup link and a card on either side are waiting idle until they are needed and the failing protected optical link is switched over to this backup link.

Link and node protection with TE is more efficient because an idle backup link for every protected link is not needed. Therefore, link and node protection used with TE is cheaper than an optical protection scheme. A backup tunnel for each protected link or node is created in advance. That means no time is wasted by having to signal the backup tunnel when the protected device fails. This time can be quite long because a path must be computed for the backup tunnel, and then it must be signaled. The following two sections explain the local protection schemes possible with TE: link protection and node protection. The two schemes have one thing in common: The repair is done as close to the point of failure as possible. Both methods provide local repair. As such, they are pretty fast and reroute the LSPs from the protected link onto the backup tunnel in tens of milliseconds. A number you might hear a lot is the 50-msec one. That is because this number is also referred to a lot when talking of the switchover time of SONET links. Link and node protection with MPLS TE is referred to as FRR.

> **NOTE**   Not only traffic should flow onto the backup tunnel when the backup tunnel is active for the rerouted TE tunnel; signaling (RSVP) messages should also take the backup tunnel so that the rerouted TE tunnel remains signaled.

FRR—Link Protection

With link protection, one particular link used for TE is protected. This means that all TE tunnels that are crossing this link are protected by one backup tunnel. This technique is also called *facility backup* because a complete link—with all its TE LSPs—is backed up. Figure 8-15 shows a simple network whereby the link R1-R2 is protected by a backup tunnel R1-R3-R2. This backup tunnel protects only the TE tunnels in the direction from R1 to R2. Therefore, to protect all tunnels crossing the link R1-R2 in *both* directions, you need another backup tunnel R2-R3-R1.

Figure 8-15 *Link Protection*

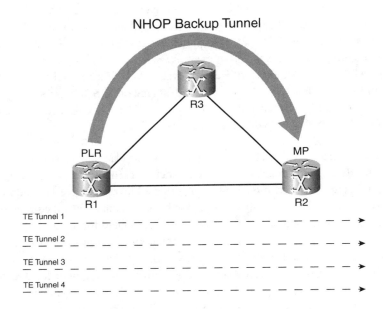

In the case of link protection, the backup tunnel is also called a *next-hop (NHOP) bypass tunnel* and always starts on the point of local repair (PLR). The PLR here is router R1. The backup tunnel for link protection always connects to the next-hop router; this means the router at the remote end of the link. This router is the merge point (MP), because this is the router where the protected tunnel and backup tunnel merge. The backup tunnel is an explicit path tunnel that RSVP signals. The backup tunnel in Figure 8-15 is only two hops, but it can be as many hops as you want. When the backup tunnel is created, RSVP signals the labels as usual. In Figure 8-16, R2 signals R3 to use label 3 (the implicit NULL label), and R3 signals R1 to use label 16 for the backup tunnel.

Figure 8-16 *RSVP Signals Labels for Backup Tunnel*

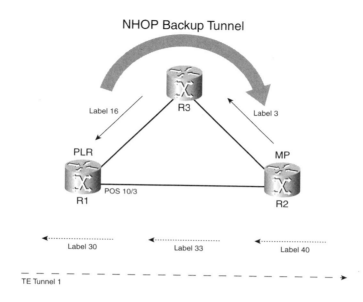

The TE tunnel 1 is crossing the link R1-R2. Look at Figure 8-17 to see the packet forwarding for tunnel 1, when the protection is not yet in use.

Figure 8-17 *Packet Forwarding for Tunnel 1*

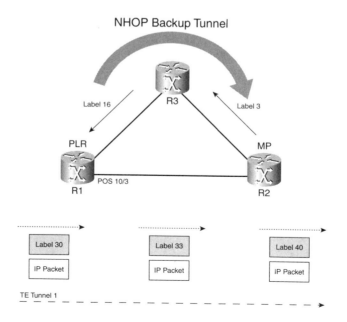

The packets on the LSP of tunnel 1 are coming in on router R1 with a label of 30. This label is swapped with label 33 when the packet leaves router R1. Finally, label 33 is swapped with label 40, outgoing from router R2. Look at Figure 8-18 to see what happens concerning the packet forwarding when the link R1-R2 fails. As soon as the link R1-R2 fails, the PLR (here R1) starts to send the traffic on TE tunnel 1 onto the NHOP backup tunnel across R3.

Figure 8-18 *Packet Forwarding for Tunnel 1 with FRR Active*

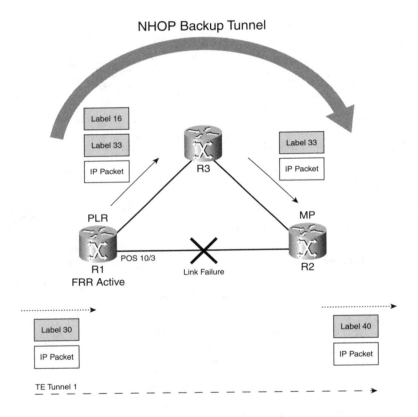

The incoming packets on R1 are label swapped as before: Label 30 is swapped with label 33. Then the additional label for the NHOP tunnel, label 16, is pushed onto the packet. The packet is label-switched on the NHOP backup tunnel until it reaches router R2 (the MP), the tail end router of the protected link. Notice that the packet arrives at R2 with label 33. When the link R1-R2 was not failing, the packet arrived at router R2 with the same label. The only difference is that now the packet arrives at R2 via another interface. Because the platform-wide label space is used, this does not cause a problem. As long as the interface uses the platform-wide label space (and not an LC-ATM interface, for example), the router does not check on which MPLS-enabled interface a labeled packet arrives.

The PLR should use this backup tunnel to carry TE LSPs only briefly. The protection is temporary, because the link failure triggers the PLR to send a PathErr to the head end router of the TE tunnel. When the head end router of the protected TE tunnel receives the PathErr, it recalculates a new path for the tunnel LSP and signals it. When the head end router completes the signaling, the whole LSP is rerouted through the network. The protected TE LSP no longer uses the backup tunnel.

NOTE   Normally, the receipt of a PathErr by the head end router makes the tunnel go down until the TE LSP is rerouted. This does not happen in the case of FRR, though. The PathErr that the PLR sends indicates that Local Repair is active. This status signals the head end router that it should not take the tunnel down while trying to find another path for the TE LSP. If the tunnel goes down, traffic is lost, which defeats the purpose of FRR.

The IGP also signals the link failure. When the PLR uses the backup tunnel to route a protected LSP, the PLR sends the PATH messages of the protected tunnel onto the backup tunnel as long as the backup tunnel is in use.

A disadvantage of using link protection is that the NHOP tunnel protects a complete link. At any time, any number of TE LSPs with a certain amount of bandwidth might be crossing the protected link. Therefore, the total protected bandwidth can vary quite a lot in time. Furthermore, the backup tunnel does not reserve bandwidth. Therefore, when protected tunnels use the backup tunnel, it is possible that not enough bandwidth is available to switch all traffic. Traffic might be dropped as a result. However, the protected tunnels should use the backup tunnel temporarily only, because the head end routers of the respective protected TE tunnels should reroute the TE LSPs while reserving enough bandwidth.

This reroute of the protected TE LSP is not possible if the head end router cannot find another feasible path. An example of such a case is a TE tunnel that has only one explicit path option and no dynamic one. If the protected link goes down, the backup link is used as long as the protected link is down, because the head end router cannot calculate another path through the network. The TE tunnel is stuck with its explicit path. To solve this, you can configure a dynamic path option with a higher number than the explicit path option. In that case, when the protected link goes down, the tunnel can use the backup tunnel until the head end router uses the dynamic path option and reroutes the tunnel via an alternative path.

The backup tunnel is preconfigured on the PLR router. You can specify the backup tunnel with the interface command **mpls traffic-eng backup-path** on the protected link. You configure the backup tunnel with an explicit path from the PLR to the next-hop router. On the head end router of the protected TE tunnel, you specify that the tunnel can use a backup tunnel (be fast rerouted) with the command **tunnel mpls traffic-eng fast-reroute**. This command sets the flag in the Session attribute object to 1, indicating that the tunnel wants local protection.

Look at Figure 8-7 again. Tunnel 1 on router paris to router rome is dynamically set up, and FRR is enabled on the tunnel interface. Router brussels has a backup tunnel 1000 protecting the link brussels-berlin. You configure this with the **mpls traffic-eng backup-path** command on the interface pos 10/3. This backup tunnel has an explicit path option routing the tunnel on the path brussels-frankfurt-berlin, thus avoiding the link brussels-berlin. Example 8-18 shows the configuration for setting up FRR link protection in this scenario. Notice that the PLR holds a FRR database. It shows, among other things, the incoming label and the outgoing label when the backup tunnel is used. When the state of the backup tunnel is *ready*, the tunnel is signaled but is not used for FRR at this moment. When the state is *active*, the backup tunnel is used to reroute a number of TE tunnel LSPs. The third possibility is the state *partial*, meaning that the backup tunnel is not signaled yet.

Example 8-18 *Backup Tunnel Configuration for Link Protection*

```
brussels#
!
interface Tunnel1000
 ip unnumbered Loopback0
 tunnel destination 10.200.254.5
 tunnel mode mpls traffic-eng
 tunnel mpls traffic-eng path-option 1 explicit name link-bru-ber
!
interface POS10/3
 ip address 10.200.211.1 255.255.255.0
 mpls traffic-eng tunnels
 mpls traffic-eng backup-path Tunnel1000
 ip rsvp bandwidth 155000
!
ip explicit-path name link-bru-ber enable
 next-address 10.200.212.2
 next-address 10.200.213.2
!

paris#
!
interface Tunnel1
 ip unnumbered Loopback0
 tunnel destination 10.200.254.6
 tunnel mode mpls traffic-eng
 tunnel mpls traffic-eng autoroute announce
 tunnel mpls traffic-eng bandwidth  155000
 tunnel mpls traffic-eng path-option 10 dynamic
 tunnel mpls traffic-eng fast-reroute
!
```

Example 8-18 *Backup Tunnel Configuration for Link Protection (Continued)*

```
brussels#show mpls traffic-eng fast-reroute database detail
LFIB FRR Database Summary:
  Total Clusters:      1
  Total Groups:        1
  Total Items:         1
Link 17: PO10/3 (Up, 1 group)
  Group 39: PO10/3->Tu1000 (Up, 1 member)
    LSP identifier 10.200.254.2 1 [1113], ready
      Input label 26, Output label PO10/3:17, FRR label Tu1000:17
```

Regular traffic should not use the backup tunnel. Therefore, the backup tunnel should not have **autoroute announce** or **forwarding adjacency** configured. See the later section titled "Forwarding Traffic onto MPLS TE Tunnels" to read up on how to forward traffic onto TE tunnels. Furthermore, make sure that the protected link and the links that the backup tunnel uses are not sharing the same infrastructure. Refer to the section titled "SRLG Used by Backup Tunnels" for more on this.

You can configure the backup tunnel as an explicit path. However, you can also configure it as an exclude path. This is an explicit path, but you only need to exclude a hop (an LSR). With backup tunnels, obviously, you must exclude the protected link from the path. Refer to the earlier section titled "IP Explicit Address Exclusion" for more information on excluding an IP address from an explicit path.

FRR—Node Protection

With FRR for Node Protection, you are not trying to protect only one link, but rather a whole router. Node protection works by creating a next-next-hop (NNHOP) backup tunnel. An NNHOP backup tunnel is not a tunnel to the next-hop router of the PLR, but to the router that is one hop behind the protected router. Therefore, in the case of node protection, the NNHOP router is the MP router. When you configure the command **tunnel mpls traffic-eng fast-reroute node-protect** on the head end of the TE tunnel, it sets the flag to 0x10 in the Session attribute of the PATH messages, indicating that it wants node protection.

Look at Figure 8-19, which has one NNHOP backup tunnel protecting the router berlin.

Figure 8-19 *Node Protection*

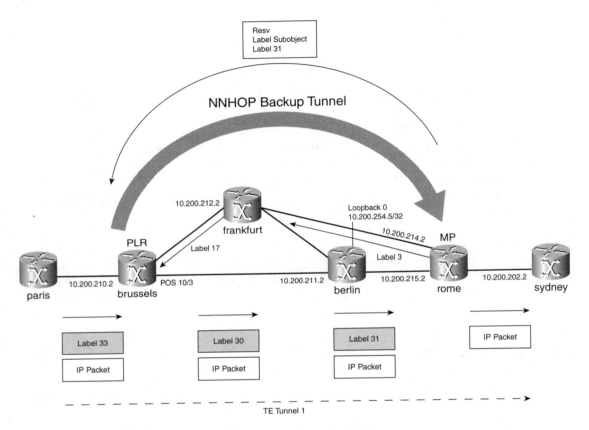

One TE tunnel goes from router paris to router sydney. An NNHOP backup tunnel 2000 goes from router brussels (the PLR) to router rome (the NNHOP and the MP). This backup tunnel avoids router berlin altogether by specifying the router berlin in the explicit path as excluded. This is done by specifying the MPLS TE router ID of router berlin as an excluded IP address in the explicit path.

Two issues make node protection a bit more complicated. The first issue is that the packets no longer arrive at the NHOP LSR, but at the NNHOP LSR. This means that the PLR somehow must learn the correct label to use for the NNHOP backup tunnel so that the packets arrive with the same top label at the NNHOP router as when the NNHOP backup tunnel is not used. To solve this problem, the label is advertised in a label subobject in an RRO object in a RESV message from the NNHOP router to the PLR router. When packets come in on the PLR on the rerouted LSP, the

PLR must swap the incoming label with this label first and then push the label of the NNHOP backup tunnel. The second issue is that the backup tunnel is avoiding a router altogether that was on the rerouted LSP. The ERO in the PATH messages still holds the IP addresses of the protected router, even though that router is bypassed. The PLR must send the PATH messages onto the NNHOP tunnel for everything to keep working correctly. Figure 8-20 shows the packet forwarding when the PLR uses the NNHOP backup tunnel to forward traffic of TE tunnel 1.

Figure 8-20 *Node Protection Active*

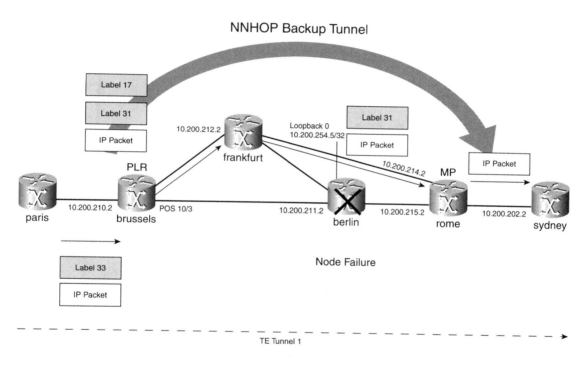

Example 8-19 shows the configuration of the NNHOP tunnel on router brussels and the TE tunnel from router paris to router sydney.

Example 8-19 *Backup Tunnel Configuration for Node Protection*

```
brussels#
interface Tunnel2000
 ip unnumbered Loopback0
 tunnel destination 10.200.254.6
 tunnel mode mpls traffic-eng
 tunnel mpls traffic-eng path-option 1 explicit name exclude-berlin
!
interface POS10/3
```

continues

Example 8-19 *Backup Tunnel Configuration for Node Protection (Continued)*

```
 ip address 10.200.211.1 255.255.255.0
 mpls traffic-eng tunnels
 mpls traffic-eng backup-path Tunnel2000
 ip rsvp bandwidth 155000
!
ip explicit-path name exclude-berlin enable
 exclude-address 10.200.254.5

paris#
!
interface Tunnel1
 ip unnumbered Loopback0
 tunnel destination 10.200.254.7
 tunnel mode mpls traffic-eng
 tunnel mpls traffic-eng autoroute announce
 tunnel mpls traffic-eng priority 7 7
 tunnel mpls traffic-eng bandwidth  1000
 tunnel mpls traffic-eng path-option 10 explicit name one
 tunnel mpls traffic-eng fast-reroute node-protect
!
ip explicit-path name one enable
 next-address 10.200.210.2
 next-address 10.200.211.2
 next-address 10.200.215.2
 next-address 10.200.202.2
!
```

Example 8-20 includes a traceroute across TE tunnel 1 to prove that the packets receive two labels instead of one when the backup tunnel is active. Also, whether the backup tunnel is in use or not, the packets on the TE tunnel 1 arrive on router rome with label 31 as the top label, even though the incoming interface is different when the TE LSP is rerouted versus when it is not.

Example 8-20 *Verifying the NNHOP Tunnel*

```
paris#show mpls traffic-eng tunnels tunnel 1 protection
paris_t1
  LSP Head, Tunnel1, Admin: up, Oper: up
  Src 10.200.254.2, Dest 10.200.254.7, Instance 1223
  Fast Reroute Protection: Requested
    Outbound: Unprotected: no backup tunnel assigned
      LSP signalling info:
        Original: out i/f: PO4/0, label: 33, nhop: 10.200.210.2
                  nhop: 10.200.215.1; nhop rtr id: 10.200.254.6
  Path Protection: None
```

Example 8-20 *Verifying the NNHOP Tunnel (Continued)*

```
brussels#show mpls traffic-eng fast-reroute database detail
LFIB FRR Database Summary:
  Total Clusters:       1
  Total Groups:         1
  Total Items:          1
Link 17: PO10/3 (Up, 1 group)
  Group 40: PO10/3->Tu2000 (Up, 1 member)
    LSP identifier 10.200.254.2 1 [1223], ready
       Input label 33, Output label PO10/3:17, FRR label Tu2000:31

brussels#show ip rsvp fast-reroute
Primary                 Protect BW        Backup
Tunnel                  I/F     BPS:Type  Tunnel:Label  State  Level    Type
------                  ------- --------  ------------- ------ -----    ------
rome_t1                 PO10/2  0:G       None          None   None
paris_t1                PO10/3  1M:G      Tu2000:31     Ready  any-unl  N-Nhop

!Traceroute when the NNHOP backup tunnel is not used
paris#traceroute 10.200.254.7

Type escape sequence to abort.
Tracing the route to 10.200.254.7

  1 10.200.210.2 [MPLS: Label 33 Exp 0] 24 msec 24 msec 24 msec
  2 10.200.211.2 [MPLS: Label 30 Exp 0] 24 msec 24 msec 24 msec
  3 10.200.215.2 [MPLS: Label 31 Exp 0] 0 msec 0 msec 0 msec
  4 10.200.202.1 8 msec *  8 msec

!Traceroute when the NNHOP backup tunnel is not used
paris#traceroute 10.200.254.7

Type escape sequence to abort.
Tracing the route to 10.200.254.7

  1 10.200.210.2 [MPLS: Label 33 Exp 0] 24 msec 24 msec 24 msec
  2 10.200.212.2 [MPLS: Labels 17/31 Exp 0] 24 msec 24 msec 24 msec
  3 10.200.214.2 [MPLS: Label 31 Exp 0] 0 msec 0 msec 4 msec
  4 10.200.202.1 8 msec *  8 msec
```

SRLG Used by Backup Tunnels

You should use SRLG when a backup tunnel can potentially be routed across a link that is on the same fiber or conduit as the protected link. If you configure the protected link and all other links that share the same fiber or conduit with the same SRLG identifier, the backup tunnel avoids those links.

> **NOTE** Backup auto tunnels, which routers automatically create, can use the SRLG of protected links to ensure that they are not routed across them. Refer to the section titled "Backup Auto Tunnels" in the Chapter 8 online supplement for more on this.

On the interfaces of the links that share the same fiber or conduit, configure the SRLG command **mpls traffic-eng srlg** *number*. *Number* is the group identifier of the SRLG.

A link can even be part of several SRLG groups at the same time. You use the following global command to indicate how to treat the SRLG concerning backup auto tunnels:

```
mpls traffic-eng auto-tunnel backup srlg exclude [force | preferred]
```

The **SRLG** command has two keywords: **force** and **preferred**. The **force** keyword ensures that a backup TE tunnel is never routed over a link that has the same SRLG as the protected link, no matter what. If a link with another SRLG is not available to the backup tunnel, the backup tunnel is not created. The **preferred** keyword indicates that if a link with another SRLG is not found first to route the backup tunnel across, the backup tunnel is created across a link with the same SRLG. Look at Example 8-21 for an example of SRLG.

Example 8-21 *Verifying SRLG Membership of TE Links*

```
paris#show mpls traffic-eng topology brief
My_System_id: 10.200.254.2 (ospf 1  area 0)

Signalling error holddown: 10 sec Global Link Generation 876

IGP Id: 10.200.254.1, MPLS TE Id:10.200.254.1 Router Node  (ospf 1  area 0)
      link[0]: Broadcast, DR: 10.200.200.2, nbr_node_id:57, gen:464
  frag_id 0, Intf Address:10.200.200.1
  TE metric:20, IGP metric:10, attribute_flags:0x0
  SRLGs: 100

IGP Id: 10.200.254.2, MPLS TE Id:10.200.254.2 Router Node  (ospf 1  area 0)
      link[0]: Broadcast, DR: 10.200.200.2, nbr_node_id:57, gen:447
  frag_id 2, Intf Address:10.200.200.2
  TE metric:10, IGP metric:10, attribute_flags:0x0
  SRLGs: None

      link[1]: Point-to-Point, Nbr IGP Id: 10.200.254.3, nbr_node_id:62, gen:876
```

Example 8-21 *Verifying SRLG Membership of TE Links (Continued)*

```
  frag_id 0, Intf Address:10.200.210.1, Nbr Intf Address:10.200.210.2
  TE metric:1, IGP metric:1, attribute_flags:0x0
  SRLGs: 1 2

paris#show mpls traffic-eng topology srlg
(ospf 1  area 0)
  SRLG:       Intf Addr:      MPLS TE Id:
  1           10.200.210.1    10.200.254.2


  2           10.200.210.1    10.200.254.2


  100         10.200.200.1    10.200.254.1
```

Multiple Backup Tunnels

Multiple backup tunnels can protect the same link or node, and they can terminate at different tail end routers. These backup tunnels can be a mix of NHOP and NNHOP. The PLR prefers an NNHOP over an NHOP backup tunnel when assigning a protected TE LSP to a backup tunnel. When the failure happens, it is possible for the TE LSPs on the protected link to switch over to several backup tunnels. Furthermore, one backup tunnel can be used to protect multiple links. This increases the scalability considerably, because it is not necessary to have a backup tunnel for every link in the network. When multiple backup tunnels are configured, each protected TE LSP is assigned to one backup tunnel. This action is evaluated periodically in Cisco IOS because conditions in the network can change. For more information on this, see the online section "Bandwidth Protection on Backup Tunnels" at www.ciscopress.com/title/1587051974.

Forwarding Traffic onto MPLS TE Tunnels

Creating a TE tunnel and having it operational is one thing. Making sure that it is used to forward traffic is another. You can enable the TE tunnel to forward traffic in six ways:

- Static routing

- Policy-based routing

- Autoroute announce

- Forwarding adjacency

- Direct mapping of AToM traffic onto TE tunnels

- Class-based tunnel selection

Static Routing

A straightforward and simple way to send traffic into the TE tunnel is to configure a static route on the tunnel head end router. You just have to configure the TE tunnel as the outgoing interface in the static route. See Example 8-22 for the configuration.

Example 8-22 *Static Routing into TE Tunnel*

```
paris#conf t
Enter configuration commands, one per line.  End with CNTL/Z.
paris(config)#ip route 10.200.254.7 255.255.255.255 tunnel 1
paris(config)#^Z
paris#show ip route 10.200.254.7
Routing entry for 10.200.254.7/32
  Known via "static", distance 1, metric 0 (connected)
  Routing Descriptor Blocks:
  * directly connected, via Tunnel1
      Route metric is 0, traffic share count is 1
```

Policy-Based Routing

Policy-based routing (PBR) uses a configured policy on the incoming interface to send traffic to a specific next hop. When using PBR, you can route traffic on criteria that differ from the usual routing based solely on the destination IP address. For instance, you can route traffic based on the source IP address or the protocol type.

Example 8-23 shows PBR with a TE tunnel as the outgoing interface. The route map *pbr* is used to switch traffic with source IP address 10.200.254.1 and destination IP address 10.200.254.7 to TE tunnel 1. While directing traffic to the output interface, you can use the route map, for example, to set the precedence of these packets. In this example, the precedence is set to 3 (flash). The default behavior is to copy the IP precedence value to the Experimental (EXP) bits in the imposed labels of the packet when the packet is forwarded onto the TE tunnel. Therefore, the EXP bits value in the labels of the packets that are policy-routed into the TE tunnel in this example is also 3. You can use PBR to send voice traffic onto the TE tunnel, for example.

Example 8-23 *Configuring Policy-Based Routing*

```
!
interface Ethernet1/1
 ip address 10.200.200.2 255.255.255.0
 ip policy route-map pbr
!
route-map pbr permit 10
 match ip address 100
```

Example 8-23 *Configuring Policy-Based Routing (Continued)*

```
 set interface Tunnel1
 set ip precedence flash
!
access-list 100 permit ip host 10.200.254.1 host 10.200.254.7

paris#show route-map pbr
route-map pbr, permit, sequence 10
  Match clauses:
    ip address (access-lists): 100
  Set clauses:
    interface Tunnel1
    ip precedence flash
  Policy routing matches: 12 packets, 720 bytes

london#traceroute
Protocol [ip]:
Target IP address: 10.200.254.7
Source address: 10.200.254.1
Numeric display [n]:
Timeout in seconds [3]:
Probe count [3]:
Minimum Time to Live [1]:
Maximum Time to Live [30]:
Port Number [33434]:
Loose, Strict, Record, Timestamp, Verbose[none]:
Type escape sequence to abort.
Tracing the route to 10.200.254.7

  1 10.200.200.2 0 msec 0 msec 0 msec
  2 10.200.210.2 [MPLS: Label 25 Exp 3] 4 msec 0 msec 0 msec
  3 10.200.212.2 [MPLS: Label 21 Exp 3] 4 msec 0 msec 0 msec
  4 10.200.214.2 0 msec 4 msec 0 msec
  5 10.200.202.1 8 msec *  8 msec
```

Autoroute Announce

Tunnel mpls traffic-eng autoroute announce is the command configured on the tunnel interface on the MPLS TE tunnel head end router so that the LSR can insert IP destinations into the routing table with the TE tunnel as next hop or outgoing interface. Basically, **autoroute announce** modifies the SPF algorithm so that the LSR can insert IP prefixes downstream of the closest TE tunnel tail end router into the routing table of the head end router with that TE tunnel as next hop. To understand what this means, look at Figure 8-21.

Figure 8-21 *autoroute announce on Several TE Tunnels*

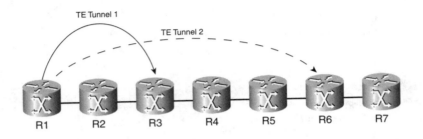

Router 1 is the head end router of the TE tunnels 1 and 2. The tail end router of tunnel 1 is router R3, and the tail end router of tunnel 2 is the router R6. With **autoroute announce** enabled for both tunnels, IP prefixes that are attached to routers R3, R4, and R5 have tunnel 1 as the next hop in the routing table of R1. IP prefixes that are attached to routers R6 and R7 have tunnel 2 as the next hop in the routing table of R1, because the tail end router of tunnel 2 (router R6) is closer than the tail end router of tunnel 1 (router R3).

Forwarding Adjacency

Forwarding adjacency is an MPLS TE feature whereby the IGP can see a TE LSP as a link. The IGP on the head end router of the TE tunnel advertises the TE LSP as a link with a certain IGP metric associated with it. Any router in the same area as the head end router then includes this link when it is running the SPF algorithm. As such, the IGP sees the total path that a TE tunnel spans as one link only. To correctly use forwarding adjacency, you must configure two TE tunnels between a pair of LSRs—one for each direction—and you must have forwarding adjacency enabled for both. The reason for this is that the link is advertised as soon as you configure forwarding adjacency on the tunnel in one direction, but the forwarding adjacency link is included in the SPF calculation of the routers only when they can see the link in both directions (this means when the forwarding adjacency is enabled on both tunnels). You can locate the pair of LSRs with the two TE tunnels between them anywhere in the MPLS TE-enabled area. The LSRs can be several hops from each other. This is the great advantage of forwarding adjacency: A pair of TE tunnels can be seen as one link and advertised as such into the IGP. This also means that routers that are not running MPLS TE but are running the IGP can see that link and consider it when running the SPF algorithm.

Because the pair of TE tunnels is advertised into the IGP as one link, it can be seen in the topology database of OSPF or IS-IS. Forwarding adjacency is enabled on the tunnel interface on the head end router with the following command:

```
tunnel mpls traffic-eng forwarding-adjacency {holdtime value}
```

The holdtime value is the time in milliseconds that the router must wait to flood, after the TE LSP has gone down. Example 8-24 shows the configuration of a TE tunnel, whereby the TE tunnel is announced as a link into OSPF. Note that IS-IS also supports forwarding adjacency. On the tail end router (10.200.254.6), you must configure a TE tunnel with this router (paris) as the tail end router and with forwarding adjacency enabled. You can see that the TE tunnel is announced as a link in OSPF. It is announced in the router LSA of the router paris, as the link with Router Interface address 0.0.0.15. This is obviously not the real IP address. Because the TE tunnel is unnumbered, OSPF cannot use the interface IP address. Instead, OSPF uses the If Index to uniquely identify the interface. OSPF identifies other unnumbered links in the same way.

Example 8-24 *Configuration of Forwarding Adjacency*

```
paris#
!
interface Tunnel1
 ip unnumbered Loopback0
 ip ospf cost 1
 tunnel destination 10.200.254.6
 tunnel mode mpls traffic-eng
 tunnel mpls traffic-eng forwarding-adjacency
 tunnel mpls traffic-eng priority 7 7
 tunnel mpls traffic-eng bandwidth  155000
!
paris#show mpls traffic-eng forwarding-adjacency
  destination 10.200.254.6, area ospf 1  area 0, has 1 tunnels
    Tunnel1     (load balancing metric 12903, nexthop 10.200.254.6)
                (flags:  Forward-Adjacency, holdtime 0)

paris#show ip ospf database router adv-router 10.200.254.2

            OSPF Router with ID (10.200.254.2) (Process ID 1)

                Router Link States (Area 0)

  LS age: 6
  Options: (No TOS-capability, DC)
  LS Type: Router Links
  Link State ID: 10.200.254.2
  Advertising Router: 10.200.254.2
  LS Seq Number: 80000039
  Checksum: 0x5DD5
```

continues

Example 8-24 *Configuration of Forwarding Adjacency (Continued)*

```
Length: 108
Number of Links: 7


  Link connected to: another Router (point-to-point)
  (Link ID) Neighboring Router ID: 10.200.254.6
  (Link Data) Router Interface address: 0.0.0.15
   Number of TOS metrics: 0
   TOS 0 Metrics: 1
...
```

Figure 8-22 shows an example where forwarding adjacency is useful.

Figure 8-22 *Forwarding Adjacency Example*

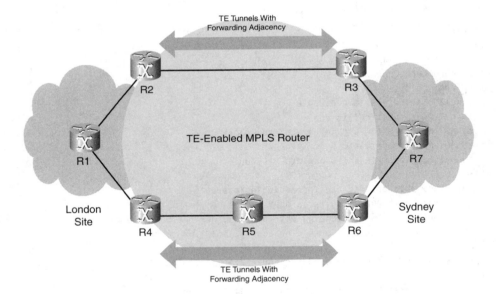

The traffic from R1 to R7—from the london site to the sydney site—takes the path R1-R2-R3-R7 because it is the shortest. If a TE tunnel were enabled from R2 to R3 and another from R4 to R6, the traffic from R1 to R7 would take the top TE tunnel, no matter how much you make the bottom TE tunnel more preferred over the top one. That is because the IP traffic can only be directed onto the TE tunnel on the head end router. The head end routers are R2 and R4 here. All other routers are unaware that the tunnel exists because it is not announced as a link in the IGP. Therefore, when R1 sends traffic to R7, it forwards the traffic to R2, which then forwards the traffic across the top TE tunnel to R3.

When forwarding adjacency is enabled on routers R2, R4, R3, and R6, the TE tunnels appear as a link on those four routers. This link is advertised via OSPF or IS-IS and is known to the routers R1 and R7. R1 includes the two links corresponding to the two TE tunnels in the SPF calculation when building its routing table. If the bottom forwarding adjacency link has the lowest IGP cost, R1 forwards traffic to R4 and over the bottom path toward R7. If the two forwarding adjacency links have the same IGP cost, R1 can even load-balance the traffic over the paths R1-R2-R3-R7 and R1-R4-R5-R6-R7. The result is that the bottom path is now utilized for the traffic between the london and sydney sites.

> **NOTE**   It is pointless to configure **mpls traffic-eng tunnels** on an MPLS TE tunnel interface, even when forwarding adjacency is enabled on it. You cannot use an MPLS TE tunnel to route other TE tunnel LSPs on it.

Direct Mapping of AToM Traffic onto TE Tunnels

A direct mapping of AToM traffic onto TE tunnels can exist. This is explained in the section titled "AToM Tunnel Selection" in Chapter 10, "Any Transport over MPLS."

Class-Based Tunnel Selection

Class-based tunnel selection (CBTS) is a TE feature whereby you can forward different class of service (CoS) traffic onto different TE tunnels. These TE tunnels can be global pool tunnels or sub-pool tunnels, but all the TE tunnels must be between the same head end and tail end routers. Furthermore, when you want to route CoS traffic onto these tunnels for one destination, you must route *all* the traffic for this destination onto these tunnels. In other words, if you have traffic for a destination routed onto the CBTS tunnels, you cannot have part of the traffic for the same destination forwarded outside of these tunnels on an LSP or as IP traffic. Basically, the LSR checks the IP precedence bits or the EXP bits value of the incoming label. Based on the value, the LSR routes the packet onto one TE tunnel that is enabled with CBTS. Because the administrator might want to change the EXP bits value of the incoming packet to a different value (for example, with MQC), the EXP bits value is checked after the MQC operation when making a decision about what TE tunnel is the next hop for the traffic.

You can directly apply the CBTS feature on TE tunnels with a PE router as the head end router and the incoming traffic from a virtual routing/forwarding (VRF) interface. You can map each EXP bits value to a particular TE tunnel. Three bits for the EXP bits give you eight levels of QoS, so you can even use eight TE tunnels between a pair of LSRs and map each EXP bits value to a different TE tunnel. The command to assign CBTS to a TE tunnel is as follows:

```
tunnel mpls traffic-eng exp [list-of-exp-values] [default]
```

The default keyword that is assigned to a TE tunnel ensures that the EXP bits that are not explicitly mapped to any other TE tunnel are mapped to that TE tunnel. Look at Example 8-25. EXP bits value 5 is mapped to tunnel 2, and all the other EXP bits values are mapped to tunnel 1.

Example 8-25   *CBTS*

```
!
interface Tunnel1
 ip unnumbered Loopback0
 tunnel destination 10.200.254.6
 tunnel mode mpls traffic-eng
 tunnel mpls traffic-eng autoroute announce
 tunnel mpls traffic-eng path-option 10 dynamic
 tunnel mpls traffic-eng exp default
!
interface Tunnel2
 ip unnumbered Loopback0
 tunnel destination 10.200.254.6
 tunnel mode mpls traffic-eng
 tunnel mpls traffic-eng autoroute announce
 tunnel mpls traffic-eng path-option 10 dynamic
 tunnel mpls traffic-eng exp 5
!
paris#show ip route 10.200.254.7
Routing entry for 10.200.254.7/32
  Known via "ospf 1", distance 110, metric 68, type intra area
  Routing Descriptor Blocks:
  * directly connected, via Tunnel2
      Route metric is 68, traffic share count is 1
    directly connected, via Tunnel1
      Route metric is 68, traffic share count is 1

paris#show mpls forwarding-table 10.200.254.7 detail
Local  Outgoing     Prefix          Bytes tag  Outgoing    Next Hop
tag    tag or VC    or Tunnel Id    switched   interface
20     Untagged     10.200.254.7/32 14848      Tu2         point2point
         MAC/Encaps=4/8, MRU=4470, Tag Stack{21}, via PO4/0
         FF030281 00015000
         No output feature configured
         Per-exp selection: 5
       Untagged     10.200.254.7/32 347134     Tu1         point2point
         MAC/Encaps=4/8, MRU=4470, Tag Stack{18}, via PO4/0
         FF030281 00012000
         No output feature configured
         Per-exp selection: 0  1  2  3  4  6  7
```

NOTE   You are not allowed to load-balance traffic with the same EXP bits value onto two different TE tunnels with CBTS.

Cost Calculation of IGP Routes over TE Tunnels

Knowing the metric for prefixes with TE tunnels as next hop might not be as straightforward as you think. This section explains how to calculate the cost of the prefixes with TE tunnels as the next hop, each time with autoroute announce enabled on the tunnel interface. When you are using autoroute announce, the cost of the TE tunnel *as used by the IGP* for the prefixes with the TE tunnel as next hop is *always* the lowest IGP total cost of the path. This cost is the path weight you see under Shortest Unconstrained Path Info when looking at a TE tunnel. The only exception to this is when you use TE metrics. See the earlier section "Dual TE Metrics" for more on this.

Default Cost Calculation

Figure 8-23 shows a network of five OSPF routers in one MPLS TE-enabled area. All links have an OSPF cost of 1 to start.

Figure 8-23 *Tunnel to Router Paris*

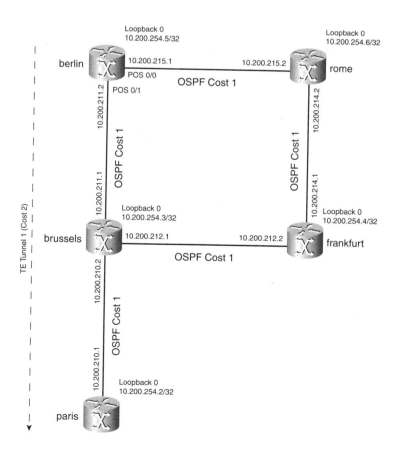

A TE tunnel exists from router berlin to router paris. The cost of the TE tunnel is 2. Because 10.200.254.2/32 is directly connected to router paris, the cost or metric for this route in the routing table of router berlin is 3. Notice in Example 8-26 that the tunnel interface on router berlin is the only next hop for that prefix. The cost via the IP path berlin-brussels-paris is also 2, but this IP path is not installed in the routing table. The general rule is that for a prefix on the tail end router, only a tunnel that ends on that tail end router is used to forward packets. No load balancing occurs between the TE tunnel and the IP path in this case. Even if the TE tunnel is not on the lowest IGP cost path (it might have an explicit path that is not on the shortest path, or it might be waiting to be reoptimized), all traffic that is destined for prefixes connected to the tail end router goes into the TE tunnel. The TE tunnel and prefix 10.200.254.2/32 are shown in Example 8-26.

Example 8-26 *TE Tunnel from Router Berlin to Router Paris*

```
berlin#show mpls traffic-eng tunnels tunnel 1

Name: berlin_t1                       (Tunnel1) Destination: 10.200.254.2
  Status:
    Admin: up        Oper: up     Path: valid     Signalling: connected

    path option 10, type dynamic (Basis for Setup, path weight 2)

  Config Parameters:
    Bandwidth: 0        kbps (Global)  Priority: 7  7   Affinity: 0x0/0xFFFF
    Metric Type: TE (default)
    AutoRoute: enabled   LockDown: disabled  Loadshare: 0        bw-based
    auto-bw: disabled
  Active Path Option Parameters:
    State: dynamic path option 10 is active
    BandwidthOverride: disabled  LockDown: disabled  Verbatim: disabled


  InLabel  :  -
  OutLabel : POS0/1, 18
  RSVP Signalling Info:
       Src 10.200.254.5, Dst 10.200.254.2, Tun_Id 1, Tun_Instance 1
    RSVP Path Info:
      My Address: 10.200.254.5
      Explicit Route: 10.200.211.1 10.200.210.1 10.200.254.2
      Record   Route:   NONE
      Tspec: ave rate=0 kbits, burst=1000 bytes, peak rate=0 kbits
    RSVP Resv Info:
      Record   Route:   NONE
      Fspec: ave rate=0 kbits, burst=1000 bytes, peak rate=0 kbits
  Shortest Unconstrained Path Info:
    Path Weight: 2 (TE)
    Explicit Route: 10.200.211.1 10.200.210.1 10.200.254.2


berlin#show ip route 10.200.254.2 255.255.255.255
```

Example 8-26   *TE Tunnel from Router Berlin to Router Paris (Continued)*

```
Routing entry for 10.200.254.2/32
  Known via "ospf 1", distance 110, metric 3, type intra area
  Routing Descriptor Blocks:
  * directly connected, via Tunnel1
      Route metric is 3, traffic share count is 1
```

Now you will change the tunnel destination to 10.200.254.4, which is the router frankfurt. If you change the link berlin-brussels to an OSPF cost 3, the dynamic TE tunnel reoptimizes to the path berlin-rome-frankfurt and has a cost of 2. You can see this in Figure 8-24.

Figure 8-24   *Tunnel to Router Frankfurt*

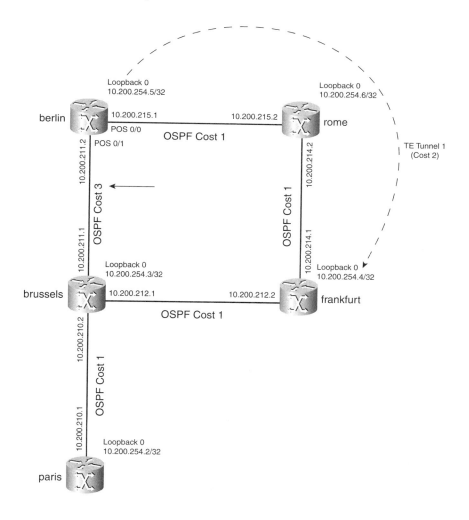

However, two paths now go to router paris. One is the IP path berlin-brussels-paris with a cost of 4, and one is the path tunnel 1{berlin-rome-frankfurt}-brussels-paris with a total cost of 2 + 1 + 1 = 4. That means that prefix 10.200.254.2/32 has two next hops in the routing table: tunnel 1 and 10.200.211.1 (brussels). As you can see in Example 8-27, for a prefix behind the tail end router of a TE tunnel, an LSR can load-balance traffic over a TE tunnel and an IP path (if the cost for both paths is equal, of course).

Example 8-27 *TE Tunnel from Router Berlin to Router Frankfurt*

```
berlin#show mpls traffic-eng tunnels tunnel 1

Name: berlin_t1                        (Tunnel1) Destination: 10.200.254.4
  Status:
    Admin: up         Oper: up      Path: valid      Signalling: connected

    path option 10, type dynamic (Basis for Setup, path weight 2)

  Config Parameters:
    Bandwidth: 0           kbps (Global)  Priority: 7  7   Affinity: 0x0/0xFFFF
    Metric Type: TE (default)
    AutoRoute: enabled   LockDown: disabled  Loadshare: 0       bw-based
    auto-bw: disabled
  Active Path Option Parameters:
    State: dynamic path option 10 is active
    BandwidthOverride: disabled  LockDown: disabled  Verbatim: disabled


  InLabel  :  -
  OutLabel : POS0/0, 17
  RSVP Signalling Info:
       Src 10.200.254.5, Dst 10.200.254.4, Tun_Id 1, Tun_Instance 7
    RSVP Path Info:
      My Address: 10.200.254.5
      Explicit Route: 10.200.215.2 10.200.214.1 10.200.254.4
      Record   Route:   NONE
      Tspec: ave rate=0 kbits, burst=1000 bytes, peak rate=0 kbits
    RSVP Resv Info:
      Record   Route:   NONE
      Fspec: ave rate=0 kbits, burst=1000 bytes, peak rate=0 kbits
  Shortest Unconstrained Path Info:
    Path Weight: 2 (TE)
    Explicit Route: 10.200.215.2 10.200.214.1 10.200.254.4

berlin#show ip route 10.200.254.2 255.255.255.255
Routing entry for 10.200.254.2/32
  Known via "ospf 1", distance 110, metric 5, type intra area
  Last update from 10.200.211.1 on POS0/1, 00:11:14 ago
  Routing Descriptor Blocks:
  * 10.200.211.1, from 10.200.254.2, 00:11:14 ago, via POS0/1
```

Example 8-27   *TE Tunnel from Router Berlin to Router Frankfurt (Continued)*

```
    Route metric is 5, traffic share count is 1
  directly connected, via Tunnel1
    Route metric is 5, traffic share count is 1
```

Keeping the OSPF cost of the link berlin-brussels at 3, the TE tunnel is fixed over the path berlin-brussels-fankfurt with an explicit path option. The cost of the tunnel is now 4, but the prefixes with this tunnel as next hop still have the IGP cost of 2. Look at Figure 8-25 for the network with the TE tunnel.

Figure 8-25   *Tunnel to Router Frankfurt over Router Brussels*

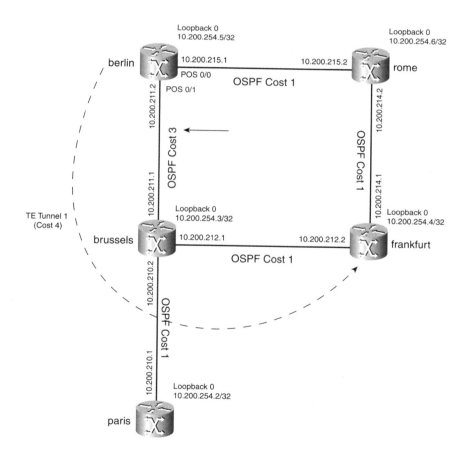

To get from berlin to paris, load balancing across the IP path berlin-brussels-paris and the path tunnel 1{berlin-brussels-frankfurt}-brussels-paris still must occur, because none of the IGP costs of the links has changed. However, the traffic going onto tunnel 1 backflows. The traffic on the tunnel arrives at frankfurt and then flows back across the link frankfurt-brussels to the router paris. That means that all the traffic that is sent onto the tunnel toward 10.200.254.2/32 from berlin crosses the link frankfurt-brussels twice. This is surely something you want to try to avoid. Even though the cost of the tunnel is 4, the cost used for the prefixes that have this tunnel as next hop is 2. The reason for this is that the cost or metric for the prefixes using the TE tunnels is calculated from the lowest IGP cost to the tunnel destination. This is true even—as in this case—when the tunnel does not take the lowest IGP cost path to the tail end router. It is this lowest IGP path cost that is used for the prefixes in the routing table that have this tunnel as next hop. Just remember the general rule mentioned in the beginning of this section regarding the cost of the tunnel as used by the IGP. The tunnel and the prefix 10.200.254.2/32 in the routing table of router berlin for Figure 8-25 are shown in Example 8-28.

Example 8-28 *Backflow*

```
berlin#show mpls traffic-eng tunnels tunnel 1

Name: berlin_t1                         (Tunnel1) Destination: 10.200.254.4
  Status:
    Admin: up          Oper: up     Path: valid     Signalling: connected

    path option 5, type explicit berlin-frankfurt (Basis for Setup, path weight 4)
    path option 10, type dynamic

  Config Parameters:
    Bandwidth: 0       kbps (Global)  Priority: 7  7   Affinity: 0x0/0xFFFF
    Metric Type: TE (default)
    AutoRoute: enabled   LockDown: disabled  Loadshare: 0        bw-based
    auto-bw: disabled
  Active Path Option Parameters:
    State: explicit path option 5 is active
    BandwidthOverride: disabled  LockDown: disabled  Verbatim: disabled


  InLabel  :  -
  OutLabel : POS0/1, 16
  RSVP Signalling Info:
       Src 10.200.254.5, Dst 10.200.254.4, Tun_Id 1, Tun_Instance 9
    RSVP Path Info:
      My Address: 10.200.254.5
      Explicit Route: 10.200.211.1 10.200.212.2 10.200.254.4
      Record   Route:   NONE
      Tspec: ave rate=0 kbits, burst=1000 bytes, peak rate=0 kbits
    RSVP Resv Info:
      Record   Route:   NONE
      Fspec: ave rate=0 kbits, burst=1000 bytes, peak rate=0 kbits
  Shortest Unconstrained Path Info:
    Path Weight: 2 (TE)
    Explicit Route: 10.200.215.2 10.200.214.1 10.200.254.4

berlin#show ip route 10.200.254.2 255.255.255.255
```

Example 8-28   *Backflow (Continued)*

```
Routing entry for 10.200.254.2/32
  Known via "ospf 1", distance 110, metric 5, type intra area
  Last update from 10.200.211.1 on POS0/1, 00:00:56 ago
  Routing Descriptor Blocks:
  * 10.200.211.1, from 10.200.254.2, 00:00:56 ago, via POS0/1
      Route metric is 5, traffic share count is 1
    directly connected, via Tunnel1
      Route metric is 5, traffic share count is 1
```

Keep the same OSPF cost on the links as before: a cost of 1 on all links and the link berlin-brussels
with an OSPF cost of 3. The TE tunnel on router berlin now has the router brussels as destination
and is explicitly routed on the path berlin-rome-frankfurt-brussels. Figure 8-26 shows the network
with this explicitly routed tunnel.

Figure 8-26   *Tunnel to Router Brussels*

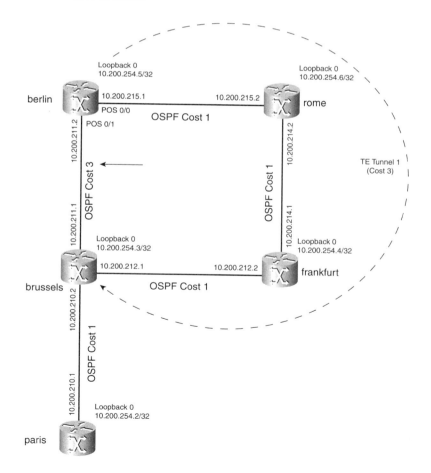

Example 8-29 shows that prefixes on the tail end router or beyond (for example, on router paris) are reachable only through the TE tunnel.

Example 8-29   *TE Tunnel from Router Berlin to Router Brussels*

```
berlin#show mpls traffic-eng tunnels tunnel 1

Name: berlin_t1                         (Tunnel1) Destination: 10.200.254.3
  Status:
    Admin: up        Oper: up     Path: valid      Signalling: connected

    path option 5, type explicit berlin-frankfurt (Basis for Setup, path weight 3)
    path option 10, type dynamic

  Config Parameters:
    Bandwidth: 0         kbps (Global)  Priority: 7  7   Affinity: 0x0/0xFFFF
    Metric Type: TE (default)
    AutoRoute: enabled   LockDown: disabled  Loadshare: 0        bw-based
    auto-bw: disabled
  Active Path Option Parameters:
    State: explicit path option 5 is active
    BandwidthOverride: disabled  LockDown: disabled  Verbatim: disabled


  InLabel  :  -
  OutLabel : POS0/0, 17
  RSVP Signalling Info:
       Src 10.200.254.5, Dst 10.200.254.3, Tun_Id 1, Tun_Instance 13
    RSVP Path Info:
      My Address: 10.200.254.5
      Explicit Route: 10.200.215.2 10.200.214.1 10.200.212.1 10.200.254.3
      Record   Route:   NONE
      Tspec: ave rate=0 kbits, burst=1000 bytes, peak rate=0 kbits
    RSVP Resv Info:
      Record   Route:   NONE
      Fspec: ave rate=0 kbits, burst=1000 bytes, peak rate=0 kbits
  Shortest Unconstrained Path Info:
    Path Weight: 3 (TE)
    Explicit Route: 10.200.211.1 10.200.254.3

berlin#show ip route 10.200.254.3 255.255.255.255
Routing entry for 10.200.254.3/32
  Known via "ospf 1", distance 110, metric 4, type intra area
  Routing Descriptor Blocks:
  * directly connected, via Tunnel1
      Route metric is 4, traffic share count is 1

berlin#show ip route 10.200.254.2 255.255.255.255
Routing entry for 10.200.254.2/32
```

Example 8-29   *TE Tunnel from Router Berlin to Router Brussels (Continued)*

```
Known via "ospf 1", distance 110, metric 5, type intra area
Routing Descriptor Blocks:
* directly connected, via Tunnel1
    Route metric is 5, traffic share count is 1
```

The cost of the shortest IGP path for the TE tunnel is 3. Therefore, the prefixes with the tunnel as next hop also receive a cost of 3, plus the cost of the path from the tail end router to the destination. Notice that both 10.200.254.3/32 and 10.200.254.2/32 have only the tunnel as the next hop. That means the prefixes at the tail end router and the prefixes beyond the tail end router have the tunnel as the only next hop. The reason the prefix 10.200.254.2/32 on router paris does not load-balance over the IP path berlin-brussels-paris and the path tunnel 1{berlin-rome-frankfurt-brussels}-paris—even though the total cost is the same (total cost = 5)—is that the tunnel tail end router crosses the IP path. The CSPF calculation on the head end router notices this and takes the TE tunnel as the only next hop for that prefix.

Adjusting the Cost Calculation

With *autoroute announce*, you can change the metric used to calculate what the next hop should be for prefixes. You can change the metric in a direct, relative, or absolute way with the following command:

```
tunnel mpls traffic-eng autoroute metric { absolute | relative } value
```

This command allows you to make the TE tunnel more or less preferred as a next hop for the prefixes as compared to other TE tunnels or IP paths. However, you still need to take the restrictions into account that were discussed in the previous section. Setting the value directly with this command does set the cost of the TE tunnel as it is announced to the IGP for all prefixes that are at the tail end router or beyond. Of course, if the prefix is several hops behind the tail end router, you also need to add the cost of that path. This is not so if you change the metric in an absolute way. In that case, all prefixes reachable through the TE tunnel receive that cost, no matter how far beyond the tail end router they might be. The relative keyword lets you change the cost of the tunnel as it is announced to the IGP in a relative way compared to the cost of the lowest cost IGP path. It allows you to adjust the cost from –10 to 10.

NOTE   Use this command with caution, because it can cause routing problems if not applied correctly.

Example 8-30 shows adjustment of the announced metric by the TE tunnel. The announced metric is adjusted by decrementing it by 2.

Example 8-30   *Adjusting Announced Metric of TE Tunnel*

```
berlin#show ip route 10.200.254.3 255.255.255.255
Routing entry for 10.200.254.3/32
  Known via "ospf 1", distance 110, metric 4, type intra area
  Routing Descriptor Blocks:
  * directly connected, via Tunnel1
      Route metric is 4, traffic share count is 1


berlin#conf t
Enter configuration commands, one per line.  End with CNTL/Z.
berlin(config)#int tunnel 1
berlin(config-if)#tunnel mpls traffic-eng autoroute metric relative -2
berlin(config-if)#^Z
berlin#show ip route 10.200.254.3 255.255.255.255
Routing entry for 10.200.254.3/32
  Known via "ospf 1", distance 110, metric 2, type intra area
  Routing Descriptor Blocks:
  * directly connected, via Tunnel1
      Route metric is 2, traffic share count is 1
```

Load Balancing

When multiple TE tunnels have the same cost, traffic can be load-balanced across them. Traffic can also be load-balanced between the native IP path and TE tunnels if the cost of the routing is the same. This situation has some restrictions, however; see the earlier section "Cost Calculation of IGP Routes over TE Tunnels." When you are load balancing over TE tunnels, the load balancing can even be unequal cost load balancing. The load balancing of traffic is weighted proportionally to the bandwidth requirement of the TE tunnels. If you have one tunnel with 80 MB and one with 20 MB of reserved bandwidth, the load-balancing ratio is 4:1, or the first tunnel should get four times more traffic than the second tunnel. However, the load-balancing ratio is an approximation, because Cisco Express Forwarding (CEF) has only 16 hash buckets. See Chapter 6, "Cisco Express Forwarding," for more on this.

When an LSR performs the load balancing over one or more IP paths and one or more TE tunnels, it is always equal cost load balancing. This means that every path gets the same amount of traffic. Multiple TE tunnels can be handy when the amount of bandwidth to be reserved between a pair of routers is more than the bandwidth capacity of the links. You can then just create multiple TE tunnels with each a piece of the required bandwidth.

MPLS TE and MPLS VPN

When you are using TE tunnels in an MPLS VPN network, you should know a few specifics.

TE Tunnels Between PE Routers

When two TE tunnels (one for each direction) exist between a pair of PE routers and the Border Gateway Protocol (BGP) next hop of the vpnv4 routes is pointing to the TE tunnels, the VRF traffic flows across the TE tunnels. The packets have two labels: The top label is the TE label, and the bottom label is the VPN label. If TE is enabled on all provider (P) routers but LDP is not, all the VRF traffic must flow over the TE tunnels; otherwise, the traffic only has the VPN label and never gets to the egress PE router. LDP does not have to be running on the TE tunnels in this case, where the PE routers are head end and tail end routers of the TE tunnels. In the next case, however, LDP must be enabled on the TE tunnels.

TE Tunnel with P Router as Tail End Router

When a P router is the tail end router of the tunnel instead of the provider edge (PE) router, you need to ensure that two things are present:

- LDP is enabled on all links.

- An LDP session exists between the head end and tail end router of the TE tunnel LSP.

The first requirement should be clear. If a TE tunnel terminates at a P router instead of the PE router, the packets still need to be label-switched up to the PE router. Otherwise, the packets become unlabeled and the IGP label and the VPN label become lost. Without the VPN label, the packets can never be switched onto the correct VRF interface. Without the IGP label, the packets cannot reach the egress PE, because an IP lookup of the destination IP address of the packet results in either the packet being dropped or the packet being incorrectly routed. This is a result of the fact that the IP VRF routes are unknown on the P routers. That is why you must make sure that LDP is running between the P routers.

The second requirement is a bit more subtle. The tail end router of a TE tunnel LSP sends an implicit NULL label to the upstream LSR for the LSP. If the tail end router is a PE router, it is okay, because the packet has one label popped off at the penultimate hop router but still arrives with the VPN label on top at the egress PE router. However, when a P router is the tail end router of the TE LSP, it causes problems. The tail end router sends an implicit NULL label to its upstream router. The result is that the packets arrive at the tail end router with the VPN label on top, so the P router either drops the packet if the label is unknown, or it forwards the packet erroneously because it might have advertised the same label, but for a different LSP.

> **NOTE** Even if the explicit NULL label is used, the packet is not forwarded correctly because the explicit NULL label is popped off and the forwarding decision is made again by looking up the VPN label in the LFIB.

The solution is to have an LDP session from the head end router to the tail end router of the TE tunnel. You can do this in two ways:

- Two tunnels between the PE (or P) and P router—one for both directions—and LDP enabled on the tunnel interfaces

- A targeted LDP session between the PE (or P) and P router

In the first case, it is enough to configure the two tunnels between the pair of routers in opposite directions and enable LDP (configuring **mpls ip**) on the tunnel interfaces. A targeted LDP session is automatically set up between the head end and tail end routers. In the second case, an LDP targeted session must be explicitly configured on the tail end router to the head end router, and **mpls ip** must be enabled on the tunnel interface on the head end router. The result is the same for both methods: The VPN packets have three labels. Figure 8-27 shows the labels on top of a VPN packet that crosses the MPLS VPN network with such a TE tunnel. The targeted LDP session advertises the LDP label from the tail end router to the head router of the TE tunnel.

Figure 8-27 *TE Tunnel with P Router as Tail End Router*

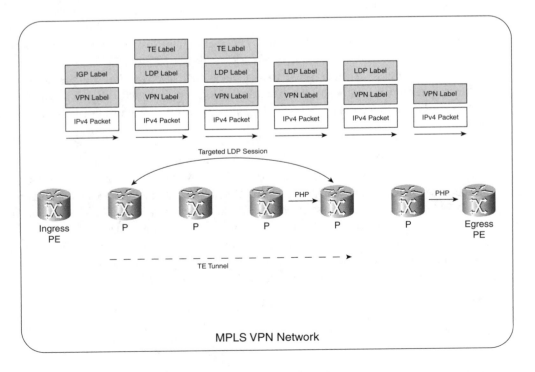

The bottom label is still the VPN label, of course. The middle label is the label that is advertised across the targeted LDP session, and the top label is the TE tunnel LSP label. The label learned from the targeted LDP session is needed to get the packet at the tail end router of the TE tunnel LSP with two labels so that it can still be forwarded toward the egress PE correctly. At the tail end router of the TE tunnel LSP, the packet arrives with two labels. The top label is the advertised label on the targeted LDP session for the BGP next-hop IP address of the vpnv4 route. This label is then label swapped with the outgoing LDP label, bound to the BGP next-hop IP address (which is on the egress PE router).

Look at Example 8-31. It shows a TE tunnel with a P router as the tail end router. When LDP is not running across the TE tunnel, the outgoing label is *Untagged* or *No Label* for prefixes behind the tail end router. When **mpls ip** is enabled on this tunnel and the tunnel in the reverse direction, a targeted LDP session is enabled—tied in with both TE tunnels. The result is that then the outgoing label is no longer *Untagged* or *No Label*, but a regular label. This tunnel starts here at router paris, which is a P router. As a result, the packet is coming in labeled, is label-swapped (with the LDP label), and an additional label (the TE label) is pushed before the packet is switched out. If MPLS VPN traffic crosses this tunnel, it has three instead of two labels.

Example 8-31 *LDP on TE Tunnel*

```
paris#show mpls forwarding-table 10.200.254.7 detail
Local  Outgoing    Prefix            Bytes tag  Outgoing   Next Hop
tag    tag or VC   or Tunnel Id      switched   interface
28     Untagged    10.200.254.7/32   1509       Tu1        point2point
       MAC/Encaps=4/8, MRU=4470, Tag Stack{33}, via PO4/0
       FF030281 00021000
       No output feature configured

paris#conf t
Enter configuration commands, one per line.  End with CNTL/Z.
paris(config)#int t
paris(config)#int tunnel 1
paris(config-if)#mpls ip
paris(config-if)#^Z
paris#
*Apr 11 20:56:39.201: %LDP-5-NBRCHG: LDP Neighbor 10.200.254.6:0 is UP
paris#
paris#show mpls forwarding-table 10.200.254.7 detail
Local  Outgoing    Prefix            Bytes tag  Outgoing   Next Hop
tag    tag or VC   or Tunnel Id      switched   interface
28     31          10.200.254.7/32   0          Tu1        point2point
       MAC/Encaps=4/12, MRU=4466, Tag Stack{33 31}, via PO4/0
       FF030281 000210000001F000
       No output feature configured
```

VRF-to-TE Tunnel Routing

What if you have an MPLS VPN network with TE enabled between the PE routers, and you want to steer VPN traffic onto TE tunnels, but different TE tunnels for different VRFs? This is possible, but consider the point of scaling: Creating one pair of TE tunnels between two PE routers for every VRF is not very scalable. However, you might want to do this in rare cases for tactical reasons. Look at Figure 8-28, which shows an example of two VRFs on the two PE routers. You can steer the VRF *cust-one* traffic onto TE tunnel 1 and the VRF *cust-two* traffic onto TE tunnel 2. A reason for this might be that you want to minimize the total delay for the traffic of VRF *cust-one* and therefore take a route where the links have a smaller delay. Delay is not an issue for the VRF *cust-two* traffic.

Figure 8-28 *VRF-to-TE Tunnel Routing*

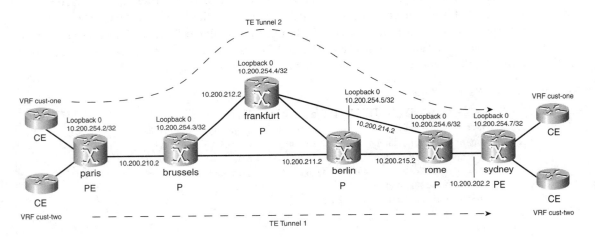

To do this, you must specify a different BGP next hop for both VRFs on the egress PE. You also must specify a static route on the ingress PE for each of those BGP next-hop addresses and point them to the respective TE tunnels. Example 8-32 shows the needed configuration.

Example 8-32 *VRF-to-TE Tunnel Routing*

```
!
hostname paris
!
ip route 10.200.254.8 255.255.255.255 Tunnel1
ip route 10.200.254.9 255.255.255.255 Tunnel2
!

!
hostname sydney
!
```

Example 8-32 *VRF-to-TE Tunnel Routing*

```
interface Loopback0
 ip address 10.200.254.7 255.255.255.255
!
interface Loopback1
 ip address 10.200.254.8 255.255.255.255
!
interface Loopback2
 ip address 10.200.254.9 255.255.255.255
!
ip vrf cust-one
 rd 1:1
 route-target export 1:1
 route-target import 1:1
 bgp next-hop Loopback1
!
ip vrf cust-two
 rd 1:2
 route-target export 1:2
 route-target import 1:2
 bgp next-hop Loopback2
!
```

NOTE   For this case, in older releases of Cisco IOS, LDP does have to be enabled on the TE tunnels, even though the TE tunnels are between the PE routers.

This chapter explained the basics of MPLS TE. For more advanced topics on MPLS TE, refer to www.ciscopress.com/1587051974. DiffServ-aware TE tunnels, auto tunnels, path protection, and interarea TE tunnels are explained there.

Summary

In this chapter, you saw how MPLS TE works. You learned that Open Shortest Path First (OSPF) and Intermediate System-to-Intermediate System (IS-IS) were extended so that they can advertise traffic engineering (TE) information, and that the signaling protocol Resource Reservation Protocol (RSVP) was also extended. You discovered how the LSR calculates the paths of TE tunnel label switched paths (LSP), how it signals them, and how it calculates their cost. Perhaps the most important section was the one explaining how to forward traffic onto TE tunnels. An important feature of TE is Fast ReRoute (FRR), where traffic on TE tunnels is protected by backup tunnels. This chapter explained in detail how FRR link protection and FRR node protection behave.

Chapter Review Questions

You can find answers to the following questions in Appendix A, "Answers to the Chapter Review Questions."

1. Name the advantages of MPLS traffic engineering.

2. What are the components of MPLS traffic engineering?

3. What are the attributes of the links enabled for traffic engineering?

4. Name the six ways how you can forward IP traffic onto a TE tunnel.

5. Name four kind of path options you can specify?

6. When you have an MPLS VPN network and TE tunnels that do not always have the PE routers as head/tail end routers, what do you need to have?

7. What is the LSR that is the head end router of a backup tunnel called?

8. Why do you need a link-state routing protocol for MPLS TE?

9. What is the feature called that has the IGP advertise TE tunnels as links?

10. How does the head end LSR of a TE tunnel know that the tunnel is fast rerouted over a backup tunnel?

What You Will Learn

By the end of this chapter, you should know and be able to explain the following:

- The necessity of having IPv6 as the successor protocol of IPv4

- The main differences between IPv4 and IPv6

- A brief overview of the IPv6 unicast routing protocols

- How to carry IPv6 across an MPLS network

- What 6PE stands for and how it operates

- What 6VPE stands for and how it operates

When you have finished this chapter, you will be able to explain the IPv6 protocol in a few sentences. You will also be able to choose the best-suited solution for an MPLS network transporting IPv6 across it.

CHAPTER **9**

IPv6 over MPLS

IPv6 is the successor to IPv4. You might think that it should be IPv5, but that one ended up as an experiment only and was dropped. IPv6 is the next-generation IP protocol. It is similar to IPv4 in many respects, but it is also different in many ways. One of the most eye-catching differences is the bigger IP addresses in IPv6 versus IPv4. That feature is the main driving force for people to move away from IPv4 and start implementing IPv6. Bigger addresses mean that you have many of them available to you. Obtaining an IPv4 address range these days is not as easy as it was 20 years ago. The official instances are reluctant when giving out new IPv4 address ranges because the available networks are slowly being depleted. IPv6, however, allows a far greater number of address ranges to be given out.

Introduction to IPv6

This section introduces the IPv6 protocol. It explains the driving forces for IPv6, the main differences between IPv6 and IPv4, and an overview of the IPv6 unicast routing protocols. The main purpose of this chapter is to explain how to carry IPv6 over an MPLS network.

The Driving Forces for IPv6

IP networks have had tremendous success in the past two decades. The Internet is the ultimate measure and summon of that success. Even though the current IP protocol—IP version 4, or IPv4—has stood the test of time, it can still be improved. The biggest reason for looking for a new IP protocol was the explosive growth of IP networks in the world. IPv4 addresses have 4 octets, or 32 bits. It soon became apparent that with the current growth of the Internet, the Regional Internet Registries would run out of IP networks to assign to companies, institutions, and organizations. For the next IP protocol—IP version 6, or IPv6—the Internet Engineering Task Force (IETF) made an IP address 128 bits long. That makes the IPv6 address four times bigger than the IPv4 address. However, this is quite a number of addresses more that can be used. The 32-bit IPv4 address provided for approximately 4.3 billion addresses. The 128-bit IPv6 address provides for approximately 3.4×10^{38} addresses. This should be enough for years to come. If, in the future, this turns out to be inadequate, a new IP protocol is likely to be engineered in time.

Perhaps the urgency for a new IP protocol for the larger addresses has been reduced because the authorities and Internet providers became a bit more cautious in assigning prefixes. Technical workarounds have also reduced the use of addresses. You can use private IP addresses and Network Address Translation (NAT) if you want to connect to the Internet. Alternatively, you can use DHCP to assign addresses dynamically when needed and retract them when the hosts are no longer present. These things have slowed the need for more addresses, but they have not cleared the need for them in the longer term. In the short term, advances in the technology might quickly increase the demand for more IP addresses. Just think of the integration of the IP network protocol into devices such as PDAs, mobile telephones, cars, TVs, and other devices and gadgets.

The bigger IP address is the most obvious improvement from IPv4 to IPv6. IPv6 has brought about other changes that are not so obvious, though. First, the IPv6 header is simpler. Some of the IPv4 fields in the header have been omitted, which has resulted in a more streamlined and more efficient header. The most noticeable deletion has been the removal of the checksum in the header. This has reduced the cost of forwarding a packet through a router.

Second, IPv6 has a fixed header size, although options are still allowed. Third, when the IETF designed IPv6, they made security a key aspect. A completely new feature of IPv6 is the Flow Label, which allows a router to identify the flow that the packet belongs to by looking only at the IP header and not deeper into the packet.

Overview of the IPv6 Protocol

The biggest changes in IPv6 compared to IPv4 are the bigger addresses and the simplified header. The next sections explain the new IPv6 header and how it is different from the IPv4 header.

The IPv6 Header

You can see the header of the IPv4 protocol in Figure 9-1. Compare that to the IPv6 header in Figure 9-2.

Figure 9-1 *IPv4 Header Format*

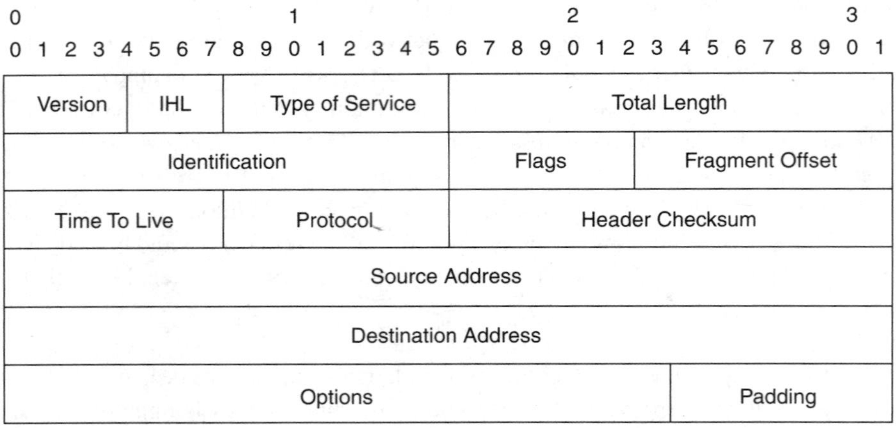

Figure 9-2 *IPv6 Header Format*

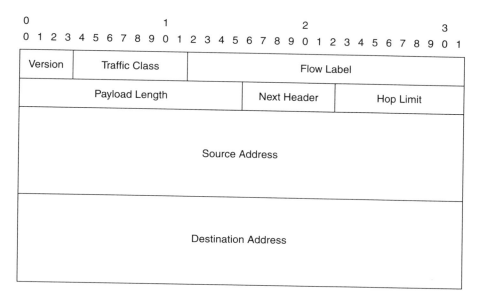

The obvious change is the length of the addresses. The source and destination address are four times bigger in the IPv6 header. Also, the header is simplified because certain fields have been omitted. For example, the header no longer has a checksum. That means you do not need to recalculate the checksum of the IP header at every hop (router) in the network, which provides a faster and simpler forwarding. The burden of checking the IP header (and payload) now lies completely with the upper layer protocols, such as TCP and User Datagram Protocol (UDP). Besides the checksum, the Fragment Offset field is gone. That is because in IPv6, the routers cannot fragment packets, as they did with IPv4. Fragmentation is avoided by the mandatory use of path MTU discovery in IPv6. The IHL (Internet Header Length) field has been removed, because the IPv6 header is always 40 bytes long. The IPv4 header was 20 bytes long but could be longer if IP options were present. With IPv6, options have been replaced by extension headers. They are similar to the IP options of IPv4 and are chained after the IPv6 header. They are present if the Next Header field in the IPv6 header indicates that an extension header follows the IPv6 header, instead of the usual TCP or UDP header. Look at Figure 9-3 to see an example of such a chain of IPv6 extension headers.

Figure 9-3 *Chain of IPv6 Extension Headers*

IPv6 Header	Routing Header	Fragment Header	
Next Header = Routing	Next Header = Fragment	Next Header = TCP	Fragment of TCP Header + Data

Other fields that were removed from the IPv4 header are the Identification, Flags, and Padding fields.

Other fields were retained from the IPv4 header. The Version field is still there, but now it indicates 6 instead of 4. The Hop Limit field has the same function as the Time To Live (TTL) field in IPv4. The Next Header field indicates what the header is that follows the IPv6 header: an IPv6 extension header or an upper-layer protocol header. It serves the same purpose as the Protocol field in the IPv4 header. The Total Length field became the Payload Length field. The Type of Service field became the Traffic Class field in the IPv6 header. The functionality is similar to the Type of Service field because it indicates the quality of service (QoS) information of the IP packet. The Traffic Class field indicates to which class the IPv6 packet belongs as used with Differentiated Services (DiffServ).

One field is completely new: the Flow Label. This field is 20 bits long and indicates the flow to which the IPv6 packet belongs. A flow in IPv4 is defined by certain parameters in the layers above the network layer (for example, the TCP ports). With this flow label, the applications that are running on the end systems can indicate the flow directly into the IPv6 header. This enables the routers to determine the flow of the packet without having to search for the information beyond the IPv6 header.

The IPv6 Addressing

Three categories of IPv6 addresses exist: unicast, anycast, and multicast. The unicast address is one IP address on one single interface. The anycast address is one address that is assigned to multiple interfaces on multiple nodes. A packet that is destined to that IPv6 address is sent to the nearest interface with that anycast address. *Nearest* means the shortest path according to the routing protocols. A multicast IP address is an address that is assigned to multiple interfaces on multiple nodes. A packet that is sent to that IPv6 address is sent to all the interfaces with that multicast address. The broadcast address did not survive the transition from IPv4 to IPv6. Multicast addresses are used now instead of the broadcast address.

The 128-bit IPv6 address is written in the following format: x:x:x:x:x:x:x:x, with each x representing a hexadecimal value of 16 bits, for a total of 128 bits of the IPv6 address. An example of such an address is 2001:DB08:7654:3210:FEDC:BA98:7654:3210.

As you can see, the textual representation of an IPv6 address is quite long compared to the short dotted-decimal representation of an IPv4 address. You can shorten the IPv6 address by replacing multiple groups of 16 bits of zeros with ::. You can do this only once in an IPv6 address, though; otherwise, the shortened address might become ambiguous. Another way to shorten the IPv6 address is to omit the leading zeros from any 16-bit field. As with IPv4 addresses, prefixes are presented in the following form: IPv6-address/prefix-length. The prefix-length is a value from 0 to 128 that indicates how long the subnet is. When the IETF created IPv6, they applied lessons that they learned from IPv4. IPv4 had network classes A, B, and C for unicast addresses. This led to classful routing and a waste of IP addresses because the big class A and B networks were never used efficiently. Later, classless routing and Variable-Length Subnet Masking (VLSM) were introduced for IPv4, but it was already too late to reassign all the IP prefixes to use a more efficient addressing scheme. IPv6 has only classless prefixes and classless routing; thus, the IPv6 addresses are used more efficiently than with IPv4.

The specific type of an IPv6 address is (similar to IPv4 addresses) indicated by the leading bits in the address. If the first three bits are 001, the IPv6 address is a global unicast address (similar to regular IPv4 addresses). The unicast address 0:0:0:0:0:0:0:1 is called the loopback address. (127.0.0.1 is used for the same purpose in IPv4.) A node might use it to send an IPv6 packet to itself. The address 0:0:0:0:0:0:0:0 is called the unspecified address. It must never be assigned to a node. It is used during initial automatic address assignment (similar to DHCP in IPv4) and indicates the absence of an address. One example of its use is in the Source Address field of any IPv6 packet that is sent by an initializing host before it has learned its own address. An IPv6 address with the first 10 bits equal to 1111111010 is a link-local unicast address. Link-local unicast addresses are constrained to one link and are never routable. They can be used only for neighbor discovery and to exchange IPv6 routing protocol updates. A link-local address is from the range FE80::/64. A multicast address is an IPv6 address with the first 8 bits equal to 11111111. A multicast address is thus from the range FF::/8. Finally, an anycast address has no specific syntax in the address. It is just a global unicast address that is assigned to multiple interfaces on multiple routers or hosts.

Other IPv6 Novelties

Besides the new header and the new address format, some other differences distinguish IPv6 from IPv4. Following are some of the differences:

- ICMPv6

- Neighbor discovery

- Router discovery

- Stateless autoconfiguration

- DHCP version 6 (DHCPv6)

- Path MTU discovery

- New Domain Name System (DNS) operation

ICMP is well known for its utilization in IPv4. It provides certain functionality, such as ping and redirects. ICMPv6 has these, as well. However, ICMP has been enlarged in IPv6 to support neighbor and router discovery (which required separate protocols in IPv4). Router discovery is functionality in IPv6 that has the routers send router advertisements so that an IPv6 node can automatically discover the routers on the local link. A link might have multiple routers. As such, the host can just pick one of the IPv6 routers on the link and use that for forwarding the IPv6 traffic; this means using it as the first gateway. The neighbor discovery in IPv6 is a way for IPv6 nodes to discover the presence of other IPv6 nodes on the same link and keep track of them. Stateless autoconfiguration is a feature whereby nodes can receive an IPv6 address from the router. DHCPv6 is the equivalent to DHCP for IPv4. DHCP allows a node to receive an IP address from a server. DHCP allows more control than stateless autoconfiguration, but it is also more complex. Path MTU discovery avoids fragmentation by the routers, which is not allowed in IPv6. Finally, DNS had to be changed to work for IPv6. A couple new DNS records were introduced: AAAA record (quad A record), which maps a host name to an IPv6 address, and the PTR record for IPv6.

Overview of IPv6 Unicast Routing in Cisco IOS

So that you can better understand how to transport IPv6 over MPLS, this section offers a brief overview of the IPv6 unicast routing protocols. Not that much has changed. The IP routing protocols have just been adapted to work for IPv6. Open Shortest Path First (OSPF) for IPv6 (OSPFv3) has changed more than any of the other protocols, but it is still similar to OSPFv2. The most significant change in configuring the IPv6 routing protocols in Cisco IOS is the change to enabling the routing protocol on the interface directly. To enable routing for IPv4, you had to specify the network command—that covers the IP addresses of the interfaces—under the router process. To enable IPv6 for Border Gateway Protocol (BGP), you must just activate the address family for IPv6.

Another change with IPv4 is the use of link-local addresses by routing protocols for IPv6. Link-local addresses are for use on a single link only. Link-local addresses are of the form FE80::/64, with the lower 64 bits being the interface ID. You can use these addresses for auto-address configuration, for neighbor discovery, or if no routers are present on the link. IPv6 packets with link-local addresses as the source or destination address are never forwarded onto another link.

IPv6 RIP (RIPng)

RIPng, or RIP next generation, is the RIP (Routing Information Protocol) for IPv6. RIP for IPv4 (originally defined in RFC 1058) was a simple distance vector routing protocol that was useful for small networks. It was later enhanced with small changes and made classless when RIP version 2 (RIPv2) was defined (RFC 2453). The limitations—such as a hop limit of 15 and the counting to infinity problem—remained, but the enhancements allowed some additional information to be carried by RIPv2. The most significant changes with RIPv2 are the use of a multicast address (224.0.0.9) as the destination address of the routing updates instead of using the broadcast address 255.255.255.255, the introduction of a subnet mask for the prefixes, the possibility for simple authentication, and route tags. Route tags are just numbers—used as an attribute—that can be used to "tag" prefixes when they are redistributed from one routing protocol into another. The RIPng routing protocol is based on the RIPv2 specification, and nothing important was changed. All of the functional aspects of RIPv2 were kept for RIPng. This means that RIPng is a limited routing protocol that is only suitable for use as a quick-and-dirty routing protocol for the smallest of networks. RIPng is described in RFC 2080.

In the Cisco IOS software implementation of RIPng, each RIPng process maintains a local database. RIPng tries to insert every nonexpired route from its local database into the master IPv6 routing information base (RIB), also known as the IPv6 routing table. If the same route has been learned from a different routing protocol with a better administrative distance than RIPng, the RIP route is not added to the IPv6 RIB, but the RIP route remains in the RIPng database. RIPng runs on top of UDP, port 521. The same timers exist in RIPng as they do in RIP: update period, route timeout period, router holddown period, and router garbage collection period.

Example 9-1 shows the basic configuration for RIPng.

Example 9-1 *Basic Configuration for RIPng*

```
!
ipv6 unicast-routing
ipv6 cef
!
interface Serial4/0
 ipv6 address 2001:DB8:4::1/64
 ipv6 enable
 ipv6 rip joene enable
!
ipv6 router rip joene
 maximum-paths 2
!
```

NOTE   Notice that **ipv6 unicast-routing** and **ipv6 cef** are not enabled by default and thus must be configured. Also notice that RIP routing processes have names and that they have to be enabled on each interface.

You can verify the RIPng database as shown in Example 9-2.

Example 9-2 *Verifying the RIPng Database*

```
new-york#show ipv6 rip joene database
RIP process "joene", local RIB
 2001:DB8:4::/64, metric 2
     Serial4/0/FE80::204:C0FF:FEF1:8820, expires in 179 secs
 2001:DB8:10::/64, metric 2, installed
     Serial4/0/FE80::204:C0FF:FEF1:8820, expires in 179 secs
```

> **NOTE**   Notice that the IPv6 routing protocols use the link-local addresses as next-hop
> addresses.

Example 9-3 shows you how to look at the IPv6 RIP prefixes in the IPv6 RIB and what the
characteristics are of the RIP process.

Example 9-3 *Verifying the RIPng Prefixes in the IPv6 RIB*

```
new-york#show ipv6 route rip
IPv6 Routing Table - 5 entries
Codes: C - Connected, L - Local, S - Static, R - RIP, B - BGP
       U - Per-user Static route
       I1 - ISIS L1, I2 - ISIS L2, IA - ISIS interarea, IS - ISIS summary
       O - OSPF intra, OI - OSPF inter, OE1 - OSPF ext 1, OE2 - OSPF ext 2
       ON1 - OSPF NSSA ext 1, ON2 - OSPF NSSA ext 2
       D - EIGRP, EX - EIGRP external
R    2001:DB8:10::/64 [120/2]
       via FE80::204:C0FF:FEF1:8820, Serial4/0

new-york#show ipv6 rip next-hops
 RIP process "joene", Next Hops
  FE80::204:C0FF:FEF1:8820/Serial4/0 [2 paths]

new-york#show ipv6 rip joene
RIP process "joene", port 521, multicast-group FF02::9, pid 146
     Administrative distance is 120. Maximum paths is 2
     Updates every 30 seconds, expire after 180
     Holddown lasts 0 seconds, garbage collect after 120
     Split horizon is on; poison reverse is off
     Default routes are not generated
     Periodic updates 9, trigger updates 0
  Interfaces:
    Serial4/0
  Redistribution:
    None
```

The multicast address used by RIPng is FF02::9. Pinging this address from a certain interface on
the router returns the IPv6 nodes running RIPng on that link. Look at Example 9-4 to see the result
of pinging the RIPng multicast address. In addition, **debug ipv6 rip** shows you the sent and
received RIPv6 updates.

Example 9-4 *Pinging the RIPng Multicast Address*

```
new-york#ping ipv6 ff02::9
Output Interface: serial4/0
Type escape sequence to abort.
```

Example 9-4 *Pinging the RIPng Multicast Address (Continued)*

```
Sending 5, 100-byte ICMP Echos to FF02::9, timeout is 2 seconds:
Packet sent with a source address of FE80::203:6CFF:FEC8:9800

Reply to request 0 received from FE80::204:C0FF:FEF1:8820, 0 ms
Reply to request 1 received from FE80::204:C0FF:FEF1:8820, 0 ms
Reply to request 2 received from FE80::204:C0FF:FEF1:8820, 0 ms
Reply to request 3 received from FE80::204:C0FF:FEF1:8820, 0 ms
Reply to request 4 received from FE80::204:C0FF:FEF1:8820, 0 ms
Success rate is 100 percent (5/5), round-trip min/avg/max = 0/0/0 ms
5 multicast replies and 0 errors.

new-york#debug ipv6 rip
RIP Routing Protocol debugging is on
new-york#
01:41:49: RIPng: response received from FE80::204:C0FF:FEF1:8820 on Serial4/0 for joene
01:41:49:       src=FE80::204:C0FF:FEF1:8820 (Serial4/0)
01:41:49:       dst=FF02::9
01:41:49:       sport=521, dport=521, length=52
01:41:49:       command=2, version=1, mbz=0, #rte=2
01:41:49:       tag=0, metric=1, prefix=2001:DB8:4::/64
01:41:49:       tag=0, metric=1, prefix=2001:DB8:10::/64
01:41:55: RIPng: Sending multicast update on Serial4/0 for joene
01:41:55:       src=FE80::203:6CFF:FEC8:9800
01:41:55:       dst=FF02::9 (Serial4/0)
01:41:55:       sport=521, dport=521, length=32
01:41:55:       command=2, version=1, mbz=0, #rte=1
01:41:55:       tag=0, metric=1, prefix=2001:DB8:4::/64
```

OSPF for IPv6 or OSPFv3

OSPFv2 is defined in RFC 2328. However, OSPF could not easily be extended to support IPv6 prefixes for the following reasons:

- OSPFv2 has rigid formatting that could not easily be extended.

- Because IPv6 is different from IPv4 in the way it works, some changes had to be made.

- The new specification for IPv6 was an opportunity to do things differently and better.

That is why OSPFv3 was specified in a completely new document (RFC 2740), but it borrowed heavily from OSPFv2. Some of the changes in OSPFv3 include these:

- Bigger addresses (128 instead of 32 bits)

- Different flooding scopes

- Per-link, instead of per-subnet protocol processing

- Use of link-local addresses

- No authentication in OSPF

- Multiple addresses possible per interface

- Changed options

Multiple IPv6 addresses per link are possible in IPv6. Different IPv6 prefixes can even exist on connecting IPv6 neighbors, without a common IPv6 prefix shared by both neighbors. That is why the protocol processing has changed from per-subnet in OSPFv2 to per-link in OSPFv3.

The use of link-local addresses in IPv6 has led to further changes in the OSPF specification. The direct result of the use of link-local addresses is the new link-local flooding scope. The link-local addresses are used for neighbor discovery, auto-configuration, and so on.

OSPFv3 does not need authentication because IPv6 provides that. OSPFv3 uses the IPv6 Authentication Header and Encapsulating Security Payload for security.

These changes have led to the differences in the newly defined OSPF packet formats. Two new link-state advertisements (LSA) also were added: Link LSA and Intra-Area LSA. The Link LSA serves three purposes:

- Advertising the link-local address to all routers that are attached to the link

- Advertising IPv6 prefixes on the link to the routers that are attached to the link

- Advertising options

The Intra-Area LSA serves either of the following two purposes:

- Associating a list of IPv6 prefixes with a transit network by referencing a network LSA

- Associating a list of IPv6 prefixes with a router by referencing a router LSA

(In OSPFv2, these prefixes were included in the router or network LSA.)

The obvious change from 32-bit to 128-bit addresses led to the redesign of the OSPF packet formats. The flooding of LSAs has changed and was made easier. Three flooding scopes are defined:

- Link-local scope

- Area scope

- Autonomous System (AS) scope

Most things that you are used to with OSPFv2 have not changed:

- OSPFv3 directly running on top of IP

- Flooding

- The discovery and maintenance of neighbor relationships, and the selection and establishment of adjacencies

- The link types, namely point-to-point, broadcast, nonbroadcast multiaccess (NBMA), Point-to-MultiPoint, and virtual links

- The interface and neighbor state machine

- Designated router (DR) election

- Area support

- Shortest Path First (SPF) calculations

- Area ID, router ID, and link-state ID as 32-bit fields

- Functionality of Hello, Database Description, Link-State Request, Link-State Update, and Link-State Acknowledgment packets

You can still use OSPFv3 in conjunction with OSPFv2. They run independently of each other. You can also run multiple instances of OSPFv3 on a single link.

Example 9-5 shows the basic configuration for OSPFv3.

Example 9-5 *Basic Configuration for OSPFv3*

```
!
ipv6 unicast-routing
ipv6 cef
!
interface Loopback0
 ip address 10.200.254.3 255.255.255.255
!
interface Serial4/0 ipv6 address 2001:DB8:4::1/64
 ipv6 enable
 ipv6 ospf 1 area 0
!
ipv6 router ospf 1
 log-adjacency-changes
 maximum-paths 2
!
```

As you can see, OSPFv3 is directly enabled on the interface, as it is done with all the IPv6 unicast routing protocols. The general OSPFv3 parameters can be configured under the ipv6 router ospf section. Example 9-6 shows how to verify the OSPFv3 neighbors.

Example 9-6 *Verifying OSPFv3 Neighbors*

```
new-york#show ipv6 ospf 1 neighbor

Neighbor ID     Pri   State         Dead Time    Interface ID    Interface
10.200.254.4     1    FULL/   -     00:00:35     10              Serial4/0

new-york#show ipv6 ospf 1 neighbor detail
 Neighbor 10.200.254.4
    In the area 0 via interface Serial4/0
    Neighbor: interface-id 10, link-local address FE80::204:C0FF:FEF1:8820
    Neighbor priority is 1, State is FULL, 6 state changes
    Options is 0x635791D9
    Dead timer due in 00:00:39
    Neighbor is up for 00:11:49
    Index 1/1/1, retransmission queue length 0, number of retransmission 1
    First 0x0(0)/0x0(0)/0x0(0) Next 0x0(0)/0x0(0)/0x0(0)
    Last retransmission scan length is 1, maximum is 1
    Last retransmission scan time is 0 msec, maximum is 0 msec
```

The OSPFv3 database is shown in Example 9-7. Notice the two new LSAs in the OSPFv3 database: Link LSA and Intra-Area LSA.

Example 9-7 *OSPFv3 Database*

```
new-york#show ipv6 ospf 1 database

            OSPFv3 Router with ID (10.200.254.3) (Process ID 1)

            Router Link States (Area 0)

ADV Router      Age       Seq#         Fragment ID  Link count   Bits
10.200.254.3    725       0x80000002   0            1            None
10.200.254.4    722       0x80000002   0            1            None

            Link (Type-8) Link States (Area 0)

ADV Router      Age       Seq#         Link ID    Interface
10.200.254.3    735       0x80000001   7          Se4/0
10.200.254.4    182       0x80000003   10         Se4/0

            Intra Area Prefix Link States (Area 0)

ADV Router      Age       Seq#         Link ID    Ref-lstype   Ref-LSID
10.200.254.3    735       0x80000001   0          0x2001       0
10.200.254.4    182       0x80000004   0          0x2001       0
```

Example 9-8 shows the OSPFv3 Link LSA in more detail.

Example 9-8 *OSPFv3 Link LSA*

```
new-york#show ipv6 ospf 1 database link

             OSPFv3 Router with ID (10.200.254.3) (Process ID 1)

                Link (Type-8) Link States (Area 0)

  LS age: 910
  Options: (V6-Bit E-Bit R-bit DC-Bit)
  LS Type: Link-LSA (Interface: Serial4/0)
  Link State ID: 7 (Interface ID)
  Advertising Router: 10.200.254.3
  LS Seq Number: 80000001
  Checksum: 0xCA4
  Length: 56
  Router Priority: 1
  Link Local Address: FE80::203:6CFF:FEC8:9800
  Number of Prefixes: 1
  Prefix Address: 2001:DB8:4::
  Prefix Length: 64, Options: None
```

Example 9-9 shows the OSPFv3 Intra-Area LSA in more detail.

Example 9-9 *OSPFv3 Intra-Area LSA*

```
new-york#show ipv6 ospf 1 database prefix

             OSPFv3 Router with ID (10.200.254.3) (Process ID 1)

                Intra Area Prefix Link States (Area 0)

  Routing Bit Set on this LSA
  LS age: 962
  LS Type: Intra-Area-Prefix-LSA
  Link State ID: 0
  Advertising Router: 10.200.254.3
  LS Seq Number: 80000001
  Checksum: 0x7879
  Length: 44
  Referenced LSA Type: 2001
  Referenced Link State ID: 0
  Referenced Advertising Router: 10.200.254.3
  Number of Prefixes: 1
  Prefix Address: 2001:DB8:4::
  Prefix Length: 64, Options: None, Metric: 64
```

Most OSPFv2 commands have the equivalent command in OSPFv3. Table 9-1 is an overview of the OSPFv3 commands versus the OSPFv2 commands.

Table 9-1   *OSPFv3 Versus OSPFv2 Commands*

OSPFv3 Command	OSPFv2 Command
show ipv6 ospf	show ip ospf
clear ipv6 ospf	clear ip ospf
debug ipv6 ospf	debug ip ospf

IS-IS for IPv6

ISO 10589 originally specified IS-IS, which specified the routing for Connectionless Network Service (CLNS). The IETF specified RFC 1195 and made IS-IS perform routing for IP.

If IS-IS runs both CLNS and IP routing, it is called dual routing. The TLV (an easy means of encoding in a Type-Length-Value fashion) encoding used throughout IS-IS ensured that the protocol was extendible from the start. Recent work is underway in the form of a draft: draft-ietf-isis-ipv6 (Routing IPv6 with IS-IS) to extend IS-IS so that it can do routing for IPv6. In essence, what is needed is the addition of a few TLVs so that IS-IS can take care of the routing for IPv6. The draft specifies the addition of two new TLVs: IPv6 Reachability and IPv6 Interface Address. The first one is the equivalent of the IP Internal Reachability Information and IP External Reachability Information TLVs, and the second is the equivalent of the IP Interface Address TLV. All of them are used for IPv4 encoding.

To configure IS-IS IPv6, you must configure the following:

- Generic IS-IS interface attributes

- IS-IS IPv6 on the interface

- Generic IS-IS router-mode attributes

- IS-IS IPv6-specific attributes under the IPv6 address-family submode of the IS-IS router mode

The generic IS-IS attributes can be the circuit type, priority, and so on configured on the interface. To configure IS-IS IPv6 on the interface, configure the command **ipv6 router isis** [*tag*]. You must enable the interface for IPv6 by having an IPv6 address on it or by having the command **ipv6 enable** on it. You can then configure any of the IPv6-specific attributes under the IPv6 address family of IS-IS. Examples are **summary-prefix** *ipv6-prefix/prefix-length* {**level-1** | **level-1-2** |

level-2} and **redistribute** *source-protocol* [*process-id*] [**include-connected**] [*target-protocol-options*] [*source-protocol-options*]. These attributes are applied only to the IPv6 routing table.

IS-IS is a link-state routing protocol. As such, it builds a database of the network topology. This database is present on all the routers. Each router must then take the IS-IS database and run a SPF calculation (or Dijkstra, after the inventor) on it. The result of this SPF calculation is the shortest path of all possible paths to all destinations or, in short, a routing table. However, when combining CLNS routing with IPv4 routing, only one SPF is performed on the IS-IS database in Cisco IOS. This means that the topologies of CLNS and IPv4 have to be the same. For a dual routing network, each interface with IS-IS routing for CLNS configured on it also has to have IS-IS routing for IPv4 configured on it. Otherwise, the topology of CLNS differs from the IPv4 topology, and routing fails in certain parts of the network.

Now that IPv6 is added as another protocol to be routed by IS-IS, the same problem can occur if the IPv4 and IPv6 topologies differ from each other. The result might be that IPv6 traffic is routed toward a non-IPv6-capable router and is thus discarded. You must take care in networks that are running IS-IS for both IPv4 and IPv6—which might still be the case for quite some time to come—that the topologies for both IP protocols are the same. Having the same topology for IPv4 and IPv6 might not always be wanted, though. They are, after all, different protocols. Cisco IOS lets you do Multi-Topology IS-IS, which allows IS-IS to run two separate SPF calculations: one for the IPv4 links, and one for the IPv6 links. This is described in the draft draft-ietf-isis-wg-multi-topology with the title "M-ISIS: Multi Topology (MT) Routing in IS-IS." This draft explains how the multi-topology IS-IS routing works and introduces the following four new TLVs for IS-IS:

- Multi-Topology TLV

- MT Intermediate Systems TLV

- Multi-Topology Reachable IPv4 Prefixes TLV

- Multi-Topology Reachable IPv6 Prefixes TLV

In Cisco IOS, you enable Multi-Topology routing in IS-IS by configuring **multi-topology** [transition] under the IPv6 address family of router IS-IS. If you do not configure this command, the default applies, which is to run one SPF for both IPv4 and IPv6, meaning that IPv4 and IPv6 topologies must be the same. The optional keyword *transition* allows the router to send and accept both Multi-Topology TLVs and the old-style IS-IS IPv6 TLVs. The network can then transition from the existing IS-IS IPv6 single SPF mode to the Multi-Topology IS-IS IPv6 mode.

NOTE   Wide metric is required to run Multi-Topology IS-IS IPv6.

Example 9-10 shows the basic configuration needed to run IS-IS for IPv6.

Example 9-10 *Basic IS-IS Configuration for IPv6*

```
!
ipv6 unicast-routing
ipv6 cef
!
interface Serial4/0
 ipv6 address 2001:DB8:4::1/64
 ipv6 enable
 ipv6 router isis
!
router isis
 net 49.0001.0001.0000.0000.0002.00
 !
 address-family ipv6
 redistribute static
 exit-address-family
!
```

Example 9-11 shows some commands to verify the correct functioning of IS-IS for IPv6.

Example 9-11 *Verifying IS-IS for IPv6*

```
new-york#show isis neighbors detail

System Id       Type Interface IP Address   State Holdtime Circuit Id
sydney          L1L2 Se4/0      10.200.202.2  UP    22       00
  Area Address(es): 49.0001.0001
  SNPA: *HDLC*
  IPv6 Address(es): FE80::204:C0FF:FEF1:8820
  State Changed: 00:02:17
Format: Phase V

new-york#show isis ipv6 topology

IS-IS IPv6 paths to level-1 routers
System Id            Metric    Next-Hop         Interface   SNPA
sydney               10        sydney           Se4/0       *HDLC*
new-york             --

IS-IS IPv6 paths to level-2 routers
System Id            Metric    Next-Hop         Interface   SNPA
sydney               10        sydney           Se4/0       *HDLC*
new-york             --

new-york#show isis ipv6 rib
IS-IS IPv6 process "", local RIB
  2001:DB8:4::/64
```

Example 9-11 *Verifying IS-IS for IPv6 (Continued)*

```
        via FE80::204:C0FF:FEF1:8820/Serial4/0, type L1  metric 20 LSP [3/4]
        via FE80::204:C0FF:FEF1:8820/Serial4/0, type L2  metric 20 LSP [4/4]
 * 2001:DB8:10::/64
        via FE80::204:C0FF:FEF1:8820/Serial4/0, type L1  metric 20 LSP [3/4]
        via FE80::204:C0FF:FEF1:8820/Serial4/0, type L2  metric 20 LSP [4/4]

new-york#show clns interface serial 4/0
Serial4/0 is up, line protocol is up
  Checksums enabled, MTU 1500, Encapsulation HDLC
  ERPDUs enabled, min. interval 10 msec.
  CLNS fast switching enabled
  CLNS SSE switching disabled
  DEC compatibility mode OFF for this interface
  Next ESH/ISH in 21 seconds
  Routing Protocol: IS-IS
    Circuit Type: level-1-2
    Interface number 0x0, local circuit ID 0x100
    Neighbor System-ID: sydney
    Level-1 Metric: 10, Priority: 64, Circuit ID: new-york.00
    Level-1 IPv6 Metric: 10
    Number of active level-1 adjacencies: 1
    Level-2 Metric: 10, Priority: 64, Circuit ID: new-york.00
    Level-2 IPv6 Metric: 10
    Number of active level-2 adjacencies: 1
    Next IS-IS Hello in 4 seconds
    if state UP
```

EIGRP for IPv6

Enhanced Interior Gateway Routing Protocol (EIGRP) is the Cisco proprietary distance vector routing protocol. It is the successor to the Interior Gateway Routing Protocol (IGRP), which was a huge success in the early days of routing. EIGRP became successful, too, especially in enterprise networks. These are the advances of EIGRP compared to IGRP:

- No periodic updates

- Classless routing

- A more efficient way in operating (for example, a more efficient use of bandwidth)

- Faster convergence

- The use of its own topology table

- Tracking of neighbors

- Guaranteed loop-free routing

- Internetwork Packet Exchange (IPX) and AppleTalk routing

The IPv4, IPX, and Appletalk routing in EIGRP are not tied together like IPv4, IPv6, and CLNS are when using IS-IS as the routing protocol. When you are adding IPv6 routing for EIGRP, it is just another addition, which is completely separate from EIGRP for IPv4. There is no linkage between EIGRP for IPv4 and EIGRP for IPv6; they are separately configured and managed.

To configure EIGRP for IPv6, you must enable IPv6 on the interface, configure **ipv6 eigrp** *as-number* on the interface, and configure **ipv6 router eigrp** *as-number*. The router ID for the EIGRP for IPv6 process is still a 32-bit field. You can find it in the same manner that you would for the EIGRP for IPv4 process. However, the **router-id** *ip-address* command can overwrite the router ID. If the router is running only IPv6 and not IPv4, make sure to configure at least one IPv4 address to serve as a router ID for EIGRP for IPv6. The main difference between EIGRP for IPv4 and EIGRP for IPv6 is that you enable EIGRP for IPv4 on an interface by having the network command cover the IPv4 address of the interface. In contrast, you enable EIGRP for IPv6 on an interface directly by configuring the command **ipv6 eigrp** *as-number* on the interface.

Example 9-12 shows a basic EIGRP for IPv6 configuration.

Example 9-12 *Basic Configuration of EIGRP for IPv6*

```
!
ipv6 unicast-routing
ipv6 cef
!
interface Loopback0
 ip address 10.200.254.3 255.255.255.255
!
interface Serial4/0
 ipv6 address 2001:DB8:4::1/64
 ipv6 enable
 ipv6 nd prefix default
 ipv6 eigrp 1
!
ipv6 router eigrp 1
 router-id 10.200.254.3
 redistribute static metric 64 2000 255 1 1500
!
```

The usual EIGRP router commands are also available for EIGRP for IPv6, as you can see in Example 9-13.

Example 9-13 *EIGRP for IPv6 Router Commands*

```
sydney(config)#ipv6 router eigrp  1
sydney(config-rtr)#?
  default              Set a command to its defaults
  default-information  Distribution of default information
  default-metric       Set metric of redistributed routes
```

Example 9-13   *EIGRP for IPv6 Router Commands (Continued)*

```
distance              Administrative distance
distribute-list       Filter networks in routing updates
exit                  Exit from IPv6 routing protocol configuration mode
log-neighbor-changes  Enable/Disable IPv6-EIGRP neighbor logging
log-neighbor-warnings Enable/Disable IPv6-EIGRP neighbor warnings
maximum-paths         Forward packets over multiple paths
no                    Negate a command or set its defaults
passive-interface     Suppress routing updates on an interface
redistribute          Redistribute IPv6 prefixes from another routing
                      protocol
router-id             router-id for this EIGRP process
shutdown              Shutdown protocol
stub                  Set IPv6-EIGRP as stubbed router
timers                Adjust routing timers
variance              Control load balancing variance
```

Example 9-14 shows how to verify whether EIGRP for IPv6 is forming neighborships.

Example 9-14   *Verifying EIGRP for IPv6 Neighbors*

```
new-york#show ipv6 eigrp 1 neighbors
IPv6-EIGRP neighbors for process 1
H   Address                  Interface       Hold Uptime   SRTT   RTO  Q   Seq
                                             (sec)         (ms)        Cnt Num
0   FE80::204:C0FF:FEF1:882 Se4/0             13 00:23:25    1    3000  0   1
```

Example 9-15 shows how to verify the EIGRP for IPv6 topology table.

Example 9-15   *Verifying EIGRP for IPv6 Topology Table*

```
new-york#show ipv6 eigrp 1 topology
IPv6-EIGRP Topology Table for AS(1)/ID(10.200.254.3)

Codes: P - Passive, A - Active, U - Update, Q - Query, R - Reply,
       r - reply Status, s - sia Status

P 2001:DB8:100::/64, 1 successors, FD is 2297856
        via FE80::204:C0FF:FEF1:8820 (2297856/128256), Serial4/0
P 2001:DB8:4::/64, 1 successors, FD is 2169856
        via Connected, Serial4/0
```

Example 9-16 shows how to check whether the EIGRP for IPv6 routes made it into the IPv6 routing table.

Example 9-16 *Verifying EIGRP for IPv6 Routes in the IPv6 Routing Table*

```
new-york#show ipv6 route eigrp
IPv6 Routing Table - 5 entries
Codes: C - Connected, L - Local, S - Static, R - RIP, B - BGP
       U - Per-user Static route
       I1 - ISIS L1, I2 - ISIS L2, IA - ISIS interarea, IS - ISIS summary
       O - OSPF intra, OI - OSPF inter, OE1 - OSPF ext 1, OE2 - OSPF ext 2
       ON1 - OSPF NSSA ext 1, ON2 - OSPF NSSA ext 2
       D - EIGRP, EX - EIGRP external
D   2001:DB8:100::/64 [90/2297856]
      via FE80::204:C0FF:FEF1:8820, Serial4/0
```

EIGRP for IPv6 transmits Hello packets with the link-local address of the transmitting interface as source address. The address of the EIGRP for IPv6 neighbor in the EIGRP neighbor table is the IPv6 link-local address. If you want to ping this link-local address, you do have to specify the output interface, because link-local addresses are only unique per interface. Multicast Hello packets have a destination address of FF02::A (the EIGRP for IPv6 multicast address). Packets sent to specific peers contain the unicast address of the peer. To test whether the EIGRP for IPv4 neighbors are listening, you can ping the EIGRP for IPv4 multicast address (224.0.0.10). For EIGRP for IPv6, ping the EIGRP for IPv6 multicast address (FF02::A) to verify which neighboring routers run EIGRP for IPv6. Look at Example 9-17 to learn how to perform this ping.

Example 9-17 *Pinging the EIGRP for IPv6 Multicast Address*

```
new-york#ping ipv6 ff02::a
Output Interface: serial4/0
Type escape sequence to abort.
Sending 5, 100-byte ICMP Echos to FF02::A, timeout is 2 seconds:
Packet sent with a source address of FE80::203:6CFF:FEC8:9800

Reply to request 0 received from FE80::204:C0FF:FEF1:8820, 4 ms
Reply to request 1 received from FE80::204:C0FF:FEF1:8820, 0 ms
Reply to request 2 received from FE80::204:C0FF:FEF1:8820, 0 ms
Reply to request 3 received from FE80::204:C0FF:FEF1:8820, 0 ms
Reply to request 4 received from FE80::204:C0FF:FEF1:8820, 0 ms
Success rate is 100 percent (5/5), round-trip min/avg/max = 0/0/4 ms
5 multicast replies and 0 errors.
```

Multiprotocol BGP Extensions for IPv6

Multiprotocol BGP (MP-BGP) is defined in RFC 2283. This RFC also defines two new attributes: Multiprotocol Reachable NLRI (MP_REACH_NLRI) and Multiprotocol Unreachable NLRI (MP_UNREACH_NLRI). The first one (MP_REACH_NLRI) carries the set of reachable destinations with the next-hop information to be used for forwarding to these destinations. The second one (MP_UNREACH_NLRI) carries the set of unreachable destinations. The first two fields in the two attributes contain the Address Family Identifier (AFI) and the Subsequent Address Family Identifier (SAFI). The first one identifies the network layer protocol for the network address advertised by BGP. The second one identifies additional information about the type of Network Layer Reachability Information (NLRI) carried by the attribute. Table 9-2 lists the AFI values and their meanings.

Table 9-2   *AFI Values and Meanings*

AFI	Meaning
1	IPv4
2	IPv6

NOTE   The address family numbers are listed at http://www.iana.org/numbers.html. The Internet Assigned Numbers Authority (IANA) is the central coordinator for the assignment of unique parameter values for Internet protocols.

Table 9-3 lists the SAFI values and their meanings.

Table 9-3   *SAFI Values and Meanings*

SAFI	Meaning
1	Unicast
2	Multicast
3	Unicast and multicast
4	MPLS Label
128	MPLS-labeled VPN

If BGP is carrying IPv6 traffic, AFI equals 2, SAFI equals 1 for Unicast, and SAFI equals 2 for multicast. When BGP peers set up their session between them, they send an OPEN message containing optional parameters. One optional parameter is **capabilities**. Possible capabilities are Multiprotocol extensions, route refresh, outbound route filtering (ORF), and so on. When the BGP peers exchange the Multiprotocol extension capability, they exchange AFI and SAFI numbers and thus identify what the other BGP speaker is capable of. When running BGP for unicast IPv6, BGP speakers exchange AFI/SAFI 2/1. In the case of 6PE, the BGP speakers exchange AFI/SAFI 2/4, indicating that they are capable of IPv6 and labels or IPv6 + label. In the case of 6VPE, the BGP speakers exchange AFI/SAFI 2/128, indicating that they are capable of VPNs for IPv6.

> **NOTE**   Both 6PE and 6VPE are schemes to carry IPv6 over MPLS. See the sections "Carrying IPv6 over an MPLS Backbone (6PE)" and "Carrying IPv6 in VPNs Across an MPLS Backbone (6VPE)" later in this chapter for more details.

Example 9-18 shows a BGP session being established between two BGP speakers that are capable of 6PE and 6VPE. In this example, the two speakers are also capable of Unicast IPv4 and IPv6 and MPLS VPN for IPv4, as indicated by the AFI/SAFI numbers.

Example 9-18   *BGP Exchanging AFI/SAFI*

```
!output has been removed for brevity
sydney#debug bgp all
BGP debugging is on for all address families
*May 18 11:51:51.192: BGP: 10.200.254.1 went from Idle to Active
*May 18 11:51:57.352: BGP: 10.200.254.1 went from Active to OpenSent
*May 18 11:51:57.352: BGP: 10.200.254.1 sending OPEN, version 4, my as: 1, holdtime 180
  seconds
*May 18 11:51:57.356: BGP: 10.200.254.1 rcv OPEN, version 4, holdtime 180 seconds
*May 18 11:51:57.356: BGP: 10.200.254.1 rcv OPEN w/ OPTION parameter len: 48
*May 18 11:51:57.356: BGP: 10.200.254.1 rcvd OPEN w/ optional parameter type 2
 (Capability) len 6
*May 18 11:51:57.356: BGP: 10.200.254.1 OPEN has CAPABILITY code: 1, length 4
*May 18 11:51:57.356: BGP: 10.200.254.1 OPEN has MP_EXT CAP for afi/safi: 1/1
*May 18 11:51:57.356: BGP: 10.200.254.1 rcvd OPEN w/ optional parameter type 2
 (Capability) len 6
*May 18 11:51:57.356: BGP: 10.200.254.1 OPEN has MP_EXT CAP for afi/safi: 2/1
*May 18 11:51:57.356: BGP: 10.200.254.1 rcvd OPEN w/ optional parameter type 2
 (Capability) len 6
*May 18 11:51:57.356: BGP: 10.200.254.1 OPEN has MP_EXT CAP for afi/safi: 2/4
*May 18 11:51:57.356: BGP: 10.200.254.1 rcvd OPEN w/ optional parameter type 2
 (Capability) len 6
*May 18 11:51:57.356: BGP: 10.200.254.1 OPEN has MP_EXT CAP for afi/safi: 1/128
*May 18 11:51:57.356: BGP: 10.200.254.1 rcvd OPEN w/ optional parameter type 2
 (Capability) len 6
*May 18 11:51:57.356: BGP: 10.200.254.1 OPEN has MP_EXT CAP for afi/safi: 2/128
*May 18 11:51:57.356: BGP: 10.200.254.1 rcvd OPEN w/ optional parameter type 2
 (Capability) len 2
*May 18 11:51:57.356: BGP: 10.200.254.1 OPEN has CAPABILITY code: 2, length 0
*May 18 11:51:57.356: BGP: 10.200.254.1 OPEN has ROUTE-REFRESH capability(new)
for all address-families
BGP: 10.200.254.1 rcvd OPEN w/ remote AS 1
*May 18 11:51:57.360: BGP: 10.200.254.1 went from OpenSent to OpenConfirm
*May 18 11:51:57.360: BGP: 10.200.254.1 went from OpenConfirm to Established
*May 18 11:51:57.360: %BGP-5-ADJCHANGE: neighbor 10.200.254.1 Up
```

CEFv6

Cisco Express Forwarding (CEF) is explained in Chapter 6, "Cisco Express Forwarding." To recap, CEF provides a prebuilt forwarding table that is derived from the IPv4 routing table. This table is used to forward IP packets either on the central processor or on the line cards/VIPs if the router has a distributed architecture. An adjacency table is used to perform the Layer 2 rewrite of the frame. For example, it can rewrite the outgoing source and destination MAC address when forwarding the Ethernet frame out of the router. CEF is required to run on the Cisco IOS router if MPLS is running because CEF is the only switching method that can impose labels on the IP packet. CEFv6 will be needed in the 6PE and 6VPE solutions that are explained later in this chapter. In both solutions, IPv6 packets will be coming in on the PE router from a customer edge (CE) router, and the IPv6 packets will be imposed with two labels before being forwarded into the MPLS backbone. Therefore, you will be able to find the IPv6 prefixes in the CEFv6 table with outgoing labels, and each IPv6 neighbor will have to be an entry in the adjacency table.

As you can see in Example 9-19, IPv6 now has an adjacency entry next to the adjacencies for IP (this is IPv4) and TAG (MPLS).

Example 9-19 *Adjacency Table*

```
london#show adjacency detail
Protocol Interface          Address
IP       Ethernet0/0/0         10.200.200.2(15)
                               0 packets, 0 bytes
                               epoch 0
                               sourced in sev-epoch 30
                               Encap length 14
                               00604700881D00024A4008000800
                               ARP
TAG      Ethernet0/0/0         10.200.200.2(9)
                               0 packets, 0 bytes
                               epoch 0
                               sourced in sev-epoch 30
                               Encap length 14
                               00604700881D00024A4008008847
                               ARP
IPV6     Serial0/1/0           point2point(11)
                               816 packets, 130848 bytes
                               epoch 0
                               sourced in sev-epoch 29
                               Encap length 4
                               0F0086DD
                               P2P-ADJ
```

IPv6 can have a CEFv6 table and CEFv6 virtual routing/forwarding (VRF) tables. The output from Example 9-20 is taken from a 6VPE network and shows the prefixes from the VRF cust-one in the CEFv6 VRF table on a PE router. Notice that some prefixes have two outgoing labels associated with them.

Example 9-20   *CEFv6 VRF Table*

```
london#show ipv6 cef vrf cust-one
2001:DB8:1:1::/64
  nexthop 2001:DB8:2::1 Serial0/1/0
2001:DB8:1:2::/64
  nexthop 10.200.200.2 Ethernet0/0/0 label 20 19
2001:DB8:3::/64
  nexthop 10.200.200.2 Ethernet0/0/0 label 20 23
```

The command **ipv6 cef** enables IPv6 CEF globally, and **ipv6 cef distributed** enables CEFv6 in distributed mode. The **show cef** commands also display IPv6 information.

This chapter could go into much more detail about IPv6, but because this is not a book on IPv6, you are encouraged to look elsewhere if you are interested in learning more about it. You can find some great books on IPv6, besides a wealth of IPv6 information on the Internet.

Carrying IPv6 over an MPLS Backbone

Because of the huge success of MPLS VPN, most service provider networks are running MPLS in their network today. If the service provider has customers connected to his network who want to run IPv6 and the service provider needs to carry IPv6 across his network, the obvious solution is to have IPv6 running on his routers, too. However, this approach has two disadvantages. First, the service provider needs to enable a new protocol (IPv6) on all his routers. Because IPv4 and IPv6 are running on the router, the router is running a dual-stack. Second, the other customers— still running IPv4—are not going away or transitioning their network to IPv6 overnight. Therefore, IPv4 and IPv6 have to run in parallel for a long time into the future.

If the service provider also wants to run MPLS for IPv6, IPv6 needs LDP support, which is not implemented yet. However, because MPLS stands for Multiprotocol Label Switching, it can transport more than just IPv4 as a payload. In networks that are running MPLS today, the labeled packets might be IPv6 packets, without the need for the P routers to run IPv6. The solutions 6PE and 6VPE are based on this.

Another method to carry IPv6 over an MPLS backbone is Any Transport over MPLS (AToM). With this solution, the MPLS payload is actually a Layer 2 frame. On the edge LSRs, the frames are labeled and then transported across the MPLS backbone through a virtual circuit or pseudowire. The transported Layer 2 frames can be Ethernet, High-Level Data Link

Control (HDLC), ATM, Frame Relay, and so on. This solution is described in Chapter 10, "Any Transport over MPLS." All three solutions have the advantage that the P routers in the MPLS backbone do not need to run IPv6 because the P routers switch only labeled packets. As such, these solutions are more popular than directly running IPv6 across the backbone. The AToM solution has two disadvantages compared to 6PE and 6VPE. The first is that the MPLS payload is made up of frames and not IPv6 packets. Therefore, an added Layer 2 header needs to be transported across the MPLS backbone. The second is that the pseudowires or virtual circuits are point-to-point in nature, whereas the 6PE and 6VPE solution are any-to-any.

One last method to carry IPv6 over an MPLS backbone is to use the MPLS VPN solution. In the case of MPLS VPN, IPv4 is carried inside VPNs over the MPLS backbone. To carry the IPv6 traffic over IPv4, the CE routers need tunnels between them. This means that the CE routers need to be dual-stack routers. These routers are the only routers that are running IPv6, because the PE routers see only IPv4 packets coming from the CE routers. In short, the advantage is that MPLS VPN is already deployed in many or most service provider networks, and the PE (and P) routers do not need to run IPv6. The disadvantage is that the CE routers need to have tunnels configured, and an extra IPv4 header adds overhead.

MPLS VPN Network Using IPv6 over IPv4 Tunnels on the CE Routers

MPLS VPN for IPv4 has seen a great success. Many service providers run it in their network. If you want to carry IPv6 over the MPLS VPN backbone, the CE routers are running IPv6 already. If the CE routers run dual-stack—meaning they also run IPv4 next to IPv6—you can implement tunnels between the CE routes to carry the IPv6 traffic. As such, the possibility of carrying IPv6 over the MPLS VPN network might seem an interesting one, because no changes need to be made on the MPLS network. The PE and P routers do not need to run IPv6 at all. The disadvantage is that the tunnels on the CE routers do not bring to IPv6 the advantage of the peer model that the MPLS VPN model has. As such, the provisioning of the CE routers is an old-style, tedious job. However, you can use several kinds of tunnels on the CE routers to carry the IPv6 traffic. Following are the tunneling methods for IPv6 that you can implement with Cisco IOS today:

- IPv6 over IPv4 GRE tunnels

- Manual IPv6 tunnels

- 6to4 tunnels

- IPv4-compatible IPv6 tunnels

- ISATAP tunnels

Figure 9-4 shows an MPLS VPN for IPv4 network with CE routers running tunnels between them to carry the IPv6 traffic across the MPLS backbone.

Figure 9-4 *MPLS VPN Network Carrying IPv6 over IPv4 Tunnels*

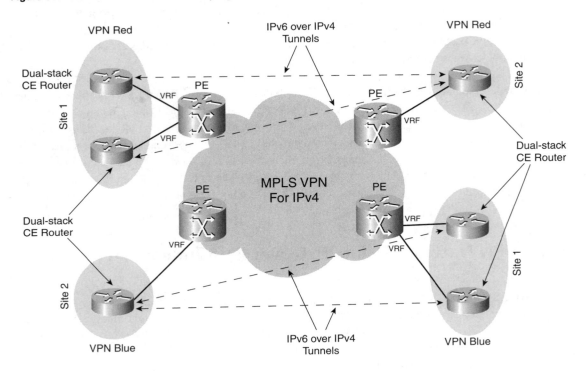

Carrying IPv6 over an MPLS Backbone (6PE)

6PE is the Cisco name for directly carrying IPv6 packets over the MPLS backbone. Note that the MPLS network does not need to run MPLS VPN. The IPv6 networks do not belong to a VPN, so no VRF interface exists on the provider edge (PE) routers. All IPv6 CE routers can see each other as 6PE runs in the global address space on the PE routers.

Operation of 6PE

In the 6PE solution, the PE routers are dual-stack, which means they run IPv4 and IPv6. The CE routers that are running IPv6 are connected to the PE router via a normal interface; the interface is not part of a VRF for IPv6 even though the same interface might be in a VRF for IPv4. The IPv6 routing distribution between the PE routers is done via MP-iBGP. At the same time, MP-iBGP distributes the label to be used for the specific IPv6 prefixes. This BGP label identifies or tags the IPv6 packet at the egress PE. The egress PE looks up this BGP label in the label forwarding information base (LFIB) and uses it to forward the IPv6 packet toward the egress CE. Look at Figure 9-5.

Figure 9-5 *6PE Network*

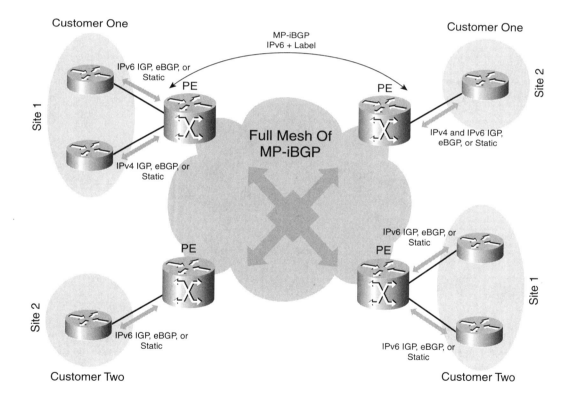

Figure 9-5 shows an MPLS network that is running 6PE. The PE routers have CE routers that are connected to them. Some of the CE routers are running IPv6, whereas others are running IPv4. The PE routers can even have a VRF interface and run MPLS VPN for IPv4 for some CE routers. The interfaces that are on the PE toward the CE routers that are running IPv6 are not in a VRF, though. The PE routers run a full mesh of MP-iBGP for IPv6. The iBGP sessions distribute the IPv6 prefixes and the associated MPLS label. This is known as IPv6 + label and is encoded according to RFC 3107. Look at Figure 9-6. It shows a network that has only two PEs running 6PE. The sydney PE router distributes the IPv6 prefix 2001:DB8:1:2::1/128 with a label of 22 to the london PE via MP-iBGP. All PE and P routers run an IGP and LDP. For packets to be forwarded to the CE router that is connected to the sydney PE, you must distribute the BGP next hop 10.200.254.4/32 with a label in the MPLS network.

Figure 9-6 *6PE Routing and Label Distribution*

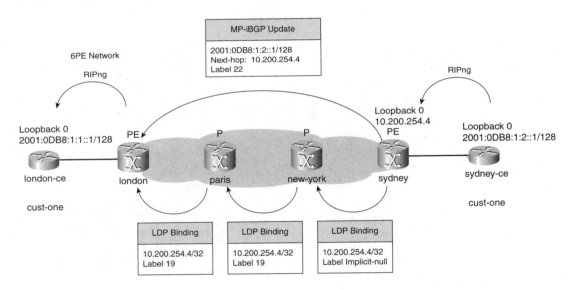

The packet forwarding is shown in Figure 9-7. You can see two labels on top of the packets: an IGP label as the top label and the BGP label as the bottom label. The IGP label is the LDP or RSVP (traffic engineering) label for the BGP next hop of the egress PE. This BGP next hop is encoded as an IPv4-mapped IPv6 address containing an IPv4 address of the egress PE router. As such, when the IPv6 packet arrives on the ingress PE and needs to be label-imposed, the IGP label used is the one associated with the IPv4 address derived from the IPv4-mapped IPv6 address. The BGP label is the label that the remote PE sent for the IPv6 prefix.

Figure 9-7 *6PE Packet Forwarding*

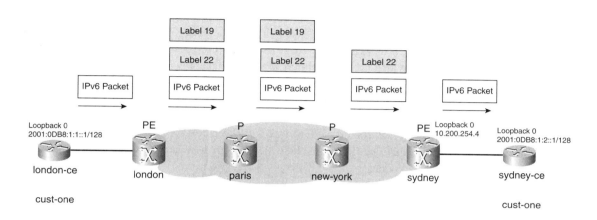

One advantage of 6PE is that the P router does not need to run IPv6 or even be IPv6 capable. Therefore, the 6PE solution can be quickly deployed over an existing MPLS backbone. A second advantage is that the IPv6 packets are directly labeled without an extra header. In the case of an AToM solution, an extra Layer 2 header is transported; in the case of IPv6 over IPv4 tunnels, an extra IPv4 header is transported. Part of the reason for the deployment of the 6PE solution is that many service providers already have an MPLS backbone because of the popularity of MPLS VPN. The operation of 6PE is similar to the operation of MPLS VPN. As such, people who are familiar with MPLS VPN quickly understand 6PE. Following are some similarities to MPLS VPN for IPv4:

■ A full mesh is needed of MP-iBGP.

■ There needs to be an IGP for IPv6 or eBGP or static routing between the PE and CE.

■ The IPv6 packets are labeled with two labels.

Perhaps most important, the 6PE solution follows the peer-to-peer VPN model that was discussed in Chapter 1, "The Evolution of MPLS," and is used in the MPLS VPN for IPv4 solution. Each CE has only one routing peer across the MPLS network, namely toward the directly attached PE router.

Because this solution involves no VPNs, no VRF interfaces exist for IPv6 on the PE routers; as such, the PE and CE routers can use any routing protocol for IPv6 in the 6PE solution. The IPv6 routing protocol does not have to be VRF-aware.

The IPv6 packet has two labels when it is forwarded through the MPLS network. Strictly taken, the IPv6 packet can be forwarded through the MPLS network with only one label on top of it. Because of penultimate hop popping (PHP), the packet would then be forwarded unlabeled between the last P router and the egress PE router. This is possible only if the last P router is IPv6-capable. If only one MPLS label and PHP are in use, the penultimate hop router must be able to know what the MPLS payload is before sending the IPv6 packet toward the egress PE router. The penultimate router must know this to set the correct protocol type in the Layer 2 header when sending the frame. Updating the IPv6 header (updating the Hop Limit and Traffic Class fields) before forwarding the IPv6 packet to the egress PE router might also be a problem. To avoid the IPv6 capability in provider (P) routers, 6PE uses two MPLS labels for forwarding. To deploy 6PE, only the edge routers need to be IPv6 capable, which is a great advantage when deploying 6PE over existing MPLS backbones.

Configuration of 6PE

The 6PE solution is simple and straightforward to configure. This section shows you that you only need to enable the iBGP neighbor under the IPv6 address family of BGP and add one extra keyword (iBGP neighbor command with the *send-label* keyword). Of course, you need to configure an IGP for IPv6 on the link between the PE and CE router. Alternatively, you can configure eBGP between the PE and CE or even static routing for IPv6.

Only two 6PE-specific commands exist:

```
neighbor ip-address send-label
```

This command activates the sending of MPLS labels via MP-BGP for the IPv6 address family and BGP peer.

```
mpls ipv6 source-interface type number
```

This command specifies the interface type and number from which MPLS takes the IPv6 address as a source address for locally generated IPv6 traffic.

When configuring 6PE, make sure **ipv6 cef** and **ipv6 unicast-routing** are configured on all routers that are running IPv6. On the PE routers, you need to redistribute the IPv6 IGP into BGP and vice versa. You need **redistribute connected** under the **address-family ipv6** of router BGP if you want the IPv6 addresses on the PE-CE link to be reachable.

Examples 9-21 to 9-24 apply to the routers that are depicted in Figure 9-6. RIPng is the IPv6 IGP between the CE and PE routers. Example 9-21 shows the configuration of the CE router london-ce.

Example 9-21 *Configuration of the CE Router London-CE*

```
!
hostname london-ce
!
ipv6 unicast-routing
```

Example 9-21 *Configuration of the CE Router London-CE (Continued)*

```
ipv6 cef
!
interface Loopback0
 ip address 10.100.1.1 255.255.255.255
 ipv6 address 2001:DB8:1:1::1/128
 ipv6 rip cust-one enable
!
interface Serial2/0
 description interface to PE london
 no ip address
 ipv6 address 2001:DB8:2::1/64
 ipv6 rip cust-one enable
!
ipv6 router rip cust-one
!
```

Example 9-22 shows the configuration of the PE router london.

Example 9-22 *Configuration of the PE Router London*

```
!
hostname london
!
ipv6 unicast-routing
ipv6 cef
!
interface Ethernet0/0
 description interface to P paris
 ip address 10.1.2.1 255.255.255.0
 ip ospf cost 1
 mpls ip
!
interface Serial2/0
 description interface to CE london
 no ip address
 ipv6 address 2001:DB8:2::2/64
 ipv6 enable
 ipv6 rip cust-one enable
!
router bgp 1
 neighbor 10.200.254.4 remote-as 1
 neighbor 10.200.254.4 update-source Loopback0
 no auto-summary
 !
 address-family ipv6
 neighbor 10.200.254.4 activate
 neighbor 10.200.254.4 send-community both
 neighbor 10.200.254.4 send-label
```

continues

Example 9-22 *Configuration of the PE Router London (Continued)*

```
 redistribute connected
 redistribute rip cust-one
 exit-address-family
 !
ipv6 router rip cust-one
 redistribute bgp 1
 !
```

Example 9-23 shows the configuration of the PE router sydney.

Example 9-23 *Configuration of the PE Router Sydney*

```
 !
hostname sydney
 !
ipv6 unicast-routing
ipv6 cef
 !
interface Ethernet0/0
 description interface to P new-york
 ip address 10.2.1.2 255.255.255.0
 ip ospf cost 1
 mpls ip
 !
interface Serial2/0
 description interface to CE sydney
 no ip address
 ipv6 address 2001:DB8:3::2/64
 ipv6 enable
 ipv6 rip cust-one enable
 !
router bgp 1

 neighbor 10.200.254.1 remote-as 1
 neighbor 10.200.254.1 update-source Loopback0
 !
 address-family ipv6
 neighbor 10.200.254.1 activate
 neighbor 10.200.254.1 send-community both
 neighbor 10.200.254.1 send-label
 redistribute connected
 redistribute rip cust-one
 no synchronization
 exit-address-family
 !
ipv6 router rip cust-one
 redistribute bgp 1
 !
```

Example 9-24 shows the configuration of the CE router sydney-ce.

Example 9-24   *Configuration of the CE Router Sydney-CE*

```
!
hostname syndney-ce
!
ipv6 unicast-routing
ipv6 cef
!
interface Loopback0
 ip address 10.100.103.1 255.255.255.255
 ipv6 address 2001:DB8:1:2::1/128
 ipv6 rip cust-one enable
!
interface Serial2/0
 description interface to PE sydney
 no ip address
 ipv6 address 2001:DB8:3::1/64
 ipv6 enable
 ipv6 rip cust-one enable
!
ipv6 router rip cust-one
!
```

Verifying 6PE Operation

Example 9-25 shows how to verify that the MP-iBGP peering sessions between the PE routers have the IPv6 + label capability.

Example 9-25   *Verifying MP-BGP for IPv6*

```
london#show bgp ipv6 unicast neighbors
BGP neighbor is 10.200.254.4,  remote AS 1, internal link
  BGP version 4, remote router ID 10.200.254.4
  BGP state = Established, up for 3d22h
  Last read 00:00:07, hold time is 180, keepalive interval is 60 seconds
  Neighbor capabilities:
    Route refresh: advertised and received(new)
    Address family IPv4 Unicast: advertised and received
    Address family IPv6 Unicast: advertised and received
    ipv6 MPLS Label capability: advertised and received
...
For address family: IPv6 Unicast
  BGP table version 5, neighbor version 5/0
  Output queue size : 0
  Index 1, Offset 0, Mask 0x2
  1 update-group member
  Community attribute sent to this neighbor
  Sending Prefix & Label
...
```

Example 9-26 shows how to check whether the IPv6 prefix 2001:DB8:1:2::1/128 made it to the PE routers and london-ce. It also shows that a traceroute from london-ce to the loopback IPv6 address of sydney-ce succeeds.

Example 9-26 *Verifying IPv6 Prefixes*

```
london#show ipv6 route 2001:DB8:1:2::1/128
Routing entry for 2001:DB8:1:2::1/128
  Known via "bgp 1", distance 200, metric 2, type internal
  Redistributing via rip cust-one
  Route count is 1/1, share count 0
  Routing paths:
    10.200.254.4%Default-IP-Routing-Table indirectly connected
      MPLS Required
      Last updated 3d22h ago


sydney#show ipv6 route 2001:DB8:1:2::1/128
Routing entry for 2001:DB8:1:2::1/128
  Known via "rip cust-one", distance 120, metric 2
  Redistributing via bgp 1
  Route count is 1/1, share count 0
  Routing paths:
    FE80::FF:FEC8:5808, Serial2/0
      Last updated 3d22h ago


london#show bgp ipv6 unicast 2001:DB8:1:2::1/128
BGP routing table entry for 2001:DB8:1:2::1/128, version 5
Paths: (1 available, best #1, table default)
  Not advertised to any peer
  Local
    ::FFFF:10.200.254.4 (metric 4) from 10.200.254.4 (10.200.254.4)
      Origin incomplete, metric 2, localpref 100, valid, internal, best,
      mpls labels in/out nolabel/22


london-ce#show ipv6 route 2001:DB8:1:2::1
Routing entry for 2001:DB8:1:2::1/128
  Known via "rip cust-one", distance 120, metric 3
  Route count is 1/1, share count 0
  Routing paths:
    FE80::A8BB:CCFF:FE00:200, Serial2/0
      Last updated 3d23h ago

!Check if the BGP label is received on the local PE.
```

Example 9-26   *Verifying IPv6 Prefixes (Continued)*

```
london#show bgp ipv6 unicast labels
   Network              Next Hop        In label/Out label
   2001:DB8:1:1::1/128
                           ::                 22/nolabel
   2001:DB8:1:2::1/128
                        ::FFFF:10.200.254.4
                                           nolabel/22
   2001:DB8:2::/64   ::                  16/nolabel
   2001:DB8:3::/64   ::FFFF:10.200.254.4
                                           nolabel/21

london-ce#traceroute
Protocol [ip]: ipv6
Target IPv6 address: 2001:DB8:1:2::1
Source address:
Insert source routing header? [no]:
Numeric display? [no]:
Timeout in seconds [3]:
Probe count [3]: 1
Minimum Time to Live [1]:
Maximum Time to Live [30]:
Priority [0]:
Port Number [33434]:
Type escape sequence to abort.
Tracing the route to 2001:DB8:1:2::1

  1 2001:DB8:2::2 28 msec
  2 ::FFFF:10.1.2.2 [MPLS: Labels 19/22 Exp 0] 20 msec
  3 ::FFFF:10.3.1.2 [MPLS: Labels 19/22 Exp 0] 28 msec
  4 2001:DB8:3::2 [MPLS: Label 22 Exp 0] 28 msec
  5 2001:DB8:3::1 28 msec
```

NOTE   Notice the ::FFFF:IPv4 address notation in the traceroute. This is an IPv4-mapped IPv6 address, because it has the format of ::FFFF:IPv4-address. It represents the address of IPv4-only nodes as an IPv6 address. This is the result of this P router not having IPv6 enabled. If this P router has IPv6 enabled and an IPv6 address on the incoming interface, a regular IPv6 address would show up in the traceroute instead of this IPv4-mapped IPv6 address. However, if the P router does not have IPv6 software, it cannot understand the IPv6 packet with the expiring TTL, and it cannot generate an ICMPv6 message. In that case, the P router drops that packet. The result is an output of * * * in the traceroute for that P router.

Example 9-27 shows how to check whether the labels are in the CEFv6 table on the ingress PE for the IPv6 prefix.

Example 9-27 *Verifying the CEFv6 Table on the Ingress PE*

```
london#show ipv6 cef 2001:DB8:1:2::1/128 detail
2001:DB8:1:2::1/128, epoch 0
  recursive via 10.200.254.4 label 22
    nexthop 10.1.2.2 Ethernet0/0 label 19
```

Example 9-28 shows how to check the LFIB on the egress PE.

Example 9-28 *Verifying the LFIB on the Egress PE*

```
sydney#show mpls forwarding-table 2001:DB8:1:2::1/128 detail
Local  Outgoing     Prefix            Bytes Label   Outgoing    Next Hop
Label  Label or VC  or Tunnel Id      Switched      interface
22     No Label     2001:DB8:1:2::1/128   \
                                      5936          Se2/0       point2point
       MAC/Encaps=4/4, MRU=1504, Label Stack{}
       0F0086DD
       No output feature configured
```

Carrying IPv6 in VPNs Across an MPLS Backbone (6VPE)

The MPLS VPN solution for IPv6 or IPv6 VPN provider edge (6VPE) is similar to the operation of MPLS VPN for IPv4. It is unnecessary to repeat all aspects again. For that reason, read Chapter 7, "MPLS VPN," before reading this section on 6VPE. The obvious difference between 6PE and 6VPE is that in 6VPE, the IPv6 customer prefixes belong to a VPN and are completely separated from the prefixes of the other customers who connect to the same MPLS VPN network.

Operation of 6VPE

The operation of MPLS VPN for IPv6 or 6VPE is similar to the operation of MPLS VPN for IPv4. 6VPE has the following key features:

- It has an MPLS core network running an IPv4 routing protocol (IGP) and a label distribution protocol (LDP or RSVP for TE).

- The edge LSRs or PE routers are capable of running IPv6.

- The edge LSRs or PE routers have VRFs that designate the VPNs toward the customer or CE routers.

- A full mesh of MP-iBGP sessions exists between the edge LSRs or PE routers and serves to distribute the IPv6 VPN prefixes and their associated labels. (These IPv6 VPN prefixes are now called vpnv6 prefixes.) This is also known as vpnv6 + label. The label encoding is done according to RFC 3107.

- The IPv6 packets are transported across the MPLS network with two labels: an IGP label as the top label and a BGP (or VPN) label as the bottom label.

- The PE and CE routers have an IPv6 routing protocol between them.

As you can see, these are similar key features to the ones for MPLS VPN for IPv4. The difference, of course, is that now the transported protocol is IPv6 and not IPv4. Notice that the PE routers must run IPv4 and IPv6 and that the P routers must not be capable of IPv6. Figure 9-8 shows the basic operation of the 6VPE solution.

Figure 9-8 *6VPE Network*

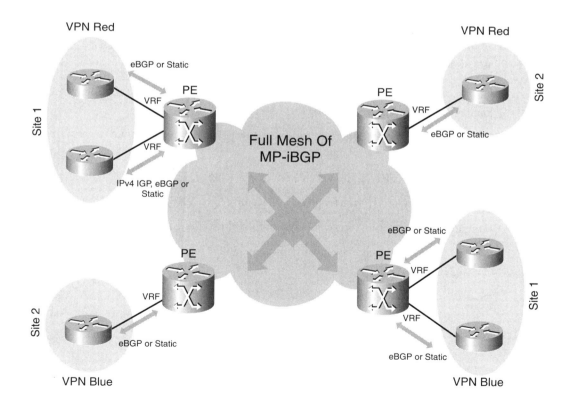

The 6VPE and MPLS VPN for IPv4 solutions are different in the following ways:

- Address family vpnv6 is used instead of address family vpnv4 for BGP; there is vpnv6 + label instead of vpnv4 + label between the PE routers.

- The next hop of the vpnv6 prefix is an IPv4-mapped IPv6 address of the egress PE.

A vpnv6 prefix is an IPv6 prefix that is prepended with a 64-bit route distinguisher (RD). This combination of an IPv6 prefix and RD makes the vpnv6 prefix unique throughout the network, allowing overlapping IPv6 prefix ranges in different VPNs, as long as those VPNs are not allowed to communicate with each other.

You can use 6VPE and MPLS VPN for IPv4 at the same time, even on the same interface on the PE router toward the CE router. You can have both an IPv6 VRF and an IPv4 VRF configured on the same interface.

Configuration of 6VPE

6VPE is similar in operation to MPLS VPN for IPv4, so similar commands are used, but now for IPv6 instead of IPv4. Following are the steps needed to configure 6VPE:

1. Configure MPLS in the IPv4 core network (this means an IPv4 unicast routing protocol and a label distribution protocol) as for MPLS VPN for IPv4.

2. Configure an IPv6 VPN routing and forwarding (VRF) instance (with route-target import and export policies) on the PE router.

3. Associate the IPv6 VRF to an interface on the PE router.

4. Configure address family vpnv6 and address family IPv6 VRF for the BGP routing protocol.

5. Configure an IPv6 routing protocol between the PE and the CE routers.

In Figure 9-9, you can see a sample network running 6VPE, with MP-eBGP as the PE-CE routing protocol.

Figure 9-9   *6VPE Sample Network*

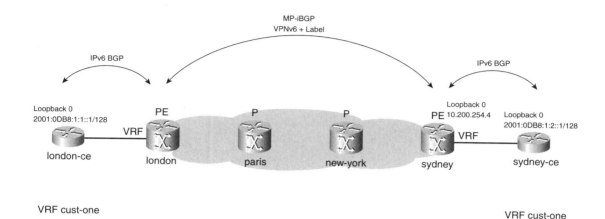

This is the basic configuration needed to have 6VPE working. In this example, there is one VRF cust-one, and the PE-CE routing protocol is MP-eBGP. On the PE routers, you must have the address family vpnv6 for BGP configured. You do not need the **send-label** keyword for the iBGP sessions, because the label is sent by default for the iBGP vpnv6 prefixes (as with the MPLS VPN for IPv4 solution). Example 9-29 shows the configuration of the london-ce router.

Example 9-29   *Configuration of the London-CE*

```
!
hostname london-ce
!
ipv6 unicast-routing
ipv6 cef
!
interface Loopback0
 ip address 10.100.1.1 255.255.255.255
 ipv6 address 2001:DB8:1:1::1/128
!
interface Serial2/0
 description interface to PE london
 ip address 10.1.1.1 255.255.255.0
 ipv6 address 2001:DB8:2::1/64
!
```

continues

Example 9-29 *Configuration of the London-CE (Continued)*

```
router bgp 65000
 bgp log-neighbor-changes
 neighbor 2001:DB8:2::2 remote-as 1
 !
 address-family ipv4
 no neighbor 2001:DB8:2::2 activate
 exit-address-family
 !
 address-family ipv6
 neighbor 2001:DB8:2::2 activate
 network 2001:DB8:1:1::1/128
 exit-address-family
 !
```

Example 9-30 shows the configuration of the london PE.

NOTE Notice the change in some commands. The VRF is now defined with **vrf definition** *vrf-name*, and it has been made address-family aware. The interface command to assign an interface to a VRF instance is **vrf forwarding** *vrf-name*.

Example 9-30 *Configuration of the London PE*

```
!
hostname london
!
ipv6 unicast-routing
ipv6 cef
!
vrf definition cust-one
 rd 1:1
 !
 address-family ipv6
 route-target export 1:1
 route-target import 1:1
 exit-address-family
!
mpls ldp router-id Loopback0 force
mpls label protocol ldp
!
interface Loopback0
 ip address 10.200.254.1 255.255.255.255
!
interface Ethernet0/0
 description interface to P paris
 ip address 10.1.2.1 255.255.255.0
```

Example 9-30   *Configuration of the London PE (Continued)*

```
 mpls ip
 !
 interface Serial2/0
  description interface to CE london
  vrf forwarding cust-one
  ipv6 address 2001:DB8:2::2/64
  ipv6 enable
 !
 router ospf 1
  log-adjacency-changes
  network 10.200.0.0 0.0.255.255 area 0
 !
 router bgp 1
  no synchronization
  bgp log-neighbor-changes
  neighbor 10.200.254.4 remote-as 1
  neighbor 10.200.254.4 update-source Loopback0
  !
  address-family ipv4
  no neighbor 10.200.254.4 activate
  exit-address-family
 !
  address-family vpnv6
  neighbor 10.200.254.4 activate
  neighbor 10.200.254.4 send-community both
  exit-address-family
  !
  address-family ipv6 vrf cust-one
  neighbor 2001:DB8:2::1 remote-as 65000
  neighbor 2001:DB8:2::1 activate
  neighbor 2001:DB8:2::1 as-override
  redistribute connected
  no synchronization
  exit-address-family
 !
```

Example 9-31 shows the configuration of the PE router sydney.

Example 9-31   *Configuration of the Sydney PE*

```
 !
 hostname sydney
 !
 ipv6 unicast-routing
 ipv6 cef
 !
 vrf definition cust-one
```

continues

Example 9-31 *Configuration of the Sydney PE (Continued)*

```
 rd 1:1
 !
 address-family ipv6
 route-target export 1:1
 route-target import 1:1
 exit-address-family
!
mpls ldp router-id Loopback0 force
mpls label protocol ldp
!
interface Loopback0
 ip address 10.200.254.4 255.255.255.255
!
interface Ethernet0/0
 description interface to P new-york
 ip address 10.2.1.2 255.255.255.0
 mpls ip
!
interface Serial2/0
 description interface to CE sydney
 vrf forwarding cust-one
 ipv6 address 2001:DB8:3::2/64
 ipv6 enable
!
router ospf 1
 log-adjacency-changes
 network 10.200.0.0 0.0.255.255 area 0
!
router bgp 1
 bgp log-neighbor-changes
 neighbor 10.200.254.1 remote-as 1
 neighbor 10.200.254.1 update-source Loopback0
 neighbor 2001:DB8:3::1 remote-as 65000
 !
 address-family ipv4
 no neighbor 10.200.254.1 activate
 exit-address-family
 !
 address-family vpnv6
 neighbor 10.200.254.1 activate
 neighbor 10.200.254.1 send-community both
 exit-address-family
 !
```

Example 9-31 *Configuration of the Sydney PE (Continued)*

```
address-family ipv6 vrf cust-one
neighbor 2001:DB8:3::1 remote-as 65000
neighbor 2001:DB8:3::1 activate
neighbor 2001:DB8:3::1 as-override
redistribute connected
no synchronization
exit-address-family
!
```

Example 9-32 shows the configuration of the sydney-ce.

Example 9-32 *Configuration of the Sydney-CE*

```
!
hostname sydney-ce
!
ipv6 unicast-routing
ipv6 cef
!
interface Loopback0
 ip address 10.100.103.1 255.255.255.255
 ipv6 address 2001:DB8:1:2::1/128
!
interface Serial2/0
 description interface to PE sydney
 ipv6 address 2001:DB8:3::1/64
 ipv6 enable
!
router bgp 65000
 bgp log-neighbor-changes
 neighbor 2001:DB8:3::2 remote-as 1
 !
 address-family ipv6
 neighbor 2001:DB8:3::2 activate
 network 2001:DB8:1:2::1/128
 exit-address-family
!
```

The supported PE-CE IPv6 routing protocols for the 6VPE solution, at the time of writing this book, are eBGP and static IPv6 routes.

Verifying 6VPE Operation

Figure 9-10 depicts the distribution of a vpnv6 prefix and label by MP-iBGP in a 6VPE network.

Figure 9-10 *Distribution of vpnv6 Prefixes and Labels*

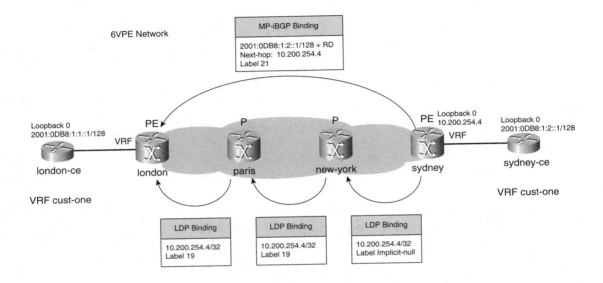

Figure 9-11 shows the same network depicting the packet forwarding of an IPv6 packet through the 6VPE network.

Figure 9-11 *Packet Forwarding Through the 6VPE Network*

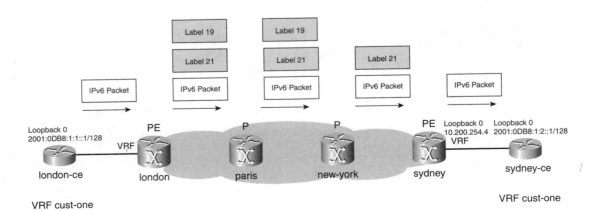

Example 9-33 shows how to check which IPv6 VRFs are running on the PE router.

Example 9-33   *Verifying IPv6 VRFs*

```
london#show vrf ipv6 cust-one
  Name                        Default RD          Protocols   Interfaces
  cust-one                    1:1                 ipv6        Serial2/0

london#show vrf ipv6 detail
VRF cust-one; default RD 1:1; default VPNID <not set>
  Interfaces:
    Serial2/0
Address family ipv6 (Table ID = 0x1E000001):
  Connected addresses are not in global routing table
  Export VPN route-target communities
    RT:1:1
  Import VPN route-target communities
    RT:1:1
  No import route-map
  No export route-map
  VRF label distribution protocol: not configured

london#show vrf ipv6 interfaces
Interface                   VRF                 Protocol    Address
Serial2/0                   cust-one            up          2001:DB8:2::2
```

Example 9-34 shows how to check whether BGP is running the capability of vpnv6.

Example 9-34   *Verifying MP-BGP for vpnv6*

```
london#show ip bgp neighbors
BGP neighbor is 10.200.254.4,  remote AS 1, internal link
  BGP version 4, remote router ID 10.200.254.4
  BGP state = Established, up for 00:29:29
  Last read 00:00:39, hold time is 180, keepalive interval is 60 seconds
  Neighbor capabilities:
    Route refresh: advertised and received(new)
    Address family VPNv6 Unicast: advertised and received
```

Example 9-35 shows how to check if on the remote PE, the IPv6 VRF prefix made it into the BGP table.

Example 9-35   *Verifying vpnv6 Prefixes*

```
sydney#show bgp vpnv6 unicast vrf cust-one 2001:DB8:1:2::1/128
BGP routing table entry for [1:1]2001:DB8:1:2::1/128, version 5
Paths: (1 available, best #1, table cust-one)
  Advertised to update-groups:
```

continues

Example 9-35   *Verifying vpnv6 Prefixes (Continued)*

```
    2
65000
   2001:DB8:3::1 (FE80::FF:FEC8:5808) from 2001:DB8:3::1 (10.100.103.1)
      Origin IGP, metric 0, localpref 100, valid, external, best
      Extended Community: RT:1:1,
      mpls labels in/out 21/nolabel
```

Notice that the RD of the vpnv6 prefixes is printed between []. vpnv6 prefixes are shown in the [RD]IPv6-network/mask-length notation. vpnv4 prefixes are printed in the RD:IPv4-network/mask-length notation. Using the same notation for vpnv6 prefixes might create problems, because the : used between the RD and the prefix is also used in the IPv6 prefix notation.

Example 9-36 shows how to check whether the IPv6 VRF prefix made it into the BGP table on the ingress PE.

Example 9-36   *Verifying vpnv6 Prefixes*

```
london#show bgp vpnv6 unicast vrf cust-one 2001:DB8:1:2::1/128
BGP routing table entry for [1:1]2001:DB8:1:2::1/128, version 7
Paths: (1 available, best #1, table cust-one)
  Advertised to update-groups:
     1
  65000
    ::FFFF:10.200.254.4 (metric 13) from 10.200.254.4 (10.200.254.4)
      Origin IGP, metric 0, localpref 100, valid, internal, best
      Extended Community: RT:1:1,
      mpls labels in/out nolabel/21
```

Example 9-37 shows how to verify the routing entries on the CE and PE routers.

Example 9-37   *Verifying Routing Entries on the CE and PE Routers*

```
london-ce#show ipv6 route 2001:DB8:1:2::1/128
Routing entry for 2001:DB8:1:2::1/128
  Known via "bgp 65000", distance 20, metric 0, type external
  Route count is 1/1, share count 0
  Routing paths:
    FE80::A8BB:CCFF:FE00:200, Serial2/0
      Last updated 00:30:29 ago

london#show ipv6 route vrf cust-one 2001:DB8:1:2::1/128
Routing entry for 2001:DB8:1:2::1/128
  Known via "bgp 1", distance 200, metric 0, type internal
  Route count is 1/1, share count 0
  Routing paths:
```

Example 9-37 *Verifying Routing Entries on the CE and PE Routers (Continued)*

```
         10.200.254.4%Default-IP-Routing-Table indirectly connected
           MPLS Required
           Last updated 00:31:17 ago

sydney#show ipv6 route vrf cust-one 2001:DB8:1:2::1/128
Routing entry for 2001:DB8:1:2::1/128
  Known via "bgp 1", distance 20, metric 0, type external
  Route count is 1/1, share count 0
  Routing paths:
    FE80::FF:FEC8:5808, Serial2/0
      Last updated 00:33:08 ago
```

You can verify the data plane by using ping and traceroute from the CE or PE router. Example 9-38 shows the traceroute and the ping from the london CE and PE router to the sydney CE router.

Example 9-38 *Traceroute and Ping*

```
london-ce#traceroute ipv6 2001:DB8:1:2::1

Type escape sequence to abort.
Tracing the route to 2001:DB8:1:2::1

  1 2001:DB8:2::2 [AS 1] 40 msec 20 msec 20 msec
  2 ::FFFF:10.1.2.2 [MPLS: Labels 19/21 Exp 0] 40 msec 40 msec  40 msec
  3 ::FFFF:10.3.1.2 [MPLS: Labels 19/21 Exp 0] 48 msec 48 msec 48 msec
  4 2001:DB8:3::2 [AS 1] [MPLS: Label 21 Exp 0] 32 msec 32 msec 32 msec
  5 2001:DB8:3::1 [AS 1] 40 msec 40 msec 40 msec

london#ping vrf cust-one ipv6 2001:DB8:1:2::1

Type escape sequence to abort.
Sending 5, 100-byte ICMP Echos to 2001:DB8:1:2::1, timeout is 2 seconds:
!!!!!
Success rate is 100 percent (5/5), round-trip min/avg/max = 4/6/8 ms

!The traceroute from the ingress PE inside the VPN:

london#traceroute vrf cust-one ipv6 2001:DB8:1:2::1

Type escape sequence to abort.
Tracing the route to 2001:DB8:1:2::1

  1 ::FFFF:10.1.2.2 [MPLS: Labels 19/21 Exp 0] 32 msec *  28 msec
  2 ::FFFF:10.3.1.2 [MPLS: Labels 19/21 Exp 0] 28 msec 28 msec 28 msec
  3 2001:DB8:3::2 [AS 1] [MPLS: Label 21 Exp 0] 28 msec 28 msec 20 msec
  4 2001:DB8:3::1 [AS 1] 32 msec 40 msec 40 msec
```

Example 9-39 shows how to verify the (two) labels for the IPv6 VRF prefix on the ingress PE router.

Example 9-39 *Verifying Labels*

```
london#show bgp vpnv6 unicast vrf cust-one labels
   Network          Next Hop      In label/Out label
Route Distinguisher: 1:1 (cust-one)
   2001:DB8:1:1::1/128
                    2001:DB8:2::1   22/nolabel
  2001:DB8:1:2::1/128
                   ::FFFF:10.200.254.4
                                   nolabel/21
   2001:DB8:2::/64  ::              23/nolabel
   2001:DB8:3::/64  ::FFFF:10.200.254.4
                                   nolabel/22


london#show ipv6 cef vrf cust-one 2001:DB8:1:2::1/128
2001:DB8:1:2::1/128
   nexthop 10.1.2.2 Ethernet0/0 label 19 21

london#show ipv6 cef vrf cust-one 2001:DB8:1:2::1/128 detail
2001:DB8:1:2::1/128, epoch 0
  recursive via 10.200.254.4 label 21
     nexthop 10.1.2.2 Ethernet0/0 label 19
```

Example 9-40 shows how to verify the label for the next hop (10.200.254.4) of the IPv6 VRF prefix on the P routers.

Example 9-40 *Verifying the LFIB on P Routers*

```
paris#show mpls forwarding-table 10.200.254.4 detail
Local  Outgoing     Prefix          Bytes Label   Outgoing   Next Hop
Label  Label or VC  or Tunnel Id    Switched      interface
19     19           10.200.254.4/32 17969         Se3/0      point2point
        MAC/Encaps=4/8, MRU=1500, Label Stack{19}
        0F008847 00013000
        No output feature configured

new-york#show mpls forwarding-table 10.200.254.4 detail
Local  Outgoing     Prefix          Bytes Label   Outgoing   Next Hop
Label  Label or VC  or Tunnel Id    Switched      interface
19     Pop Label    10.200.254.4/32 26473         Et0/0      10.2.1.2
        MAC/Encaps=14/14, MRU=1504, Label Stack{}
        AABBCC000700AABBCC0005008847
        No output feature configured
```

Example 9-41 shows how to verify the incoming VPN label of the IPv6 VRF prefix in the LFIB on the egress PE router.

Example 9-41   *Verifying the LFIB on the Egress PE Router*

```
sydney#show mpls forwarding-table vrf cust-one 2001:DB8:1:2::1/128 detail
Local   Outgoing     Prefix        Bytes Label   Outgoing   Next Hop
Label   Label or VC  or Tunnel Id  Switched      interface
21      No Label     2001:DB8:1:2::1/128[V]   \
                                   9360          Se2/0      point2point
        MAC/Encaps=0/0, MRU=1504, Label Stack{}
        VPN route: cust-one
        No output feature configured
```

The outgoing label is *No label*, which is correct for an IPv6 VRF prefix learned from the CE router.

IPv6 Internet Access Through 6VPE

RFC 4364 specifies how to access the Internet from within a VPN. These methods for accessing the Internet from CE routers belonging to a VPN that is built from the MPLS VPN for IPv4 architecture are described in detail in Chapter 7. You can use the same three methods that are discussed in Chapter 7 to provide Internet access for VPNs that are built from the 6VPE architecture. These three methods are as follows:

■ Non-VRF Internet access

■ VRF Internet access

■ Static and static VRF routes providing Internet access

In the first method, the non-VRF access method, one or more CE routers can access the Internet by using a (sub)interface or GRE tunnel that is a non-VRF interface. The routers connect to the Internet directly over that interface. The second method, the VRF Internet access method, is accomplished by putting the Internet routes into one VRF. When a CE router connects to that VRF, it has Internet access. The third method uses static and static VRF routes. Basically, both static routes are configured on the PE router and give the CE router Internet access. The static VRF route with global keyword on the PE router points to a next hop in the global routing table. This causes the traffic from the CE router to flow toward the Internet gateway router, because the lookup of the IPv6 destination address for the traffic from the CE now happens in the default routing table on the PE router. The return traffic—coming from the Internet toward the CE—has to make it back to the CE router. This is done by configuring a static IPv6 route on the PE router in the global routing table and pointing it toward the CE router.

Supported Features for 6VPE

6VPE supports additional features. These are features that have been available for MPLS VPN for IPv4. Following are some of these features:

- Site-of-Origin (SOO)

- Route Target rewrite

- VRF-aware ping and traceroute

- VRF-aware telnet

- Allowas-in and as-override

- Multipath eBGP, iBGP, eiBGP multipath, and dmz-link-bandwidth-based load balancing for vpnv6 prefixes

- VRF route limit

- VRF-aware route dampening

- TE tunnel between PE routers

- VRF-aware syslog

These features are explained in Chapter 7.

You can find an overview of Inter-Autonomous Systems 6VPE and Carrier's Carrier (CsC) through 6VPE in "Chapter 9 Supplement" at http://www.ciscopress.com/1587051974.

Remarks for Both 6PE and 6VPE

Following are some remarks that apply equally well to the 6PE and 6VPE solutions.

Route Reflectors

You can implement route reflectors (RR) for both 6PE and 6VPE. 6PE needs an **address-family IPv6** under the router bgp process on the RRs. You must also configure the **send-label** keyword on the neighbor commands toward the route reflector clients. For the 6VPE solution, you need to configure the **address-family vpnv6** under the router bgp process on the RRs. The **send-label** keyword is not needed for the iBGP neighbors because sending a label with the vpnv6 prefix is the default behavior for iBGP sessions.

Turning Off TTL Propagation on the PE Routers

Turning off **mpls ip propagate-ttl** on the PE routers removes the P routers from the IPv6 traceroute for both the 6PE and 6VPE solutions. This behavior is the same as turning off **mpls ip propagate-ttl** for a network that is running MPLS VPN for IPv4. This behavior is explained in detail in Chapter 13, "Troubleshooting MPLS Networks."

> **NOTE**   Chapter 13 also explains that when tracerouting in an MPLS network and the TTL expires on a P router, the ICMP message "TTL exceeded" is forwarded along the LSP until the end of the LSP. The same happens for an IPv6 traceroute. Therefore, the P router does not look up the source IPv6 address of the TTL-expiring IPv6 packet in the global routing table to return the ICMPv6 message. This P router might not even have an IPv6 routing table. The P router forwards the ICMPv6 message along the LSP to the egress LSR of that LSP so that eventually the ICMPv6 message can get to a router—the egress PE or CE router—that can send the ICMPv6 message back to the router or host that sent the original packet.

Load Balancing Labeled IPv6 Packets

Newer Cisco IOS software that is also capable of running IPv6 can do load balancing based on the source and destination address in the IPv6 header of labeled packets. Non-IPv6-capable Cisco IOS routers load-balance labeled IPv6 packets based on the value of the bottom label. The hashing algorithm is the one that CEF uses.

PHP

PHP is the default behavior for MPLS Cisco IOS networks. Therefore, a labeled IPv6 packet is forwarded from the last P router to the egress PE router with only one label on top of it, both in a 6PE and a 6VPE network.

BGP Functionality

Several specific features of BGP are available in the 6PE and 6VPE solution. Following are some of them:

- ASN override

- Allowas-in

- BGP prefix-lists

- BGP AS path filtering

- BGP route refresh

These features are explained in detail in Chapter 7.

Summary

The new IP protocol out there is IP version 6. One day or another, you will come across it.

Both the 6PE and 6VPE solution require PE routers that are capable of IPv6. Both solutions use the peer-to-peer model with its benefits: one routing peer for the customer edge (CE) router across the MPLS backbone—namely, the connected PE router—and an easy provisioning model. The provisioning model is the same as the one in the MPLS VPN for IPv4 solution: Adding a site requires a change in configuration only on the local PE router, but not on the remote PE routers or on the remote CE routers.

Many people are familiar with the MPLS VPN for IPv4 solution because of its popularity. This makes the introduction of the 6PE or 6VPE solution into their network relatively easy, because the operation of these solutions is similar to the operation of the MPLS VPN for IPv4 solution. The following items are seen in the 6PE and 6VPE solution, but also in the MPLS VPN for IPv4 solution:

- Label switching of packets

- A label stack of two labels

- A full mesh of MP-iBGP between the PE routers

- An Interior Gateway Protocol (IGP), eBGP, or static routing between PE and CE routers

- A peer-to-peer model

- The P routers only label switch packets (no need for added intelligence such as VRF awareness or IPv6 awareness on the P routers)

The obvious difference between the 6PE and 6VPE solution is the lack of VPNs in the 6PE solution. You can use both the 6PE and 6VPE solutions in conjunction with the other MPLS solutions in the MPLS network.

Chapter Review Questions

You can find answers to the following questions in Appendix A, "Answers to the Chapter Review Questions."

1. Name three reasons to have a new IP protocol.

2. How many bits does an IPv6 address have?

3. What happened to IP protocol version 5?

4. Name the five ways a service provider can carry IPv6 packets across the backbone network?

5. What is the routing protocol OSPF for IPv6 also called?

6. Which field in the IPv6 header is the equivalent to the Type of Service field in the IPv4 header for the Differentiated Services (DiffServ) model?

7. What routing protocols are supported on the PE-CE links of the 6PE solution?

8. How many labels are put on top of the IPv6 packet in a 6PE network?

9. How can you quickly see the difference between the 6PE and 6VPE solution by looking at the configuration of a PE router?

10. Why are the 6PE and 6VPE solutions the best ones for carrying IPv6 traffic across an MPLS backbone?

What You Will Learn

By the end of this chapter, you should know and be able to explain the following:

■ The purpose and architecture of AToM

■ The Layer 2 encapsulation types that can be carried across the MPLS backbone

■ How to implement Ethernet over MPLS

■ How to use QoS to enhance the AToM network functionality

■ How to interwork between different Layer 2 encapsulation types

CHAPTER 10

Any Transport over MPLS

Any Transport over MPLS (AToM) was developed years after the huge success of MPLS VPN. MPLS VPN is the virtual private network (VPN) solution to carry customer IP traffic over a shared MPLS service provider backbone. However, the leased lines, ATM links, and Frame Relay links still generate a lot of money for service providers. Many customers lease ATM or Frame Relay virtual circuits from a service provider and use them to carry their traffic between their sites, across the infrastructure provided by the service provider. The customer has routers or other networking devices in each site, and the devices are interconnected via the leased lines, ATM virtual circuits (VCs), or Frame Relay VCs.

The service provider has a specific network built to carry the Layer 2 traffic from the customers. The routers from the customer are interconnected at Layer 3, but they do not interact with the equipment of the service provider at Layer 3. With the success of MPLS VPN, the service provider has an MPLS backbone set up, but the service provider still has the legacy network to carry the Layer 2 traffic from the customers. AToM provides a solution whereby the MPLS backbone also carries the Layer 2 traffic from the customers, thereby eliminating the need to run two separate networks side by side. Thus, the service provider can provide an existing service (ATM, Frame Relay, and so on) over the MPLS backbone. Using only one network infrastructure to provide both MPLS VPN and AToM services enables the service provider to save money. Customers are unwilling to migrate to the MPLS VPN solution for two reasons. The first reason is that they want to retain complete control over their network and the way it is built. The second reason is that they have legacy equipment (for example, IBM FEP) running protocols that cannot be carried over IP.

Whereas MPLS VPN provides a service of creating VPNs at Layer 3, AToM creates VPNs at Layer 2 and is sometimes referred to as L2VPN. The AToM intelligence is limited to the provider edge (PE) routers. Therefore, AToM is an edge technology—like MPLS VPN—that uses an MPLS backbone. However, AToM is limited to creating a Layer 2 point-to-point service, which is referred to as virtual private wire service (VPWS). You can also use MPLS to create a Layer 2 point-to-multipoint service. This service is referred to as Virtual Private LAN Service (VPLS), which is described in Chapter 11, "Virtual Private LAN Service." This chapter covers only AToM, the Layer 2 point-to-point service.

Understanding the Need for AToM

AToM is the Cisco name for the Layer 2 transport service over an MPLS backbone. The customer routers interconnect with the service provider routers at Layer 2 (Ethernet, High-Level Data Link Control [HDLC], PPP, ATM, or Frame Relay). This eliminates the need for the legacy network from the service provider carrying these kinds of traffic and integrates this service into the MPLS network that already transports the MPLS VPN traffic.

AToM is an open standards-based architecture that uses the label switching architecture of MPLS and can be integrated into any network that is running MPLS. The advantage to the customer is that they do not need to change anything. Their routers that are connecting to the service provider routers can still use the same Layer 2 encapsulation type as before and do not need to run an IP routing protocol to the provider edge routers as in the MPLS VPN solution. As such, the move from the legacy network that is running ATM or Frame Relay to the network that is running AToM is completely transparent to the customer.

The service provider does not need to change anything on the provider (P) routers in the core of the MPLS network. The intelligence to support AToM sits entirely on the PE routers. As such, the core and edge technologies (MPLS and AToM, respectively) are decoupled. The core label switching routers (LSRs) only switch labeled packets, whereas the edge LSRs impose and dispose of labels on the Layer 2 frames. This is similar to the MPLS VPN solution, in which the P routers switch only labeled packets and the PE routers need the intelligence to impose and dispose of labels on the IP VPN traffic from the customers.

Transporting Layer 2 Frames

Two solutions are available for transporting Layer 2 frames across a packet-switched network (PSN):

- Carry the traffic across an MPLS backbone, which is the AToM solution.

- Carry the traffic across an IP backbone, which is the Layer 2 Tunneling Protocol version 3 (L2TPv3) solution.

NOTE   Both solutions are implemented in Cisco IOS, but because this book focuses on MPLS, only the AToM solution is explained here.

L2TPv3 is the Layer 2 transport service over an IP network. The Layer 2 frames are encapsulated with an L2TPv3 header and are transported across the IP network. Similar to AToM, L2TPv3 can carry ATM, Frame Relay, HDLC, PPP, Ethernet, ATM, and others.

Both the AToM and L2TPv3 solutions use the same architecture, but the network that is carrying the service is different. The architecture is based on pseudowires. The pseudowires carry the customer Layer 2 traffic from edge to edge across the packet-switched backbone network, whether it is an MPLS or an IP-based backbone. The pseudowire is a connection between the PE routers and emulates a wire that is carrying Layer 2 frames. Pseudowires use tunneling. The Layer 2 frames are either encapsulated into an IP packet (L2TPv3) or are labeled (MPLS). The result is that the specific Layer 2 service—its operation and characteristics—is emulated across a PSN. The Internet Engineering Task Force (IETF) specifies the architecture and encapsulation in several RFCs and drafts. In Figure 10-1, you can see the pseudowire emulation edge-to-edge reference model, as specified by the IETF.

Figure 10-1 *Pseudowire Emulation Edge-to-Edge Reference Model*

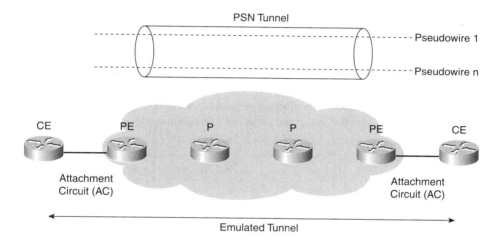

In Figure 10-1, you see a PSN tunnel between the two service provider edge routers. The PSN can be either an IP or an MPLS-based network. Inside the PSN tunnel might be one or more pseudowires that connect the attachment circuits (ACs) on the PE routers to each other. The AC can be ATM, Frame Relay, HDLC, PPP, and so on. Frames that the PE receives on the AC are encapsulated and sent across the pseudowire to the remote PE router. The egress PE router receives the packets from the pseudowire and removes their encapsulation. The egress PE extracts and forwards the frames to the AC.

Before the pseudowire is ready to switch the frames, the PE routers must set it up between them. During the setup, the PE routers exchange the necessary information so that they agree what the service is. For example, the PE routers must agree on the encapsulation method and what to do if they receive out-of-order frames. The result of the AToM service is that the customer edge (CE) routers or CE switches see themselves as directly connected to each other on Layer 2, even though a pseudowire separates them. If the CE routers or switches are running Cisco Discovery Protocol (CDP), for example, they see each other as CDP neighbors. If they are routers, they can directly form a routing protocol adjacency between them because the CE routers are seen as directly connected at Layer 2.

AToM Architecture

In networks that use AToM, all the routers in the service provider network run MPLS, and the PE routers have an AC toward the CE router. The PE router receives Layer 2 frames on the AC and encapsulates them with labels before sending them onto the PSN tunnel toward the remote PE. At the remote PE, the label(s) are removed and the frames are sent toward the remote CE.

In the case of AToM, the PSN tunnel is nothing other than a label switched path (LSP) between two PE routers. As such, the label that is associated with that LSP is called the *tunnel label* in the context of AToM. The LSRs can signal that LSP in different ways. First, the Label Distribution Protocol (LDP) can signal the LSP hop-by-hop between the two PEs. Second, the LSP can be an MPLS traffic engineering (TE) tunnel that the Resource Reservation Protocol (RSVP) signals with the extensions needed for TE. With this tunnel label, you can identify to which PSN tunnel the carried customer frame belongs. This tunnel label also gets the frames from the local or ingress PE to the remote or egress PE across the MPLS backbone. To multiplex several pseudowires onto one PSN tunnel, the PE router uses another label to identify the pseudowire. This label is called the VC or PW label because it identifies the virtual circuit or the pseudowire that the frame is multiplexed onto. Figure 10-2 shows the pseudowire emulation edge-to-edge reference model, but translated to a network where the PSN is an MPLS network.

Figure 10-2   *Pseudowire Emulation Edge-to-Edge Reference Model for an MPLS Network*

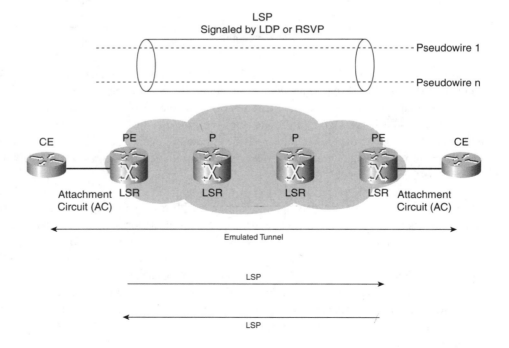

An LSP is unidirectional. Therefore, for a pseudowire to be set up, two LSPs must exist between a pair of PE routers, one for each direction.

Data Plane of AToM

As the ingress PE receives a frame from the CE, it forwards the frame across the MPLS backbone to the egress LSR with two labels: the tunnel label and the VC label.

In an AToM network, each pair of PE routers must run a targeted LDP session between them. The targeted LDP session signals characteristics of the pseudowire and most importantly advertises the VC label. The VC label is always the bottom label in the label stack. It identifies the egress AC on the egress PE. The tunnel label is the top label in the label stack and tells all intermediate LSRs to which egress LSR the frame must be forwarded. Figure 10-3 shows a typical setup with a pseudowire between two PE routers.

Figure 10-3 *Forwarding of AToM Packet*

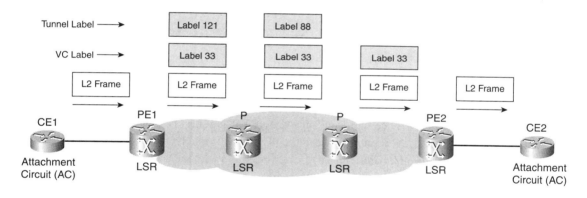

The ingress PE router PE1 first pushes the VC label (label 33) onto the frame. Then it pushes the tunnel label. The tunnel label is the label that is associated with the Interior Gateway Protocol (IGP) prefix identifying the remote PE. This prefix is specified by the configuration of AToM. The MPLS packet is then forwarded according to the tunnel label, hop by hop, until the packet reaches the egress PE, PE2.

Notice that when the packet reaches the egress PE, the tunnel label has already been removed. This is because of the penultimate hop popping (PHP) behavior between the last P router and the egress PE. The egress PE then looks up the VC label in the label forwarding information base (LFIB), strips off the VC label, and forwards the frame onto the correct AC.

The P routers never need to look at the VC label; therefore, they do not need the intelligence to be able to do anything with the VC label. The P routers are completely unaware of the AToM solution.

Because the tunnel label is simply the LDP or RSVP-learned label, no special label distribution protocol has to be set up for AToM on the P routers. The MPLS backbone normally is already using either label distribution protocol. The VC label, however, needs to be associated with a certain AC and advertised to the remote PE. A targeted LDP session performs this job, as explained in the next section.

Example 10-1 shows the LFIB on the egress PE router. As you can see, the VC label points to a Layer 2 circuit entry in the LFIB with the specific virtual circuit identifier (VCID) and also points to an outgoing interface or VC.

Example 10-1 *LFIB Entry for AToM on Egress PE*

```
PE2#show mpls forwarding-table interface serial 4/0/0
Local   Outgoing    Prefix         Bytes tag  Outgoing   Next Hop
tag     tag or VC   or Tunnel Id   switched   interface
33      Untagged    l2ckt(100)     2138118    Se4/0/0    point2point
```

> **NOTE** The Time To Live (TTL) in the tunnel label is always set to 255, and the TTL in the VC label is always set to 2.

Signaling the Pseudowire

A targeted LDP session between the PE routers signals the pseudowires. In essence, the signaling protocol LDP sets up and maintains the pseudowires between the PE routers, as shown in Figure 10-4. LDP has been extended with new Type Length Value fields (TLVs) to perform this job. The main purpose of this LDP session between the PE routers is to advertise the VC label that is associated with the pseudowire. This label is advertised in a Label Mapping message using the downstream unsolicited label advertisement mode.

Figure 10-4 *Signaling by Targeted LDP Session*

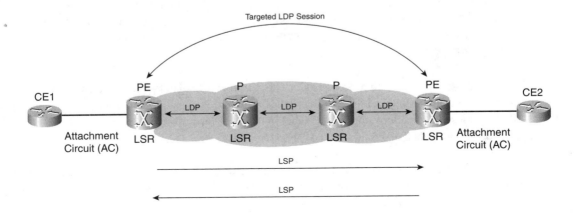

You can see in Figure 10-5 how the VC and tunnel labels are advertised. The VC label is advertised by the egress PE to the ingress PE for the AC (VC ID 100) over the targeted LDP session. The tunnel label is the label advertised for the egress PE router to the ingress PE by LDP. Notice that the egress PE advertises label 3, which indicates that PHP is used.

Figure 10-5 *Advertised Labels for AToM*

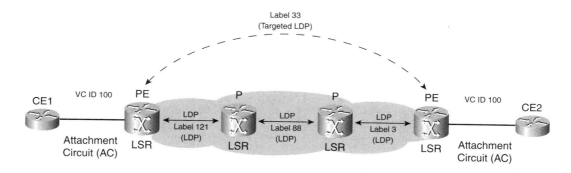

The Label Mapping message that is advertised on the targeted LDP session contains some TLVs:

■   Pseudowire identifier (PW ID) FEC TLV

■   Label TLV

The PW ID FEC TLV identifies the pseudowire that the label is bound to. The Label TLV is the TLV that LDP uses to advertise the MPLS label.

The PW ID FEC TLV contains the following elements:

■   C-bit

■   PW Type

■   Group ID

■   PW ID

■   Interface Parameters

Figure 10-6 shows the format of the PW ID FEC TLV.

Figure 10-6   *The PW ID FEC TLV*

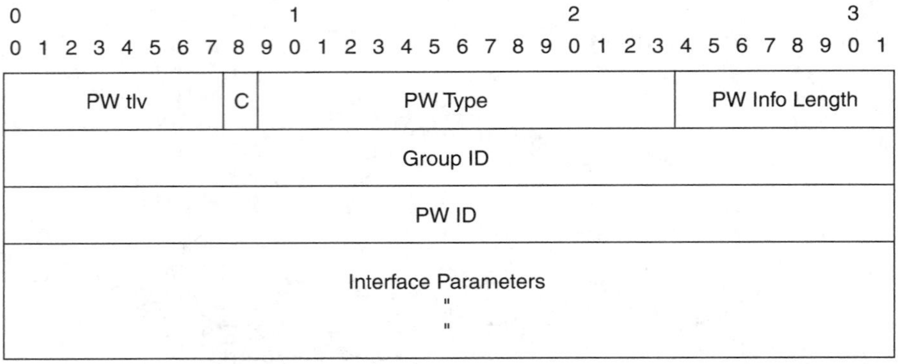

The PW TLV value is set to 128 to indicate that this is the PW ID FEC TLV.

C-Bit

The C-bit—if set to 1—indicates that a control word is present. Refer to the section "The Control Word" for an explanation on the control word.

PW Type

The PW Type is a 15-bit field that represents the type of the pseudowire. Table 10-1 lists the assigned values for the PW Type field.

Table 10-1   *PW Type Assigned by IANA*

PW Type	Description
0x0001	Frame Relay DLCI[1]
0x0002	ATM AAL5 SDU[2] VCC[3] transport
0x0003	ATM transparent cell transport
0x0004	Ethernet Tagged Mode
0x0005	Ethernet
0x0006	HDLC
0x0007	PPP
0x0008	SONET/SDH CEM[4]
0x0009	ATM n-to-one VCC cell transport
0x000A	ATM n-to-one VPC cell transport

Table 10-1   *PW Type Assigned by IANA (Continued)*

PW Type	Description
0x000B	IP Layer 2 Transport
0x000C	ATM one-to-one VCC cell mode
0x000D	ATM one-to-one VPC cell mode
0x000E	ATM AAL5 PDU[5] VCC transport
0x000F	Frame-Relay Port mode
0x0010	SONET/SDH CEP[6]
0x0011	Structure-Agnostic E1 over Packet (SAToP)
0x0012	Structure-Agnostic T1 (DS1) over Packet (SAToP)
0x0013	Structure-Agnostic E3 over Packet (SAToP)
0x0014	Structure-Agnostic T3 (DS3) over Packet (SAToP)
0x0015	CESoPSN[7] basic mode
0x0016	TDMoIP[8] basic mode
0x0017	CESoPSN TDM[9] with CAS[10]
0x0018	TDMoIP TDM with CAS
0x0019	Frame Relay DLCI

[1] DLCI = data-link connection identifier

[2] SDU = service data unit

[3] VCC = virtual channel connection

[4] CEM = Circuit Emulation Service over MPLS

[5] PDU = protocol data unit

[6] CEP = Circuit Emulation over Packet

[7] CESoPSN = Circuit Emulation Service over Packet Switched Network

[8] TDMoIP = time-division multiplexing over IP

[9] TDM = time-division multiplexing

[10] CAS = channel associated signaling

Many pseudowire types can be configured. You can recognize the widely used protocols HDLC, PPP, Ethernet, ATM, and Frame Relay. Others refer to the possibility to carry time-division multiplexing (TDM) and circuit emulation service (CES) over MPLS. This book does not cover these last two services.

Group ID

The Group ID identifies a group of pseudowires. Cisco IOS assigns the same Group ID to all ACs on the same interface. The PE can use the Group ID to withdraw all of the VC labels that are associated with that Group ID in one LDP Label Withdraw message. This is referred to as a *wild card label withdrawal.*

PW ID

The PW ID is a 32-bit connection identifier that together with the PW Type completely identifies the pseudowire. You can specify the PW ID in Cisco IOS on both PE routers with the **xconnect** *peer-router-id vcid* interface command. The PW ID is the VC ID as seen in the output of Cisco IOS commands.

Interface Parameters

The Interface Parameters describe some interface-specific parameters such as maximum transmission unit (MTU) of the interface toward the CE router, an optional interface description string, requested VLAN ID, and so on. If the MTU parameter does not match on both sides, the pseudowire is not signaled.

Because an LSP is unidirectional, a pseudowire can be formed only if another LSP exists in the opposite direction between the same pair of PE routers. The PW ID FEC TLV is used to identify and match the two opposite LSPs between a pair of PE routers.

Signaling the Status of the Pseudowire

After the PE routers have set up the pseudowire, the PE can signal the PW status to the remote PE. The PE routers can achieve this using two methods:

- Label Withdraw

- PW Status TLV

The Label Withdraw method is the older of the two methods. A PE router can withdraw the label mapping either by sending a Label Withdraw message or by sending the Label Mapping Release message, in case the imposing router wants to restart forwarding frames with sequence one. If the AC goes down, the PE router signals this by sending a Label Withdraw message to the remote PE. If a physical interface goes down, the Label Withdraw message contains the Group ID to signal that all ACs of the interface are down.

When the PE routers use the second method, the PW Status TLV follows the LDP Label Mapping TLV when the pseudowire is signaled. This indicates that the PE router wants to use the second method. If the other PE router does not support the PW Status TLV method, both PE routers revert back to the Label Withdraw method. After the pseudowire is signaled, the PW Status TLV is carried in an LDP notification message. This PW Status TLV allows for more states to be signaled than just the down notification with the first method.

The PW Status TLV contains the 32-bit Status Code field. Table 10-2 specifies the specific status codes for pseudowires that have been defined so far.

Table 10-2   *Status Codes*

PW Status Code	Description
0x00000000	Pseudowire forwarding (clear all failures)
0x00000001	Pseudowire not forwarding
0x00000002	Local AC (ingress) receive fault
0x00000004	Local AC (egress) transmit fault
0x00000008	Local PSN-facing PW (ingress) receive fault
0x00000010	Local PSN-facing PW (egress) transmit fault

Because individual bits set these status codes, the PE router can set multiple bits to signal multiple faults at the same time.

The Control Word

The control word is a 32-bit field that is inserted between the VC label and the transported Layer 2 frame in the case of AToM. It is required for some Layer 2 protocols but optional for others. The control word carries extra information such as protocol control information and a sequence number and does this in a compressed format. This information is needed to correctly and efficiently carry the Layer 2 protocol across the MPLS network. The ingress PE router adds the control word, and the egress PE router strips it off after processing it. Whether the control word is used can be signaled by the PE routers or can be configured. In both cases, the egress PE router knows that it should expect the presence of the control word after the MPLS label stack. Figure 10-7 shows the generic format of the control word.

Figure 10-7   *Generic Format of the Control Word*

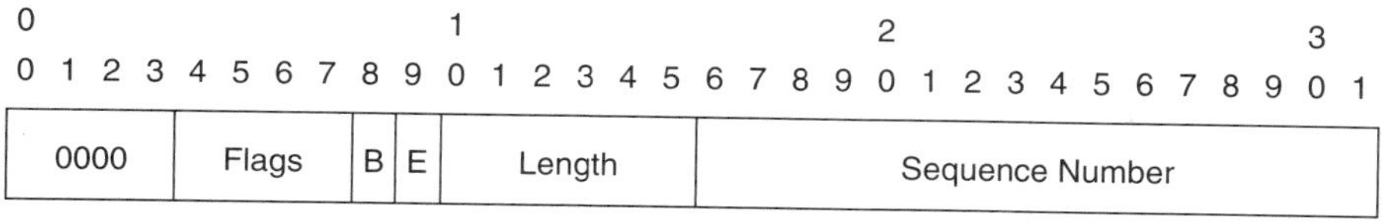

Figure 10-8 shows the control word placed between the MPLS labels and the transported Layer 2 frame.

Figure 10-8   *Placement of the Control Word*

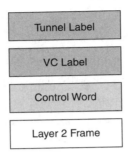

Control Word Functions

The control word has the following five functions:

- Pad small packets

- Carry control bits of the Layer 2 header of the transported protocol

- Preserve the sequence of the transported frames

- Facilitate the correct load balancing of AToM packets in the MPLS backbone network

- Facilitate fragmentation and reassembly

Pad Small Packets

Sometimes the transmitted labeled AToM packet is smaller than the required minimum length for the specific encapsulation type. An example is Ethernet, where the required minimum length of the frame is 64 bytes. If the AToM packet does not meet this minimum length, the frame is padded to meet the minimum length on the Ethernet link. Because the MPLS header (the label stack) has no length field that indicates the length of the frame, the control word holds a length field indicating the length of the frame. If the received AToM packet on the egress PE router has a control word with a length field that is not 0, the router knows that padding was added and can correctly remove the padding before forwarding the frame.

Carry Control Bits of the Layer 2 Header of the Transported Protocol

The second reason for a control word is the carrying of the control bits that are set to certain Layer 2 protocol flags. The flags that are copied to the control word depend on the carried protocol. For Frame Relay, the forward explicit congestion notification (FECN), backward explicit congestion notification (BECN), discard eligible (DE), and command/response (C/R) bits are carried in the control word as control bits. For ATM, the Explicit Forward Congestion Indication (EFCI) and cell loss priority (CLP) bit can be copied to the control word. For the PPP and HDLC protocols, no control bits are copied, but the fragmentation bits can be set.

Preserve the Sequence of the Transported Frames

The third reason for the presence of the control word is to carry the sequence number. With this sequence number, the receiver can detect out-of-sequence packets. The first packet sent onto the pseudowire has a sequence number of 1 and increments for each subsequent packet by 1 until it reaches 65,535, at which point it wraps around back to 1.

If such out-of-sequence packets are detected, they are dropped. Reordering for out-of-sequence AToM packets is not done in Cisco IOS on the PE routers.

In Cisco IOS, sequencing is disabled by default. You can enable it under the pseudowire-class configuration. You can use a pseudowire-class in Cisco IOS to specify AToM-specific configuration. You can enable sequencing in the transmit or receive direction or both, as shown in Example 10-2.

Example 10-2 *Enabling Sequencing*

```
PE#
!
pseudowire-class one
 encapsulation mpls
 sequencing both
!

PE1#show mpls l2transport vc 100 detail
Local interface: Se0/1/0 up, line protocol up, HDLC up
  Destination address: 10.200.254.4, VC ID: 100, VC status: up
    Output interface: Et0/0/0, imposed label stack {19 23}
    Preferred path: not configured
    Default path: active
    Tunnel label: 23, next hop 10.200.200.2
  Create time: 00:00:01, last status change time: 00:00:00
  Signaling protocol: LDP, peer 10.200.254.4:0 up
    MPLS VC labels: local 22, remote 19
    Group ID: local 0, remote 0
    MTU: local 1500, remote 1500
    Remote interface description:
  Sequencing: receive enabled, send enabled
  VC statistics:
    packet totals: receive 153, send 12352
    byte totals:   receive 14984, send 1259492
    packet drops:  receive 0, send 0
```

Facilitate the Correct Load Balancing of AToM Packets in the MPLS Backbone Network

The fourth reason for the control word is the correct load balancing of AToM packets in the MPLS network. Routers can perform MPLS payload inspection to determine what the payload is. Based on the type of payload, the router can decide how to load-balance the traffic. Some implementations—such as Cisco IOS—look at the first nibble behind the label stack. If that nibble is a 4, the router assumes that this is an IPv4 packet, because the first nibble of an IPv4 packet is always 4. However, sometimes the first nibble is 4 but the MPLS payload is not an IPv4 packet. For example, an Ethernet frame might start with 4. The insertion of the control word between the label stack and the MPLS payload provides certainty that the first nibble after the MPLS label stack is not 4. The generic control word—as depicted in Figure 10-7—starts with a nibble with value 0, and the control word used for Operation and Maintenance (OAM) data starts with a nibble with value 1. Refer to Chapter 14, "MPLS Operation and Maintenance," to see a second definition of the control word, where the first nibble is always 1.

Facilitate Fragmentation and Reassembly

The fifth reason for the control word is the correct functioning of the fragmentation and reassembly of the frames. The PE routers can indicate whether they support fragmentation by signaling it when they advertise the VC label, or you can configure them to do fragmentation and reassembly. If the PE routers do support fragmentation, they can correctly reassemble received fragments if the control word is present. In the control word, the fragmentation is performed by using the Beginning (B) and Ending (E) bits. Fragmentation and reassembly uses the sequence number in the control word to indicate a group of fragments. You can see in Figure 10-7 where the bits B and E and the sequence number are put in the control word.

If the combined label stack, AToM payload, and pseudowire header (like the control word) result in an AToM packet whose MTU is bigger than the MTU in the MPLS network, the packet is dropped somewhere in the network. P routers do not support fragmenting AToM packets.

On the other hand, the AToM packet might be forwarded if it is fragmented and reassembled. The fragmentation of the AToM packet occurs on the ingress PE router, whereas the reassembly occurs on the egress PE router of the MPLS network.

Table 10-3 shows the values of the B and E bits and their meanings.

Table 10-3   *B and E Bit Values*

B and E Bit	Description
00	Indicates that the entire (unfragmented) payload is carried in a single packet
01	Indicates the packet carrying the first fragment
10	Indicates the packet carrying the last fragment
11	Indicates a packet carrying an intermediate fragment

Fragmentation can affect the performance, so avoid it whenever possible. You can avoid fragmentation by carefully selecting the MTU and MPLS MTU values on the links in the MPLS backbone, as described in the next section.

MPLS MTU in the MPLS Backbone

In AToM networks, if the two PE routers are not directly connected, at least two labels are added to each frame that is transported across the pseudowire. This increases the packet size with at least 8 bytes. Another 4 bytes are added if the control word is used. The payload that is transported with AToM is not just an IP packet as with MPLS VPN, but a Layer 2 frame. Therefore, when calculating the biggest possible AToM packet, you must add the number of bytes for the Layer 2 frame header. Take Ethernet over MPLS as an example. If the transported frame is an Ethernet II frame carrying an IP packet of 1500 bytes, the AToM payload is 1514 bytes. The added 14 bytes are the 6 bytes for Source and Destination MAC Address each and the 2 bytes for the Ethertype. If, however, the transported frame is 802.1Q, you need to add another 4 bytes for the VLAN tag. If the transported frame is a QinQ frame, you need to add another 8 bytes.

To ensure that fragmentation is not needed, check that the MTU of the core links is bigger than the maximum-sized transported AToM packets. If this is not the case, you can increase the MTU for MPLS packets with the interface command **mpls mtu**. MTU problems surface regularly where Ethernet links exist in the MPLS core. The default MPLS MTU value is the default MTU value for that link. On an Ethernet, this is 1500 bytes. Therefore, assuming that the transported Layer 2 payload is 1500 bytes and the default MTU or MPLS MTU value remains unchanged, you will run into trouble. If you take an IP packet of 1500 bytes that is transported across an Ethernet over MPLS (EoMPLS) pseudowire with one VLAN header, the MPLS packet is 1530 bytes long if the control word is used.

The 1530 bytes in this example break up as follows:

■   1500 bytes for IP

■   8 bytes for the two MPLS labels

■   4 bytes for the control word

■   4 bytes for the Ethernet VLAN header

■   14 bytes for the transported Ethernet II frame header (no FCS)

Thus, the MPLS MTU on all MPLS interfaces in the core network should be at least 1530 bytes to avoid fragmentation. The alternative is to use path MTU discovery throughout the network.

The Basic AToM Configuration

The basic configuration for AToM is pretty straightforward. You must first select the encapsulation type of the customer-facing (CE-facing) interface on the PE with the following command:

```
Router(config-if)# encapsulation encapsulation-type
```

Then you enable AToM by specifying the **xconnect** command on the CE-facing interface, as follows:

```
Router(config-if)# xconnect peer-router-id vcid encapsulation mpls
```

The *peer-router-id* is the LDP router ID of the remote PE router. The *vcid* is the identifier that you assign to the pseudowire. The VCID has to be unique per pair of PE routers. As soon as you configure this command on the interface—on both PE routers—the targeted LDP session is established between the two PE routers. The specification of the MPLS encapsulation is optional, because you can also specify it in the pseudowire class. The pseudowire class is not required on the PE router to configure AToM, but it is necessary if you need to specify more than just the encapsulation to be MPLS. In the pseudowire class, you can specify certain characteristics of the pseudowires. Interworking, preferred-path, and sequencing are such configurable characteristics, besides the encapsulation type. The only other encapsulation type available besides MPLS is L2TPv3. Interworking, preferred-path, and sequencing are explained in following sections of this chapter.

Figure 10-9 shows a basic example of an AToM network with two PE routers that provide an AToM service to the two CE routers, CE1 and CE2. The transported Layer 2 protocol is HDLC.

Figure 10-9 *AToM Example for HDLC*

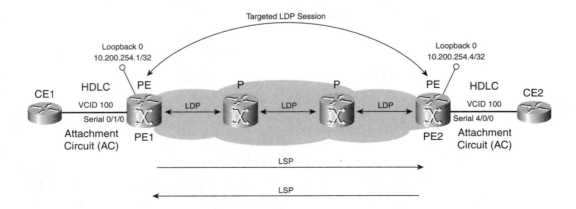

You can see the basic configuration needed on the PE routers for AToM in Example 10-3.

Example 10-3 *Basic AToM Configuration of PE1 and PE2*

```
PE1#
!
mpls ldp router-id Loopback0 force
mpls label protocol ldp
pseudowire-class one
 encapsulation mpls
!
interface Serial0/1/0
 no ip address
 encapsulation hdlc
 xconnect 10.200.254.4 100 pw-class one
!

PE2#
!
mpls ldp router-id Loopback0 force
mpls label protocol ldp
pseudowire-class one
 encapsulation mpls
!
interface Serial4/0/0
 no ip address
 encapsulation hdlc
 xconnect 10.200.254.1 100 pw-class one
!
```

NOTE   The default encapsulation for a serial interface in Cisco IOS is HDLC, so it is normally not displayed in the configuration. It is shown here for clarity.

Example 10-4 shows that you can verify the state of the pseudowire with the **show mpls l2transport** command.

Example 10-4 *Verifying AToM on PE1 and PE2*

```
PE1#show mpls l2transport vc 100

Local intf     Local circuit          Dest address     VC ID      Status
------------   --------------------   ---------------  ---------- ----------
Se0/1/0        HDLC                   10.200.254.4     100        UP

PE1#show mpls l2transport vc 100 detail
Local interface: Se0/1/0 up, line protocol up, HDLC up
```

continues

Example 10-4 *Verifying AToM on PE1 and PE2 (Continued)*

```
   Destination address: 10.200.254.4, VC ID: 100, VC status: up
     Output interface: Et0/0/0, imposed label stack {19 23}
     Preferred path: not configured
     Default path: active
     Tunnel label: 23, next hop 10.200.200.2
   Create time: 01:11:35, last status change time: 00:03:31
   Signaling protocol: LDP, peer 10.200.254.4:0 up
     MPLS VC labels: local 24, remote 19
     Group ID: local 0, remote 0
     MTU: local 1500, remote 1500
     Remote interface description:
   Sequencing: receive disabled, send disabled
   VC statistics:
     packet totals: receive 54, send 44
     byte totals:   receive 4964, send 4483
     packet drops:  receive 0, send 0


PE2#show mpls l2transport vc 100

Local intf     Local circuit         Dest address     VC ID      Status
------------   --------------------  ---------------  ---------  ----------
Se4/0/0        HDLC                  10.200.254.1     100        UP

PE2#show mpls l2transport vc 100 detail
Local interface: Se4/0/0 up, line protocol up, HDLC up
   Destination address: 10.200.254.1, VC ID: 100, VC status: up
     Preferred path: not configured
     Default path: active
     Tunnel label: 22, next hop point2point
     Output interface: Se5/0, imposed label stack {22 24}
   Create time: 00:12:23, last status change time: 00:03:51
   Signaling protocol: LDP, peer 10.200.254.1:0 up
     MPLS VC labels: local 19, remote 24
     Group ID: local 0, remote 0
     MTU: local 1500, remote 1500
     Remote interface description:
   Sequencing: receive disabled, send disabled
   Sequence number: receive 0, send 0
   VC statistics:
     packet totals: receive 50, send 64
     byte totals:   receive 4578, send 6984
     packet drops:  receive 0, seq error 0, send 0

PE1#show mpls l2transport binding 100
   Destination Address: 10.200.254.4,  VC ID: 100
     Local Label:  24
```

Example 10-4   *Verifying AToM on PE1 and PE2 (Continued)*

```
        Cbit: 1,    VC Type: HDLC,    GroupID: 0
        MTU: 1500,   Interface Desc: n/a
        VCCV Capabilities: Type 1, Type 2
    Remote Label: 19
        Cbit: 1,    VC Type: HDLC,    GroupID: 0
        MTU: 1500,   Interface Desc: n/a
        VCCV Capabilities: Type 1, Type 2
```

To see which AToM features the interface supports for each encapsulation type, use the **show mpls l2transport hw-capability** command, as shown in Example 10-5.

Example 10-5   *Verifying AToM Features*

```
PE1#show mpls l2transport hw-capability interface serial 0/1/0
Interface Serial0/1/0

Transport type FR DLCI
  Core functionality:
    MPLS label disposition supported
    Distributed processing supported
    Control word processing supported
    Sequence number processing not supported
    VCCV Type 1 processing supported
  Edge functionality:
    MPLS label imposition supported
    Distributed processing supported
    Control word processing supported
    Sequence number processing not supported

Transport type ATM AAL5
  Core functionality:
    MPLS label disposition supported
    Control word processing supported
    Sequence number processing not supported
    VCCV Type 1 processing supported
  Edge functionality:
    Not supported

Transport type ATM CELL
  Core functionality:
    MPLS label disposition supported
    Control word processing not supported
    Sequence number processing not supported
    VCCV Type 1 processing not supported
  Edge functionality:
    Not supported
```

continues

Example 10-5 *Verifying AToM Features (Continued)*

```
Transport type Eth VLAN
  Core functionality:
    MPLS label disposition supported
    Distributed processing supported
    Control word processing supported
    Sequence number processing not supported
    VCCV Type 1 processing supported
  Edge functionality:
    Not supported

Transport type Ethernet
  Core functionality:
    MPLS label disposition supported
    Distributed processing supported
    Control word processing supported
    Sequence number processing not supported
    VCCV Type 1 processing supported
  Edge functionality:
    Not supported

!output omitted for brevity
```

Transported Layer 2 Protocols

AToM supports several Layer 2 protocols that can be transported across the MPLS network. This section shows an overview of the needed configuration for each of these Layer 2 protocols. In addition to that, you learn what the exact payload is of the AToM packets for each protocol. Note that the ACs on both sides of the MPLS network are of the same encapsulation type. This is referred to as like-to-like functionality.

HDLC

For HDLC, the customer-facing interface on the PE router needs the **encapsulation hdlc** command. Example 10-6 shows the basic AToM configuration for HDLC.

Example 10-6 *AToM Configuration for HDLC Encapsulation*

```
PE#
!
pseudowire-class one
 encapsulation mpls
!
interface Serial0/1/0
 no ip address
 encapsulation hdlc
 xconnect 10.200.254.4 100 pw-class one
!
```

The AToM payload is the HDLC frame, minus the flags and the frame check sequence (FCS) field. The egress PE router adds the FCS field and flags before sending the frame to the CE.

PPP

For PPP, the customer-facing interface on the PE router needs the **encapsulation ppp** command, as shown in Example 10-7.

Example 10-7 *AToM Configuration for PPP Encapsulation*

```
PE1#
!
pseudowire-class one
 encapsulation mpls
 !
interface Serial0/1/0
 no ip address
 encapsulation ppp
 xconnect 10.200.254.4 100 pw-class one
 !

PE1#show mpls l2transport vc 100

Local intf     Local circuit         Dest address      VC ID      Status
------------   -------------------   ---------------   ---------- ----------
Se0/1/0        PPP                   10.200.254.4      100        UP
```

The AToM payload is the PPP frame, minus flags, address, control field, and FCS field. The egress PE router adds the flags, address, control field, and FCS field before sending the frame to the CE.

Frame Relay

Frame Relay can be carried across the MPLS network in two fashions: DLCI-to-DLCI or port-to-port. In the DLCI-to-DLCI method, one VC is carried over one pseudowire. In the port-to-port method, all VCs on one port are carried over one pseudowire. You can use both the Frame Relay encapsulation types of Cisco or the IETF (RFC 1490) for the DLCI-to-DLCI and the port-to-port methods.

DLCI-to-DLCI

In the DLCI-to-DLCI method, each VC is carried across the MPLS network over one pseudowire. Frame Relay VCs to pseudowires have a one-to-one mapping. The DLCI-to-DLCI method gives you some flexibility because each VC can be tunneled to different PE routers if needed, which is what you usually need when connecting customer sites with Frame Relay. In the DLCI-to-DLCI method, the transported frame is the Frame Relay payload. The flags and FCS field are stripped off. The Frame Relay header is also stripped off, but the control bits FECN, BECN, DE, and C/R are copied into the control word as the F, B, D, and C bits, respectively. The control word for Frame Relay over MPLS is depicted in Figure 10-10.

Figure 10-10 *Control Word Format for Frame Relay over MPLS*

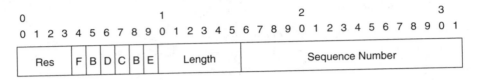

An additional header is added between the control word and the Frame Relay payload indicating the Ethertype. Ethertype is a field that indicates the Layer 2 or Layer 3 protocol of the payload. For example, the Ethertype value of 0x0800 indicates that the payload is IP. The remote PE router receives a labeled packet with the VC label on top. The VC label is looked up and used to indicate the VCID. When the VC label is stripped off, the information inside the control word is used to construct the Frame Relay header before sending the frame toward the CE router. Figure 10-11 shows the DLCI-to-DLCI Frame Relay over MPLS (FRoMPLS) frame format for Cisco encapsulation.

Figure 10-11 *DLCI-to-DLCI FRoMPLS Frame Format for Cisco Encapsulation*

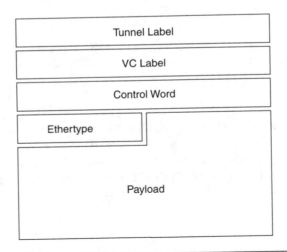

NOTE   When you use IETF encapsulation instead of Cisco, Frame Relay uses the NLPID field instead of the Ethertype field.

In this mode, you cannot transport the Local Management Interface (LMI) messages across the MPLS network; they are terminated at the PE router. However, when the PE router terminates the LMI messages, the LMI status can dictate the status of the pseudowire. When LMI indicates the presence of a VC, for example, a VC label advertisement is sent to the remote PE router. When the VC is not present, a VC label withdraw is sent.

Port-to-Port Mode (Port Trunking)

Cisco IOS also supports port-to-port FRoMPLS. This means that instead of carrying an individual Frame Relay VC over one pseudowire, you can carry a whole trunk of VCs over one pseudowire, which is what you would do to replace the core of an existing Frame Relay network with MPLS. A many-to-one mapping of VCs to pseudowire exists. On the PE side, the encapsulation that you use to transport Frame Relay in the port-to-port mode is HDLC. Figure 10-12 shows the port-to-port FRoMPLS frame format for Cisco encapsulation and a detailed look at the Frame Relay header.

Figure 10-12   *Port-to-Port FRoMPLS Frame Format for Cisco Encapsulation*

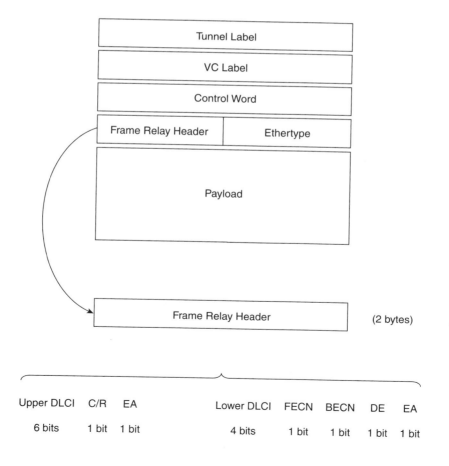

> **NOTE** When you use IETF encapsulation instead of Cisco, Frame Relay uses the NLPID field instead of the Ethertype field.

In port-to-port mode, the pseudowire carries the Frame Relay header—after stripping off the flags and FCS field. In this mode, the LMI messages can be transported transparently across the MPLS network; they appear as regular HDLC frames to the PE routers. The AToM control word cannot hold the Frame Relay control bits (FECN, BECN, DEC/R); they are 0. However, the original Frame Relay control bits are transported transparently as part of the AToM HDLC payload to the remote CE router.

This is a method suited, for example, to reach a remote Frame Relay access site across an MPLS network. Example 10-8 shows the configuration of the CE and PE routers for FRoMPLS in port-to-port mode. For demonstration purposes, two DLCIs were configured on the CE routers toward the PE routers. The PE routers PE1 and PE2 were configured with HDLC as encapsulation on the interfaces toward the CE routers and thus also for HDLC over MPLS.

Example 10-8 *Frame Relay over MPLS Port-to-Port Example*

```
!
hostname PE1-ce
!
interface Serial0/1
 no ip address
 encapsulation frame-relay
 frame-relay intf-type nni
!
interface Serial0/1.1 point-to-point
 ip address 10.100.101.1 255.255.255.0
 frame-relay interface-dlci 17
!
interface Serial0/1.2 point-to-point
 ip address 10.100.102.1 255.255.255.0
 frame-relay interface-dlci 1007
!

!
hostname PE1
!
pseudowire-class one
 encapsulation mpls
!
interface Serial0/1/0
 no ip address
 encapsulation hdlc
```

Example 10-8 *Frame Relay over MPLS Port-to-Port Example (Continued)*

```
  xconnect 10.200.254.4 200 pw-class one

 !

 !
hostname PE2
 !
pseudowire-class one
 encapsulation mpls
 !
interface Serial4/0/0
 no ip address
 encapsulation hdlc
 xconnect 10.200.254.1 200 pw-class one
 !

 !
hostname PE2-ce
 !
interface Serial0/0
 no ip address
 encapsulation frame-relay
 frame-relay intf-type nni
 !
interface Serial0/0.1 point-to-point
 ip address 10.100.101.2 255.255.255.0
 frame-relay interface-dlci 17
 !
interface Serial0/0.2 point-to-point
 ip address 10.100.102.2 255.255.255.0
 frame-relay interface-dlci 1007
 !

PE1#show mpls l2transport vc 200

Local intf     Local circuit          Dest address     VC ID      Status
------------   ---------------------  ---------------  ---------- ----------
Se0/1/0        HDLC                   10.200.254.4     200        UP

PE1#show mpls l2transport vc 200 detail
Local interface: Se0/1/0 up, line protocol up, HDLC up
  Destination address: 10.200.254.4, VC ID: 200, VC status: up
    Preferred path: not configured
    Default path: active
    Tunnel label: 23, next hop 10.200.200.2
    Output interface: Et0/0/0, imposed label stack {23 19}
  Create time: 2d16h, last status change time: 2d15h
```

continues

Example 10-8 *Frame Relay over MPLS Port-to-Port Example (Continued)*

```
Signaling protocol: LDP, peer 10.200.254.4:0 up
  MPLS VC labels: local 16, remote 19
  Group ID: local 0, remote 0
  MTU: local 1500, remote 1500
  Remote interface description:
Sequencing: receive disabled, send disabled
Sequence number: receive 0, send 0
VC statistics:
  packet totals: receive 36498, send 35542
  byte totals:   receive 762468, send 842039
  packet drops:  receive 10, seq error 0, send 0
```

ATM

Carrying ATM over MPLS (ATMoMPLS) is possible with the ATM adaptation layer 5 (AAL5) encapsulation whereby ATM cells are used to transport larger frames. Another possibility is ATM cell relay mode. In ATM cell relay mode each individual ATM cell is transmitted over the MPLS network or multiple cells are packed together if cell packing is used.

ATM AAL5

Each received ATM AAL5 service data unit (SDU) (RFC 1483/2684) from the AC is labeled and sent onto the MPLS network. Before labeling, the header is removed and control information is copied into the control word. The egress PE router then looks up the VC label, strips it off, constructs the outgoing AAL5 SDU, and forwards the frame. The control information copied from the header is the Explicit Forward Congestion Indication (EFCI), the Cell Loss Priority (CLP), and possibly the Frame Relay C/R bit if Frame Relay to ATM Interworking is done.

With ATM AAL5 service, you can also transport the OAM cells. If the PE router does not support the forwarding of OAM cells, you can use OAM cell emulation to terminate the OAM locally. You do this by configuring the command **oam-ac emulation-enable** on the AC of the PE router. Figure 10-13 shows the frame format for carrying ATM AAL5 over MPLS.

Figure 10-13 *ATM AAL5 over MPLS Frame Format*

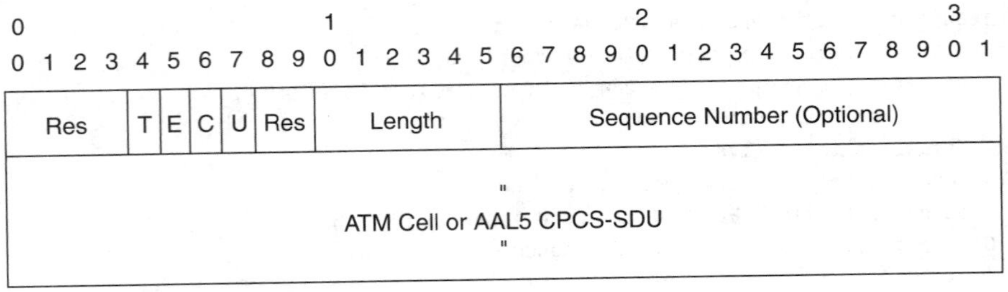

The T, E, C, and U bits of the control word have the following meaning:

- **T (transport type) bit**—The T bit indicates whether the packet contains an ATM admin cell or an ATM AAL5 payload. If T=1, the packets contain an ATM admin cell.

- **E (EFCI) bit**—The E bit is set to 1 if the EFCI bit of the final cell of the AAL5 CPCS-SDU or of the single cell is set to 1.

- **C (CLP) bit**—The C bit is set to 1 if the CLP bit of any of the ATM cells that transported the AAL5 CPCS-SDU is set to 1.

- **U (Command/Response field) bit**—The U bit is used when FRF 8.1 Frame Relay to ATM PVC service Interworking is used. The CPCS-UU Least Significant Bit (LSB) of the AAL5 CPCS-PDU might contain the Frame Relay C/R bit and should be copied to the U bit in the control word.

Example 10-9 shows the configuration of an AToM network that is transporting ATM AAL5 frames over MPLS.

Example 10-9   *ATM AAL5 over MPLS Example*

```
hostname PE2-ce
!
interface ATM3/0
 ip address 10.150.1.1 255.255.255.0
 pvc 10/100
  encapsulation aal5snap
 !
!
hostname PE1-ce
!
interface ATM2/0
 ip address 10.150.1.2 255.255.255.0
 pvc 10/100
  encapsulation aal5snap
 !
!

hostname PE1
!
pseudowire-class one
 encapsulation mpls
!
interface ATM8/0/0
 no ip address
 pvc 10/100 l2transport
  encapsulation aal5
  xconnect 10.200.254.4 1000 pw-class one
```

continues

Example 10-9 *ATM AAL5 over MPLS Example (Continued)*

```
!
!
hostname PE2
!
pseudowire-class one
 encapsulation mpls
!
interface ATM0/0/0
 no ip address
 pvc 10/100 l2transport
  encapsulation aal5
  xconnect 10.200.254.1 1000 pw-class one
 !
!

PE1#show xconnect peer 10.200.254.4 1000

VC ID       Peer Address    Encap    Status  Interface
1000        10.200.254.4    MPLS     up      AT8/0/0

PE1#show mpls l2transport vc 1000

Local intf    Local circuit            Dest address     VC ID      Status
------------  -----------------------  ---------------  ---------  ----------
AT8/0/0       ATM AAL5 10/100          10.200.254.4     1000       UP

PE1#show mpls l2transport vc 1000 detail
Local interface: AT8/0/0 up, line protocol up, ATM AAL5 10/100 up
  Destination address: 10.200.254.4, VC ID: 1000, VC status: up
    Preferred path: not configured
    Default path: active
    Tunnel label: 23, next hop 10.200.200.2
    Output interface: Et0/0/0, imposed label stack {23 35}
  Create time: 01:00:17, last status change time: 00:11:22
  Signaling protocol: LDP, peer 10.200.254.4:0 up
    MPLS VC labels: local 25, remote 35
    Group ID: local 0, remote 0
    MTU: local 4470, remote 4470
    Remote interface description:
  Sequencing: receive disabled, send disabled
```

Example 10-9 *ATM AAL5 over MPLS Example (Continued)*

```
   Sequence number: receive 0, send 0
   VC statistics:
     packet totals: receive 27, send 26
     byte totals:   receive 2864, send 2936
     packet drops:  receive 0, seq error 0, send 0

PE1#show atm pvc 10/100
ATM8/0/0: VCD: 1, VPI: 10, VCI: 100
UBR, PeakRate: 149760
AAL5 L2transport, etype:0xF, Flags: 0x10000C2E, VCmode: 0x0
OAM Cell Emulation: not configured
Interworking Method: like to like
Remote Circuit Status = No Alarm, Alarm Type = None
InPkts: 2677, OutPkts: 27, InBytes: 140580, OutBytes: 2756
!output omitted for brevity
```

ATM Cell Relay

With ATM cell relay, ATM cells are labeled and transported across the MPLS network. Every single cell is transported across the network, including the OAM cells. With ATM cell relay, you have two options—single cell relay mode and packed cell relay mode—as you learn about in the next sections.

Single Cell Relay Mode

With single cell relay, each ATM cell is separately labeled and carried across the MPLS network. The disadvantage of single cell relay is the created overhead of adding two MPLS labels, a control word (optional), and an ATM cell header to every cell that is transported. The payload of the AToM packet is the 48 bytes of the cell payload. Because of AToM transporting the cells, each cell gets at least the additional overhead of 12 bytes: 8 bytes for the two MPLS labels and 4 bytes for the ATM cell header.

As you can see in Figure 10-14, the AToM packet consists of 4 bytes of the control word, 4 bytes for the ATM cell header, which consists of virtual path identifier (VPI), virtual channel identifier (VCI), Payload Type Identifier (PTI), and Cell Loss Priority (CLP)—or just C here—information, and the 48 bytes of the ATM cell payload. Although the 5 bytes of the ATM header are removed, the VPI and VCI information is put in a new ATM cell header between the control word and the ATM cell payload. The Header Error Control (HEC) field is removed from the ATM header. The

PTI bits and C bit (CLP bit) are copied from the ATM header. Figure 10-14 shows the control word format. The control bits in the control word should be 0.

Figure 10-14 *Single Cell Relay Packet Format*

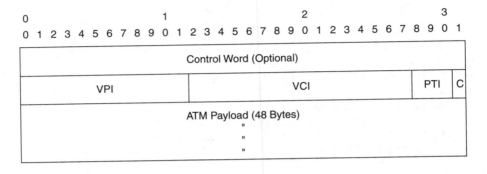

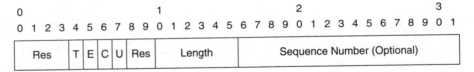

Example 10-10 shows the configuration of an AToM network transporting ATM cells over MPLS in single cell relay mode. The AAL used is AAL0 on the PE routers for cell relay.

Example 10-10 *ATM Single Cell Relay Mode Example*

```
!
hostname PE1-ce
!
interface ATM2/0.1 point-to-point
 ip address 10.100.100.2 255.255.255.0
 pvc 10/100
  encapsulation aal5snap
 !
!
```

Example 10-10 *ATM Single Cell Relay Mode Example (Continued)*

```
!
hostname PE2-ce

!
interface ATM3/0.1 point-to-point
 ip address 10.100.100.1 255.255.255.0
 pvc 10/100
  encapsulation aal5snap
 !
!


!
hostname PE1
!
interface ATM8/0/0
 mtu 1500
 no ip address
 pvc 10/100 l2transport
  encapsulation aal0
   xconnect 10.200.254.4 1000 pw-class one
 !
!


!
hostname PE2
!
interface ATM0/0/0
 no ip address
 pvc 10/100 l2transport
  encapsulation aal0
   xconnect 10.200.254.1 1000 pw-class one
 !
!


PE1#show mpls l2transport vc 1000

Local intf     Local circuit           Dest address    VC ID     Status
------------   ---------------------   ---------------  --------  ----------
AT8/0/0        ATM VCC CELL 10/100     10.200.254.4     1000      UP

PE1#show mpls l2transport vc 1000 detail
Local interface: AT8/0/0 up, line protocol up, ATM VCC CELL 10/100 up
  Destination address: 10.200.254.4, VC ID: 1000, VC status: up
    Preferred path: not configured
    Default path: active
    Tunnel label: 23, next hop 10.200.200.2
    Output interface: Et0/0/0, imposed label stack {23 24}
```

continues

Example 10-10 *ATM Single Cell Relay Mode Example (Continued)*

```
     Create time: 01:21:52, last status change time: 00:06:36
     Signaling protocol: LDP, peer 10.200.254.4:0 up
       MPLS VC labels: local 20, remote 24
       Group ID: local 0, remote 0
       MTU: local n/a, remote n/a
       Remote interface description:
     Sequencing: receive disabled, send disabled
     Sequence number: receive 0, send 0
     VC statistics:
       packet totals: receive 231, send 676
       byte totals:   receive 13860, send 40560
       packet drops:  receive 0, seq error 0, send 0
```

You also can configure cell relay in Virtual Path (VP) mode or Port mode.

The following shows the configuration for cell relay in VP mode:

```
!
interface ATM8/0/0
 no ip address
 atm pvp 11 l2transport
   xconnect 10.200.254.4 1000 pw-class one
 !
```

This is the configuration for cell relay in Port mode:

```
!
interface ATM8/0/0
 no ip address
   xconnect 10.200.254.4 1000 pw-class one
 !
```

Packed Cell Relay Mode

To have ATM cell relay but overcome the disadvantage of the added overhead by labeling every cell separately, use cell packing, which allows the packing of several cells and their labeling in one AToM packet. The packet format is the same as with single cell relay, except that multiple cells are in one frame. Therefore, after the control word, you see multiple occurrences of the VPI/VCI/PTI/C fields and the ATM cell payloads. This means that for each ATM cell transported, the labeled packet will have 52 bytes. Figure 10-15 shows the packing of multiple cells into one frame.

Figure 10-15 *Packed Cell Relay Packet Format*

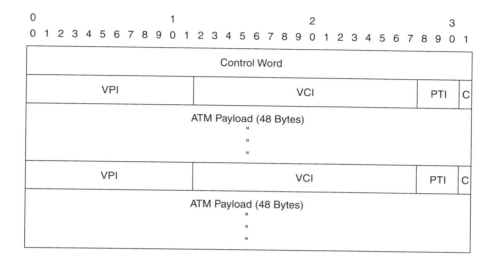

Figure 10-15 depicts two cells, but you can have more. As with single cell relay, the HEC field is removed from the ATM header. The maximum number of cells for one frame is 28. The interface command **cell-packing** *cells* **mcpt-timer** *timer* lets you configure how many cells maximum should be packed into one frame and in which time (in microseconds). MCPT stands for Maximum Cell Packing Timeout. The *timer* keyword lets you specify which timer to use.

You can configure three timers per ATM interface with the command **atm mcpt-timers**. Each timer governs how long to wait before sending the frame. When the timer expires, no more cells are packed into the frame, and the frame is sent onto the pseudowire. Per PVC configured on one interface, you can then choose one of the three timers to use for packing the cells into the frame. Example 10-11 shows the configuration needed on the PE router to enable packed cell relay. A debug command is also available for packed cell relay.

Example 10-11 *ATM Packed Cell Relay Mode Example*

```
!
hostname PE1
!
interface ATM8/0/0
 mtu 1500
 no ip address
```

continues

Example 10-11   *ATM Packed Cell Relay Mode Example (Continued)*

```
atm mcpt-timers 200 300 400
pvc 10/100 l2transport
 encapsulation aal0
 cell-packing 28 mcpt-timer 3
 xconnect 10.200.254.4 1000 pw-class one
!
!

PE1#show atm cell-packing
                          average               average
      circuit       local nbr of cells    peer  nbr of cells   MCPT
      type          MNCP  rcvd in one pkt MNCP  sent in one pkt (us)
ATM8/0/0      vc  10/100  28       22      28       22          400

PE1#debug atm cell-packing
ATM Cell Packing debugging is on
```

Ethernet

The AToM solution to carry Ethernet over MPLS is strictly point-to-point. In essence, all Ethernet frames are carried from one ingress PE to one egress PE router. This is the equivalent of LAN-to-LAN bridging over point-to-point WAN links. The connection is not multipoint, so no emulation of a LAN-like functionality occurs whereby one frame enters the ingress PE and is broadcast to all PE routers that belong to the same Layer 2 VPN. A LAN-like solution across MPLS in one VPN is possible; it is called VPLS, and it is covered in Chapter 11.

The AC can be an Ethernet port or an 802.1Q (dot1q) VLAN. For each of the two types of ACs, LDP signals a different VC Type or PW type in the PW ID FEC TLV via the targeted session between the PE routers. VC Type 5 is used for Ethernet Port mode, and VC Type 4 is used for Ethernet VLAN mode. In the Ethernet VLAN mode, a VLAN header that has some meaning to the PE routers is always present. In other words, the PE routers look at the VLAN header. In Ethernet Port mode, a VLAN header might or might not be present on the frame. In any case, if a VLAN header does exist, the PE router does not inspect it; rather, it carries the frame transparently. Running EoMPLS in Ethernet Port mode allows a complete Ethernet trunk to be transported over one pseudowire. To run Ethernet VLAN mode, configure the **xconnect** command on the VLAN interface or on the Ethernet subinterface.

This section describes some issues that pertain only to EoMPLS.

Ethernet Frame Format

Figure 10-16 shows the Ethernet II frame format. The first one is the Ethernet II frame. The second is the Ethernet II frame with an 802.1Q VLAN header. The 802.1Q VLAN header consists of the tag protocol identifier (TPID) and tag control information (TCI) fields. These 4 extra bytes are referred to as the VLAN tag.

Figure 10-16 *Ethernet II and Ethernet II with 802.1Q Frame Format*

Ethernet II Frame Format

Preamble	SFD	DA	SA	Ethertype	Data	FCS
7 Bytes	1 Byte	6 Bytes	6 Bytes	2 Bytes	46-1500 Bytes	4 Bytes

Ethernet II With 802.1Q Frame Format

Preamble	SFD	DA	SA	TPID	TCI	Ethertype	Data	FCS
7 Bytes	1 Byte	6 Bytes	6 Bytes	2 Bytes	2 Bytes	2 Bytes	46-1500 Bytes	4 Bytes

The 4 bytes of the VLAN header are further divided into the following:

■   TPID (16 bits)—The TPID is set to 0x8100 to identify the tagged protocol as 802.1Q.

■   TCI (16 bits)—The TCI consists of the following fields:

> Priority (3 bits)—The 3 priority bits are used as quality of service (QoS) bits to prioritize the Ethernet frames.

> CFI (1 bit)—The canonical format indicator indicates whether the MAC address is in canonical format.

> VID (12 bits)—The VID is the VLAN identifier. It is the number of the VLAN.

EoMPLS Forwarding

When the ingress PE router receives the Ethernet frame, it strips off the preamble, Start of Frame Delimiter (SFD), and FCS fields, adds a control word, labels the frame, and forwards it across the MPLS network. If the Ethernet frame is tagged with an 802.1Q tag, this tag is kept, too. On the egress PE router, the VC label is stripped off, the control word is removed, the Ethernet FCS is added, and the frame is sent toward the CE router or switch.

VLAN ID Rewrite

VLAN ID Rewrite is the feature whereby the 802.1Q tag might be rewritten in Ethernet VLAN mode if the 802.1Q VLAN ID is different at both sides of the AToM network. You might have VLAN 100 on the ingress PE router and VLAN 200 on the egress PE router, for example. The VLAN ID rewrite happens either on the imposition side or on the disposition side. The VLAN ID Rewrite is an automatically enabled feature, so no configuration is needed to enable it.

EoMPLS Scenario Examples

This section gives you an overview of some of the scenarios to create EoMPLS services. Notice that EoMPLS is either done in Ethernet Port mode or in Ethernet VLAN mode. In the examples, the *Ethernet* refers to Ethernet Port mode, and *Eth VLAN* refers to Ethernet VLAN mode.

EoMPLS Carrying Simple Ethernet

The PE routers are configured with the **xconnect** command on the main Ethernet interface and carry the nontagged Ethernet frames received from the CE routers over the pseudowire. The PE routers run EoMPLS in Ethernet Port mode. In Figure 10-17, you can see that the pseudowire with VCID 2000 carries the Ethernet frames across the MPLS network.

Figure 10-17 *EoMPLS Carrying Simple Ethernet*

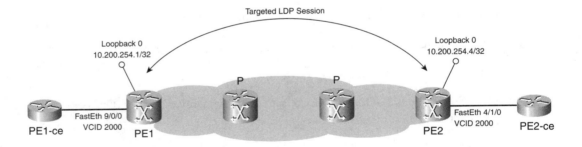

Example 10-12 shows the configuration needed for the network in Figure 10-17. The **xconnect** commands on the Ethernet interfaces of the PE routers specify the loopback IP address of the remote PE router as peer-router-id. The configured VCID is 2000.

Example 10-12 *EoMPLS Carrying Simple Ethernet Example*

```
PE1-ce
!
interface FastEthernet0/1
 ip address 10.100.100.1 255.255.255.0
!

PE2-ce
!
```

Example 10-12 *EoMPLS Carrying Simple Ethernet Example (Continued)*

```
interface FastEthernet0/1
 ip address 10.100.100.2 255.255.255.0
!


!
hostname PE1
!
pseudowire-class one
 encapsulation mpls
!
interface FastEthernet9/0/0
 no ip address
 xconnect 10.200.254.4 2000 pw-class one
!


!
hostname PE2
!
interface FastEthernet4/1/0
 no ip address
 xconnect 10.200.254.1 2000 pw-class one
!


PE1#show mpls l2transport vc 2000

Local intf     Local circuit          Dest address     VC ID      Status
------------   ----------------------   ---------------   ---------   ----------
Fa9/0/0        Ethernet                 10.200.254.4     2000       UP

PE1#show mpls l2transport vc 2000 detail
Local interface: Fa9/0/0 up, line protocol up, Ethernet up
  Destination address: 10.200.254.4, VC ID: 2000, VC status: up
    Preferred path: not configured
    Default path: active
    Tunnel label: 23, next hop 10.200.200.2
    Output interface: Et0/0/0, imposed label stack {23 35}
  Create time: 00:02:26, last status change time: 00:02:26
  Signaling protocol: LDP, peer 10.200.254.4:0 up
    MPLS VC labels: local 25, remote 35
    Group ID: local 0, remote 0
    MTU: local 1500, remote 1500
    Remote interface description:
  Sequencing: receive disabled, send disabled
  Sequence number: receive 0, send 0
  VC statistics:
    packet totals: receive 107, send 67
    byte totals:   receive 10736, send 7818
    packet drops:  receive 0, seq error 0, send 0
```

EoMPLS Carrying an Ethernet Trunk

When the AC is an Ethernet trunk, the configuration on the PE routers is the same as in Example 10-12. The difference is that the CE routers are configured with 802.1Q subinterfaces; therefore, the Ethernet frames are tagged when the PE router receives them. The result is that the PE routers carry the whole 802.1Q trunk across the MPLS network in one pseudowire. The transported Ethernet frames across the pseudowire have the 802.1Q tags.

Figure 10-18 shows the two PE routers running EoMPLS in Ethernet Port mode. The CE routers have two subinterfaces: one for VLAN 100 and one for VLAN 200. Both VLANs are carried across the MPLS network over the pseudowire with VCID 2000.

Figure 10-18 *EoMPLS Carrying an Ethernet Trunk*

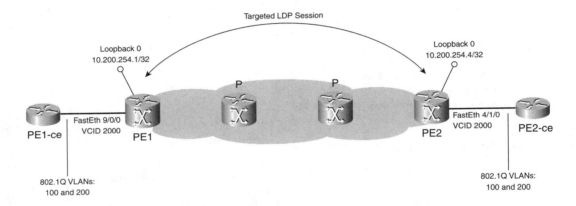

The PE routers are running EoMPLS in Ethernet Port mode, indicated by the VC Type being Ethernet, as shown in Example 10-13.

Example 10-13 *EoMPLS Carrying an Ethernet Trunk Example*

```
PE1-ce
!
interface FastEthernet0/1
 no ip address
!
interface FastEthernet0/1.1
 encapsulation dot1Q 100
 ip address 10.100.100.1 255.255.255.0
!
interface FastEthernet0/1.2
 encapsulation dot1Q 200
 ip address 10.100.200.1 255.255.255.0
!

PE2-ce
```

Example 10-13 *EoMPLS Carrying an Ethernet Trunk Example (Continued)*

```
!
interface FastEthernet0/1
 no ip address
!
interface FastEthernet0/1.1
 encapsulation dot1Q 100
 ip address 10.100.100.2 255.255.255.0
!
interface FastEthernet0/1.2
 encapsulation dot1Q 200
 ip address 10.100.200.2 255.255.255.0
!


PE1#show mpls l2transport vc

Local intf     Local circuit           Dest address     VC ID    Status
------------   ----------------------  --------------   ------   ----------
Fa9/0/0        Ethernet                10.200.254.4     2000     UP

PE1#show mpls l2transport vc detail
Local interface: Fa9/0/0 up, line protocol up, Ethernet up
  Destination address: 10.200.254.4, VC ID: 2000, VC status: up
    Preferred path: not configured
    Default path: active
    Tunnel label: 23, next hop 10.200.200.2
    Output interface: Et0/0/0, imposed label stack {23 21}
  Create time: 00:01:04, last status change time: 00:00:19
  Signaling protocol: LDP, peer 10.200.254.4:0 up
    MPLS VC labels: local 24, remote 21
    Group ID: local 0, remote 0
    MTU: local 1500, remote 1500
    Remote interface description:
  Sequencing: receive disabled, send disabled
  Sequence number: receive 0, send 0
  VC statistics:
    packet totals: receive 50, send 39
    byte totals:   receive 5712, send 5389
    packet drops:  receive 0, seq error 0, send 0

PE1#show mpls l2transport binding
  Destination Address: 10.200.254.4,  VC ID: 2000
    Local Label:  24
        Cbit: 1,    VC Type: Ethernet,    GroupID: 0
        MTU: 1500,   Interface Desc: n/a
        VCCV Capabilities: Type 1, Type 2
    Remote Label: 21
        Cbit: 1,    VC Type: Ethernet,    GroupID: 0
        MTU: 1500,   Interface Desc: n/a
        VCCV Capabilities: Type 1, Type 2
```

EoMPLS Carrying One VLAN

In the scenario of EoMPLS carrying one VLAN, you have an 802.1Q trunk between the CE and the PE routers. Each VLAN is mapped to one pseudowire. The advantage of this scenario compared to the previous scenario is that each VLAN has its own pseudowire and can be routed differently through the MPLS network, or the different pseudowires can be between different PE routers. Figure 10-19 shows an example of the two PE routers running two pseudowires between them, one for VLAN 100 and one for VLAN 200.

Figure 10-19 *EoMPLS Carrying One VLAN*

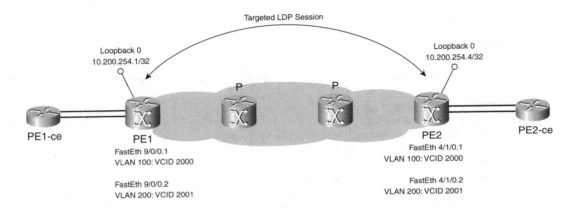

The PE routers are running EoMPLS in VLAN mode, indicated by the VC Type being Eth VLAN, as shown in Example 10-14.

Example 10-14 *EoMPLS Carrying One VLAN Example*

```
!
hostname PE1
!
interface FastEthernet9/0/0
 no ip address
!
interface FastEthernet9/0/0.1
 encapsulation dot1Q 100
 xconnect 10.200.254.4 2000 pw-class one
!
interface FastEthernet9/0/0.2
 encapsulation dot1Q 200
 xconnect 10.200.254.4 2001 pw-class one
!
```

Example 10-14 *EoMPLS Carrying One VLAN Example (Continued)*

```
!
hostname PE2
!
interface FastEthernet4/1/0
 no ip address
!
interface FastEthernet4/1/0.1
 encapsulation dot1Q 100
 xconnect 10.200.254.1 2000 pw-class one
!
interface FastEthernet4/1/0.2
 encapsulation dot1Q 200
 xconnect 10.200.254.1 2001 pw-class one
!

PE1#show mpls l2transport vc

Local intf    Local circuit          Dest address     VC ID    Status
------------  ---------------------  ---------------  -------  ----------
Fa9/0/0.1     Eth VLAN 100           10.200.254.4     2000     UP
Fa9/0/0.2     Eth VLAN 200           10.200.254.4     2001     UP

PE1#show mpls l2transport vc 2001 detail
Local interface: Fa9/0/0.2 up, line protocol up, Eth VLAN 200 up
  Destination address: 10.200.254.4, VC ID: 2001, VC status: up
    Preferred path: not configured
    Default path: active
    Tunnel label: 23, next hop 10.200.200.2
    Output interface: Et0/0/0, imposed label stack {23 22}
  Create time: 00:10:33, last status change time: 00:03:46
  Signaling protocol: LDP, peer 10.200.254.4:0 up
    MPLS VC labels: local 24, remote 22
    Group ID: local 0, remote 0
    MTU: local 1500, remote 1500
    Remote interface description:
  Sequencing: receive disabled, send disabled
  Sequence number: receive 0, send 0
  VC statistics:
    packet totals: receive 91, send 43
    byte totals:   receive 8686, send 4906
    packet drops:  receive 0, seq error 0, send 0

PE1#show mpls l2transport binding
  Destination Address: 10.200.254.4,  VC ID: 2000
    Local Label:  20
        Cbit: 1,    VC Type: Eth VLAN,    GroupID: 0
        MTU: 1500,    Interface Desc: n/a
```

continues

Example 10-14   *EoMPLS Carrying One VLAN Example (Continued)*

```
            VCCV Capabilities: Type 1, Type 2
    Remote Label: 21
        Cbit: 1,    VC Type: Eth VLAN,    GroupID: 0
        MTU: 1500,    Interface Desc: n/a
        VCCV Capabilities: Type 1, Type 2
Destination Address: 10.200.254.4,  VC ID: 2001
    Local Label:  24
        Cbit: 1,    VC Type: Eth VLAN,    GroupID: 0
        MTU: 1500,    Interface Desc: n/a
        VCCV Capabilities: Type 1, Type 2
    Remote Label: 22
        Cbit: 1,    VC Type: Eth VLAN,    GroupID: 0
        MTU: 1500,    Interface Desc: n/a
        VCCV Capabilities: Type 1, Type 2
```

Dot1q Tunneling (QinQ) over AToM

Dot1q tunneling, or QinQ, refers to a technique whereby Ethernet frames are double tagged—that is, the Ethernet frames have two 802.1Q tags. This is done by configuring the interface in dot1qtunnel mode with an access VLAN instead of the normal access VLAN mode or trunk mode. The received frames on the interface that is configured for dot1qtunnel are left intact and another 802.1Q tag is put onto the frame. This 802.1Q tag refers to the VLAN number that is configured on the dot1qtunnel interface. If the frames that the router receives are already 802.1Q tagged, they receive another 802.1Q tag.

You can use dot1q tunneling to transport VLANs inside a VLAN across a switched network. You also can use dot1q tunneling to transport the customer VLANs across the MPLS network inside a VLAN of the service provider. If the PE router is configured with a dot1qtunnel interface to the CE router, and the CE router is configured with a trunk toward the PE router, the PE router adds a second 802.1Q tag to the Ethernet frames before labeling them and forwarding them onto the MPLS network.

In Figure 10-20, you can see that this technique carries the 50 customer VLANs from one site to another site across the MPLS network with the AToM solution. The CE router is configured with a trunk port carrying the 50 VLANs, whereas the CE-facing interface on the PE router is configured with the access VLAN 800 and dot1qtunnel. Therefore, all frames are tagged with VLANs 1 to 50 and are "encapsulated" into VLAN 800 of the service provider on the PE router. The result of this is that the service provider needs only one VLAN—VLAN 800—to carry all the VLANs from this customer for that site. The other sites have a configuration that is similar to this site.

Figure 10-20 *Dot1q Tunnel Example*

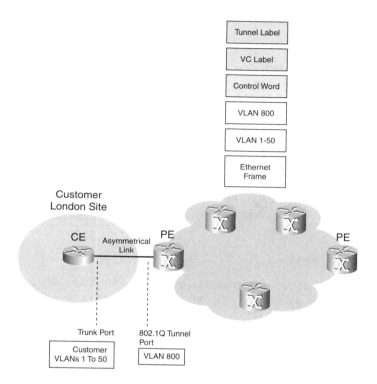

Example 10-15 shows a possible configuration for the CE and PE routers to have dot1q tunneling over AToM.

Example 10-15 *Dot1q Tunnel Configuration Example*

```
CE#
interface FastEthernet0/1
 no ip address
!
interface FastEthernet0/1.1
 encapsulation dot1Q 1
 ip address 10.1.2.2 255.255.255.0
!
interface FastEthernet0/1.2
 encapsulation dot1Q 2
 ip address 10.1.4.2 255.255.255.0
...

PE#
vlan dot1q tag native
```

continues

Example 10-15 *Dot1q Tunnel Configuration Example (Continued)*

```
interface FastEthernet2/3
 no ip address
 switchport
 switchport access vlan 800
 switchport mode dot1qtunnel
 spanning-tree bpdufilter enable
!
interface Vlan800
 no ip address
 mpls l2transport route 2.2.2.5 800
```

NOTE The **mpls l2transport route** *destination vc-id* command is the equivalent but older command for the command **xconnect** *peer-router-id vcid* **encapsulation mpls**.

AToM Tunnel Selection

The AToM Tunnel Selection feature enables you to steer the AToM traffic through the MPLS network over a path that you specify. For this to work, you need to set up an MPLS TE tunnel from the PE to the PE router and then specify that the AToM traffic should take the TE tunnel instead of the default shortest labeled path. In addition, you can specify whether fallback to the default path is desirable when the TE tunnel fails.

Figure 10-21 shows an MPLS network with MPLS VPN and AToM customers. The CE routers CE1 and CE2 are part of one MPLS VPN network, whereas CE3 and CE4 are two CE routers that are connected through AToM. Normally, all labeled traffic follows the top path because it is the shortest path through the MPLS backbone. If you want to separate the AToM from the VPN traffic in the MPLS network, you can create two TE tunnels between the two PE routers (one for each direction) to carry the AToM traffic. This might be desirable if you want to ensure a certain delay in the network for each kind of traffic, without the direct use of QoS. Another driver might be the guarantee of seamless service via the use of Fast ReRouting (FRR) or bandwidth protection when using TE.

Figure 10-21 *Example of Tunnel Selection*

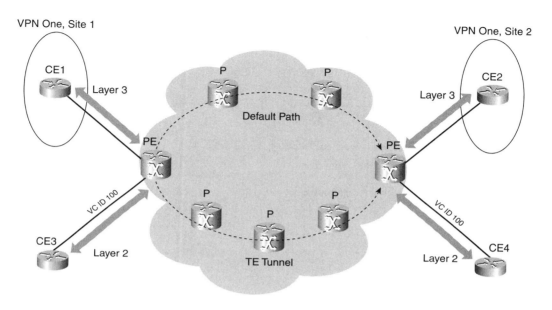

If the purpose is to separate the AToM traffic from all the other MPLS traffic, do not configure **autoroute announce** on the TE tunnel because that steers *all* the traffic onto the TE tunnel. Example 10-16 shows how to configure tunnel selection. You have to configure **preferred-path** under the pseudowire class and create a TE tunnel between the PE routers without the **autoroute announce** command.

Example 10-16 *Tunnel Selection Example*

```
pseudowire-class pw1
 encapsulation mpls
 preferred-path interface Tunnel1
!
interface Tunnel1
 ip unnumbered Loopback0
 tunnel source Loopback0
 tunnel destination 10.1.1.2
 tunnel mode mpls traffic-eng
 tunnel mpls traffic-eng path-option 1 dynamic
!
interface FastEthernet2/6
 no ip address
 xconnect 10.1.1.2 100 pw-class pw1
```

To verify that the tunnel selection is working, look at the pseudowire with the command **show mpls l2transport vc** [**vcid** *vc-id*] | [*vc-id-min vc-id-max*] [**interface** *name* [*local-circuit-id*]] [**destination** *ip-address* | *name*] [**detail**]. Example 10-17 shows this.

Example 10-17 *Verifying Tunnel Selection*

```
PE#show  mpls l2transport vc 100 detail
Local interface: Fa2/6 up, line protocol up, Ethernet up
  Destination address: 10.1.1.2, VC ID: 100, VC status: up
    Preferred path: Tunnel1,  active
    Default path: ready
    Tunnel label: 3, next hop point2point
    Output interface: Tu1, imposed label stack {12307 20}
  Create time: 00:00:11, last status change time: 00:00:11
  Signaling protocol: LDP, peer 10.1.1.2:0 up
    MPLS VC labels: local 21, remote 20
    Group ID: local 0, remote 2
    MTU: local 1500, remote 1500
    Remote interface description:
  Sequencing: receive disabled, send disabled
  VC statistics:
    packet totals: receive 1, send 6
    byte totals:   receive 368, send 0
    packet drops:  receive 0, send 0
```

Following is the full syntax of the preferred path command:

```
preferred path [interface tunnel tunnel-number | peer {ip address | host name}]
[disable-fallback]
```

Instead of specifying a TE tunnel, you can specify an IP address (or host name) of the remote PE router. You should choose a different IP address on the remote PE router from the one the default LSP uses. The path to that IP address must be an LSP, but you can route it differently through the MPLS network than the default path, used by the labeled traffic between the two loopback IP addresses on the PE routers. Tunnel selection uses fallback, meaning that if the preferred path (TE tunnel or the specific IP address) becomes unavailable, the AToM traffic is sent across the default path. You can, however, disable it by specifying the **disable-fallback** keyword on the **preferred-path** command, as shown in Example 10-18.

Example 10-18 *Fallback Disabled Example*

```
pseudowire-class pw1
 encapsulation mpls
 preferred-path interface Tunnel1 disable-fallback
!
PE#show mpls l2transport vc 100 detail
Local interface: Fa2/6 up, line protocol up, Ethernet up
  Destination address: 10.1.1.2, VC ID: 100, VC status: up
```

Example 10-18 *Fallback Disabled Example (Continued)*

```
    Preferred path: Tunnel1,  active
    Default path: disabled
    Tunnel label:  3, next hop point2point
    Output interface: Tu1, imposed label stack {12307 20}
  Create time: 00:00:13, last status change time: 00:00:13
  Signaling protocol: LDP, peer 10.1.1.2:0 up
    MPLS VC labels: local 16, remote 20
    Group ID: local 0, remote 2
    MTU: local 1500, remote 1500
    Remote interface description:
  Sequencing: receive disabled, send disabled
  VC statistics:
    packet totals: receive 2, send 6
    byte totals:   receive 189, send 0
    packet drops:  receive 0, send 0
```

AToM and QoS

You can use QoS in MPLS networks to prioritize certain packets, just as you would prioritize IP packets. In the case of IP, you set the precedence or DiffServ Codepoint (DSCP) bits in the IP header to prioritize the IP packet. In the case of MPLS, you prioritize the packet by setting the Experimental (EXP) bits to a value between 0 and 7. The MPLS payload is a frame instead of an IP packet in the case of AToM. Three possibilities exist for marking the EXP bits:

- Statically configuring the setting of the EXP bits

- Marking the EXP bits according to the IP precedence bits

- Using information from the frame header to set the EXP bits

You can statically configure the EXP bits by using Modular QoS Command Line Interface (MQC) on the router. You must configure a policy on the ingress interface (customer CE-facing interface) that sets the MPLS EXP bits. It is important to note that the EXP bits are set in both the tunnel and the VC label. This is important in the (default) case of PHP where, at the last P router, the tunnel label is removed, and the packet arrives at the egress PE with only the VC label in the label stack. Therefore, you must also set the EXP bits in the VC label if you want to preserve the QoS information that is encoded in MPLS all the way to the egress PE router.

The examples in this section show setting the EXP bits in the case of EoMPLS. Example 10-19 shows an example of a policy that is configured with MQC on the ingress interface of the ingress PE router to set the EXP bits to 4.

Example 10-19 *Setting EXP Bits with MQC*

```
PE1#
!
class-map match-all EXP
  match any
!
policy-map set-EXP
  class EXP
    set mpls experimental 4
!
interface FastEthernet9/0/0
 no ip address
 xconnect 10.200.254.4 100 pw-class one
 service-policy input set-EXP
!
```

You can set the EXP bits according to the precedence bits of the IP header only if the frame payload is IP. The information from the frame header that is used to set the EXP bits in the MPLS labels could be, for example, the priority bits (P bits) from the 802.1Q header. If the values of the experimental bits are not assigned, the priority bits in the 802.1Q header tag control information field are copied by default into the EXP bit fields.

Example 10-20 shows the configuration of a router where the EXP bits are set to 1 if the 802.1Q priority bits of the received frames are set to 1, 2, or 3. In addition, traffic shaping is applied on the ingress interface of the ingress PE router.

Example 10-20 *Setting EXP Bits with MQC According to the 802.1Q Priority Bits*

```
PE1#
!
interface Vlan50
 no ip address
 mpls l2transport route 1.1.1.1 100
 service-policy input exp-one
end
!
class-map match-all blue
  match cos  1  2  3
!
policy-map exp-one
  class blue
    set mpls experimental 1
```

Example 10-20 *Setting EXP Bits with MQC According to the 802.1Q Priority Bits (Continued)*

```
  class class-default
    shape average 2000000 8000 8000
!
PE1#show policy-map exp-one
 Policy Map exp-one
  class  blue
   set mpls experimental 1
  class  class-default
   shape average 2000000 8000 8000

PE1#show class-map blue
 Class Map match-all blue (id 3)
   Match cos  1  2  3

PE1#show policy-map interface vlan 50

 Vlan50

  service-policy input: exp-one

    class-map: blue (match-all)
      match: cos  1  2  3
      set:
       mpls experimental 1

    class-map: class-default (match-any)
      0 packets, 0 bytes
      5 minute offered rate 0 bps, drop rate 0 bps
      match: any
        0 packets, 0 bytes
        5 minute rate 0 bps
      queue size 0, queue limit 250000
      packets input 0, packet drops 0
      tail/random drops 0, no buffer drops 0, other drops 0
      shape: cir 2000000,  Bc 8000,  Be 8000
        input bytes 0, shape rate 0 bps
```

Up to this point in the chapter, the ACs on both sides were of the same encapsulation type, which is also referred to as *like-to-like functionality*. L2VPN Interworking is an AToM feature that allows different encapsulation types at both sides of the AToM network. The Interworking feature then "translates" one Layer 2 encapsulation to another.

L2VPN Inter-Autonomous Networking provides an AToM service across multiple autonomous systems, each capable of providing AToM service.

L2VPN Pseudowire Switching allows the stitching of two pseudowire segments.

Local Switching is a feature whereby the PE router switches Layer 2 frames from one AC to another without sending the frames across the MPLS network.

For more information on L2VPN Interworking, L2VPN Inter-Autonomous Networking, L2VPN Pseudowire Switching, or Local Switching, refer to "Chapter 10 Supplement" at http://www.ciscopress.com/1587051974.

Summary

In this chapter, you saw how to build Layer 2 virtual private networks (VPNs) over an MPLS infrastructure. You can build these VPNs by constructing pseudowires between PE routers that carry the Layer 2 frames from the attachment circuits (ACs) that are attached to the PE router. ACs can have a variety of encapsulation types, including High-Level Data Link Control (HDLC), PPP, Frame Relay, ATM, and Ethernet. Frame Relay can be transported in DLCI-to-DLCI mode or in port-to-port mode. ATM can be transported in AAL5, single cell relay, or packed cell relay mode. Finally, you saw some specific Any Transport over MPLS (AToM) issues related to maximum transmission unit (MTU), quality of service (QoS), and AToM Tunnel Selection.

Chapter Review Questions

You can find answers to the following questions in Appendix A, "Answers to the Chapter Review Questions."

1. Name the advantages of AToM for the service provider.

2. Name the advantages of AToM for the customers of the service provider.

3. How many labels are used to forward AToM traffic, and what is the use of each of those labels?

4. Name three of the five functions of the control word.

5. Ethernet over MPLS can be done in two modes. What are they called?

6. Which two modes exist to carry Frame Relay over MPLS?

7. What is the command to limit the number of ATM cells going into one frame in Packed Cell Relay mode?

8. Which VC types (PW types) can EoMPLS use?

9. What is the AToM signaling protocol between PE routers?

10. What does the C-bit in the PW ID FEC TLV indicate?

What You Will Learn

By the end of this chapter, you should be able to do the following:

- Explain what VPLS stands for

- Explain how VPLS emulates an Ethernet switched network over MPLS

- Configure VPLS

When you are able to do these tasks, you will have a thorough understanding of VPLS.

CHAPTER 11

Virtual Private LAN Service

Virtual Private LAN Service (VPLS) emulates a LAN segment across the MPLS backbone across pseudowires or virtual circuits. VPLS creates one or more LANs for each customer who is using the service from the service provider. Each LAN, of course, is completely separate from the other emulated LAN segments—hence the "P" for "Private" in VPLS. When the customer with different Ethernet sites connects to an MPLS backbone where VPLS is deployed, it appears as if all the sites are interconnected through a virtual Ethernet switch. Two options are available to interconnect these Ethernet sites: either Spanning Tree Protocol (STP) bridge protocol data units (BPDU) are not allowed to pass through the virtual switch, or they are allowed to pass. In the first case, the spanning tree in each Ethernet site terminates at the provider edge (PE) router. In the second case, the spanning tree crosses the MPLS backbone (the virtual switch), and one STP runs through all sites. An Ethernet LAN is a Layer 2 domain. As such, Ethernet frames are transported across the MPLS backbone. This is the same as for Ethernet over MPLS (EoMPLS). However, EoMPLS is a service that is point-to-point in nature, whereas VPLS—emulating a LAN—is point-to-multipoint in nature and as such must support replicating broadcast and multicast frames. Finally, VPLS must perform some features that are inherent to an Ethernet switch—such as MAC address learning and aging—if the virtual switch is to be emulated.

The Need for VPLS

VPLS is a service that emulates an Ethernet LAN. The need for VPLS arose because MPLS VPN is a service that is IP centric. No other Layer 3 traffic can be carried across the MPLS backbone with this service. Any Transport over MPLS (AToM) allows you to carry all Layer 3 protocols as AToM carries the Layer 2 frames across the MPLS backbone; thus, AToM is not limited to carrying IP. The disadvantage of AToM is that it is point-to-point. Between each pair of PE routers is a pseudowire (two LSPs, one for each direction) that carries the Layer 2 frames. Metro Ethernet networks have seen a tremendous rise in popularity in the past few years because Ethernet is cheap, flexible, omnipresent, and easy to provision.

If a customer wants to connect his Ethernet segments from different sites across an MPLS backbone from a service provider, he could use the EoMPLS service, but that would connect the segments in a point-to-point fashion. If the different Ethernet sites are located in proximity, the customer could connect them by deploying an Ethernet switch between the segments. The

Ethernet switch would forward the unicast frames and replicate the packets to different outgoing ports for the forwarding of multicast and broadcast frames. If the different sites are not in close proximity, a switch could not be put directly between the different sites to interconnect the sites at Layer 2. VPLS would provide that functionality by emulating an Ethernet LAN or acting as a logical bridge over MPLS.

Figure 11-1 shows some Ethernet sites from one customer in different cities. The different LAN segments are interconnected by the service provider that runs the VPLS service. The VPLS service that runs over MPLS emulates an Ethernet switch that has different ports leading to the different Ethernet sites. A port can be a physical Ethernet port or a pseudowire.

Figure 11-1 *VPLS: Logical Bridge*

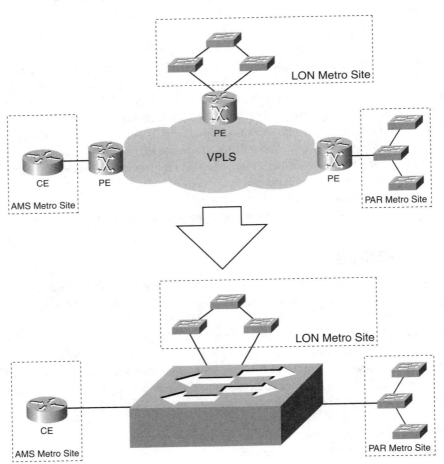

VPLS Architecture

A VPLS service emulates a LAN or the functionality of an Ethernet switch. An Ethernet switch has the following characteristics:

- Forwarding of Ethernet frames

- Forwarding of unicast frames with an unknown destination MAC address

- Replication of broadcast and multicast frames to more than one port

- Loop prevention

- Dynamic learning of MAC addresses

- MAC address aging

VPLS should also have these characteristics. Ethernet frames receive two MPLS labels before they are forwarded across the MPLS backbone. This forwarding of Ethernet frames is the same as in Chapter 10, "Any Transport over MPLS." An imposed virtual circuit (VC) label always serves as a demultiplexing label and indicates the VC that the frame belongs to. The tunnel label is the top label that indicates how the frame is forwarded from the ingress PE to the egress PE router.

If the PE router receives a frame that has an unknown destination MAC address, the frame is replicated and forwarded to all ports that belong to that LAN segment. The LAN segment on an Ethernet switch might be a collection of ports belonging to the same VLAN. When configuring VPLS, you must specify which VPLS instance a particular port or VLAN belongs to. The frames with unknown destination MAC addresses are forwarded to all ports belonging to that VPLS instance. On a true Ethernet switch, the port would just be a physical interface. However, with VPLS, it might be a physical interface, but it could also be a pseudowire to another PE router. Look at Figure 11-2, which shows the PE routers involved with the VPLS instance named cust-one for one customer. The customer has several sites, all of which are connected to a PE router. The PE routers have pseudowires between them to carry the Ethernet frames. Each pseudowire consists of two label switched paths (LSPs), one for each direction.

Figure 11-2   *VPLS Reference Model*

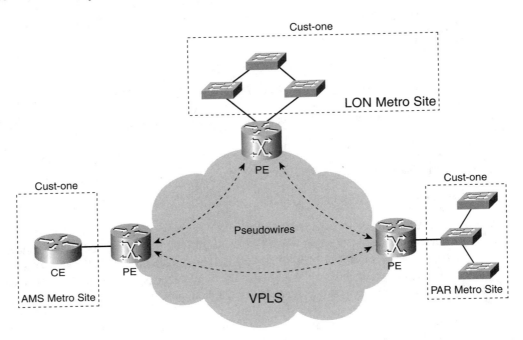

If the CE router or switch sends a broadcast frame to the PE router, the frame is replicated and forwarded to all physical ports on that PE router belonging to that VPLS instance, but also to all pseudowires associated with that VPLS instance. Multicast frames are replicated and forwarded to all physical ports that are part of the multicast group and to all pseudowires (the underlying WAN ports). When forwarding broadcast frames, it is important to flood the frame throughout the broadcast domain. If the PE routers are not fully meshed for one VPLS instance, a spanning tree protocol is required to keep the Layer 2 topology loop free. However, a simpler mechanism was chosen to keep the forwarding free of loops. The PE routers need to be in a full mesh of pseudowires, and the PE routers perform split-horizon in Layer 2 forwarding. Split-horizon here means that a flooded frame that is received on one pseudowire will never be forwarded to other pseudowires.

NOTE   Split-horizon is on by default. You can turn it off if needed. See the section "Hierarchical VPLS" for such an example.

As with Ethernet switches, the PE routers of the VPLS network should perform MAC address learning and aging. This means that the PE routers will notice the source address of received frames and associate them with a physical port or pseudowire. Similar to an Ethernet switch, the MAC addresses are aged out after a certain period of not receiving a frame from that MAC address. The aging time is refreshed after receiving a frame.

VPLS Data Plane

In the data plane, the transported frames look the same as Ethernet frames in the AToM model. Two labels are imposed on the Ethernet frame. The top label or tunnel label identifies the tunnel (LSP) that the frame belongs to. In other words, it forwards the frame from the local or ingress PE to the remote or egress PE. The bottom label is the VC label, and it identifies the pseudowire. In other words, the egress PE looks at the VC label; it uses the VC label to determine to which attachment circuit (Ethernet port or VLAN interface) the frame should be forwarded onto. Figure 11-3 shows the Ethernet frame with two MPLS labels as it is transported across the MPLS network.

Figure 11-3 *VPLS Data Plane*

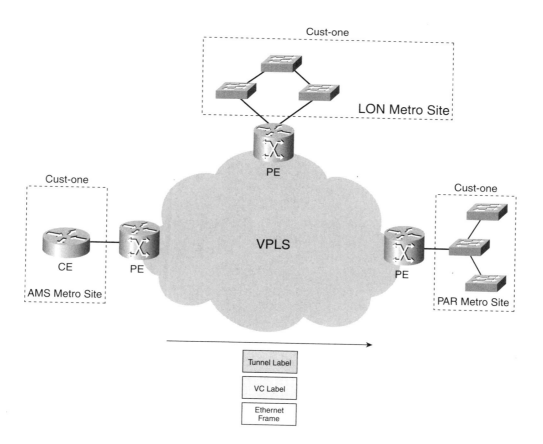

The transported frame is the Ethernet frame without an 802.1Q tag; this tag is stripped before the frame is forwarded into the MPLS network. The PE router builds a MAC table as any regular Ethernet switch. This MAC table forwards Ethernet frames to and from the physical Ethernet ports and to and from the pseudowires. In Cisco IOS, each customer who is connected to the MPLS backbone has a virtual forwarding instance (VFI). VFI is the collection of data structures that

Cisco IOS uses to forward Ethernet frames onto the Ethernet Attachment Circuits (the physical Ethernet ports) and the virtual circuits or pseudowires. Control plane and data plane information feed the VFI. The control plane information is the configuration on the PE router and the signaling protocol LDP that signals the pseudowires. It can populate the VFI with VC membership and VC label information. The data plane information is the data derived from frame forwarding, such as the MAC address learning information. Look at Figure 11-4 to see the VPLS PE router with physical Ethernet ports and pseudowires into the MPLS network.

Figure 11-4   *VPLS PE Router*

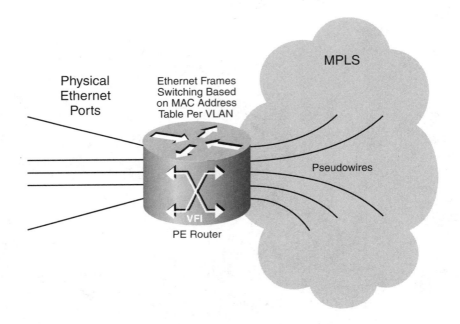

VPLS Signaling

VPLS requires a full mesh of pseudowires between PE routers for each VPLS instance. When you configure the VPLS instance on the PE router, you must also specify the VPLS neighbors of this PE router. That means you must specify all the remote PE routers for this PE router for that one VPLS instance. The PE routers then form a targeted LDP session between them in a full mesh. The targeted LDP session signals each VC or pseudowire between a pair of PE routers and advertises the VC labels. If a VPLS instance is assigned to a VLAN interface on the local PE router, a local VC ID is assigned to the VPLS instance. The VC ID is the VPN Identifier (VPN ID) that you must assign to a VPLS instance by means of configuration. Each pseudowire between a pair of PE routers for that VPLS instance has that VC ID. However, the local VC label that the router assigns for that VPLS instance is different for each pseudowire. Figure 11-5 shows the VPLS signaling.

Figure 11-5 *VPLS Signaling*

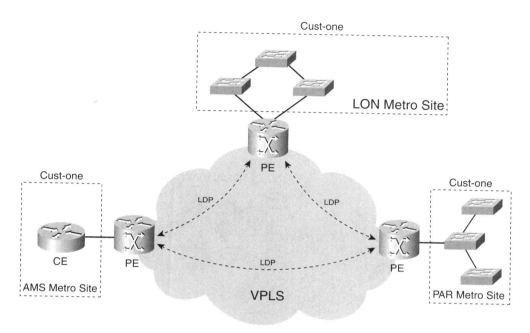

Targeted LDP Sessions Between PE Routers

The Basic VPLS Configuration

The configuration for VPLS is simple. First, you must configure a VPLS instance with the global **l2 vfi** command. The VFI needs to have a unique name on the PE router.

```
Router(config)#l2 vfi name manual
```

Then you need to specify a unique VPN ID number for that VFI.

```
Router(config-vfi)#vpn id number
```

Configure as neighbors all the egress PE routers of the full mesh of that VPLS.

```
Router(config-vfi)#neighbor remote-router-id encapsulation mpls
```

After you define the VFI, associate the VLAN interfaces belonging to that VFI with the VFI. You do this with the interface command **xconnect vfi**.

```
Router(config-if)#xconnect vfi name
```

Consider the following VPLS network example depicted in Figure 11-6.

Figure 11-6 *VPLS Example Network*

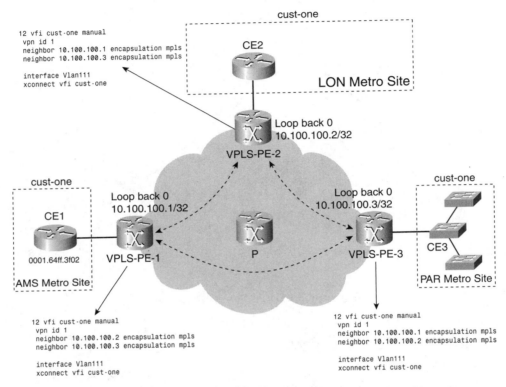

Figure 11-6 shows three PE routers. Three sites are connected for the VPLS instance cust-one. The configuration of the PE router VPLS-PE-1 is shown in Example 11-1. VLAN 111 is associated with VPLS instance cust-one.

Example 11-1 *VPLS Configuration of VPLS-PE-1*

```
!
hostname VPLS-PE-1
!
mpls label protocol ldp
mpls ldp router-id Loopback0 force
l2 vfi cust-one manual
 vpn id 1
 neighbor 10.100.100.2 encapsulation mpls
 neighbor 10.100.100.3 encapsulation mpls
!
interface FastEthernet4/2
 no ip address
```

Example 11-1 *VPLS Configuration of VPLS-PE-1 (Continued)*

```
 switchport
 switchport access vlan 111
 spanning-tree bpdufilter enable
!
interface POS5/1
 ip address 10.10.1.1 255.255.255.0
 mpls ip
 mls qos trust dscp
!
interface Vlan111
 no ip address
 xconnect vfi cust-one
!
```

When the set of VFIs are configured on all PE routers for one VPLS customer, the VPLS instance is configured.

Verifying the VPLS Operation

The output of Example 11-2 is taken on the router VPLS-PE-1 depicted in Figure 11-6. You use the **show vfi** command to verify the existence and state of the VFI cust-one.

Example 11-2 *show vfi*

```
VPLS-PE-1#show vfi cust-one
VFI name: cust-one, state: up
  Local attachment circuits:
    Vlan111
  Neighbors connected via pseudowires:
    10.100.100.2  10.100.100.3
```

The **show mpls ldp neighbor** command verifies the existence of the targeted LDP sessions between all PE routers for the VFI cust-one. In Example 11-3, VPLS-PE-1 has two targeted LDP sessions for the two remote PEs and one direct LDP neighbor: a P router.

Example 11-3 *show mpls ldp neighbor*

```
VPLS-PE-1#show mpls ldp neighbor
    Peer LDP Ident: 10.100.100.4:0; Local LDP Ident 10.100.100.1:0
        TCP connection: 10.100.100.4.11046 - 10.100.100.1.646
        State: Oper; Msgs sent/rcvd: 4438/4481; Downstream
        Up time: 2d16h
        LDP discovery sources:
          POS5/1, Src IP addr: 10.10.1.2
```

continues

Example 11-3 *show mpls ldp neighbor* (Continued)

```
        Addresses bound to peer LDP Ident:
           10.48.70.71     10.100.100.4    10.10.2.2        10.10.1.2
           10.10.3.2
    Peer LDP Ident: 10.100.100.2:0; Local LDP Ident 10.100.100.1:0
        TCP connection: 10.100.100.2.11526 - 10.100.100.1.646
        State: Oper; Msgs sent/rcvd: 4423/4424; Downstream
        Up time: 2d16h
        LDP discovery sources:
           Targeted Hello 10.100.100.1 -> 10.100.100.2, active, passive
        Addresses bound to peer LDP Ident:
           65.9.65.1       10.48.72.194    10.100.100.2    10.10.2.1
    Peer LDP Ident: 10.100.100.3:0; Local LDP Ident 10.100.100.1:0
        TCP connection: 10.100.100.3.11001 - 10.100.100.1.646
        State: Oper; Msgs sent/rcvd: 33/37; Downstream
        Up time: 00:18:24
        LDP discovery sources:
           Targeted Hello 10.100.100.1 -> 10.100.100.3, active, passive
        Addresses bound to peer LDP Ident:
           10.100.100.3    10.10.3.1
```

Example 11-4 shows that the **show mpls l2transport** commands verify the existence of the VCs associated with the VFI cust-one (VC ID 1).

Example 11-4 *show mpls l2transport* Commands

```
VPLS-PE-1#show mpls l2transport summary
Destination address: 10.100.100.2, total number of vc: 1
  0 unknown, 1 up, 0 down, 0 admin down
  1 active vc on MPLS interface PO5/1
Destination address: 10.100.100.3, total number of vc: 1
  0 unknown, 1 up, 0 down, 0 admin down
1 active vc on MPLS interface PO5/1

VPLS-PE-1#show mpls l2transport vc 1 detail
Local interface: VFI cust-one up
  Destination address: 10.100.100.2, VC ID: 1, VC status: up
    Tunnel label: 17, next hop point2point
    Output interface: PO5/1, imposed label stack {17 18}
  Create time: 2d17h, last status change time: 01:04:54
  Signaling protocol: LDP, peer 10.100.100.2:0 up
    MPLS VC labels: local 16, remote 18
    Group ID: local 0, remote 0
    MTU: local 1500, remote 1500
    Remote interface description:
  Sequencing: receive disabled, send disabled
  VC statistics:
    packet totals: receive 23964, send 23699
```

Example 11-4 *show mpls l2transport Commands (Continued)*

```
        byte totals:    receive 2440105, send 2511957
        packet drops:   receive 0, send 0

Local interface: VFI cust-one up
  Destination address: 10.100.100.3, VC ID: 1, VC status: up
    Tunnel label: 18, next hop point2point
    Output interface: PO5/1, imposed label stack {18 16}
  Create time: 2d17h, last status change time: 00:16:02
  Signaling protocol: LDP, peer 10.100.100.3:0 up
    MPLS VC labels: local 17, remote 16
    Group ID: local 0, remote 0
    MTU: local 1500, remote 1500
    Remote interface description:
  Sequencing: receive disabled, send disabled
  VC statistics:
    packet totals: receive 105057, send 123145
    byte totals:   receive 103022139, send 105052493
    packet drops:  receive 0, send 0

VPLS-PE-1#show mpls l2transport binding
  Destination Address: 10.100.100.2,  VC ID: 1
    Local Label:  16
        Cbit: 0,    VC Type: Ethernet,     GroupID: 0
        MTU: 1500,   Interface Desc: n/a
    Remote Label: 18
        Cbit: 0,    VC Type: Ethernet,     GroupID: 0
        MTU: 1500,   Interface Desc: n/a
  Destination Address: 10.100.100.3,  VC ID: 1
    Local Label:  17
        Cbit: 0,    VC Type: Ethernet,     GroupID: 0
        MTU: 1500,   Interface Desc: n/a
    Remote Label: 16
        Cbit: 0,    VC Type: Ethernet,     GroupID: 0
        MTU: 1500,   Interface Desc: n/a
```

You can verify the presence of the local VC labels in the MPLS forwarding table with the **show mpls forwarding-table** command on the PE router (see Example 11-5).

Example 11-5 *show mpls forwarding-table*

```
VPLS-PE-1#show mpls forwarding-table
Local  Outgoing    Prefix          Bytes tag  Outgoing    Next Hop
tag    tag or VC   or Tunnel Id    switched   interface
16     Untagged    l2ckt(1)        2469636    Et3         point2point
17     Untagged    l2ckt(1)        104971374  Et3         point2point
18     Pop tag     10.10.2.0/24    0          PO5/1       point2point
```

continues

Example 11-5 *show mpls forwarding-table (Continued)*

```
19    Pop tag    10.10.3.0/24        0    PO5/1    point2point
20    17         10.100.100.2/32     0    PO5/1    point2point
21    Pop tag    10.100.100.4/32     0    PO5/1    point2point
22    18         10.100.100.3/32     0    PO5/1    point2point
```

VPLS and Tunneling Layer 2 Protocols

With VPLS, you can tunnel certain Layer 2 control protocols. As you can see in Example 11-6, you can configure the PE router to tunnel Cisco Discovery Protocol (CDP), STP, or VLAN Trunking Protocol (VTP). In that case, the control packets of those protocols are transparently tunneled across the MPLS network, without the PE routers participating in those protocols. To tunnel these protocols across VPLS, configure the command **l2protocol-tunnel** on all the customer-facing physical Ethernet interfaces on the PE routers.

Example 11-6 *l2protocol-tunnel Command*

```
VPLS-PE-3#conf t
Enter configuration commands, one per line.  End with CNTL/Z.
VPLS-PE-3(config)#int fas 8/2
VPLS-PE-3(config-if)#l2protocol-tunnel ?
  cdp                  Cisco Discovery Protocol
  drop-threshold       Set drop threshold for protocol packets
  shutdown-threshold   Set shutdown threshold for protocol packets
  stp                  Spanning Tree Protocol
  vtp                  Vlan Trunking Protocol
<cr>
```

Tunneling Cisco Discovery Protocol

Example 11-7 shows the output of **show cdp neighbor** on CE1 when VPLS-PE-1 is not configured for tunneling CDP for VPLS instance cust-one. The router CE1 sees the PE router VPLS-PE-1 as a CDP neighbor.

Example 11-7 *CDP Neighbors on CE1 Without Tunneling CDP*

```
CE1#show cdp neighbors
Capability Codes: R - Router, T - Trans Bridge, B - Source Route Bridge
                  S - Switch, H - Host, I - IGMP, r - Repeater


Device ID          Local Intrfce      Holdtme   Capability   Platform    Port ID
VPLS-PE-1          Fas 2/2            175        R S I        WS-C6506   Fas 4/2
```

Example 11-8 shows the output of the CDP command on router CE1 after enabling tunneling CDP on all physical ports that are associated with VPLS instance cust-one on the PE routers. Now router CE1 sees router CE2 and the Catalyst switch at the third site as CDP neighbors. The PE routers do not inspect the CDP packets coming from the CE routers; instead, they forward them onto the other ports or pseudowires of the VPLS instance.

Example 11-8   *CDP Neighbors on CE1 with Tunneling CDP*

```
CE1#show cdp neighbors
Capability Codes: R - Router, T - Trans Bridge, B - Source Route Bridge
                  S - Switch, H - Host, I - IGMP, r - Repeater


Device ID             Local Intrfce        Holdtme   Capability    Platform    Port ID
BTL3-CAT-304-0        Fas 2/2              146          S I        WS-C2950-2Fas 0/9
CE2                   Fas 2/2              150          R          C10720      Fas 2/6
```

Tunneling Spanning Tree Protocol

By default, VFI does not forward the STP BPDUs on the PE routers. As such, the STP tree in the metro Ethernet site stops at the PE router. The data frames are forwarded across the MPLS network. The frames cannot loop, however, because of the Layer 2 split-horizon rule imposed by the PE routers, which do not forward frames onto the pseudowires if the frames were received from the pseudowires. Because of this split-horizon rule, all PE routers must be in a full mesh for each particular VPLS instance. If the VPLS network were a hub-and-spoke design, certain frames would need to be received and forwarded on the pseudowires, which would not allow for the split-horizon rule to be enforced. To keep such a network loop free, the service provider needs to resort to a protocol—such as STP—to do the job. STP is not needed in the service provider network because the split-horizon is on by default.

In some cases, you need to enable end-to-end STP. The CE routers then run STP across the MPLS backbone. For instance, multihomed customer sites to two PE routers or more require the end-to-end enabling of STP to keep the network loop free. To have end-to-end STP, you need to configure the PE routers to tunnel the STP BPDUs. To tunnel the STP BPDUs, configure the following interface command on the PE routers on the physical Ethernet interfaces.

```
VPLS-PE-1(config-if)#l2protocol-tunnel stp
```

You must tunnel STP BPDUs throughout the network consistently to avoid severe network problems and instability.

Look at the network in Figure 11-6. Bridging is enabled on the CE routers and on the CE switch. Before the tunneling of STP BPDUs is enabled on the PE routers, CE2 sees VPLS-PE-2 (MAC address 00d0.041b.906f) as the root of the spanning tree (see Example 11-9). No other bridges participate in this spanning tree.

Example 11-9 *VPLS-PE-2 Is Root*

```
CE2#show spanning-tree 1

 Bridge group 1 is executing the IEEE compatible Spanning Tree protocol
  Bridge Identifier has priority 32768, address 0001.64ff.4186
  Configured hello time 2, max age 20, forward delay 15
  Current root has priority 8192, address 00d0.041b.906f
  Root port is 10 (FastEthernet2/6), cost of root path is 10
  Topology change flag not set, detected flag not set
  Times:  hold 1, topology change 35, notification 2
          hello 2, max age 20, forward delay 15
  Timers: hello 0, topology change 0, notification 0
  bridge aging time 300

Port 10 (FastEthernet2/6) of Bridge group 1 is forwarding
    Port path cost 10, Port priority 128
    Designated root has priority 8192, address 00d0.041b.906f
    Designated bridge has priority 8192, address 00d0.041b.906f
    Designated port is 130, path cost 0
    Timers: message age 1, forward delay 0, hold 0
    BPDU: sent 4, received 1436
```

Now the tunneling of STP BPDUs is enabled on the three PE routers. CE1, CE2, and CE3 participate in one spanning tree that spans the three metro Ethernet sites. The output in Example 11-10 shows that CE2 now sees CE1 (MAC address 0001.64ff.3f02) as the root of the spanning tree.

Example 11-10 *CE1 Is Root*

```
CE2#show spanning-tree 1

 Bridge group 1 is executing the IEEE compatible Spanning Tree protocol
  Bridge Identifier has priority 32768, address 0001.64ff.4186
  Configured hello time 2, max age 20, forward delay 15
  Current root has priority 32768, address 0001.64ff.3f02
  Root port is 10 (FastEthernet2/6), cost of root path is 10
  Topology change flag set, detected flag not set
  Times:  hold 1, topology change 35, notification 2
          hello 2, max age 20, forward delay 15
  Timers: hello 0, topology change 0, notification 0
  bridge aging time 15

Port 10 (FastEthernet2/6) of Bridge group 1 is forwarding
```

Example 11-10   *CE1 Is Root (Continued)*

```
      Port path cost 10, Port priority 128
      Designated root has priority 32768, address 0001.64ff.3f02
      Designated bridge has priority 32768, address 0001.64ff.3f02
      Designated port is 5, path cost 0
      Timers: message age 1, forward delay 0, hold 0
      BPDU: sent 6, received 1475
```

Trunk Port Between the CE and PE

In the basic VPLS configuration example, the customer-facing Ethernet port on the PE router is configured as an access port. You can also configure this interface as an 802.1Q trunk. Additional configuration on the interface allows certain customer VLANs to be transported over VPLS (one VLAN per VFI instance). For each allowed customer VLAN (VLAN 111 and 222 in Example 11-11), you must configure a VFI with a unique name and VPN ID and associate it with the appropriate VLAN interface.

Example 11-11   *Trunk Port VPLS Configuration*

```
VPLS-PE-1#
!
interface FastEthernet4/2
 no ip address
 switchport
 switchport trunk encapsulation dot1q
 switchport trunk allowed vlan 111,222
 switchport mode trunk

l2 vfi cust-one-111 manual
 vpn id 1
 neighbor 10.100.100.1 encapsulation mpls
 neighbor 10.100.100.3 encapsulation mpls
!
l2 vfi cust-one-222 manual
 vpn id 2
 neighbor 10.100.100.1 encapsulation mpls
 neighbor 10.100.100.3 encapsulation mpls
!
interface Vlan111
 no ip address
 xconnect vfi cust-one-111
!
interface Vlan222
 no ip address
 xconnect vfi cust-one-222
!
```

Hierarchical VPLS

With Hierarchical VPLS (H-VPLS), the PE routers are no longer directly attached to the customer equipment. Hierarchy is introduced by adding another layer in the access layer toward the customer equipment. H-VPLS has two forms:

- H-VPLS with dot1q tunneling in the access layer

- H-VPLS with MPLS in the access layer

Figure 11-7 shows H-VPLS.

Figure 11-7   *H-VPLS*

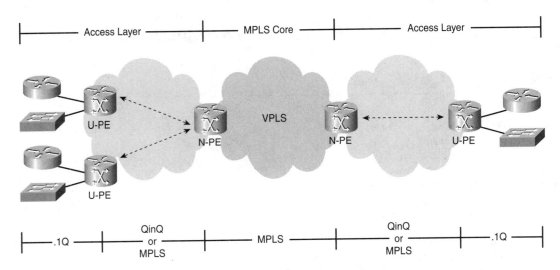

There are now N-PE and U-PE routers. The N-PE routers are network-facing PE routers, whereas the U-PE routers are user-facing PE routers. The hierarchy provides the benefits of less signaling in the MPLS core network and less packet replication on the N-PE routers. The U-PE routers have an aggregation role and do some packet replication and MAC address learning.

H-VPLS with Dot1q Tunneling (QinQ) in the Access Layer

As in the case of EoMPLS, dot1q tunneling (QinQ) is possible with VPLS. This means that the customer VLANs can be *encapsulated* into another VLAN (the provider VLAN, or P-VLAN), allowing a multi-VLAN switched customer network to be transparently transported between multiple sites connected to an MPLS network. This P-VLAN is mapped to one VFI on the N-PE router. If the CE equipment is a router, you can configure the Ethernet interface toward the PE router as a trunk interface by configuring 802.1Q subinterfaces, each with a specific VLAN number. If the CE equipment is an Ethernet switch, you can configure the Ethernet interface toward the PE router as an 802.1Q trunk interface with a certain number of VLANs. Look at the network in Figure 11-8. The customer VLANs are 200 to 250. These VLANs are tunneled into VLAN 111 (the P-VLAN) on the service provider side by configuring dot1q tunneling and access VLAN 111 on the Ethernet interface that faces the CE.

Figure 11-8 *H-VPLS with Dot1q Tunneling in the Access Layer*

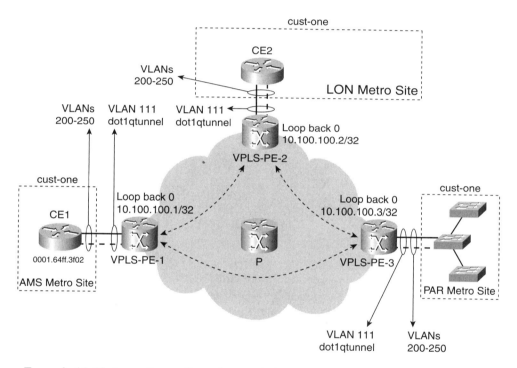

Example 11-12 shows the configuration needed on the PE router for dot1q tunneling.

Example 11-12 *Dot1q Tunneling*

```
VPLS-PE-1#show running-config interface fas 4/2
!
interface FastEthernet4/2
 no ip address
 switchport
 switchport access vlan 111
 switchport mode dot1q-tunnel
 spanning-tree bpdufilter enable
```

The VFI is configured for VLAN 111 on the PE router. The frames are then transported across the MPLS network with one 802.1Q tag (VLAN 200–250) and two MPLS labels. Because the VFI is configured per VLAN and all the VLANs of one customer are encapsulated into one service provider VLAN, the service provider needs to use only one VLAN per customer when using the dot1q tunneling method in combination with VPLS. The big advantages for the service provider in deploying dot1q tunneling are saving VLANs and transporting customer VLANs transparently, so that the service provider does not know which VLANs need to be transported and to which remote sites.

H-VPLS with MPLS in the Access Layer

Look at Figure 11-9 to see H-VPLS with MPLS in the access layer.

Figure 11-9 *H-VPLS with MPLS in the Access Layer*

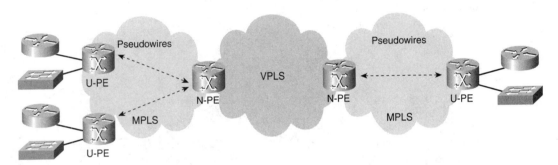

With MPLS in the access layer, point-to-point virtual circuits will exist between the N-PEs and U-PEs. You need to disable the default split-horizon behavior on the N-PEs because an N-PE must forward Layer 2 frames received on the pseudowires from another N-PE onto the pseudowires toward the U-PEs and vice versa. You can achieve this with the following command:

```
neighbor remote router id encapsulation mpls no-split-horizon
```

Quality of Service

As with AToM, you can use quality of service (QoS) with VPLS. By default, the 802.1Q priority bits are copied to the Experimental (EXP) bits of the MPLS labels. If the service provider wants to change the QoS, he can deploy Modular QOS Command Line Interface (MQC). On the VLAN interface, the service provider can configure MQC to color and police the traffic. You can directly set the EXP of the imposed MPLS labels to a certain value and shape the traffic to a certain average rate. This is especially important when the access interfaces to the customer are high-speed Ethernet links. Example 11-13 shows a configuration example in which the Ethernet traffic is shaped on the VLAN interface and the EXP bits in the MPLS labels are set to a value of 3.

Example 11-13 *VPLS QoS Example*

```
!
hostname VPLS-PE-1
!
class-map match-all red
  match any
!
policy-map VPLS
  class red
   set mpls experimental 3
    shape average 100000000 400000 400000

!
interface Vlan111
 no ip address
 xconnect vfi cust-one
 service-policy output VPLS
!


VPLS-PE-1#show policy-map interface vlan 111 output
 Vlan111
  Service-policy output: VPLS
    Class-map: red (match-all)
      1082 packets, 1036414 bytes
      30 second offered rate 0 bps, drop rate 0 bps
      Match: any
      queue size 0, queue limit 0
      packets output 1082, packet drops 0
      tail/random drops 0, no buffer drops 0, other drops 0
      QoS Set
        mpls experimental 3
          Packets marked 1082
      shape (average) cir 100000000 bc 400000 be 400000
      target shape rate 100000000

    Class-map: class-default (match-any)
      0 packets, 0 bytes
      30 second offered rate 0 bps, drop rate 0 bps
      Match: any
```

Limiting MAC Addresses

If the metro Ethernet sites have many hosts/switches, you need to prevent the PE routers from learning too many MAC addresses from the customers. You also need to protect the PE router from possible denial-of-service (DoS) attacks involving MAC address learning. You can limit the maximum number of MAC entries per VLAN on the PE router by entering the following command:

```
mac-address-table limit [vlan vlan] [maximum num] [action {warning | limit | shutdown}]
[flood]
```

The options are to warn when the maximum number of MAC addresses is reached, limit them, or shut down the VLAN altogether. Example 11-14 shows what happens if more than the maximum number of MAC addresses is learned on VLAN 111 and the action is to shut down the VLAN.

Example 11-14 *Limiting MAC Addresses*

```
VPLS-PE-3(config)#mac-address-table limit vlan 111 maximum 5 action shutdown

VPLS-PE-3#
Jul 26 15:06:04.326: %SYS-5-CONFIG_I: Configured from console by console
Jul 26 15:06:04.521: %MAC_LIMIT-SP-4-VLAN_EXCEED: Vlan 111 with configured limit 5 has
 currently 6 entries
Jul 26 15:06:10.522: %MAC_LIMIT-SP-4-VLAN_DROP: Vlan 111 with configured limit 5 has
 currently 0 entries
```

Routing Peering

As with AToM, all CE routers see each other as directly connected across the MPLS network at Layer 3. The advantage for the service provider is that he does not have to worry about Layer 3 routing protocols because no peering (no routing peering) takes place between the PE and the CE equipment at Layer 3 as it does with MPLS VPN. This is clearly an advantage of VPLS over MPLS VPN. The advantage of VPLS over EoMPLS for the customer is that the routing peering between CE routers happens simply over an (emulated) LAN and not over a full mesh of point-to-point circuits. This simplifies the configuration on the CE equipment considerably and makes certain migrations a lot easier to perform when necessary.

Summary

In this chapter, you saw that Virtual Private LAN Service (VPLS) emulates a LAN and interconnects several LAN segments by acting as a virtual Ethernet switch spanning the MPLS backbone. A VPLS instance can be configured for each customer or each VLAN of a customer. The Ethernet frames are forwarded across the MPLS backbone with a tunnel and a virtual circuit (VC) label. Each VPLS instance creates a full mesh of pseudowires between all PE routers that are participating in the VPLS instance. The PE routers are capable of replicating and forwarding broadcast and multicast frames. You saw how to configure and troubleshoot VPLS on Cisco routers and how to tunnel certain Layer 2 control protocols across the MPLS network. Finally, you learned about Hierarchical VPLS (H-VPLS).

Chapter Review Questions

1. As which kind of port type can the customer-facing Ethernet interface on the PE router be configured?

2. How many labels are used to forward VPLS traffic, and what is the use of each of those labels?

3. What does VFI stand for?

4. Which Layer 2 control protocols can be tunneled across the VPLS network?

5. Why do the PE routers need to be in a full mesh of pseudowires in VPLS?

6. Name the six functions that VPLS performs in emulating an Ethernet switch.

7. In which two ways can H-VPLS be implemented?

What You Will Learn

By the end of this chapter, you should know and be able to explain the following:

- How QoS information is propagated in MPLS networks

- Which kind of DiffServ tunneling models are available

- How to implement the different DiffServ tunneling models in Cisco IOS

CHAPTER 12

MPLS and Quality of Service

Quality of service (QoS) has become popular the past few years. Few networks have unlimited bandwidth, so congestion is always a possibility in the network. QoS is a means to prioritize important traffic over less important traffic and make sure it is delivered.

The Internet Engineering Task Force (IETF) has designated two ways to implement QoS in an IP network: Integrated Services (IntServ) and Differentiated Services (DiffServ). IntServ uses the signaling protocol Resource Reservation Protocol (RSVP). The hosts signal to the network via RSVP what the QoS needs are for the flows of traffic that they send. DiffServ uses the DiffServ bits in the IP header to qualify the IP packet to be of a certain QoS. The routers look at these bits to mark, queue, shape, and set the drop precedence of the packet. The big advantage of DiffServ over IntServ is that the DiffServ model needs no signaling protocol. The IntServ model uses a signaling protocol that must run on the hosts and routers. If the network has many thousands of flows, the routers must keep state information for each flow passing through it. This is a serious scalability issue, which is why IntServ has not proven to be popular.

A good example where QoS is needed is VoIP traffic. VoIP traffic needs to be delivered within a certain time to the destination, or it becomes obsolete. Therefore, QoS should prioritize the VoIP traffic to ensure that it is delivered within a certain time constraint. To achieve this, it is possible within Cisco IOS to queue VoIP with a higher priority than FTP or HTTP traffic and to make sure that if congestion occurs, FTP or HTTP traffic is dropped ahead of the VoIP traffic. Cisco IOS has several mechanisms to do this on a router. Refer to Table 12-1 for examples of QoS functions and features in Cisco IOS.

Table 12-1   *QoS Functions and Corresponding Cisco IOS-Enabling Features*

QoS Functions	Cisco IOS-Enabling Features
Traffic classification	Access control list matching
Traffic marking	IP Precedence bits
	IP DSCP[1]
	MPLS EXP[2] field

continues

Table 12-1 *QoS Functions and Corresponding Cisco IOS-Enabling Features (Continued)*

QoS Functions	Cisco IOS-Enabling Features
Congestion management	LLQ[3]
	CBWFQ[4]
Congestion avoidance	WRED[5]
Traffic conditioning	Shaping and policing

[1] DSCP = DiffServ Codepoint

[2] EXP = Experimental

[3] LLQ = low-latency queuing

[4] CBWFQ = class-based weighted fair queueing

[5] WRED = weighted random early detection

You can set the priority of an IP packet either in the IP Precedence field (three bits) or in the six bits of the DiffServ Codepoint field (DSCP). Originally, only three bits of the Type of Service field (TOS) in the IP header were reserved for QoS. The number of bits in the IP header that could be used for QoS was later increased to six with the introduction of DiffServ QoS.

DiffServ with IP Packets

Refer to Figure 12-1 to refresh your memory about what the IP header looks like.

Figure 12-1 *IP Header Fields*

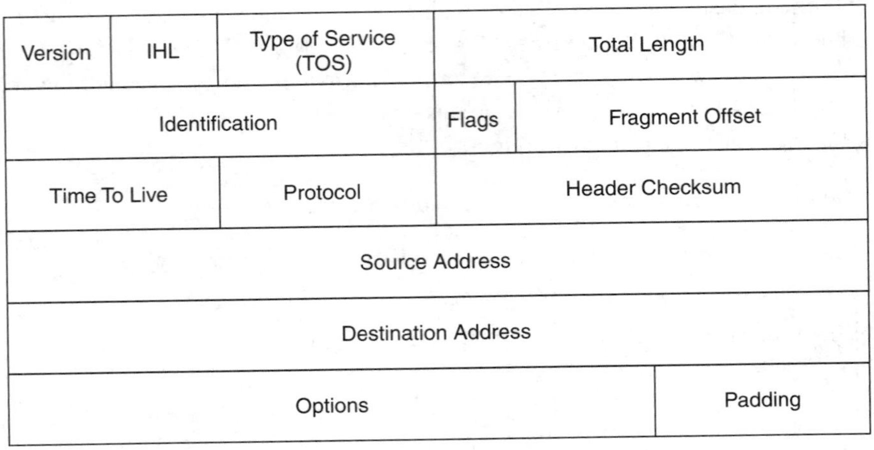

Version	IHL	Type of Service (TOS)		Total Length	
Identification			Flags	Fragment Offset	
Time To Live		Protocol		Header Checksum	
Source Address					
Destination Address					
Options				Padding	

Figure 12-2 shows you how the TOS field is divided.

Figure 12-2 *The TOS Byte of the IP Header Defining the Precedence Bits*

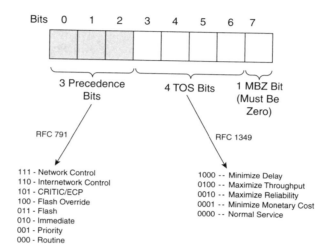

The usage of the precedence bits for QoS is now widely used throughout the world for many networks. The drawback of the precedence bits, however, is that only three exist, which means you can have only eight levels of service. Therefore, the IETF decided to dedicate more bits for QoS. The four TOS bits were deprecated, and three of them were assigned to DiffServ QoS, in addition to the three precedence bits. DiffServ ended up with six bits, providing more than enough levels of QoS. Figure 12-3 shows you which bits of the TOS byte are used for DiffServ.

Figure 12-3 *The TOS Byte of the IP Header Defining the DSCP per RFC 2474*

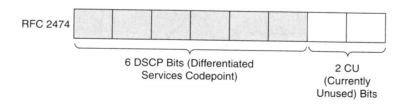

Two types of forwarding classes within the DiffServ model are defined: expedited forwarding (EF) and assured forwarding (AF). EF is a low loss, low latency, low jitter, assured bandwidth, end-to-end service through a DiffServ domain. AF defines different services of forwarding assurances through a DiffServ domain. Four classes of AF are defined, each with three drop precedence. AF classes are noted as AFij, with i being 1 to 4 for the class and j being 1 to 3 for the drop precedence. The first three bits of the six-bit DSCP field define the class, the next two bits define the drop precedence, and the last bit is reserved. The higher the drop precedence inside a class, the more likely the packet is to be dropped, relative to the other packets with lower drop precedence when congestion occurs. Four classes exist for the traffic, and three levels exist for drop precedence. AF23, for example, denotes class 2 and drop precedence 3. Table 12-2 shows the recommended values for the four assured forwarding classes.

Table 12-2 *Recommended Values for the Four AF Classes*

Name	DSCP (binary)	DSCP (decimal)
AF11	001010	10
AF12	001100	12
AF13	001110	14
AF21	010010	18
AF22	010100	20
AF23	010110	22
AF31	011010	26
AF32	011100	28
AF33	011110	30
AF41	100010	34
AF42	100100	36
AF43	100110	38

Table 12-3 shows you the four AF classes, each with three drop precedence.

Table 12-3 *Four AF Classes and Three Drop Precedence*

Drop Precedence	Class 1	Class 2	Class 3	Class 4
Low	001010	010010	011010	100010
Medium	001100	010100	011100	100100
High	001110	010110	011110	100110

If you are using EF, the recommended DiffServ field is 101110 (decimal 46). The default class is 0 or 000000 in binary. In Cisco IOS, you can find all these values when configuring QoS with the

Modular QoS Command Line Interface (MQC). Example 12-1 shows how to configure the router to match a certain DSCP in a class map on a router.

Example 12-1 *Matching DSCP in a Class Map*

```
router(config-cmap)#match ip dscp ?
  <0-63>   Differentiated services codepoint value
  af11     Match packets with AF11 dscp (001010)
  af12     Match packets with AF12 dscp (001100)
  af13     Match packets with AF13 dscp (001110)
  af21     Match packets with AF21 dscp (010010)
  af22     Match packets with AF22 dscp (010100)
  af23     Match packets with AF23 dscp (010110)
  af31     Match packets with AF31 dscp (011010)
  af32     Match packets with AF32 dscp (011100)
  af33     Match packets with AF33 dscp (011110)
  af41     Match packets with AF41 dscp (100010)
  af42     Match packets with AF42 dscp (100100)
  af43     Match packets with AF43 dscp (100110)
  cs1      Match packets with CS1(precedence 1) dscp (001000)
  cs2      Match packets with CS2(precedence 2) dscp (010000)
  cs3      Match packets with CS3(precedence 3) dscp (011000)
  cs4      Match packets with CS4(precedence 4) dscp (100000)
  cs5      Match packets with CS5(precedence 5) dscp (101000)
  cs6      Match packets with CS6(precedence 6) dscp (110000)
  cs7      Match packets with CS7(precedence 7) dscp (111000)
  default  Match packets with default dscp (000000)
  ef       Match packets with EF dscp (101110)
```

You can match any of the 64 DSCP values (0–63) just by configuring that DSCP value. You can also match the AF classes, the Class Selector (CS)—if you only want to match the first three bits of the DSCP—, the default class, and the EF class.

DiffServ with MPLS Packets

Remember the syntax of a label from Chapter 2, "MPLS Architecture"? Figure 12-4 is a refresher.

Figure 12-4 *Syntax of an MPLS Label*

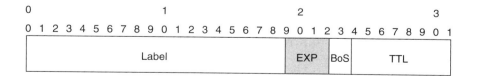

As you can see, there are three EXP, or experimental, bits. They are called experimental, but they are really used only for QoS. You can use these bits in the same way that you use the three precedence bits in the IP header. If you use these three bits for QoS, you can call the label switched path (LSP) an E-LSP, indicating that the label switching router (LSR) will use the EXP bits to schedule the packet and decide on the drop precedence. However, when you are using MPLS, you have another option for implementing QoS for the labeled packets. An LSP is a signaled path through the network between two routers. You can use the label on top of the packet to imply part of the QoS for that packet. However, then you need one label per class for each flow of traffic between the two endpoints of the LSP. Therefore, the signaling protocol has to be able to signal a different label for the same LSP or prefix. Such an LSP is called an L-LSP, indicating that the label implicitly holds part of the QoS information. With an L-LSP, the EXP bits still hold part of the QoS, but only the drop precedence, whereas the label indicates the class. With an E-LSP, the EXP bits hold both the class and the drop precedence information. Because Cisco IOS implements only E-LSPs, this chapter looks only at E-LSPs when describing how to implement QoS in MPLS networks.

When an LSR forwards a labeled packet, it needs only to look up the top label in its label forwarding table (LFIB) to decide where to forward the packet. The same is true for the QoS treatment. The LSR needs only to look at the EXP bits of the top label to determine how to treat this packet. Remember that QoS constitutes traffic marking, congestion management, congestion avoidance, and traffic conditioning and that you can use low-latency queuing (LLQ), class-based weighted fair queueing (CBWFQ), weighted random early detection (WRED), policing, and shaping to implement this for IP packets. You can use the same features to implement QoS based on the EXP bits for labeled packets. For example, WRED has been modified to look at the EXP bits to determine the drop precedence of labeled packets when being queued. The preferred way to configure MPLS QoS in Cisco IOS is by means of the Modular Quality of Service Command Line Interface (MQC). MQC is an easy, straightforward way of configuring the different QoS building blocks on the router.

Default MPLS QoS Behavior in Cisco IOS

In Cisco IOS, the default behavior when imposing one or more labels on an IP packet is to copy the precedence value to the EXP bits of all imposed labels. This is called TOS reflection, because nothing regarding QoS changes by default. If, however, the six bits of the DSCP field are used, only the first three bits of DSCP are copied to the EXP bits of the labels. This leads to the first MPLS QoS rule.

MPLS QoS Rule 1: By default, in Cisco IOS, the precedence bits or the first three bits of the DSCP field in the IP header are copied to the EXP bits of all imposed labels at the ingress LSR.

Forwarding a labeled packet is a bit more complicated. You have to distinguish two cases: swapping a label, and possibly imposing one or more labels on the one hand and disposing one or more labels on the other hand. In the case of swapping an incoming label with an outgoing label on the LSR, the EXP bits are copied from the incoming label to the outgoing label. The same is true when swapping a label and then imposing one or more labels. The value of the EXP bits is copied from the incoming label to the swapped outgoing label and also to the labels that are then pushed on top of the swapped label. However, forwarding a labeled packet in the disposition mode, meaning that a label is popped, is quite different. When the router forwards a labeled packet and issues a pop, the value of the EXP bits is not copied to the newly exposed label or to the IP Precedence field (or possibly the DSCP field) of the IP header, if the packet becomes unlabeled. This means that, by default, in Cisco IOS, the EXP bits of the newly exposed label or the IP precedence/DSCP field of the newly exposed IP header remains unchanged and dictate the new QoS of the packet. This leads to the second, third, and fourth MPLS QoS rule.

MPLS QoS Rule 2: By default, in Cisco IOS, the EXP bits of the incoming top label are copied to the swapped outgoing label and to any label pushed onto that.

MPLS QoS Rule 3: By default, in Cisco IOS, the EXP bits of the incoming top label are *not* copied to the newly exposed label when the incoming label is popped.

MPLS QoS Rule 4: By default, in Cisco IOS, the EXP bits of the incoming top label are *not* copied to the precedence bits or DSCP bits when the label stack is removed and the IP header becomes exposed.

Furthermore, when you use MQC to change the QoS of the labeled packet, only the top label and possible pushed labels receive the new value for the EXP bits. The labels underneath the top label in the label stack do not receive the new value for the EXP bits. The precedence bits or DSCP bits do not change either. This means that when you manually change the QoS of a labeled packet on a certain LSR, that packet changes its QoS value sometime later in the network. Namely, when the label is popped off, the value of the EXP bits of the incoming top label is not copied to the newly exposed label, following MPLS QoS Rule 3. That means that the old QoS value of the packet is now active again. This actually happens frequently, because penultimate hop popping (PHP) is the default behavior in Cisco IOS. It happens by default in many MPLS networks and is something to watch out for. If you want to keep the new QoS value of the packet, you need to configure Cisco IOS commands to make sure that the QoS is copied down at disposition time. You will read more about that later in this chapter. This leads to the fifth MPLS QoS rule.

MPLS QoS Rule 5: When you change the EXP bits value through configuration, the value of the EXP bits in labels other than the top label, the swapped label, or the imposed labels and the precedence bits or DSCP bits in the IP header remain unchanged.

MPLS QoS Rules 4 and 5 lead to the fact that QoS tunneling becomes available. This means that the QoS value of the IP packet is transported through the MPLS network without change.

Look at Figure 12-5. You can see a Label Switch Router (LSR) with two interfaces. The left interface is the ingress interface, and the right is the egress interface. An IP packet or labeled packet comes in on the left interface and leaves the router on the right interface. This chapter uses this simple drawing throughout to clearly show the behavior of the EXP bits when a packet goes through the router. In each figure, the IP packet is the rectangle in the clear, and a label is one gray rectangle on top of the IP packet. In the IP packet, the QoS information is shown as the DSCP value. Each label also shows the EXP bits value.

Figure 12-5 *Sample LSR Drawing with an Ingress and an Egress Interface*

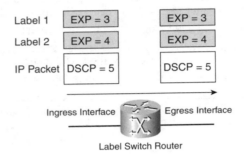

Figure 12-6 shows you the default treatment by Cisco IOS of the EXP bits in the label(s) when imposing, swapping, or disposing of labels. When you imply the five MPLS QoS rules, you get the default forwarding treatment that is shown in Figure 12-6.

Figure 12-6 *Default Treatment by Cisco IOS of the EXP Bits When Imposing, Swapping, and Disposing of MPLS Labels*

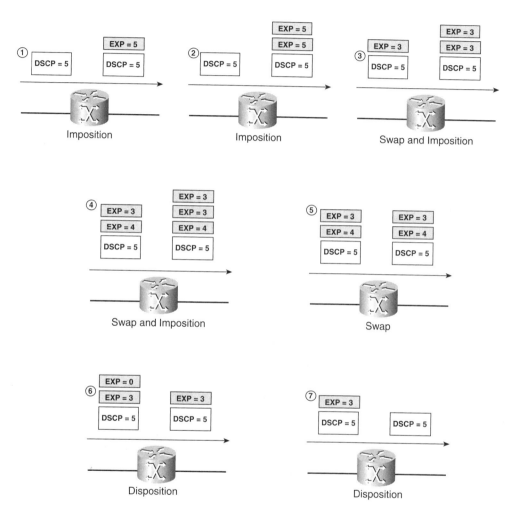

The first two pictures show you TOS reflection. By default, the IP precedence (or first three bits of DSCP) is copied to the imposed labels. This is MPLS QoS Rule 1. The third picture shows you that the EXP bits of the top label of the incoming packet are copied to the swapped label and the pushed label(s). This is MPLS QoS Rule 2. The fourth and fifth pictures are again examples of MPLS QoS Rule 2, but now they show that the EXP bits of the labels, which are below the top label at the ingress interface, are not changed (MPLS QoS Rule 5). The sixth picture shows you an example of MPLS QoS Rule 3, and the seventh picture is an example of MPLS QoS Rule 4.

DiffServ Tunneling Models

MPLS QoS Rule 4 causes an interesting behavior: Regardless of what the MPLS EXP value was changed to at the ingress LSR or any other LSR, that value is not copied to the exposed IP packet at the egress LSR of the MPLS network. In effect, this enables the operator of the MPLS cloud to carry the QoS value of the IP packet transparently through the MPLS network. No matter how many times the EXP bits are changed, by default, the IP precedence or DSCP bits of the IP packet are preserved; the value at the egress LSR is the same as when the IP packet entered the MPLS network. You can now tunnel the DiffServ value of the IP packet through the MPLS network (hence the name DiffServ Tunneling). The obvious advantage is that the MPLS network can have a different QoS scheme than the customers who connect to it, because the MPLS QoS scheme can be independent from the IP QoS scheme of the customers. The IETF has defined three models to tunnel the DiffServ information. All three models are distinct and have their own merits. Furthermore, the distinction between the three models is only at the edge LSRs. The P routers do not come into play with regard to the different DiffServ tunneling models.

Consider Figure 12-7.

Figure 12-7 *General Operation of the MPLS DiffServ Tunneling Models*

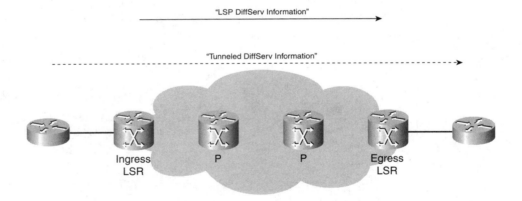

The Tunneled Diffserv information is the QoS of the labeled packets or the precedence/DSCP of the IP packets coming into the ingress LSR of the MPLS network. The LSP DiffServ information is the QoS (the value of the EXP bits) of the MPLS packets transported on the LSP from the ingress LSR to the egress LSR. The Tunneled DiffServ information is the QoS information that needs to get across the MPLS network transparently, whereas the LSP DiffServ information is the QoS information that all LSRs in this MPLS network use when forwarding the labeled packet.

Pipe Model

In the Pipe model, the following rules apply:

■ The LSP DiffServ information is not necessarily (but might be) derived from the Tunneled DiffServ information on the ingress LSR.

■ On an intermediate LSR (a P router), the LSP DiffServ information of the outgoing label is derived from the LSP DiffServ information of the incoming label.

■ On the egress LSR, the forwarding treatment of the packet is based on the LSP DiffServ information, and the LSP DiffServ information is not propagated to the Tunneled DiffServ information.

> **NOTE** Forwarding treatment here means classifying the packet for scheduling and discarding behavior at the output interface.

If the MPLS network is receiving IP packets on the ingress LSR and the MPLS network is using E-LSPs only, the Pipe model becomes a bit easier to explain. The Tunneled DiffServ information is the precedence bits or the DSCP of the IP packet. The LSP DiffServ information is the EXP bits value of the labels in the MPLS network. The forwarding treatment (classifying and discard behavior) of IP packets is based on the precedence bits or DSCP in the IP header. This is called the IP PHB (per-hop behavior) hereafter. The forwarding treatment op MPLS packets is based on the EXP bits. This is called the MPLS PHB (per-hop behavior) hereafter.

The rules for the Pipe model now translate into the following:

■ The EXP bits can be copied from the IP precedence or set through configuration on the ingress LSR.

■ On a P router, the EXP bits are propagated from incoming label to outgoing label.

■ On the egress LSR, the forwarding treatment of the packet is based on the MPLS PHB (EXP bits), and the EXP bits are not propagated to the IP precedence.

Short Pipe Model

The Short Pipe model is similar to the Pipe model, with one difference. The forwarding treatment on the egress LSR is different for the Short Pipe model. Therefore, the third bullet becomes this:

■ On the egress LSR, *the forwarding treatment of the packet is based on the Tunneled DiffServ information*, and the LSP DiffServ information is not propagated to the Tunneled DiffServ information.

If the MPLS network is receiving IP packets on the ingress LSR, that third bullet becomes this:

■   On the egress LSR, *the forwarding treatment of the packet is based on the IP PHB (IP precedence)*, and the EXP bits are not propagated to the IP precedence.

Uniform Model

The Uniform model is quite different from the Pipe or Short Pipe model. In the Uniform model, the following rules apply:

■   The LSP DiffServ information *must* be derived from the Tunneled DiffServ information on the ingress LSR.

■   On an intermediate LSR (a P router), the LSP DiffServ information of the outgoing label is derived from the LSP DiffServ information of the incoming label.

■   On the egress LSR, the LSP DiffServ information must be propagated to the Tunneled DiffServ information.

Notice the change in the first bullet: The LSP DiffServ information *must be* derived from the Tunneled DiffServ information on the ingress LSR. On the egress LSR, the Tunneled DiffServ information is derived from the LSP DiffServ information. This means that a packet belongs to the same QoS class at any time. The QoS information is always present in the topmost label or in the IP header if the packet is not labeled. The MPLS network does not have an impact on the QoS information, but it does switch the packets through the MPLS network, of course.

You can instruct the router to change the EXP bits of the top label(s) through configuration (by using MQC in Cisco IOS) anywhere in the MPLS cloud. This only changes the outer QoS information, or the LSP DiffServ information. This change in the LSP DiffServ information is not propagated down to the Tunneled DiffServ information in the Pipe model and Short Pipe model on the egress LSR. It is, however, propagated on the egress LSR when you are using the Uniform model.

In Cisco IOS, the configuration that you need to enable one of the three DiffServ Tunneling models is MQC. MQC is configurable per interface. Therefore, you can choose the DiffServ Tunneling model per interface—hence, per customer connecting to the MPLS network. The only LSRs where this configuration is needed are the ingress and egress LSRs. On those routers, the specific DiffServ Tunneling model is determined.

Figure 12-8 shows you the three tunneling models in the case of an MPLS virtual private network (VPN). The packets that are entering and exiting the MPLS VPNs are IP packets. Therefore, the Tunneled DiffServ information translates to the DSCP bits in the IP header, and the LSP DiffServ information translates to the EXP bits in the MPLS labels.

Figure 12-8   *Three DiffServ Tunneling Models for MPLS VPN*

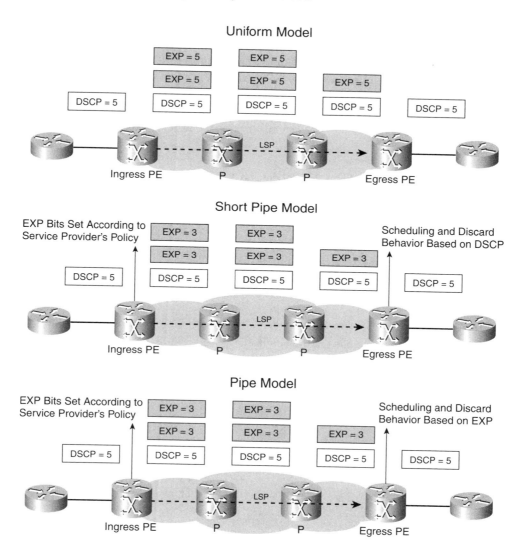

Advantages of the DiffServ Tunneling Models

The usefulness of the Uniform model is that there is only one DiffServ information for a packet. This is the DiffServ information encoded in the top label. Whether this is different from the underlying DiffServ information is not important, because the top DiffServ information is propagated down at the egress LSR of the LSP.

The advantage for both the Short Pipe model and the Pipe model is that the original Tunneled DiffServ information is preserved when the packet leaves the MPLS network. That means that the IP DiffServ information or the tunneled MPLS DiffServ information remains unchanged. When customers connect to the MPLS network, their QoS information is tunneled transparently through the MPLS network. Furthermore, if customers have their own rules for QoS, the MPLS service provider, who imposes his own rules on the packets at the ingress LSR without changing the original QoS of the packet, can ignore the customers' rules. This is a lot more scalable than catering for the QoS of each customer. Because a label has only three EXP bits, the MPLS service provider has to fit each QoS level of every customer into one of a maximum of eight levels of QoS in the MPLS network.

The difference between the Short Pipe model and the Pipe model is visible only at the egress LSR. The egress LSR forwards packets according to the LSP DiffServ information when you have the Pipe model and according to the Tunneled DiffServ information when you have the Short Pipe model. This means that in the Short Pipe model, the packets are forwarded on the egress LSR according to some QoS that is different for each customer. In the Pipe model, the packets are forwarded on the egress LSR according to the QoS of the LSP of the MPLS network. This latter model greatly reduces the QoS configuration because it is the same for all traffic. In contrast, with the Short Pipe model, you need a different QoS configuration for each customer (or for each outgoing link).

The Pipe model does have one requirement for it to work. The egress LSR must forward the packets based on the LSP DiffServ information. That means that the implicit NULL label cannot be used in the case of plain IP-over-MPLS (in this case the labeled packets have only one label in the label stack), as explained in the paragraphs that follow. In Figure 12-9, you can see a plain IP-over-MPLS network with the implicit NULL label.

Figure 12-9 *Plain IP-over-MPLS with Implicit NULL Label*

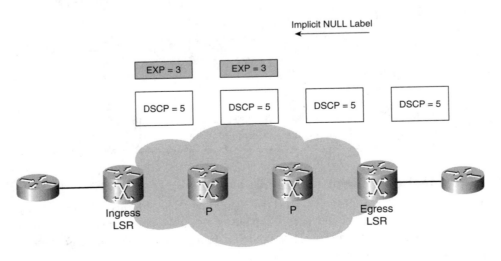

From Chapter 3, "Forwarding Labeled Packets," you know that using the implicit NULL label is called PHP and that it causes the penultimate LSR to forward the packets with one label fewer, because of a pop operation. If this is a plain IP-over-MPLS network, only one label is on top of the incoming packets on that LSR, so the packets are then forwarded to the last LSR as IP packets. If you are running the Pipe model, the egress LSR cannot forward the packet based on the MPLS EXP bits (the LSP DiffServ information) because the packet no longer has a label. Furthermore, if you are running the Uniform model, you can no longer copy the EXP bits value from the label into the IP precedence or DSCP bits on the egress LSR. The obvious solution for this problem is to use the explicit NULL label instead of the implicit NULL label, which Cisco IOS uses by default. Then the egress LSR signals an explicit NULL label toward the penultimate LSR. As you have seen already, both LDP and RSVP (for traffic engineering) can signal the explicit NULL label. The only function of the explicit NULL label is to carry the QoS information in the EXP bits. Figure 12-10 shows the same network as Figure 12-9, but now with the explicit NULL label.

Figure 12-10 *Plain IP-over-MPLS with Explicit NULL Label*

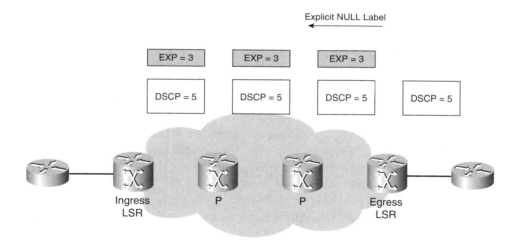

The problem is not present only with plain IP-over-MPLS. What if you have an MPLS VPN network? By default, it also has PHP. What if someone alters the EXP bits on a P router? The result will be that the top label will have a different value for the EXP bits than the label underneath. That is okay as long as no labels are popped off. However, when a label is popped off at the penultimate LSR, the value of the EXP bits is not copied to the newly exposed label. Therefore, in the case of MPLS VPN and PHP, the label on top of the packet on the egress LSR is the VPN label, and it has the EXP bits that were set on the ingress PE. That means the alteration of the EXP bits on a P router is lost. Also, in the case of MPLS VPN, the solution is to have the egress PE advertise the explicit NULL label. In that instance, the packet arrives at the egress PE with two labels. The top label is the explicit NULL label that holds the MPLS QoS information.

How to Implement the Three DiffServ Tunneling Models

The distinction between the three models is made only on the ingress and egress LSR. For the three models, no configuration is needed on the ingress LSR assuming that the service provider is willing to accept the DiffServ information set by the customer as the LSP DiffServ information in the MPLS core. The reason for that is MPLS QoS Rules 1 and 2. However, for the Uniform model, this is a requirement, whereas for the Pipe and Short Pipe models, the ingress LSR could set other values for the EXP bits. Because the customer connecting to the MPLS service provider could set the DiffServ information of the packets to anything, the service provider would most likely choose to set the EXP bits at the ingress LSR to values he has chosen.

On the egress LSR, all three models are distinct. For the Uniform model, the LSP DiffServ information *must* be propagated to the Tunneled DiffServ information. This is not done by default in Cisco IOS. Therefore, you have to configure qos-group on the router by using MQC. You can match the EXP bits on the ingress interface of the egress LSR and set the qos-group respectively. In contrast, on the egress interface of the egress LSR, you match the qos-group and set the EXP bits of the outgoing labeled packet or the IP precedence/DSCP of the outgoing IP packet. This propagation of the EXP bits must also be done on P routers in the case of a pop label operation if the EXP bits were changed somewhere upstream. The propagation on the egress LSR cannot be done for the Pipe and Short Pipe models because then the original Tunneled DiffServ information would be overwritten by the LSP DiffServ information.

For the Pipe model, make sure that the egress LSR forwards the packets based on the LSP DiffServ information. That means you can either use the explicit NULL label in order to avoid PHP; or, if you do use the implicit NULL label, use qos-group on the penultimate LSR to copy the EXP bits of the incoming label to the exposed label after the pop operation. This is needed when the EXP bits were changed somewhere upstream. In the case of plain IP-over-MPLS, there is only one label in the label stack, and therefore you must avoid PHP.

For the Short Pipe model, the egress LSR forwards the packet based on the Tunneled DiffServ information. In that case, you can use implicit NULL, because the egress LSR no longer needs the LSP DiffServ information to forward the packet.

Recoloring the Packet

The MPLS network can encounter congestion, so the operator might want to recolor some packets. This recoloring means the router configuration is used to change the LSP DiffServ information of the packet on any LSR. In effect, the top label gets a new value for the EXP bits. This is allowed, but make sure that this change in QoS is propagated when a label is popped off. A label is popped off when using implicit NULL for PHP. PHP does not happen only at the egress LSR of the MPLS network. A label can also be popped at the tail LSR of a TE tunnel, which is not necessarily the egress LSR of the MPLS network. In the case of popping a label at an LSR, you can configure qos-group to propagate the QoS information. You need to do this for all three models if the pop operation is on an intermediate LSR.

In addition, for the Uniform model, make sure that at the egress LSR, you copy the QoS information to the labeled or IP packet that is leaving the egress LSR.

Figures 12-11 and 12-12 show examples of a packet being recolored on a P router in an MPLS VPN network.

Figure 12-11 *Recoloring a Packet in an MPLS VPN Network for the Pipe and Short Pipe Models*

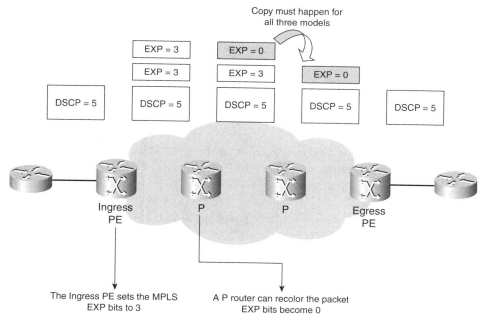

Figure 12-12 *Recoloring a Packet in an MPLS VPN Network for the Uniform Model*

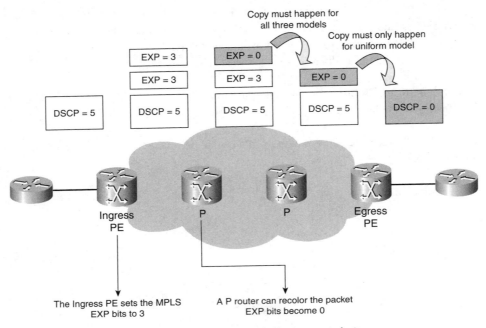

The Uniform model needs extra configuration on the egress PE. The EXP bits of the top label of the received packet must be propagated to the IP precedence or DSCP bits. You can accomplish this by configuring qos-group on the egress PE.

Table 12-4 shows an overview of the three Tunneling models regarding the label operation for plain IP-over-MPLS, MPLS traffic engineering, and MPLS VPN. Consider these three cases:

- **IP-to-Label**—The packet is received as an IP packet and forwarded labeled (ingress PE).

- **Label-to-Label**—The packet is received labeled and forwarded labeled (P router).

- **Label-to-IP**—The packet is received labeled and forwarded as an IP packet (egress PE).

Table 12-4   *Overview of the Three Tunneling Models for Plain IP-over-MPLS, MPLS Traffic Engineering, and MPLS VPN*

Tunneling Model	IP-to-Label	Label-to-Label	Label-to-IP
Uniform	Copy IP precedence/ DiffServ to MPLS EXP	MPLS EXP copied	Copy MPLS EXP to IP precedence/DiffServ
Pipe	MPLS EXP set according to service provider policy	MPLS EXP copied	Preserve IP precedence/DiffServ *Forwarding treatment based on MPLS EXP*
Short Pipe	MPLS EXP set according to service provider policy	MPLS EXP copied	Preserve IP precedence/DiffServ *Forwarding treatment based on IP precedence/DiffServ*

With plain IP-over-MPLS, MPLS traffic engineering, and MPLS VPN, the incoming packet is an IP packet. However, in the case of Carrier's Carrier (CsC) and Inter-Autonomous MPLS VPN, the incoming packet on the ingress LSR is already labeled. Then both the Tunneled and the LSP DiffServ information are MPLS EXP bits, but in different labels in the label stack. Thus, it is possible to have hierarchical levels of MPLS DiffServ tunnels.

MQC Commands for MPLS QoS

Cisco IOS lets you change the EXP bits to a new value or implement the behavior of copying the EXP bits to the exposed IP precedence/DSCP bits on the egress LSR. In Cisco IOS, you can use the Modular QoS Command Line Interface (MQC) or Committed Access Rate (CAR) for this. However, MQC is the newest implemented feature and the one with the most capabilities, so it is the only one mentioned here.

You can use two commands in MQC to change the EXP bits of labels. The following command sets the EXP bits in the topmost label:

```
set mpls experimental topmost value
```

You can use it in an input or an output service policy.

The next command sets the EXP bits in the pushed label(s):

```
set mpls experimental imposition value
```

You can use it only in an input service policy.

The *value* for both commands is between 0 and 7.

To make the impact of these two commands easier to understand, Figures 12-13 through 12-17 show you the result of these commands when you apply them to the input or output interface of a router. The LSP is left to right, so the input interface is the left interface and the output interface is the right interface. The examples demonstrate the impact of the commands in terms of imposition, swapping labels, or disposition of labels. Pay close attention to when the EXP bits of a certain label change.

Figure 12-13 *Set MPLS Experimental Commands with Imposition*

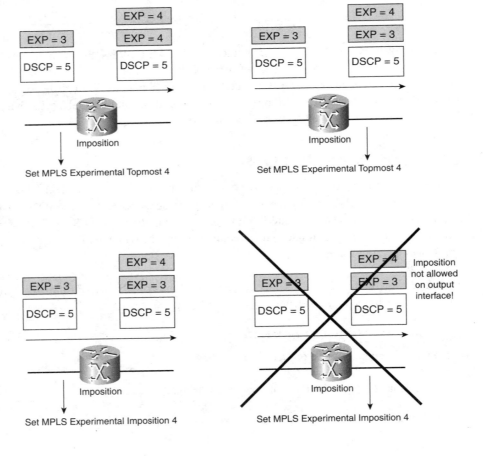

Remember MPLS QoS Rule 2 for the imposition case.

Figure 12-14   *Set MPLS Experimental Commands When Swapping Labels*

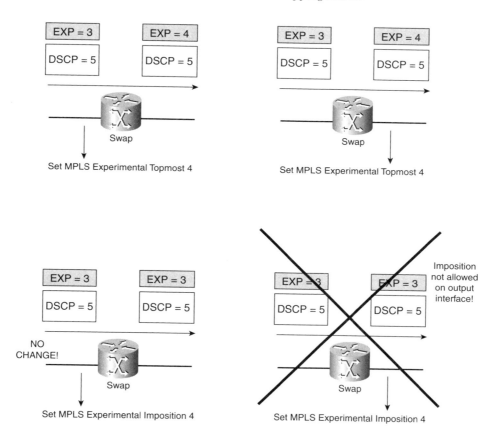

Remember MPLS QoS Rule 2 for the swap case.

Figure 12-15 *Set MPLS Experimental Commands with Disposition*

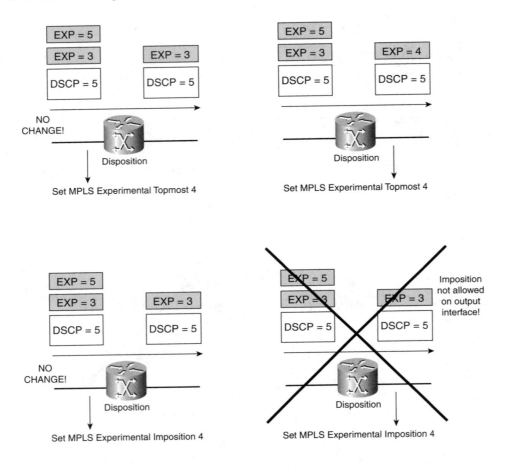

Remember MPLS QoS Rule 3 in the case of pop.

Figure 12-16 shows an interesting use of the set MPLS experimental commands. You can use the commands on the incoming and outgoing interface at the same time. The top illustration shows you that this gives you an interesting possibility—namely, to recolor the EXP bits of the two labels to a different value. The incoming EXP bits are changed to four by the MQC command on the swapped and pushed labels is on the input interface, and the EXP bits are changed to five only on the top label on the output interface. The bottom illustration in Figure 12-16 is not a very useful one, because you can change the EXP bits by one command on the input or output interface. You do not need to have both commands here, except to show what happens if you do configure both. Clearly, the command on the input or the output interface suffices.

Figure 12-16 *Set MPLS Experimental Commands on Input and Output Interfaces*

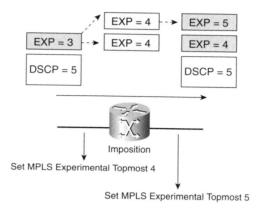

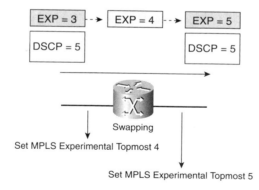

Figure 12-17 shows the commands in the case of IP-to-Label imposition.

Figure 12-17 *Set MPLS Experimental Commands with IP-to-Label Imposition*

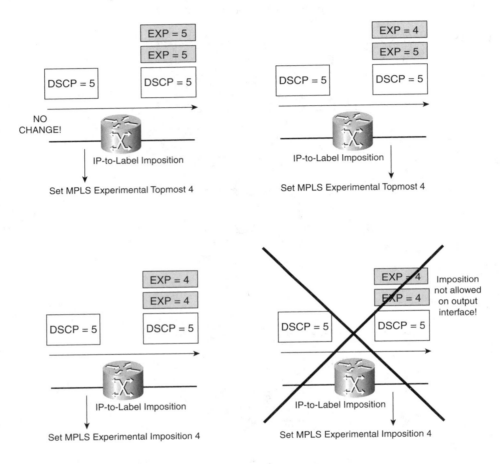

Remember MPLS QoS Rule 1 for the IP-to-Label case.

Moving MPLS QoS from the PE to the CE Router

These DiffServ Tunneling models are popular for MPLS VPN networks. However, the PE routers have some work to do, including running BGP, labeling packets, running LDP, running routing protocols over the virtual routing/forwarding (VRF) interfaces to the customer CE routers, and so on. If the MPLS VPN network also does one of the DiffServ models, the PE must have some MQC configuration. To make matters worse, the DiffServ models are configurable per interface—hence, per customer connecting to the MPLS VPN network. This considerably increases the needed amount of QoS configuration on the PE. One solution is to move the MPLS QoS to the CE routers. That means at a minimum that the CE routers will be the first routers encapsulating the IP packets with labels. You can use CsC for this. However, this entails running LDP between the PE and CE router—when the PE-CE routing protocol is an IGP, which is not always wanted.

If the only thing you need on the CE routers is to have the EXP bits conveying the MPLS QoS from CE to PE, you can use the explicit NULL label. A new interface command was invented to do just that: **mpls ip encapsulate explicit-null**. You need to configure this command on the interface of the CE router toward the PE. It encapsulates all IP packets, leaving the interface with one explicit NULL label. The PE router receives the explicit NULL-labeled packet on the VRF interface and forwards the packet in the normal manner into the MPLS network to the remote PE router. However, the PE router must have **mpls ip** configured on that VRF interface; otherwise, the explicit NULL-labeled packets are dropped. The PE router automatically copies the EXP bits from the incoming explicit NULL label to the EXP bits of all outgoing labels (without changing the precedence/DSCP of the IP packet). If you want to use MQC to implement one of the three DiffServ models, you can configure it now on the CE router. Thus, the QoS configuration per customer on the PE router is no longer needed. This greatly increases the scalability of the design. However, you do need to run newer Cisco IOS software (minimum 12.2[13]T) on the PE router so that the PE can automatically copy the EXP bits from the incoming explicit NULL label to the outgoing labels. If this is not possible, you can use the qos-group feature.

Figure 12-18 shows an example of using the explicit NULL label on the CE router toward the PE.

Figure 12-18 *Explicit NULL Label on CE Router*

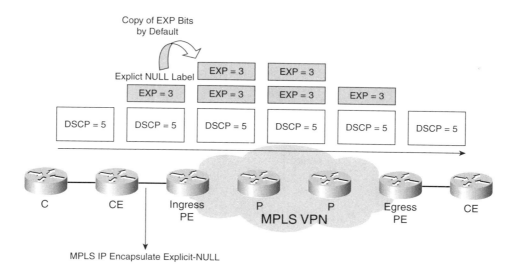

As already mentioned, you can also move the MPLS QoS from the PE to the CE by using CsC. This does involve using the signalling protocol LDP between the PE and the CE. An alternative to LDP is eBGP as the signalling protocol. External BGP is the preferred protocol anyway between different autonomous systems today. However, using the explicit NULL label between the PE and CE implies that LDP is not needed when the PE-CE routing protocol is an IGP.

Implementing the DiffServ Tunneling Models in Cisco IOS

This section gives an overview of implementing the different MPLS DiffServ Tunneling models in Cisco IOS. The sample network used here is an MPLS VPN network, because this is the MPLS application used most often today. The configuration shown pertains to only one or two values of the MPLS experimental bits or the IP precedence bits to keep the configuration small. In a real-world network, this configuration might need to be expanded to cover all EXP and precedence bits (DSCP levels).

Example 12-2 shows how to implement the MPLS DiffServ Uniform model in Cisco IOS and demonstrates the configuration needed on the ingress PE. Only precedence 4 is being matched. Precedence 4 is mapped to EXP bits value 4 by the policer, unless the bandwidth is exceeded, in which case the EXP bits are recolored to the value 2. The egress interface configuration is not needed for the MPLS DiffServ Uniform model, but it is added to show how to perform QoS on the EXP bits.

Example 12-2 *Ingress PE: MPLS DiffServ Uniform Model*

```
!Ingress interface:

class-map IP-AF11
 match ip precedence 4
!
policy-map set-MPLS-PHB
  class IP-AF11
    police cir 8000
      conform-action set-mpls-exp-transmit 4
      exceed-action set-mpls-exp-transmit 2
!
interface ethernet 3/1
 service-policy input set-MPLS-PHB

!Egress interface:

class-map MPLS-AF1
 match mpls experimental topmost 2 4
!
policy-map output-qos
 class MPLS-AF1
```

Example 12-2 *Ingress PE: MPLS DiffServ Uniform Model (Continued)*

```
    bandwidth percent 40
    random-detect
!
interface ethernet 3/0
 service-policy output output-qos
```

For the Uniform model, you must copy the precedence bits to the EXP bits on the ingress PE.

Example 12-3 shows the configuration of an intermediate P router.

Example 12-3 *P Router: MPLS DiffServ Uniform Model*

```
!Ingress interface:

!Nothing needed because the EXP bits are copied to the swapped outgoing label by default.


!Egress interface:

class-map MPLS-AF1
 match mpls experimental topmost 2 4
!
policy-map output-qos
 class MPLS-AF1
   bandwidth percent 40
   random-detect
!
interface ethernet 3/0
 service-policy output output-qos
```

Example 12-4 shows the configuration of the PHP P router.

Example 12-4 *PHP P Router: MPLS DiffServ Uniform Model*

```
!Ingress interface:

class-map mpls-in
 match mpls experimental topmost 2 4
!
policy-map policy2
 class mpls-in
   set qos-group mpls experimental topmost
!
interface ethernet 3/1
 service-policy input policy2
```

Example 12-4 *PHP P Router: MPLS DiffServ Uniform Model (Continued)*

```
!Egress interface:

class-map qos-group-out
 match qos-group 2
 match qos-group 4
!
policy-map policy3
 class qos-group-out
  set mpls experimental topmost qos-group
  bandwidth percent 40
  random-detect
!
interface ethernet 3/1
 service-policy output policy3
```

On the PHP router, qos-group ensures that the EXP bit values 2 and 4 are copied to the exposed outgoing top label after popping the incoming label.

Example 12-5 shows the configuration of the egress PE.

Example 12-5 *Egress PE: MPLS DiffServ Uniform Model*

```
!Ingress interface:

class-map mpls-in
 match mpls experimental topmost 2 4
policy-map foo
 class mpls-in
  set qos-group mpls experimental topmost
!
interface ethernet 3/0
 service-policy input foo


!Egress Interface:

class-map qos-out
 match qos-group 2
 match qos-group 4
!
policy-map foo-out
 class qos-out
  set precedence qos-group
  bandwidth percent 40
  random-detect
!
interface ethernet 3/1
 service-policy output foo-out
```

On the egress PE, copy the EXP bits to the precedence bits by using qos-group.

The following configuration is an example of how to implement the MPLS DiffServ Pipe model in Cisco IOS. Only the egress PE is shown, because this LSR has a different configuration from the previous example. For the Pipe and Short Pipe DiffServ model, however, the ingress PE can change the EXP bits according to the policy of the service provider. In Example 12-6, the egress LSR does not copy the EXP bits to the precedence bits of the outgoing IP packet. The scheduling of the packets on the egress interface is still done indirectly on the EXP bits as qos-group is being used. Example 12-6 shows the configuration of the egress PE for the MPLS DiffServ Pipe model.

Example 12-6 *Egress PE: MPLS DiffServ Pipe Model*

```
!Ingress interface:

class-map mpls-in
 match mpls experimental topmost 2 4
!
policy-map foo
 class mpls-in
   set qos-group mpls experimental topmost
!
interface ethernet 3/0
 service-policy input foo

!Egress Interface:

class-map qos-out
 match qos-group 2
 match qos-group 4
!
policy-map foo-out
 class qos-out
   bandwidth percent 40
   random-detect
!
interface ethernet 3/1
 service-policy output foo-out
```

The following configuration is an example of how to implement the MPLS DiffServ Short Pipe model in Cisco IOS. Only the egress PE is shown, because this LSR has a different configuration from the previous example. Namely, the egress LSR forwards the packet based on the precedence or DSCP bits of the IP packet after removing the labels. The egress LSR does not copy the EXP bits to the precedence bits of the outgoing IP packet.

Example 12-7 shows the configuration of the egress PE for the MPLS DiffServ Short Pipe model.

Example 12-7 *Egress PE: MPLS DiffServ Short Pipe Model*

```
!Egress Interface:

class-map IP-AF1
 match ip precedence 2 4
!
policy-map output-qos
 class IP-AF1
  bandwidth percent 40
  random-detect precedence-based
!
interface ethernet 3/0
 service-policy output output-qos
```

Example 12-8 shows another configuration you can use for the egress PE in the Pipe model. In this configuration, the experimental bits 0 and 1 are mapped into qos-group 1, but with a different discard-class, discard-class 1 and 2, respectively. The different discard-class provides a different drop precedence. The experimental bits 2 and 3 are mapped to qos-group 2, with discard-class 1 and 2, respectively. On the egress interface, the packets from one qos-group go into one queue, but in that queue are packets that have two different drop precedence levels.

Example 12-8 *Egress PE: MPLS DiffServ Pipe Model*

```
!Ingress interface:

class-map MPLS-AF11
 match mpls experimental topmost 0
!
class-map MPLS-AF12
 match mpls experimental topmost 1
!
class-map MPLS-AF21
 match mpls experimental topmost 2
!
class-map MPLS-AF22
 match mpls experimental topmost 3
!
policy-map set-MPLS-PHB
 class MPLS-AF11
  set qos-group 1
  set discard-class 1
 class MPLS-AF12
  set qos-group 1
  set discard-class 2
 class MPLS-AF21
```

Example 12-8   *Egress PE: MPLS DiffServ Pipe Model (Continued)*

```
    set qos-group 2
    set discard-class 1
class MPLS-AF22
    set qos-group 2
    set discard-class 2
!
interface ethernet 3/0
 service-policy input set-MPLS-PHB


!Egress interface:

class-map IP-AF1
 match qos-group 1
!
class-map IP-AF2
 match qos-group 2
!
policy-map output-qos
 class IP-AF1
   bandwidth percent 20
   random-detect discard-class-based

 class IP-AF2
   bandwidth percent 30
   random-detect discard-class-based

!
interface ethernet 3/1
 service-policy output output-qos
```

The Table-Map Feature

The *table-map* is a conversion table between the different types of QoS that a packet can have. It allows you to map IP precedence, DSCP, MPLS EXP bits, qos-group, and Layer 2 cos information (the 802.1Q priority bits) via an MQC command. For example, you can map the IP precedence in the incoming IP packet to the EXP bits value of the outgoing labeled packet by using this table instead of specifying an MQC command for each value to be mapped. Table 12-5 shows the categories of QoS information that you can map and their values.

Table 12-5   *Categories of QoS Information for Table-Map*

Packet Marking Category	Value Range
Cos	0 to 7
IP precedence	0 to 7
DSCP	0 to 63

continues

Table 12-5 *Categories of QoS Information for Table-Map (Continued)*

Packet Marking Category	Value Range
Qos-group	0 to 99
MPLS EXP imposition	0 to 7
MPLS EXP topmost	0 to 7

Table 12-6 shows the To and From types that you can use in a table-map.

Table 12-6 *To and From Packet-Marking Types*

To Packet-Marking Type	From Packet-Marking Type
Precedence	CoS
	QoS group
DSCP	CoS
	QoS group
CoS	Precedence
	DSCP
QoS group	Precedence
	DSCP
	MPLS EXP topmost
MPLS EXP topmost	QoS group
MPLS EXP imposition	Precedence
	DSCP

The commands in Example 12-9 show the **set** commands that you can use to apply a table-map. The first argument is the To type, and the second is the From type. You can also apply the **set** commands without a table-map. The command **set mpls experimental topmost qos-group**, for example, means that the qos-group packet-marking category is used to set the MPLS EXP value in the top label.

Example 12-9 *set Commands to Apply a Table-Map*

```
set precedence cos table table-map-name
set dscp cos table table-map-name
set cos precedence table table-map-name
set cos dscp table table-map-name
set qos-group precedence table table-map-name
set qos-group dscp table table-map-name
```

Example 12-9 *set Commands to Apply a Table-Map (Continued)*

```
set mpls experimental topmost qos-group table table-map-name
set mpls experimental imposition precedence table table-map-name
set mpls experimental imposition dscp table table-map-name
set qos-group mpls exp topmost table table-map-name
set precedence qos-group table table-map-name
set dscp qos-group table table-map-name
```

The global command to configure the table-map in Cisco IOS is **table-map** *table-map-name* **map from** *from-value* **to** *to-value* [**default** *default-action-or-value*]. The default keyword and default-action-or-value argument sets the default value (or action) to be used if a value is not explicitly designated.

Example 12-10 shows an example of a table-map. The qos-group is set via an input policy on the incoming interface according to the precedence value. The EXP bits are set on the outgoing topmost label—derived from the qos-group—via the table-map command that specifies that the values 0 and 3 are swapped and sets all other values to 7. So, for example, precedence 0 is copied to qos-group 0, and qos-group 0 is copied to MPLS EXP bits 3 through the table *map-out*.

Example 12-10 *Example of a Table-Map*

```
table-map map-out
 map from 0 to 3
 map from 3 to 0
 default 7
!
 class-map match-all class-in
  match any
 class-map match-all class-out
  match any
 policy-map in
  class class-in
   set qos-group precedence
 policy-map policy-out
  class class-out
   set mpls experimental topmost qos-group table map-out
!
interface Ethernet1/0
 ip address 10.1.1.1 255.255.255.252
 service-policy output policy-out
 mpls ip
!
interface Ethernet1/1
 ip vrf forwarding one
 ip address 192.168.1.2 255.255.255.252
 service-policy input in
```

The Use of MPLS QoS for Ethernet over MPLS

So far in this chapter, the packet for which the QoS was set was an IP packet or a labeled packet. However, in the case of Ethernet over MPLS (EoMPLS), the forwarded packet is actually an Ethernet frame. If the frame is a non-VLAN Ethernet frame, it does not have QoS information embedded. If the frame is an 802.1Q frame, though, the Priority bits (P bits) in the 802.1Q header designate a QoS value. If a service provider carries the 802.1Q Ethernet frames over an MPLS network as in the case of point-to-point EoMPLS or VPLS, it would be nice if he could police the traffic and recolor it, if needed. You can do this in Cisco IOS. You can match the 802.1Q Priority bits in MQC by matching cos values in the class map. In Example 12-11, the EXP bits are set to 1 on the tunnel and VC label on the ingress PE, if the 802.1Q P bits are 1, 2, or 3.

Example 12-11 *MPLS QoS for EoMPLS*

```
interface Vlan50
 no ip address
 !
 mpls l2transport route 1.1.1.1 100
 service-policy input foo
 !
class-map match-all foo-class
  match cos  1  2  3
 !
policy-map foo
  class foo-class
    set mpls experimental 1
  class class-default
    shape average 2000000 8000 8000
```

As you can see, the service provider can use traffic shaping to limit the rate of transmitted data to an average rate or committed information rate (CIR). This is useful in the EoMPLS application where the service provider limits the amount of traffic that a customer can send over the Ethernet interface toward the MPLS network.

Summary

Today the usage of quality of service (QoS) has become widespread. Most networks use some kind of QoS at some routers. MPLS networks could not stay behind for long. Most MPLS networks already have QoS, or the network administrators have started to implement QoS. The propagation of QoS in MPLS networks is done through the usage of the experimental bits in the labels.

The Experimental (EXP) bits in the top label in the label stack determine the QoS of the packet and how it will be treated when a label switching router (LSR) forwards it. This chapter explained how the propagation of the QoS information works for labeled packets. It also explained what happens to the EXP bits value when a label is popped, swapped, or pushed. This chapter continued by describing how this QoS behavior by LSRs can be used to implement one of the three MPLS DiffServ Tunneling models in Cisco IOS.

You saw how to make your MPLS network more scalable by moving the MPLS QoS from the PE to the CE router. You also saw how to use MQC to change the MPLS QoS information on an LSR and how this affects the propagation of the MPLS QoS information on the LSRs that are downstream of this router.

Chapter Review Questions

1. How many bits in the IP header can be used for QoS?

2. How many AF classes exist?

3. Name the three MPLS DiffServ models.

4. What is the difference between the Pipe and Short Pipe models?

5. What is the interface command to encapsulate all IP packets with an explicit NULL label?

6. What is TOS reflection?

7. What feature is used in Cisco IOS to alter the EXP bits?

8. What is the problem with PHP and QoS?

9. What is the solution to the problem in question 8?

10. On which labels can you change the EXP bits value?

What You Will Learn

By the end of this chapter, you should know and be able to do the following:

- Know how many labels to expect on a packet at a particular link in any MPLS network

- Use the traceroute tool in Cisco IOS to help determine problems with the forwarding of MPLS packets

- Solve a typical MPLS MTU problem

- Explain the propagation of the Time To Live (TTL) value by labeled packets

- Tackle a problem with load balancing labeled packets

- Explain what the command **mpls ip propagate-ttl** does and what its typical use is

- Use MPLS-aware Netflow to better troubleshoot MPLS forwarding problems

When you are able to do these, you are ready to troubleshoot MPLS problems in a proper and efficient manner.

Troubleshooting MPLS Networks

To troubleshoot MPLS networks, you need to be able to troubleshoot the control plane and the data plane. You should be able to troubleshoot the control plane at this point in the book if you have been reading chapters in order, because those chapters explain how the control plane works. You have seen the various control protocols Label Distribution Protocol (LDP), Resource Reservation Protocol (RSVP), and Border Gateway Protocol (BGP) and how they operate in signaling and advertising labels. Earlier chapters also explained how to troubleshoot the protocol by using the various **show** and **debug** commands that are available for each control protocol. What the other chapters in this book did *not* cover extensively is how to troubleshoot the data plane of MPLS networks. This chapter does.

Label Stack Depth

To detect problems with labeled packets in the data plane, you need to know how many labels are present in the label stack of the packets at each point in the network. Only then can you figure out if the labeled packets have the right number of labels and if it is the correct label in the right place in the label stack. Therefore, you need to know for your network how many labels a labeled packet has at each link. The number of labels present in the label stack depends on the MPLS network design you have. Each network design has a particular number of labels associated with it. Look at some examples. Following are the simple scenarios and the number of labels associated with them:

1. Plain IPv4-over-MPLS: 1
2. MPLS VPN or Any Transport over MPLS (AToM) or 6PE or 6VPE: 2
3. Traffic engineering (TE): 1
4. TE with Fast ReRouting (FRR) "in use": 2

You can combine certain scenarios. The number of labels might increase, or it might not. In any case, it is not as simple as just adding the number of labels of each scenario. Assume that you combine scenarios 2 and 4. Each scenario has two labels, but the combined scenario of 2 and 4 will not have 4 labels, but only 3! Following are a few possible combined scenarios:

- LDP session "over" MPLS TE, if the TE tunnel ends at the P router: 2
- Scenario 2 + 3 : 2

- Scenario 2 + 4 : 3

- Scenario 2 + 5 : 3

- Inter-autonomous MPLS VPN: 2 or 3 (IPv4 + label), depending on the exact scenario

Verifying Label Switched Path

A label switched path (LSP) can fail at any given place in the network. You can verify the LSP step by step by looking at the IP routing protocols and label distribution protocols (LDP, RSVP, and BGP) and by looking at the Cisco Express Forwarding (CEF) table and label forwarding information base (LFIB) on the provider edge (PE) and provider (P) routers. At a minimum, the LSP must never be interrupted; this means that the LSP must always have an incoming label and an outgoing label in the LFIB pointing to the correct next-hop label switching router (LSR). As soon as the outgoing label is "No Label" (Untagged) at an LSR that is not the egress LSR, the packets are forwarded unlabeled, and the packet forwarding fails for this LSP. You check the LSP by looking at the CEF table (the global or the virtual routing/forwarding (VRF) table) on the ingress LSR of the LSP. On all the other routers—up to and including the egress LSR—on the LSP, you need to check the LFIB entry for the LSP.

When a problem indicates that packets are not arriving at the intended destination, you need to identify the troubled LSP. The LSP might be the path from ingress PE to egress PE in an MPLS VPN network, the path that a TE tunnel takes, or the path from a CE router to the remote customer edge (CE) router in the case of Carrier's Carrier (CsC). After you have identified the LSP, verify the forwarding entries in the LSRs of the LSP for the specific prefix. At the first hop, check whether the CEF table has the correct outgoing label(s). A plain IPv4-over-MPLS network has only one outgoing label. An MPLS VPN network has at least two outgoing labels: one Interior Gateway Protocol (IGP) and one virtual private network (VPN) label. A TE tunnel has one label. In the case of AToM, it is not necessary to check the outgoing labels on the ingress PE in the CEF table because the transported data is not IP, but you should check them with the **show mpls l2transport** command. Starting with the first P router on an LSP, up to the egress LSR, you should check the labels in the LFIB. You must be able to match the outgoing label in the LFIB for a prefix on an LSR, with the incoming label in the LFIB of the next LSR. The traceroute tool, which is explained in the next section, can help you in determining whether the labels are correct. That tool has been enhanced to display the MPLS labels in the output.

Tracerouting in MPLS Networks

Tracerouting is a special tool that is widely used because it is so powerful. Soon you will learn how tracerouting behaves in an MPLS network, but to understand this, you must first understand how tracerouting works in an IP network.

Tracerouting in an IP Network

In Cisco IOS, when you issue the **traceroute** command on a router, it sends probes to the particular destination IP address that you specify. The probes sent out are UDP packets with a high destination UDP port. The first probe sent out has its IP TTL set to 1, the second probe has its IP TTL set to 2, and so on. In Cisco IOS, the high destination UDP port is a number that is greater than 30,000. Because the first probe sent out has a TTL of 1, the TTL of the packet expires on the next-hop router. Figure 13-1 shows what happens with the first probe when tracerouting.

Figure 13-1   *Tracerouting in an IP Network: Probe 1*

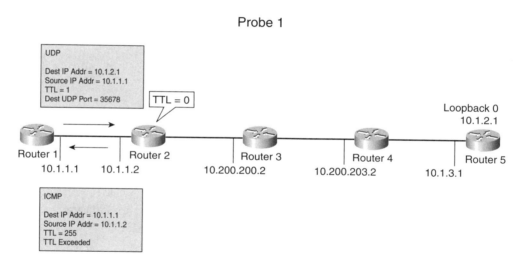

As you can see, Router 2 creates an Internet Control Message Protocol (ICMP) message of the type "TLL exceeded" (ICMP type 11, code 0) and sends it to the originator of the packet. At that point, you get the first line in the output of the traceroute, displaying the IP address of the router that generated the ICMP message. You can see this in Example 13-1.

NOTE   In Cisco IOS, three probes are sent by default for each TTL value.

Router 1 then sends a probe with TTL set to 2. This packet has its TTL expire on the third router. This router returns an ICMP "TTL exceeded" message, and the second line in the output of the traceroute appears. This is displayed in Figure 13-2.

Figure 13-2 *Tracerouting in an IP Network: Probe 2*

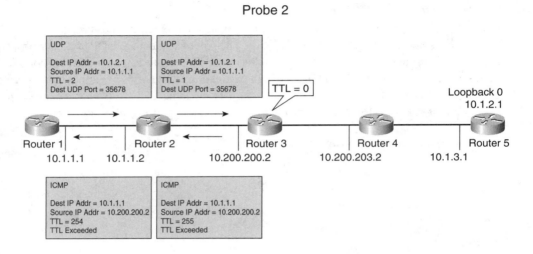

The process continues like this until a probe hits the destination—a router or host—with the IP address you provided in the traceroute command. The destination device receives the packet (the TTL is not expiring), notices that it is an UDP packet, but also notices that it does not have an application running for that particular UDP port. The reason for choosing such a high UDP port is that it is unlikely that an application on the destination device is using it and that the destination device will generate an ICMP message. The destination generates an ICMP "port unreachable" (ICMP type 3, code 3) message and sends it to the originator. Figure 13-3 illustrates the behavior of the last probe.

Figure 13-3   *Tracerouting in an IP Network: Probe 4*

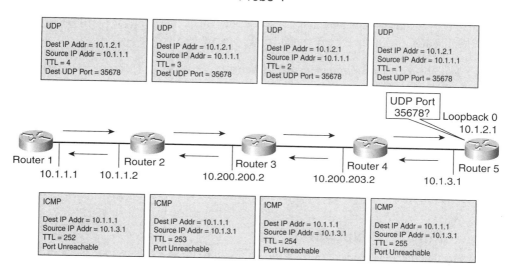

At this point, the traceroute stops, and the output looks like the one in Example 13-1.

Example 13-1   *Example of a Traceroute in an IP Network*

```
Router1#traceroute 10.1.2.1

Type escape sequence to abort.
Tracing the route to 10.1.2.1

  1 10.1.1.2 4 msec 0 msec 4 msec
  2 10.200.200.2 28 msec 28 msec 32 msec
  3 10.200.203.2 28 msec 28 msec 28 msec
  4 10.1.3.1 16 msec 20 msec 16 msec
```

Label-Aware ICMP

Tracerouting in an MPLS network is similar to tracerouting in an IP network. One difference is that the LSR on which the TTL of the labeled packet expires generates an ICMP message with a new extension. The ICMP message that the LSR generates is still a "TTL exceeded" ICMP message, but it is extended to hold the full MPLS label stack of the original packet received by the LSR that is the cause for the ICMP message being generated. This means that when you perform a traceroute from an LSR, the ICMP messages received from each LSR hold the label stack. This label stack is then printed in the output of the traceroute on the LSR, which makes troubleshooting in an MPLS network much easier.

Example 13-2 shows the new output of a traceroute when performed in an MPLS network. The label value along with the Experimental (EXP) bits value is printed.

Example 13-2 *Example of a Traceroute in an MPLS Network*

```
Router2#traceroute 10.200.254.4

Type escape sequence to abort.
Tracing the route to 10.200.254.4

  1 10.200.200.2 [MPLS: Label 17 Exp 0] 24 msec 24 msec 28 msec
  2 10.200.203.2 [MPLS: Label 16 Exp 0] 24 msec 24 msec 24 msec
  3 10.200.202.2 12 msec *  8 msec
```

TTL Behavior in MPLS Networks

The way that the TTL propagates from the IP header to the label stack and vice versa and the way that the TTL field in the label stack is treated can be summarized in the following rules:

- When an IP packet is first labeled, the TTL value is copied from the IP header to the TTL fields of all the labels in the imposed label stack after being decremented by 1.

- When a label *swap* forwards the labeled packet, the TTL field of the incoming top label is copied to the outgoing top label after being decremented by 1.

- When the labeled packet is forwarded by a label *pop*, the TTL field of the incoming top label is copied to the newly exposed top label after being decremented by 1, unless the newly exposed label has a TTL value that was smaller than the incoming top label. In the latter case, the outgoing TTL is the TTL of the newly exposed label after being decremented by 1.

- When the labeled packet is forwarded and one or more labels are pushed onto it, the TTL field of all the pushed labels is the TTL value of the incoming top label after being decremented by 1.

- When the label stack is removed, the TTL value of the top label is copied to the TTL field in the IP header unless the TTL value of the incoming label was greater than the IP TTL value in the underlying IP packet. In the latter case, the IP TTL value is retained when the IP packet is switched out.

- An LSR never changes the TTL value of nonexposed labels (not the top label).

- If a packet is label switched, the TTL value in the underlying IP header is never changed.

If the TTL of the top label in the label stack expires when it reaches 0, the following happens:

- The label stack is stripped off.

- The underlying IP packet (IPv4 or IPv6) is examined, and an ICMP message "TTL exceeded" with a destination IP address equal to the source IP address of the packet for which this ICMP message is generated is created. The TTL is set to 255 in the IP header and in all labels of the label stack of the ICMP message. The label stack put on the ICMP packet is the original label stack with the label operation performed on it according to the LFIB.

- The ICMP message "TTL exceeded" is forwarded along the LSP until the end of the LSP. The router does not look up the source IP address in the global routing table to return the ICMP message. This rule has one exception, which is explained in the section "**mpls ip ttl-expiration pop** Command."

The reason for this behavior is that in MPLS networks, the P routers are likely not to have the knowledge needed to forward the ICMP message directly back to the originator of the packet for which the ICMP message is generated. Take the example of an MPLS VPN network. The P routers do not have the IP VRF routing tables in memory. The only routers that have the VRF routing tables are the PE routers on the edge of the MPLS network. Therefore, the P routers are left with two options: Either drop the packets silently without generating an ICMP message, or forward the ICMP message along the LSP to the egress LSR of that LSP so that the ICMP message will eventually get to a router that can send the ICMP message to the router or host that sent the original packet. In the case of MPLS VPN, such a router that could return the ICMP message would be the egress PE or CE router. In Cisco IOS, the latter option was chosen as the default behavior.

Tracerouting in MPLS Networks

Tracerouting in an MPLS network is a bit different compared to tracerouting in an IP network. The probes sent are the same, but the routers that are running MPLS treat the ICMP messages differently. Look at Figure 13-4, which shows an MPLS VPN network that will be used to show how tracerouting works in an MPLS network.

Figure 13-4 *Tracerouting in an MPLS Network: Network*

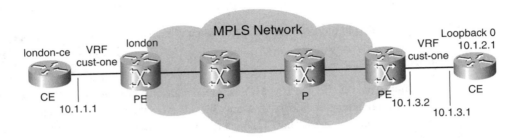

This network has two CE routers, two PE routers, and two P routers. The traceroute is done on the left CE router toward the right CE router. The packets that the CE router sends are still UDP packets with high destination UDP ports. The first probe has IP TTL set to 1 and is received on the VRF interface on the ingress PE router. The TTL of the packet expires on the ingress PE, and it sends an ICMP message "TTL exceeded" back to the CE. This is the same behavior as tracerouting in an IP network. Figure 13-5 shows the first probe.

Figure 13-5 *Tracerouting in an MPLS Network: Probe 1*

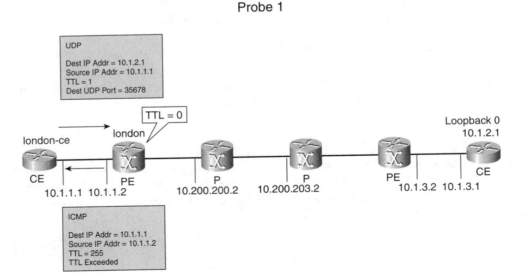

The CE sends the second probe. The ingress PE receives it, lowers the TTL by 1, and adds two labels: the VPN label, followed by the IGP label on top. The TTL of both labels is set to 1, in compliance with the rules mentioned in the previous section. The ingress PE forwards this packet to the next LSR, a P router. This P router sees the TTL in the top label expiring. It removes the label stack, examines the IP header of the underlying packet, and creates an ICMP message "TTL expired." Because this is a new packet, the IP TTL and the TTL in the labels are set to a value of 255. The source IP address is the IP address on the incoming interface of the P router. This ICMP message is not sent directly to the originator of the packet. Instead, a label stack is put onto the ICMP message—as if this were the original packet being forwarded according to the LFIB—and forwarded along the original LSP toward the egress LSR. On the egress PE router, the labels are stripped off, and the IP packet is forwarded. Because the IP destination of the *original* packet was not directly connected to the egress PE router, the outgoing label on the egress PE is "No Label." As such, the unlabeled IP packet is directly forwarded—without an IP lookup—toward the CE router. That CE router has the destination IP address of the ICMP message in its routing table and returns the ICMP message. Eventually, the CE router on the left receives the ICMP message. Figure 13-6 shows the path of this second probe.

Figure 13-6   *Tracerouting in an MPLS Network: Probe 2*

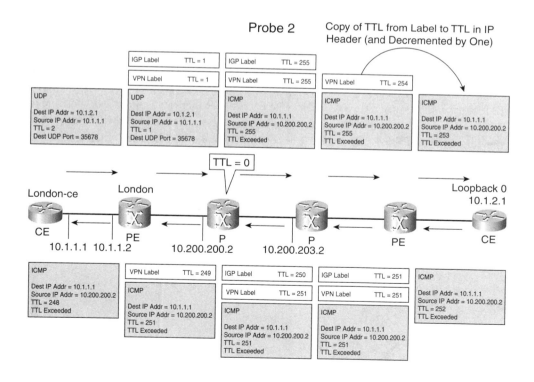

This behavior is the same for all probes: All ICMP messages are forwarded along the original LSP and are not sent back directly to the originator.

Example 13-3 shows the result of this traceroute.

Example 13-3 *Example of Traceroute in MPLS Network*

```
london-ce#traceroute 10.1.2.1

Type escape sequence to abort.
Tracing the route to 10.1.2.1

  1 10.1.1.2 4 msec 0 msec 4 msec
  2 10.200.200.2 28 msec 28 msec 32 msec
  3 10.200.203.2 28 msec 28 msec 28 msec
  4 10.1.3.2 16 msec 20 msec 16 msec
  5 10.1.3.1 12 msec 12 msec 12 msec
```

There can be a small difference in the output of the traceroute if you perform a traceroute for a destination for which the outgoing label is "Aggregate" in the LFIB of the egress LSR. There is an "Aggregate" outgoing label if the destination is either directly connected to that egress LSR or if it is an aggregate BGP route.

If the outgoing label is "Aggregate," the labels are stripped off after the LFIB lookup, and the packet receives an additional IP lookup so that the egress LSR can determine where the IP packet needs to be sent. As the egress LSR recognizes the incoming label as a VPN label, it performs the IP lookup in the appropriate VRF table. The egress LSR then sends the ICMP message directly back to the originator and does not forward it to the CE router on the right side, as in the case of the outgoing label being "No Label." This obviously makes a difference when troubleshooting a problem; in one case, the packets are forwarded over an extra link. Figure 13-7 shows the packet path for the second probe when tracerouting with the outgoing label "Aggregate" on the egress LSR.

Figure 13-7   *Tracerouting in an MPLS Network: Outgoing Label Is "Aggregate"*

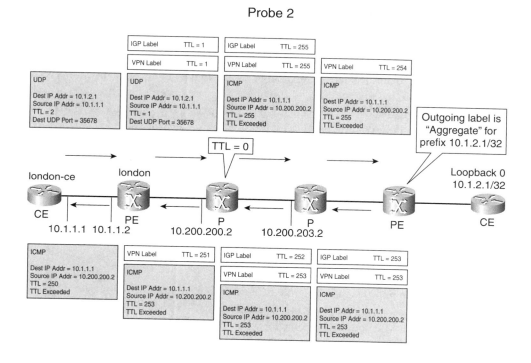

Problems with Tracerouting in MPLS Networks

Tracerouting in an MPLS network is similar to tracerouting in an IP network. However, the path that the ICMP messages take is not the same in an MPLS network as in an IP network. All ICMP messages are forwarded to the egress router on the LSP. The result of this behavior is that tracerouting becomes less efficient. Take the example of the link between the two P routers in the previous network, when it is no longer forwarding labeled packets. For example, LDP is failing between the two P routers. You can see the result of the traceroute in Example 13-4.

Example 13-4   *Example of a Broken Link in an MPLS Network*

```
london-ce#traceroute 10.1.2.1

Type escape sequence to abort.
Tracing the route to 10.1.2.1

 1 10.1.1.2 4 msec 0 msec 4 msec
 2 * * *
```

Example 13-4   *Example of a Broken Link in an MPLS Network (Continued)*

```
  3   *   *   *
 ...
 10   *   *   *
```

As you can see in the output, it appears that the problem is already happening between the ingress PE and the first P router because there is only one line in the output; in reality, however, the problem is between the first and second P router. The same traceroute in this network without MPLS enabled would show the problem at the correct place. The traceroute in an MPLS network is flawed if the result is a failure because all ICMP messages are forwarded along the LSP instead of being sent back directly. As such, the ICMP messages can be dropped anywhere along the LSP, and the correct place of failure in the data plane will not be shown in the output of the traceroute. In other words, wherever a problem occurs in the MPLS VPN network, the CE-to-CE traceroute starts to fail from the second probe onward. This renders the traceroute tool useless when the forwarding path has a problem. The solution to this is to use MPLS LSP traceroute, as described in Chapter 14, "MPLS Operation and Maintenance."

mpls ip ttl-expiration pop Command

One command can improve the use of the traceroute tool, at least in some cases. The command **mpls ip ttl-expiration pop** *labels* can make a difference. The value of *labels* is between 1 and 6. This command lets you control the behavior when an ICMP TTL expired message is generated. The default behaviour is to forward the ICMP message along the original LSP. With this command, you can specify the behavior when the TTL of a labeled packet expires, according to the number of labels in the label stack. If the configured number of labels is not exceeded, the default behavior is overridden. In that case, the generated ICMP message is forwarded after looking up the source IP address in the global routing table. If the configured number of labels is exceeded, the default forwarding behaviour is used. As an example, take a plain IPv4-over-MPLS network. This means that MPLS is enabled for all IGP prefixes in the global routing table. Traffic has only one label. If you perform a traceroute and configure the command **mpls ip ttl-expiration pop 1** on all the LSRs, all generated ICMP messages are sent back directly to the source of the original packet.

Look at Figure 13-8. It shows the first probe of a traceroute from the left PE in a simple MPLS network. The command **mpls ip ttl-expiration pop 1** is configured on all LSRs. The ICMP message is sent directly to the router that initiates the traceroute, if the packet has only one label. The probe has only one label because the destination IP address is in the global routing table.

Figure 13-8   *Tracerouting in an MPLS Network:* **mpls ip ttl-expiration pop** *Command*

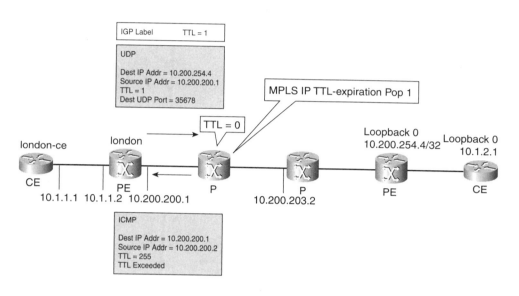

The egress PE router receives packets with only one label with the default penultimate hop popping (PHP) behaviour in MPLS VPN networks. If the command **mpls ip ttl-expiration pop 1** is configured on that PE router and a packet is received with its TTL expiring, the label is removed, and the IP lookup happens in the correct VRF table (the VRF table that is associated with the VPN label) to return the packet immediately.

no mpls ip propagate-ttl

When the IP packet first becomes labeled on the ingress PE router, the following rule is observed:

■   When an IP packet is first labeled, the TTL field is copied from the IP header to the TTL fields of all the labels in the label stack after being decremented by 1.

You can change that default behavior with the command **no mpls ip propagate-ttl [forwarded | local]**. The command **no mpls ip propagate-ttl** stops the copying of the IP TTL to the TTL fields in the MPLS labels. In that case, the TTL fields in the labels are set to 255. The result of this is that for a traceroute on the local CE router to the remote CE router, the topology of the MPLS network is hidden from the customer because the MPLS routers (except the ingress PE) are skipped. By default, the traceroute from the local CE router to the remote CE router looks like the output in Example 13-5.

Example 13-5 *Example of Traceroute in MPLS VPN Network*

```
london-ce#traceroute 10.1.2.1

Type escape sequence to abort.
Tracing the route to 10.1.2.1

  1 10.1.1.2 4 msec 0 msec 4 msec          ingress PE
  2 10.200.200.2 28 msec 28 msec 32 msec   P
  3 10.200.201.2 28 msec 28 msec 28 msec   P
  4 10.1.3.2 16 msec 20 msec 16 msec       egress PE
  5 10.1.3.1 12 msec 12 msec 12 msec       remote CE
```

If you configure **no mpls ip propagate-ttl** on the PE routers, the output of the traceroute looks like Example 13-6. The P routers and egress PE router are removed from the traceroute. As such, the customer in the VPN cannot see the P routers when tracerouting through the MPLS network.

Example 13-6 *Example of Traceroute in MPLS VPN Network with* ***no mpls ip propagate-ttl***

```
london-ce#traceroute 10.1.2.1

Type escape sequence to abort.
Tracing the route to 10.1.2.1

  1 10.1.1.2 4 msec 4 msec 0 msec          ingress PE
  2 10.1.3.1 16 msec 12 msec 12 msec       remote CE
```

The TTL propagates throughout the MPLS network in the labels, as shown in Figure 13-9.

Figure 13-9 *Tracerouting in an MPLS VPN Network: **no mpls propagate-ttl**: Probe 2*

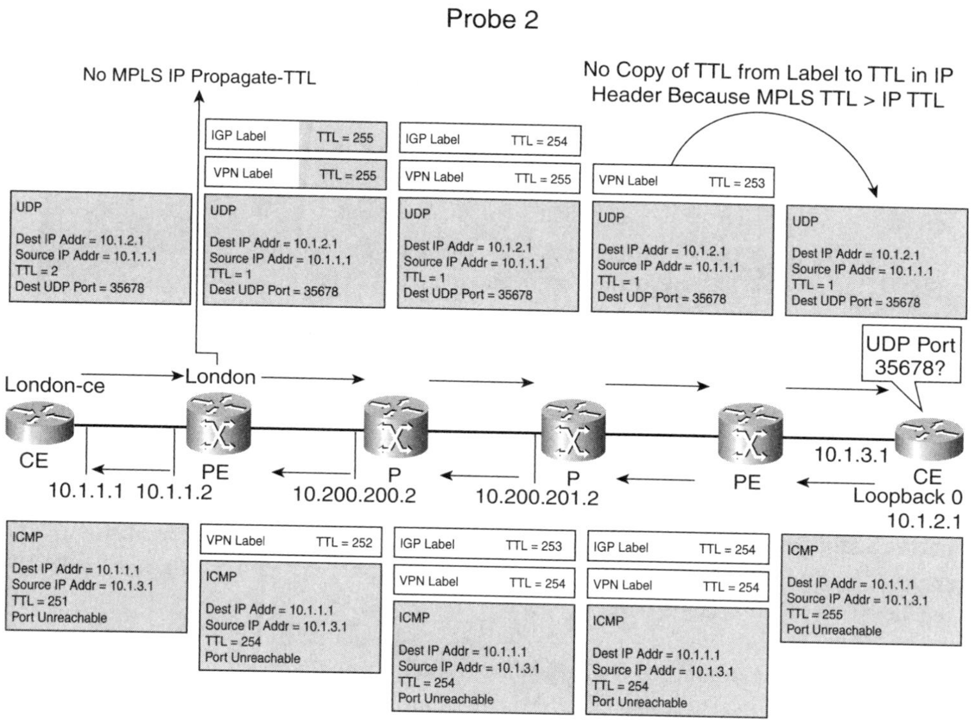

Probe 2

No MPLS IP Propagate-TTL

No Copy of TTL from Label to TTL in IP
Header Because MPLS TTL > IP TTL

IGP Label	TTL = 255

IGP Label	TTL = 254

VPN Label	TTL = 255

VPN Label	TTL = 255

VPN Label	TTL = 253

UDP

Dest IP Addr = 10.1.2.1
Source IP Addr = 10.1.1.1
TTL = 2
Dest UDP Port = 35678

UDP

Dest IP Addr = 10.1.2.1
Source IP Addr = 10.1.1.1
TTL = 1
Dest UDP Port = 35678

UDP

Dest IP Addr = 10.1.2.1
Source IP Addr = 10.1.1.1
TTL = 1
Dest UDP Port = 35678

UDP

Dest IP Addr = 10.1.2.1
Source IP Addr = 10.1.1.1
TTL = 1
Dest UDP Port = 35678

UDP

Dest IP Addr = 10.1.2.1
Source IP Addr = 10.1.1.1
TTL = 1
Dest UDP Port = 35678

UDP Port
35678?

London-ce   London

CE   PE

10.1.1.1 10.1.1.2

P

10.200.200.2

P

10.200.201.2

PE

10.1.3.1

CE
Loopback 0
10.1.2.1

ICMP

Dest IP Addr = 10.1.1.1
Source IP Addr = 10.1.3.1
TTL = 251
Port Unreachable

VPN Label	TTL = 252

ICMP

Dest IP Addr = 10.1.1.1
Source IP Addr = 10.1.3.1
TTL = 254
Port Unreachable

IGP Label	TTL = 253

VPN Label	TTL = 254

ICMP

Dest IP Addr = 10.1.1.1
Source IP Addr = 10.1.3.1
TTL = 254
Port Unreachable

IGP Label	TTL = 254

VPN Label	TTL = 254

ICMP

Dest IP Addr = 10.1.1.1
Source IP Addr = 10.1.3.1
TTL = 254
Port Unreachable

ICMP

Dest IP Addr = 10.1.1.1
Source IP Addr = 10.1.3.1
TTL = 255
Port Unreachable

You can see now that the second probe already triggers an ICMP message "port unreachable" on the remote CE router. This causes the traceroute to terminate after sending the second probe.

NOTE   You can see in Example 13-6 that the egress PE is not shown in the CE-to-CE traceroute, when **no mpls ip propagate-ttl** is configured on the ingress PE router. Since Cisco IOS 12.3(13), 12.3(13)T, and 12.0(31)S, the egress PE router is shown even when **no mpls ip propagate-ttl** is configured on the ingress PE router. When the egress PE router has the preceding Cisco IOS and the MPLS TTL is greater than or equal to the IP TTL, the egress PE checks the TTL value of the IP packet even when the outgoing label is "No Label." If the IP TLL is 1 or 0, the egress PE generates the ICMP TTL expired message. If the IP TTL is greater than 1, the IP TTL is decremented by 1, and the packet is forwarded.

The result is basically that the customer in his VPN sees the MPLS cloud as only one hop when tracerouting through it. In Figure 13-9, you can also see that the TTL value from the label is not copied into the TTL field of the IP header on the egress PE router. That is because the MPLS TTL value is greater than the TTL value in the IP header. Imagine that the MPLS TTL value *is* copied into the IP header on the egress PE router. In that case, the IP TTL value becomes 252. If that packet again arrives on the ingress PE router because of a routing loop, the MPLS TTL value is set to 255 again. That packet loops forever because neither the MPLS TTL nor the IP TTL ever reaches 0, and the packet is never dropped.

A drawback of this command is that when the service provider performs a traceroute in his network (from ingress PE to egress PE), he has the same result and sees his own network as only one hop. This obviously makes troubleshooting a bit painful. Therefore, it might be better for the service provider to configure **no mpls ip propagate-ttl forwarded** on his PE routers. Disabling TTL propagation of forwarded packets allows only the structure of the MPLS network to be hidden from customers, but not the service provider in an MPLS VPN network. If **no mpls ip propagate-ttl forwarded** is used, the TTL value from the IP header is not copied into the TTL fields of the labels for the packets that are switched through the ingress LSR. The TTL value is, however, copied for the locally generated packets on the ingress LSR. An illustrative example of the latter case is an MPLS VPN network with **no mpls ip propagate-ttl forwarded** configured on the ingress PE. The TTL value is not copied for packets that are received from the CE router, but it is copied into the labels for packets that are locally generated on the ingress PE router, such as for a traceroute in the VRF on the ingress PE router. Example 13-7 illustrates this. The first traceroute is what the customer sees from the CE router, and the second traceroute is what the service provider sees from the PE router.

Example 13-7 *Example of Traceroute in an MPLS VPN Network with **no mpls ip propagate-ttl forwarded***

```
london(config)#no mpls ip propagate-ttl forwarded

london-ce#traceroute 10.1.2.1

Type escape sequence to abort.
Tracing the route to 10.1.2.1

  1 10.1.1.2 0 msec 0 msec 0 msec
  2 10.1.3.1 12 msec 12 msec 12 msec

london#traceroute vrf cust-one 10.1.2.1

Type escape sequence to abort.
Tracing the route to 10.1.2.1

  1 10.200.200.2 [MPLS: Labels 19/28 Exp 0] 28 msec 28 msec 28 msec
  2 10.200.203.2 [MPLS: Labels 16/28 Exp 0] 32 msec 28 msec 28 msec
  3 10.1.3.2 [MPLS: Label 28 Exp 0] 16 msec 20 msec 16 msec
  4 10.1.3.1 12 msec 12 msec 12 msec
```

NOTE   The command **mpls ip propagate-ttl** really only makes sense on edge LSRs or PE routers, because the command only affects copying the IP TTL to the TTL field in the labels. The label imposition of customer IP packets happens only on edge LSRs, so configuring this command on all your P routers is not really beneficial.

The IP address that you notice in the output of the traceroute command is the source IP address of the ICMP packet. The router that generates the ICMP message uses the IP address of the interface on which the original packet was received as the source IP address of the ICMP message. An exception to this rule occurs when performing a traceroute from within a VRF. The egress PE router does not use the IP address of the incoming interface because this IP address is in the global routing table. Rather, the egress PE router uses an IP address of the VRF as the source IP address of the ICMP message. This means that the output of the traceroute does not show IP addresses from inside the MPLS cloud if a traceroute is performed from a CE router through the MPLS cloud and the PE routers have **no mpls ip propagate-ttl** or **no mpls ip propagate-ttl forwarded** configured.

MPLS MTU

The maximum transmission unit (MTU) of a link determines whether a labeled packet is too big to be transmitted across a link. Note that a link has a physical MTU value and an IP MTU value. Take the example of an Ethernet link on a Cisco IOS router. The MTU value is 1500 bytes. That is the Layer 3 MTU value of the packet. Therefore, an IP packet up to 1500 bytes can be transmitted across the Ethernet link without having to be fragmented. Typically, when MPLS is used, the IP packet of 1500 bytes receives one or two labels. It might be more, such as when CsC is deployed, but two labels are the maximum for this example. Therefore, 2 labels are added to the IP packet, or 2 times 4 bytes, which makes 8 bytes. The maximum size of the labeled packet is 1508 bytes. However, the MTU of the Ethernet link was 1500 bytes, meaning that IP packets of 1493 to 1500 bytes now have to be fragmented because they are labeled. Because sending maximum-sized packets is common (for example, for FTP), this might lead to fragmenting a huge part of the traffic and problems down the road.

To prevent fragmentation in the first place, you can do three things: lower the MTU for the IP packets to 1492 bytes, use Path MTU discovery, or create a new MTU, specifically for MPLS. The first solution works only if the MTU is lowered consistently throughout the network. Also, if you do not lower the MTU values of the end stations throughout the network, the traffic that enters the MPLS cloud might still be 1500 bytes, leading to fragmentation on the edge LSRs. Lowering the MTU value on the end stations is usually not practical because of their abundance. Also, the end stations usually belong to a different company than the one owning the MPLS network, as with the example of an MPLS VPN network, in which you usually have a service provider and customers.

The second solution, using Path MTU discovery, involves the end stations sending packets and lowering the maximum size of the packet when necessary. However, this is a viable solution only if all the end stations use Path MTU discovery. Even if the end stations do use Path MTU discovery, the ICMP messages needed to make it work might be dropped by access lists or firewalls, which occurs more and more these days. Fortunately, most end stations now support Path MTU discovery and have it enabled by default. The remark regarding the end stations belonging to a different company from the one owning the MPLS network also applies here.

Cisco IOS has the third solution as a new MTU value was introduced for the labeled packets: MPLS MTU. This MTU is the size of the Layer 3 packet, including the labels stack. Therefore, in our example, for an IP packet that is 1500 bytes and has two labels in the label stack, you need to set the MPLS MTU to 1508 on the Ethernet interface. This solution has one problem. The Ethernet specification allows for a Layer 3 payload of only 1500 bytes. With the addition of two labels, the total size of the packet is 1508 bytes. Cisco IOS now allows a slightly bigger packet than the 1500 bytes maximum. These frames that are slightly bigger than the maximum allowed size are called *baby giant frames*. The advantage of setting the MPLS MTU is that you need to configure it only in the MPLS network.

> **NOTE**   MPLS MTU is a configurable value in Cisco IOS. It is the maximum allowed size for a packet *after* labeling. The Internet Engineering Task Force (IETF) specified a value called maximum initially labeled IP datagram size (MILIDS). However, this is the maximum allowed size of the packet *before* labeling.

MPLS MTU is an interface configuration command. If you do not configure it, the default MPLS MTU value is the same as the MTU value of the interface.

Ping

The ping tool in Cisco IOS provides a few features that can help with troubleshooting:

- Attaching an IP option

- Specifying the MTU

- Sweeping

With ping, you can specify to add an IP option such as timestamp or record route to the packet. If you add an IP option, all intermediate routers have to process-switch the IP packet. This can exclude problems in the fast path forwarding (CEF). Because ping allows you to specify the MTU value as the size of the packet, you debug certain MTU problems that might exist in the MPLS cloud. Ping lets you sweep, or use a variable packet size for the ping. You can specify a range of packet sizes and see which sized ping is lost.

Debug MPLS Packets

You can debug the forwarding of MPLS packets, just as you can debug the forwarding of IP packets. The command is **debug mpls packets**. However, if you turn on this debug command without further specifying anything, it returns debug output for all label switched packets. This is something that is probably fine in a lab environment, but not in a production network. Fortunately, you can specify an access list that limits the output to certain labeled packets.

> **WARNING**   Debugging the forwarding of (labeled) packets can consume many CPU cycles on the router and as such is a dangerous thing to do. When debugging in the data plane—such as **debug mpls packets**—, be sure you know what you are doing and take the necessary precautions in case the router cannot keep up with the debugging. One thing you should do to limit the risk is to turn off the console logging on that router.

The command **debug mpls packets** generates output for every packet that is processed. Example 13-8 shows that you can limit the output by specifying an MPLS access list or an interface. The access list needs to be within the range 2700 to 2799, identifying it as an MPLS access list.

Example 13-8   *Example of **debug mpls packets** with Access List*

```
event#debug mpls packets ?
  <2700-2799>          MPLS label access list
  Async                Async interface
  BVI                  Bridge-Group Virtual Interface
  CTunnel              CTunnel interface
  Dialer               Dialer interface
  EsconPhy             ESCON interface
  Ethernet             IEEE 802.3
...
event(config)#access-list 2700 permit ?
  WORD   mpls label table name or 'any'

event(config)#access-list 2700 permit any ?
  <16-1048575>  mpls label number
  any           any label number
  <cr>

event(config)#access-list 2700 permit any 16 ?
  <0-7>  mpls exp value
  any    any exp value
  <cr>

event(config)#access-list 2700 permit any 16 any ?
  <0-1>  mpls eos value
  any    any eos value
  <cr>

event(config)#access-list 2700 permit any 16 any any ?
  <cr>
```

You can specify the MPLS label table, the label number, the EXP value, and the EOS value. The MPLS label table is the LFIB that is being used. This is either the global LFIB or a specific VRF LFIB. The MPLS EOS value is the EoS (end-of-stack) or BoS (bottom-of-stack) bit. If you specify 1 for EOS, the debug information displays packets with only one label in the stack. If the top label has the BoS bit set, it is the only label in the stack.

Example 13-9 shows the output when enabling MPLS packet debugging.

Example 13-9   *Example of **debug mpls packets***

```
event#debug mpls packets 2700
Packet debugging is on with ACL 2700
```

Example 13-9   *Example of debug mpls packets (Continued)*

```
event#
1d02h: MPLS turbo: Et3/1: rx: Len 122 Stack {16 0 253} {24 0 254} - ipv4 data
1d02h: MPLS turbo: Se4/0: tx: Len 108 Stack {24 0 252} - ipv4 data
```

> **NOTE**   Depending on what router this debugging is performed on, the debug might or might not show the debugging information. On a distributed platform, the packets are switched from line card to line card and do not pass the central CPU of the router. As such, the debugging on the central CPU does not show packets being switched.

The packet enters the router on interface Ethernet3/1 and leaves on interface Serial4/0. The whole label stack is presented as each label is printed between { }. The label information printed is {label EXP TTL}. The label is just the value of the label (20 bits). EXP is the value of the Experimental bits, and TTL is the Time To Live of the label. The BoS bit is not printed. At the end, the underlying data type is displayed; in this case, it is an IPv4 packet. If it were an IPv6 packet, ipv6 data would be printed. Remember that labeled packets are switched based on the label value in the top label. This label value must match the value in the LFIB. The packet that entered the router had two labels, but it had only one when it left. This is confirmed by the LFIB shown in Example 13-10.

Example 13-10   *LFIB Entry for Incoming Label 16*

```
event#show mpls forwarding-table labels 16
Local   Outgoing      Prefix          Bytes Label   Outgoing   Next Hop
Label   Label or VC   or Tunnel Id    Switched      interface
16      Pop Label     10.200.254.4/32 154802        Se4/0      point2point
```

The packet that is being switched is an MPLS VPN packet; that is why it has two labels. Because the **debug mpls packets** was turned on on a penultimate LSR, one label is popped off from the label stack of the packet when it is forwarded through the router. In the case of an AToM packet, the output looks like Example 13-11.

Example 13-11   *debug mpls packets of an AToM Packet*

```
1d05h: MPLS turbo: Et3/1: rx: Len 122 Stack {16 0 254} {26 0 2} CW {0 0 0}
1d05h: MPLS turbo: Se4/0: tx: Len 108 Stack {26 0 2} CW {0 0 0}
```

You can see that CW, or the control word, is displayed, indicating that the MPLS payload is an AToM packet. The syntax of the control word as displayed in the output of the **debug mpls packets** command consists of three fields and is the following: {flags length sequence-number}. Refer to Chapter 10, "Any Transport over MPLS," to understand the meaning of these fields in the control word.

Debugging Load Balancing of Labeled Packets

The algorithm for load balancing labeled packets is as follows:

■ If the MPLS payload is an IPv4 packet, the load balancing is done by hashing the source and destination IP address of the IPv4 header.

■ If the MPLS payload is an IPv6 packet, the load balancing is done by hashing the source and destination IP address of the IPv6 header.

■ If the MPLS payload is not an IPv4 or IPv6 packet, the load balancing is done by load balancing the MPLS packets based on the value of the bottom label.

The hashing algorithm for labeled packets is the one that CEF uses. For CEF, you use the command **show ip cef** [**vrf** *vrf-name*] **exact-route** *source-address destination-address* to figure out to which outgoing link a packet will be switched for a particular source and destination IP address. You can use a similar command to figure out the outgoing link for labeled packets in the case of load sharing. The command is **show mpls forwarding-table labels** *label* **exact-path**. Because the load balancing algorithm for CEF and labeled packets is the same, you need to specify the source and destination IP address of the IPv4 payload with this command so that the correct outgoing link can be displayed. Look at Figure 13-10.

Figure 13-10 *Usage of* **exact-path** *Command When Load Balancing Labeled Packets*

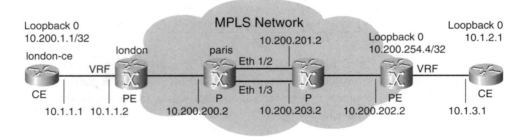

You can perform a traceroute from the CE router on the left to the destination IP address 10.1.2.1 on the remote CE router with two different source IP addresses. For each traceroute, the first P router uses a different outgoing link in the MPLS cloud. You can find the exact link being used for a specific pair of source and destination IP addresses by using the **show mpls forwarding-table**

labels *label* **exact-path** command on that P router (router paris in the example). The two traceroutes are shown in Example 13-12.

Example 13-12 *Example of **exact-path** Command*

```
london-ce#traceroute
Protocol [ip]:
Target IP address: 10.1.2.1
Source address: 10.1.1.1
...
Tracing the route to 10.1.2.1

  1 10.1.1.2 0 msec 0 msec 4 msec
  2 10.200.200.2 28 msec 32 msec 32 msec
  3 10.200.203.2 28 msec 32 msec 28 msec
  4 10.1.3.2 20 msec 20 msec 16 msec
  5 10.1.3.1 12 msec 12 msec 12 msec

london-ce#traceroute
Protocol [ip]:
Target IP address: 10.1.2.1
Source address: 10.200.1.1
...
Tracing the route to 10.1.2.1

  1 10.1.1.2 4 msec 0 msec 4 msec
  2 10.200.200.2 28 msec 32 msec 28 msec
  3 10.200.201.2 32 msec 32 msec 28 msec
  4 10.1.3.2 20 msec 20 msec 16 msec
  5 10.1.3.1 12 msec 12 msec 12 msec

paris#show mpls forwarding-table labels 19 exact-path ipv4 10.1.1.1 10.1.2.1
10.1.1.1 -> 10.1.2.1 : Et1/3 (next hop 10.200.203.2) Label stack: 16
paris#show mpls forwarding-table labels 19 exact-path ipv4 10.200.1.1  10.1.2.1
10.200.1.1 -> 10.1.2.1 : Et1/2 (next hop 10.200.201.2) Label stack: 16

paris#show mpls for labels 19
Local   Outgoing    Prefix          Bytes tag  Outgoing    Next Hop
tag     tag or VC   or Tunnel Id    switched   interface
19      16          10.200.254.4/32 4554904    Et1/3       10.200.203.2
        16          10.200.254.4/32 3310       Et1/2       10.200.201.2

paris#show mpls forwarding-table labels 19 exact-path ?
  <1-4294967295>  Label stack entry 2
  ipv4            IPv4 payload
```

Note that the IPv4 addresses that are specified in the command of Example 13-12 are actually IP addresses belonging to the VPN and are not known in the global routing table on the P routers.

This is not a concern because the IP addresses that are specified do not need to be known in the routing table of the P routers. The P routers just perform the algorithm on both IP addresses to decide which link to use to switch the packet out hashing from a set of possible outgoing links. The set of outgoing links is still determined by the lookup of the top label in the incoming label stack on the packet.

In some cases—if the MPLS payload is not an IPv4 or IPv6 packet—the load balancing of labeled packets is not done on the IP addresses underneath the label stack. In those instances, the load balancing is done on the bottom label. However, the label stack might be too deep. This means that there are too many labels, and a specific type of router cannot read the bottom label. In that situation, a label at a specific depth (for example, the third label from the top) is chosen to do the load balancing on. That is why the command lets you specify the complete label stack by letting you specify the label stack entries from 2 to 8. Cisco IOS then figures out which label to use from the user-specified labels and displays the results of the load balancing algorithm on that specific label.

Verifying MPLS on the Interface

You can verify a few MPLS interface parameters with the command **show mpls interfaces detail**. First, you can verify whether LDP is enabled on the interface. Second, you can verify whether the interface is enabled for RSVP with extensions so that a TE tunnel can cross the interface. Third, you can verify whether BGP with MPLS label advertisement is enabled on the interface. Finally, you can determine the MPLS MTU value of the interface, which is mentioned in the output. Look at Example 13-13 to see the output of the **show mpls interfaces detail** command.

Example 13-13 *Example of show mpls interfaces detail*

```
london#show mpls interfaces detail
Interface Ethernet0/0/0:
        IP labeling enabled (ldp):
          Interface config
        LSP Tunnel labeling enabled
        BGP labeling enabled
        MPLS operational
        Optimum Switching Vectors:
          IP to MPLS Turbo Feature Vector
          MPLS Feature Vector
        Fast Switching Vectors:
          IP to MPLS Fast Feature Switching Vector
          MPLS Feature Vector
        MTU = 1508
```

Verifying Number of Bytes Label Switched

One way of tracking the level of traffic switched for a certain LSP is by looking at the accounting in the LFIB for that LSP. The LFIB has a column for Bytes Tag Switched that keeps track of the amount of label switched bytes. This can indicate whether the level of traffic for a certain LSP is anywhere near the level of traffic you expect. If that counter is 0 when you expect it to be far higher than that, the LSP is experiencing a problem. You can also keep an eye on the counter to see if it is increasing when you know that traffic should be passing through on the LSP and hence that a particular top label should be used for forwarding traffic. Example 13-14 shows the output of the LFIB and the accounting per LSP.

Example 13-14 *Example of Accounting in LFIB*

```
london#show mpls forwarding-table
Local  Outgoing     Prefix          Bytes tag  Outgoing    Next Hop
tag    tag or VC    or Tunnel Id    switched   interface
16     Untagged     l2ckt(100)      33837024   none        point2point
17     Untagged     10.48.0.0/16    4878       Et0/0/7     10.48.70.1
20     Pop tag [T]  10.200.202.0/24 0          Tu1         point2point
26     16       [T] 10.100.200.0/24[V]   \
                                     0          Tu1         point2point
27     Pop tag      10.200.200.2/32 0          Et0/0/0     10.200.200.2
28     Aggregate    10.1.1.0/24[V]  172690752
29     Untagged     10.200.1.1/32[V] 0         Se0/1/1     point2point
30     Pop tag      10.233.1.1/32   12869      Et0/0/0     10.200.200.2

[T]    Forwarding through a TSP tunnel.
       View additional tagging info with the 'detail' option
```

You can track traffic in the LFIB only if the traffic is entering the router labeled. If the traffic is entering the router on the head end of the LSP and it is IP traffic, CEF switches it. Therefore, you need to check the CEF table (either the global CEF table or the VRF CEF table). However, in Cisco IOS, the traffic measurement is not enabled by default for CEF. Therefore, you must configure CEF accounting on the router. At that point, the number of packets and bytes switched by the CEF table for a certain destination becomes visible. Example 13-15 shows the CEF accounting.

Example 13-15 *Example of IP CEF Accounting*

```
london(config)#ip cef accounting per-prefix

london#show ip cef vrf cust-one 10.200.1.2 detail
10.200.1.2/32, version 30, epoch 0, cached adjacency to Tunnel1
100 packets, 10000 bytes
  tag information set, all rewrites owned
    local tag: 39
    fast tag rewrite with Tu1, point2point, tags imposed {21 16 28}
  via 10.200.254.4, 0 dependencies, recursive
```

Example 13-15 *Example of IP CEF Accounting (Continued)*

```
    next hop 10.200.254.4, Tunnel1 via 10.200.254.4/32 (Default)
    valid cached adjacency
    tag rewrite with Tu1, point2point, tags imposed {21 16 28}
```

MPLS-Aware Netflow

Useful on certain occasions is the MPLS-aware Netflow feature. MPLS-aware Netflow collects statistics for labeled packets and can report them on a label position in the label stack. You can specify up to three label positions in the label stack to keep track of. The command to enable MPLS-aware Netflow globally is this:

> ip flow-cache mpls label-positions [*label-position-1* [*label-position-2*
>
> [*label-position-3*]]] [mpls-length] [no-ip-fields]

You can specify up to the sixth label in the label stack. A prerequisite for this feature is enabling Netflow on the interface with the command **ip route-cache flow [input]**. To view a snapshot of the MPLS-aware Netflow cache on the router, use the command **show ip cache verbose flow**.

Figure 13-11 shows the six label positions that Netflow can keep track of.

Figure 13-11 *Six Label Positions*

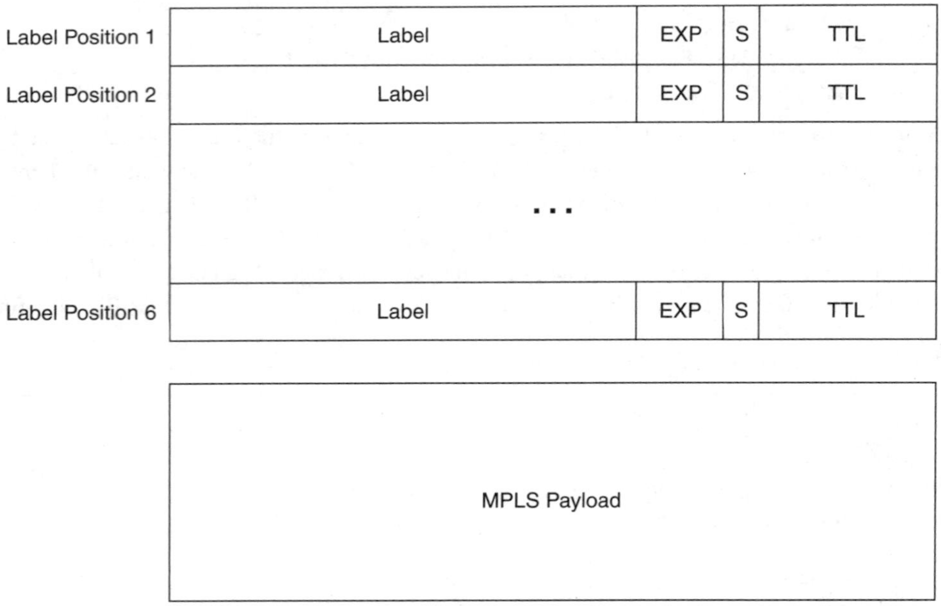

The command is useful for troubleshooting MPLS problems in the data path, particularly on the P routers. You can identify these kinds of problems by enabling **debug mpls packets** on the LSR, but using the **debug** command outside of the lab environment is dangerous. However, you can use the MPLS-aware Netflow feature on any LSR without significantly increasing the load of the CPU. For instance, you can enable MPLS-aware Netflow on any P router between two PE routers and look at the second label. If your network is running MPLS VPN or AToM, the second label is the VPN or AToM label and is otherwise difficult to track on P routers. Netflow can then prove whether the packets with a certain label in the second label position passed through the LSR.

The MPLS-related output shown in the Netflow cache is the label value, the EXP bits, the end-of-stack bit, and—if it is the top label—the label type. The label type can be LDP, VPN, AToM, BGP, or TE tunnel midpoint. Example 13-16 shows the output of the command **show ip cache verbose flow**. The label information is displayed as *Pos:Lbl-Exp-S*. *Pos* is the position, *Lbl* is the label value, *Exp* is the Experimental bits, and *S* is the end-of-stack bit. Between rounded brackets, notice the label type and the prefix associated with the label. If it is an AToM label or a label that is associated with a TE tunnel, the prefix is displayed as 0.0.0.0.

Example 13-16   *Example of MPLS-Aware Netflow*

```
ip flow-cache mpls label-positions  1 2
!
interface Ethernet1/1
 ip address 10.200.200.2 255.255.255.0
 ip route-cache flow input
 mpls ip
!
sydney#show ip cache verbose flow
IP packet size distribution (52385 total packets):
   1-32   64    96   128   160   192   224   256   288   320   352   384   416   448   480
   .000 .008 .000 .991 .000 .000 .000 .000 .000 .000 .000 .000 .000 .000 .000

   512   544   576  1024  1536  2048  2560  3072  3584  4096  4608
   .000 .000 .000 .000 .000 .000 .000 .000 .000 .000 .000

IP Flow Switching Cache, 4456704 bytes
  4 active, 65532 inactive, 84 added
  4840 ager polls, 0 flow alloc failures
  Active flows timeout in 30 minutes
  Inactive flows timeout in 15 seconds
  last clearing of statistics never
Protocol         Total    Flows   Packets Bytes  Packets Active(Sec) Idle(Sec)
--------         Flows    /Sec    /Flow  /Pkt    /Sec    /Flow       /Flow
TCP-BGP             19     0.0        1     50     0.0      0.1        15.3
TCP-other           60     0.0        1     48     0.0      3.2        15.4
Total:              79     0.0        1     49     0.0      2.5        15.4
```

Example 13-16 *Example of MPLS-Aware Netflow (Continued)*

```
SrcIf           SrcIPaddress    DstIf          DstIPaddress    Pr TOS Flgs  Pkts
Port Msk AS                     Port Msk AS    NextHop             B/Pk  Active
Se5/0           0.0.0.0         Se4/0/1        0.0.0.0         00 00  10     5250
0000 /0  0                      0000 /0  0     0.0.0.0                 112 1170.0
Pos:Lbl-Exp-S 1:27-0-1 (ATOM/0.0.0.0)
Se5/0           0.0.0.0         Se4/0/0        0.0.0.0         00 00  10      46K
0000 /0  0                      0000 /0  0     0.0.0.0                 104 1017.0
Pos:Lbl-Exp-S 1:28-0-1 (VPN/10.200.1.2)
Et0/0/1         10.140.100.1    Et0/0/0        10.233.1.1      01 00  10        5
0000 /0  0                      0800 /0  0     0.0.0.0                 100   0.0
Pos:Lbl-Exp-S 1:30-0-1 (BGP/10.233.1.1)
Et0/0/0         10.200.200.2    Et0/0/1        10.140.100.1    01 C0  10        2
0000 /0  0                      0303 /0  0     0.0.0.0                  56   3.0
Pos:Lbl-Exp-S 1:26-6-1 (LDP/10.140.100.1)
Et1/3           10.200.254.3    Et1/1          10.200.244.1    01 00  10        5
0000 /0  0                      0800 /0  0     0.0.0.0                 100   0.0
Pos:Lbl-Exp-S 1:21-0-1 (TE-MIDPT/0.0.0.0)
```

Example 13-17 shows the output of MPLS-aware Netflow monitoring label positions 1, 2, and 3. An example of a labeled packet with one, two, and three labels is shown.

Example 13-17 *Example of One, Two, and Three Reported Labels by MPLS-Aware Netflow*

```
ip flow-cache mpls label-positions 1 2 3 mpls-length

horizon#show ip cache verbose flow
...
SrcIf           SrcIPaddress    DstIf          DstIPaddress    Pr TOS Flgs  Pkts
Port Msk AS                     Port Msk AS    NextHop             B/Pk  Active
Et1/2           10.200.254.3    Et1/1          10.200.254.1    11 C0  10       50
0286 /0  0                      0286 /0  0     0.0.0.0                  66 403.9
Pos:Lbl-Exp-S 1:23-6-1 (TE-MIDPT/0.0.0.0)
Et1/1           10.200.254.1    Et1/2          10.200.254.4    06 C0  18        3
2B0F /0  0                      00B3 /0  0     0.0.0.0                  54   4.5
Pos:Lbl-Exp-S 1:21-6-0 (TE-MIDPT/0.0.0.0) 2:16-6-1
Et1/1           10.1.1.1        Et1/2          10.200.1.2      01 00  10      731
0000 /0  0                      0800 /0  0     0.0.0.0                 112  16.2
Pos:Lbl-Exp-S 1:21-0-0 (TE-MIDPT/0.0.0.0) 2:16-0-0 3:28-0-1
```

MPLS-aware Netflow reports the label type and associated prefix of only the top MPLS label. The reason for this is that this router—on which you configure MPLS-aware Netflow—assigns only the top label. The router has no idea which protocol assigned the other labels. However, when you are troubleshooting the MPLS network, you must know what labels you are expecting in which label position so that you can use MPLS-aware Netflow intelligently.

Summary

In this chapter, you saw how to troubleshoot problems in the forwarding or data path of MPLS networks. Tools such as the well-known traceroute and ping are useful in pinpointing a problem, but you must be aware how to use them and how to interpret the data. This chapter reviewed specific MPLS commands that have a relationship with tracerouting. It covered other typical MPLS issues, such as MTU problems and load balancing of labeled packets. Finally, it explained MPLS-aware Netflow and indicated how it could help you in troubleshooting certain forwarding problems. Chapter 14 covers MPLS operation and maintenance (OAM)-specific tools that you can use to troubleshoot problems in the MPLS network.

Chapter Review Questions

1. What would you configure on the PE routers if you wanted to be able to see the LSRs in the output of the traceroute command from the PE routers, but not the customers performing the traceroute from the CE routers?

2. When is the MPLS TTL not copied to the IP TTL when disposing of the labels? Why?

3. What kind of packets are sent when you traceroute in Cisco IOS?

4. Why does it not make much sense to configure **no mpls ip propagate-ttl** on P routers?

5. How can you verify which outgoing interface is taken when load balancing labeled packets?

6. What information about the labels can MPLS-aware Netflow provide?

7. Which access lists can you associate with the command **debug mpls packets**?

What You Will Learn

By the end of this chapter, you should know and be able to explain the following:

- What MPLS OAM entails

- Why MPLS LSP ping and MPLS LSP traceroute are far more powerful troubleshooting tools than IP ping and IP traceroute

- How IP SLA can perform MPLS network performance measurement

- How Netflow accounting can be used and deployed in MPLS networks

- How SNMP can be used in MPLS networks and how it has been made MPLS VPN aware

CHAPTER 14

MPLS Operation and Maintenance

You can use MPLS Operation and Maintenance (OAM) to detect operational failures, but also for accounting and performance measurement in the MPLS network. Problems on the control plane can be reported by traps or seen by polling the Management Information Base (MIB). This might suffice for IP networks, but it is more difficult to detect the problems that are purely in the data plane when the network is running MPLS. MPLS OAM is a set of protocols that detects problems in the MPLS network more easily and more quickly and keeps track of measurements that are important in networks that have service level agreements (SLAs) with customers or other companies. The goal of MPLS OAM is to detect, report, and fix a problem before a user calls it in.

Requirements of MPLS OAM

The requirements of MPLS OAM are the following:

- Detection and diagnosis of control and data plane defects

- Detection of a defect in a label switched path (LSP)

- OAM packets flowing on the same path as MPLS data traffic

- Path characterization

- Measurement of SLAs

- OAM Interworking

- MIBs

- Accounting

The following sections explain in detail what these requirements entail.

Detection and Diagnosis of Control and Data Plane Defects

Common problems for MPLS networks are packets arriving at a label switching router (LSR) with a specific top label for which the LSR has no forwarding information or incorrect forwarding information. This problem can be detected by the control information that Label Distribution Protocol (LDP), Resource Reservation Protocol (RSVP), IP routing protocols, routing table, label information base (LIB), and label forwarding information base (LFIB) provide. However, the problem only becomes apparent if actual traffic is flowing and fails at some LSR. A more subtle and more difficult-to-detect problem is the one in which the control plane information is correct but the data plane fails. It is possible for the control plane software to behave correctly, with the problem undetected by **show** commands on the router, while the data plane drops or mistreats the packet, which might result in a forwarding failure. For instance, an ASIC that performs the forwarding of labeled packets in hardware on the LSR might treat the TTL value wrongly. In that case, the packets might fail at this LSR or at an LSR that is further downstream. You will see later in this chapter that LSP ping and LSP traceroute are tools that can detect problems in the MPLS control and data planes.

Detection of a Defect in a Label Switched Path (LSP)

Another common problem is the failure of a label advertisement between two LSRs. For instance, the LDP peer neighborship might be down between two LSRs, which causes the packets to be dropped or forwarded without a label stack. For instance, if MPLS transports Layer 2 traffic that becomes unlabeled on a provider (P) router, it is dropped. Similarly, if IPv4 traffic becomes unlabeled, it might be forwarded according to the global routing table. If no route for the destination IP address exists, the packet is dropped. If a routing entry exists, the packet is forwarded. In that case, two things can happen: The packet might actually make it and be forwarded to the destination, or it might be forwarded to the wrong destination. The packet might be dropped later on, or the return packet might be dropped.

Another commonly seen problem in MPLS networks is MTU problems. Because of the added label stack, the size of the packet increases by n times 4 bytes—where n is the number of labels in the label stack. If the control word is present between the label stack and the MPLS payload, another 4 bytes is added. This can cause MTU problems on certain routers, either because they cannot support greater MTU sizes or because of a configuration error. In either case, as long as smaller packets are forwarded, the problem goes undetected. The problem is detected the first time larger packets are transmitted.

In networks that have equal cost multi paths (ECMP), some problems can go unnoticed as long as one path of the ECMP paths is not used. However, as soon as traffic flows across that one failing path, the problem becomes apparent. It is best to detect these problems before a customer calls them in. MPLS OAM was developed with this is mind.

OAM Packets Flowing on the Same Path as MPLS Data Traffic

It is important that the OAM packets follow the same path as the real user data to detect the errors in the data plane of the LSR. Therefore, the MPLS OAM traffic is simple User Datagram Protocol (UDP) traffic and not a special data type that the routers might treat differently. For instance, Internet Control Message Protocol (ICMP) traffic might be forwarded differently on routers than common TCP or UDP traffic. The forwarding in the data plane plays an important role here. Some hardware forwarding is different depending on the type of traffic, or sometimes it is bypassed, with the software forwarding the traffic.

Path Characterization

OAM traffic can determine the path characteristics of the MPLS traffic. These characteristics can include the following:

- Quality of service (QoS) treatment

- Time To Live (TTL) treatment

- Latency

- Jitter

- ECMP behavior

- Maximum transmission unit (MTU) along the path

- Packet loss

It is important when looking at the treatment of traffic along an LSP or traffic belonging to a specific Forwarding Equivalence Class (FEC) that you measure the correct characteristics. It is, for instance, important that voice traffic has a small latency and jitter value along the path, whereas this is not so important for Internet data traffic. An excellent tool to characterize the data path is IP SLA, which is discussed later in this chapter.

Measurement of SLAs

If SLAs apply to the MPLS network, the characteristics of the LSPs should correspond to the predefined SLAs. As such, MPLS OAM should provide a mechanism to measure the characteristics of the LSPs. For SLAs, the latency, jitter, round-trip-time (RTT), and packet loss are important characteristics to measure for each LSP. You can look at MIB information to achieve this, or you can actively measure it by sending probes onto the LSPs. IP SLA can send probes to measure the performance of the network ad hoc or at regular intervals.

OAM Interworking

When you transport Layer 2 frames across the MPLS cloud (AToM), each provider edge (PE) router has attachment circuits (AC). These ACs can have Layer 2 protocols with their own OAM messages and error packets. MPLS OAM must support the translation or mapping of these native Layer 2 protocol OAM messages (or at least a subset of them) into newly defined MPLS OAM messages. In the opposite way, specific MPLS error conditions that affect the pseudowires must be mapped to the native OAM messages of the AC protocols on the PE routers.

MIBs

Management always plays an important role in networking. This is no different for MPLS networks. Management and MIBs play an important role in tracking the status of a network and provide an early warning when things go wrong. Specific MIBs for MPLS have been developed, and new ones are still being worked on. In the light of OAM for MPLS networks, management needs much attention, and its importance is often forgotten or understated.

Accounting

Accounting is important for network measurements and billing purposes. Netflow can provide accounting in Cisco IOS. Netflow has been made MPLS aware to account labeled traffic per LSP and even finer than that, because any label in the label stack can be tracked. Netflow is explained later in this chapter.

Router Alert Option and Router Alert Label

IP packets can have a Router Alert option appended to the IP header. This option is an IP option indicating that the router should inspect the packet further when forwarding the packet, even though the packet is not directly addressed to that router. The transit router for the packet should not just forward the packet by doing an IP lookup, but the router should inspect it further before forwarding it. What this inspection means is not defined and is up to the software implementation on the router. The Router Alert option is an IP option like the Timestamp, Loose Source Route, and Strict Source Route options are. The Router Alert option is defined in RFC 2113. An IP option is encoded as a Type Length Value (TLV). Look at Figure 14-1 to see the Type definition of an IP option.

Figure 14-1 *IP Option Type Definition*

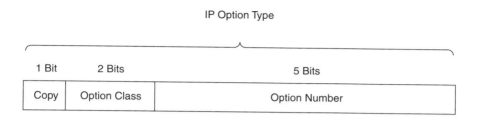

IP Option Type

1 Bit	2 Bits	5 Bits
Copy	Option Class	Option Number

- Copy
  - 0   Do Not Copy
  - 1   Copy To Fragment
- Option Class
  - 0   Datagram Or Network Control
  - 1   Reserved
  - 2   Debugging and Measurement
  - 3   Reserved

Figure 14-2 shows the IP option with the values for the IP Router Alert option.

Figure 14-2 *IP Router Alert Option*

Type	Length	Value
10010100	00000100	2-Octet Value

- IP Option Is Copied To Fragments (COPY =1)
- Option Class = 0
- Option Number = 20
- Length = 4
- Value
  - − 0   Router Shall Examine Packet
  - − 1–65535   Reserved

This Router Alert option works only if the packet is an IP packet. If the packet were labeled and as such forwarded by the LFIB on the LSR, the LSR would not even know that the packet had the Router Alert option present. Of course, you could program the LSR to perform deep packet inspection and always look at the IP header information of labeled packets to determine whether the Router Alert option were present. However, that could lead to a serious forwarding performance impact on the LSR, so it is not the best solution. It might not even be possible to do this in hardware forwarding engines, or it might be too costly. A better solution is to use a special MPLS label as the top label in the label stack of the packets that the LSRs need to examine. This special label is MPLS label 1, which is called the Router Alert label.

Router Alert Label

The Router Alert label has a value of 1, and it can be present anywhere in the label stack except at the bottom. When an LSR receives a packet with label 1 as the top label, it knows that it must further examine the packet. Therefore, the LSR removes label 1 and examines the packet. The LSR then looks at the exposed new top label in the label stack and makes a forwarding decision by looking up this label in the LFIB. This forwarding decision makes the LSR perform a swap, pop, or push operation on the label stack and returns the outgoing interface and next hop for the packet. Before switching the packet out of the LSR, the LSR puts label 1 back as the top label in the label stack and forwards the packet. Therefore, having the Router Alert label as the top label does not influence the forwarding decision made on the packet; it solely indicates that the LSR must examine the packet. On routers that are running Cisco IOS, packets that have the Router Alert label are forwarded in software, which means the hardware forwarding engines are bypassed. The use of the Router Alert label for labeled packets is analogous to the use of the Router Alert option for IP packets.

NOTE   RFC 3032, "MPLS Label Stack Encoding," describes the Router Alert label.

Because the Router Alert label forces the LSR to treat a labeled packet in a different manner than when the labeled packet has no Router Alert label as the top label when forwarding the packet, its use is not directly helpful for MPLS OAM. Remember that one of the requirements was for the MPLS user data traffic and the MPLS OAM traffic to be forwarded in the same way. This is clearly not the case for traffic whose top label is the special label 1. Therefore, the Router Alert label is not used to send the MPLS OAM packets when testing an LSP. It can, however, be used for the return OAM traffic. Because an LSP is unidirectional, MPLS OAM traffic is verifying the LSP in only one direction. This means that the return traffic verifies nothing; it just needs to get back to the source. The return traffic can be sent with the Router Alert option so that it bypasses the hardware forwarding engines and has a better chance of getting back to the source. If the return traffic is labeled, it also has the Router Alert label, so the hardware forwarding engines are bypassed.

OAM Alert Label

In Chapter 3, "Forwarding Labeled Packets," you saw a specific MPLS label called the Operation and Maintenance Alert label that has a value of 14. This label is specified by the ITU-T Recommendation Y.1711 and RFC 3429. You insert this OAM Alert label in the label stack just below the label(s) of the LSP under test. Cisco IOS does not use this special MPLS label anywhere. That is because the introduction of a special label in the label stack can influence the treatment of the packet when being forwarded. An example of this is the case of load balancing labeled packets, where the change in the label stack can introduce a different forwarding behavior. As such, the real user data traffic and the OAM traffic can be forwarded in a different way, rendering the OAM testing useless in some cases. A second example is the use of penultimate hop popping (PHP) in a plain IP-over-MPLS network. In this case, the packet arrives on the egress LSR with just the OAM Alert label in the label stack where otherwise it would arrive without a label stack. None of the OAM techniques discussed in this chapter and used by Cisco IOS uses the OAM Alert label.

MPLS LSP Ping

MPLS LSP ping is the name for an MPLS echo request and MPLS echo reply. Ping is a well-known troubleshooting tool for IP networks that is used to figure out if the object is there. If it is, you see an echo. It is like using SONAR on a submarine. Ping uses ICMP, which was designed to augment the IP protocol because it can signal error conditions (destination unreachable, time exceeded, and so on) and send informational advertisements (redirect, address mask, and so on). Ping uses ICMP to carry echo request and echo reply packets. The echo request packet is sent toward the destination, which should then reply with an echo reply packet. The source receiving the echo reply indicates that the two hosts can see each other on the network level (Layer 3).

Because MPLS cannot work without IP on the network level, you can still use the IP ping when the network is running MPLS. The ping packets are labeled and label-switched throughout the network. Why invent MPLS LSP ping? Well, IP ping is insufficient for verifying the correctness of the MPLS LSP. Although it can verify whether the connectivity is present on the IP level, it does not verify whether the LSP is broken. If you have a plain IP-over-MPLS network and LDP is broken between two LSRs, ping indicates that there is no problem as the echo request makes it to the destination and the echo reply makes it back to the source. Between the two LSRs where the LDP session is broken, the packets are no longer labeled. The ping indicates falsely that everything is okay, when in reality the LSP is broken.

To see that this can lead to useless troubleshooting, imagine that you are switching Any Transport over MPLS (AToM) traffic across that LSP, and the two LSRs with the broken LDP session are P routers in an AToM network. Refer to Figure 14-3 for the network.

Figure 14-3 *Broken LSP in AToM Network*

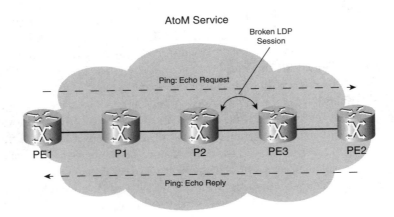

If the LSP is broken, the AToM traffic becomes unlabeled between LSRs P2 and P3. Because those two LSRs do not know how to forward those frames, they are dropped. A ping from PE to PE router across the LSP would be successful, but the AToM traffic would fail. To have a similar protocol to the IP ping protocol indicate specific problems with MPLS LSPs, MPLS LSP ping was invented.

LSPs can break for any number of reasons, while the IP connectivity remains fine. Following are some reasons an LSP could be broken:

- The LDP session is down.

- MPLS is not enabled on an LSR (or one interface).

- The LFIB has a wrong entry for that LSP (wrong in/out label or wrong outgoing next-hop information).

- The software and hardware LFIB have a discrepancy.

For some of these problems, the packets become unlabeled; others are label-switched, but in a wrong way. That is why you need a mechanism to test the LSP end to end and give some helpful feedback when the LSP is broken. When you are troubleshooting the LSP, it is good to know where the LSP is broken and what the error is. MPLS LSP ping detects problems in the forwarding plane, but it also checks the control plane against the information in the data plane.

LSP Ping Protocol Details

LSP ping is similar to IP ping in that it also uses an echo request and echo reply. That is where the similarities stop, though. MPLS LSP ping has different packet formats altogether and returns more troubleshooting information. An MPLS echo request is sent by the sender and tests one particular FEC. The echo request holds the FEC stack indicating which FEC is being tested. The FEC stack can hold one or more labels that the receiver is to verify. The receiver then verifies that the FEC stack on the echo request is the correct one for the FEC. Also, the data plane information for the FEC is verified with the control plane information.

An MPLS echo request is a UDP packet with a destination port of 3503 and a source port chosen by the sender. It has a Router Alert option. To prevent the packet from switching any further as an IP packet if the LSP is broken but the IP path is still fine, the IP TTL of the packet is set to 1 and the destination IP address of the packet is from the range 127.0.0.0/8. The address range 127.0.0.0/8 is for local IP addresses to the host; thus, packets that have a destination IP address from this range should never be seen on the network wires. An LSR never forwards such an IP packet if the LSP is broken, and neither does the egress LSR of the LSP. The egress LSR sends the packet to the UDP software module running on the router listening to UDP port 3503. The source IP address is just a chosen IP address of the sender. Figure 14-4 shows the format of an MPLS echo request.

Figure 14-4 *MPLS Echo Packet Format*

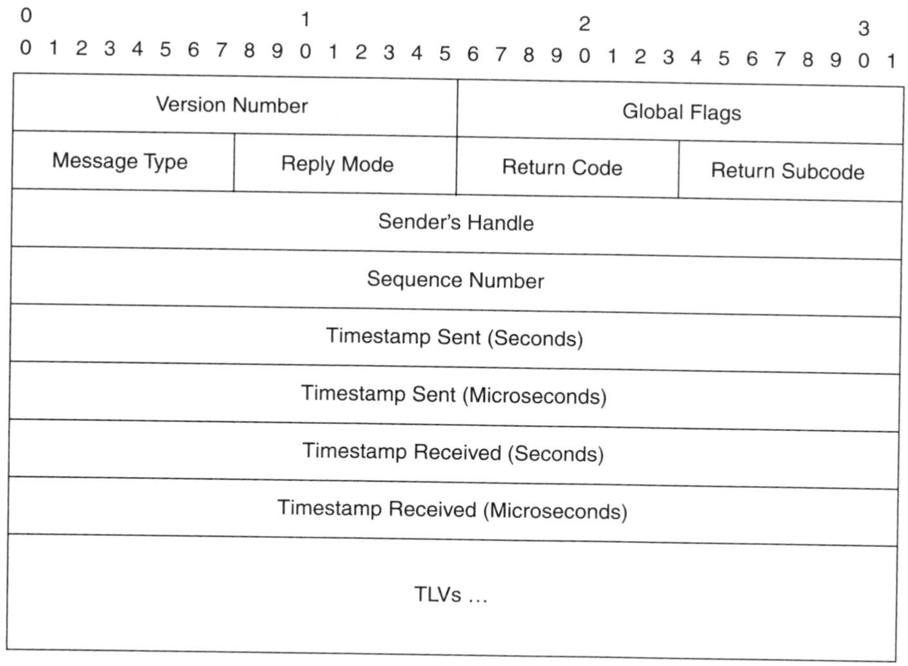

The version number is 1. The Global Flags field currently has only one defined bit. The LSB is the V (Validate FEC Stack) flag. If the V flag is set, the sender wants the receiver to validate the FEC stack. The Message Type is either 1 for an MPLS echo request or 2 for an MPLS echo reply. The Reply mode indicates how the MPLS echo reply should be returned. Four possibilities exist, as you can see in Table 14-1.

Table 14-1   *Reply Mode*

Value	Meaning
1	Do not reply
2	Reply via an IPv4/IPv6 UDP packet
3	Reply via an IPv4/IPv6 UDP packet with Router Alert
4	Reply via an application-level control channel

Reply Mode 1 is to be used only if Echo Replies do not need to be returned. It might be that someone is monitoring the destination by means of a software component to see if the MPLS echo requests make it, so returning the Echo Replies is unnecessary. Reply Mode 2 is the regular reply mode.

Reply Mode 3 is the same as Reply Mode 2, but the echo reply packets are returned with the Router Alert option. As explained in the previous section, you can use this to ensure that the packet has the highest degree of certainty to get back, in the case of forwarding problems along the return path. Reply Mode 4 is a reply mode out of band. Note that MPLS LSP ping tests one LSP. Because LSPs are unidirectional, only the echo requests are testing the MPLS LSP. The echo reply packets are not testing anything anymore; they are simply required to get the information back to the sender. As such, the network does not need to return the echo reply packets along the same path in the opposite direction. The network also does not need to return them labeled. The network can send them back as IP packets.

The Sender's Handle is just that: a handle or number indicating who the sender is. The Sequence Number identifies subsequent echo requests and echo replies sent by the same LSR. The Timestamps are composed of two fields: one in seconds and one in microseconds. The Timestamp Sent indicates the time of day that the sender sent the echo request, and the Timestamp Received indicates the time of day that the receiver received the echo request. For the timestamps to be useful, you need to synchronize the clocks of the sender and receiver. The last fields transport the TLVs.

You can see the possible values of the return code in Table 14-2. RSC refers to the return subcode. The return subcode indicates the stack depth for which the return code is applicable. The stack depth is 1 for the bottom label, 2 for the label above, and so on.

Table 14-2   *Return Codes*

Value	Meaning
0	No return code
1	Malformed echo request received
2	One or more of TLVs misunderstood
3	Replying router is egress for the FEC at stack depth <RSC>
4	Replying router has no mapping for the FEC at stack depth <RSC>
5	Downstream mapping mismatch
6	Upstream interface index unknown
7	Reserved
8	Label-switched at stack depth <RSC>
9	Label-switched but no MPLS forwarding at stack depth <RSC>
10	Mapping for this FEC is not given label at stack depth <RSC>
11	No label entry at stack depth <RSC>
12	Protocol not associated with interface at FEC stack depth <RSC>
13	Premature termination of ping due to label stack shrinking to a single label

The sender always sets the return code to 0. The receiver can set the return code as feedback to the sender of the echo request. If the receiver were indeed the proper egress LSR for the FEC under test, it would return the echo reply packet with a return code of 3. That is the return code you would see if the MPLS ping worked fine. A receiver would know if it were the proper egress LSR by comparing the information in the FEC stack of the echo request with the actual information on the LSR. Return code 8 means that the packet has a label stack indicating that a pop or swap operation is performed and it is okay to forward a labeled packet. A return code of 9 indicates a label operation, but that labeled packets cannot be switched out. A return code of 4 means that the label in the stack is unknown to the LSR. A return code of 5 means that the downstream mapping object provided by the upstream LSR is not what the downstream LSR expected.

NOTE MPLS LSP ping is specified in RFC 4379, "Detecting Multi-Protocol Label Switched (MPLS) Data Plane Failures." The return code values of 6 and 7 had a different meaning in previous versions of the draft leading up to this RFC. Return code 6 meant, "Replying router is one of the downstream routers, and its mapping for this FEC on the received interface is the given label." Return code 7 meant, "Replying router is one of the downstream routers, but its mapping for this FEC is not the given label."

Finally, the MPLS echo packet has TLVs. Table 14-3 lists the various TLVs that can be carried by the MPLS echo packets.

Table 14-3 *TLVs*

Type	Value Field
1	Target FEC Stack
2	Downstream Mapping
3	Pad
4	Not Assigned
5	Vendor Enterprise Number
6	Not Assigned
7	Interface and Label Stack
8	Not Assigned
9	Errored TLVs
10	Reply TOS Byte

The PAD TLV pads the Echo packet up to a certain size. This can be useful if you are testing the MTU of a complete LSP. The echo request packet is then padded up to the size you can specify. The Vendor Enterprise Number allows vendors to privately extend the packets with vendor-specific information. The more interesting TLVs with respect to troubleshooting purposes are the Target FEC Stack TLV, the Downstream Mapping TLV, and the Interface and Label Stack TLV.

Target FEC Stack

An MPLS echo request indicates which FEC is under test with the Target FEC Stack TLV. The Target FEC Stack TLV is a list of sub-TLVs. Each sub-TLV indicates one entry in the label stack.

The first entry in the list corresponds to the top label in the label stack, and so on. Look at Table 14-4 for a list of the sub-TLVs.

Table 14-4   *Target FEC Stack Sub-TLVs*

Type	Meaning
1	LDP IPv4 prefix
2	LDP IPv6 prefix
3	RSVP IPv4 LSP
4	RSVP IPv6 LSP
5	Not Assigned
6	VPN[1] IPv4 prefix
7	VPN IPv6 prefix
8	L2 VPN endpoint
9	"FEC 128" Pseudowire (deprecated)
10	"FEC 128" Pseudowire
11	"FEC 129" Pseudowire
12	BGP[2] labeled IPv4 prefix
13	BGP labeled IPv6 prefix
14	Generic IPv4 prefix
15	Generic IPv6 prefix
16	Nil FEC

[1] VPN = virtual private network

[2] BGP = Border Gateway Protocol

The LDP IPv4 prefix is a FEC whereby LDP has advertised an IPv4 prefix. RSVP IPv4 LSP is a FEC that a traffic engineering (TE) tunnel maps. A virtual private network (VPN) IPv4 prefix is a vpnv4 prefix as advertised by Border Gateway Protocol (BGP). A FEC 128 pseudowire is a FEC used for a virtual circuit (VC) in AToM. Finally, a FEC can be an IPv4 prefix with the label as advertised by BGP. The Target FEC Stack carried by the MPLS echo packet can be composed of any combination of these sub-TLVs. In any case, each sub-TLV indicates what is to be verified. It might be an IPv4 prefix, a vpnv4 prefix, a pseudowire, a TE tunnel, or a BGP labeled IPv4 prefix. Each sub-TLV holds the information to uniquely identify what object is under test. For an IPv4 prefix, this information is only the IPv4 prefix and its prefix length. For a VPN IPv4 prefix, this is the prefix, its prefix length, and the route distinguisher (RD). For a TE tunnel, the following information is included:

- IPv4 tunnel end point address

- Tunnel ID

- Extended tunnel ID

- IPv4 tunnel sender address

- LSP ID

For a pseudowire as used in Cisco IOS, the following information is included:

- Address of sender PE

- Address of remote PE

- VC ID (pseudowire ID)

- VC type (pseudowire type)

The generic IPv4 and IPv6 prefix sub-TLVs are used when the protocol that is advertising the label is unknown. For instance, the sender of the LSP ping in one autonomous system does not know the label protocol for this prefix in the other autonomous system, when the LSP crosses two or more autonomous systems. For these sub-TLVs the information that is carried is the IPv4 or IPv6 prefix and prefix length. The Nil FEC is used for the reserved labels, such as the Router Alert label or the Explicit NULL label. The information that the Nil FEC carries is just the label value.

Downstream Mapping

The Downstream Mapping object is an optional TLV that indicates who the downstream LSR is, which downstream or outgoing label is used, by which protocol the label was assigned, and some Multipath information. The Downstream Mapping object is not used if the replying LSR is the egress LSR for the FEC. As such, this TLV is not used when you perform an MPLS ping on the LSR. However, MPLS echo request and reply packets are also used for MPLS traceroute, and this TLV can provide valuable information there. Refer to the section "MPLS Traceroute in Cisco IOS" for more details. Figure 14-5 shows the Downstream Mapping object.

Figure 14-5 *Downstream Mapping Object*

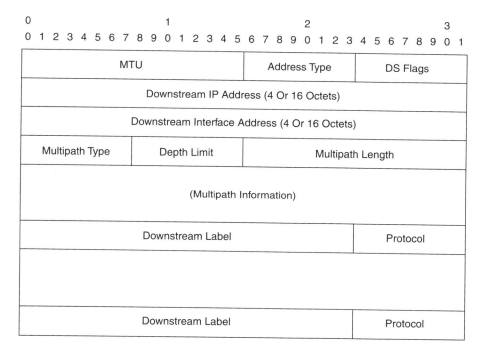

The MTU is the MTU value of the outgoing link. The Address Type indicates an IPv4, an IPv6, or an unnumbered address. The DS Flags field currently has two defined bits. The two least significant bits are the I and N bits. The I bit indicates whether the replying router should include an Interface and Label Stack object in the echo reply packet. If set, the N bit indicates that the packet should be treated as a non-IP packet. This is important when LSRs determine if the packets are IP or non-IP. It could influence the load balancing in the case of ECMP, for example. If the sender uses this echo request to diagnose a non-IP flow, it sets this bit. The downstream IP address is either the IPv4 (4 octets) or IPv6 (16 octets) address of the downstream LSR. This address is the LSR router ID of the downstream LSR or the interface address. The end of the TLV has room for several downstream labels. This set of labels is the stack of labels that is the outgoing label stack on this LSR. If the LSR forwards out this packet, that label stack is pushed onto the packet. Each label has 24 bits per label available. This means that next to the 20 bits for the label value, 4 bits remain. These four bits indicate the Experimental (EXP) bits of the label and the End-of-Stack bit.

The protocol is the protocol that assigned the label. Table 14-5 shows the possible protocols assigning labels.

Table 14-5   *Protocol Values*

Protocol Number	Signaling Protocol
0	Unknown
1	Static
2	BGP
3	LDP
4	RSVP-TE

You use the multipath type and multipath information only for load balancing. The responder LSR of the echo request can indicate how it performs load balancing to the sender of the echo request. You do not use the multipath type and multipath information when performing a regular LSP ping or LSP traceroute. You use it as an extension to detect all possible paths in the case of load balancing. Table 14-6 shows the possible multipath types and the multipath information for each type.

Table 14-6   *Multipath Types*

Key	Type	Multipath Information
0	No multipath	Empty (Multipath Length = 0)
2	IP address	IP addresses
4	IP address range	Low/high address pairs
8	Bit-masked IP address set	IP address prefix and bit mask
9	Bit-masked label set	Label prefix and bit mask

Type 0 means that no load balancing exists, and all packets are forwarded out this one interface. Types 2, 4, 8, and 9 supply specific information on the load balancing hashing that is performed. You can encode the multipath information in different ways according to the multipath type. The multipath information holds the IP addresses and labels of the packets that will use this interface on the responding LSR.

Interface and Label Stack TLV

Figure 14-6 shows the TLV format of the Interface and Label Stack TLV. Its purpose is to notify the sender of the echo request on which interface the packet was received and which labels were in the label stack.

Figure 14-6 *Interface and Label Stack TLV*

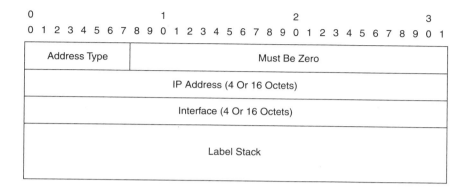

The Address Type indicates an IPv4, an IPv6, or an unnumbered address. The IP Address and Interface indicate where the packet entered the LSR. The label stack is the label stack of the MPLS echo request packet as it was *received* by the receiver.

Errored TLVs TLV

The receiver might send this TLV to the sender of the echo request packet. It holds the TLVs that the receiver found to be unsupported or containing an error.

Reply TOS Byte

The sender of the echo request can use this TLV to tell the receiver to set the TOS byte of the echo reply to a certain value.

LSP Ping Operation

The MPLS echo request for an MPLS ping holds the following information:

- MPLS Echo Header

- Target FEC Stack TLV

- A PAD TLV (optional)

The echo reply holds the following information:

- MPLS Echo Header

- An Error Code TLV (optional)

- A PAD TLV (optional)

- The Target FEC Stack TLV from the echo request (optional)

The MPLS echo request for an MPLS ping is forced into the right FEC at the sender. The LSR does not do this via a simple lookup of the IP address in the CEF table. The destination IP address is from the range 127.0.0.0/8 anyway, so this is not even possible. The destination of the packet is derived from the IP address that the user command or a software component provides. This determines which label stack is pushed onto the packet. The packet is switched out of the LSR according to this information. At a minimum, the TTL of the top label is set to 255. When the receiver receives the MPLS echo request, it must perform the following tasks:

- Check for format errors on the echo request

- Note the interface that the packet was received on

- Note the label stack of the packet as it entered the LSR

- Check whether the label stack on the packet is the same as the one in the Target FEC Stack TLV

- Check whether the LSR is indeed the egress LSR for this FEC

- Check whether the FEC distribution protocol is associated with the incoming interface

- Send an echo reply, unless Reply Mode is 1

If the reply mode is Reply via an IPv4/IPv6 UDP Packet with Router Alert, the IP Router Alert option must be present. This means that if the echo reply is labeled, the packet has the Router Alert label as the top label. The destination IP address of the echo reply packet is the source IP address of the echo request packet. The IP TTL is set to 255, and the UDP ports are 3503.

LSP Verification

LSP verification (LSPV) is the Cisco IOS subsystem that is responsible for anything related to MPLS LSP ping and traceroute. The duties of LSPV include these:

- Encoding and decoding of MPLS echo requests and MPLS echo replies

- Maintaining a database of outstanding MPLS echo requests

- Providing the command-line interface (CLI) for MPLS LSP ping and traceroute

- Interfacing with IP, MPLS, and AToM on the LSR to send and receive the echo requests and replies

- Listening to UDP port 3503

- Handling packets with MPLS TTL expiring and packets with the MPLS Router Alert label

It is important to note that in Cisco IOS, even if MPLS is not enabled on the router, LSPV still functions. The reasoning behind this is that stray packets might still arrive on a router that is not running MPLS because of a malfunctioning on another router. To ensure that echo reply packets are created in response to the erroneously forwarded echo requests, every router in the network should be running LSPV. This ensures that a response is created in the face of problems, rather than no response at all.

On a Cisco router that is running LSPV, the following LSPV debugs are available:

■ Debug mpls lspv error

■ Debug mpls lspv event

■ Debug mpls lspv packet data

■ Debug mpls lspv packet error

■ Debug mpls lspv tlv

MPLS Ping in Cisco IOS

In Cisco IOS, you can send an MPLS LSP ping with the **ping mpls** command. In Example 14-1, you can see that three options exist: IPv4, traffic-eng, and pseudowire. The pseudowire option is for Virtual Circuit Connection Verification (VCCV), which is explained later in this chapter. The IPv4 option is for sending an echo request for an LSP that is bound to an IPv4 prefix. The FEC is chosen by specifying the IPv4 prefix (network and mask). As such, the corresponding label stack for this IPv4 prefix is put on the echo request. The destination IP address of the echo request is by default 127.0.0.1. Therefore, the router uses the target FEC address you type in to figure out which label stack to put on the packet and on which LSP to forward the packet; it is not used as the real destination IP address in the IP header.

Example 14-1 *MPLS LSP Ping*

```
new-york#ping mpls ?
  ipv4        Target specified as an IPv4 address
  pseudowire  Target VC specified as an IPv4 address and VC ID
  traffic-eng Target specified as TE tunnel interface
  <cr>

new-york#ping mpls ipv4 ?
  A.B.C.D  {/nn || A.B.C.D}  Target FEC address with mask

new-york#ping mpls ipv4 10.200.254.4 ?
  A.B.C.D  {/nn || A.B.C.D}  IP prefix and prefix mask
```

continues

Example 14-1 *MPLS LSP Ping (Continued)*

```
new-york#ping mpls ipv4 10.200.254.4/32 ?
  destination              Destination address or address range
  dsmap                    Request dsmap from replying router
  exp                      EXP bits in mpls header
  flags                    Flag options
  force-explicit-null      force an explicit null label to be added
  interval                 Send interval between requests in msec
  output                   Output options
  pad                      Pad TLV pattern
  repeat                   Repeat count
  reply                    Reply mode
  revision                 Echo Packet TLV versioning
  size                     Packet size
  source                   Source specified as an IP address
  sweep                    Sweep range of sizes
  timeout                  Timeout in seconds
  ttl                      Time to live
  verbose                  verbose output mode
  <cr>
```

In Example 14-1, you can see additional options for the LSP ping for a FEC that is bound to an IPv4 address. You can change the destination address from the default 127.0.0.1 to any IP address. The destination IP address in Cisco IOS can be anything, although theoretically it should be from the range 127.0.0.0/8. You can change the experimental bits value with the **exp** keyword. This makes it easy to test the QoS treatment of labeled packets along an LSP. The **pad** keyword allows you to specify the pad filling of the packet. An MPLS LSP ping sends five echo requests by default, but you can change this with the **repeat** keyword. The **size** and **sweep** keywords let you specify the size of the packet. As such, you can test the MTU of the LSP. It is important to note that the router sets the Don't Fragment (DF) bit in the IP header of the echo request packet; that way, an LSR does not fragment the packet if the MTU of a link is not big enough to forward the packet. The Reply mode lets you specify how the echo reply packets are to be sent back. Example 14-2 shows the three possible Reply modes for LSP ping in Cisco IOS.

Example 14-2 *MPLS LSP Ping Reply Modes*

```
new-york#ping mpls ipv4 10.200.254.4/32 reply mode ?
  ipv4           Send reply via IPv4
  no-reply       Send no reply
  router-alert   Send reply via IPv4 UDP with router alert
```

The **ipv4** keyword is the default; it indicates that the echo reply packet is sent back as a regular IPv4 packet. If the return path is actually an LSP, the echo reply packet is sent back as a labeled packet. This is not something that the sender of the MPLS LSP ping can control. The **no-reply** keyword indicates that no echo reply packet should be sent back. It might be that you can account for the packets received in another way, such as by another application running on the receiving LSR. The **router-alert** keyword indicates that the echo reply packet has the IP Router Alert option.

If that echo reply packet is returned labeled, it also has the Router Alert label. This indicates intermediate LSRs to intercept and investigate the packet. The Verbose mode provides additional information. The return code and source IP addresses of the echo reply packets are printed in Verbose mode.

Look at Figure 14-7 for the network topology used for the remainder of this chapter.

Figure 14-7 *Network Topology*

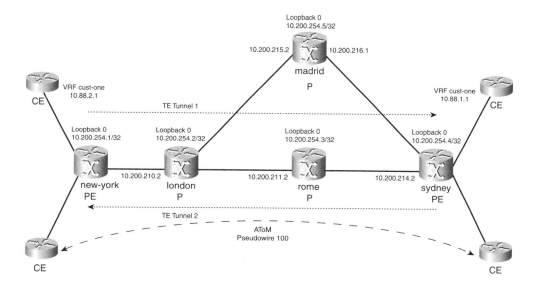

Look at Example 14-3 for a successful MPLS LSP ping. The return code 3 indicates that the egress LSR for the FEC returned the echo reply. The MPLS LSP ping was thus successful, as indicated by the exclamation marks (!).

Example 14-3 *Successful MPLS LSP Ping*

```
new-york#ping mpls ipv4 10.200.254.4/32 verbose
Sending 5, 100-byte MPLS Echos to 10.200.254.4/32,
     timeout is 2 seconds, send interval is 0 msec:

Codes: '!' - success, 'Q' - request not sent, '.' - timeout,
  'L' - labeled output interface, 'B' - unlabeled output interface,
  'D' - DS Map mismatch, 'F' - no FEC mapping, 'f' - FEC mismatch,
  'M' - malformed request, 'm' - unsupported tlvs, 'N' - no label entry,
  'P' - no rx intf label prot, 'p' - premature termination of LSP,
  'R' - transit router, 'I' - unknown upstream index,
  'X' - unknown return code, 'x' - return code 0

Type escape sequence to abort.
!    size 100, reply addr 10.200.214.2, return code 3
```

continues

Example 14-3 *Successful MPLS LSP Ping (Continued)*

```
!    size 100, reply addr 10.200.214.2, return code 3
!    size 100, reply addr 10.200.214.2, return code 3
!    size 100, reply addr 10.200.214.2, return code 3
!    size 100, reply addr 10.200.214.2, return code 3

Success rate is 100 percent (5/5), round-trip min/avg/max = 60/72/92 ms
```

Look at Example 14-4. It shows the same MPLS LSP ping, but with a TTL of 2. Because the egress LSR is three hops away, the TTL of the echo request packets expires at the penultimate hop LSR on the LSP. That LSR sends back an echo reply packet with a return code of 8, indicating that the packet was correctly labeled but that it is not the target router for this FEC (the egress LSR). This is indicated with an L in the output.

Example 14-4 *Early Terminated MPLS LSP Ping*

```
new-york#ping mpls ipv4 10.200.254.4/32 ttl 2 verbose
Sending 5, 100-byte MPLS Echos to 10.200.254.4/32,
     timeout is 2 seconds, send interval is 0 msec:

Codes: '!' - success, 'Q' - request not sent, '.' - timeout,
  'L' - labeled output interface, 'B' - unlabeled output interface,
  'D' - DS Map mismatch, 'F' - no FEC mapping, 'f' - FEC mismatch,
  'M' - malformed request, 'm' - unsupported tlvs, 'N' - no label entry,
  'P' - no rx intf label prot, 'p' - premature termination of LSP,
  'R' - transit router, 'I' - unknown upstream index,
  'X' - unknown return code, 'x' - return code 0

Type escape sequence to abort.
L    size 100, reply addr 10.200.211.2, return code 8
L    size 100, reply addr 10.200.211.2, return code 8
L    size 100, reply addr 10.200.211.2, return code 8
L    size 100, reply addr 10.200.211.2, return code 8
L    size 100, reply addr 10.200.211.2, return code 8

Success rate is 0 percent (0/5)
```

NOTE In Table 14-2, return code 6 is "Upstream Interface Index Unknown." In Cisco IOS versions that use an MPLS OAM implementation released before RFC 4379 was finalized, return code 6 is frequently seen in the output of **ping mpls**. A few implementations were based on the drafts leading up to RFC 4379. In these older Cisco IOS versions, return code 6 meant, "Replying router is one of the 'Downstream Routers,' and its mapping for this FEC on the received interface is the given label." This corresponds to return code 8 in the RFC. You can choose to use a certain revision of the draft/RFC by using the **revision** keyword for the **ping mpls** and **traceroute mpls** commands.

A prerequisite for receiving any echo reply is that the LSR that is receiving the echo request must run LSPV. If the LSR does not run LSPV, it drops all packets that are destined for UDP port 3503, and the MPLS LSP ping times out, which is indicated by a period (.) in the output. The receiver sends an ICMP message "time exceeded" (TTL expired)—because the destination IP address is 127.0.0.1—, but this is not shown in the "ping mpls" output.

You can also use MPLS LSP ping to verify a TE LSP. On the head end router of the TE tunnel, the echo request packet is forced onto the TE tunnel. Note that the TE tunnel does not need to have autoroute announce or forwarding adjacency. Without either configured, the TE tunnel does not actually forward IP traffic. The great advantage of MPLS LSP ping is that it can verify the TE tunnel before it attracts data to be forwarded. Example 14-5 shows an MPLS LSP ping onto a TE tunnel.

Example 14-5 *MPLS LSP Ping onto TE Tunnel*

```
new-york#ping mpls traffic-eng Tunnel 1 verbose
Sending 5, 100-byte MPLS Echos to Tunnel1,
      timeout is 2 seconds, send interval is 0 msec:

Codes: '!' - success, 'Q' - request not sent, '.' - timeout,
  'L' - labeled output interface, 'B' - unlabeled output interface,
  'D' - DS Map mismatch, 'F' - no FEC mapping, 'f' - FEC mismatch,
  'M' - malformed request, 'm' - unsupported tlvs, 'N' - no label entry,
  'P' - no rx intf label prot, 'p' - premature termination of LSP,
  'R' - transit router, 'I' - unknown upstream index,
  'X' - unknown return code, 'x' - return code 0

Type escape sequence to abort.
!    size 100, reply addr 10.200.214.2, return code 3
!    size 100, reply addr 10.200.214.2, return code 3
!    size 100, reply addr 10.200.214.2, return code 3
!    size 100, reply addr 10.200.214.2, return code 3
!    size 100, reply addr 10.200.214.2, return code 3

Success rate is 100 percent (5/5), round-trip min/avg/max = 60/69/88 ms
```

MPLS LSP Traceroute

The goal of traceroute is to test the path, whereas the goal of ping is to test the connectivity. The goal of MPLS LSP traceroute is to test the path of the LSP and verify the control and data plane on every LSR along the path of the LSP.

An MPLS LSP traceroute is nothing more than an MPLS echo request. The difference with MPLS LSP ping is that MPLS LSP traceroute sends several MPLS echo request packets with increasing MPLS TTL. The first MPLS LSP traceroute probe has MPLS TTL 1, and for every subsequent probe, the TTL is increased by 1. One additional TLV that is included with the echo request for

MPLS LSP traceroute is the Downstream Mapping TLV. If an LSR receives the MPLS echo request with TTL 1, it replies to it. If the LSR is not the egress LSR for the FEC and everything checks out fine, the LSR replies as one of the downstream routers. Therefore, it replies with a return code of 8 and the appropriate downstream TLV information (MTU, Address Type, Downstream IP Address, Downstream Interface Address, Multipath information, Downstream Label, and Protocol) filled in. If the LSR is the egress LSR for the FEC, it does not need to fill in the Downstream Mapping information but should reply with a return code of 3.

The MPLS echo request for an MPLS traceroute holds the following information:

- MPLS Echo Header

- Target FEC Stack TLV

- Downstream Mapping TLV

- A PAD TLV (optional)

The echo reply will hold the following information:

- MPLS Echo Header

- An Error Code TLV (optional)

- A PAD TLV (optional)

- Downstream Mapping TLV

The sender of the MPLS LSP traceroute packets copies the received Downstream Mapping TLV into the next echo request he is sending. As such, at each hop, the expected label(s)—as reported by the LSR one hop upstream—is tested with the label(s) on the received packet on the downstream LSR.

MPLS Traceroute in Cisco IOS

Example 14-6 shows an MPLS traceroute example for the IPv4 prefix 10.200.254.4/32, which is three hops away from the router new-york.

Example 14-6 *MPLS LSP Traceroute*

```
new-york#traceroute mpls ?
  ipv4         Target specified as an IPv4 address
  traffic-eng  Target specified as TE tunnel interface
  <cr>
```

Example 14-6   *MPLS LSP Traceroute (Continued)*

```
new-york#traceroute mpls ipv4 ?
  A.B.C.D   {/nn || A.B.C.D}  Target FEC address with mask

new-york#traceroute mpls ipv4 10.200.254.4/32 ?
  destination         Destination address or address range
  exp                 EXP bits in mpls header
  flags               Flag options
  force-explicit-null force an explicit null label to be added
  output              Output options
  reply               Reply mode
  revision            Echo Packet TLV versioning
  source              Source specified as an IP address
  timeout             Timeout in seconds
  ttl                 Maximum time to live
  verbose             verbose output mode
  <cr>

new-york#traceroute mpls ipv4 10.200.254.4/32 verbose
Tracing MPLS Label Switched Path to 10.200.254.4/32, timeout is 2 seconds

Codes: '!' - success, 'Q' - request not sent, '.' - timeout,
  'L' - labeled output interface, 'B' - unlabeled output interface,
  'D' - DS Map mismatch, 'F' - no FEC mapping, 'f' - FEC mismatch,
  'M' - malformed request, 'm' - unsupported tlvs, 'N' - no label entry,
  'P' - no rx intf label prot, 'p' - premature termination of LSP,
  'R' - transit router, 'I' - unknown upstream index,
  'X' - unknown return code, 'x' - return code 0

Type escape sequence to abort.
  0 10.200.210.1 10.200.210.2 MRU 1500 [Labels: 44 Exp: 0]
L 1 10.200.210.2 10.200.211.2 MRU 1500 [Labels: 37 Exp: 0] 100 ms, ret code 8
L 2 10.200.211.2 10.200.214.2 MRU 1504 [Labels: implicit-null Exp: 0] 60 ms, ret code 8
! 3 10.200.214.2 64 ms, ret code 3
```

The MPLS traceroute returns every hop with the code, maximum receive unit (MRU), and the label stack. The code is L when a downstream router sends the echo reply. The label stack holds the label value and the EXP bits value for each label. The first hop is actually hop 0, which is the router sending the echo requests. At hop 0, you can see that the outgoing packet has label 44 as the top label for this FEC (20.200.254.4/32 and EXP = 0) being tested.

Enabling **debug mpls lspv tlv** on the router new-york shows exactly what is sent and received with the echo requests and echo replies for the MPLS traceroute in Example 14-6. Example 14-7 shows this debug output.

Example 14-7 *debug mpls lspv tlv*

```
new-york#debug mpls lspv tlv
tlv debugging is on

new-york#
LSPV: Echo Hdr encode: version 1, msg type 1, reply mode 2, return_code 0, return_subcode
0, sender handle 387CC538, sequence number 1, timestamp sent 15:48:48 UTC Wed Jun 28 2006,
timestamp rcvd 00:00:00 UTC Mon Jan 1 1900
LSPV: Cisco ext subTLV encode: type 1, length 4, tlv revision 0x4
LSPV: LDP IPv4 prefix encode: destaddr 10.200.254.4/32
LSPV: ds map encode: addr_type 1, rtr_id 10.200.210.2, mtu 1500, intf_addr 10.200.210.2,
flags 0x0, hashkey 0, depth limit 0, multipath length 0, [44]
LSPV: Echo Hdr decode: version 1, msg type 2, reply mode 2, return_code 8, return_subcode
1, sender handle 387CC538, sequence number 1, timestamp sent 15:48:48 UTC Wed Jun 28
2006, timestamp rcvd 15:48:48 UTC Wed Jun 28 2006
LSPV: Vendor Private, tlvtype 0xFC00, tlvlength 0xC
LSPV: Cisco ext Enterprise TLV decode
LSPV: type 1, length 4, tlv revision 0x4
LSPV: Downstream Mapping, tlvtype 0x2, tlvlength 0x14
LSPV: Downstream Mapping decode: addr_type 1, rtr_id 10.200.211.2, mtu 1500 intf_addr
10.200.211.2, flags 0x0, hashkey 0, multipath length 0, [37]
LSPV: Echo packet decoded assuming tlv version 4
00:14:31: LSPV: Echo Hdr encode: version 1, msg type 1, reply mode 2, return_code 0,
return_subcode 0, sender handle 387CC538, sequence number 2, timestamp sent 15:48:48 UTC
Wed Jun 28 2006, timestamp rcvd 00:00:00 UTC Mon Jan 1 1900
00:14:31: LSPV: Cisco ext subTLV encode: type 1, length 4, tlv revision 0x4
00:14:31: LSPV: LDP IPv4 prefix encode: destaddr 10.200.254.4/32
00:14:31: LSPV: ds map encode: addr_type 1, rtr_id 10.200.211.2, mtu 1500, intf_addr
10.200.211.2, flags 0x0, hashkey 0, depth limit 0, multipath length 0, [37]
00:14:31: LSPV: Echo Hdr decode: version 1, msg type 2, reply mode 2, return_code 8,
return_subcode 1, sender handle 387CC538, sequence number 2, timestamp sent 15:48:48 UTC
Wed Jun 28 2006, timestamp rcvd 15:48:49 UTC Wed Jun 28 2006
00:14:31: LSPV: Vendor Private, tlvtype 0xFC00, tlvlength 0xC
00:14:31: LSPV: Cisco ext Enterprise TLV decode
00:14:31: LSPV: type 1, length 4, tlv revision 0x4
00:14:31: LSPV: Downstream Mapping, tlvtype 0x2, tlvlength 0x14
00:14:31: LSPV: Downstream Mapping decode: addr_type 1, rtr_id 10.200.214.2, mtu 1504
intf_addr 10.200.214.2, flags 0x0, hashkey 0, multipath length 0, [3]
00:14:31: LSPV: Echo packet decoded assuming tlv version 4
00:14:31: LSPV: Echo Hdr encode: version 1, msg type 1, reply mode 2, return_code 0,
return_subcode 0, sender handle 387CC538, sequence number 3, timestamp sent 15:48:48 UTC
Wed Jun 28 2006, timestamp rcvd 00:00:00 UTC Mon Jan 1 1900
00:14:31: LSPV: Cisco ext subTLV encode: type 1, length 4, tlv revision 0x4
00:14:31: LSPV: LDP IPv4 prefix encode: destaddr 10.200.254.4/32
```

Example 14-7   *debug mpls lspv tlv (Continued)*

```
00:14:31: LSPV: ds map encode: addr_type 1, rtr_id 10.200.214.2, mtu 1504, intf_addr
10.200.214.2, flags 0x0, hashkey 0, depth limit 0, multipath length 0, [3]
00:14:31: LSPV: Echo Hdr decode: version 1, msg type 2, reply mode 2, return_code 3,
return_subcode 1, sender handle 387CC538, sequence number 3, timestamp sent 15:48:48 UTC
Wed Jun 28 2006, timestamp rcvd 15:48:48 UTC Wed Jun 28 2006
00:14:31: LSPV: Vendor Private, tlvtype 0xFC00, tlvlength 0xC
00:14:31: LSPV: Cisco ext Enterprise TLV decode
00:14:31: LSPV: type 1, length 4, tlv revision 0x4
00:14:31: LSPV: Echo packet decoded assuming tlv version 4
```

Each time you see `encode`, it means that this router builds the echo request to be sent. Each time you see `decode`, it means that this router is decoding a received echo reply. Therefore, the router new-york first sends an echo request with message type 1 and reply mode 2 `Reply via an IPv4/IPv6 UDP packet`. It has the Target FEC Stack 10.200.254.4/32 and a Downstream Mapping TLV (see `ds map encode`) with Router ID 10.200.210.2, MTU 1500, interface address 10.200.210.2, and label 44. These addresses are on the next-hop router london, and label 44 is the outgoing label for this LSP on router new-york. The echo reply received (message type 2 and reply mode 2) from the router london indicates a return code of 8. It holds a Downstream Mapping TLV (see `ds map decode`) with label 37. Router new-york then sends the second echo request with this Downstream Mapping TLV included. The echo reply for this echo request has return code 8 again and a new Downstream Mapping TLV with label 3, indicating the implicit NULL label. Router new-york sends the third echo request with this received Downstream Mapping TLV from the second-hop LSR. The third LSR responds with an echo reply with return code 3, indicating that it is the egress LSR for this FEC. The echo reply from the egress LSR does not hold a Downstream Mapping TLV.

That MPLS LSP ping can indicate a problem while IP ping cannot is shown in the next example. Router rome has just been taken offline. The traffic from router new-york to router sydney should go via router madrid. However, a problem exists, as you can see in Example 14-8.

Example 14-8   *MPLS LSP Failing*

```
new-york#ping 10.200.254.4

Type escape sequence to abort.
Sending 5, 100-byte ICMP Echos to 10.200.254.4, timeout is 2 seconds:
!!!!!
Success rate is 100 percent (5/5), round-trip min/avg/max = 20/24/32 ms

new-york#traceroute 10.200.254.4

Type escape sequence to abort.
Tracing the route to 10.200.254.4
```

continues

Example 14-8 *MPLS LSP Failing (Continued)*

```
  1 10.200.210.2 [MPLS: Label 44 Exp 0] 20 msec 20 msec 32 msec
  2 10.200.215.2 20 msec 20 msec 20 msec
  3 10.200.216.2 32 msec *  20 msec

new-york#ping mpls ipv4 10.200.254.4/32 verbose
Sending 5, 100-byte MPLS Echos to 10.200.254.4/32,
      timeout is 2 seconds, send interval is 0 msec:

Codes: '!' - success, 'Q' - request not sent, '.' - timeout,
  'L' - labeled output interface, 'B' - unlabeled output interface,
  'D' - DS Map mismatch, 'F' - no FEC mapping, 'f' - FEC mismatch,
  'M' - malformed request, 'm' - unsupported tlvs, 'N' - no label entry,
  'P' - no rx intf label prot, 'p' - premature termination of LSP,
  'R' - transit router, 'I' - unknown upstream index,
  'X' - unknown return code, 'x' - return code 0

Type escape sequence to abort.
B    size 100, reply addr 10.200.210.2, return code 9
B    size 100, reply addr 10.200.210.2, return code 9
B    size 100, reply addr 10.200.210.2, return code 9
B    size 100, reply addr 10.200.210.2, return code 9
B    size 100, reply addr 10.200.210.2, return code 9

Success rate is 0 percent (0/5)

new-york#traceroute mpls ipv4 10.200.254.4/32 verbose
Tracing MPLS Label Switched Path to 10.200.254.4/32, timeout is 2 seconds

Codes: '!' - success, 'Q' - request not sent, '.' - timeout,
  'L' - labeled output interface, 'B' - unlabeled output interface,
  'D' - DS Map mismatch, 'F' - no FEC mapping, 'f' - FEC mismatch,
  'M' - malformed request, 'm' - unsupported tlvs, 'N' - no label entry,
  'P' - no rx intf label prot, 'p' - premature termination of LSP,
  'R' - transit router, 'I' - unknown upstream index,
  'X' - unknown return code, 'x' - return code 0

Type escape sequence to abort.
  0 10.200.210.1 10.200.210.2 MRU 1500 [Labels: 44 Exp: 0]
B 1 10.200.210.2 10.200.215.2 MRU 1504 [No Label] 80 ms, ret code 9
B 2 10.200.210.2 10.200.215.2 MRU 1504 [No Label] 72 ms, ret code 9
B 3 10.200.210.2 10.200.215.2 MRU 1504 [No Label] 88 ms, ret code 9
...
B 30 10.200.210.2 10.200.215.2 MRU 1504 [No Label] 80 ms, ret code 9
```

As you can see, the problem is at the first hop, at router london. It returns no outgoing label. It turns out that the cause of the problem is on the router madrid, which advertised the prefix 10.200.254.4/32 with no label to router london.

Router Alert Label

When an MPLS LSP ping or traceroute is issued, the echo request has the IP Router Alert option on it. The echo reply does not have it, by default. When you use the command **ping mpls** or **traceroute mpls** with the keyword **reply mode router-alert**, the echo reply has the IP Router Alert option. If the return path is an LSP, the echo reply is labeled and has the top label 1 (the Router Alert label. The label 1 ensures that the packet is inspected at each LSR. The LSR at each hop removes the Router Alert label, the LSR makes a forwarding decision on the label underneath, the LSR performs a label operation, the LSR pushes the Router Alert label onto the label stack again, and the LSR forwards the packet. Figure 14-8 shows an example where a P router has a hardware forwarding error. The LFIB entry in hardware is wrong for the echo reply packet on the router P2. The echo reply packet is erroneously forwarded to router P4 instead of router P1. As such, the echo reply packet does not make it back to router PE1. The user is unsure whether it was the echo request packet or the echo reply packet that did not make it. If the echo reply packet has the Router Alert label in the label stack, the hardware on P2 does not forward the packet; it is forwarded correctly to router P1 and reaches PE1.

Figure 14-8 *Echo Reply with Router Alert Label*

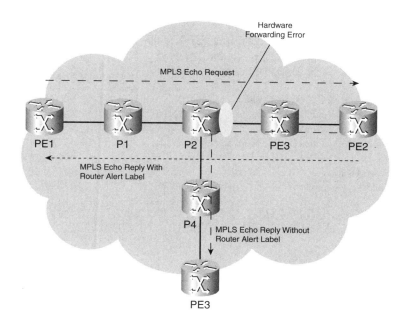

Example 14-9 shows the output of **debug mpls packet** for the echo Reply packet, with the Router Alert Label as the top label.

Example 14-9   *MPLS LSP Ping with Reply Mode Router Alert*

```
00:01:39: MPLS: Se4/0: recvd: CoS=6, TTL=254, Label(s)=1/24
00:01:39: MPLS: Et3/1: xmit: CoS=6, TTL=253, Label(s)=1/26
```

Load Balancing

The paths london-rome-sydney and london-madrid-sydney are made equal cost. When you are sending traffic with the same source and same destination IP address from new-york to sydney, all traffic takes the same path. At router london, all this traffic is forwarded out onto only one of the two possible paths. That is because of the load-balancing treatment of labeled packets in Cisco IOS. The default behavior in Cisco IOS is to look at the IP header underneath the label stack and use the same hashing algorithm as CEF to determine the load balancing. Because the default is CEF per destination load balancing, all traffic that has the same pair of source and destination IP address is switched out of the LSR onto the same path. With MPLS echo request, the default destination IP address is 127.0.0.1 in Cisco IOS. To determine the correct functioning of all possible paths on the LSRs, use different destination IP addresses. An easy way to use different destination IP addresses in the echo requests is to specify a range. Look at Example 14-10, where subsequent echo requests are sent out with a destination IP address from the range 127.0.0.1 to 127.0.0.10.

Example 14-10   *MPLS LSP Ping with Destination Range*

```
new-york#ping mpls ipv4 10.200.254.4/32 destination 127.0.0.1 127.0.0.10 repeat 1
Sending 1, 100-byte MPLS Echos to 10.200.254.4/32,
     timeout is 2 seconds, send interval is 0 msec:

Codes: '!' - success, 'Q' - request not sent, '.' - timeout,
  'L' - labeled output interface, 'B' - unlabeled output interface,
  'D' - DS Map mismatch, 'F' - no FEC mapping, 'f' - FEC mismatch,
  'M' - malformed request, 'm' - unsupported tlvs, 'N' - no label entry,
  'P' - no rx intf label prot, 'p' - premature termination of LSP,
  'R' - transit router, 'I' - unknown upstream index,
  'X' - unknown return code, 'x' - return code 0

Type escape sequence to abort.
Destination address 127.0.0.1
!
Destination address 127.0.0.2
...
Destination address 127.0.0.10
!
```

Example 14-10   *MPLS LSP Ping with Destination Range (Continued)*

```
Success rate is 100 percent (10/10), round-trip min/avg/max = 60/82/128 ms

new-york#ping mpls ipv4 10.200.254.4/32 destination 127.0.0.1 verbose
Sending 5, 100-byte MPLS Echos to 10.200.254.4/32,
      timeout is 2 seconds, send interval is 0 msec:

Codes: '!' - success, 'Q' - request not sent, '.' - timeout,
  'L' - labeled output interface, 'B' - unlabeled output interface,
  'D' - DS Map mismatch, 'F' - no FEC mapping, 'f' - FEC mismatch,
  'M' - malformed request, 'm' - unsupported tlvs, 'N' - no label entry,
  'P' - no rx intf label prot, 'p' - premature termination of LSP,
  'R' - transit router, 'I' - unknown upstream index,
  'X' - unknown return code, 'x' - return code 0

Type escape sequence to abort.
!    size 100, reply addr 10.200.214.2, return code 3
!    size 100, reply addr 10.200.214.2, return code 3
!    size 100, reply addr 10.200.214.2, return code 3
!    size 100, reply addr 10.200.214.2, return code 3
!    size 100, reply addr 10.200.214.2, return code 3

Success rate is 100 percent (5/5), round-trip min/avg/max = 60/68/80 ms

new-york#ping mpls ipv4 10.200.254.4/32 destination 127.0.0.4 verbose
Sending 5, 100-byte MPLS Echos to 10.200.254.4/32,
      timeout is 2 seconds, send interval is 0 msec:

Codes: '!' - success, 'Q' - request not sent, '.' - timeout,
  'L' - labeled output interface, 'B' - unlabeled output interface,
  'D' - DS Map mismatch, 'F' - no FEC mapping, 'f' - FEC mismatch,
  'M' - malformed request, 'm' - unsupported tlvs, 'N' - no label entry,
  'P' - no rx intf label prot, 'p' - premature termination of LSP,
  'R' - transit router, 'I' - unknown upstream index,
  'X' - unknown return code, 'x' - return code 0

Type escape sequence to abort.
!    size 100, reply addr 10.200.216.2, return code 3
!    size 100, reply addr 10.200.216.2, return code 3
!    size 100, reply addr 10.200.216.2, return code 3
!    size 100, reply addr 10.200.216.2, return code 3
!    size 100, reply addr 10.200.216.2, return code 3

Success rate is 100 percent (5/5), round-trip min/avg/max = 60/62/72 ms
```

You can see that changing the destination IP address from 127.0.0.1 to 127.0.0.4 changes the path taken for the echo request. The first packet is received on the interface with IP address 10.200.214.2 on LSR sydney, whereas the second echo request is received on the interface with IP address 10.200.216.2.

MPLS traceroute with the destination range shows you the different paths taken depending on the destination IP address. You can see that two different paths are discovered in Example 14-11.

Example 14-11 *MPLS LSP Traceroute with Destination Range*

```
new-york#traceroute mpls ipv4 10.200.254.4/32 destination 127.0.0.1 127.0.0.10
Tracing MPLS Label Switched Path to 10.200.254.4/32, timeout is 2 seconds

Codes: '!' - success, 'Q' - request not sent, '.' - timeout,
  'L' - labeled output interface, 'B' - unlabeled output interface,
  'D' - DS Map mismatch, 'F' - no FEC mapping, 'f' - FEC mismatch,
  'M' - malformed request, 'm' - unsupported tlvs, 'N' - no label entry,
  'P' - no rx intf label prot, 'p' - premature termination of LSP,
  'R' - transit router, 'I' - unknown upstream index,
  'X' - unknown return code, 'x' - return code 0

Type escape sequence to abort.
Destination address 127.0.0.1
  0 10.200.210.1 MRU 1500 [Labels: 44 Exp: 0]
I 1 10.200.210.2 MRU 1500 [Labels: 37 Exp: 0] 68 ms
I 2 10.200.211.2 MRU 1504 [Labels: implicit-null Exp: 0] 100 ms
! 3 10.200.214.2 80 ms
...
Destination address 127.0.0.4
  0 10.200.210.1 MRU 1500 [Labels: 44 Exp: 0]
I 1 10.200.210.2 MRU 1500 [Labels: 41 Exp: 0] 80 ms
I 2 10.200.215.2 MRU 1504 [Labels: implicit-null Exp: 0] 60 ms
! 3 10.200.216.2 68 ms
...
Destination address 127.0.0.10
  0 10.200.210.1 MRU 1500 [Labels: 44 Exp: 0]
I 1 10.200.210.2 MRU 1500 [Labels: 37 Exp: 0] 80 ms
I 2 10.200.211.2 MRU 1504 [Labels: implicit-null Exp: 0] 68 ms
! 3 10.200.214.2 92 ms
```

The first probe (destination IP address 127.0.0.1) of the MPLS LSP traceroute takes the path london-rome-sydney, whereas the second probe (destination IP address 127.0.0.4) takes the path london-madrid-sydney.

VCCV

VCCV has been specified to test and verify the data plane of pseudowires. VCCV entails procedures to create a control channel between the PE routers that provide the AToM service. The network layer might actually be MPLS, L2TPv3, or IP. Because this book covers only MPLS, it hereafter deals only with MPLS as the network layer when looking at VCCV. If MPLS is the network layer, VCCV re-uses MPLS LSP ping to verify the connectivity of pseudowires. VCCV creates a control channel between PE routers whereby the VCCV packets are sent across as IP packets. You can use three kinds of control channels:

- Inband VCCV

- Out-of-band VCCV

- TTL expiry VCCV

The first method uses the inband VCCV. Packets on the inband VCCV carry a control word. AToM data can carry a control word between the label stack and the MPLS payload. The first nibble of that control word is then 0000. For the OAM packets on the control channel, however, the first nibble of the control word is 0001. The control word then acts as the payload identifier (or protocol ID field). The protocol identifier is 0x21 for IPv4 or 0x57 for IPv6 packets. However, the presence of the control word is not enforced, so this option is not always possible.

The second method uses the out-of-band VCCV. The out-of-band VCCV does not rely on the presence of the control word but rather on the presence of the Router Alert label immediately above the VC label. The problem with this approach is that implementations that determine the load balancing decision based on a label at some depth in the label stack might alter that decision because of the presence of the label with value 1. If the AToM data traffic and the AToM OAM traffic—the VCCV traffic—take a different path, the testing is not really valid.

The third and last method uses TTL expiry. In essence, the TTL value of the VC label is set to 1 so that the TTL of the labeled packet expires at the egress PE router, and that LSR has to inspect the packet because it will be further processed. However, the TTL of the VC label might be overwritten when the tunnel label is popped off. Therefore, the third method is not advisable. The first method is the one that Cisco IOS uses.

> **NOTE** Cisco IOS does not overwrite the TTL value of 1 in the VC label when the tunnel label is popped off at the penultimate hop LSR.

VCCV uses the MPLS LSP ping packet header and TLVs. The Target FEC Stack TLV is used; it indicates a pseudowire. FEC 128 Pseudowire (new) is used for VCCV in Cisco IOS.

The capability to support a control channel and the type of that channel are signaled between PE routers. This is done by a VCCV parameter TLV in a VC FEC Interface TLV for LDP. LDP is the signaling protocol between PE routers for AToM. The VCCV Parameter TLV holds a Control Channel (CC) Type and a Control Verification (CV) Type. The CC indicates any of the following:

■ A control word with the first nibble being 0001 and a payload identifier

■ The MPLS Router Alert label

■ A VC label with TTL set to 1

The CV Type indicates any of the following:

■ ICMP ping

■ LSP ping

■ Bidirectional Forwarding Detection

■ VCCV uses ICMP ping when the network protocol is IP or L2TPv3. VCCV uses LSP ping when the network protocol is MPLS, as it is for AToM. Finally, VCCV can use Bidirectional Forwarding Detection (BFD)—a lightweight protocol that detects connectivity failures between platforms—to verify the session between the two PE routers. BFD can be used for any of the three network protocols.

Cisco IOS uses the first method when sending AToM VCCV packets, the one with the control word with the first nibble being 0001 and a payload identifier. Look at Example 14-12 for a **ping mpls pseudowire** (or a VCCV) example in Cisco IOS.

Example 14-12 *MPLS Ping for VCCV*

```
new-york#ping mpls pseudowire 10.200.254.4 100 verbose repeat 1
Sending 1, 100-byte MPLS Echos to 10.200.254.4,
      timeout is 2 seconds, send interval is 0 msec:

Codes: '!' - success, 'Q' - request not sent, '.' - timeout,
  'L' - labeled output interface, 'B' - unlabeled output interface,
  'D' - DS Map mismatch, 'F' - no FEC mapping, 'f' - FEC mismatch,
  'M' - malformed request, 'm' - unsupported tlvs, 'N' - no label entry,
  'P' - no rx intf label prot, 'p' - premature termination of LSP,
  'R' - transit router, 'I' - unknown upstream index,
  'X' - unknown return code, 'x' - return code 0

Type escape sequence to abort.
!    size 100, reply addr 10.200.214.2, return code 3
```

Example 14-12 *MPLS Ping for VCCV (Continued)*

```
Success rate is 100 percent (1/1), round-trip min/avg/max = 68/68/68 ms

new-york#
01:12:08: LSPV: Echo Hdr encode: version 1, msg type 1, reply mode 2, return_code 0,
return_subcode 0, sender handle 1333CD0B, sequence number 1, timestamp sent 09:03:04 UTC
Tue Jun 27 2006, timestamp rcvd 00:00:00 UTC Mon Jan 1 1900
01:12:08: LSPV: Cisco ext subTLV encode: type 1, length 4, tlv revision 0x4
01:12:08: LSPV: FEC 128 Pseudowire (new) encode: sender addr 10.200.254.1, remote addr
10.200.254.4, vcid 100, vctype 6
01:12:08: LSPV: Echo Hdr decode: version 1, msg type 2, reply mode 2, return_code 3,
return_subcode 1, sender handle 1333CD0B, sequence number 1, timestamp sent 09:03:04 UTC
Tue Jun 27 2006, timestamp rcvd 09:03:03 UTC Tue Jun 27 2006
01:12:08: LSPV: Vendor Private, tlvtype 0xFC00, tlvlength 0xC
01:12:08: LSPV: Cisco ext Enterprise TLV decode
01:12:08: LSPV: type 1, length 4, tlv revision 0x4
01:12:08: LSPV: Echo packet decoded assuming tlv version 4
```

The Target FEC Stack indicates a pseudowire. The sender IP address is 10.200.254.1, and the remote PE address is 10.200.254.4. The VCID is 100, and the VC Type is 6, which indicates an encapsulation type of HDLC.

Example 14-13 shows an intermediate router with the output of **debug mpls packet**. The AToM packet now has a control word (CW) with value 0x10000021. The first nibble is thus 0001, and the payload identifier is 0x21, which indicates IPv4.

Example 14-13 *Debug MPLS Packet*

```
MPLS turbo: Et0/1/3: rx: Len 130 Stack {21 0 255} {52 0 255} CW {0x10000021}
MPLS turbo: PO5/0/0: tx: Len 120 Stack {18 0 254} {52 0 255} CW {0x10000021}
```

It is important to note that the pseudowire is tested in only one direction. The VCCV traffic in the to direction is on the pseudowire, but the traffic in the from or return direction is not. That means that in a typical AToM network, where the top label is the LDP derived label and the second label is the AToM VC label, the VCCV packets have two labels in the to direction but only one label in the return direction.

In Cisco IOS, VCCV capabilities that are exchanged between PE routers indicate which Control Channel Type is being used. Cisco IOS advertises both Type 1 and Type 2. Type 1 (inband method) is the usage of the control word with the protocol ID field. Type 2 (out-of-band method) is the usage of the MPLS Router Alert label above the VC label. As you can see in Example 14-14, Types 1 and 2 are signaled by LDP between the AToM-capable PE routers. Cisco IOS signals that both types are understood, but it only sends AToM VCCV packets with the Type 1 method.

Example 14-14 *VCCV Capabilities*

```
new-york#show mpls l2transport binding 100
   Destination Address: 10.200.254.4,  VC ID: 100
    Local Label:  72
         Cbit: 1,    VC Type: HDLC,    GroupID: 0
         MTU: 1500,    Interface Desc: n/a
         VCCV: CC Type: CW [1], RA [2]
               CV Type: LSPV [2]
    Remote Label: 47
         Cbit: 1,    VC Type: HDLC,    GroupID: 0
         MTU: 1500,    Interface Desc: n/a
         VCCV: CC Type: CW [1], RA [2]
               CV Type: LSPV [2]
```

You can use VCCV as a diagnostic tool. In that case, the VCCV packets are sent only when the user types the command **ping mpls pseudowire** in Cisco IOS CLI. You can also use VCCV as a fault detection tool, if the VCCV packets are periodically sent under the control of a specific software component.

IP Service Level Agreement

The Cisco IP Service Level Agreement (IP SLA) is a network performance measurement tool that is embedded in Cisco IOS. IP SLA allows the network operator to monitor the network performance-wise and see if the SLAs are adhered to. The network characteristics that you can monitor include jitter, one-way delay, RTT, and packet loss. These measurements can be done per class-of-service. IP SLA measures the network by sending periodic probes. The probes can be various protocol packets, such as ICMP, UDP, TCP, HTTP, Domain Name System (DNS), FTP, DHCP, and so on. The measurement of jitter and RTT can be particularly important if the network has Voice-over-IP (VoIP) traffic, because this type of traffic requires a small jitter value. You can also use IP SLA as a troubleshooting tool, because it can gather measurement information from the network in real-time throughout the network. As such, the network operator can pinpoint the problem with greater speed than when no IP SLA is present.

> **NOTE**   IP SLA was formerly known as Cisco Service Assurance Agent (SAA).

IP SLA requires an IP SLA source and a destination device to work. The source device is always a Cisco router, but the destination device does not need to be; it can be any IP host. However, you can gather the most useful information if the destination device is a Cisco router that acts as an IP

SLA responder. The IP SLA performance statistics are also available via SNMP through the Response Time Monitor MIB (CISCO-RTTMON-MIB).

In Example 14-15, IP SLA is enabled on two customer edge (CE) routers: new-york-ce and sydney-ce. Two types of IP SLAs are monitored by configuring two probes: rtr 1 and rtr 2. The router new-york-ce is the source, and sydney-ce is the destination. Rtr 1 and rtr 2 are configured on new-york-ce. Rtr 1 is simply ICMP traffic, so the destination does not need to be a responder. However, rtr 2 is measuring jitter with UDP packets. For this, the destination must be a responder.

Example 14-15 *Configuration of IP SLA Source*

```
!
hostname new-york-ce
!
rtr 1
 type echo protocol ipIcmpEcho 10.88.1.1 source-ipaddr 10.88.2.1
 request-data-size 1000
 frequency 10
rtr schedule 1 start-time now
rtr 2
 type jitter dest-ipaddr 10.88.1.1 dest-port 5000
 request-data-size 400
rtr schedule 2 start-time now
!
```

Example 14-16 shows the needed configuration to enable a Cisco router to be an IP SLA responder.

Example 14-16 *Configuration of IP SLA Destination*

```
!
hostname sydney-ce
!
rtr responder
!
```

> **NOTE**   The Cisco IOS IP SLA commands start with rtr, because Response Time Reporter (RTR) was the original name of IP SLA.

Example 14-17 shows the IP SLA statistics collected by the new-york-ce router for rtr 1 and rtr 2.

Example 14-17 *show rtr collection-statistics*

```
new-york-ce#show rtr collection-statistics
Entry number: 1
Start Time Index: 13:19:29.166 UTC Wed Jan 12 2005
Number of successful operations: 59
Number of operations over threshold: 0
Number of failed operations due to a Disconnect: 0
Number of failed operations due to a Timeout: 0
Number of failed operations due to a Busy: 0
Number of failed operations due to a No Connection: 0
Number of failed operations due to an Internal Error: 0
Number of failed operations due to a Sequence Error: 0
Number of failed operations due to a Verify Error: 0
RTT Values:
RTTAvg: 271      RTTMin: 271      RTTMax: 275
NumOfRTT: 59     RTTSum: 16004    RTTSum2: 4341176

Entry number: 2
Start Time Index: 13:19:29.535 UTC Wed Jan 12 2005
Number of successful operations: 10
Number of operations over threshold: 0
Number of failed operations due to a Disconnect: 0
Number of failed operations due to a Timeout: 0
Number of failed operations due to a Busy: 0
Number of failed operations due to a No Connection: 0
Number of failed operations due to an Internal Error: 0
Number of failed operations due to a Sequence Error: 0
Number of failed operations due to a Verify Error: 0
RTT Values:
NumOfRTT: 100    RTTAvg: 150      RTTMin: 115      RTTMax: 185
RTTSum: 15009    RTTSum2: 2297675
Packet Loss Values:
PacketLossSD: 0 PacketLossDS: 0
PacketOutOfSequence: 0  PacketMIA: 0    PacketLateArrival: 0
InternalError: 0        Busies: 0
Jitter Values:
MinOfPositivesSD: 6      MaxOfPositivesSD: 11
NumOfPositivesSD: 90     SumOfPositivesSD: 677    Sum2PositivesSD: 5167
MinOfNegativesSD: 0      MaxOfNegativesSD: 0
NumOfNegativesSD: 0      SumOfNegativesSD: 0      Sum2NegativesSD: 0
MinOfPositivesDS: 1      MaxOfPositivesDS: 1
NumOfPositivesDS: 18     SumOfPositivesDS: 18     Sum2PositivesDS: 18
MinOfNegativesDS: 1      MaxOfNegativesDS: 1
NumOfNegativesDS: 18     SumOfNegativesDS: 18     Sum2NegativesDS: 18
Interarrival jitterout: 0       Interarrival jitterin: 0
One Way Values:
```

Example 14-17   *show rtr collection-statistics (Continued)*

```
NumOfOW: 0
OWMinSD: 0      OWMaxSD: 0      OWSumSD: 0      OWSum2SD: 0
OWMinDS: 0      OWMaxDS: 0      OWSumDS: 0      OWSum2DS: 0
```

The `MinOfPositivesSD` parameter represents the smallest positive jitter from source to destination. The `MaxOfPositivesDS` parameter represents the biggest positive jitter from destination to source and so on.

VRF-Aware IP SLA

IP SLA has been made VRF aware. This means that it can run inside a VRF on PE routers. Therefore, you can use IP SLA to measure the network performance inside the VPN from the PE routers. IP SLA can, for instance, measure the RTT between PE routers inside the customer VRF. From the PE router, the IP SLA probes are forwarded using the VRF routing table. Equally, the IP SLA can run on multi-VRF CE routers. To make IP SLA run over MPLS VPN, you must put the rtr probe into the correct VRF. Look at Figure 14-9 to see a network in which the IP SLA source has been put on the PE router. You can put the IP SLA in multiple VRF instances and measure the network performance toward the remote CE routers or the PE routers if you put the IP SLA responder in the appropriate VRF.

Figure 14-9   *IP SLA for MPLS VPN*

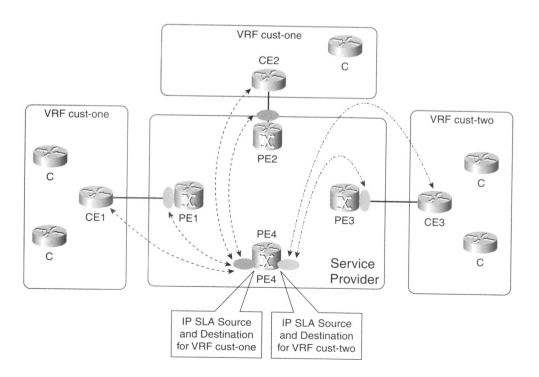

In Example 14-18, the rtr 1 probe has been put in VRF cust-one.

Example 14-18 *IP SLA for a VRF*

```
!
rtr 1
 type jitter dest-ipaddr 10.10.100.1 dest-port 5000 source-ipaddr 10.11.11.1
 vrf cust-one
 request-data-size 100
rtr schedule 1 start-time now
!
```

For accuracy of the measurements, it is advisable that you use dedicated routers for IP SLA. These routers are often referred to as *shadow routers*. Because these routers are dedicated to IP SLA, they are not involved in packet forwarding and can spend all of their CPU processing on IP SLA. If the shadow routers are attached to PE routers as CE routers and you have one shadow router per point of presence (POP), you can measure the performance of the MPLS VPN backbone from every POP to every other POP. If these routers are attached to PE routers as multi-VRF CE routers, they can actually perform CE-to-CE measurements across the MPLS VPN network for several VPNs. It then suffices to have one shadow router per POP in the network. Look at Figure 14-10 for an MPLS VPN network with shadow IP SLA CE routers measuring the performance POP to POP.

Figure 14-10 *Shadow IP SLA CE Routers*

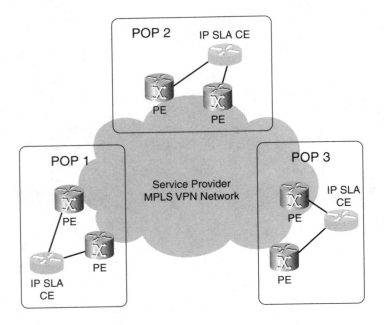

Netflow Accounting

Netflow provides a means to do accounting in IP networks, which can be used for network management, planning, and billing. The data gathered is a set of traffic statistics, such as protocol, port, and QoS information. You can export the information that you gather on network flows to a Netflow collector to analyze and further process. A flow is unidirectional and is defined as the set of source IP address, destination IP address, source port, destination port, protocol, TOS byte, and input interface. Netflow provides accounting in IP networks, but it can also provide accounting in MPLS networks. Look at Figure 14-11 for an overview of where Netflow can operate in MPLS networks.

Figure 14-11   *Netflow in MPLS Networks*

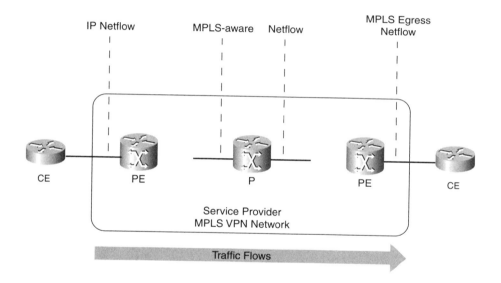

Netflow can also track IP-to-label flows on the ingress LSR. It does not matter whether the incoming interface is a regular global IP or a VRF interface. At the egress LSR, Netflow can provide egress Netflow accounting for packets that enter the LSR as labeled packets and leave the LSR as IP packets; this is the label-to-IP path. It is called *egress Netflow* because the packets are disposed of the label stack on their way out of the router. The egress interface on the LSR can be a regular global IP interface or a VRF interface. Therefore, you can find egress Netflow on the egress PE routers in MPLS VPN networks. Finally, Netflow can do accounting in the label-to-label path. In other words, it can perform accounting for labeled packets on P routers in MPLS networks. The data can be exported in the Netflow version 9 export format. In addition to the usual data that you can gather, you can track up to three MPLS labels from the label stack. The tracked information is the value of the labels, the experimental bits value, the MPLS application (MPLS VPN, AToM, MPLS TE, and so on) that is associated with the top label, and the prefix that is associated with the top label. It is important that the MPLS payload does not have to be IP. MPLS-aware Netflow can track labeled packets that carry non-IP payload, such as AToM packets.

To enable Netflow accounting on a router, you must configure the command **ip route-cache flow** on the input interface. You can see the Netflow statistics on the router with the command **show ip cache [verbose] flow**. On the ingress LSR of an MPLS network, you can configure **ip route-cache flow** on the ingress interface, even if it is a VRF interface.

To configure egress Netflow accounting, you must configure the interface command **mpls netflow egress** on the egress interface of the egress LSR.

To configure MPLS-aware Netflow, configure the global command **ip flow-cache mpls label-positions [label-position-1 [label-position-2 [label-position-3]]] [mpls-length] [no-ip-fields]**. You can specify the label position as being up to the sixth label in the label stack. A prerequisite for this feature is to enable Netflow on the interface with the command **ip route-cache flow [input]**. To view a snapshot of the MPLS-aware Netflow cache on the router, you must use the command **show ip cache verbose flow**.

> **NOTE** Chapter 13, "Troubleshooting MPLS Networks," talks more about MPLS-aware Netflow.

SNMP/MIBs

SNMP is a protocol that provides the communication between an SNMP manager (usually the management station) and the SNMP agent in IP networks. The SNMP agent is a software component that runs on a device to be managed. SNMP provides a standardized framework for managing devices in the network. Part of the framework is the MIBs and the Structure of Management Information (SMI). The SMI provides the mechanisms to define the MIB. Plenty of MIBs are available, and new ones are always being defined. Most protocols have their own MIBs. However, other MIBs are not tied to a certain protocol, but rather to a certain software component on the SNMP agent. You can access SNMP MIBs by using a simple command on a management station or by a complicated piece of software with a graphical user interface running on the management station managing up to thousands of devices in the network. The MIB is actually composed of a collection of objects that refer to a managed entity on the device. The value of the objects can be read by a **GET** or **GETNEXT** command issued from the management station. In some cases, you can set the managed object with a **SET** command from the management station. Look at Figure 14-12 for an overview of the SNMP protocol.

Figure 14-12 *SNMP Protocol Overview*

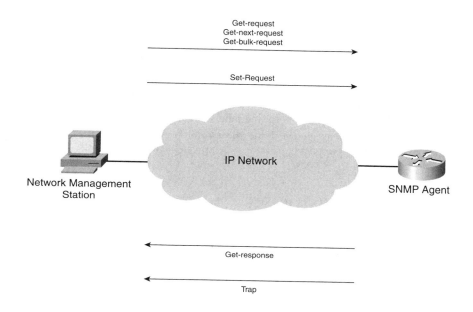

SNMP can manage nodes in the network in two fashions: a polling fashion and an interrupt-driven fashion. In the polling fashion, a management station periodically polls or queries the devices in the network. A problem is the frequency to poll the devices when monitoring the status of the network devices—such as the routers. If a problematic event occurs, such as an interface going down, it might take a while before the polling station notices the event. Therefore, the second fashion is interrupt-driven. As soon as an event occurs on the managed device, SNMP sends a trap to the management station informing it of the change.

A MIB is a collection of managed objects, each with a name (value), status, access, and syntax. Many MIBs are available, some of which are defined by standard bodies and some of which are proprietary or enhanced with proprietary information. This book lists only the MIBs that are related to MPLS and that are supported in Cisco IOS. Following are the MIBs that fit into that category:

■   MPLS-LDP-MIB

■   MPLS-LSR-MIB

■   MPLS-TE-MIB

■   MPLS-VPN-MIB

- CISCO-IETF-PW-MIB

- CISCO-IETF-PW-MPLS-MIB

- CISCO-IETF-PW-TC-MIB

It should be obvious what most MIBs represent by looking at their name. The MPLS-LDP-MIB is the MIB that has objects related to LDP. It holds objects that are related to the LDP router ID, LDP peer information, and sessions. The MPLS-LSR-MIB holds objects that are related to counters, the LFIB, incoming and outgoing labels, and so on. In short, the MPLS-LSR-MIB can give the same information as seen with the **show mpls forwarding-table** command. The MPLS-TE-MIB is the MIB that holds objects related to TE. The MPLS-VPN-MIB is the MIB that deals with VRF-specific objects.

The PW in some MIBs stands for pseudowire; these MIBs are related to AToM if the underlying network protocol is MPLS. IF-MIB is the name of the interface MIB. It has been enhanced in Cisco IOS to support the MPLS layer. As such, statistics can be polled for labeled traffic that is being forwarded through the router. You can check the operational status of MPLS on an interface and the MPLS MTU of an interface by using this MIB.

Some MIBs that are related to routing are not really related to MPLS directly. However, without routing, MPLS is not possible; therefore, when talking about managing MPLS networks, it is necessary to manage IP routing, too. That is why if you are running OSPF in your network, you will be interested in the OSPF-MIB. If you are running MPLS VPN, the MIBs BGP4-MIB and CISCO-BGP4-MIB will be attractive. When you are running MPLS TE, the RSVP-MIB will captivate you.

Now is a good time to look at an example from the MPLS-TE MIB. An object tracks the state transitions of the TE tunnel. The object name is mplsTunnelStateTransitions, and the Object Identifier (OID) is 1.3.6.1.3.95.2.2.1.26. This OID uniquely defines the object. It defines which organization assigns the MIB, which MIB it is, and which object it is from that MIB. The OID is a list of integers, read from left to right, that uniquely indicates the managed object. Figure 14-13 shows the OID tree of the object mplsTunnelStateTransitions.

Figure 14-13   *OID of mplsTunnelStateTransitions*

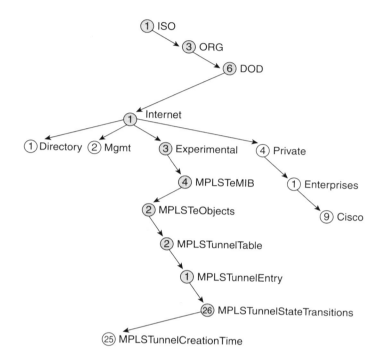

All OIDs of all MIBs can be represented in such an OID tree. In this example,
1.3.6.1.3.95.2.2.1.26 translates to iso (1) . org (3) . dod (6) . internet (1) . experimental (3) .
mplsTeMIB (95) . mplsTeObjects (2); mplsTunnelTable (2); mplsTunnelEntry (1);
mplsTunnelStateTransitions (26). The MPLS TE objects are defined in RFC 3812, which defines
the MPLS TE MIB. Example 14-19 shows how the RFC defines the OID 1.3.6.1.3.95.2.2.1.26.

Example 14-19   *OID 1.3.6.1.3.95.2.2.1.26*

```
mplsTunnelStateTransitions OBJECT-TYPE
      SYNTAX        Counter32
      MAX-ACCESS    read-only
      STATUS        current
      DESCRIPTION
         "Specifies the number of times the state
            (mplsTunnelOperStatus) of this tunnel instance
             has changed."
      ::= { mplsTunnelEntry 33 }
```

The access permission is read-only, its status is current, and its type is counter32. This OID allows you to track the number of state transitions of the TE tunnel. In other words, you can track the state changes (up/down) on the head end router for the TE tunnel interface. On the management station, you can retrieve this information with an **snmpwalk** or **snmpget** command. Look at Example 14-20 for the output from the **snmpwalk** command for the object mplsTunnelStateTransitions.

Example 14-20   *snmpwalk of OID 1.3.6.1.3.95.2.2.1.26*

```
nms{1}1249: snmpwalk -c cisco 10.48.70.116 1.3.6.1.3.95.2.2.1.26
SNMPv2-SMI::experimental.95.2.2.1.26.1.0.180944385.180944388 = Counter32: 9
SNMPv2-SMI::experimental.95.2.2.1.26.1.543.180944388.180944385 = Counter32: 0
```

The TE tunnel changed its state nine times on the LSR with IP address 10.48.70.116.

Another example is the retrieval of the LSR identifier that LDP uses. Example 14-21 shows how the mplsLdpLsrId object is defined in the MPLS LDP MIB.

Example 14-21   *mplsLdpLsrId*

```
mplsLdpLsrId OBJECT-TYPE
          SYNTAX      MplsLsrIdentifier
          MAX-ACCESS  read-only
          STATUS      current
          DESCRIPTION
              "The Label Switching Router's Identifier."
          ::= { mplsLdpLsrObjects 1 }
```

As you can see, the object name or OID is not the most readable term and not the easiest to find when you are looking for a specific management object. It can be a tedious job, but www.cisco.com has "Cisco IOS MIB Tools," which can help you find the right object and translate the object name into the OID and vice versa. In Example 14-22, you can see the output of the SNMP Object Navigator on www.cisco.com of the mplsLdpLsrId object.

Example 14-22   *mplsLdpLsrId by SNMP Object Navigator*

```
Object        mplsLdpLsrId
OID           1.3.6.1.4.1.9.10.65.1.1.1
Type          MplsLsrIdentifier
Permission    read-only
Status        current
MIB           MPLS-LDP-MIB
Description   The LSR's Identifier.
```

Example 14-23 shows the **snmpwalk** for the object mplsLdpLsrId on the router new-york.

Example 14-23   *snmpwalk of OID 1.3.6.1.4.1.9.10.65.1.1.1*

```
nms{1}1164: snmpwalk -c cisco 10.48.70.116 1.3.6.1.4.1.9.10.65.1.1.1
SNMPv2-SMI::enterprises.9.10.65.1.1.1.0 = Hex-STRING: 0A C8 FE 01
```

The returned value of mplsLdpLsrId is the LSR identifier in hexadecimal. The value 0A C8 FE 01 in hexadecimal is 10.200.254.1 in dotted decimal.

Example 14-24 shows that object mplsOutSegmentOctets (OID 1.3.6.1.3.96.1.7.1.1) returns the number of octets (bytes) switched out on this segment or LSP. It matches the number of Bytes Label Switched for each LSP, as seen in the LFIB on this LSR.

Example 14-24   *snmpwalk of OID 1.3.6.1.3.96.1.7.1.1*

```
nms{1}1239: snmpwalk -c cisco 10.48.70.109 1.3.6.1.3.96.1.7.1.1
SNMPv2-SMI::experimental.96.1.7.1.1.8705 = Counter32: 0
SNMPv2-SMI::experimental.96.1.7.1.1.9217 = Counter32: 0
SNMPv2-SMI::experimental.96.1.7.1.1.9729 = Counter32: 0
SNMPv2-SMI::experimental.96.1.7.1.1.10241 = Counter32: 1009
SNMPv2-SMI::experimental.96.1.7.1.1.10753 = Counter32: 6423184
SNMPv2-SMI::experimental.96.1.7.1.1.11265 = Counter32: 0
SNMPv2-SMI::experimental.96.1.7.1.1.11777 = Counter32: 0
SNMPv2-SMI::experimental.96.1.7.1.1.12289 = Counter32: 0
SNMPv2-SMI::experimental.96.1.7.1.1.12801 = Counter32: 0
SNMPv2-SMI::experimental.96.1.7.1.1.13313 = Counter32: 6826536
SNMPv2-SMI::experimental.96.1.7.1.1.13825 = Counter32: 0


london#show mpls forwarding-table
Local  Outgoing    Prefix          Bytes Label  Outgoing   Next Hop
Label  Label or VC or Tunnel Id    Switched     interface
16     No Label    10.9.9.5/32     0            Fa0/0/0    10.48.70.106
17     Pop Label   10.200.214.0/24 0            PO5/0/0    point2point
18     16          10.200.216.0/24 0            PO5/0/0    point2point
19     17          10.200.217.0/24 0            PO5/0/0    point2point
20     Pop Label   10.200.254.3/32 1009         PO5/0/0    point2point
21     18          10.200.254.4/32 6423184      PO5/0/0    point2point
22     19          10.200.254.5/32 0            PO5/0/0    point2point
23     20          10.200.254.6/32 0            PO5/0/0    point2point
24     Pop Label   10.200.254.4 1 [543]   \
                                   0            Et0/1/3    10.200.210.1
25     28          10.200.254.1 1 [9]    \
                                   0            PO5/0/0    point2point
26     Pop Label   10.200.254.1/32 6826536      Et0/1/3    10.200.210.1
27     22          44.44.44.44/32  0            PO5/0/0    point2point
```

Traps are unsolicited information sent via SNMP. Informs are also unsolicited information sent via SNMP; the difference is that informs are acknowledged, whereas traps are not. For MPLS, you can enable three kinds of traps: LDP, TE, and VPN. Example 14-25 shows the possible MPLS traps in Cisco IOS.

Example 14-25 *Traps for MPLS in Cisco IOS*

```
london(config)#snmp-server enable traps mpls ?
  ldp            Allow SNMP MPLS label distribution protocol traps
  traffic-eng    Allow SNMP MPLS traffic engineering traps
  vpn            Allow SNMP MPLS Virtual Private Network traps

london(config)#snmp-server enable traps mpls ldp ?
  pv-limit       Enable MPLS LDP path vector limit mismatch traps
  session-down   Enable MPLS LDP session down traps
  session-up     Enable MPLS LDP session up traps
  threshold      Enable MPLS LDP threshold exceeded traps
  <cr>

london(config)#snmp-server enable traps mpls traffic-eng ?
  down     Enable MPLS TE tunnel down traps
  reroute  Enable MPLS TE tunnel reroute traps
  up       Enable MPLS TE tunnel up traps
  <cr>

london(config)#snmp-server enable traps mpls vpn ?
  illegal-label  Enable MPLS VPN illegal label threshold exceeded traps
  max-threshold  Enable MPLS VPN maximum threshold exceeded traps
  mid-threshold  Enable MPLS VPN middle threshold exceeded traps
  vrf-down       Enable MPLS VPN vrf down traps
  vrf-up         Enable MPLS VPN vrf up traps
  <cr>
```

To send SNMP notification messages to a server within a VRF, use the VRF keyword for the **snmp-server** command on the PE. Example 14-26 shows this command in action.

Example 14-26 *VRF-Aware **snmp-server** Command*

```
!
snmp-server host 10.254.9.40 vrf cust-one Cisco
!
```

Context-Based Access for SNMP over MPLS VPN

So far, SNMP access to devices has been global, meaning that the SNMP access has been for the whole device. However, with the introduction of MPLS VPN, you see the concept of VPNs and VRFs on the PE routers. The VPN provides a VRF routing table, VRF CEF table, and VRF interfaces on the PE routers. The VRF is not part of the global context of the PE router, but rather the VRF context. The problem is when the SNMP traffic comes into the PE router via the VRF interfaces or when traps leave the PE router via the VRF interfaces. The management stations inside the customer VPNs can access the whole management context of the PE router, even if the SNMP requests come into the PE router via a VRF interface. Customer management stations in the VPN should not be allowed to view the whole of the PE router or the global context of the router via the management protocols.

To enable the VPN customer to access only the MIB data that pertains to the VRF of that customer, the service provider can configure an SNMP context for that VRF. Consequently, the customer can only access the SNMP data in that context and cannot access MIB data from other VPN customers on the same PE router. The context keyword under the IP VRF configuration is used to associate a read, write, or notify SNMP view within an SNMP context. You can also restrict the access to certain MIB trees. It is important to note that for context-based access for SNMP over MPLS VPN to work for a certain MIB, that MIB needs to have been made context-aware.

Example 14-27 shows the configuration of a PE router with a VRF *cust-one*. The service provider wants to restrict the SNMP requests coming in on the PE router on the VRF *cust-one* interfaces. The PE router should only send SNMP responses back concerning the VRF *cust-one*. As you can see, a context is associated with the VRF *cust-one* and is applied to the group *cust-one-group*. A view with community string *comm-one* is associated with that context. The view is restricted to the routing table, because the only MIB that is included is the IP-FORWARD-MIB.

Example 14-27 *Context-Based Access for SNMP over MPLS VPN*

```
!
hostname new-york
!
ip vrf cust-one
 rd 1:1
 context context-cust-one
 route-target export 1:1
 route-target import 1:1
!
interface Ethernet1/0
 ip vrf forwarding cust-one
 ip address 10.48.70.116 255.255.255.0
!
```

continues

Example 14-27 *Context-Based Access for SNMP over MPLS VPN (Continued)*

```
snmp-server group cust-one-group v1 context context-cust-one read view-cust-one
snmp-server view view-cust-one ipForward included
snmp-server user comm-one cust-one-group v1
snmp-server context context-cust-one
snmp mib community-map  comm-one context context-cust-one target-list comm-one-vpn
snmp mib target list comm-one-vpn vrf cust-one
!
```

The network management station in the *cust-one* VPN can look at the complete VRF *cust-one* routing table with all its parameters (route, mask, next hop, metric, and so on) by performing an SNMPWALK for the object ipCidrRouteEntry (1.3.6.1.2.1.4.24.4.1) from the IP-FORWARD-MIB. Example 14-28 shows the SNMPWALK for the object ipCidrRouteEntry on the PE router new-york from the network management station in the VRF cust-one. This is the same information as the output from the command **show ip route vrf cust-one** on the new-york PE router. Note that the SNMP packets are entering the PE router on an interface belonging to VRF *cust-one*.

Example 14-28 *Context-Based Access for VRF Routing Table*

```
nms{1}2056: snmpwalk -v1 -c comm-one 10.48.70.116 1.3.6.1.2.1.4.24.4.1
IP-MIB::ip.24.4.1.1.0.0.0.0.0.0.0.0.10.48.70.4 = IpAddress: 0.0.0.0
IP-MIB::ip.24.4.1.1.10.10.10.0.255.255.255.0.0.10.48.70.118 = IpAddress: 10.10.10.0
IP-MIB::ip.24.4.1.1.10.10.10.12.255.255.255.0.0.10.48.70.4 = IpAddress: 10.10.10.12
IP-MIB::ip.24.4.1.1.10.10.11.0.255.255.255.0.0.10.48.70.4 = IpAddress: 10.10.11.0
...
```

MPLS VPN MIBs

The MIB that is specifically used to set or get objects related to MPLS VPN is MPLS-VPN MIB. The MPLS-VPN MIB has objects related to the VRFs on the PE router. Such objects are related to the VRF, the VRF interfaces, the VRF routing table, and BGP information. For instance, the object mplsVpnVrfRouteTable with OID 1.3.6.1.3.118.1.4.1 allows the network management station from the service provider to get the VRF routing tables from the PE routers. This information includes the prefix, route metric, next-hop information, protocol, and so on from the VRF routing tables. Another example is the description of the VRF on the PE router. If you have configured a description for the VRFs on the PE routers, you can retrieve it with the object mplsVpnVrfDescription. This object is defined in Example 14-29.

Example 14-29 *Object mplsVpnVrfDescription*

```
Object       mplsVpnVrfDescription
OID          1.3.6.1.3.118.1.2.2.1.2
Type         SnmpAdminString
Permission   read-create
```

Example 14-29   *Object mplsVpnVrfDescription (Continued)*

```
Status          current
MIB             MPLS-VPN-MIB
Description     The human-readable description of this VRF.
```

Look at Example 14-30 to see what an **snmpwalk** returns for OID 1.3.6.1.3.118.1.2.2.1.2 from the
PE router new-york configured with two VRFs, each with its own description.

Example 14-30   *snmpwalk of 1.3.6.1.3.118.1.2.2.1.2*

```
!
hostname sydney
!
ip vrf cust-one
 description customer-one
 rd 1:1
 route-target export 1:1
 route-target import 1:1
!
ip vrf cust-two
 description customer-two
 rd 2:2
 route-target export 1:1
 route-target import 2:2
!

nms{1}2116: snmpwalk -v1 -c cisco 10.48.70.118 1.3.6.1.3.118.1.2.2.1.2
SNMPv2-SMI::experimental.118.1.2.2.1.2.8.99.117.115.116.45.111.110.101 = STRING:
"customer-one"
SNMPv2-SMI::experimental.118.1.2.2.1.2.8.99.117.115.116.45.116.119.111 = STRING:
"customer-two"
```

Syslog

Syslog is a method to send messages from the router to a host that is running a syslog daemon.
However, you can also store the syslog messages locally on the router. If you send the syslog
messages to a host collecting the messages from all the devices in the network, you see a global
overview, and you can store the messages securely and manage them better. You can look at and
manipulate the syslog file so that it provides better management and troubleshooting. The syslog
messages have a number between 0 and 7, representing the severity of the message. You can use

this number to limit the number of messages sent to the syslog server according to the importance of the message. Table 14-7 gives an overview of the severity levels of the syslog messages.

Table 14-7 *Logging Priorities*

Severity Level Number	Severity Level Name	Description
0	Emergencies	System unusable
1	Alerts	Immediate action needed
2	Critical	Critical conditions
3	Errors	Error conditions
4	Warnings	Warning conditions
5	Notifications	Normal but significant condition
6	Informational	Informational messages only
7	Debugging	Debugging messages

The highest priority level is 0, and the lowest is 7. If you specify a level of severity, messages with that severity number and lower are sent to the syslog server or stored locally. If, for example, you specify level 3 for the level of the messages sent to the syslog server, all messages that have a severity level of 3, 2, 1, and 0 are sent. The syslog message format follows:

```
DATE-TIME-%FACILITY-SEVERITY-MNEMONIC : Message-text
```

Example 14-31 shows the syslog messages for an LDP session flapping. The first message indicates that the LDP session is going down. The second syslog message for LDP indicates that the LDP session came up again.

Example 14-31 *Syslog Messages for LDP Peer Neighbor Changes*

```
!
logging history debugging
logging trap debugging
logging source-interface Loopback0
logging 10.254.9.40
!
london#show logging
Syslog logging: enabled (0 messages dropped, 2 messages rate-limited, 0 flushes, 0
overruns, xml disabled, filtering disabled)
    Console logging: level debugging, 951085 messages logged, xml disabled,
                     filtering disabled
    Monitor logging: level debugging, 6 messages logged, xml disabled,
                     filtering disabled
    Buffer logging: level debugging, 951082 messages logged, xml disabled,
```

Example 14-31 *Syslog Messages for LDP Peer Neighbor Changes (Continued)*

```
                          filtering disabled
        Exception Logging: size (4096 bytes)
        Count and timestamp logging messages: enabled

No active filter modules.

    Trap logging: level debugging, 347 message lines logged
        Logging to 10.254.9.40, 51 message lines logged, xml disabled,
              filtering disabled

Log Buffer (65536 bytes):

*Jan 11 10:07:20.201: %LDP-5-NBRCHG: LDP Neighbor 10.200.254.5:0 is DOWN
*Jan 11 10:07:40.125: %OSPF-5-ADJCHG: Process 1, Nbr 10.200.254.5 on Ethernet0/1/2 from
FULL to DOWN, Neighbor Down: Dead timer expired
*Jan 11 10:08:14.277: %LDP-5-NBRCHG: LDP Neighbor 10.200.254.5:0 is UP
*Jan 11 10:08:27.049: %OSPF-5-ADJCHG: Process 1, Nbr 10.200.254.5 on Ethernet0/1/2 from
LOADING to FULL, Loading Done
```

You can see that the LDP neighbor change messages are sent with a priority level of 5.

You can send syslog messages to a server that is located in a VPN. Look at Example 14-32 to see how the **logging host** command has been made VRF-aware.

Example 14-32 *Configuration of VRF-Aware Syslog*

```
!
service timestamps log datetime msec
!
logging host 10.254.9.40 vrf cust-one
!
```

OAM Message Mapping

OAM Message Mapping is important in the case of AToM. In AToM networks, pseudowires or VCs transport Layer 2 frames across the MPLS cloud. Toward the native Layer 2 clouds on either side of the MPLS network are ACs with the particular Layer 2 encapsulation. One important aspect when managing this service is the mapping of the OAM messages of the ACs onto newly defined pseudowire OAM messages on the pseudowires and vice versa. Specific alarm indications can be transported between the PE routers, indicating the state of the pseudowires and the ACs. Each Layer 2 protocol on the AC can have its own set of alarms and defects messages. ATM, for example, has more fault management indications than Frame Relay. Each of these native messages—as defined by each Layer 2 protocol—should be mapped onto newly defined pseudowire OAM messages. These pseudowire OAM messages are transported across the pseudowires between PE routers and can indicate the state of the ACs or the pseudowires. This mapping is needed to provide an emulated service of the native Layer 2 protocols end to end across the MPLS network. This mapping is important when the native Layer 2 circuits are terminated on the PE routers. When the Layer 2 circuits are *not* terminated on the PE routers—for example, Frame Relay in port mode over MPLS—the native OAM messages are transported across the pseudowires transparently. In that case, it is not necessary to map the OAM messages at the PE routers.

The PE router can receive alarms from the ACs indicating problems, or the state of the circuit or the link can simply be down. The router must transport this state across the pseudowire. The pseudowire can be down or fail for any number of reasons. The router must then translate this state in OAM messages that are sent onto the ACs. The PE router can directly detect a problem with the pseudowire if the underlying interface is down or if the VC label has a problem, for instance. However, it can also detect it through another protocol, such as LSP ping. The goal is ensuring end-to-end monitoring of the network. For instance, if a PE router detects that the local attached Frame Relay PVC is inactive, it can map this to a pseudowire status message, which is sent to the remote PE router. The remote PE router should then translate this pseudowire status message into corresponding Frame Relay alarms that are sent out onto the egress Frame Relay PVC.

ATM uses the following OAM cells:

- Loopback cells

- Continuity Check (CC) cells

- Alarm Indication Signal (AIS) cells

- Remote Detection Indication (RDI) cells

AIS cells are sent downstream of the failure, and RDI cells are sent upstream. The PE routers must look at these alarms and map them into pseudowire status messages and vice versa. In Cisco IOS, the PE routers can respond to End OAM cells if **oam-ac emulation-enable** is enabled; otherwise, they are transparently sent across the pseudowire. The PE routers can respond to the segment OAM cells if the OAM Segment Endpoint feature is configured. The needed configuration command for this is **oam-ac segment endpoint**.

Summary

You saw in this chapter what the OAM requirements for MPLS networks are. You learned about MPLS LSP ping and LSP traceroute, and you saw specific examples of their use in Cisco IOS. This chapter explained Virtual Circuit Connection Verification (VCCV) and how it is used to test the data plane of AToM networks. It also gave an overview of the measurement tool IP SLA and provided some examples. In addition, it touched on the MPLS-awareness of IP SLA. This chapter also explored accounting for MPLS networks, with a look at Netflow in Cisco IOS. It reviewed network management in MPLS networks and highlighted the SNMP access, MIBs, traps, and syslog for MPLS VPN networks specifically. Finally, this chapter included a short section on OAM message mapping, which is the mapping of native Layer 2 protocol messages onto the pseudowire OAM messages.

Chapter Review Questions

You can find answers to the following questions in Appendix A, "Answers to the Chapter Review Questions."

1. What does MPLS LSP ping provide that IP ping does not?

2. Name three MPLS-specific MIBs.

3. What does a ping mpls or traceroute mpls with reply mode router-alert do?

4. What is the name for the Cisco IOS subsystem that is responsible for processing MPLS echo request and echo reply packets?

5. What MPLS-related information can you see with MPLS-aware Netflow?

6. What prevents an MPLS echo request packet from being forwarded as an IP packet after it becomes unlabeled?

7. What is IP SLA?

8. If Type 1 VCCV is used, how is the packet identified as being an AToM VCCV packet?

9. Why would you want to change the default destination IP address of 127.0.0.1 in the IP header of LSP ping packets if the packets are label-switched anyway?

10. What is context-based access for SNMP?

What You Will Learn

This chapter will give you an insight into the near future of MPLS. The future is always difficult to predict, but some enhancements will most certainly be made to MPLS. In the next few pages, you will read about a few enhancements to MPLS that are likely candidates for deployment in networks. There are other candidate enhancements, as well, that I do not mention, and there are the enhancements and new developments that nobody has thought of yet.

CHAPTER 15

The Future of MPLS

MPLS has become popular and has seen many implementations and deployments by service providers. The original idea for inventing MPLS was a better integration of IP in ATM networks. However, MPLS—or Tag Switching as it was called originally—has seen success that has surprised many people in the networking industry. A big part of the sensation is the result of the huge success of MPLS VPN in the industry. Service providers quickly recognized the great benefits of MPLS VPN and deployed it quickly while features for it were still being developed. These days even enterprise customers are looking at MPLS VPN with interest. They might have already deployed MPLS VPN for the benefit of a greater scalability. Other benefits to them is the separation of departments, or the easier deployment of PE and CE routers. Today, Any Transport over MPLS (AToM), MPLS traffic engineering (TE), and VPLS are experiencing a growing interest from the industry, and service providers are deploying these MPLS applications. Because most service provider networks are already running MPLS for the MPLS VPN service, the operators and technical support people have the experience in deploying and troubleshooting MPLS. It then becomes a smaller step to deploy one of the other MPLS applications. MPLS will have more development and the proliferation will continue to happen. For now, MPLS can still grow in those two areas.

New MPLS Applications

MPLS VPN is by far the most popular and mature MPLS application. MPLS TE has also matured greatly, because it has been around even longer than MPLS VPN, at least in Cisco IOS. Other MPLS applications such as AToM, Virtual Private LAN Service (VPLS), and MPLS Operation and Maintenance (OAM) will improve and see more deployments. AToM might end up with more supported encapsulations and more control information applied. VPLS has just started to take off. The introduction of hierarchy in VPLS will make it more scalable.

MPLS OAM is the technology that needs the most development to mature. The operation and maintenance aspects of a protocol are usually the last to be implemented. It is no different for MPLS. First, there is the rush to bring out the protocol specifications, while the operation and management details are worked out later. The fact that the specifications for MPLS OAM have been nailed down is a sign that MPLS has reached the stage of maturity. LSP Ping and LSP Traceroute have been finalized, and new OAM protocols (for example, Bidirectional Forwarding Detection (BFD) for MPLS LSPs and Label Switch Router Self-Test, both briefly summarized in the "OAM Protocols" section in this chapter) are very likely to be deployed. Finally, because quality of service (QoS) is still gaining momentum, it will certainly see more deployments and better definitions in the MPLS networks.

Work at IETF

Much work is still going on regarding MPLS topics at the Internet Engineering Task Force (IETF). Many RFCs on MPLS have already been published, but drafts are still being written. Some of these drafts might become important, whereas others will experience less demand. This section lists a few topics that are likely to receive interest from the networking industry.

MPLS Control Word

The control word (the MPLS header) is used today in AToM networks to carry protocol control information across the MPLS network to support the correct operation of pseudowires. Networks can also use the MPLS control word for the fragmentation of AToM traffic. Another use of the control word is as Pseudowire Associated Channel Header. This stems from the fact that MPLS has no protocol identifier field to indicate the payload type. The Pseudowire Associated Channel Header indicates that the MPLS payload is not the normal AToM data traffic. One example of such traffic is the MPLS OAM traffic. The future might bring more examples of traffic types that need to be identified as something other than data traffic. If the first nibble of the MPLS control word is 0, the packet is mere data traffic. If the first nibble of the MPLS control word is 1, the packet is not data traffic but instead belongs to a pseudowire-associated channel. The Associated Channel Type in the control word indicates what the payload protocol is.

Figure 15-1 shows the control word when used as a Pseudowire Associated Channel Header.

Figure 15-1   *Pseudowire Associated Channel Header*

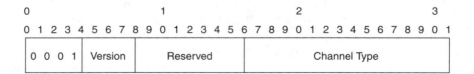

One important use of the Pseudowire Associated Channel Header is to let the intermediate label switching router (LSR) (the P routers) know what the payload is, at least if those LSRs perform deep packet inspection. Doing so enables intermediate LSRs to treat the MPLS packet accordingly. One important use of deep packet inspection is the correct load balancing according to some fields in the payload of the MPLS packet.

NOTE   RFC 4385 describes the usage of the control word in an MPLS network.

FCS Retention

Currently, in AToM networks, the frame check sequence (FCS) of Ethernet, Frame Relay, High-Level Data Link Control (HDLC), and PPP Layer 2 frames is removed before AToM sends the frames across the pseudowire. At the remote end of the pseudowire, the egress PE inserts the FCS by calculating it over the received Layer 2 frame. This behavior might lead to problems if intermediate LSRs introduce a problem whereby they change the payload of the MPLS packet. This problem can go undetected until the packet reaches its destination host. That also makes troubleshooting the problem more difficult, because you first have to identify where the problem happens. A draft is currently within the IETF (draft-ietf-pwe3-fcs-retention) that describes FCS retention and how it can be signaled between PE routers so that the PE routers can decide whether to retain the original FCS. When the original FCS is retained, it guarantees the transparent behavior of the pseudowire for the Layer 2 frames.

AToM Fragmentation and Reassembly

Fragmentation is generally not good because it places a greater workload on the platform that is performing the fragmentation. Therefore, avoid it if possible. Path MTU Discovery and careful usage of the IP MTU and MPLS MTU commands generally get you far. Sometimes fragmentation is unavoidable, as in the case of Path MTU Discovery not working because of firewalls blocking the ICMP messages needed for Path MTU Discovery to work properly. If the payload is IP traffic, the ingress PE router can fragment the IP packet before it enters the pseudowire. In that case, the destination host reassembles the packet. If the frame payload is not IP, the ingress PE router can perform the fragmentation on the frame before it enters the pseudowire and the egress PE router reassembles the frame. The IETF draft "draft-ietf-pwe3-fragmentation" describes this procedure. Even if the MPLS MTU is sufficient in the MPLS cloud for the AToM traffic, you still might want to fragment frames to ensure a low latency transmission on the pseudowire. The receiving PE router should signal its capability to reassemble the fragments toward the ingress PE in the Virtual Circuit FEC element. The fragmentation is handled through the control word, present below the label stack of the MPLS packet.

Circuit Emulation

There is still an enormous amount of time-division multiplexing (TDM) private lines and legacy equipment using these TDM services. Therefore, it makes sense to carry TDM over MPLS to support the legacy services using T1, E1, T3, E3, N × 64, and V.35. The advantage of carrying these types of services over MPLS is that one common network—the MPLS network—can carry the IP/AToM traffic and the TDM traffic. With TDM Circuit Emulation, the TDM bit stream is carried across the MPLS cloud over an MPLS pseudowire. The difficult part is the emulation of the TDM circuit. Examples include the clock recovery and procedures for alarm signaling. The egress PE router can recover the clock by using timestamps that the ingress PE router sets. Synchronous Digital Hierarchy/Synchronous Optical Network (SDH/SONET) circuit emulation over MPLS is another area of development. SONET and SDH are standards that describe a digital hierarchy to carry synchronous data on fiber networks. They are both popular—SONET in the United States and SDH in Europe.

GMPLS

Generalized MPLS (GMPLS) is based on MPLS TE, but it has added extensions that make it work on a newer set of platforms. These new platforms are dense wavelength-division multiplexing (DWDM) systems, Photonic Cross-Connects (PXC), and Optical Cross-Connects (OXC), among others. These platforms that run GMPLS are not just routers or ATM switches that have MPLS enabled. These nonrouter platforms run GMPLS in the control plane, while MPLS is absent from the data plane. That is because these new platforms do not switch packets that can be labeled, neither do they switch ATM cells. They switch wavelengths (lambdas), time-division channels (Synchronous Optical Network and Synchronous Digital Hierarchy: SONET/SDH), and complete physical ports or fibers.

The building blocks of GMPLS are the same as those of regular MPLS TE in the control plane: the IPv4 protocol, a link state routing protocol, and Resource Reservation Protocol (RSVP) with the TE extensions. One new protocol required to run GMPLS is the Link Management Protocol (LMP), which was developed to manage the links easier. GMPLS needs LMP because these newer platforms can have a huge number of wavelengths between them, which makes the management of the links cumbersome. LMP takes care of the management and link connectivity verification on these links. GMPLS—like MPLS TE—distributes network constraints of the physical media to all the platforms that participate in GMPLS. You can then use these constraints to build LSPs throughout the network that might—like regular MPLS TE—deviate from the shortest path. The constraints are different from those used by MPLS TE, because the physical media is different. Different link capacity, protection, and restoration constraints are involved.

OAM Protocols

BFD is a new, lightweight, media independent protocol that detects faults in the data plane between two devices. It has been specifically developed to be routing protocol and media independent and to quickly detect data communication failures. The "quickly" stands for subsecond detection. SONET has alarms that can detect and notify problems quickly. Most media, however, have no such fast detection mechanisms. BFD quickly detects all failures between routers instead of relying on the hello mechanism of the routing protocols. The routing protocols can perform the same function, but they are slower and less scalable if the number of interfaces is large.

BFD also detects data plane failures for MPLS LSPs. Although LSP Ping can do this, it also checks information from the control plane against the data plane. BFD for MPLS LSPs does not do this; therefore, it is lighter in design and can be implemented easier in hardware. A BFD session is established between the ingress and egress LSR, and BFD control packets are sent across. As such, BFD tracks the liveliness of the MPLS LSP and detects failures in the data plane for the LSP. Because BFD for MPLS LSPs is lighter than LSP Ping, it is more scalable. You can use BFD on more LSPs, and it detects failures more quickly.

One problem with MPLS is often that the control plane looks fine but the data plane does not. Label Distribution Protocol (LDP), RSVP, or Border Gateway Protocol (BGP) might indicate the correct incoming and outgoing labels, but the forwarding plane—the LFIB or the ASIC that is programmed with the LFIB—might be doing the wrong forwarding, resulting in the packet being misrouted or dropped. Although the solutions discussed in Chapter 14, "MPLS Operation and Maintenance," can help to identify the problem, they are often not scalable in large networks. A solution for this problem is an LSR testing its own data plane information. This functionality is called the Label Switching Router Self-Test.

Look at Figure 15-2 for an overview of the LSR Self-Test.

Figure 15-2 *LSR Self-Test Overview*

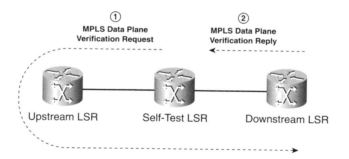

The LSR doing the testing sends a special packet called an MPLS Data Plane Verification Request to its upstream neighbor. This packet holds the incoming label stack that the LSR doing the testing expects on packets coming from its upstream neighbor. This upstream LSR then forwards the labeled packet to the downstream neighbor of the LSR under test. The LSR doing the testing performs normal label forwarding on the packet and hence is testing the correctness of one LSP in its data plane. In other words, the LSR doing the testing performs the normal label operation (pop, push, or swap) on the labeled packet and forwards it to its downstream neighbor. The downstream neighbor intercepts the packet and sends an MPLS Data Plane Verification Reply to the LSR doing the testing. The MPLS Data Plane Verification Reply packet indicates the interface on the downstream neighbor on which the packet was received and the label stack. The LSR doing the testing can then verify this information. This LSR Self-Test functionality is based on the LSP Ping functionality, but extensions were added to it.

MPLS Labeled Multicast

Recent developments have been made on MPLS labeled multicast. IP multicast is a known architecture that is proven in the industry. Many want multicast traffic to be MPLS labeled. The label switched paths (LSP) encountered in this book are point-to-point. You could make them point-to-multipoint or even multipoint-to-multipoint. MPLS TE and RSVP for TE have been extended to be able to create point-to-multipoint LSPs. LDP can also create these point-to-multipoint LSPs for the people who do not need TE or who already have a deployed MPLS network with LDP. LDP has been extended to provide these point-to-multipoint and multipoint-to-multipoint LSPs.

Even though you can use downstream label distribution with MPLS labeled multicast, it introduces upstream label distribution. MPLS networks so far have not used upstream label distribution. When transporting multicast as MPLS labeled packets, one LSR can forward a single copy of one labeled packet on a multiaccess link to multiple downstream LSRs. The LSR can only do this if it supports Upstream Label Distribution mode, because then it distributes one label to its downstream LSRs for one point-to-multipoint LSP. In Downstream Label Distribution mode, each downstream LSR assigns independently a different label for the same point-to-multipoint LSP. This prohibits the upstream LSR from sending a single copy of one labeled packet on the point-to-multipoint LSP on the multiaccess link.

One of the most interesting applications of labeling multicast traffic is carrying MPLS VPN multicast traffic across the MPLS backbone on point-to-multipoint LSPs.

The Proliferation of MPLS

MPLS is no longer solely used by service providers, but more and more by enterprise networks that have a larger network diameter or that have specific needs. Furthermore, MPLS has already moved from the core of the network closer to the edge. An example of this is the extensions of the LSPs onto the CE router for the easier deployment of QoS in MPLS VPN networks.

Although MPLS VPN autonomous systems are still interconnected via IP most of the time, in the future, more and more MPLS VPN networks will be interconnected via MPLS, and the packets will be sent labeled toward the other autonomous system. The interconnection between MPLS networks will not be limited to interconnecting MPLS VPN networks but will also be used to switch AToM or IPv6 traffic from one provider to another. This trend of more labeled packets in places where they are not today will most likely continue.

MPLS has spread from being solely used on IP routers and ATM switches to being used in the control plane of OXCs, DWDM systems, and TDM switches. MPLS most definitely still has to mature in this area.

Summary

This chapter presented an overview of recent or new MPLS developments. These developments might or might not be implemented in the near future. Even if they are implemented, however, it is not guaranteed that they will become successful and see many deployments. The more distant future is much harder to predict. Nevertheless, you are sure to see more developments in MPLS, with it spreading further into networks that have no MPLS today.

MPLS is a mature technology that has many deployments and people who have experience in operating, maintaining, designing, and troubleshooting its networks. As for the future, we will see what it brings...

Appendixes

Answers to Chapter Review Questions

Chapter 1

1. What are the MPLS applications mentioned in this chapter?

   Answer: Traffic engineering, MPLS VPN, AToM, and VPLS are the MPLS applications mentioned in this chapter.

2. Name three advantages of running MPLS in a service provider network.

   Answer: The advantages of running MPLS in a service provider network include the following:

   — Better integration of IP over ATM

   — A network that is running a BGP-free core

   — Easy deployment of a peer-to-peer VPN model (MPLS VPN)

   — One unified network infrastructure

   — Optimal flow of traffic

   — Traffic engineering enables the steering of traffic through the network on a path different than the least cost path computed by the dynamic routing protocol

3. What are the advantages of the MPLS VPN solution for the service provider over all the other VPN solutions?

   Answer: MPLS VPN allows for easy provisioning of sites and allows for optimal traffic flow in the backbone network at all times.

4. Name the four technologies that can be used to carry IP over ATM.

    Answer: The four technologies that can be used to carry IP over ATM are as follows:

    — RFC 1483

    — LANE

    — MPOA

    — MPLS

5. Name two pre-MPLS protocols that use label switching.

    Answer: ATM and Frame Relay are two pre-MPLS protocols that use label switching.

6. What do the ATM switches need to run so that they can operate MPLS?

    Answer: The ATM switches need an IP routing protocol and a label distribution protocol to operate MPLS.

7. How do you ensure optimal traffic flow between all the customer sites in an ATM or Frame Relay overlay network?

    Answer: The connectivity between the customer sites needs to be a full mesh of virtual circuits.

Chapter 2

1. Name the four fields that are part of a label.

    Answer: The four fields that are part of a label are a 20-bit label value, 3 experimental bits, 1 Bottom of Stack bit, and an 8-bit TTL field.

2. How many labels can reside in a label stack?

    Answer: Any number of labels can reside in a label stack.

3. In which layer does MPLS fit in the OSI reference model?

    Answer: MPLS fits in no category of the OSI reference model. The best description for MPLS would be Layer 2.5.

4. Which table does an LSR use to forward labeled packets?

    Answer: The LSR uses the LFIB table to forward labeled packets.

5. What type of interfaces in Cisco IOS use the Downstream-on-Demand label distribution mode and the per-interface label space?

    Answer: LC-ATM interfaces use the Downstream-on-Demand label distribution mode and the per-interface label space.

6. Why does the MPLS label have a Time To Live (TTL) field?

    Answer: As the packets are labeled, the IP TTL can no longer be used. A mechanism is still needed to avoid a packet circulating in a loop forever.

Chapter 3

1. What does the push operation do on a labeled packet?

    Answer: The push operation replaces the top label with another and then pushes one or more labels onto the label stack.

2. Which Cisco IOS command do you use to see what the swapped label is and which labels are pushed onto a received packet for a certain prefix?

    Answer: show mpls forwarding-table [*network* {*mask* | *length*}] [**detail**]

3. What does the outgoing label entry of "Aggregate" in the LFIB of a Cisco IOS LSR mean?

    Answer: The outgoing label entry "Aggregate" means that the LSR removes the label and does an IP lookup to be able to determine where the packet needs to be forwarded.

4. What label value signals the penultimate LSR to use penultimate hop popping (PHP)?

    Answer: The label with value 3, known as the implicit NULL label, signals the penultimate LSR to use PHP.

5. What are the value and the function of the Router Alert label?

    Answer: The value of the Router Alert label is 1 and its function is to make sure that all LSRs forwarding this packet take a closer look at it.

6. Why does an LSR forward the ICMP message "time exceeded" along the LSP of the original packet with the TTL expiring instead of returning it directly?

    Answer: The LSR—or an intermediate LSR—might not have the information it needs to return the ICMP message, so it forwards it along the LSP in the hope that the packet reaches a router that can return the ICMP message to the sender of the original packet.

7. Is using Path MTU Discovery a guarantee that there will be no MTU problems in the MPLS network?

    Answer: No, the ICMP messages might not make it back to the originator of the packet for various reasons.

8. Why is MTU or MRU such an important parameter in MPLS networks?

    Answer: The MRU is so important in MPLS networks because the addition of a label stack increases the size of a frame slightly. As such, the size of the frame might become more than the maximum allowed size of a frame on the data link. Especially on Ethernet links, care must be taken that such frames can still be forwarded. Such frames are known as baby giant frames.

Chapter 4

1. What is the fundamental purpose of LDP?

    Answer: The fundamental purpose of LDP is to distribute label bindings.

2. Name the four main functions that LDP takes care of.

    Answer: The four main functions that LDP takes care of include the following:

    — The discovery of LSRs that are running LDP

    — Session establishment and maintenance

    — Advertising of label mappings

    — Housekeeping by means of notification

3. How can you reduce the number of label bindings on an LSR?

    Answer: To reduce the number of label bindings on an LSR, you can either control the advertisement of label bindings via LDP in the outbound direction, or you can filter the incoming label bindings.

4. What problem does MPLS LDP-IGP synchronization solve?

    Answer: MPLS LDP-IGP synchronization solves the problem of labeled packets being dropped when the LDP information is out of sync with the IGP.

5. How many LDP sessions are established between two LSRs that have six links between them, of which two links are LC-ATM links and four are frame links?

    Answer: Three LDP sessions are established in that case.

6. What do you need to configure to protect the LDP sessions against attacks?

Answer: You need MD5 authentication for the LDP neighbor.

7. What trick does MPLS LDP-IGP Synchronization employ to ensure that the link is not used to forward traffic while the LDP session is unsynchronized?

Answer: MPLS LDP-IGP Synchronization has the IGP advertise the link with the maximum metric.

8. What does LDP Session Protection use to protect an LDP session?

Answer: LDP Session Protection uses a targeted LDP session.

Chapter 5

1. In what ways is an ATM LSR different from a frame-based LSR?

Answer:

— The label value is encoded in the VPI/VCI fields.

— ATM LSRs forward cells.

— ATM LSRs are not capable of decrementing the TTL.

— LDP runs in Downstream-on-Demand label advertisement mode on ATM LSRs.

2. What is the default control VC for LDP?

Answer: 0/32 is the default control VC for LDP.

3. What is the preferred control mode for LDP on the ATM LSRs?

Answer: Ordered Control mode is the preferred mode for LDP on the ATM LSRs.

4. Name two ways that LDP can detect loops.

Answer: LDP can detect loops in the following two ways:

— By means of a Hop Count TLV

— By means of a Path Vector TLV

5. Which two features must an ATM switch have in the control plane to become an ATM LSR?

Answer: An ATM LSR must have an IGP and a label distribution protocol.

6. Which label space is used on an LC-ATM interface?

   Answer: Per-interface label space is used on an LC-ATM interface.

7. What IP precedence values are by default mapped to the standard LVC type with Multi-VC TBR?

   Answer: Precedence values 1 and 5 are mapped by default to the standard LVC type with Multi-VC TBR.

8. What would be the reason to disable the head end VCs on an LSC?

   Answer: You might disable the head end VCs on an LSC to reduce the number of LVCs through the ATM network.

9. Why does the Cisco equipment not advertise bound IP addresses of the LSR on LC-ATM interfaces with LDP?

   Answer: The Cisco equipment does not advertise these addresses because they are not needed when the LSRs are running LDP on LC-ATM links. Mapping the received label to the downstream LDP peer is clear.

10. What is the advantage and disadvantage of VC-Merge?

    Answer: The advantage of VC-Merge is the reduction of LVCs; the disadvantage is the buffering of the cells, which implies the need for more memory on the LSR.

Chapter 6

1. Name the two components of CEF.

   Answer: The two components of CEF are the adjacency table and the FIB or CEF table.

2. Name the three most common packet switching methods in Cisco IOS.

   Answer: Process switching, fast switching, and CEF switching are the three most common packet switching methods in Cisco IOS.

3. Why does MPLS use CEF?

   Answer: MPLS uses CEF because it is the only switching method in Cisco IOS that implements labeling of incoming IP packets.

4. What is the adjacency table used for?

    Answer: The adjacency table takes care of the Layer 2 rewrite of the frames that are switched by the router.

5. What fields of the IP header does CEF use to load-balance IP packets?

    Answer: CEF uses the destination IP address and the source IP address to load-balance IP packets.

6. How does CEF perform equal and unequal cost load balancing?

    Answer: CEF uses a hashing algorithm that looks at the source and destination IP address of the packet. The hash result points to one or more of the 16 hash buckets, which in turn indicates which adjacency to use to forward the packet.

7. How does a prefix in the CEF table get the imposed label stack?

    Answer: Each label in the imposed label stack can be assigned directly via LDP, BGP, or RSVP, or it can be inherited from recursion.

8. How is load balancing of labeled packets performed in Cisco IOS?

    Answer: If the MPLS payload is an IPv4 or IPv6 packet, CEF hashing is performed on the source and destination IP address. If the MPLS payload is anything else, the load balancing is determined by the value of the bottom label in the label stack.

9. Name two reasons *not* to use CEF per-packet load balancing.

    Answer: Two reasons for not using CEF per-packet load balancing are these:

    — Receipt of out-of-sequence packets, resulting in reordering of the packets or dropping of the packets

    — Jitter (variable delay)

10. Name two huge differences between the fast switching and the CEF switching methods.

    Answer: Fast switching and CEF switching are different in the following two ways:

    — Fast switching uses an on-demand route cache, whereas the CEF switching table is prebuilt.

    — The CEF table holds the MPLS label information to label IP packets before switching them out of the router; fast switching does not.

Chapter 7

1. What is a route distinguisher?

   Answer: A route distinguisher is a 64-bit value—chosen by the service provider—that is appended to the IPv4 routes of the customer and makes the routes unique.

2. How is a packet that is coming from the CE router identified as to which VRF it belongs?

   Answer: The packet is identified as belonging to a VRF by the VRF configuration on the interface.

3. What is the purpose of RTs?

   Answer: You use RTs to import vpnv4 routes into the VRF routing table and to export the vpnv4 routes to VRF sites that accept the RT.

4. What is an RR group?

   Answer: An RR group can be configured on route reflectors to filter vpnv4 routes.

5. What is the BGP neighbor command with as-override used for?

   Answer: The BGP speaker checks the as-path of the BGP route and replaces all occurrences of the autonomous system number of the BGP peer in the as-path with his own autonomous system number.

6. When would you use different route distinguishers for routes of the same VPN?

   Answer: You would use different route distinguishers for hub-and-spoke topologies and when you need to make different vpnv4 routes from the same IPv4 route when sites are dual homed to PE routers and the MPLS VPN network has route reflectors.

7. What command should you configure on a Multi-VRF CE router that is running OSPF?

   Answer: You should configure **capability vrf-lite** on a Multi-VRF CE router that is running OSPF.

8. What three characteristics does an OSPF sham link have?

   Answer: An OSPF sham link has the following characteristics:

   — Unnumbered

   — Point-to-point

   — Demand-circuit

9. Why do MPLS VPN packets have two MPLS labels?

   Answer: P routers use the IGP label to forward the packet to the correct egress PE router. The egress PE router uses the VPN label to forward the IP packet to the correct CE router.

10. Which BGP extended community can prevent routing loops from occurring in MPLS VPN networks?

    Answer: Site-of-Origin (SOO) can prevent routing loops from occurring in MPLS VPN networks.

Chapter 8

1. Name the advantages of MPLS traffic engineering

   Answer: The advantages of MPLS traffic engineering include the following:

   — Steering traffic so that all links in the network are used optimally

   — Routing traffic around hotspots in the network

   — Fast rerouting traffic around link and node failures

2. What are the components of MPLS traffic engineering?

   Answer: Following are the components of MPLS traffic engineering:

   — OSPF or IS-IS with TE extensions enabled

   — RSVP

   — Link attributes

   — CSPF on the head end router

   — TE Tunnel (Trunk) attributes

   — Link manager

3. What are the attributes of the links enabled for traffic engineering?

   Answer: The attributes of the links that are enabled for traffic engineering include these:

   — Maximum reservable bandwidth

   — Maximum reservable sub-pool bandwidth

   — SRLG

   — Attribute flags

   — Traffic engineering metric

4. Name the six ways how you can forward IP traffic onto a TE tunnel.

Answer: You can forward IP traffic onto a TE tunnel by using the following:

— A static route

— Policy-based routing

— Forwarding adjacency

— Autoroute announce

— Direct mapping of AToM traffic onto TE tunnels

— CBTS

5. Name four kind of path options you can specify.

Answer: You can specify the following path options:

— Explicit

— Explicit with exclude address

— Explicit with loose next address

— Dynamic

6. When you have an MPLS VPN network and TE tunnels that do not always have the PE routers as head/tail end routers, what do you need to have?

Answer: When you have an MPLS VPN network and TE tunnels that do not always have the PE routers as head/tail end routers, you need the following:

— LDP enabled on the links

— LDP targeted session on the TE tunnel if the tail end router is a P router

7. What is the LSR that is the head end router of a backup tunnel called?

Answer: The point of local repair (PLR) is the LSR that is the head end router of a backup tunnel.

8. Why do you need a link-state routing protocol for MPLS TE?

Answer: You need a link-state routing protocol for MPLS TE because the head end LSR needs to know the attributes and available bandwidth of all links.

9. What is the feature called that has the IGP advertise TE tunnels as links?

   Answer: Forwarding adjacency is the feature that has the IGP advertise TE tunnels as links.

10. How does the head end LSR of a TE tunnel know that the tunnel is fast rerouted over a backup tunnel?

    Answer: The head end LSR of a TE tunnel knows that the tunnel is fast rerouted over a backup tunnel because it receives a PathErr message from the PLR, indicating that Local Repair is active.

Chapter 9

1. Name three reasons to have a new IP protocol.

   Answer: Following are some of the reasons for having a new IP protocol:

   — Bigger addresses

   — More streamlined and more efficient IP header

   — Fixed IP header size

   — Flow Label field

2. How many bits does an IPv6 address have?

   Answer: An IPv6 address has 128 bits.

3. What happened to IP protocol version 5?

   Answer: IPv5 was experimental and was dropped.

4. Name the five ways a service provider can carry IPv6 packets across the backbone network.

   Answer: A service provider can carry IPv6 packets across the backbone network in these ways.

   — Run a dual stack (IPv4 and IPv6) on the backbone routers.

   — Run AToM and transport IPv6 packets on pseudowires.

   — Use the MPLS VPN for IPv4 solution with the CE routers running dual stack, and carry IPv6 over IPv4 tunnels.

   — Use 6PE.

   — Use 6VPE.

5. What is the routing protocol OSPF for IPv6 also called?

   Answer: OSPFv3 is another name for the routing protocol OSPF for IPv6.

6. Which field in the IPv6 header is the equivalent to the Type of Service field in the IPv4 header for the Differentiated Services (DiffServ) model?

   Answer: The Traffic Class field in the IPv6 header is equivalent to the Type of Service field in the IPv4 header for the Differentiated Services (DiffServ) model.

7. What routing protocols are supported on the PE-CE links of the 6PE solution?

   Answer: All IPv6 unicast routing protocols are supported on the PE-CE links of the 6PE solution.

8. How many labels are put on top of the IPv6 packet in a 6PE network?

   Answer: Two labels are put on top of the IPv6 packet in a 6PE network.

9. How can you quickly see the difference between the 6PE and 6VPE solution by looking at the configuration of a PE router?

   Answer: The configuration of 6VPE shows VRFs for IPv6 and an address family vpnv6 for BGP on the PE router.

10. Why are the 6PE and 6VPE solutions the best ones for carrying IPv6 traffic across an MPLS backbone?

   Answer: The IPv6 packets are transported across the MPLS backbone natively. This means that there is no added Layer 2 frame header or IPv4 header.

Chapter 10

1. Name the advantages of AToM for the service provider.

   Answer: Following are the advantages of AToM for the service provider:

   — You can apply AToM over the existing MPLS infrastructure and protect existing investments.

   — You can provision AToM easily, because you do not need to deploy IP routing with the customer routers.

   — You decouple edge and core technologies in the MPLS network. No changes are needed for the P routers, and only the PE routers need to have the intelligence to run AToM.

2. Name the advantages of AToM for the customers of the service provider.

Answer: AToM has several advantages for the customers of the service provider:

— The customer can keep the virtual leased line-like service between his routers.

— The customer needs to make no configuration changes when migrating from the legacy network to the MPLS network.

— The customer does not have to interact with the service provider at Layer 3 (IP routing). As such, the Layer 3 protocol of the customer can be anything; it is not limited to IP.

3. How many labels are used to forward AToM traffic, and what is the use of each of those labels?

Answer: Two labels forward AToM traffic. The top label, or tunnel label, identifies the PSN Tunnel (LSP) of the frame. In other words, it forwards the frame from the ingress PE to the egress PE. The bottom label, the VC label, identifies the pseudowire. In other words, the egress PE looks at the VC label; it uses the VC label to determine to which AC the frame should be forwarded.

4. Name three of the five functions of the control word.

Answer: The control word has five functions:

— Padding small packets

— Carrying control bits of the Layer 2 header of the transported protocol

— Preserving the sequence of the transported frames

— Facilitating the correct load balancing of AToM packets in the MPLS backbone network

— Facilitating fragmentation and reassembly

5. Ethernet over MPLS can be done in two modes. What are they called?

Answer: The two modes of Ethernet over MPLS are Ethernet Port mode and Ethernet VLAN mode.

6. Which two modes exist to carry Frame Relay over MPLS?

Answer: DLCI-to-DLCI mode and Port-to-Port mode carry Frame Relay over MPLS.

7. What is the command to limit the number of ATM cells going into one frame in Packed Cell Relay mode?

    Answer: cell-packing *cells* **mcpt-timer** *timer* limits the number of ATM cells going into one frame in Packed Cell Relay mode.

8. Which VC types (PW types) can EoMPLS use?

    Answer: EoMPLS can use VC types 4 and 5.

9. What is the AToM signaling protocol between PE routers?

    Answer: (Targeted) LDP is the AToM signaling protocol between PE routers.

10. What does the C-bit in the PW ID FEC TLV indicate?

    Answer: If the C-bit is set, it indicates the use of the control word.

Chapter 11

1. As which kind of port type can the customer-facing Ethernet interface on the PE router be configured?

    Answer: The customer-facing Ethernet interface on the PE router can be configured as any of the following:

    — An access port

    — An 802.1Q trunk port

    — A dot1qtunnel port

2. How many labels are used to forward VPLS traffic, and what is the use of each of those labels?

    Answer: Two labels are used to forward VPLS traffic. The top label, or tunnel label, identifies the tunnel (LSP) that the frame belongs to. In other words, it forwards the frame from the local or ingress PE to the remote or egress PE. The bottom label is the VC label. It identifies the pseudowire. In other words, the VC label is looked at by the remote PE; it uses the VC label to determine which attachment circuit the frame should be forwarded onto.

3. What does VFI stand for?

    Answer: VFI stands for virtual forwarding instance.

4.   Which Layer 2 control protocols can be tunneled across the VPLS network?

     Answer: CDP, STP, and VTP can be tunneled across the VPLS network.

5.   Why do the PE routers need to be in a full mesh of pseudowires in VPLS?

     Answer: The PE routers need to be in a full mesh of pseudowires in VPLS because the chosen mechanism to prevent the looping of frames in the MPLS network is Layer 2 split-horizon, meaning that received frames on the pseudowires cannot be forwarded out on the pseudowires again.

6.   Name the six functions that VPLS performs in emulating an Ethernet switch.

     Answer: VPLS performs the following six functions in emulating an Ethernet switch:

     — Forwarding of Ethernet frames

     — Forwarding of unicast frames with an unknown destination MAC address

     — Replication of broadcast and multicast frames to more than one port

     — Loop prevention

     — Dynamic learning of MAC addresses

     — MAC address aging

7.   In which two ways can H-VPLS be implemented?

     Answer: H-VPLS can be implemented by using dot1q tunneling (QinQ) or MPLS pseudowires between the N-PEs and U-PEs in the access layer.

Chapter 12

1.   How many bits in the IP header can be used for QoS?

     Answer: Three bits in the IP header can be used for QoS if the precedence bits are used, and six bits can be used if the DSCP bits are used.

2.   How many AF classes exist?

     Answer: Four AF classes exist.

3.   Name the three MPLS DiffServ models.

     Answer: Uniform model, Pipe model, and Short Pipe model are the three MPLS DiffServ models.

4. What is the difference between the Pipe and Short Pipe models?

   Answer: The only difference between the two models is the forwarding treatment of the packets on the egress LSR. The egress LSR forwards packets based on the LSP DiffServ information in the Pipe model. The egress LSR forwards packets based on the Tunneled DiffServ information in the Short Pipe model.

5. What is the interface command to encapsulate all IP packets with an explicit NULL label?

   Answer: mpls ip encapsulate explicit-null is the interface command to encapsulate all IP packets with an explicit NULL label.

6. What is TOS reflection?

   Answer: TOS reflection is the default behavior of copying the precedence value of an IP packet to the EXP bits of all imposed labels.

7. What feature is used in Cisco IOS to alter the EXP bits?

   Answer: MQC is used in Cisco IOS to alter the EXP bits.

8. What is the problem with PHP and QoS?

   Answer: The problem with PHP and QoS is that the EXP bits value is not copied to the newly exposed MPLS label or precedence/DiffServ bits in the IP header, if the packet becomes unlabeled.

9. What is the solution to the problem in question 8?

   Answer: The solution is to copy the EXP bits value by using qos-group or the explicit NULL label.

10. On which labels can you change the EXP bits value?

    Answer: You can change the EXP bits value only on the top label and the pushed label(s).

Chapter 13

1. What would you configure on the PE routers if you wanted to be able to see the LSRs in the output of the traceroute command from the PE routers, but not the customers performing the traceroute from the CE routers?

   Answer: In that case, you would configure **no mpls ip propagate-ttl forwarded.**

2. When is the MPLS TTL not copied to the IP TTL when disposing of the labels? Why?

Answer: When MPLS TTL > IP TTL, the MPLS TTL value is not copied into the IP header. This rule prevents packets from looping forever when the command **no mpls ip propagate-ttl (forwarded)** is configured on the ingress PE routers/LSRs.

3. What kind of packets are sent when you traceroute in Cisco IOS?

Answer: The packets that are sent when tracerouting in Cisco IOS are UDP packets with a high destination UDP port, with increasing TTL values, starting at 1.

4. Why does it not make much sense to configure **no mpls ip propagate-ttl** on P routers?

Answer: no mpls ip propagate-ttl hides the topology of the MPLS core for the customers who are connecting to the MPLS VPN network. This command takes effect only when the IP packets are imposed with labels. This imposition occurs only for the customers' packets at the PE routers.

5. How can you verify which outgoing interface is taken when load balancing labeled packets?

Answer: To verify which outgoing interface is taken when load balancing labeled packets, use the command **show mpls forwarding-table labels** *label* **exact-path**.

6. What information about the labels can MPLS-aware Netflow provide?

Answer: MPLS-aware Netflow can provide the following information:

— Label position

— Label value

— Experimental bits value

— End-of-Stack bit

— Label type (label-associated protocol)

— The prefix that the label is bound to

7. Which access lists can you associate with the command **debug mpls packets**?

Answer: You can associate access lists from the range 2700 to 2799.

Chapter 14

1. What does MPLS LSP ping provide that IP ping does not?

   Answer: IP ping verifies only IP connectivity, whereas LSP ping also verifies whether the LSP is broken.

2. Name three MPLS-specific MIBs.

   Answer: MPLS-specific MIBs can include any three of the following:

   — MPLS-LDP-MIB

   — MPLS-LSR-MIB

   — MPLS-TE MIB

   — MPLS-VPN-MIB

   — CISCO-IETF-PW-MIB

   — CISCO-IETF-PW-MPLS-MIB

   — CISCO-IETF-PW-TC-MIB

3. What does a ping mpls or traceroute mpls with reply mode router-alert do?

   Answer: The return packet has the IP Router Alert option. The Router Alert label is present if the return packet is labeled.

4. What is the name for the Cisco IOS subsystem that is responsible for processing MPLS echo request and echo reply packets?

   Answer: LSPV is the Cisco IOS subsystem that is responsible for processing MPLS echo request and echo reply packets.

5. What MPLS-related information can you see with MPLS-aware Netflow?

   Answer: With MPLS-aware Netflow, you can see the following MPLS-related information:

   — Value of the labels

   — Experimental bits value

   — MPLS application that is associated with the top label

   — Prefix that is associated with the top label

   — Label position

   — End-of-Stack bit

6.   What prevents an MPLS echo request packet from being forwarded as an IP packet after it becomes unlabeled?

Answer: The IP TTL is set to 1, and the destination IP address is from the range 127.0.0.0/8.

7.   What is IP SLA?

Answer: IP SLA is an embedded tool in Cisco IOS that does network performance measurement. It can measure jitter, one-way delay, round-trip-time (RTT), and packet loss by sending probes that can be of different protocols.

8.   If Type 1 VCCV is used, how is the packet identified as being an AToM VCCV packet?

Answer: If Type 1 VCCV is used, the control word below the label stack has the first nibble equal to 1.

9.   Why would you want to change the default destination IP address of 127.0.0.1 in the IP header of LSP ping packets if the packets are label-switched anyway?

Answer: If you have load-balanced paths in the MPLS network, changing the destination IP address can change the path that the packet takes.

10.   What is context-based access for SNMP?

Answer: A context can be associated with a VRF on a PE router to enable only hosts in the VPN to access the MIB data on the PE router that pertains only to that VRF.

Index

Numerics

6PE, 354
    BGP features, 379
    configuring, 358–361
    similarities to MPLS VPN for IPv4, 357
    verifying operation, 361–364
6VPE, 364
    BGP features, 379
    comparing with MPLS VPN for IPv4, 366
    configuring, 366–371
    features of, 364
    IPv6 Internet access, 377
    RR, implementing, 378
    supported features, 378
    verifying configuration, 372–377

A

AAL (ATM Abstraction Layer), 107
abbreviating IPv6 addresses, 332
address families, configuring, 191–192
    vpnv4, 196
addresses (IPv6), abbreviating, 332
adjacency table, 151, 351
adjusting
    LDP session keepalive timer, 73
    metrics with autoroute announce, 319–320
**administratively down links, preventing with
    LDP Session Protection, 100**
advertising label bindings, 77–81
    in UD mode, 78
    label withdrawal, 81–83
Advisory Notifications (LDP), 83
AF (assured forwarding), 459
aggregate labels, 131

aggregate operation, 47
applying table maps, 488–489
APS (automatic protection switching), 291
architecture of VPLS, 437–438
areas (OSPF), 215
**ASICs (application-specific integrated
    circuits), 7, 147**
    PSAs, 155–156
ASN (autonomous system number), 179
ATM (Asynchronous Transfer Mode), 7
    AAL, 107
    cells, 106
        GFC field, 107
        interleaving, 132
    control VC, verifying, 115
    Frame mode, configuring, 143–144
    label advertisement, 111–114
        control modes, 122–123
    LDP bindings, viewing, 118–119
    LSRs, 109
        aggregation, 131
        transit LSRs, 120
        VC-merge, 132, 135
    non MPLS-aware switches, 135–138
    OAM cells, 576
    OSPF neighborships, verifying, 114
    overlay model, 107, 174
    peer networks, 108
    transporting across MPLS networks, 408
    VCs, 111
**ATM AAL5, transporting across MPLS
    networks, 408–411**
**ATM cell relay, transporting across MPLS
    networks, 411–415**
    packed cell relay mode, 414–416
    single cell relay mode, 411–414

C

F

T

CISCO SYSTEMS

Cisco Press

CCIE PROFESSIONAL DEVELOPMENT
RESOURCES FROM EXPERTS IN THE FIELD

CCIE Professional Development books are the **ultimate resource for advanced networking professionals**, providing practical insights for effective network design, deployment, and management. **Expert perspectives, in-depth technology discussions, and real-world implementation advice** also make these titles essential for anyone preparing for a CCIE® exam.

CISCO SYSTEMS

CCIE® Professional Development
Routing TCP/IP
Volume I

A detailed examination of interior routing protocols

ciscopress.com   Jeff Doyle, CCIE No. 1919

1-57870-041-8

Look for CCIE Professional Development titles at your favorite bookseller

Cisco BGP-4 Command and Configuration Handbook
ISBN: 1-58705-017-X

Cisco OSPF Command and Configuration Handbook
ISBN: 1-58705-071-4

Inside Cisco IOS® Software Architecture
ISBN: 1-57870-181-3

Network Security Principles and Practices
ISBN: 1-58705-025-0

Routing TCP/IP, Volume I
ISBN: 1-57870-041-8

Troubleshooting IP Routing Protocols
ISBN: 1-58705-019-6

Troubleshooting Remote Access Networks
ISBN: 1-58705-076-5

Coming in Fall 2005
Cisco LAN Switching, Volume I, Second Edition
ISBN: 1-58705-216-4

Routing TCP/IP, Volume I, Second Edition
ISBN: 1-58705-202-4

Visit **www.ciscopress.com/series** for details about the CCIE Professional Development series and a complete list of titles.

Learning is serious business.
Invest wisely.

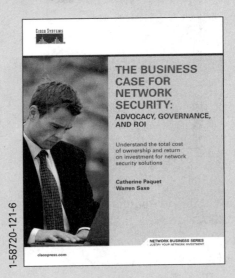